ALSO BY WILLIAM GADDIS

The Recognitions

J R

JR

BY

WILLIAM
GADDIS

ALFRED A. KNOPF   NEW YORK   1975

THIS IS A BORZOI BOOK
PUBLISHED BY ALFRED A. KNOPF, INC.

Copyright © 1971, 1974, 1975 by William Gaddis

All rights reserved under International and Pan-American
Copyright Conventions. Published in the United States by
Alfred A. Knopf, Inc., New York, and simultaneously in Canada
by Random House of Canada Limited, Toronto. Distributed by
Random House, Inc., New York.
Portions of this book were first published in *The Dutton
Review, Antaeus,* and *Harper's* magazine, June 1975 issue.
The author wishes to acknowledge assistance given him toward
the completion of this work by the Rockefeller Foundation and
the National Endowment for the arts.

Library of Congress Cataloging in Publication Data

Gaddis, William, [Date]
J R

I. Title.
PZ4.G124Jac   [PS3557.A28]   813'.5'4   75–8230
ISBN 0-394-49550-0   0-394-73142-5 (pbk.)

Manufactured in the United States of America

FIRST EDITION

J R

—Money . . . ? in a voice that rustled.

—Paper, yes.

—And we'd never seen it. Paper money.

—We never saw paper money till we came east.

—It looked so strange the first time we saw it. Lifeless.

—You couldn't believe it was worth a thing.

—Not after Father jingling his change.

—Those were silver dollars.

—And silver halves, yes and quarters, Julia. The ones from his pupils. I can hear him now . . .

Sunlight, pocketed in a cloud, spilled suddenly broken across the floor through the leaves of the trees outside.

—Coming up the veranda, how he jingled when he walked.

—He'd have his pupils rest the quarters that they brought him on the backs of their hands when they did their scales. He charged fifty cents a lesson, you see, Mister . . .

—Coen, without the h. Now if both you ladies . . .

—Why, it's just like that story about Father's dying wish to have his bust sunk in Vancouver harbor, and his ashes sprinkled on the water there, about James and Thomas out in the rowboat, and both of them hitting at the bust with their oars because it was hollow and wouldn't go down, and the storm coming up while they were out there, blowing his ashes back into their beards.

—There was never a bust of Father, Anne. And I don't recall his ever being in Australia.

—That's just what I mean, about stories getting started.

—Well, it can't help repeating them before a perfect stranger.

—I'd hardly call Mister Cohen a stranger, Julia. He knows more about our business than we do ourselves.

—Ladies, please. I haven't come out here simply to dig into your intimate affairs but since your brother died intestate, certain matters will have to be dealt with which otherwise might never come up at all. Now to return to this question of . . .

—I'm sure we have nothing to hide. Lots of brothers don't get on, after all.

—And do come and sit down, Mister Cohen.

—You might as well tell him the whole story, Julia.

—Well, Father was just sixteen years old. As I say, Ira Cobb owed him some money. It was for work that Father had done, probably repairing some farm machinery. Father was always good with his hands. And then this problem came up over money, instead of paying Father Ira gave him an old violin and he took it down to the barn to try to learn to play it. Well his father heard it and went right down, and broke the violin over Father's head. We were a Quaker family, after all, where you just didn't do things that didn't pay.

—Of course, Miss Bast, it's all . . . quite commendable. Now, returning to this question of property . . .

—That's what we're discussing, if you'll be a little patient. Why, Uncle Dick, Father's older brother, had walked all the way back to Indiana, every step of the way from the Andersonville prison.

—And after that business of the violin, Father left home and went to teaching school.

—The one thing he'd wanted, all his life, was to own as far as he could see in any direction. I hope we've cleared things up for you now.

—We might if he came back here and sat down. He won't find anything gazing out the window.

—I had hoped, said Mister Coen from the far end of the room, where he appeared to steady himself against the window frame, —I expected Mrs Angel to be with us here today, he went on in a tone as drained of hope as the gaze he had turned out through evergreen foundation planting just gone sunless with stifling the prospect of roses run riot only to be strangled by the honeysuckle which had long since overwhelmed the grape arbor at the back, where another building was being silently devoured by rhododendron before his eyes.

—Mrs Angel?

—The daughter of the decedent.

—Oh, that's Stella's married name isn't it. You remember, Julia, Father used to say . . .

—Why, Stella called earlier, you told me yourself Anne. To say she was taking a later train.

—That name was changed from Engels, somewhere along the way . . .

—I'm afraid I'll miss her then, I have to be in court . . .

—I scarcely see the need for that, Mister Cohen. If Stella's husband is so impatient he's hiring lawyers and running to court . . .

—You're losing a button here, Mister Cohen. Thomas had the same trouble when he got stout. He couldn't keep a crease in anything either.

—Miss . . . Bast. I'm afraid I haven't made myself clear. My court appearance today has nothing whatsoever to do with this matter. There is no reason for any of this to ever come into court. In fact, believe me Miss Bast . . . both of you ladies, the last thing I would wish would be to . . . to see you ladies in court. Now. You must understand that I am not here simply as Mister Angel's attorney, I am here as counsel for General Roll . . .

—You remember back when Thomas started it, Julia? And we thought it was a military friend he'd made?

—Of course it was James who had friends in the military.

—Yes, he'd run off to war, you know, Mister Cohen. A drummer boy in the Spanish war.

—The . . . Spanish war? he murmured vaguely, braced against the back of the Queen Anne chair before the empty hearth.

—Yes. He was only a child.

—But . . . the Spanish war? That was 'thirty-seven, wasn't it? or 'thirty-eight?

—Oh, not so long ago as that. I think you mean 'ninety-seven, or 'ninety-eight was it, Anne? When they sank the Maine?

—Who? That's one I never heard. Do you feel unwell, Mister Cohen?

—Yes, Thomas ran off right after James did, but he was too small for the war of course. He joined a Tom show passing through town, playing clarinet in the entreact and they also let him look after the dogs, finding livery stables to put them up in. You might have noticed his scar, Mister Cohen, where one of the bloodhounds tore open his thumb. He carried it with him right into the grave, but you're not leaving us so soon, Mister Cohen? Of course if we've answered all your questions, I know you must be a busy man.

—Mister Cohen might like a nice glass of cold water.

—No, it isn't . . . water that I need. If you ladies, you . . . just for a moment, if you'll give me your undivided attention . . .

—We have no objection at all, Mister Cohen. We're telling you everything we can think of.

—Yes but, some of it is not precisely relevant . . .

—If you'll simply tell us what it is you want to know, instead of wandering around the room here waving your arms. We want to see this settled as much as anyone.

—Yes . . . thank you, Miss Bast. Precisely. Now. As we are all aware, the bulk of your brother's estate consists of his controlling share in the General Roll Corporation . . .

—Share! I think Thomas had at least forty shares, or forty-five was it Anne? Because we have . . .

—Precisely, Miss Bast. Since its founding, General Roll has been a closely held company owned by members of your family. Under the guidance of the decedent, and more recently that of his son-in-law Mister Angel, General Roll has prospered substantially . . .

—You certainly wouldn't know it from the dividends, Mister Cohen. There simply have not been any.

—Precisely. This is one of the difficulties we face now. Since your brother, and more recently his son-in-law, have wished to build the company larger rather than simply extract profits from it, its net worth has grown considerably, and with that growth of course have come certain obligations which the company right now is being hard pressed to satisfy. Since no buy-sell arrangement had been made with the decedent prior to his death, no cross-purchase plan providing life insurance on each of the principals or an entity plan that would have allowed the company itself to buy up his interest, in the absence of any such arrangements as these, the money which will be required to pay the very substantial death taxes . . .

—Julia, I'm sure Mister Cohen only is complicating things unnecessarily . . .

—Crowned by the complications inherent in any situation in which the decedent dies intestate . . .

—Julia, can't you . . .

—Further complicated by certain unresolved and somewhat delicate aspects of the family situation which I have come out here today to discuss with . . .

—Mister Cohen, please! Do sit down and come to the point.

—Yes, after all Julia, you remember. Charlotte died without leaving a will and Father simply sat down and parceled things out. Of course I think that James always felt . . .

—Yes, James made it quite clear how he felt. Do sit down here, Mister Cohen, and stop waving that piece of paper around.

—It's . . . simply the waiver I mentioned, he said giving it up and seating himself in the Queen Anne chair whose arm came off in his hand.

—Julia? I thought Edward had fixed that.

—It was the side door latch he fixed, Anne.

—It didn't work when I let Mister Cohen in. He had to come round by the back.

—I thought you came in at the side, Mister Cohen.

—Well I let him in, Julia. After all.

—I thought Edward had . . .

—Let him in?

—No. Fixed the latch.

Mister Coen, finished fitting the arm of the chair back into place, leaned carefully away from it. —That is the waiver I brought out for your nephew Edward to sign, he said resting his elbows on the scarcely more firm support of his knees. —A, a mere formality in this case. Of course, where there's a will . . .

—There's a way. You're quite witty today Mister Cohen, but believe me Anne I think this is Thomas' will, the tangle things are in right now.

—Yes, just look at these obituaries, and why Mister Cohen ever brought them out unless to tangle things up still further. To read them it's hard even knowing who's dead. Did you see this one? It's all about James. James, and no mention of Thomas at all.

—I simply included it because . . . he began in a tone that seemed to echo the deep, as he fixed the newspaper streamer flown before his glazed eyes. —Word comes in to a newspaper of a death, if someone there is in a hurry and just hears the last name, he might grab the obituary that's already written on someone like your brother James, as prominent as your brother James, they keep one written and up to date against the day . . .

—But James isn't dead! he's just away . . .

—Abroad, accepting some sort of award.

—Yes, yes in fact, I think if you'll read that clipping . . .

—That seems to be about all James does now, going about to accept awards.

—It's not as though he didn't deserve them, Julia. Don't give Mister Cohen the wrong idea, there's no telling the stories he'll carry back with him.

—I . . . ladies I assure you, all I wish to carry back is this waiver with your nephew's signature. Since your brothers were not, ahm, especially close, and the decedent died intestate, the cooperation of the survivors is . . .

—You make us sound like a shipwreck, Mister Cohen.

—Well now that you speak of it, Miss Bast . . .

—I think I know what he's trying to say. He's going to drag up those old stories about James and Thomas not getting on.

—I don't think he could sit there and name two brothers who went out of their way for one another as often as James and Thomas did. Neither of them had a single job that the other didn't claim to have got for him.

—The Russian Symphony . . .

—And Sousa's Band? Of course there was a certain competitive spirit between the boys. No one denies that, Mister Cohen. We had a family orchestra, you know, and they practiced three and four hours a day. Every week Father gave a dime to the one who showed the most improvement. From the time they were six, until they left home . . .

—Yes, Julia played the . . . where are you going now, Mister Cohen? If you'll just sit still for a minute, I'm sure we can find some black thread. I can sew that button back on while we're chatting.

—While I wait to talk with your nephew Edward . . .

—Whatever that paper is you've brought there, I don't think he'll be in any hurry to sign it.

—Yes, I remember Father telling us to never sign anything we didn't read carefully.

—But . . . ladies! I want him to read it, I urge him to read it. I urge you to read it! It's only a few lines, the merest formality, a waiver to permit the appointment of the decedent's daughter, one Stella, Mrs Angel, as administrator of her father's estate, so that we may submit to the court . . .

—Mister Cohen, you distinctly said that you hoped to keep us all out of court. Didn't you hear him say that, Anne?

—Yes, I certainly did. And I'm not at all sure what James will say about these goings on.

—James has a great instinct for justice, Mister Cohen, and in spite of his being a composer he knows more than a little about the law. If we're all obliged to end up in court in order to settle what's right and wrong here . . .

—Madam, Miss Bast, please I . . . I implore you, there is no such issue at stake, and there is no reason there ever should be. The law, Miss Bast, let me tell you, the law . . .

—Do be careful of that lamp, Mister Cohen.

—There's no question of justice, or right and wrong. The law seeks order, Miss Bast. Order!

—Now Mister Cohen, if you'll just sit still. I've found some black thread right here in the basket.

—And an agreement within a legal framework is made for the protection of all concerned. Now . . .

—Perhaps you would like to take off your jacket. I'm just afraid you will spill those papers.

—Yes. Thank you. No. Now . . .

—It's carpet thread, and should hold quite well. It will probably outlast the suit itself.

—Let me assure you that signing this waiver will not in any way affect any claim your nephew may have upon the estate of the decedent. But because of his somewhat equivocal position . . .

—I got it for Father's overcoat buttons. It always outlasted the coats themselves.

—I don't know what you're inferring, Mister Cohen, but . . .

—This is as I understand it, Miss Bast, your nephew Edward's position in the family. His mother, who was known as Nellie . . .

—She wasn't simply known as Nellie. That was Nellie's Christian name, even though a lot of people thought it was a nickname. But I see no reason to start prying . . .

—I think when James is done his memoirs, can you raise your arm a little Mister Cohen? A lot of prying people will have surprises, and after all the gossip that followed . . .

—Ladies, I am not here to pry! But in the legal disposition of your brother's estate, his relationship to Nellie and your nephew Edward is extremely pertinent. Now as I understand it, your brother Thomas had one child, Stella, by his first wife, who then died . . .

—I wouldn't really say who then died, Mister Cohen. Why, she was still alive when . . .

—Of course, forgive me. At any rate Thomas remarried, one Nellie, who in due course appears to have separated from him, in order to cohab . . . ahm, to . . .

—Yes, to marry James. Precisely. But I would hardly say in due course, Mister Cohen. I think we were all really quite surprised.

—I don't know, Anne. Nellie was flighty.

—I remember James using that word, now that you say it. It was when Rachmaninoff was visiting, I remember because he'd just had his fingers insured. Hand me those scissors please, Mister Cohen?

—However, yes, thank you, here . . . now, however, in the absence of any record of legally contracted marriage between the said Nellie and James . . .

—My dear Mister Cohen . . .

—Or indeed any evidence of legal and binding divorce between the aforesaid Nellie and the decedent . . .

—It scarcely seems necessary . . .

—And although it appears to have been known that this Nellie aforesaid was the, living as the, ahm, the wife of the decedent's brother James at the time she bore her son Edward, and had been so living for some indefinite time prior to that event, nonetheless in the continued absence of a birth certificate attesting to those circumstances of his, ahm, provenience, Edward is in a position to exert a substantial claim upon the estate in question, and therefore . . .

—I scarcely understand a word you've said, Mister Cohen, and where you got that piece of paper you're reading from . . .

—But I wrote it, Miss Bast, it's . . .

—His glasses are rather like the ones that James lost that summer up near Tannersville, aren't they Julia.

—And the idea of digging up all this gossip again. Why, Edward's been perfectly happy here, and James has been a fine father to him, there's never been any question at all, why . . .

—But I don't question that, Miss Bast. The point is simply that in regards to your brother's estate, until his position is clearly established, he . . . what . . .

—Just a little thread here still hanging, if you'll hold still . . .

—Yes, thank you again for the button, Miss Bast, but . . .

—Are you leaving so soon?

—No I simply hope I think may be . . . maybe think better on my feet . . .

—He's spilling those papers there, Julia.

—Miss Bast, and . . . yes, thank you Miss Bast, and therefore . . .

—After Nellie died, Mister Cohen.

—To the contrary notwithstanding . . .

—James brought him here then, you know, and we've practically brought him up ourselves. James' work has always made such demands. That's his studio there at the back, you can see it right out that side window, and we'd often miss him for days at a time . . .

—But the point, the point Miss Bast, the point of law at issue here is . . .

—Julia, I think I heard something, it sounded like hammering, someone hammering . . .

—The presumption, you see, the presumption of legitimacy while not conclusive and rebuttable in the first instance remains one of the strongest presumptions known to the law, and will not fail, Miss Bast, yes, where is it, Hubert versus Cloutier, it will not fail unless common sense and reason are outraged by a holding that it abides . . .

—There's no question that at the time, Julia, we all thought James' behavior outrageous . . .

—In general this presumption is not even overcome by evidence of the wife's adultery, in regard to your nephew's claim even when this adultery is established as of about the commencement of the usual period of gestation, as held in Bassel versus the Ford Motor Company . . .

—Mister Cohen please, Edward has nothing against the Ford Motor Company or anyone else, now . . .

—I am merely stating the legal position open to him, Miss Bast, in the event he should elect to pursue . . .

—Hammering, didn't you hear it?

—Possibly your testimony and that of your brother James regarding the period of his cohabitation with the said Nellie prior to Edward's birth, since there is merely a prima facie presumption that, just a moment, here, yes, that a child born in wedlock is legitimate where husband and wife had separated and the period of gestation required, in order that the husband may be the father, while a possible one, is exceptionally long and contrary to the usual course of nature, you see? Now in bringing a proceeding to establish the right to the property of a deceased person, the burden is on the claimant to show his kinship with the decedent, where kinship is an issue, of course, as in this instance of basing a claim on the alleged fact that claimant is decedent's child, and . . . yes, that while in the first instance, where is it yes, proof of filiation from which a presumption of legitimacy arises will sustain the burden and will establish the status of legitimacy and heirship if no evidence tending to show illegitimacy is introduced, the burden to establish legitimacy does not shift and claimant must establish his legitimacy where direct evidence, as well as evidence of potent . . . is this word potent? potent, yes potent circumstances, tending to disprove his claim of heirship, is introduced. Now, regarding competent evidence to prove filiation . . .

—Mister Cohen, I assure you there is no need to go on like this, if . . .

—Ladies, I have no choice. In settling an estate of these proportions and this complexity it is my duty to make every point which may bear upon your nephew's legal rights absolutely crystal clear to you and to him. Now.

—It's kind of him, Julia, but I must say . . .

—You understand that to proceed without taking into consideration your nephew's possible rights in this estate would be to jeopardize the status of everyone concerned, since to hold a child a bastard is not permissible unless there is no judicial escape from that conclusion . . .

—Mister Cohen!

—And it is incumbent upon the party assuming the fact of illegitimacy to disprove every reasonable possibility to the contrary, and as apparently obtains here, in the case of a child conceived or born in wedlock, it must be shown that the husband of the mother could not possibly have been the father of the child.

—Crystal clear indeed Mister Cohen!

—Crystal clear, and while I am aware that you ladies may find certain legal terms somewhat obscure, nonetheless in pursuing other evidence tending to support illegitimacy, a declaration of the deceased mother, for example, might be admissible, or any similar characterizations of family relationships tending, as part of a series of res gestae, to throw light . . .

—Nellie was never one to write letters.

—Or photographs, he came on in a flourish of papers at the wall behind him —for the purpose of comparing the physical characteristics of the child with those of the husband and such other man . . .

—Just behind your left shoulder Mister Cohen, that's always been my favorite picture of James. There, the two men sitting in the tree, the other one was Maurice Ravel. It shows James' profile off so nicely, though he always felt that our Indian blood . . .

—I don't think that's anything to get into now, Anne.

—It's quite all right, ladies. I have it here somewhere . . .

—Really, Anne . . .

—Yes, here, even where territorial statute provides for the legitimacy of the issue of marriages null in law, the issue of a white man and Indian woman has been held illegitimate . . .

—It is Cherokee blood you understand, Mister Cohen. They were the only tribe to have their own alphabet.

—Notwithstanding that the alleged marriage may have been conducted in accordance with the customs of the Indians on an Indian reservation within the territory and that, I think, should settle that. It's not an area to meddle in, Miss Bast.

—He might like to see that picture of Charlotte in the headdress, when she was touring with . . .

—Now. There appears to be another sister somewhere. Carlotta.

—That's precisely who Anne is talking about. She's right behind you there, Mister Cohen.

—She what? who . . . ?

—Do be careful, you're going to break something. She's there, just above the building with the dome. That's one of James' Masonic lodges. Charlotte's wearing a green felt hat, but of course the color doesn't show in the picture. She bought it to get married in.

—She did this place over you know, Mister Cohen. After her stroke, which was why she left the stage. She made quite a name on the Keith Circuit where she introduced . . . what was that song, Julia. I know the sheet music is around somewhere, probably over in James' studio. She's wearing a hat made to look like a daisy. That was why she took the name Carlotta, of course.

—And she died of the stroke?

—Why, certainly not. She carried right on, with a beaded bag on her withered arm, and except for a slight limp when she was tired you'd never know what she had gone through. She spent most of her winters in Cairo.

—Cai . . . ro? that . . . that would be, Egypt? Perhaps . . . The tremor seemed to pass through his voice right out his arm snagged in mid-air upon his wristwatch, —when I've talked with your nephew Edward, will he be down . . .

—If Mister Cohen would just come to the point here, we might not need to bother Edward at all.

—Yes, Mister Cohen. If you'll just tell us how we can work things out for him . . .

—Work things out for him? He's not an infant, is he?

—Infant! He's bigger than you are, Mister Cohen, and you scarcely need shout.

—Taller, Julia, but I wouldn't say bigger. I just took in the waist on those gray trousers . . .

—By . . . by infant I meant merely a, an infant in law, a, someone under the age of twenty-one.

—Edward? Let me think, Julia. Nellie died the year that James finished his opera, and . . .

—No, she died the year he started it, Anne. Or rather he started it the year she died, and so that would make . . .

—His opera Philoctetes. Maybe you know it, Mister Cohen?

—There's no way he could, Anne. It's never performed.

—Well, there was the winter when James was in Zurich. Perhaps Mister Cohen has . . .

—Ope! dropped his glasses . . .

—I hope they didn't break? That's a good way to take off weight, Mister Cohen. Bending up and down from the floor like that. I met the woman who told me about it in the ladies' room at A and S's. She was doing it with a deck of cards. She threw the whole deck out on the floor, and then stooped to pick them up one by one. I'm sure some of the weight goes in perspiration, but perhaps Mister Cohen . . .

—Mister Cohen seems to perspire quite freely . . .

—If we're patient with him a little bit longer, I think that all he really is after is Edward to sign this piece of paper.

—You have nothing else up your sleeve, Mister Cohen?

—I . . . thank you for your patience, yes all I need is a copy of his birth certificate.

—There. You see, Anne?

—To establish his parenthood and his age. I had, I assumed he had passed his majority and fervently hope so, so, so that I won't have to deal . . . to inconvenience you ladies further, the validity of his signature, you see, of course, on this waiver, depending upon his legal capacity to contract, although of course a minor may be emancipated . . .

—Emancipated! I assure you Mister Cohen . . .

—Which entitles him to keep his own earnings, but . . .

—Every penny that Edward earns . . .

—In no way enlarges his capacity to contract, as in Masus vernon Manon, I mean Mason versus Wright, yes, the contracts of an infant being voidable by him but not void, though this may not apply to necessaries, these however being relative. Now, comparing the voidable contract which is in itself not void to that of a lunatic, when of course his contract is made before he has been judicially declared incompetent, you ladies deserve . . .

—Oh Julia.

—Poor Edward.

—You see? You ladies deserve every protection, because the infant himself is the only one who can take advantage of infancy. The defense of infancy is not available to the adult, and this infant may disaffirm any time he likes. His mere intention to disaffirm is sufficient. In an action brought against him by creditors, assignees by purchase or in bankruptcy, sureties, or anyone else with a collateral interest in the contract, the mere setting up of infancy as a defense is sufficient, and none of them has available the defense of the infant, which is that of infancy.

—As far as his age goes, Edward himself . . .

—For your own protection, ladies. This birth certificate. Because this infant, ladies, this infant may disaffirm any time he wishes to, even if he has misrepresented his age in the first place in order to get the other party to contract with him, remember that ladies. Remember Danziger versus the Iron Clad Realty Company.

—I think he's going for a glass of water, Julia.

—That door, Mister Cohen.

—Failing any adoption papers, which could of course change the picture substantially, since the adopted child has the same legal rights as the blood child. Therefore if the child were the natural child of the decedent's brother but had been adopted by the decedent, he would of course have every right to participate in this estate. If on the other hand he . . .

—He's going to get into Reuben, Julia.

—James never really adopted Reuben.

—In the distribution of this estate that is to say, since in order to satisfy taxes part of this estate will have to be sold . . .

—They're after our trees right now.

—I suppose it does look like an estate to them, Julia, stuck in their tiny pasteboard houses on little shirttails of land.

—Forcing your holdings to go public . . .

—They take for granted everything's for sale.

—Proper evaluation will have to be made, of course, in terms of the prevailing market . . .

—That's what the water people said, when they went into court and swore up and down that back in our trees was the only place they could possibly put up their pumping station.

—Since no part of the estate involved has ever been offered publicly before.

—I heard hammering out there last night, Julia.

—I thought I heard the sound of a truck myself.

—Or a tractor, the kind they knock down trees with.

—Would they do that? even the water people? come in knocking down our trees at night?

—They were there this morning.

—The water people? Why didn't you call me!

—No the trees Anne, the trees.

—I'm glad you saw them. I didn't really look.

—I can't say I did either. But I know that passing the kitchen window I would have missed them if they'd been gone.

—Perhaps Mister Cohen looked when he came in.

—The oaks, Mister Cohen?

—And some locust?

—It's the oaks, though, Anne, that really stand out.

—Before the advent of such a sale, you would, of course, receive adequate notice.

—What Mister Cohen considers adequate, I can't even read them without a glass, Anne? have you seen the latest one? I had it here just a moment ago.

—It's right there on the mantel, a picture of a castle? James' hand has never been easy Mister Cohen, and he tries to get so much on one postcard . . .

—Anne I'm talking about the local paper, Mister Cohen means these legal notices they tuck off in the back in type so small that no one can read it, in language no one can understand. In fact if he has a moment now, he might be willing to translate something . . .

—But Julia he's just broken his glasses.

—Here it is yes, yes this second column here Mister Cohen. No, right down here. It looks to me like they're up to something with the old Lemp home.

—Do they have a picture of it there? It was always the grandest house in town, and when we were just girls Mister Cohen . . .

—This is simply a legal notice, Anne. They don't print pictures in a legal notice. Can you see through the breakage, Mister Cohen?

—It's a shame that Mister Cohen can't see it, a white Victorian with a tower and a porte cochere along one side, and those copper beeches on the lawn. When Julia and I were girls Mister Cohen we used to imagine living there. We dreamt that some great stroke of fortune would . . .

—So far as I can make out here Miss Bast, this is simply a petition for a zoning change to turn the place into a nursing home . . .

—Old Mrs Lemp never was well of course, was she.

—It's her son we mentioned earlier Mister Cohen, the attorney you should be taking all this up with.

—But Julia someone should warn Mister Cohen, when he says the law has no interest in justice . . .

—Ladies I, please I seem to be having difficulty making myself clear but I assure you . . .

—He made himself quite clear didn't he Julia but I think he should be forewarned, if Mister Lemp took no interest in justice Father would never have chosen him.

—Even James holds him in high regard, and James can be most critical.

—Yes and Thomas, Julia, after all, he had Mister Lemp begin the suit against that dreadful little man who started that musical instrument company and stole every idea Thomas had.

—They're not instruments at all, Mister Cohen. The Jubilee Musical Instrument Company is what he calls it but all they make are machines that play tunes, and that lawsuit, Anne, I think it was really James' idea. He was someone James held in great contempt.

—He had something to do with that awful family, that politician out west somewhere whose family owned stock in the little company Thomas took on there may even be some there in the drawer, when he was looking for sheeps' intestines to . . .

—We needn't go into that right now Anne, if Mister Cohen has no more questions . . .

—But ladies I, this newspaper here I understood it was the local paper . . .

—Well of course it is it comes every week, it's the only way we keep up with things.

—But it's, I just noticed it's from a town in Indiana I'm afraid when you said local I thought, your attorney Mister Lemp is, is in Indiana?

—Did you think he would be in Timbuctoo?

—No no I, I simply meant that if, that a nearby lawyer who might be more familiar with local situations . . .

—He's quite familiar with them thank you Mister Cohen. I wrote him last week about this bingo parlor, Anne.

—But I meant, to go back to your nephew ladies some clue possibly regarding his age just, on your income taxes for instance do you recall listing him as a deduction?

—You talk about adequate notice Mister Cohen, this went up right under our noses. The holy name of something or other, they play there every Wednesday night and park their cars right up in our hedge.

—I see yes because if he is that would indicate he is still a minor though I, I trust he's not disabled?

—We'd better be thankful to still have the hedge. It deadens the noise from the road, James says.

—You might tell Mister Cohen about those two women who came pounding on the door last week, staring in through these living room windows they thought it would make a nice teen center.

—I see yes you see your nephew ladies, your nephew Edward, in the event he is still a minor, he . . .

—Looking in from the road they said it looked empty. Just what were they doing looking in from the road?

—To protect his interests as well as your own re, recalling Egnaczyk versus Rowland where the infant sought to recover his car and disaffirm the repair contract the infant lost out in this case ladies, the defense of infancy in this case ladies, in this case the court refused to permit it, using infancy as a sword instead of a shield . . . there! I heard something. Don't I hear him now? your nephew coming downstairs at last?

—Edward?

—Hammering, Julia.

—Yes, it couldn't be Edward. He left long ago, didn't he Anne?

—I think I heard him leave when I was sewing that button on. He has class today you know, Mister Cohen. At the Jewish temple, rehearsing Wagner . . .

—He's . . . left? You mean, while I've been waiting, you just let him go? He . . . I don't understand . . .

—We don't interfere with his comings and goings but don't think we haven't wondered ourselves. Why he wants to teach at the Jewish temple.

—And what's got into them, doing Wagner.

—That table Mister Cohen, do be careful . . .

—You're not leaving us?

—I'm, yes, leaving . . . leaving this waiver for him, for you . . . somebody to sign, and your, I mean his birth certificate, here is his card, if you will give it to me, I mean if you will give him my card Miss Bast and urge him to get in touch with me so I won't have to . . . to inconvenience you further . . .

—Our counterfeit quarter, Julia, we wanted to show it to Mister Cohen. It was such a crude job, Mister Cohen, the copper showing right through at the edges, and one of our own tradesmen passed it on us. Can you see it, there on the mantel?

—I don't think he can see a thing, Anne. But it wasn't on the mantel this morning.

—That one sticks, Mister Cohen. You'd best use the side.

—It's the side that sticks, Julia. He'd better use the back. Out through the kitchen Mister Cohen . . .

—And Mister Cohen . . . ? Once you're out there if you'll just take a look? in the back? for the trees?

—And he might listen, Julia . . . pursued him through the presence of potatoes and green beans with strings like packing thread disintegrating with a smoked pork butt on the kitchen stove since near dawn, followed him as far as the corner of the house where a hanging gutter streaked clapboards and glass whenever it rained.

—I don't think he's paid us any attention. Just see him out there, my! He is in a hurry.

Avoiding an apple tree, its entire top blown out the year before, which redeemed itself now with a bumper crop of tasteless fruit in brave colors and curious shapes, —he looks like someone's chasing him.

—He was certainly full of gossip, for a perfect stranger.

—I do wonder what James will have to say.

—James will say what he's always said. He knows I've never believed it, for one.

—But even if you are right, Julia. If they weren't married till Edward was born, he's been Edward's father all these years.

—You remember what Father used to say, the devil paying the piper for all the good tunes.

—Yes. There he goes now . . . The car crept up the drive past trees which appeared to stagger without even provocation of a breeze, rearing their splintered amputations in all directions, an atmosphere of calamity tempered, to the south, by a brooding bank of oak, by several high locusts serenely distinct against the sky in the west. —It was naughty of James.

—I hope he gets out through the hedge all right.

—Did you hear that crash last night? and the sirens? It's a wonder they aren't all killed.

—Listen . . . !

To the squeal of brakes, the car burst out into the world trailing a festoon of privet, swerved at the immediate prospect of open acres flowered in funereal abundance to regain the pavement and lose it again in a brief threat to the candy wrappers and beer cans nestled along the hedge line up the highway, that quickly out of sight to the windows' half-shaded stare from the roof pitches frowning over the hedge to where it ended, and a yellow barn took up, and was gone in a swerving miss for the pepperidge tree towering ahead, past shadeless windows in a naked farmhouse sprawl at the corner where the road trimmed neatly into the suburban labyrinth and things came scaled down to wieldy size, dogwood, then barberry, becomingly streaked blood-red for fall.

Past the firehouse, where once black crêpe had been laboriously strung in such commemoration as that advertised today on the sign OUR

DEAR DEPARTED MEMBER easy to hang and store as a soft drink poster, past the crumbling eyesore dedicated within recent memory as the Marine Memorial, past the graveled vacancy of a parking lot where a house, ravined by gingerbread, had held out till scarcely a week before, and through the center of town where all allusion to permanence had disappeared or was being slain within earshot by shrieking electric saws, and the glint of chrome that streaked the glass bank front across the resident image of bank furniture itself apparently designed to pick up and flee at a moment's notice doors or no doors, opened, as they were now, to dispense the soft music hovering aimlessly about a man pasteled to match the furniture, crowding the high-bosomed brunette at the curb with —something, Mrs Joubert, something I'd meant to ask you but, oh wait a moment, there's Mister Best, or Bast is it? Mister Bast . . . ? He's music appreciation, you know.

—He?

—What? Oh there, coming out? No, no that's Vogel. Coach Vogel. You know him, the coach? Coach? Good morning . . .

—Good what? Oh, Whiteback. Good morning, didn't see you. I just robbed your bank.

—I didn't see you, called Mister Whiteback, and waved. —He what did he do? The sun in my eyes . . . It caught him flat across the lenses, erasing any life behind them in a flash of inner vacancy as he returned to —here, this young man coming here is Bast, you could probably tell he's in the arts, can't you. Mister Bast? I was just telling Mrs Joubert here, if she thinks she's pressed for space you've had to rehearse all the way over to the Jewish temple since we had to take the cafeteria over for the driver training, right? Mister Bast is helping out Miss Flesch on her Ring to have it ready for Friday, the Foundation is sending out a team to give our whole in-school television program the once over and giving them a look at Miss Flesch's Ring will give a real boost to the cultural aspect of, things. Not to slight your efforts Mrs Joubert. She has the new television course in, is it sixth grade social studies Miss Joubert? What's in the paper bag, you haven't robbed the bank, Mrs Joubert?

—This? No, it's just money, she said, and shook the paper sack. —Not mine, my class. It's what they've saved to buy a share in America. We're taking a field trip in to the Stock Exchange to buy a share of stock. The boys and girls will follow its ups and downs and learn how our system works, that's why we call it our share . . .

—In what.

—In America, yes, because actually owning it themselves they'll feel . . .

—No, I mean what stock.

—That's our studio lesson today deciding which one, if you want to look in on our channel. We have a resource film from the Exchange itself, too.

—Teaching our boys and girls what America is all about . . .

—Stick 'em up!

Bast's elbow caught Mrs Joubert a reeling blow in the breast, she dropped the sack of coins and he stood for an instant poised with raised hand posed in pursuit of that injury before the flush that spread from her face to his sent him stooping to recover the sack by the top, spilling the coins from its burst bottom into the unmown strip of grass, and left him kneeling down where the wind moved her skirt.

—Poor child, why they let him run around loose . . .

—It's the testing . . . Mister Whiteback withdrew a foot where his clocked ankle was nudged in pursuit of a dime, glancing down as it prospered to a quarter under Mrs Joubert's expensively shod instep, and his voice was sheared off by an inhuman scream.

—What was that! . . . oh Mister Bast, I'm sorry, I didn't hurt you . . . ? She withdrew her heel from the back of his left hand as Bast got the nickel with his right, looking up from her flexed knee to start to speak.

—Those saws, they're doing the trees in the next block, widening Burgoyne Street, said Mister Whiteback above. —I'll drop you, if . . . Mister Bast? he retired in the box step of the rhumba now spilling from the bank out across the walk and into the grass where Bast was going at it as though finding money lost by someone else, —if you can just pick the rest of it up and drop it off for Mrs Joubert's studio lesson?

—It was twenty-four dollars . . .

—And still get to your rehearsal, Mister Bast. To have it ready for Friday, we want to show this Foundation team how we're motivating this cultural drive in our youngsters, it's all in preparation for the cultural festival next spring you know, Miss Joubert . . . watch his hand there yes, to show we can make this cultural drive pay off like never before in mass consumers, mass distribution, mass publicity, just like automobiles and bathing suits . . .

—And sixty-three cents, Mrs Joubert finished, a gentle bulge rippling from her knee as she shifted her weight in departure to disappear in the swirl of her skirt as the quarter bounding from the billowing trouser cuff drew Bast in a headlong lunge after the exhaust of Whiteback's car shearing from the curb, rounding the corner into Burgoyne Street to course through the shrieks of saws and limbs dangling in unanesthetized aerial surgery, turning at last into the faculty parking lot and into Gibbs' limited vista from a second floor classroom window watching Mrs Joubert alight and come toward the portal beneath him, knuckles gone white where he grasped the cold radiator staring down into the loose fullness of her approach till it was gone beneath the sill, and he turned back to the darkened classroom to face the talking face in flattened animation on the screen itself until the tension of watching without listening broke the surface in a slight twitch of his own lip and turned him back to the window looking down, now into the wide eye of a camera aimed up at himself and the frieze of teachers similarly abandoned in windows surmounting the dedication of the school hewn over the entrance.

—ΕΒΦΜ ΣΑΟΗ ΑΘΘΦΒΡ . . .

—Oh, can you read it? asked the young man with the camera, lowering it to join the congregation of cameras, meters, and accessories strung from what convenient protrusions his lank figure afforded.

—Not exactly read it, said his companion, a scrap of paper spread on the back of a heavy book in the crook of his arm. —But I thought I'd copy it down, it might make a good epigraph for the book when I find out what it means. And get some of those blank faces. There, the one at that window having a smoke in the boys' washroom while his class is being taught by television, speaking of technological unemployment.

—I don't think that's a point the Foundation wants you to stress, particularly. But it's your book.

—But you're paying for it.

The camera snapped and joined the others, swinging to their stride as they passed in beneath the sill and out of the view of Mister Gibbs, molested from behind by words,

————Energy may be changed but not destroyed . . .

From a basement door Mister Leroy rose into the sunlight bearing a pail and his smile, intimate even at the distance turned directly up to Gibbs before there was chance to evade it, as he glided over the gravel in the silence of the boxing shoes laced tightly to the image of nonviolence his passage insisted everywhere he went.

————Scientists believe that the total amount of energy in the world today is the same as it was at the beginning of time . . .

—Turn that off . . .

—But wait Mister Gibbs it's not over, that's our studio lesson we'll be tested on . . .

—All right let's have order here, order . . . ! he'd reached the set himself and snapped it into darkness. —Put on the lights there, now. Before we go any further here, has it ever occurred to any of you that all this is simply one grand misunderstanding? Since you're not here to learn anything, but to be taught so you can pass these tests, knowledge has to be organized so it can be taught, and it has to be reduced to information so it can be organized do you follow that? In other words this leads you to assume that organization is an inherent property of the knowledge itself, and that disorder and chaos are simply irrelevant forces that threaten it from outside. In fact it's exactly the opposite. Order is simply a thin, perilous condition we try to impose on the basic reality of chaos . . .

—But we didn't have any of this, you . . .

—That's why you're having it now! Just once, if you could, if somebody in this class could stop fighting off the idea of trying to think. All
right, it all comes back to this question of energy doesn't it, a concept that
can't be understood without a grasp of the second law of, yes? Can't you
hear me in the back there?

—This wasn't in the reading assignment and that . . .

—And that . . . he paused to align pencils on his desk all pointing in
the same direction before he looked up to her far in the back bunched
high and girlish by a princess waist, bangs shading the face pancaked into
concert with her classmates in the shadowless vacancy of youth, —that
is why I am telling it to you now. Now, the concept we were discussing
yesterday, first a definition . . . ?

—The tendency of a body which when it is at rest to . . .

—Never mind, next . . . ?

—And which when it is in motion to re . . .

—I said never mind! No one . . . ? Does anyone dare try to spell it
then . . . ? He turned reaching high enough on the board to pull up his
jacket for a glimpse of blue drawers through a hole in the trouser seat,
wrote e and waited.

—E?

—Yes e, obviously. What comes next.

—N?

Gibbs repeated —n, and wrote it.

—D? as the bell rang.

—Correct, t, r, o, p, y, he finished the word and broke the chalk in
emphatic underline, turning past the toss of blonde hair repeated in the
thighs as she stood up and joined the surge of disorder at his back, his
lower lip now caught between his teeth in a way that seemed to dam his
spirit as he regained the window and the open parking lot below where
now, all continent and unaware of fragmentation in another mind's eye,
Mister diCephalis came carrying a child's umbrella in the congruous
fashion it feigned here in the small, rolled, black, its handle a curve of
simulated birch hooked on his wrist as he passed under the inscribed
lintel and pushed at the glass door that never yet had opened in and did
not now, stopped to unlimber the umbrella, pulled the door open, and
moved at home through crowd and noise toward a door of wood and
thick as his wrist which swung lightly closed behind him, not for being
well hung but because its hollow core reduced it to a swinging sign for
the word Principal and a sounding board diffusing the racket in the hall
into the presence of moderation and benign achievement themselves
diffused, along with the Horatio Alger award and fifty-six honorary degrees when hung, high in the confines of a single face framed cheaply on
the wall in witness "that confidence, a belief in ourselves, individually
and collectively, is a very important feature in the degree of activity you
normally anticipate in our economy," resolve that "if we have the cour-

age, if we have got, you might say, the widely held determination to move courageously, there is no question in my mind but that it would be helpful," only the eyes tinged with alert vexation over "whether or not a campaign for bringing about this kind of confidence is the best thing, I haven't thought of that as a public relations problem that has yet come to me . . ."

—The fear psychology, the drills, all that stuff and junk, came the voice of Miss Flesch hacking through the diffusion that bore him on toward the inner office, eyes lowered from initial confrontation where she'd look at him, at anyone, her own eyes wide and wild as though she'd been touched privately or slapped. —It's not the kids, they think the drills are a game, crawling under their desks and everything, they have a ball. It's the parents that make the trouble, she concluded through bread, the gone bite in her seed roll smeared with lipstick like the coffee cup at her knee on the desk, and the cigarette, raised quivering now her contact lenses were in focus and she looked at him with neither that precipitate outrage nor, in fact, much interest at all, as he surreptitiously rid himself of the umbrella, hooked it on the rim of a metal school wastebasket, before advancing to shake hands.

—Dan? Mister Hyde, on our new school board. This is Dan diCephalis, Mister . . .

—Major Hyde, Dan. Good meeting you . . . loomed worsted with a bluish tinge in arbitrary sway over the pastel arrangement behind the desk, cordially drawing Mister diCephalis half out of a sleeve of knife edge pressed nondescript. —We all know Dan here from the school television. Driver training, right Dan?

—That, ah, yes I started giving that course but . . .

—Did a fine job too Major, but Vogel's taken that chore on now. Vogel, the coach, he has a real sense of ahm, of cars, yes and doing a very fine job. We've saved Dan's talents here for . . .

—Some elementary math and physics . . .

—On tape, Miss Flesch closed in and bit and scarred her bun and smiled the lipstick on her teeth.

—Dan's our school psychologist now, or psycho . . . psycho . . .

—metrician. Psycho . . .

—Psychometrician, yes. In charge of all our testing and, and doing a fine job, yes. That's why I wanted him in on this ahm, these budget questions, this equipment, some of the new testing equipment . . .

—We're talking about the new testing equipment, Dan.

—It's quite a budget item, yes. Now the need to justify the test results, of course, in order to justify the test results in terms of the ongoing situation, in other words, this equipment item is justified when we testor tailing, tailor testing to the norm, and since the only way we can establish this norm, in terms of this ongoing situation that is to say, is by the testing itself, somebody's going to get left out in the cold, right?

A boy who scores out at the idiot-genius level, this music-math correlation, perfectly consistent but he's running around town sticking people up with a toy pistol. Then here's one with no future at all on the standard aptitudes, but I was told . . .

—It isn't the equipment it's the holes, in this computerized scoring the holes that have been punched in some of the cards don't, aren't consistent with forecasts in the personality testing, the norm in each case should . . .

—Right Dan, the norm in each case supporting, or we might say being supported, substantiated that is to say, by an overall norm, so that in other words in terms of the testing the norm comes out as the norm, or we have no norm to test against, right? So that presented in these terms the equipment can be shown to justify itself, in budgetary terms that is to say, would you agree, Major?

—I'll say one thing Dan, if you can present it at the budget meeting the way Whiteback's just presented it here no one will dare to argue with you, and I don't think you need to bring up these problems with your holes Dan. Might be misunderstood, lead you right back into questions about all this teaching equipment you people bought here last year that's not even unpacked.

—There's nothing wrong with it at all it's just that we, that nobody understands how to use it.

—How to utilize it yes, but . . .

—What you can't get through people's heads, when you're dealing with these grants and aid federal, state, foundations whatever it is, if you don't spend you don't get. See it at the corporate level all the time, mention an initial outlay and they grab for their wallets take this shelter idea now . . .

—Major Hyde headed up our Civil Defense Program here Dan, you may remem . . .

—Before it turned into a milksop rescue outfit and lost sight of the basics Dan, we're talking about bringing your mobile tv unit over and giving these youngsters a looksee at my shelter, show them what . . .

—Yes well of course Dan may have ahm, may not have been living here yet when it was built back in the ahm, and did a very fine job of course when it was built before the . . .

—Before the whole country lost sight of the basics Dan, we all saw it spread right up to the national level and giving these fine youngsters a good looksee at my shelter will get them off to a fresh start, show them what America's all about, what we have to protect . . .

—Yes well the youngsters of course are ahm, are youngsters yes but incorporating this shelter proposal in the new budget may not ahm, Vern that is to say, I don't think Vern will . . .

—I don't think Vern's head's screwed on Whiteback, if you're going to let a District Superintendent like Vern dictate to the parents of these future citizens that they can't exercise their democratic right to vote on an issue that may decide the whole . . .

—Yes well of course I think Senator ahm, Congressman Pecci he's dropping by to fill us in on the chances for locating this new Cultural Center here and of course his ahm, yes is that him?

—Tell him to wait, said Miss Flesch through bread, and banged the phone down.

—Wait we can't keep him waiting, he's . . .

—It's not him no it's Skinner, this textbook salesman Mister Skinner . . . she knotted her knees, —for me.

—I'm sorry Major yes Miss Flesch here, Miss Flesch doubles in brass you might say, our top studio teacher you know that and our curriculum specialist too, she's . . .

—Glad to see somebody who's not afraid of work. Getting this budget across is going to take everything we can give it, they'll be there with their hands on their wallets and their youngsters' educations will be the last thing on their minds, take this shelter proposal if they have a good look at one before they pile in and tear the idea to pieces they . . .

—Hello . . . ? Yes, yes send him right in . . .

—Mister . . .

—Congressman . . . ?

—No it's only, it's Mister Skinner . . . she recovered her balance and her knees one to the other —I'll be right out, she called at the figure retreating through the door weighted by a briefcase of Gladstone bag design past the threat of pinstripe coming up behind.

—Come in Senator come in, I know it's still Congressman just getting in the habit . . .

—Mister . . .

—Whiteback, Major . . .

—diCephalis, Dan, the school . . .

—Great pleasure . . .

—Congressman . . .

—And Miss Flesch here kind of doubles in brass you might say, right Whiteback? Handles the curriculum, and she's shaping up as a real video personality on the school tv. We're just checking out a few items before the taxpayers get their teeth into this budget, Hyde went on as the blue stone ring borne on Pecci's hand ceased darting about in handshakes and withdrew to highlight his pinstripe presence. —The only thing on their minds is their tax rate and most of them don't even know that, right Whiteback? As president of the bank and principal of this school setup Whiteback here gets a grandstand look at both sides of the coin, take the whole idea of locating this Cultural Center here, I don't see why we can't tie it right in with . . .

—Once we have their confidence . . .

—Now whether or not a campaign for bringing about this kind of confidence is the best thing, I haven't thought of that as a public relations problem, but let's not forget above all things the need of confidence, and that . . .

—Of course, I think nationally, it's what you and I think of the prospects . . .

—PRwise it can't hurt us educationwise, Miss Flesch got in through bread.

—In fact, tie it all right into this shelter item too, let people have a look with your mobile tv unit. My boy could give it sort of a tour in fact, he knows it inside out. Wall thickness, ventilation, food storage waste disposal get in a little about what America really is, what we . . .

—Just give them an inch, like with the religious holidays if they all get off Good Friday the Jewish parents want them off Seder too . . .

—Is Seder a holiday? I thought it was a . . .

—Fight over prayers in the school and that gets us right into the transportation mess, they vote against busing the Catholic kids to parochial school and we can get thirteen hundred of them dumped on us over night, then where are we?

—And take this one, custodial salaries, two hundred and thirty-three-odd thousand, up from two seventeen . . .

—Ask Mister Leroy, that's his baby.

—Right. You mention education and they grab for their wallets. Now here's thirty-two thousand six hundred and seventy for blacktopping the parking lot over to the tv studio.

—That's the only bid that came in.

—And there's this twelve thousand dollars item for books.

—That's supposed to be twelve hundred, the twelve thousand should be paper towels. Besides, there's already that bequest for books for the library.

—Did it say books in so many words? No. It's just a bequest for the library.

—Use it for a pegboard. You need a pegboard in a library. Books you don't know what you're getting into.

—Right. Remember Robin Hood? That man Schepperman . . .

—Schepperman! That reminds me that lettering over the front door, Gibbs' idea . . .

—It's worked so far but it can't work forever, sooner or later somebody will show up who reads Greek. Then where are we?

—Up the creek, Miss Flesch obliged with a promptness that lost her some coffee down her chin, —like the smut mail.

—There's an issue. The smut mail rise.

—My boy sent off for a ball glove and what he got back in the mail was . . .

—Mouthpiece puller, sleigh bells, strobotuner, choir risers, tympanies, marching bell and stand, two thousand five hundred and . . . what's all that for?

—Breakage. Here, replacing glass, repairing doors, painting, refinishing and so forth, thirty-three thousand two eighty-five. Thirty-three thousand dollars for breakage, isn't that what we're really talking about? Plain unvarnished vandalism? And another fourteen thousand plus item down here, repairs and replacement, chairs, desks, project tables, pianos, same thing isn't it? Breakage . . . ?

—But two thousand dollars for filmstrips and five more on filmstrip projectors, movie projectors, record players, tape recorders, projection carts . . .

—It's already on the books . . .

—That's what I mean books, Miss Flesch scattered seeds. —All this audio-visual bla bla bla and we've practically promised Duncan and Company a textbook order to Mister Skinner for . . .

—Thirty-three and fourteen, that's forty-three, forty-seven thousand on breakage.

—Waffle iron, sixty dollars?

—Predictable, deliberate, you might even say prescheduled breakage . . .

—And doing a very fine job, too.

—I see it at the corporate level all the time. Now, getting back to the point, how about Friday for bringing your mobile tv over for a looksee at my shelter, get across the remote capabilities of microwave transmission with a good cable system . . .

—But not Friday, Friday we're getting a visit from the Foundation. They're sending out a team, a program specialist and a writer, to give our whole in-school television setup here the real once over for a book. I don't hardly need to say that the point in all this is to show them how we're using, utilizing this new media to motivate the cultural drive in these youngsters should give things a nice boost right up their . . .

—Up their alley, check. My shelter . . .

—My Ring . . . Miss Flesch got in at a bite.

—My wife . . . ventured Mister diCephalis, who had been busy responding to Mister Pecci's stylish appearance by squaring the handkerchief in his own breast pocket, leaving it with apparent satisfaction and a clean margin showing between the pocket's edge and the line of dirt that had distinguished the initialed fold on view there now for some weeks.

And as though calculating the effect, Hyde stepped from the window and reduced the figure behind the desk to the less pungent proportions of natural lighting. —The Foundation is committed up to its, it's deeply committed. They've sunk seventy or eighty million into this school tv project nationwide and they're not pulling out and leaving setups like this one holding the bag. The point like I've been saying from the start is that in-school tv, to be in-school tv, it has to be in-school tv with lessons piped into school receivers in school classrooms for school kids in school classes, a simple interference-free closed-circuit school setup where every Tom Dick and Harry can't tune in on the kind of open-circuit broadcast you've got now and write letters telling you off on the new math.

—Educationwise it isn't hurting us PRwise, I'll say that, Miss Flesch said it, and mashed out her cigarette.

—Now the Senator here, Assembleyman Pecci that is, he has a bill he's introducing that makes all this mandratory, it will get this in-school television out of the community entertainment field and back into the school, and the only squawk we'll get from the Foundation is because they stuck you with this whole open-circuit setup in the first place.

—I don't get mail telling me off . . . Miss Flesch threatened with a buttered thumb. —I get all this mail . . .

—She gets all this fan mail.

—All this fan mail you could call it even, she pursued from the desk top to Mister Pecci who seemed, just then, to realize that from where he sat he might appear to be looking up her skirt, and lowered his eyes to adjust a gold tieclasp representing an unfurled American flag to match his cuff links. —Not just mail from kids' parents but from shut-ins, jobless, old retired people and everybody like just last week I got this letter of commendation from the Senior Citizens, you need popular support to run a school system and you don't get that without the support of the community look at this budget vote coming up and all that bla bla bla, they want to see where their money goes. I got nothing to hide, she came on, and pinioned a passing eye with the barest movement urging —my Ring, you take my Ring . . .

—We take her Ring, Pecci responded to this invitation, and then raised his eyes to the others, —there might even be some way to tie it into the cultural, something cultural?

—Let's give Pecci here an A for breakthrough. Tie it in with this Culture Center, locating it here, bring in your Spring Arts Festival expanded with a few remote specials stressing the patriotic theme, you might even do one on my shelter, what America's all about, waste disposal and all, and wrap it all up with the whole in-school television program once that's on a good interference-free closed-circuit system bring in a little Foundation backing and you're on your way.

—Once we have their confidence . . .

—Now whether or not a campaign . . .

—I think nationally . . .

—PRwise . . .

The telephone rang. —Hello . . . ? Oh. Yes. Long distance, for you Mis . . .

—Me? Oop! my coffee . . .

—My office . . . Pecci inclined across the desk avoiding the puddle. —I told them where to reach me if . . . Hello?

—And something else, Whiteback reclined with a squeak, —this young man what's his name, Bast? He's a composer, he writes music, he's here from the Foundation or rather they placed him here, in this pilot program. Handed to us on a platter, he's ahm . . .

—Me? paid to me? No, it was paid to the law firm, my partner. Just say twenty-five thousand paid for consultation, representation, and what? No, say legal services, rendered by Ganganelli during this legislative session in conjunction with . . . no, conjunction, conjunk, junk . . .

—Motivating the music appreciation drive in these youngsters, we have him helping out Miss Flesch while we work something up for him maybe with the high school band.

—In conjunction with certain amendments to the state law relating to highway construction standards, just say standards in highway construction.

—I talked to him about it on the way over this morning, motivating this cultural drive and seeing it pay off in mass consumers, mass distribution . . .

—No, standards. I said standards, standards, with a d . . .

—Like automobiles and bathing suits.

—Law! They can't pull that law on him tell him, it wasn't even passed till after he wasn't reelected . . . Goodbye, call me if there's any snag.

—On her Ring, yes and, and doing a very fine job . . .

—He helps some, rehearsing and all that stuff and junk but he hasn't got much personality for it . . . here, gimme one of those, will you? She swooped at Mister diCephalis quietly disposing of a cigarette package in the wastebasket.

—No, I . . . they're candy, he blurted. —The children's. I picked them up by mistake, they look just like mine, the package . . .

She laughed at him.

The telephone rang.

—Hel . . . oh, what? Now? They're here from the Foundation? They can't be, this isn't Friday. Well try and stall them . . .

—Gimme the phone, my . . .

—My boy's in this thing of hers, Hyde dropped to Pecci, —quite the little musician. No piano or violin, nothing pansy. Trumpet.

—My wife's taping something this morning, Mister diCephalis got in abruptly. —A resource program . . .

—Let's just turn on the tube and see what we've got to show them.

—Taping? what, said Miss Flesch over the rim of the telephone.

—A resource program. On silkworms, she has her own Kashmiri records . . .

—If your Ring isn't ready, your Wagner, what is there?

—My Mozart. She hung up the telephone and dialed again. —No answer, I'll call and see if my visuals are ready . . . and she found her bun, washed in another bite with cold coffee and chewed into the mouthpiece, listening.

——gross profit on a business was sixty-five hundred dollars a year. He finds his expenses were twenty-two and one half percent of this profit. First, can you find the net profit?

—What's that? demanded Hyde, transfixed by unseeing eyes challenging the vacant confine just over his head.
—Sixth grade math. That's Glancy.

——percent this would be of the entire sales, if the sales were seventy thousand dol . . .

—Sixth? That?
—Glancy. They're doing percents.

——merchant, and this merchant sold a coat marked fifty dollars at ten percent discount . . .

—Glancy reading cue cards. You can tell.
—Don't show them that, just Glancy writing on a blackboard.

——that this merchant still made a twenty percent profit, let's find the cost of the original . . .

—Try switching to thirty-eight.

——original cost of the . . . combustion ir. these thousands of little cylinders in our muscle engines. Like all engines, these tiny combustion engines need a constant supply of fuel, and we call the fuel that this machine uses, food. We measure its value . . .

—Even if the Rhinegold is ready it's Wagner, isn't it? But if the Mozart is scheduled the classroom teachers, they're ready with the followup material from their study guides on the Mozart. They can't just switch to the Wagner.

——the value of the fuel for this engine the same way, by measuring how much heat we get when it's burned . . .

—That's a cute model, it gets the idea right across. Whose voice?
—Vogel. He made it himself out of old parts.
—Whose.
—Parts?
—Some of them might never even have heard of Wagner yet.
—No, the voice.
—That's Vogel, the coach.

——that we call energy. Doing a regular day's work, this human machine needs enough fuel equal to about two pounds of sugar . . .

—If they thought it was Mozart's Rhinegold and get them all mixed up, so you can't really switch.
—He put it together himself out of used parts.

——fuel in a regular gasoline engine, and converts about twelve percent into the same amount of real work.

—To forty-two, try forty-two.

——that the engine has an alimentary system just like the human machine. When you pull up at the gas pump and ask for ten gallons the fuel is poured through an opening, or mouth, and goes into the gas tank, the engine's stomach . . . who earns a hundred and twenty-five dollars a month pays four percent of it to the Social Security . . .

—I said forty-two, try forty-two. I think Mrs Joubert has something.

——how much he's paid to the Social Security Board at the end of ten years, and . . . American Civil War, that was fought to free the slaves, and . . . in the carburetor, where the fuel is digested and . . .

—Omigosh! Miss Flesch erupted into the mouthpiece. Her free hand dug for a tissue —they're what? Over at the temple? Not the Rhinegold, the Wagner no, the . . . No m, m like Mary. O. Yeah like zebra . . . she wiped her mouth, —What do you mean will I play the piano the only prop I've got is a . . . no a book, a book . . . A book yeah so it looks like I'm reading from this book and don't forget the music for my singalong, I always sign off with a singalong . . .

—Go back to whatever that was about the Civil War, I think that's history . . .

——that we wouldn't like the taste of gasoline but luckily our car engine . . .

—Or Social Studies.

——the American Indian, who is no longer segregated on the reservation, but encouraged to take his rightful place at the side of his countrymen, in the cities, in the factories, on the farm . . .

—Just hang on, I'm coming over there anyway. Yeah, driving, I'll get a ride over if . . . she banged down the phone, dismounting the desk in an open slide toward Mister Pecci. —Is Skinner's car still out front? It's a green one, this textbook salesman. He'll ride me over . . .

—My wife, said Mister Pecci withdrawing a knee from the sweep of her heel, —she was one of the original Miss Rheingolds, maybe she still has a specialty number she could help you out with introducing your Rhinegold story . . . ?

—See you all on the hungry eye, said Miss Flesch winking one of her own and threatening one of Mister Pecci's with a sweep of the umbrella under her arm, and whether Mister diCephalis was making a last grab for it or fending it off was not clear as she passed him for the door that banged hollowly on her call to —Skinner, Mister Skinner, can you ride me over . . .

Mister diCephalis had by now reached and dialed the telephone, where he kept in undertone —Yes I know it that's why I'm calling, because . . . from the Foundation yes they're here now, that's what they're coming for, to . . . what? The silkworms, yes, the Kashmiri . . .

cultural aspect of . . . yes. But I do want them to see you, that's why I'm calling . . .

—They must be out there now they, we can't keep them waiting . . . Whiteback inclined to meet the screen's glassine stare with his own reaching the channel selector, —if there's something on while we're waiting for the, for Miss Flesch something in the, something . . .

——about money . . . to free the slaves and . . . typifying the grandeur of our natural resources and the national heritage that makes all of us proud to be Amer . . .

—That's good, there . . .

—What is it Dan, what's . . .

—I'm cleaning up this coffee she wait, wait this must be hers this book about Mozart Mozart's letters, she . . .

—Look out you're spilling those what's all that it looks like her script, part of her script get it over to her, there's a page under the . . .

—Mind moving your foot . . .

—There's another one . . .

——the mighty Sequoia, which may reach a height of three hundred fifty feet and be almost thirty feet at the base. An age of a thousand years old is still young for the mighty Sequoia . . .

—Wait the pages are getting mixed up she'll be . . .

—Let her straighten them out just get it over to her wait there's one under the desk, have you got your car Dan?

——national parks. In the vast public domain, the federal government owns one hundred seventy million acres in our glorious west . . .

—No just hurry Dan, hurry up or she'll come in! We thought you'd never get here . . . and he opened the door full on the two figures standing there as the wall clock beyond them dropped its longer hand with a click for the full minute and hung, poised to lop off a fragment of the next as Gibbs passed, looked up and saw that happen, fingering the change in his pocket on his way to the outside door and the cloudless sky filled with the even passage of the sun itself in brightness so diffuse no shadow below could keep an edge on shaded lawns where time and the day came fallen through trees with the mottled movement of light come down through water, spread up an empty walk, over gravel and empty pavement, and lawn again, lending movement to the child motionless but for fragmenting finger and opposable thumb opening, closing, the worn snap of an old change purse, staring in through the glass with an expression of unbroken and intent vacancy.

Beyond the glass, the boy inside darted a glance from his newspaper out into the purse snapped open; snapped shut, he smoothed the porous fold of the obituary page away from him, nagged his lip with a pencil and then scratched his knee with it before his foot returned to forcing back, and forth, and back, the idle vent on a floor grating, shut, open, shut, as the light on his paper dimmed with the sun abruptly pocketed in a cloud and what shadow the child beyond had cast was lost beneath the trees where she sought the greenest leaves fallen from the pin oaks shading the grass around her. The largest she found, she folded its dark face in, creasing across the veins, then folded another as carefully chosen over it, pausing with one blown here from a maple and slightly discolored, the green already run from its edges but folded at last with the others stained back outside and snapped all together into the purse, as a wind rustled those on the ground around her and touched the trees above, the cloud past, their movement scattering the sunlight against the glass, never disturbing those within.

—Rhine . . . G O L D! they howled into the glare of footlights, cowering round the empty table at the center of the stage.

—Rhinemaidens! . . . The baton rapped sharply through their declining wail. —This is your shout of triumph. A joyful cry! Bast thumped out the theme again on the piano, missed a note, winced, repeated it. —Can't you sound joyful, Rhinemaidens? Look, look around you. The river is glittering with golden light. You're swimming around the rock where the Rhinegold is. The Rhinegold! You love the Rhinegold Rhinemaidens, you . . .

—So where's the Rhinegold?

—We're pretending it's on the table there, you're all swimming around . . .

—No like she means we can pretend we're out here swimming like around this old table which we can even pretend it's this big rock but there's nothing on it, like there's nothing which we can pretend it's this here Rhinegold.

Again he tapped the baton against the music stand. —The art department has promised the real Rhinegold for Friday, so today you'll just have to pretend. Pretend it's there shimmering and glittering, you're swimming around it protecting it, but you don't dream it's in danger. You don't dream anyone would dare try to steal it, even when the dwarf appears. The dwarf Alberich, who comes first seeking love . . . what's the matter there?

—Like if we're all so beautiful who would want to love this here lousy little dwarf?

—Well, that . . . that's what happens, isn't it. You don't. You laugh at his . . . his advances, and that hurts him, it hurts him so deeply that he decides he'll take the Rhinegold instead, so that he can . . . where is he now, Alberich the dwarf, where is he . . . ? Bast rattled the baton briskly against the music stand, and a trumpet blast shattered the comparative quiet. —What was that!

A salute stirred from the shadows in the wings. —That's where I come in here with the trumpet when you hit that thing with your stick, answered a martial miniature advancing into the glare with a clatter of knife and ax, flashlight, whistle, compass, and a coil of rope crowding his small waist.

—You come in when I point the baton right at you, and you come in playing the Rhinegold motif. Now what was that you think you just played?

—The Call to the Colors, anybody knows that. Besides I don't even know this here Rhinegold thing and my father said I probly should play this anyway because it's the best thing I can play.

—Well, what else can you play.

—Nothing.

Bast rested his head on his right hand, weakly flexing his left and studying the gouge on its back as a smart slap of salute wheeled the trumpeter off in the general direction of Valhalla, and he gave them the key with a chord.

—And like right here Miss Flesch said might be a good place for our specialty numbers, like we already have ballet tap and toe and if we're on the school tv and all . . .

—You . . . straighten that out with her.

—She's going to be here today?

—That's a good question, Bast muttered. —Has anyone seen her?

—I seen her, came a voice from the wings.

—This morning? Where.

—No, last night in this green car parked up in the woods with this here . . .

—That's enough! Bast, and the crack of his baton, severed that response and the billow of tittering it rode out on, breaking against the banks of empty seats; he struck the chord and with the power of music set their brittle limbs undulating in unsavory suggestion, bony fronts heaving with nameless longing straining the garlands of streaked paper and seamed up remnants of other cultural crusades, here the gold fringe of an epaulette quivered, there a gold tassel shook as, revived by Bast's flailing arm, the cry of —R H I N E gold . . . ! filled the hall, brought up short by the Call to the Colors: down the keyboard Bast darted as though fleeing that, into the Ring motif, and now more faintly, the last to realize that the stage had been taken over by one enthralling bellow. Undismayed by lack of piano accompaniment, or now the peremptory rattle of the baton, this baying augmented as the apparition drew up at the footlights for breath.

—She's being Wotan, a Flosshilde offered in awe.

—Wotan isn't on yet. You're not on yet! Bast shouted at this eruption freely adorned with horns, feathers, and bicycle reflectors, the helmet hung askew over a face where mascara awash in perspiration descended a bad complexion to streak the imbrications of silvered cardboard cover-

ing the padded bosom below. Simulated fox tails dangled at the flanks.
The spear sagged forward. —I thought you all knew, there was to be no
makeup until your actual performance, he said, and as Wotan obediently
drew a glistening forearm across that face he looked away, noting apparently for the first time the epaulettes and gold tassels trimming jackets
tailored to imaginary bosoms, the gold piped shorts cloistering assorted
hams. —What's that you're wearing there? And you . . . ?

—She's wearing her mother's falsies in there, said one Wellgunde,
delivering a Woglinde a punch in the bloated chest, bringing blushes and
brays of laughter.

—No, those gold tassels, those costumes . . .

—We got twirling after.

—You have what?

—Twirlingafter! . . . he don't even understand plain English.

—That bulletin about your costumes. Did you read it?

—We couldn't hardly. You know? Like there were all those words
in it which we didn't have them yet.

—What grade English are you in? What year?

—English?

—Like he means Communications Skills only we didn't get those
words yet, we maybe won't get them till Language Arts even.

—All right, all right, you can . . . take your places, Bast said, drawing
both hands down his face in imitation of sepulchrous calm which
promptly provoked —Uh, say there . . . from behind, and swung him
round dropping his hands to face an elderly figure being weighed unsteadily forward by the saxophone strung to his neck.

—Where do I sit?

—Sit?

—Up on the stage? or down here with you.

—Sit? You've . . . come to watch?

—Not today, no, today I'll play right along, said his guest eagerly,
fingers quivering over the keys of the saxophone. —Keep at it the doc
told me last night, just keep at it and you'll have the old muscular coordi-
nation back like a well-oiled machine in no time. You're loosening up the
old fingers yourself, eh? Your hand there? That's a nasty one, he said with
solicitous relish, drawing a folding chair nearer the piano.

But Bast had escaped to the edge of the stage where he called in a
choked tone —all right! the dwarf now, who is Alberich, the dwarf?

—That's supposed to be that boy J R, said Wotan sidling up, wiping
both hands on a fox tail. —He's only being it to get out of gym anyway,
this here little dwarf. He don't even have a costume yet.

—Well . . . where is he! Find him!

—He was reading the paper over at that window.

—He was in the front office, I seen him when I went to the girls'
room playing with the telephone in there.

—I got a cold, that's why my eyes look like this, said Wotan with a rheumy stare that sent Bast up the aisle and out the pastel hall, looking in doors till he reached the last one: there in a swivel chair a boy sat, back to the door, his cheerless patterned sweater of black diamonds on gray hunched over the desk, and a hand with a pencil stub rose over one narrow shoulder to scratch where his hair stood out in a rough tag at the nape.

—What are you doing in here! Playing with the . . .

—Playing? The chair lurched, then swung round slowly as the boy recovered the wad of a soiled handkerchief from the telephone mouthpiece as he hung it up. —Boy you scared me.

—Scared you! What are you doing in here, aren't you in this rehearsal? What are you doing here playing with the telephone . . .

—Playing? But no I was just . . . it rang. He reached for it.

—Give me that!

—But it's probably . . .

—Here! . . . What? hello? . . . Miss Flesch here? now? No, I haven't seen her all morning, she . . . Me? Bast, Edward Bast, I'm . . . What do you mean are we ready? Ready for what . . . The telephone pressed at his ear, Bast stared blankly at the boy's foot twisting under the chair's pedestal, the seam split up the back of the sneaker, and abruptly put out his hand to stop the repetition of the chair tipping forth, and back, and the boy shrugged, recovered a grimy envelope with figures penciled on its back to stuff it, with his pencil stub and wadded handkerchief, into a pocket, looped a knee over the chair arm and began to wedge the toe of his sneaker into a desk-drawer handle. —You mean right now? today? Of course it's not ready today, no. No, and listen. An old man just showed up here with a saxophone, he . . . what? What class in music therapy, where? Hello? Hello? He banged down the telephone, swerved the chair round to face the door saying —Come along, and was almost out when it rang again. —Give me that! he said catching his balance. —Hello? Who? No . . . No he's not and what's more this telephone is not . . . what? He banged it down again.

—Why'd you want to do that? the boy came hurrying out ahead of him. —It was just . . .

—Come along! Bast pressed him down the hall, eyes on the shoulders narrowed in a shrug and held there by the sweater, which was too small. —You're supposed to be up on that pile of chairs in back, Bast pursued him down the aisle —while the Rhinemaidens swim around down in front, do you know your part?

—He don't even have a costume yet grumbled Wotan, drooping in the lee of the piano like some lost sport sulking in a corridor of prehistory.

—And hunch down up there, Bast called after him. —You're supposed to look small, like a dwarf.

—He's already littler than us, Wotan obliged, swelling. —He's only in sixth grade which that's why he could be in it to be this here little dwarf which he's only being it anyway to . . .

—Get up on the stage, out of sight. Now, we . . . Bast halted. Behind him the saxophone wavered tentatively around C-flat. —Wait a minute! Where is it! That paper bag that was here on the piano.

—You always carry your money like that?

—It's not mine, that money. It belongs to Mrs Joubert's class. Where is it!

—Hey, see? here? a Rhinemaiden giggled from the stage. —See? Like for the Rhinegold, with real money so we can really pretend, see?

—That one's my type, the saxophonist confided over Bast's shoulder as he sat to the piano. —Maybe you can . . . but he was cut off as Bast came down with an E-flat chord that sent the boy scaling the peak of the stacked chairs and the Rhinemaidens wriggling and howling by turns below, arching limbs and brazening impertinent bodies in what quite rightly they believed to be lewd invitation, whispering, perspiring, cowering to the blast of the Call to the Colors obliterating a brief saxophone chorus of Buffalo Gals while, in sinister pianissimo, making good use of his unimpaired hand, Bast echoed the Ring motif oblivious, staring, up into the stage illumination on the dwarf's uncostumed threadbare scaffolded above the caterwauling, and he pounded an open way for his desperate crew through the rhythms of the Nibelungs, hand drawn up in twinges each time a finger struck among those sharp cadences teeming with injury.

—Look! Who's that up in the back there, came in a stage whisper.

—The lights, I can't see nothing . . .

—It's that fruit Leroy.

—He's too little, it's that Glancy.

—Running . . .

Faster, Bast played now as though hurrying to catch a train, straining toward the crescendo of its arrival till this, with pain that streaked to his elbow sharp as the chord he struck, was all he heard, and the cry of the dwarf was lost, —Hark floods! Love I renounce forever! . . . lost, if it was ever made at all, the figure running down the aisle reaching the piano as it crashed with the Rhinegold motif that brought the pile of chairs cascading to the stage and scattered the Rhinemaidens in disheveled pursuit of the dwarf, who seemed indeed to know his part, and had got off with the Rhinegold.

—I told you . . . ! shouted Wotan bursting out into the sun, bearing down on the only figure in sight who watched this extravagant onslaught without alarm; but all they wrested from her was the change purse, its nickeled clasp worn down to brass from being closed, and opened, and closed, opened now and on dead leaves at that, flung back to the ground indistinguishable from the leaves they trampled, drawing up in garish clumps of recrimination.

—Where'd he go? that lousy little . . .

—Look!

—Look out!

Gravel sprayed them from the drive.

—In the car, that's Mister Bast. They're chasing him in the car.

—Whose? Driving . . .

—Glancy. That big lardass Glancy . . .

—It wasn't either that's deSyph, that old junk heap that's deSyph's . . . and they drifted off to tell, over groundswells of lawn heaving with the slow rise, and fall, of light broken by the gentle sway of trees on winds bearing news, from higher up, of a used car sale blown down on retching waves of the tune Clementine to the wailing counterpoint of the saws in Burgoyne Street, where the used car plunged among the dangling limbs.

—The lesson's all set up, the visuals everything right from the teacher's guide . . . and the brief prospect of a straightaway freed his hand from the wheel to turn on the radio. —The script that's her script and that book, that's to pretend like you're reading it it's a prop . . .

—But this money, the boy who ran off with that paper bag we were using it in the Rhinegold rehears . . .

—You don't need it no, for the Mozart that Rhinegold bag it would throw off everything the testing, the whole . . .

—It's not that it's the money, it's the money . . .

Steel teeth overhead shredded a descending bloat of Clementine as the radio warmed to Dark Eyes, and the driver shifted in a seated schottische overshooting a turn to the right. —My wife will help you out don't worry, she's waiting for us I already called her and I told you about the singalong, don't forget the singa . . .

—But then maybe your wife could . . .

—Help out yes she has a resource program on right after, she's in the arts too maybe you know her? B'hai, folk song, preColumbian sculpture . . . he cut short with a grimace that might have been merely the effort of swerving to a halt at the door where he promptly resumed the catalog in introducing —my wife Ann Mister Bast, she had the Senior Citizens' class in clay sculpture too, the ones with arthritis here, wait! don't forget the script . . . before leaving Bast in a spray of gravel, where Mrs diCephalis took his hand and kept it.

—In this way, she led him, raising the folds of a many-colored sari to pick her way over the maze of cables, into —an intimate medium, it really is, because when you look into the camera you're looking each child right in the eye, she said flashing him a blacked sweep of hers over a shoulder. —When I'm on camera, I just keep repeating to myself I am speaking to a single child. I am speaking to a single child, over and over. That's what makes it intimate . . . She stopped abruptly in the shadow of a stage flat so that he ran up against her and discreetly lowered his eyes from the caste mark that had begun to run on her forehead, past the distinct lashes, nose shadowed retroussé and white teeth, to come up short on a gape in the sari where her brassiere strap hung errant and anomalous. —I do my own makeup but these are my own eyelashes, I'm naturally dark, she said, taking his attempt to withdraw his hand as provocation to hold it in both of hers. —You see, I am a talented woman, Mister Bast, who has never been allowed to do anything . . . Somewhere a bell rang but she held him in an instant longer, with peristaltic reluctance let him slip away —in there, we'll look in there first. It's where the director monitors the programs.

On the screen was Smokey Bear.

——pledge as an American to save and faithfully to defend from waste, the natural resources of my country, its soil and minerals, its forests, waters, and wildlife.

—The youngsters find it reassuring, said Hyde looking up from Smokey Bear. —Like seeing a commercial.

—Yes, in terms of implementing the study material, Whiteback continued as his guests came to rest on the small sofa under their litter of cameras, coats, pamphlets, brochures and notepaper, —into a meaningful learning experience . . .

——a series of collapsible pipes, called the intestines . . .

—Thirty-seven thousand five hundred, came Pecci's voice from the inner office, —for legislative services rendered in conjunction with proposition thirteen on the referendum on pay subscription televis, you'd better call me back on this . . .

——of America, the free enterprise system, and man's modern industrial know-how, have forged a two edged sword which at one fell swoop has severed the barrier between . . .

—What's that?

—The American flag, said Mister Pecci joining them, glittering at the cuff.

—Oh, the film. It's on film, a resource film on ahm, natural resources, Mister Hyde's company was kind enough to provide . . .

—What America is all about, said Hyde standing away from the set with a proprietary air. —What we have to . . .

—To use, or rather utilize . . .

——like the iceberg, rising to a glittering peak above the surface. For like the iceberg, we see only a small fraction of modern industry. Hidden from our eyes is the vast . . .

—Gibbs? Is that you? Come in, come in.

—No, don't let me disturb you . . .

—Yes come in, we have some people here from the Foundation, Whiteback insisted. —Their Program Specialist Mister Ford . . . An arm rose from the clutter of cameras, —and Mister Gall here. Mister Gall here is a writer. Mister Gibbs here is the what you might call chief cook and bottle washer on our science program and . . . doing a fine job, yes. Mister Gall here is getting material together on the Foundation's whole in-school television support program, Gibbs. They're going to publish it in book form.

—Bitten off quite an assignment, Mister Gall. I imagine you need all the information you can get, said Hyde abruptly threatening him with a thick brochure from above. —I just happened to have this research report with me. It's a pretty good rundown of long-term operating cost estimates on closed-circuit cable setups, compared to what you run into trying to carry a full lesson load on open-circuit broadcasting. I picked it up to show the Senator here, Congressman, Pecci . . .

——energy still locked in the vast shale oil deposits beneath thousands of barren mountain peaks jutting from the sea of the public domain, two thirds of the state of Utah . . .

—Structuring the material in terms of the ongoing ahm, situation yes, on Mozart's, ah, Ring, is it?

—I noticed something here . . . Mister Ford spoke for the first time with the commanding indifference of an old-school drawl, running his finger down a catalogued list —here, The Rhinegold is it?

—Oh, you have one of our schedules, we . . . having trouble locating one, this use of, utilization of . . .

—Schepperman?

—Schepperman? Yes well he, ahm, it was his idea originally. This doing this Ring, before he, before we replaced him. He, ah, painted, taught painting, that was before we replaced him of course, a little trouble over the loyalty oath provision . . .

—Little? Mister Pecci repeated, opening pinstripe over his glittering tieclasp in a campaign gesture. —Like being a little bit pregnant, eh?

—Yes well of course the, on the cultural aspect of the arts we have a studio teacher now, Whiteback came on at the brightness control, —a video personality that motivates a really meaningful learning experience in these youngsters . . .

——Everybody has a laughing place, to go, hol hol

The face of Wolfgang Amadeus Mozart shimmered on the screen.

——To go hol hol

—Here she is now yes, I think she taped this audio part, introducing this, music appreciation this is, in terms of closed-circuit capabilities this . . .

—In terms of tangibilitating the full utilization potential of in-school television . . .

—Something for the pit and something for the gallery, murmured Mister Ford.

—Making the artist really come alive for these youngsters. Humanizing them, the artists that is to say, motivating . . .

—Warm bodies . . .

——Today, boys and girls . . .

—Who's that?

—The Mozart. It's . . .

—No. The voice . . .

——fairy tale life of the composer Wolfgang Amadeus Mozart. Even his name, Amadeus, or in German, Gottlieb, means beloved by the gods . . .

—Remind me to call him later, about the fire sprinklers, Whiteback inclined toward Hyde in undertone.

—Call who.

—Gottlieb, about the fire sprinklers.

——darling of the gods, this little Peter Pan of music who never really grew up, a real life fairy tale that takes us from the glittering courts of Europe to a scene in a great thunderstorm. There's even a mysterious messenger of death in this tale, filled with magic and enchantment . . .

—That's not Dan, is it? the voice? muttered Hyde, as the camera shuddered down the spangle-decked embroidery of a sleeve to fingers drawn poised on a keyboard.

——apple cheeks, dressed in silks of lilac and gold, was barely seven years old when he played for the court in Vienna and the Emperor called him my little magician. In Naples the superstitious Italians even made him take off a ring he was wearing, to prove it wasn't a magic ring that gave him his magical powers . . .

And in response to a querulous growl from Mister Pecci the still picture on the screen gave way to a face staring directly at the viewers, glistening with perspiration.

——playing and composing music since the age of four. By the time he was fourteen Mozart had written sonatas, a symphony, even an opera . . .

—This is our, our composer in residence, Whiteback blurted with what sounded like relief. —He's been working with our ahm curriculum specialist she thought he needed, must have thought he needed exposure to the ahm, to do a very fine job of course we have you Foundation people to thank . . .

——rich people who commissioned work from artists and gave them money. Mozart wrote beautiful music for his patron until he left the Archbishop's house to marry a beautiful girl named Constanze. Later Mozart told a friend, when my wife and I were married we both burst into tears, and that shows us what a really human person this great genius really was doesn't it boys and girls. His wife's name Constanze means constancy, and she was constant to her dear childlike husband all the rest of his, of his, his cheap coffin in the rain that . . .

—A little heavy on the talking face, came murmured from the heap of cameras on the sofa —and you want a little more spontaneity here where he's shuffling pages around like that, come in close on the way his hands are shaking, it looks a little forced . . .

———the um, constant yes she, she constantly spent what little money they had on luxuries and she, she was constantly pregnant and she, finally she was constantly sick so you can see why she, why Mozart burst into tears when he married her. He was always the, this little darling of the gods he'd supported his whole family since he was a child being dragged around by his father and shown off like a, like a little freak . . .

—He, he seems to be departing somewhat from the ahm, the . . .
—They needed a stronger key light on that waist shot when he threw out the script, get across a lot more spontaneity without it . . .

———money, he wrote three of his greatest symphonies in barely two months while he was running around begging for loans wherever he . . .

—Yes Miss ah, Miss Flesch will probably take over any minute she, it's her program, studio lesson that is to say of course on our budget we can't go all out on ahm, on these enrichment programs in music, just in music alone we're already spending just on band uniforms alone . . .

———three more piano concertos, two string quintets, and the three finest operas ever written, and he's desperate, undernourished, exhausted, frantic about money while his wife runs up doctor bills and he's pawning everything in sight just in order to work, to keep working . . .

—You've got to watch those hot lights on these close shots.
—Yes he, he needs a haircut . . . and the full face on the screen dissolved to a wigged profile where the camera sought something of interest in the composer's baleful eye.

———think he was childish, she was twice as childish and, and oh yes this mysterious stranger dressed all in gray who Mozart thought was a messenger of death, it was really just a messenger from a crackbrain named Walsegg who wanted some music for his dead wife. He couldn't write a requiem so he wanted to hire Mozart to, and then pretend he'd written it himself. What else could Mozart do? He's sick, worn out, used up, he's only about thirty-five and he's been supporting everybody in sight for thirty years, but he sets to work again. He's having trouble breathing, having fainting spells, he's emaciated, his legs and hands swell up and he finally thinks somebody is trying to poison him that's a, a real life fairy tale all right boys and girls, now the storm. It's December, rain and sleet howling through the night. I'm already tasting death, he says, and shivers his lips in the, in a little drum passage from his requiem . . .

—Sorry, if someone could tell me where the men, the boys' room is . . . ?

—Out yes out to the right Mister Gall it's ahm, it's marked boys yes maybe we've all seen enough of this to ahm, in terms of structuring the material that is to . . .

—What's their camera there an Arie? Looks like they've got the wrong lens . . .

———spent about four dollars for his funeral but that, that might spoil our nice fairy tale boys and girls his few friends following the cheap coffin in the rain and turning back before it ever reached the pauper's grave nobody could ever find again is, do you know what a pauper is boys and girls? It means a very poor person and and, yes and we don't like to think about poor people no, no let's try to remember this little, little unspoiled genius in his happy moments when he, when he um, yes when he wrote happy letters to people, yes . . .

—I'd stay away from prop shots like this one too, they're liable to pick up the book upside down.

—Yes we've had ahm, had trouble with books yes . . .

———that here's um, yes here's one he wrote to a girl cousin about the time he was writing his Paris symphony he says, he apologizes to her for not writing and he says Do you think I'm dead? Don't believe it, I implore you. For believing and shitting are two very different things . . .

—Did you, did I . . . hear that?

The cameras heaved patiently. —You find the sound systems on these commercial receivers are pretty uniformly poor . . .

———um, his um playful sense of humor yes he tells her you wouldn't be able to resist me much longer and our arses will, will um, will be the symbols of our peacemaking and then he, then he tells her down here about an imaginary village called Tribsterill where the, where the muck runs down to the sea . . .

—It's that switch on the left yes the one that says off, turn it off, off . . .

———village called Burmesquik where the crooked arseholes are manufactured and um, in the um, his um playful sense of humor yes we, it shows us what a really human person this great genius was doesn't it boys and um, and girls and, and you you, single child out there his letters help you, help make him somebody you can understand too . . .

—No on the left Congressman, the one on the left . . . !

—Sorry . . . Gibbs recovered an elbow from the maze of camera straps where he hung over the back of the sofa staring at the blur on the screen abruptly cropped across chin and hairline, replaced by an American flag, a vista of redwood forest, the music rising as though to carry off the voice.

———to humanize him because even if we can't um, if we can't rise to his level no at least we can, we can drag him down to ours . . .

—See what I mean, there's too much bass in these commercial sets . . . and the foot was withdrawn as Hyde tripped over it on his way to the set where Mister Pecci stood with a control knob that had just come off in his hand.

————what the um, what democracy in the arts is all about isn't it boys and girls and, and you, you . . .

—Wait, hello? I said get Mister Leroy right in here to make a small repair hello? Don't put any more calls through on this line . . .

—An interesting effect . . . Mrs Joubert's face peered from the screen over Hyde's shoulder —but their synch is off . . . and a white-maned man erect in bed, a white-maned man seated in a wicker chair, a white-maned man in plaster replica passed in rapid sequence. —Sounds like a crossed wire there . . . and words and music were restored abruptly over the image of a giant redwood tree.

————of America's beloved humorist whose real name wvrrrrrk fairy tales boys and girls like, like Franz Schubert dying of typhus at thirty-two yes or, or Robert Schumann being hauled out of a river so they could cart him off to an asylum or the, or Tchaikowski who was afraid his head would fall off if . . .

—Do something pretty fast where the, God damn it! came from under the planter where Hyde sought the plug on hands and knees.

—You're in trouble when your music level is up so high it fights the voice like this . . .

————tell you about our favorite American composer sitting on the floor cutting out paper dolls, Edward Mac . . .

—Can you ahm, yes can you pull the plug just pull the plug . . .

—What the . . . hell do you think I'm . . . trying to . . . came from the shadows behind the set where now a biceped Valkyrie bearing a dead warrior aloft gave way to an amazon Brünnhilde in massive concentric breastplates as the voice rose to challenge the stabbing rondo of the D-minor piano concerto of Wolfgang Amadeus Mozart.

————fairy tale isn't it, that his life was a fairy tale that's the real fairy tale isn't it and in um, yes in the singalong to end our fairy tale today we can um, maybe we can find some of his own words in a letter for, to sing along with Amadeus Ah, muck! Sweet word! Muck! chuck!

—You'd better watch your recordings on this open-circuit broadcasting you know. Royalty problems . . . The telephone rang. The door opened, closed, opened again to admit Mister Gall with the final allegro, assai.

————muck! suck, oh charmante, muck, suck! That's what I like! Muck, chuck and suck! Chuck muck and . . .

An expletive broke from under the window planter as the sound cut off, leaving the screen filled with a face perspiring with silent imperative until the reassuring countenance of Smokey Bear restored one faltering note and then another of song.

———a laughing place, to go, hol hol

—Sen, Congressman? It's for you, it's Parentucelli . . .

—Who . . . Gibbs muttered immobile, eyes returning the fixity of the ursine stare from the screen—just who, exactly, was that.

———to go hol hol

—That, yes, well, the young com, ahmposer in, yes in residence, composer in residence from the Foundation. Placed with us by the Foundation that is, in the, an in-depth pilot program in the arts, that is to say a grant. Maybe Mister Ford can explain it more, more in depth?

———hol hol

—No, no, quite a different administrative area, Mister Ford sprawled easily. —Only about three percent of the Foundation's budget goes on the arts, after all.

—A quarter, they want a quarter a yard maybe we get them down to twenty-two, twenty-three cents, Mister Pecci's voice reached in. —No, it's Flo-Jan. The Flo-Jan Corporation, that's f, l, o . . .

—Did I miss something? Mister Gall appeared with his pencil.

—Technical difficulties creep in, trouble with their framing there a few times and they need some practice with their lenses but once you've got good hardware that's all it takes. Practice.

Behind him Gibbs came slowly erect against the wall. —You can't fault us on hardware, he said turning, as they all did, to Mister diCephalis' entrance. —What goes into it, of course . . .

Gall wrote software? and waited, as Mister diCephalis with some effort pushed the frail door closed behind him to have it bob open again for Mister Leroy in his boxing shoes carrying a pail which he set down. —The control knobs here, Whiteback started as Leroy closed in silently, indicating the pail with a theatrical glance. —Well don't, don't bring it in here, don't . . . just get rid of it! it's not why I called for you, I just want you to fix the knobs on this set . . . ! And they parted for Mister Leroy moving between them with his smile, fitting the knobs back on, pocketing his screwdriver and leaving the screen awash with a rain of dollar bills. —Yes now here we, wait you're not leaving? Because we ahm, this lesson in sixth grade social studies yes we wanted you to see this lesson in terms of structuring the ahm . . . and his pastel flurry indicated a map of the United States mounting in distended animation toward the templed splendor of the Stock Exchange to disappear in a whirr of lines, —opening with this resource film . . .

—Lost their loop, Mister Ford obliged rising in his maze of cameras.

—But you both ahm, Mister Gall yes you might want to see this next lesson in terms of a good deal less ahm, less unplanlessness than the one we've just . . .

—No I meant to ask though, that line over the main entrance here? in Greek? I thought, is it Plato? or . . .

—————someone to tell us what we mean by our share in America . . . ?

—Yes well Mister Gibbs here might ahm, here she is now . . . he waved at Mrs Joubert's image as though she might wave back.
—You might try Empedocles.
—Oh . . . ? he juggled papers, book, pencil. —that's e? m . . . ?
—And if you could stay for the next studio lesson? came between them, —a re, resource program on, silkworms . . .
—I think it's a fragment from the second generation of his cosmogony, maybe even the first . . .
—We're yes we're trying something new here the, combining the studio lesson with the classroom portion . . .
—When limbs and parts of bodies were wandering around everywhere separately heads without necks, arms without shoulders, unattached eyes looking for foreheads . . .

—————and that's the difference between our country and Russia isn't it class . . .

—The youngsters themselves become part of the teaching process for a truly meaningful learning experience utilizing the ahm, the youngsters themselves . . .
—Never read it? In the second generation these parts are joining up by chance, form creatures with countless hands, faces looking in different directions . . .

—————and that's what owning a share in a corporation means too doesn't it, the right to vote, just like being an Am . . .

—In the third generation of course you begin to get . . .
—Yes well that doorway is ahm, I don't think you need to bother with the inscription there Mister Gall it's ahm, we're having the whole thing replaced that is to say . . . and he seized a hand extended from the maze of camera straps for any who cared to take it.
—That literature on closed-circuit systems I gave you there Mister Gall my card's right in it there, Hyde, if you want any more inforlook! Wait look there's my boy! the one, no that arm's in the way. There, that's his hand. See this boy in front in the diamond check sweater he's right behind him, see the arm sticking up?

—————while our volunteers count up our investment capital because our money isn't doing anybody any good here, is it. Money that isn't out working and earning something is just like a lazy partner who . . .

The door banged hollow. The telephone rang. —Better just take that phone off the hook and leave it Whiteback, you're going to be flooded with calls from every jobless welfare retired freeloading jackass in the district who sits home and . . .

—But my office, my office is calling me back, said Mister Pecci through gum, —on this proposition thirteen . . .

————in the bowel, where this raw material is converted for use as . . . all kinds of raw silk . . .

—Wait Dan you, you're not changing that are you?

————this raw silk that can't be wound and is called silk waste . . .

—It's this, just this resource program my wife . . .

—Yes well I think we ought to get back to that social service lesson there Dan looks like she's giving these youngsters a sense of real values, my boy there . . .

————when the silkworm starts to spin it discharges a colorless . . . that happens in the large bowel before . . . billions of dollars, and the market value of shares in public corporations today has grown to . . .

—Getting some feedback on that enrichment program you just broadcast to half the world, Whiteback?

—That? on the phone? No, no it's that textbook salesman he claims he had an accident on the school property out there, he says Leroy signaled him right out that blind corner in front of a truck, one of those big asphalt trucks . . .

—He wasn't out there just now when they took her away, he . . .

—Who Dan took who away, where . . .

—To the hospital Miss Flesch they, didn't you know what happened? He was riding her over . . .

—Sorry to miss that, was she . . .

—Will you just let him tell it Gibbs? And this foulmouthed whoever this was that just took over her lesson how'd he get in there.

—Well I thought he, he tied right in didn't he? Yes I gave him the script and . . .

—Why didn't you just take the ahm, take on the lesson yourself Dan you had the script didn't you?

—Or Vogel, you could have grabbed Vogel couldn't you? Real masculine man's way of putting something over we just had him on here, his voice . . .

—Yes but you can't use Vogel live no those ahm, those scars yes that's why his lessons are all taped that is to say, voice over with models and visuals but his face, we got him from the New York City schools and ahm, and doing a very fine job of course but you can't use him live . . .

————to buy stock from a broker as we'll see on our field trip, now. Our volunteers have counted up twenty-four dollars and sixty-three cents so let's look at the closing prices on the . . .

—But the lesson, the Mozart? Did, nothing went wrong did it? that could affect the testing I mean, it's all preprogrammed state-wide . . .

—Yes well Dan he ahm, he departed pretty severely from the curriculum.

——a point that's right, when we talk this special investors' language we don't say dollar do we, we say . . .

—But I heard he's in music I gave him her script and he, she set it up right from the teacher's guide he . . .

—Yes well they had some ahm, some technical difficulties Dan this program specialist from the Foundation pointed out several ahm . . .

——railroads we could buy three shares of Erie Lackawanna, or cars? We can't afford General Motors can we, but . . .

—In simple straightforward terms Dan, you might say that he structured the material in terms of the ongoing situation to tangibilitate the utilization potential of this one to one instructional medium in such a meaningful learning experience that these kids won't forget it for a hell of a long time, how's that Whiteback.

—Yes well that's ahm, I think Mister Gibbs has put it quite clearly Dan of course . . .

——for Disney at forty and a half we'd have Mick . . .

—What he said about superstitious Italians, you heard that.

—I certainly did Senator, you heard that didn't you Gibbs? Mister Gibbs?

—Oh I certainly did Major, I . . .

—Well what are you sitting there with a, looking like you think something's funny about all this, you think our Congressman came all the way out here to be insulted?

—Know just how he must feel Major, that's your car out there Congressman? The white Cadillac with the bumpersticker that says keep God in America?

——or Campbell Soup at twenty-seven . . . ?

—Now look Gibbs . . .

—Didn't know he was trying to get out Major, that's all I . . .

—Look Whiteback, this has . . .

—Wouldn't blame him of course but . . .

—Yes well I think what Mister Gibbs means is ahm . . .

—All right then just tell me this, what about this report he's leaving under God out of his proscribed openings, what about it Gibbs.

——or be part owners of a movie company . . .

—Afraid I can't help you, it sounds a little more like Dan's . . .

—Dan's what I'm not talking about Dan's anything, I'm talking about a report that you use a proscribed opening for your class like the pledge of allegiance you leave out under God, one nation under God I'm talking about all these smart remarks you've been making, I'm trying to have a serious discussion with these Foundation people on closed-circuit broadcast and you butt in with arms and legs flying around somebody's eyes looking for their forehead what was all that supposed to be!

—He was asking about one of the preSocratics, Major, the rule of love and the rule of strife in the cosmic cycle of Emp . . .

—They didn't come here to talk about comic cycles look at this. Just one budget item, look at this. Camera, film chains, test equipment, videotape, needed to replace obsolete equipment prevent breakdowns and lost instructional time and improve lesson quality, ninety-two thousand four hundred and you think that's a comic cycle? The taxpayers what do you think they think it is!

——Someone said chewing gum? Well Wrigley at thirty-nine is a little out of our reach, let's . . .

—That pail Major be, be careful yes of course the ahm, that lintel over the entrance I think Mister Gibbs was explaining the lettering over the ahm, the Greek letters that is to say since of course he's the only one who can ahm, who suggested that solution to Mister Schepperman's unfortunate ahm, of course since he recommended Mister Schepperman to us in the first place yes or was it Mister Schepperman who ahm, who's no longer with us that is to say yes he's probably just ahm, probably still . . .

—Been selling his blood for money to buy paint.

—That's disgusting Gibbs, sounds like somebody you'd bring in, now let's get back to this budget . . .

—Why because his work, because he thinks one painting's worth more than his own . . .

—Fine let him! Who asked him to paint it anyhow!

—That's the point, Major. Nobody.

——mond Cable or some other growth stock . . .

—What did she say? what stock?

—But without them where do you get art.

—Get it? Art? You get it where you get anything you buy it, listen Gibbs don't try to tell me in this day and age there isn't enough around for everybody great art, pictures music books who's heard all the great music there is, you? You read all the great books there are? seen all these great pictures? Records of any symphony you want reproductions you can get them that are almost perfect, the greatest books ever written you can get them at the drugstore your friend here selling his blood he's crazy that's all, like the one that just enriched the countryside here with the Mozart, pick up the paper the only time you read about them they're making trouble for somebody, for themselves or somebody else that's the only time you hear about them.

—The only time you hear about anybody.

——that we're ready to vote for our share in Am . . .

—What do you mean do I go around with narcotics signing petitions painting slop writing books full of dirty words with a beard? They just want something for nothing half of them are crazy anyhow what about the one he just said he was afraid his head would fall off? Or your big name painter that cut off his ear what about him.

—But that's what I said, without them where do you get the . . .

—Wait be quiet!

—Yes well of course we don't really ahm . . .

—Look that's my company! Did you hear that? They're buying a share in my company Diamond Cable did you see that? That's my company . . . !

—I saw it, from the show of hands it looked like they wanted to buy the . . .

—The what Gibbs, the what. The show of hands you didn't even see it, you've been standing there trying to look down her dress they bought what they wanted to buy. You saw it Whiteback?

——why we call it corporate democracy isn't it class . . .

—There did you hear that? Corporate democracy did you hear that Gibbs? This share in America it's my company they just bought a share in my company, I didn't get where I am slopping paint on the floor and cutting off my ear either run this school system along corporate lines Whiteback you'd have these strike threats complaints over harassment cleared up in no time, you'd . . .

—Yes well of course Vern ahm, I don't think Vern would . . .

—That's what they're whining about isn't it Dan? this harassment?

—The, the yes the directives the forms, the rules, regulations, guidelines . . .

—Yes well of course the ahm, you teachers get them from me, I get them from the District Superahm, Vern that is to say yes and he gets them from . . .

—Start an investigation find out who's behind it, the . . .

—The harassment?

—No behind the complaints, the . . .

—And of course we all get them from the state and the state gets them from the federal education office in . . .

—The complaints?

—No the directives that is to say, guidelines, forms, regulations, Title Four . . .

—Title Four's a hell of a big investment the government's just protecting their investment see it at the corporate level all the time, that's what you're . . .

—Yes well of course we ahm, in terms of the ongoing situation in order to correlate the ahm, correlations Dan you can ahm . . .

—The, the correlations the correlations require standardization which, which requires standards . . .

—Go ahead Dan I'm listening, just let me get Whiteback's phone in there . . .

—The standards yes establishing the standards in, just in the scoring area, some of the cards they have holes punched in them that don't make any sense at all, on these tests for instance the ones to classify potential failures . . .

—Good, get them early. Hello? Weed out the bad risks . . . what . . . ? he listened, spoke a crude syllable into the phone and laid it ranting on the desk. —Father Haight over at the parochial school letting us know they didn't miss anything, lift your lessons right off the air and . . .

—When a boy that boy with the cap pistol, when he scores top on the music math index and then you check up his holes and find they don't fit . . .

—Yes well of course he's ahm, all we can do that is to say is to ahm . . .

—Send him back to Burmesquik.

—What was that Gibbs? Hyde sank back on the desk corner, where the telephone miniature continued to rant into his trouser pocket.

—I said maybe he hears a different drummer, Major.

—Nothing pansy about that, my boy's as good on the drums as he is on trumpet. You've got a hole in the seat of your pants there too, Gibbs.

—Too? like this boy with the cap pistol? He launched a sudden step backwards, —let him step to the music which he . . .

—Look out!

—My, God . . .

—What was in it!

—That, that Leroy that idiot Leroy . . . Whiteback snatched up a blue cuff in a quick two step, —he brought the whole pailful to show me what was stopping up the plumbing in the junior high be careful, they're all over the floor . . .

—But the, the junior high?

—There's programming for you . . . Gibbs knocked a shoe against the baseboard, —speak of tangibilitating unplanlessness where'd you pick up that language, Whiteback?

—You, you have to speak it when you talk to them here Senator we, this way, we'll get some paper towels in the boys' room, Dan? Can you just reach over and, reach that? turn that thing off?

——treatment of waste silk, called discharging . . .

—Still want to get together on this remote special Whiteback, put it on tape for these Foundation people after this disgraceful exhibition you put on here today we might be able to cut our losses . . .
—I said off Dan, not up . . .

——beautiful colors, but the smell of this waste silk fermenting is so offensive that . . .

—Send your remote unit out to my shelter, tie the whole thing in with what we . . .
—Off, the knob marked off . . .

——improving production knowhow and eliminating waste in the cause of human better . . .

—Leroy must have got these knobs on backwards.

——elimination of waste and is fitted with a muscular mechanism, or sphincter . . .

—Out to the right, Whiteback led them in order of importance.
—Remember . . . ? said Gibbs over diCephalis' shoulder, glancing up at the portrait as he reached to close the door behind them —when Eisenhower's doctor told the press this country is very interested in bowel movements?
—It's marked boys . . .
The door swung the word Principal hollow behind their backs, leaving the only voice chiding in miniature from the desk where the telephone lay, the only face, where nothing had happened framed high on the wall there all this time to change the expression unchanged by a boy's lifetime at the country's helm "focusing on ideas rather than phrasing" with the plea "let's not forget, above all things, the need of confidence and that, of course, I think nationally, it is what do you and I think of the prospects, do we want to go buy a refrigerator or something that is going to, that we think is useful and desirable in our families, or don't we? And it is just that simple in my mind."
Dead before their eyes, the clock severed another of the minutes that lacked the hour, —oh. Coming out? asked diCephalis and then, paused pulling at the lateral handle of the door under the word push, —can I ride you somewhere?
—I'd rather you didn't, Gibbs said holding the door opened for him, stopping to find a cigarette, to pat pockets for the rattle of matches in a box, gazing up at the Greek letters over the portal as he lit it and then back after the diminuendo of diCephalis' retreat until that reared off in the form of a car aiming its impressively gathered speed at its crippled mate in green parked just outside the gate where with a reassuring look around the blind corner, Leroy motioned him, full career ahead, a course

halted shudderingly abrupt as from the green wreck at the curb emerged the amorphous figure of its owner holding a small rolled black umbrella by its handle of simulated birch, recoiling, at that instant, from the flamboyant arrival of diCephalis on the one hand and, on the other, a mail truck from the blind corner that passed like a shot.

—Gosh!

—That, that's mine, that umbrella.

—This? Gosh . . . And it was handed over on a note of apology given cyclopean definition by the loss of a lens.

—She took it by mistake. Not mine exactly, my little boy's, diCephalis shouted as the roar of his engine rose. —I took it by mistake . . . and as he swerved into the open Leroy's smile hung in the rearview mirror, down the block, through the arboreal slaughterhouse of Burgoyne Street, he kept looking up to the mirror as though it might still be there, even glancing into a wall mirror passing through the studio corridor as if to find it and reflecting no recognition for the face he saw instead, none in fact till he came on three versions of his wife on as many monitoring screens doing what, in another costume and to other music, might have been the concluding swoop of a tango, prompting the director to select a static bit of folk art so that her program ended with an endearing gesture that never left the room.

Telephones right and left lay on desks, hung from cords, berating one another. —I'm looking for this Mister Bast . . . ?

—You are, eh?

He backed out of the man's way, turned by his wife's emergency and swept in its wake back the way he had come. —Well? What did they have to say? she asked as he swung the car door open for her.

—Who?

—Who! And now look what you've done, torn my sari. Who do you think? she pulled a silk fragment from a tear in the door steel, —the Foundation people, who! About my lesson, my . . . they saw it didn't they?

—Well not, not exactly all of it, they . . . he drowned his own voice with a roar of the engine.

—They what? Did they see any of it?

—Well they, of course, yes that part about the waste, the silk waste . . . ? The engine quieted, absorbed by its engagement with the gears which mounted the shift column in a rhythmical shimmy as the radio warmed.

—Waste! Then they didn't see, why didn't they? Why didn't they see all of it!

—Well you see they, there were some technical difficulties . . . he began, shifting in the seat as the space around them took life with a Clementi trio from the radio.

—Technical! tell me technical! Technical like you or one of that crew of Whiteback's switching channels, technical! And turn off that noise. Noise, you'll hide in noise any chance you get . . . look out!

—But I called you to tell you they were there from the Foundation, he said as one of Burgoyne Street's limbs swung past her window. —If I didn't want them to see you would I even have called?

—Unless you manage to kill me first . . . she ducked away from her window, —no, you knew I'd find out they'd been there even if you didn't tell me ahead so this way you played it safe, technical! You think I can't see what you'd do to keep them from seeing me? Because you're afraid they might have seen some talent, they might have seen somebody creative and I might get that Foundation grant and then where would you be? I'd be in India and where would you be!

—Well, I . . .

—Do you think . . . look out! Yes unless you kill me first, you're going to tell me you didn't see that limb? Do you think they didn't notice it? That you picked the dullest part of my lesson to show them and then switched to something else? What. That Glancy at the blackboard? or your scarface friend with the machines? Which one. Or that Miss Money-bags with the social studies and the fake French name and the bazooms, which one?

—But, moneybags . . . he started, and then appeared to concentrate on the prospect of a curve distantly ahead.

—I thought so, with that front of hers that's all you can look at, those French suits with nothing on under you don't dress like that on a tea-cher's salary. But don't get worried I'm not asking you for anything, if you think I'd ask for your support on anything at least of all in the arts, not after this performance. Not that it's anything different than the way you've always been, when I was having modern dance . . .

—But those lessons . . .

—And voice culture, singing . . .

—But those lessons . . .

—And painting, when I had it with Schepperman the support I got from you . . .

—But those lessons, I paid him for those lessons . . .

—Paid him! You paid him six months later as if that's even the kind of support I mean, paid him! I mean some kind of plain understanding of somebody that wants to express themself and he had more inspiration in one finger . . .

—Finger . . . muttered diCephalis, maneuvering the curve.

—What? Yes, mock me, go ahead. Just repeat what I say, go ahead. If you knew how childish it sounds this jealousy of yours, because that's all it is. Jealousy. You're afraid somebody else may try to do something, aren't you. With your book, just because you're having trouble writing your book, you're afraid somebody else may do something creative, aren't you. Aren't you . . . !

—But no, my book . . .

—Aren't you. Can't you answer me? Aren't you?

—But my book, no. It isn't. Creative I mean, it isn't supposed to be it's just on measurement, measuring things, it's nothing to do with creative, my book . . .

—My book! My book! That's all we ever hear from you my book, well let me just tell you something that's to don't be surprised if somebody else has a book, that's all. Just don't be surprised! And she fixed unflinching on the passing gantlet of apartment house existences dismantled and laid out side by side on aprons of grass affording the embattled privacy of city stoops, sheltered by awnings of rippling yellow plastic blazoning heraldic initials in old world black letter, mounting names discreetly hidden a bare year since in the Brooklyn telephone directory on sentry carriage lamps, ships' lanterns in authentic replica, a livid pastel wagon wheel swooning at a rustic angle, a demented wheelbarrow choked with stalked memories of flowers, a family of metal flamingoes, of ducks, of playful elves, till with a narrow miss for the cast iron potbellied stove painted pink and sporting a naked geranium stem from its lid the car left the pavement. —Just don't act too surprised.

—Yes, well, we're home, he said motionless.

—Home! The car wavered into silence. She sat staring out, long lashes sticking at the corners. —If you'd ever, even, just given me that.

He hesitated, swallowed, and got out, to round the back of the car in no hurry until, approaching the other side of it, he opened her door in a lively manner as though he might have been waiting here to deliver her from a drive with someone neither of them cared for. —That young man, he said briskly now, —the one I brought over? You were going to give him some pointers before he went on, did you . . . see him? His lesson, I mean . . . ?

—I certainly did not. I was getting my own ready. Do you think there's nothing to it but standing in front of a camera? Why.

—Why? what . . .

—Why what! You asked me if I saw his lesson. No. Why. I suppose you're going to tell me he could have given me some pointers.

—No in fact, I didn't see it either and I heard, I heard there were some technical difficulties.

Safe ahead, she stopped. —I could have told you that, the minute they see talent or sensitivity they sabotage it with technical difficulties and from talking to that young man if you look at his eyes, you can tell a person by their hands haven't I said that? And he has more artistic sensitivity look out, if you step on this . . .

—In one finger, he muttered behind her on the flagstone path, restraining the umbrella.

—Finger. Yes in one finger. You're doing it again and it's childish, a child could see through you the way your jealousy sticks out because you're afraid of everything aren't you, afraid of life, living, anything that lives and grows . . .

—Finger, he muttered reaching for the aluminum frame door that bore his initials in the large as it slammed with the sound of a shot.

An elderly dog eyed him from under the table but did not move.

—Hello Dad, he said, and hooked the umbrella to a room divider supporting the old man and several sculptured primitives, all eminently male, that locked that wistful gaze beyond the silent rise and fall of fingers parading the sweeter for being unheard melody up and down the saxophone, propped erect in this mad pursuit of whatever men or gods those were to prompt a halt with —She has a dirty mind.

—Who? diCephalis asked vaguely, his hands now filling with the contents of an inside pocket, a tape measure, an automatic pencil calibrated in centimeters, a notebook thumb indexed with attached pen bearing magnifying glass or, as it turned in his hand, magnifying glass bearing pen, digits, holes, and the legend Do not fold or mutilate borne on a green card, an orange card, on two, three, four white cards, a length of string, a length of twine, a wallet glazed with soiled attentions, a linen counter, a perforation guage, a letter with a four place number as its return address.

—I wouldn't let her bring things like that into any house of mine, muttered the old man shifting from one ham to the other beneath the belittling thrust of a primitive insistence particularly African. —Nobody's built like that. They couldn't walk around. What . . . ? He looked up, —yes the dog, the dog smells something terrible today, don't he . . . and he settled back to the spirit ditty of no tone struggling to escape his fingers on the saxophone erect, as diCephalis started a round of turning off lights. Foyer, hall, bathroom, foyer, closet, side door, snap, snap, snap snap he made his way along stuffing his pockets again with everything but the letter and a newspaper clipping stuck to it, snap, snap, into the bedroom.

—What are you doing?

—We don't need all these lights on in rooms nobody's in.

—All these lights, she said to her streaked image in the glass, removing lashes.

—Are you using the typewriter?

—Do I look like I'm using the typewriter?

—Well no, I meant, just these papers . . .

—Just these papers! Throw them out. It's just my project summary for the Foundation grant throw it out! What are all those papers you're dumping there.

—Nothing. A questionnaire I'm filling out.

—Nothing. I'll bet nothing. For a job? Your name must be as well known in personnel offices as Santy Claus.

—But in this one there's no name it's, they use computers. He brandished a flyer carrying a man's face eradicated by punched holes and numbers. —They use, they call it coded anonymity, where they can make more meaningful evaluations of qualifi . . .

—What do you need to put your anonymity in code for?

—Respecting the dignity of the private individ . . .

—Nobody knows who you are anyway. Nora! Stop that racket! what in God's name are they doing, can't you stop them? And what's this, right in with my face creams. More papers.

—Oh that, I've been looking for that.

—Well this is a good place for it, nobody would steal it here.

—Who would steal it anywhere? It's for refinancing our mortgage.

—Refinancing? What's that, you're borrowing more?

—We have to, we owe . . .

—We? That last time they hauled the car in? She looked up to catch him in the mirror but he clung to a shoulder strap. —Or the time before, every time. Is that we?

—No I didn't mean, what I meant, I meant to ask you, do you remember that last towing charge? how much it was?

—Fifty cents? something . . . ow!

—It couldn't have been that little, it . . .

—So maybe it was four fifty, six fifty, I distinctly remember the fifty cents Nora, stop it! What in God's name are you doing? Nora! Can't you stop them? Instead of standing in here arguing about fifty cents? This thing you have about money you have a real thing about it. The way you plunge the house into darkness the minute you walk in going around turning off all the lights, turning down the heat every time you pass it, fifty cents! You get a break you're scared to keep it, like that tax refund for three hundred dollars, and you send it back.

—Daddy! Dad . . . !

—No, it was three hundred twenty thirty-six and the refund I filed for was only thirty-seven ten so I couldn't . . .

—Quick, a penny! Gimme another penny quick!

—I couldn't keep it, and I couldn't just . . .

—Quick!

—What for, Nora?

—Quick. Donny is this machine which I have to put a penny in him to make him go, to make it go.

—What it would have done to their records if I'd cashed it, what kind of machine?

—A jumping machine. Didn't you hear it? Quick I have to put in another penny before he runs out.

—Wait! Wait a minute, to put in where? What do you mean another penny, where!

—In his mouth, this penny I found on your dresser it . . . wait! Wait . . . ! What are you . . . what are you doing to him? Look out, you'll break him! You'll . . . upside down, he'll . . . Mama! Mama! . . . There, see? I told you!

—Well, don't . . . don't step in it! Get a rag. Donny! Come here, don't touch your mother's . . .

—My God! and all over my sari! Let go, let me go! Nora, take him!

Can't one of you take him? The smell will never come out. Don't just stand there Nora! Get a rag!

—Daddy, I got your penny back. Here . . .

—A rag I said, don't wipe it on your dress! And look at my sandals! she got past them, rounded the corner and shook the bathroom door. —Dad! Are you in there? A rude sound responded promptly from within, and here she came again. —All of you! You're all against me, all of you . . . !

The side door banged. Somewhere a clock with a broken chime had a try at striking the hour, and Mister diCephalis hurried to the telephone resetting his watch, to dial and stand looking out the window at something his wife had said was a snowball bush hidden openly against others as shapeless as they were nameless she'd said only needed trimming, ignoring the tug at his trouser leg, —See, Donny? Daddy's not mad, he just wanted his penny back . . . for the recorded remonstrance he listened to through to the end before lowering his eyes from that hostile spectacle of growth to dial again, and raise them again to his wife out there scrubbing her sari with water from the garden hose squatted like some Gangetic laundress, numbed stare fixed on the remotely male privilege of the hunt as it prospered, here, past frilled ironwork made of aluminum to appear new and new lengths of post and rail treated to appear old, in the form of Bast near a gallop behind prey in a heedless trot more secure, with each step, in the protective drab of black patterned on gray, frayed, knotted, and unshorn in other details, as the intervals between bayberry keeping mown distance from mimosa alerted by Insurance, Chiropodist, This desireable property For Sale, God Answer's Prayer, gave way to depths of locust long stunted in internecine struggle now grappling with woodbine, and the sidewalk itself finally disappeared under grass at the designated site by God's grace of an edifice for worship by the people of Primitive Baptist Church on a sign about to be reclaimed by the undergrowth.

—Stop!

—What?

—I said wait a minute . . . !

—No you said . . .

—Where's that money you, you stole.

—I what? Oh. Oh, hi.

—Where is it!

—In that paper bag, that? That was our class money.

—It was Miss, Mrs what's her name . . .

—Joubert, Mrs Joubert. That's my class, six J.

—Well where is it!

—The money? his shoulders hunched in the shift of books, a black zippered portfolio, a newspaper and mail in assorted sizes from one arm to the other. —I told you, I had to hurry up to class from that rehearsal thing with it, he said stooping for a dropped envelope, pausing down there to add a knot to the lace in his sneaker. —You can ask her.

—You . . . you're sure?

—Sure ask anybody. Hey wait, I mean you're not mad are you hey? Books and papers threatening to right and left, he trotted up beside Bast. —Where you going.

—Home.

—Oh. You live out this way?

—Yes.

—Up the main road?

—Yes but . . .

—I'll walk you.

—I'm in a hurry.

—That's okay. He hurried along bumping Bast's thigh with his armload. —How far up do you live, past that big corner?

—Right off it.

—Like across from where they're building this here new shopping center, right?

—They're not building anything.

—I mean like where they're going to.

—Going to what. Who.

—You live in that big old place right after that old empty farmhouse if you turn left, right? This here old house with these little pointy windows and this like big barn in back by the woods? with this big high scraggly hedge out front like?

Bast's steps had slowed as a small clearing opened abruptly on their right where mangled saplings and torn trunks and limbs still bearing leaves engaged a twisted car fender, a split toilet seat, a chair with one leg and a variety of empty tin cans surrounding a sign Clean Fill Wanted with a telephone number. —How did you know that.

—That's the only place up there, right? And like right across from it where that guy that raises flowers which used to live in the farmhouse, where he has all those flowers that's where they're having this here new shopping center, you know?

—No. Who told you that.

—It's right in the paper here about the zoning change . . . and in his effort to keep stride and dig into that armload, everything went. —I . . . oh, thanks. You don't have to help me, I mean I just wanted to show you . . .

—Damn it!

—What. The mud? It brushes off when it gets dry. I just . . .

—Whose is all this? said Bast stooped, picking up Gem School of Real Estate, Amertorg International Trading Corp., Cushion-Eez Shoe Company, National Institute of Criminology, Ace Match Company, —this mail.

—It's today's. I just went to the post office.

—This is yours? your mail?

—Sure, you just send away, J R said without looking up from the skidding surfaces of the magazines he was pulling together, Success Secrets, Selling, Success, the abrupt appearance of a bared breast crowding a full page, —it's mostly free, you know? He gathered in the breast without a glance, and stood.

—What are those magazines? Bast said, staring.

—Just things where you get to send away, you know? Like I thought I had the town paper here but it's the wrong one, about zoning this improved property and all.

Bast stood slowly, cleared his throat muttering —improved! and kicked an empty catfood can at the twisted fender.

—Like all they need here is fill and they, hey wait up . . . J R dug in a pocket, came up with the handkerchief wad, the pencil stub. —They pay like seven dollars a yard for clean fill, you know hey? he said looking at the sign, scratching the pencil stub on a magazine margin. —Have you got a pencil?

—No, and here. Bast handed over the mail and turned away. —I'm in a hurry.

—But just, okay but sometime could we, hey . . . ? J R stood by the mangled clearing biting at the point of the pencil stub, trying it for a mark, biting again. —Hey Mister Bast? he called, and Bast half raised an arm without lifting his eyes from his lengthening steps toward the main road opening ahead, where the voice barely reached him as he crossed its unkempt shoulder. —I just mean like maybe we can use each other some time, okay . . . ?

Pursuing nothing, unpursued, a police car appeared, sheared past him, its siren tearing the day to pieces out of sight beyond the firehouse and the crumbling plaza of the Marine Memorial behind him as he turned up the highway and crossed, stepping over ruts, tripping against cragged remnants of sidewalk in block lengths allotted by rusted poles still bearing aboveground indecipherable relics of street signs that had signaled a Venetian bent real estate extravaganza in the twenties, until even those limbs of rust lay twisted to earth and naked of any sign of place, of any suggestion of the tumbled column and decollated plaster Lion of St Mark's moldered smooth there in the high browned grass where he turned in, any memory at all but these weeds recalled by the aged as Queen Anne's laces lining ruts which led back into the banks of oak, no cars but those seeking seclusion for the dumping of outmoded appliances, fornication, and occasional suicide, and those far fewer and on foot who knew it for a back entrance to the Bast property.

—Those woods were filled with people that summer, 'twenty-five was it, Julia? or 'twenty-six? You recall Charlotte was just back from Europe, men dressed up in gondoliers' hats they actually had a gondola too, down at the creek at that little bridge. A white pitched bridge going absolutely nowhere and how she laughed, she had just come from Venice.

—She stopped when she saw James out in the midst of it, selling waterfront lots to those poor people. They'd been brought out from town on special trains free.

—Waterfront . . . ?

—They were told it would be waterfront, Stella. With docks for ships coming in from Europe and canals like Venice, and they believed it.

—I don't think James tried to deceive them, Julia. James took it all as rather a lark.

—A lark? People losing their whole life's savings? Most of them had been domestics, they could hardly speak English.

—Is this Uncle James? here, in this hat? Stella asked absently, mirrored in the picture's glass, her back to them in a simple curve of gray tailored to the grave decline of her shoulders.

—No, James, James didn't put on one of those getups. The gondolier's hat and all the rest of it, none of that was his idea at all. He was simply selling lots on commission for Doc what was his name, when he went to jail . . .

—No, no, Anne. She means that picture over there, James in some sort of academic costume. An honorary something he got somewhere after that first performance of his . . .

—And where is he now?

—There's a card from him Stella, it's there on the mantel. A picture of a castle.

—This? with the corner cut off it? There's no way to know . . .

—James' hand is impossible to read. The only way we can write to him is to cut off the return address and paste it on to the front of a letter, and since we never really know where . . . there! Just hold still for a moment, Stella. Do you see it now, Julia? The resemblance to James?

—If she'd raise her chin a little. A little, perhaps, around the mouth but . . . is that a scar? Around the throat, it must be the light in here but it looks . . .

—Julia! I wouldn't . . .

—It's all right, said Stella, turning from them what might have become a smile to draw up her throat's long and gentle curve. —You see? It goes right around, she seemed to finish, and turned back to the photographs framed on the wall.

—It almost looks . . .

—You, you might want to wear a necklace, Stella. There was one that belonged to Charlotte, somewhere. Who did that go to Julia? the one with the . . .

—Oh, I don't try to hide it . . . she brought them forward with the dull calm in her voice. —The children in our apartment building, do you know what they say? That I'm a witch, that I can screw my head on and off. They think that this one comes off at night and I put on another . . .

—Stella! that's . . . you, you're a beautiful girl!

—One that would turn them to stone if they saw it, she went on, all they could see of her expression its movement in the glass, and then —there were beautiful witches after all, she finished with a slight tremor that might have been a laugh.

—What . . .

—What was it? An operation. Thyroid.

—It's a shame you . . . you've never had children, Stella. Children of your own, you and . . . oh, I can never recall his name.

—Whose.

—Why, your husband, Mister . . .

—Norman, oh, said Stella in the same dead calm, and then —and this? turned again to a picture. —Sitting at the piano beside Uncle James, this little boy. It's not Edward, is it?

—That? No. No, that's not Edward, no.

—Is it . . . anyone?

—It's . . . no, it's a boy. A boy James took in for lessons.

—Reuben? Stella turned abruptly, and stood there as the turn had left her, one foot cocked on a heel. —The boy he adopted?

—He didn't. James never adopted him. There. Do you see? the stories that get started?

—Yes, that Mister . . . this lawyer who was here. Prying and gossiping, trying to bring Reuben into things too, saying the adopted child has the same rights as the blood child and so forth, why . . .

—Here, his card's here somewhere. Cohen, here it is. You see? he said they'd left out the h. You would think he'd want to get new cards printed.

—Perhaps he doesn't care to spend the money. It might be cheaper just to change his name, you remember Father saying . . .

—Why your husband had to send him out here Stella, as though things weren't confused enough.

—I'm sorry I missed him. When Norman's secretary said he was coming out to see you and Edward and help clear things up . . .

—Clear things up? Waving his arms around, breaking furniture, tossing papers every which way? And his language!

—I'm sure that Norman never meant him to . . .

—Crystal clear but he couldn't speak simple English, unless you call profanity crystal clear. Be careful of that chair arm, he broke that too.

—Perhaps Edward can fix it, Julia.

—Yes he warned us against Edward, if you can imagine.

—But I'm sure Mister Coen didn't mean . . .

—Referring to Edward as an infant . . .

—A lunatic . . .

—Talking about suing the Ford Motor Company, using infancy as a sword instead of a shield whatever that means, he kept repeating it. Remember Danziger, he said, versus the Ironclad Realty Company. I won't forget them in a hurry after that performance, but heaven knows why. I never heard James mention either of them.

—Or Father either, why Mister Cohen even wanted to hear that old story about Father and the violin.

—And that picture of Charlotte in the Indian headdress to prove some notion about resemblances, that gossip about our Indian blood and talking about emancipation, Edward being emancipated! as though we were all a family of . . . well!

—We even had to sew a button on for him. Where do you suppose that picture is, Julia? The one on the song sheet. It was when she opened at the New Montauk Theater . . .

—It must be over in James' studio with everything else.

—With everything else, yes. It's a good thing he never got loose over there. When he started to pry into James' income tax returns, asking if James took Edward as an exemption . . .

—There's no reason he shouldn't. I've heard James say myself that as long as Edward is a fulltime student . . .

—That Bryce boy, the one they called the young planter, he was still in high school at the age of twenty-nine.

—That was quite a different story, Anne.

—Wasn't Reuben an orphan? Stella said abruptly over them.

—No. Certainly not.

—I thought I'd heard my father say . . .

—Just because James found him in an orphanage. The boy's mother had died and his father couldn't look after him and put him in an orphanage where he'd get decent care. That's where James found him, giving music lessons. The Masons did charity work, you know, and James was giving lessons in a Jewish orphanage. He thought the boy had talent and, well, that it should be developed.

—But he brought him home, didn't he?

—James brought him home to teach, simply that. It's . . . it was all so many years ago and I'm sure the only reason your Mister Cohen brought it up was to try to stir up those old stories about James and your father. About James and Thomas not getting on, simply because of . . . of what's at stake.

And Stella's turn and movement from them in her gray took a melancholy dimension from the fading streaks of the fall sun mottling the glass. —What's that, she said.

—Why, the business. After all.

—After all, it was James who helped him get started. When Thomas first talked about music publishing . . .

—I'd hardly call it music publishing, Anne. When Thomas first talked about making piano rolls, James said he thought that playing reed instruments all those years had loosened something in Thomas' head.

—Nevertheless I would not have imagined there was still so much money in piano rolls, but your Mister Cohen says it's doing very well. I thought people had radios and things today. It's not as though James has no stake in it, after all.

—But he still owns his stock, said Stella from the pictures. —And you both do too?

—You certainly wouldn't know it from the dividends.

—Not that it's all just a matter of money.

—Then what is it . . . ? What light there was was gone, pocketed above, leaving Stella in her turn matching her stare to those fallen to the empty floor and left there, as though something only a moment before had been there, moving, and fled.

—Why, why simply I think James simply felt that Thomas took . . . took certain advantages. Musician friends of his, of James, they showed up here on concert tours and James had scarcely introduced them when he found that Thomas had them out there in Astoria cutting piano rolls.

—Who was that, Anne?

—Well, Saint-Saëns was one. When he was here touring . . .

—I think James thought that Saint-Saëns was rather silly, with his theosophy and all the rest of it.

—I think James really liked Saint-Saëns, Julia. It was Saint-Saëns' music that James thought was rather silly, he thought that it was trite. Yes, it must have been the music, because it wasn't when Saint-Saëns himself was here at all, it was when Paderewski was here playing Saint-Saëns.

—Steinway brought Paderewski over here years before, Herbert Hoover was mixed up in that somewhere making money to get himself through college and I don't think it was Saint-Saëns' theosophy, Anne. I think you're thinking of what James used to say about Scriabin and Madame Blavatsky before he had that tumor and died. He never wrote songs.

—Was it true? said Stella from over there, —that my father and Uncle James once met on the street in some city abroad where they'd both just arrived, and without a word they put down their suitcases and started to fight?

—The boys didn't actually fight. It was more of a philosophical dispute, Thomas insisting the magic touch of these virtuosos could be preserved on his piano rolls, and James . . .

—If there was anything that drove James wild it was the idea of talent going to waste, being lost, suppressed. It drove him wild.

—And that was why he took the boy in from the Jewish orphanage?

—Yes, he was a very shy, quiet little boy. He didn't really look like a Jew to us.

—Not a jewy Jew, no.

—In those days we thought Jews all had hooked noses but he was almost blond, wasn't he Julia. And blue eyes.

—But he took our name, didn't he?

—Oh, borrowed it, Stella, borrowed it and used it and just never returned it. He had such admiration for James.

—Well, James loved him, and . . .

—No, not the boy. Not James. It was the talent James loved, he took him out of that orphan asylum because he thought the boy should be spending every minute with music, studying, practicing, working on his music, James drove him as hard as he drove himself. That was the reason he took the child in, to live with him when Edward came here with us.

—Oh? Stella turned, her arms akimbo. —When do you expect him back?

—Look at that card. Around Thanksgiving, from what I could make of it.

—I meant Edward, didn't you say he's just teaching? somewhere nearby . . . ?

—Yes, James was going to try to arrange something for him through some connections he used to have, being a composer in residence somewhere, but we don't know whatever became of that project. When it comes to returning a kindness some people have such short memories, you know.

—He was quite taken with you, you know, Stella. He had the kind of crush that little boys have, all those years ago.

—Well, Stella must have seemed quite grown up to him. When you're that age, a matter of six or eight years . . .

—I don't want to miss him but I can't stay much longer, you don't mind if I call for a cab?

—No, there on the secretary. The number's somewhere.

Then casually, without a glance back, —What was it, Stella asked, —that Mister Coen wanted of Edward?

—That's a good question!

—He wanted Edward to sign . . .

—Something he wanted Edward to sign, but we'd best wait to see what James has to say about it.

—And he wanted Edward's birth . . .

—Pardon? Stella was dialing.

—Some nonsensical notions he had, questioning James as Edward's father and heaven knows what else!

—James was always a lovely father to Edward.

—Well he certainly tried Anne, but James has never been the easiest person in the world to live with when he's working. He can seem plain morose and irritable when he's preoccupied with work.

—His Philoctetes, yes. When he was working on that, he didn't speak to a soul for days at a time, he . . . what, Stella?

—She's phoning, Anne. And Anne . . . in a voice that rustled, out over the floor stretching bare the length of the room toward Stella as sun, spilling in again, brought it to faded life. —I wouldn't go into all kinds of details right now, before we hear what James has to say.

—But Julia . . .

—You got your cab, Stella? The name is there somewhere. A Jewish name, but I can't recall it.

—It's Italian, Julia. It's painted right on the taxi door.

—The next train, yes . . . came Stella's murmur at the phone. —Mrs Angel . . .

—Well, you know how cheap names are.

—Stella . . . ? You got your taxi? It's a shame you have to leave. You've scarcely sat down since you came.

Stella stood tracing an edge of sun with the point of her shoe. —It was Edward's birth certificate that Mister Coen wanted? she said finally.

—He, he mentioned it, yes.

—But if there's any question, Edward himself must wonder . . .

—Wonder?

—What he's . . . inherited.

—Why he's, what he'll have from James, heaven knows. I'm sure James doesn't. His work is always money going out not coming in, having scores prepared and getting them copied, the parts for each instrument . . .

—And James was never one for writing little trios. He likes lots of brass.

—And voices.

—Voices, yes. What it would cost to do his Philoctetes! Hiring musicians to play his compositions, getting them recorded and all the rest of it his royalty checks aren't a drop in the bucket, even these awards seem to cost twice what they bring in. When the time comes there won't be much for Edward.

—It wasn't money I meant, said Stella quietly, and then, her voice as casual as her step, —was Nellie talented?

—Nellie?

—Talented?

—I . . . I don't think the question ever came up.

—In all these pictures with Uncle James, Stella murmured clouding the glass of one with her closeness, —there's none . . .

—That's the one of him with Kreisler, isn't it?

—But this says Siegfried Wagner, nineteen twen . . .

—Oh. That was Siegfried Wagner, yes. He used to be around Bayreuth and charge twenty-five cents for his photograph, simply because he was Wagner's son.

—But in all these pictures with women, there's none . . .

—That was that Teresa what was her name, Julia. She was over here touring during the war. She'd been married to that, I can't recall him either. During the war even though he was British, he made such a scene about being German but what was his name, a French name, but what was it. He was married a good half dozen times. She was known as the Valkyrie of the keyboard, she came from Argentina or some such.

—There's no picture of Nellie? Stella got in abruptly, turning her back on those frames and faces. —Didn't she take lessons of Uncle James? after he was sick, and she'd come to nurse him back?

—I think you have it twisted, Stella. She was sick and, yes and James . . .

—There's no reason to stir it all up again. That Mister Cohen, repeating gossip . . .

—But now that we speak of it, Julia, do you think we have Edward's birth certificate?

—I suppose it's right there in the top drawer. That little Martha Washington sewing table.

—Here? said Stella, trying it. —But it's locked.

—Yes. The key is right there in the bottom drawer. Yes, there . . . let me see that, Stella. It's a picture of Nellie with the Gloria Trumpeters when they led that welcome home parade for Charles Lindbergh, down Fifth Avenue.

—I think they went up Fifth Avenue, Anne. And you certainly can't make out Nellie in this. I think it was before her time, at that.

—Then why would we ever have kept the clipping?

—Nellie played . . . trumpet?

—You knew that, Stella. You knew James gave her lessons.

—But not, trumpet. No, I just thought, just music.

—Yes, or was it cornet, Julia.

—And I thought Uncle James just wouldn't waste time on people without talent.

—Well, but after all, Stella.

—Nellie wasn't well, Stella, after all. She had consumption. You knew that, didn't you? It wasn't as though James set out to make her the finest cornetist in the world. The doctors said she must build up her lungs, and that was why she came for these lessons. But she came too late.

Closer, over the sewing table fitting its key, Stella's hand rose as it might have in scorn, lost to her forehead tucking a strand of hair. —Oh?

—That's . . . but you knew that, didn't you? Stella?

—Knew?

—Knew that . . . that that was how Nellie died.

Motionless, eyes taking all, giving nothing, Stella said —Was it?

—Why, why . . .

—Yes, why yes Stella . . .

Their looks suspended three sides of a broken triangle which crumbled, shifting on different planes. —I'm sure that Thomas has told her, Anne. Perhaps it's just slipped her mind for the moment.

And two sides of the triangle rose again, querying, seeking confirmation in the third; but Stella's eyes stayed down, kept the distance in her voice. —There's nothing here but stock certificates, securities . . .

—Yes, that's what James always says isn't it. Bonds are for women, and . . .

—Stocks are for men. But that was Father.

—Listen. I think I hear hammering somewhere.

—You might as well stop looking there, Stella. It's probably over in James' studio, though I'd hate to be the one to look. Digging through all that, pictures, clippings, deeds and tax bills, song sheets, scores and all those piano rolls . . .

—Julia . . . now? Don't you hear it? Hammering?

—Edward?

—Oh, it's Edward?

—Edward . . . but what's that he's carrying?

—It looks like a can.

—A beer can!

—In the living room? What in the world!

—You, we said he was upset Stella, but . . .

—If he could see himself . . .

But only the wallpaper's patient design responded to his obedient query, glancing from habit to an unfaded square of wall where no mirror had hung in some years. —It's empty . . . he brandished the can, —I just thought I'd . . .

—You recall the time James came home so late from the Polish legation his hand, what's happened to Edward's hand?

—And his coat hem all out in the back.

—It's nothing it's just an empty beer can, I came in . . .

—Well don't wave it around. We can smell it over here.

—I came in the back way by the studio and picked it up on the lawn out there, just to throw it away . . .

—We don't care to have it seen in our trash, thank you. He'll have to throw it out somewhere else. Did I hear Stella's cab outside?

—No I have a minute before it comes, I thought Edward could show me the studio? I don't think I've ever seen it, and we might find that paper . . . ?

—Yes wasn't there something we meant to tell Edward?

—He had a telephone call this morning.

—That was some wretched woman selling dance lessons, Anne.

—They don't mind how they run up our telephone bill. Why we don't simply have it taken out . . .

—Well it's certainly outlived its usefulness, why we ever had it put in in the first place . . .

—When we bought all that telephone stock Julia, I think we felt we should give them our business.

—No I think it was the other way round, Anne. I think we decided to buy their stock because they already had our business, and if we're having it taken out they may as well have their stock back too.

—We might let Edward just take it in to town and sell it to someone at the Stock Exchange, I'm sure someone down there would be happy to have it. Did you see it in the drawer there Stella?

—Where, they must have gone out. Waving that beer can, if he could have seen himself . . .

—That hem's out again where I mended it. I wish he could get a nice blue suit.

—She certainly was full of questions, wasn't she. You remember how she spread those stories about Thomas and James, about James and Nellie, that summer, she was still just a child. It all came back through that Mrs, Mrs, fat, she had part of one finger missing, who spread it all over the countryside.

—And did you notice? I don't think she was wearing a girdle.

—No, it's something about her eyes. They don't match her face.

—Now, the hammering, hammering . . .

While with the effort of being contested from the other side by the robust emanation from the simmering tenderloin he'd got the door closed against its pursuit and set off on his own where Stella moved over the grown grass with the assurance of a nurse up corridors as though she'd brought the indoors with her, past the invalid trees and that horticultural Laocoön of honeysuckle, grape and roses, pausing inured at an excruciating attempt by Japanese crabapple to espalier its unpruned limbs against the studio's shingles to call —this way . . . ? and then lead on, returning his eyes to her sawing haunches rounding yew overgrown at the brick terrace that fronted the place against the lowering threat of oak. He fumbled the beer can, digging in pockets. —But it's open . . .

—Open? the door . . . ?

—Here . . . She thrust a thigh against the heavy door pushing it in on its hinges, showing the neatly broken pane with a thrust of her elbow, crushing glass underfoot with her entrance, asking —is there a light? and as surely finding the switch, dropping the heavy shadows of overhead beams down upon them, bringing the brooding outdoors in, paused, as he came up short behind her, apparently indifferent to the lingering collision of his free hand in its glide over the cleft from one swell to the other brushing up her waist to the elbow, where only the tremor of uncertainty in his grasp moved her on into the vacant confines of the room to murmur —it needs airing . . .

—That's the, it's damp yes it's the stone floor, he came on off balance as though trying to get around her, gesturing the beer can at chance meetings of beam and scantling that niched the walls haphazard —it used to be a barn it's, they say it was the first wet wash laundry on Long Island it's always been a, breaking in who would break in . . .

—But nothing's missing?

—That's not the . . .

—Or broken . . . ? she'd paused at the piano, came around to open its keyboard and tap C —they didn't run off with this . . .

—It's not funny it's, wait! behind you my phonograph, is it still there? he came toward her all motion, provoked no more than a drop of her hand to switch the thing on sending its arm moving over the turning record with an ominous assurance taken up, as she turned, by strings foreboding in a minor key. —That's not the point! if nothing's gone or broken it's the idea of somebody in here somebody I've never, I don't even know, it's like finding somebody's broken into the one place I, where nothing happens, where I work where nothing else happens can't you understand that! he came on loudly against the rising threat of strings sundering the eaves above —do you think music is just, composing do you think it's just writing down notes? he brandished the beer can at the studio windows —just part of, of all that out there . . . ? and the strings receded quelled by plaintive oboes seeking dialogue, severed by the stab of C under her finger.

—Is this F-sharp? she ran a finger along the stave, bent closer, struck it turning him on his heel as her left hand rose to bracket C two octaves down in tremolo.

—No wait what are you . . .

—All the spirit deeply dawning in, is this what you're working on?

—It's no it's nothing! he pulled the pages from the rack —it's just, it's nothing . . . and left her standing, the strings patterning their descent in the slope of her shoulders to remain there, as she bent to close the keyboard, in the remnant of a shrug.

—They told me you've been teaching Edward, is it . . .

—Well I'm not! he'd dropped the pages in a chair behind him, sat on its arm clutching the beer can —I was but I'm not I, something just happened something as stupid as this, this breaking in here . . . he withdrew his foot abruptly, raised his eyes to her ankles' approaching amble, turn and pass toward a bull's eyed door beyond the fireplace.

—What's in there . . . she found the switch and snapped it, peering through.

—Nothing just, just papers, programs old scores what's . . .

—Uncle James'? he worked over here?

—Well he, of course he did yes I, because it's one place it's the one place an idea can be left here you can walk out and close the door and leave it here unfinished the most, the wildest secret fantasy and it stays on here by itself in that balance between, the balance between destruction and and realization until . . .

—He said this? Uncle James?

—What?

—From him, it just sounds quite romantic . . . she'd snapped the room beyond back into darkness and came from behind him with that ease of drift that brought his eyes up once she'd passed, —his music's always so . . .

—Well why why shouldn't he have said that something like that he, that he could come back the next day a week a month later he could open the door and find it here this same unfinished vision here just like he'd left it, this same awful balance waiting undisturbed just like he'd left it here to, to tip it and, the gray days I've come in here and built a fire to shut it all out so I could work those summers I, I haven't even seen you since those summers . . .

—You can't stay here though can you . . . she turned from the empty black of the fireplace —working? You couldn't stay anyhow . . .

—What?

—With no heat here?

—With, here? I, I don't know I . . .

—And if you've . . .

—I said I don't know! he was up, took the steps after her she'd turned toward the stairs as counterpoint wove the strings toward extinction, —Stella . . .

—What happened.

—That you, just that you're really standing right here in . . .

—No your music . . . she turned her head, caught his breath on her cheek —what happened to . . .

—No that's what I was trying to find something like the, like Beethoven took Egmont his incidental music for Egmont I tried to, I found that long poem of Tennyson's Locksley Hall of Tennyson's I remembered it from school and I've been trying to work out something like, it's something like an operatic suite that part you picked up there that line, those lines that open trust me cousin, the whole current of my being sets to, is that what you . . .

—No just that record, I thought something had happened to it.

—What the, that? that record?

—What happened. It just stopped.

—That it's nothing it's just a practice record it's, that's where the solo comes in the D-minor concerto without the piano part I thought you meant my, what I'm working on I . . .

—I didn't think you wanted to talk about it.

—Well why shouldn't I! what's, why shouldn't I talk about it . . .

—I don't really know, Edward. What's up there.

—The what?

—Up there, upstairs . . .

—Up, what! did you hear something?

—No, no I just meant what's up there . . . she nodded up to shadows where the strings lurked again in ambush for their solo antagonist —up on that balcony . . .

—Nothing just, just the same things papers, old letters scores piano rolls wait . . . he came after her, after the mounting insinuation of her thighs' rise, rest, and rise in the ravening ease of her climb caught that suddenly off balance where she stopped half turned on the landing and he caught at the rail, at her waist where he'd run head on and a hand of hers caught his with the beer can and steadied him, held him off there with no way to know if her glance had missed the knotted length of rubber stretched like a dead thing on the stair. —Wait! wait if, if somebody's up there . . . he stooped to snatch the thing up and force it into the beer can's cleft crowding her on, —if they just did it . . .

—Did what Edward, if who . . .

—No no broke in I mean if, if they just broke in and they're still up here, hiding . . .

—Don't be silly there's no one . . . she paused at the top, thrust aside with her foot a packet of letters tied with a shoelace to push the door opening off the balcony, —it would be hopeless wouldn't it . . .

—No what's, what . . .

—All these papers, to start looking for any they need for this estate in all this . . . she passed through without pausing her glance at the bed's faded coverlet ripped half to the floor, turning up to the skylight —do you sleep up here too?

—Too . . . ? the can quivered at her back, —sometimes yes I, all the times I've tried to imagine what it would be like but I, it's still like you're not really here all the times I've been working when I've thought about you when I, even when I try not to I do Stella what you saw on the piano down there in the dark of, those lines I even thought I'd play that how she turned her, her bosom shaken with a sudden storm of sighs . . .

—Edward . . . her turn that close dropped his eyes to the sighing fall of her breast against his wrist there, —I don't . . .

—All the spirit deeply dawning in the, the dark of hazel eyes that's why I, what I've always remembered your eyes when you smiled I've always remembered your smile but your, how sad your eyes are when you smile that's why I, what I'm working on that's why it's . . .

—You'll let me hear it won't you, when it's finished? She brushed past him for the door where the strings rose again, gaily framing an empty trap in the eaves beyond, —it sounds charming . . .

—Charming is that all you, old-fashioned is that what you mean old-fashioned? Is . . .

—Oh a bit perhaps, but . . .

—It doesn't matter no I just said you wouldn't understand anyhow if you couldn't even . . .

—But I've never heard it, how could . . .

—I said it doesn't matter! he plunged after her jamming the bubbled knot into the beer can as she gained the stairs, —that's why you laughed isn't it why you're laughing at me you're not even laughing, you . . .

—Edward please, you're not being . . .

—What I'm not being what, I said you wouldn't understand it anyhow that's why I, what it's about that's what this is about if you'll listen . . .

—I can't stay now Edward, my . . .

—Why not because you don't want to hear it, because that's what it's about that, when you married that . . .

—But . . . she paused as he broke from the foot of the stairs behind her —you, you've never met him Edward, what ever could have given you the . . .

—What given me the what I, those summers when we . . .

—But Edward really what ever could have given you the idea that I . . .

—Why couldn't it! he came on as the strings sounded now in gashes from the eaves above them —that's why you, why you're smiling you just smiled it's not even a smile it's just, that last summer once when we all went swimming up on the mountain that stream with the deep pool where we, where you went to the one above it you went up there alone to wash your hair I thought you'd just, I came up to bring you something a towel or something you were taking off your bathing suit and I, I can still, that night I couldn't sleep that night and I can still . . .

—But, is that all? Above them the strings withdrew for a long-due trouncing by the solo, filling the space around her with the presence of empty sound. —And Edward after all, you've grown up since then haven't you and . . .

—There! you, there it's not even a smile no you let people try to do something they can't you know all the time they can't you let them try anyhow you just watch and, and then when it's too late and you smile that sad smile and it's still in your eyes that you knew all the time that's why it's wait, wait where . . .

—My cab's out there Edward, I . . .

—Your what? what's . . .

—My cab, I called a cab for the next train and it's . . .

—Cab you didn't tell me you called a cab wait . . .

—I can't, really . . .

—No but, wait wait I'll ride over with you . . . he came still clutching the beer can, crowding her for the front door, leading her the way so anyone watching might have thought it was she pursuing him over the grown grass, through light ending the day with a lustrous quality that brought to vivid life the yellows in what green remained past the crucified crabapple and torment of honeysuckle, grape and rose, toward the drive where he got the cab's door opened for her, stared at the can in his hand and then jammed it in the corner of the seat starting to follow.

—But Edward . . .

—No wait . . . ! Behind them, in exultant pursuit of its routed enemy, the orchestra burst full tilt from the studio —wait let me run back and turn that off just a second, wait . . .

—But driver . . .

—You wait a second now lady, you'll wait two hours for the next train.

—All right . . . The door slammed with the cab's lurch, —hurry then. Hurry . . . And she was swept down that arboreal veterans' ward, its splintered inmates staggered at parade rest for her plunge out the hedge, flung round the corner past the scarred pepperidge tree and hurled up the open highway in the careering interior teeming with static the entire way to the station where he turned to indicate the can couched in the corner of the seat.

—You don't want to leave something like that in my cab, lady . . .

The only trash basket in sight was one metal and smashed flat, the only voice one spilling urgency from the radio of a police car parked emptily by. Unseen now, unpursued, she rose to the elevated platform with steps as ponderous as the concrete stairs that took her to the top but one, and there stopped dead. He'd looked at her full before he'd turned away, before her voice brought him round again, books and papers disheveled under one arm wrapped outside with the Turf Guide and appearing in his shoulders' sag to grow heavier each slow step toward her. —Hello Stella . . . He stopped out of reach.

—Jack? She paused, and took the last step up. —How are you.

—Stella Bast . . . his arm fell from a gesture of wellbeing —I'm, as you see . . .

—Yes it's, it's Stella Angel now I . . .

—Way it's supposed to be Stella, honest oaf get half the kingdom too?

—But what . . .

—Old king having trouble with his price earnings ratio offers his beautiful daughter and half his kingdom for somebody to straighten things out, the halfbaked prince botches it some honest oaf crawls out of the woodwork gets the production lines humming and taps the old king for . . .

—Jack please he, he just died and . . .

—And you're on the next train out.

—Why would you say that.

—Just figured you'd done it Stella, put him out of action and . . .

—It was my father who died Jack he, you're still drinking aren't you . . .

—And you? been out here to a party? He was staring at the thing in her hand, its contents dangling —or you the new Miss Rheingold . . .

The platform shuddered with a train going through in the wrong direction and a tremor lingered in her frame, turning away, following its

lights receding as though desperate to lose distinction among lights signi-
fying nothing but motion, movement itself stilled by distance spreading
to overwhelm the eye with the vacancy of punctuation on a wordless
page. She reached an empty trash bin and dropped the can clattering
into it. —I'd forgotten what you could be like.

—Tried to myself but I gave that up too. I said some cruel things to
you then didn't I Stella.

—Yes but, I'd forgotten almost, you don't need to feel . . .

—No, no I meant every word.

—Jack, you . . .

—What? he followed her again.

—No, nothing . . . she stood staring out where burning neon forced
the eye to read. —How did you end up in a place like this.

—I haven't ended up.

—I heard you'd married.

—Did you.

—I thought, Jack what a waste I always knew you cared so, so
strongly so bitterly I just never knew what it was you cared about . . .

—It would take a woman to say that wouldn't it, something like that.

—I didn't mean, no, no never mind I'm, I'll wait up there for the
train you'll want to sit back here won't you, in the smoker, it was nice
to see you . . .

—Sorry I bothered you Stella, next time . . .

—Please, stop it!

—What, the minute you see me you start to . . .

—Well what are you doing here! What are you doing in a town like
this the first time I've seen you in, in all this time and you're wandering
around a train platform with your old books and papers your hair messed
and your, a hole in your trouser seat you look . . .

—Tell you the truth Stella it's a little embarrassing I'm, you see I'm
out here with a repertory company plays, you know, same God damned
plays over and over I'm just coming from rehearsal's why I'm still in this
costume . . .

—What a waste . . .

—Little comedy we're putting on now I could probably get you the
ingenue lead just get up there and play yourself, doing it right down here
at the firehouse it's sort of a grim fairy tale called Our Dear Departed
Mem . . . she put a hand on his arm as the train shuddered in beside them
and he turned and looked at her, down the length of her. —All right
come on, he passed his hand down her waist —I'll ride you into town
. . . and they entered the car out of sight behind its filthy windows as its
lights too receded and became mere punctuations in this aimless spread
of evening past the firehouse and the crumbling Marine Memorial, the
blooded barberry and woodbine's silent siege and the desirable property
For Sale, up weeded ruts and Queen Anne's laces to finally mount the

sky itself where another blue day brought even more the shock of fall in
its brilliance, spread loss like shipwreck on high winds tossing those oaks
back in waves blown over with whitecaps where their leaves showed
light undersides and dead branches cast brown sprays to the surface,
straining at the height of the pepperidge tree and blowing down the
open highway to find voice in the screams of the electric saws prospering
through Burgoyne Street —like the Erinyes . . . came in a mutter up the
stepped concrete to the station platform where Mrs Joubert, hemming
her throng between the arriving shudder of the train and a billboard
freshly inscribed Party tonite at Debbys cespool breng youre own spoon
and straws, caught her lapels against a gust.

—All right boys and girls stay together, the car on the left here stop
pushing! Can't you get the door oh, can you help us? Mister . . .

—Bast yes, yes I'd be . . .

—That door there yes thank you, if you can help me get them
settled? or are you with the others . . .

—Me? No the other what, I'm . . .

—Up ahead there, the other teachers it's a conference or something,
she said seated now, smoothing the skirt toward her knee with long
fingers, —why they couldn't spare anyone to help with this field trip I
think it's something to do with the union . . .

—No I'm not with them no, no I'm not with anybody . . . he came
down beside her and peaked his trousers at the knee as though to rouse
some memory of a crease there —in fact I'm, I mean after what happened yesterday I guess I'm not really even with the school anymore, if
you . . .

—That? Her profile broke with a smile turned full on him, —why it
was just a silly accident Mister Bast, who could . . .

—No I know it but, well I mean some people might think I did it on
purp . . .

—I'm sure no one would dream of it and I haven't even thanked you
have I, for picking it all up it was only three pennies short.

—Oh the, that money yes is that what you . . .

—It's for this trip today and I do appreciate your help . . .

—I'm glad to . . . he came to slow rest against her unyielding thigh,
—I'm just going in for . . .

—Boys sit down up there! If you'd just sit up there behind those two
boys, I don't know what they're up to but to keep anything from starting.

—Oh. You mean now?

—Yes just to keep, oh! Never mind I'll get it . . . the shuddering glide
of the train drew her hand after the lipstick rolling under the seat ahead.

—Hey quick look.

—What.

—I saw one again, watch when she's bending down . . .

—So what you, oh hi Mister Bast? You going in with us?

—No.

—Where you going.

—I'm just going in.

—How come.

—Some business I have to take care of.

—What kind of business.

—Just my own business now turn around and face the front.

—No but I just wanted to ask you, what does maneuver mean? It's m, a, n . . .

—It means to, to do something in a certain way to get something done. Now turn around.

—Oh, J R muttered, sinking back so that all of him evident over the seat was a pencil stub digging at the rough tag of hair lapping his collar. —He doesn't know either . . . and the complex of legs, feet tapping, twisting, wedged into seat hinges, hands scratching, picking, resumed as the train slipped forward.

—Where does it say it.

—Brilliantly executed K'ung-p'a maneuvers require no bodily contact, and yet K'ung-p'a can be deadly, crippling . . .

—That's a lot of crap.

—Oh yeah? Then look, you pay nothing if you can't disarm one hoodlum, send another flying through the air, and slam a third into the ground, all in a split second of . . .

—Well, maybe . . .

—Because K'ung-p'a is deadly beyond imagination, and since attack as well as defense is taught, only a small limited edition has been printed for serious students who must vow never to use it as an aggressor but only as self-defense to protect himself, his friends and his family. We don't ever want a criminal or hoodlum to be able to buy it because of its deadly power . . .

—Okay, what do you want for it.

—What'll you give me.

—This? Yes I want to learn the piano without hours of okay then this, look. Millions of dollars have been paid for rare coins, now you can learn the rare dates and how to identify the rare coins in your possession by obtaining our catalogue, okay?

—Okay. That and what else.

—Rush full information plus three free cosmetic samples, no obligation. Okay?

—Okay.

—Okay, if you give me Scientific method builds powerful muscles hey wait wait, look at that!

—What. That tit?

—No, down here. Original factory-packed new thirty caliber fifteen shot wait no it must be this government surplus crap . . .

—You want it?

—No I already sent for it, I got it here. It's mostly crap . . . and the two heads submerged together over the papers massed on the seat between them, knees rising, feet twisting, fingers gone from picking and scratching to dig through envelopes marked Personal, Here is the Information You Requested, Bonus Offer Inside; flyers headed Immediate Cash Commissions Paid on Every Sale, Prospects and Customers Everywhere, How to Make Big Profits Overseas; letters opening Dear Friend, Dear Sir, Is You Future Worth Five Minutes? Take a Good Look in the Mirror, closing Cordially, Yours for Success, —this one?

—Let's see.

—Let's see.

—See? Defense Surplus Sales Office, Fleet Station San Diego, it's mostly crap. Like what I wanted was this here surplus tank, so they send me this and you look up where it says tank it just says Tank, tip, fuel, four fifty gal, aluminum, aircraft, repairs required. It's just this lousy used airplane gas tank, see?

—Let's see, what's all that stuff. .

—That's these old shoes. Shoes, service, Field, leather, composition soles and heels, natural and dark brown, sizes nine C to fifteen FF a thousand seven hundred eighty-seven pairs see it's all just crap look, cable, telephone, eighteen hundred conductors nine hundred pair solid twenty-two AWG or like here, Misc hardware consisting of an estimated two thousand pieces including cups, casters, washers, screws, nuts, clamps, latches, snap hooks, rings, they just have all this crap to get rid of see? What'll you give me for it.

—Nothing.

—I got more of them too.

—Who wants them. What's this.

—Crap.

—. . . many Jews in the Holy Land should have to refuse to enter hospitals for necessary treatment because they fear that if they die their bodies will be mutilated! Furthermore, what did you want to send for this for?

—Who sent for it. It just came by itself.

—I know, I got this other one just like it only this it's about cutting up these here animals . . .

The train hung poised on a hum of escaping power, shuddered and lurched backward to a halt that jolted Bast's elbow from the sill where he had pressed it in an apparent attempt to cushion his head against the dirty pane and doze.

—Dear Future Investigator. Thank you for your inquiry in regards to the investigation profession. By responding to our advertisement, you have shown the initiative necessary to better your earning capacity and social standing. With the increasing crime rate . . .

—What are you going to put where it says are you married? if you have an automobile? What part of the world would you like to work in?

—I can put something and look. A Gold Sealed Diploma, suitable for framing . . .

—How much do they want.

—I know, that's what I'm looking for.

—What's that one.

—Never before has a career in art offered so many exciting opportunities for success and high income. Original hand painted pictures are being sought today by more and more interior decorators, homeowners, and . . .

—Boy, what crap. That's all you've got is crap. What's this.

—It's this club you can join if I recommend you.

—What kind of a club.

—It's this club, see? You step inside and suddenly excitement surrounds you! You enter a world highlighted by the soft, flickering glow of open-hearth fireplaces . . . the attentive rustle of beautiful Bunnies, the bright colors of original . . .

—Bunnies? What kind of a club is that.

—and a heady houseparty atmosphere that seems to prevail . . .

—What, these are bunnies? these girls with their ass sticking in this guy's face? Where do you join it.

—Dear Friend. If you are now a Playboy Club keyholder or if this is your second invitation to join the Playboy Club, please accept our apologies. In each area where Playboy Clubs are being placed in operation there exists a certain select group of individuals . . .

—How much does that say, twenty-five cents? You a member?

—Dollars. No.

—Crap. I got almost the same thing only it's free. Look. Dear Friend. This month Rancho Hacienda Estates is ushering in the season with a succession of gala banquets. Look at the delicious, full-course dinner menu enclosed, to which you are invited as our distinguished guest. There is no cost or obligation to you. In order to make this gala evening an even more memorable event in your life, our entertainment plans for you include a private showing of the new color film Golden Evenings, which we believe will cast the same haunting glow over this festive occasion that can light the golden evening years of your life at Rancho Hacienda Estates. May we make reservations for yourself and your spouse . . .

—What's a spouse?

—What's the difference. It's free.

—Well what is it.

—How am I supposed to know. Hey Mister . . .

—Leave him alone hey, he's asleep . . .

—Dear Friend. How soon can you get started in Import-Export?

What do you need to know? How much does it cost? What products can you import? The answers to these questions may determine your entire future . . .

—No but look the thing is it's still all crap because I mean look hey, like where this thing says yes I want to make More Money selling Advertising Book Matches. Please send the starting Portfolio and information about Sales Plans Premiums and handsome Professional Carrying Case then tell us briefly your age and selling experience what are you going to put, right? I mean like this here shoe thing Dear Friend. You have been recommended for the opening we have in your territory for a man who wants to increase his income then like what do you do where it says on this here little card I am interested in your offer to set me up in my own shoe business I wear shoe size like what are you going to put where it says here be sure to give size? I mean like if you put in your real size they know right off how big you are they won't send you shit, or if you put some grownup size then you're like going along these here traveled highways where every place of business is your prospect and potential book match customer carrying this here handsome Professional Carrying Case selling these matches wearing this demonstrator pair of these here grownup size shoes like some crazy looking . . .

—Okay then look, what do you want for those surplus Army stuff catalogs.

—Nothing. All you've got is crap.

—You said they were crap too.

—Yeah but they're better crap than your shoe stuff and your match thing what's in there, let's see. Dead men do tell tales, often the fingerprint expert is called upon . . . What do you want for it. And this wait, this guy with his fingers all grown together fingerprinting and identification magazine look, I'll give you this surplus stuff catalog for all this stuff, okay?

—What, that one lousy thing for all this?

—No but wait I got more. Look. Department of Defense, Sealed Bid Sale offering tab cards, tires, crane engines . . .

—What else.

—Look. General Services Administration, Region Seven, sales of civilian agency surplus property, see? Automotive, Medical, clothing, hand tools and wait hey look, Spot Bid Sale, Defense Logistics Services Center, pipe fittings, valves, hardware, generator sets, test sets and stands, electrical . . .

—Is that all?

—All what do you mean, all, there's six of them here with this look, this Reference Guide about how you get all this . . .

—Okay look what do you want for it, look I'll . . .

—We can't hey, we're there . . .

—Boys and girls? Let's wait till everyone gets out . . .

—Boy this train should have had a wreck hey look at all the lousy teachers on it . . .

—When we can't even get room in the cafeteria for driver training because they took the Senior Citizens' painting class out of the gym when they started the prenatal care program there what's going to happen to the adult hobby show?

—For the kind of evaluative criterions you find in these kind of enviremental settings . . .

—With the educational discount a lawnmower like that should be about forty-two dollars, so I said . . .

—When they tried to tell me I didn't know enough math to teach it I showed them enough units for the certificates and you should have seen their faces . . .

—Like they do it in Russia so I said . . .

—Like it says here to gain the creative tension necessary to make deadline negotiations meaningful you need an impending social crisis like . . .

—Seeing her in the hospital and she says Leroy motioned them right out in front of that truck so I said you better get a better story to tell your insurance company . . .

—With the textbook and the workbook and the tests and the answer key but no teacher manual how do they expect . . .

—A short story out of it which if I published it somewheres there's three semester hours credit right there . . .

—Boys and girls? I think everyone's out, stand and file out the front and wait on the platform here, get your feet off the seat, who has the money for our share in, there it is yes Mister Bast maybe you wouldn't mind taking it? Mister Bast is joining us today boys and girls . . .

—No but wait . . .

—Can we stop at the girls' room Mrs Joubert? Like this one on the train the door was stuck and . . .

—Mrs Joubert what about lunch . . .

—Watch the stairs there don't push!

—Wait I'm sorry I didn't mean, I thought you just meant on the train . . .

—Nine, eleven twelve are there? thirteen? You didn't happen to count them Mister Bast?

—No but no but I'm sorry I thought you just meant to help you on the train I, I have to go somewhere I came in today to look for a job and, and wait maybe I could do it tomorrow I . . .

—It's my fault no I wouldn't think of it we'll be, stop that running! We'll be fine Mister Bast really we, oh the money yes . . .

—But I, maybe on the way back maybe I can . . .

—Our train's around four yes and thank you, oh and I hope your job works out boys and girls stay together . . . ! they dodged ahead through the flood of hats, haircuts, briskly folded newspapers, —five, six one at a time now one at a time . . . ! engulfed in the roar of the subway until they burst from the pavement where the sun cut a path across Trinity Church —eight, nine I should have counted wait for the light!

—Hey look at the graveyard . . .

—Boys and girls? yes look at the tombstones some of them are over two hundred years old oh look, look at that one with the weeping cherub carved on it isn't it dear . . . and they gaped obediently at the bird dropping coursing down that weathered angel's cheek until the light changed and released them across Broadway and down Wall in disheveled Indian file staggered seriatim by a stench rising from the sidewalk grating at No. 11 until George Washington's extended hand flung their attention fragmented round the corner into Broad where the lofty pediment at No. 20 threatened to spill its stone comedy of naked labor yoked, high above their heads, to the lively dominion seething within, buffeted by the anxiety of lifetimes' savings adrift in windbreakers and flowered hats toward the visitors' gallery where football field hyperbole addressed them in a voice strategically boxed along the rail.

—on the Exchange floor which is made of solid maple . . .

—Boy what a mess.

—Hey I thought we're going to the Museum of Natural History.

—thousand brokers who have the privilege of trading stocks on the floor . . .

—We getting tested on this Mrs Joubert?

—that look like hieroglyphics on the ticker tape band you see running high above the . . .

—See that little guy waving down there hey? I bet if I spit . . .

—stock of companies that provide jobs for millions of Americans in every walk of . . .

—Where we going hey, Mrs Joubert? We're supposed to go buy this here stock off somebody down in that . . .

—No this way, this way, someone from the company's meeting us here . . . she quested through the modest playland of corporation exhibits off the gallery where questions posed fabricated to answers that flashed at the touch of a button, racks offered free picture postcards, pamphlets, booklets, brochures on Investment Facts, The Language of Investing, How to Invest on a Budget, A Glossary of Investment Terms —I think I see him, Mister Davidoff? We're over here . . .

—So these are our new owners!

—Boys and girls this is Mister Davi . . .

—Better keep the profits coming in hadn't we, he elbowed his way toward her from a height whose precise statistical average left him looking shorter than any adult he approached —look like a pretty shrewd bunch . . . he paused there taking them in at a glance as he seemed to anything that moved —well! We all set?

—Nine, ten oh there . . . she turned at a glimpse of diamond-patterned sweater dodging from push button information on How To Read a Stock Table, —come along now let's follow Mister Davidoff . . .

—I got sixteen postcards wha'd you get . . .

—Quit pushing . . . the elevator doors gasped closed like the breath held till they opened —where we going now hey . . .

—Icecream, there's a guy out there selling icecream hey . . .

—Where we going now . . .

—Right up here everybody . . . Mister Davidoff wheeled her off balance toward the figure ahead commanding the Treasury steps whose greeting he returned with a wave of bonhomie and introduced all round —standing here in the cradle of American history boys and girls where he took the oath as our first president . . . he threatened passersby with instructive left jabs —under a buttonwood tree back in seventeen ninety-two when merchants met there to buy and sell securities and over here, here look right over here the pits in this wall boys and girls, see them here . . . ? But her gaze, shifting, evading the stabs of his free hand, rose to rest on the magnificent chandelier glittering serene through the lazy drift of a full American flag reflected from the fortress behind them rising, falling back on gentle billows, shifting planes of reflection and reality where the still points of light pierced the engulfing warmth of the sun —left by a bomb planted by a Russian anarchist that killed a dozen innocent people right where you youngsters are standing right now, and when J P Morgan heard what's the matter . . .

—Nothing no, I was just a little dizzy.

—Shall I get you a . . .

—No I'm quite all right I, I haven't felt awfully well all day if you'll get them across . . .

And Davidoff found himself standing alone —on the northernmost line of defense of this tiny Dutch settlement, and once we cross Wall Street boys and girls, he led in a brave stride off the curb, —we're in Indian country . . . pausing past the dark mass of —an Italian Renaissance palace in Italy, but it's really the Federal Reserve Bank and there are millions of dollars right under your feet, in vaults five stories down in bed rock . . . and they kicked at the filthy pavement experimentally, eddying round him finally as he stopped at a portal plaqued Crawley & Bro. over vicious chevaux-de-frise, to allot them to the elevators within.

—Boy, hey . . .

—Look at that one . . . !

—Boy hey what would you do if they were all alive?

But of all the eyes fixed on them only the blue ones moved, as the blonde behind the desk ahead looked up; the others simply stared with hapless fixity relieved, in the wild hog, by some remembered ferocity, by rue in an antelope —like a regular jungle hey . . .

—What I told you, the Museum of Nat . . .

—Where's the snakes? They got any snakes Mrs Joubert?

But she'd sunk back on a leather bench, left the assault to their guide's officious requests for —the photographer, has he showed up yet? Nobody from my office here? One of our PR boys was, oh and Shirl has Monty called? I'm expecting a call from Monty here and the cars, the limousines . . .

A loud buzz cut him off. She pushed her nail polish aside and responded to the box at her elbow. —Yes sir, yes sir . . . oh and Mister Crawley, Mister Davidoff is here with . . . yes sir.

—And Shirl, tell him . . .

—He'll be right out, she said, as an unencumbered massive panel behind her proved to be a door.

—What in God's . . . !

—I want you to meet a real live stock broker boys and girls, this is Mister Crawley, he came on with the sweep he had used to introduce them to the father of their country —oh and Crawley, he added in a hoarse aside, —don't try any fast ones on them. They're a pretty shrewd bunch!

—We'll try not to take a lot of your time, Mister Crawley, said Mrs Joubert. —We just wanted the class to learn something about actually buying stock through a broker . . .

—No trouble no trouble at all, for you. Shirley? Get that Diamond Cable certificate out, the one . . .

—Yes sir. Telephone.

—For me . . . ? Davidoff's arm shot out and the reach of heavy tweed over his shoulder came near garroting him with its cord. —If it's Monty better let me . . .

—Crawley here. What? No, I don't know what the hell's going on there nobody does . . . What? no, it's not just two or three stocks, it's the whole market . . . do what? Certainly not. If you want to quote me you can say the long overdue technical readjustments taking place in our present dynamic market situation offer no convincing evidence of the sort that has characterized long-term deterioration in past major business downturns. What might appear at this ah, this juncture as conflicting behavior, the conflicting behavior of prevailing economic forces . . . right. Expect a certain leveling off period when . . . right. Right. Any time . . . Shirley? any more papers call tell them I'm out, he finished handing back the phone, turning, —now. These young ladies and gentlemen are here to buy some stock are they?

—Right this way boys and girls.

—They, wait a minute here . . . !

—Just want to get them inside for the pictures.

—Pictures?

—It's Mister Moncrieff, sir.

—Oh here, wait! sorry . . . Davidoff let the door go in their faces —he said he'd call me here if . . .

—Monty? Crawley here.

—Tell him I . . .

—Hold on a minute. Just get them settled in there will you Dave? I'll be right along. Now, Monty? You did, eh? So did I. Nobody knows what the hell's going on over there . . . Box? How the hell would he know he's right in the midst of it, he . . . you will? What time do you leave for Washington, I'll be . . . close that door there will you Shirley? I said I'll be . . .

—Boy!

—More!

—Still no snakes?

—What's that skinny one up there with the great big eyes, it looks sad.

—You'd be sad too if you . . .

—It says kudu.

—Well now, said Davidoff sitting, —we're a long way from that old buttonwood tree aren't we, boys and girls . . . and he'd barely shot his cuffs, treating them all to a double bolt of sapphires, when the panel door easing open brought him to his feet. —What is it, Shirl . . . ? But the blonde stopped a step inside to bend over Mrs Joubert, who nodded and excused herself. —Yes, well . . . he sat again slowly watching the door ease closed, —are there, does anybody have a question?

A sweatered arm shot up from a distant bastion of brown leather. —What's a warrant?

—A stock warrant, eh? I think that had better wait until you boys and girls know a little more about the price of apples, you with me? Now first off, what's the whole point of this stock market, anyhow. It's to bring together people who want to buy with people who want to sell. Now if you're selling something, something definite . . . He shaped the space before him with empty hands into —a basket, baskets let's say. You may have a tough time finding somebody that wants to buy exactly your kind of baskets. But if you own stock in a company that makes baskets, you can sell it in a minute. There's always a buyer waiting somewhere, maybe five thousand miles away, somebody you don't know and never even have to see. Are you with me?

—Yeah but what about all these baskets? Like suppose this here company makes all these baskets which they can't sell them either?

—Well, we start right off with the old law of supply and demand don't we, they probably wouldn't have started making baskets in the first place unless . . .

—They're stuck with all these here lousy baskets they made which nobody wants to buy them, so who wants their stock?

—Yes, well, something like that would cause the price of the stock to decline wouldn't it, and the old law . . .

—So this old law of supply and decline with all these baskets happens with their stock too so what's the difference? Like everybody's buying it and selling it which they all want to get rid of it at once so like how does anybody know how much it's worth? Like we saw all these guys tearing up all this paper all over the floor which nobody knew what they were doing, so like now we buy this stock of Diamond Cable with our money so what if there's all this here cable nobody wants like nobody that didn't buy all those baskets so it just ends up all these guys are running around tearing up paper all over the floor like where does that leave us?

—Hold on now, hold on. First, you're not going to get stung with Diamond Cable, you can take my word for it. Second, every one of those guys out on the Stock Exchange floor knows what he's doing, he knows to the penny where the stocks he handles stand. And third, stock prices don't just fly out of control because a lot of those guys, as you call them, those men out on the floor of the Exchange, a lot of them are what are called specialists . . .

—Sorry there . . . Crawley held the door wide for Mrs Joubert before he strode in to pause at eye level with a bighorn and match profiles. —Well, boys and, you little . . . ladies and gentlemen, getting right down to business, eh? That's what brings us all together, eh? Business, Dave why don't you just sit right down over there. That's what brings people together, eh? Now then . . . He came crowding the blotter where Davidoff's hands untangled ducking the reach for a button, —Shirley . . . ?

—Better have her check on that photographer . . .

—Shirley? Where's that Diamond Cable certificate? These young people are here on business, let's not waste their time.

—I'll bring it right in sir, her boxed voice blurted at the fist doubled on the blotter.

—Yes the, time is money, isn't it. I guess you've, we've all heard that haven't we . . . hands opening and grasping closed on nothing he glanced up and sought refuge from one blank face in the next till he found Mrs Joubert's —maybe the ahm, your little people have some questions while we're waiting . . . ? he drummed off the blotter's limits.

—I think they'd like to hear what you . . .

—Did you kill all these animals yourself Mister Crowley?

—Crawley . . .

—That tv on your desk is it color tv?

—This, this is called a Quotron. Just by pressing a button or two I can ask it for the latest information on any stock, number of shares traded, latest bid and asked prices . . .

—Is that you in that picture up there with that dead horse you just shot?

—Horse? horse? That's a, a hunter's hartebeest, got it in Kenya there's its head right over there, yes. Now then . . .

—What are futures?

—Futures? Crawley reared his chin toward the dim recess of dark leather.

—Here where it says the effect on nickel futures of the new government cobalt stockpile requirements which . . .

—What are you reading there!

—Nothing just, just this here let . . .

—Mister Beaton returning your call sir, the box blurted as Davidoff rounded the turn with the papers scooped from the low table in the corner to drop them on the desk blotter blinding the oval of burnished gold at Crawley's cuff with a burst of sapphire, confiding —better let me have a word with him, Monty wants . . .

—Beaton? Crawley here, what's . . . the what . . . ? No still got one certificate down here, this last option he picked up it's . . . that's right . . . he paced a step away from the desk, two steps back as though chained there before the eyes fixed on him from all directions as his own rose to the door panel abruptly jarring the dismal black on gray pattern backed against it, breaking out with an arm reaching the scrimshaw handed through. —That's right just call it a blind trust, better than going in there with this public disclosure drag things out for a month and . . . probably will yes I'll send it up . . . and he got the phone down before Davidoff's lurched —Monty wants . . . could reach it.

—Now then, you've got your certificate all we need is the . . .

—Excuse me Mister Crawley perhaps they'd all like to hear what it says before we . . .

—Sure it says, holy, it says two hundred ninety-three thousand shares it says this is to certify that the Emily Cates Moncrieff Founda . . .

—Here give me that!

—Give me that!

Davidoff rounded one end of the desk, Crawley the other sweeping open the door as he caught the certificate in mid-air, —Shirley! . . .

—But holy . . .

—The telephone's lighting up hey . . .

—Hello? Davidoff here . . . He does? He did . . . ? It is? Tell him I'm on my way, he hung up taking both hands to jam the Italian knit constriction at his throat still tighter, —brush fire, the boss wants me to get right up there I'd better take one of the cars, I think you can all fit into the other two they'll be waiting downstairs, I'll have everything on deck when you get there. Oh and Shirl . . .

Crawley got the door closed with his back against it. —Here's our certificate, now do any of you little, you young people know what it's worth?

A hand going up caught him in the ribs as he crossed the room. —The closing price of it was twenty-four dollars and sixty-three cents each.

—Twenty-four sixty-three, he muttered with a pencil, —plus the twelve and a half cents odd-lot differential . . .

—The what?

—The, stocks are usually bought and sold in round lots, a hundred shares. When we deal in less than that we call it an odd lot and there's a little price differential yes, plus the broker's commission . . .

—How much do you get?

—We'll make it one percent, eh? Plus four cents . . .

—Mister Crawley, this might be an opportunity to show the boys and girls how your Quotron works, you might just push Diamond and see what's happening to it?

—Mphh . . .

—Holy, two hundred eighty thousand that's dollars?

—No no that's, number of shares traded so far today yes quite a, quite an active issue.

—What's that minus sign two and an eighth.

—Yes, off two and an eighth points, isn't it.

—Dollars?

—Well yes in a, in a manner of speaking . . .

—So now it's only twenty-two fifty and a half cents so we saved two dollars and twelve and a half . . .

—And who are you? said Crawley looking up abruptly as the door cracked slowly. —If you're here to clean the typewriters they're out there.

—I'm a, I'm the photographer are you Mister Davidoff?

—My God no. Come in, over there.

—But I was told that a Mister Davidoff . . .

—Come in if you're coming and hurry up. Now then. Three, six, ten. Nine. That's twenty-two ninety . . .

—That four cents, what was that four cents?

—What four cents.

—When you added in four cents.

—Four cents? Tax. Stock transfer tax.

—Oh. Hey Mrs Joubert how come he . . .

—Let's not worry about it now boys and girls. You . . . she motioned to the slight figure strung with cameras, —if you'll just get this, Mister Crawley? If you would just stand holding out the certificate to, yes that boy there and, yes, the money, get the money on the desk in . . .

—Like that . . . Good . . . Once more. All right. Now just once more looking this way, once more . . .

—Get off that table!

—Yes sir.

—I'm sure we have enough thank you, we've taken enough of Mister Crawley's valuable time and, here, this way. Don't forget our stock certificate and, no just leave the money there. I don't think we have any more questions, do we . . . ?

—Did you shoot that there pig Mister Crowley?

—Pig? That's wild hog. A mean customer, wild hog.

—Would he hurt you?

—Hurt you? He killed three fine dogs.

—So that's why you shot him?

—No, hunting. Hunt them with lances that's right, right out that way . . . he came on, herding them along, —a mean customer . . . as the cropped head cupped in his hand turned sharply and he pulled back as though bitten.

—What kind of gun have you got?

—Gun? Got twenty of them. Here, keep with the others . . . what's that you've got there.

—Nothing just, I just wondered if I could take a pamphlet or something, came from behind him —like this thing Capital Gains and Losses, and this . . .

—Take it. Take it.

—Mister Crawley he's taking . . .

—stock guide, and this stock commission calculator . . .

—Take it, take them just come along . . . !

—Five, six, seven, Mrs Joubert counted at the elevator.

—What kind of a gun did you kill that thing with those horns with?

—Mannlicher here, look out there! Get off that desk . . . !

—Yes sir, I just wanted one more picture of . . . oh! I'm sorry, I'll pick it up . . .

—Just leave it! leave it! don't, hold things up . . .

—There goes a nickel.

—ten, eleven . . .

—A penny went back of that chair back there hey . . .

—Now are we all, J R? Come along you've got quite enough . . .

—This could I just have this too it says Investment Barometer . . .

—Take it along, take it . . . Crawley breathed heavily, blocking them packed in the small elevator and paused, as though to be certain the doors would close on them before turning with —get this money picked up in there, Shirley. And count it while you're at it . . . bending for the dime gone under her chair as the doors closed on his tweed seat expanse, —should be twenty-two dollars and ninety cents . . .

They plummeted.

—I think I just need some air, said Mrs Joubert, and drew her fingertips across her forehead.

—Where we going now.

—Did we eat yet?

—Out this way everyone, into those two cars there.

—The big black ones?

—Why, do you see a red one dopey?

—Who's that guy saluting to.

—That's a chauffeur what do you think it is, that's because we're an owner now right Mrs Joubert?

—Look out. Sit on somebody else, will you?

—Where we going to eat?

—Boy hey look back there, that guy lying in that doorway? He didn't have any hands, did you see him?

—Boy did you see his face?

—He didn't have any either hey what's that, a radio? Turn it.

—It's a cigarette lighter, dopey.

—Push it.

—Where we going now.

—All right now, let's just try to sit quietly and act a little more like . . .

—But Mrs Joubert he's taking up the whole seat with all those papers and stuff how's anybody supposed to sit anyplace . . .

—Let's try to act a little more like grownup shareowners in a large corporation . . . She gathered her lap from the cascade threatening from the knees beside her —until we . . . get there . . . and she stared out of the window.

—Get where.

She stared out of the window until they got there.

—Hey look they beat us, they're here already.

A piece of newspaper came blown ankle high along the curb and clung. —Six, seven . . . her pointing finger trembled, she kicked the bit of newspaper away, —eight . . .

—But that says Typhon International Building the company our stock is is . . .

—Just go in, go in! It's the right place, hurry.

—More elevators.

—We'll find our company on the fifteenth floor boys and girls. Push fifteen, someone . . . ?

—Lemme push it.

—Hey listen. That music, hear that music? Where's it coming from. Listen.

—What are we stopping for.

The doors opened silently. No one went and no one came. Nothing moved but notes of Dardanella. The doors closed.

—Can I stay on the elevator and listen to the music awhile Mrs Joubert?

—Here we are, now try to act . . .

—Hey look they beat us, they're here already.

—Hey did you have music in your elevator too?

—And look hey, here comes that same little guy again.

Shooting rights and lefts as though fighting his way through a horde to receive them Davidoff burst upon the elevator bank putting on his jacket, closing the generous bills of his collar with the mean knot of the tie in a sweep of opening a door where there was none. —Your new bosses . . . his gesture ended in a fling toward a girl packed in yellow coming up behind, his expression in a wink —boys and girls, one of our topflight secretaries. Oh and Carol . . . he stopped short piling them up on his abrupt authority, —tell Mister Eigen I need him in the board room immediately and Carol, bring in a dozen copies of the Annual Report, I told Eigen to put a little kit together for these youngsters . . . he poised long enough to keep her off balance, and then —this way, he stepped out with a rewarding report each time a heel hit the hard floor, mounting the corridor to the door opened off it just short of where blue carpeting began, and they piled up at shore's edge to crane for a glimpse of —my office in here . . . composition seated chairs vacantly attending the cater-cornered command of a paper-littered metal desk —oh and Florence, get a mailroom boy into the board room to run that projector, and those box lunches . . .

—Yes sir. I'm looking for the . . .

—And where's Mister Eigen? I need him in the board room.

—He's working on the new draft of Mister Moncrieff's speech Mister Davidoff, he needs that corrected third draft . . .

—Check. If the fire bell rings I'll be in the board room, right through here everybody . . . he turned and, in a single stride, dropped his stature into the blue that swallowed his course in silence toward the walnut bulwark ahead where he touched the metal doorknob and quaked, —not scared of a little static electricity . . . ? he dipped and crested, swung the door, and they came through bobbing, streaming, running downwind in the seaway stretched before them where, dead ahead, beating his course close-hauled, hat turned up all round, white handkerchief puffed next to the hearing aid made fast to the leach of light gray flannel, the immaculate specter approaching eased off abruptly to make the walnut piling on a beam reach, luff unsteadily, and begin to gather sternway.

—Oh here Governor, here . . . Davidoff veered full throttle cutting across vagaries of wind and sail and the dictates of labored metaphor, threatening capsize on all hands —our new, some of our new shareowners sir they've, this is Governor Cates boys and girls, he's a director of the company. They've just bought a share of company stock, sir.

—Which company? The Governor sought mooring.

—Diamond, a share of Diamond Cable, sir . . . Davidoff tipped side to side on the blue ripple of carpet as they scudded past. Governor Cates rocked gently. —Can't go wrong with that can they sir, he looked back for Mrs Joubert, —here, here . . . ! Governor Cates had begun to gather headway. —This way . . . Davidoff waved them on in a wide berth, getting the last of them by as the Governor made mid-channel dead in her course.

—Amy . . . ?

—Good morning, Uncle John.

—Good, come along with me for a minute, Amy.

She took his arm, —oh Mister Davidoff . . . ? over his shoulder as Davidoff got the last of them through a door ahead and swung back.

—Take your time, we've got a presentation all set up for them.

—And the lunches?

—And the lunches . . . He listed in a bow and hurried back up the corridor to enter the board room with —Well! You've just had an opportunity not many youngsters experience. When you go home tonight you can tell your families you met one of your country's outstanding Americans.

—You mean you?

—Governor Cates is one of the men who opened the frontiers of America as we know it today, Davidoff leaned knuckled under on the expanse of walnut stretched before him, pad, pencils, ashtray, pad, pencils, ashtray, —he . . .

—Him? He was this frontiersman?

—Not like Daniel Boone if that's what you're thinking of, no. He opened America's industrial frontiers, her natural resources that make us the wealthiest country in the world. He's a man presidents come to for advice, and you can be proud . . .

—Is he rich?

—Well after all, a man who has contributed so greatly to his country's wealth and power would deserve . . .

—What are all these here pads and pencils for?

—This is the board room, where your board of directors meets. They sit right in the very chairs you're sitting in and, oh Carol just bring those in and pass them around. This is your company's Annual Report boys and girls, we put it out because we believe that you, and all the other company owners, have a right to know all about your company and the activities it's engaged in Carol tell him to get that projector going, the many varied ways your company serves our great country with cable of every kind you can imagine from the defense industry to communications of every sort, the . . .

————ubbb . . . vvvv . . . vvawwwwg . . .

—Carol . . . ! Light splashed over the map and drapes behind him. —He's got that on backwards, tell him to . . .

—He's rewinding it, he . . .

—Oh and Carol where's Mister Eigen, I said I wanted him in here to handle this presentation find him and send him right in here. Communications of every sort, from interpersonal messages to the vast and growing television audience, whether it be the family gathered at home for the finest in entertainment or the student in the remote classroom absorbing the lesson of the master, whose wisdom can be shared with more fertile young minds in a single hour today than Plato, Aristotle, and the renowned teachers of antiquity reached in their entire we about ready in there? Momentarily blinded, he turned to reach behind the tasteful gold-on-blue arrangement of denarii, ducats, shekels, and similar bright testaments to long submerged mercantile struggles that formed the pattern of the drapes.

—Boy hey, look!

—Hey that's real neat. Look hey.

The map rose silently and disappeared, revealing a horizontal bar graph in gay shades of orange labeled Plant Investment and Accumulated Depreciation (in Millions), which followed the map to expose Sources of Capital (in Millions) in vertical yellows, Sales Projections by Continent (in Millions) in assorted aggressive hues, and two, three, four more with the haste of snapping window shades, to lay bare an empty screen.

—Reached, in their entire lives. Lifetimes. Now, in just a moment now, you'll have a close look at the many and varied contributions your company's products are making toward a growing America, and your share in helping our great country to turn the promise of tomorrow into the reality of today, as the tide of human ready in there? He braced back, doubled fists on his hips in a commanding stance of out-of-doors to look up the length of the table's sheen broken by balled sweaters, a candy wrapper, elbows and whole arms and even a head or two, chairs swiveled and legs slung outboard twisting, tapping, —we may have time for a question or two somebody might have about the Annual Report. Your board of directors wants every shareowner to, yes?

—Are you one?

—A shareowner? Of course and I'm proud to . . .

—No I mean like a director, said the girl wadding her sweater.

—Oh, Davidoff inclined restraining his glasses to contain his wink, —maybe some day, if you'll vote for me. Because, he straightened up —that's what people's capitalism is, isn't it everybody. As one of the company's owners you elect your directors in a democratic vote, and they hire men to run the company for you the best way possible. When you vote next spring . . .

—With one share we get like one vote?

—You certainly do, and what's more you're entitled to . . .

—And like if I owned two hundred ninety-three thousand shares then I'd get like two hundred ninety-three thousand votes?

—That's not fair! Like we get this one lousy vote and he gets like two hun . . .

—What's so not fair! You buy this here one share so you've got like this lousy twenty-two fifty working for you where I've got like six thou, wait a second . . . the pencil stub came up to scratch, —nought times nought is . . .

—He couldn't could he?

—I could so boy I could even vote two hundred ninety-three thousand times for myself for a director if I wanted to couldn't I?

—I mean like that's democracy? It sounds like a bunch of . . .

—Slow down now slow down, before a family squabble starts here let's come to this little lady's rescue . . . she cringed from Davidoff's wink behind the sweater wad, —every shareowner wants profits whether you've got one share or a million, right? So you'll all want to vote for directors that will hire topflight management like your company here's got to keep those profits rolling in and if they're not, this little lady with her one share has just as much right to question the directors and management as somebody with a million shares because they're working for her too, aren't they. If she thinks they're not running things for her and all the other owners she can even take them to court and start a lawsuit for damages to make sure they're obeying all the company's rules, that's why we put a copy of the company's bylaws in your little kit there. Those are the company's rules and anybody who breaks one has to answer to this little lady, like a regular club boys and girls and those are the club's rules one for all and all for one, I think that's a pretty good little lesson in democracy that film about ready in there?

—Could I just ask if . . .

—Looks like we've got another minute . . . he looked past the arm straining the sweater's dreary pattern in front of him, —look right in the back of your Annual Report there and you'll see the pictures of your directors, that's Governor Cates up in the corner you can say you've actually met him can't you, and the big man right under him you might have heard about in your history books about the war let's speed it up in there we can't take all day, General Box, he was the famous armored division commander who stopped the whole German army in the big winter Ardennes . . . they startled to a blare of music and he shielded his eyes, —all right boys and girls I think we're ready to see . . .

—Could I just ask back here where it says eight hundred sixty-seven thousand shares . . .

—Turn that sound down! What is it Carol . . .

—These eight hundred sixty-seven thousand shares which it says here they were under option at an aggregate price of . . .

———of tomorrow, presented by . . .

—Down turn it down! Look, he seized the narrow shoulder where the sweater's seam gaped —it would take a month to explain all that arithmetic it's just what we call the consolidated financial statement, don't worry about it. Now, get those lights somebody . . . ?

—I'm not worried about it I just wondered who . . .

———our natural resources, and the national heritage that makes us all proud to be . . .

—What's this Carol.

—The update on Mister Moncrieff's biography before it's sent out and Mister Eigen wondered if that press release . . .

—Where is he I said I wanted him up here, that press release can wait I'd better check this bio out with Monty get Eigen right up here to keep an eye on things, boys and girls? I've got to get on deck for a brush fire, he came on over their heads loosening his tie —oh and Carol make sure the board room's cleaned up in there when they're done . . . and his lips continued to move silent as his stride up the corridor, round an alcove, touching the doorknob his wince became a grimace associated with tightening his tie passing with a nod toward an unoccupied desk —Boss wants to see me . . . tapping briskly on the door ahead and opening it, slow, on Mrs Joubert sitting knees clenched reading through tortoise shell glasses, looking up just then elsewhere to ask —must I read all this now? elsewhere the weather side of Cates hunched, back to the door, reading papers with a look pinched through gold rims that rose abruptly and glanced off hers to cross the desk lusterless with —just the cobalt? where Moncrieff's glance over heavy black half frames and the huddled permanent of a secretary had already passed them both and returned, to leave Davidoff standing like the cry of fire! in an empty theater.

—The cobalt's what they want. The cobalt's what they're getting. He took off the glasses, folded in their straight black bows and sat back molding the bridge of his nose. —Why drag in anything else.

—Like to see things spelled out Monty, spell them out now you don't end up trying to spell them out for some damn subcommittee.

A light glowed on the desk's button-studded console and a naked arm braceleted with the time came up for the telephone. —Mister Beaton, sir.

—Just tell him . . . staring beyond them, Moncrieff's finger coursed the ridge of his nose as though the face where his eyes were fixed, dropped back to profile and none of its aloofness lost, even lowered, prompted comparison. —Here . . . he took the telephone, —bring in everything on this smaltite contract, and Beaton? My daughter's here waiting to sign those powers of attorney. What's holding things up. He handed back the telephone still looking beyond where her profile broke again, turning to him, slipping off the tortoise shells, dangling them.

—Must I read all this now? The children . . .

—Just sit still for a minute, Amy. What is it Dave.

Davidoff came forward as though he had just entered. —Your youngsters are fine, he skirted the thrust of her ankle as she crossed her knees —in there watching the presentation we put together for the spring stockholders' meeting getting a real kick out of it, he came rounding the corner of the desk in a generous turn that included them all in his audience, lowering his tone on arrival for the confidence —We'd better watch our step Boss, they're a pretty shrewd bunch . . .

A light glowed. Up came the phone, and a murmur —the press calling for the statement . . .

—He's got it right here, just read it off to them here Dave.

From the tangle of arms naked, silk-and-mohair, the acrylic sheen of Davidoff's rose with the telephone. —Hello? You'll have the statement first thing tomorrow, he said, and handed the phone back.

—What's this, then. Where's the statement.

—Being typed up sir, said Davidoff, briskly tossing the paper clip from his papers into the empty wastebasket. —This is your biography, I wanted to check it out before we release it . . .

—I want this press statement out today.

—Yes sir and on this bio, I thought we might want . . .

—Let me see that . . . Cates straightened up from the wastebasket to drop the paper clip into a vest pocket.

—Yes sir. Oh and Miss Bulcke, she can run off a draft right now Boss save us time, just take this . . . he nodded to her blank pad. —The long overdue technical readjustments taking place in our present dynamic market situation offer . . .

—Who the devil cares whether you played football against Brown, Monty.

—We felt sir, in creating Mister Moncrieff's image as an aggressive competitive team player . . .

—Image! Cates' laugh cleared his throat, —they ought to see you running around with that damn butterfly net Monty.

—Will you read back, Miss . . .

—market situation offer . . .

—offer no convincing evidence of the kind that has characterized long-term deter . . . A light glowed. The pencil stopped.

—Ever see your father with that butterfly net, Amy?

—Senator Broos returning your call, sir.

—long-term deterioration . . .

—Broos? Hold on a minute. Come in Beaton. Amy? Just sit still for a minute. Broos . . . ?

—deterioration. In the past . . .

—Finish that up outside Dave. Broos? Beaton's right here yes, what's the story down there . . .

Davidoff avoided Beaton's approach with a badly choreographed sidestep, recovered his balance as Beaton drew a chair to the desk and his evenly dulled black shoes neatly together without a glance up from the papers he opened before him.

—Hold on. What time is my plane?

—What airport, said Cates behind her.

—I don't know sir.

—Well you'd better know, damn cab fare to Kennedy's twice the fare to LaGuardia.

—Yes sir.

—They want to know if there's any way we can put off signing this contract till next week, Moncrieff said away from the phone. Beaton leaned close and spoke in a low tone. —Hello? No it's impossible, my resignation here's effective at the close of today's business, hold on . . . a light glowed and he handed over the phone.

—It's General Blaufinger sir.

—Tell him to hold on.

—He's a damned old woman, Cates muttered making figures on the back of an envelope.

—He's calling from Bonn sir.

—Let him hold on . . . he recovered the phone, —Broos? Where's the problem . . . Have you got a copy of it in front of you? All right first, in clause four. For the purposes of cobalt stockpiling, national security and so forth and so forth, that during the life of this contract as stated in clause one supra the government hereby agrees to purchase from Typhon International five point two thousand tons of contained cobalt annually, at the guaranteed price of four dollars sixty seven cents per pound, now. Down in seven. In order to expedite this and so forth and so forth the government agrees to advance to Typhon International the sum of thirty-nine point seven million dollars to construct a smaltite processing plant for the extraction of contained cobalt and then down in eleven, the government agrees to sell, at cost, to the processing plant to be erected operated and so forth by Typhon International in the country of Gandia, sufficient smaltite ore to yield at a minimum the amount of contained cobalt as set forth in clause four supra and for which purposes this contract shall be deemed to be . . . what? Because if they wanted to buy nickel they would have said nickel. They didn't come to us to buy nickel. They didn't come to us to buy iron or arsenic they came to buy cobalt and cobalt occurs in smaltite, if we come across nickel or iron or anything else in the ore reduction that's . . . well let them scream giveaway they . . . I know he does, I say if we spell things out here we're the ones who are shouting giv . . . No he's right here . . .

—Broos . . . ? the phone came up clenched to a deaf ear, —no damn time to start nitpicking, if this contract's not signed sealed and delivered while Monty's still running things here his signature on it's no more damn good than Jefferson Davis', already got enough damn problems left-wing press adding two and two getting five sounds like a few blacks jumped the gun over there blew up a damn bridge or something, Blaufinger on the phone here first damn thing he'll want to know's if there's any talk about sending in troops to stabilize the situation. The answer'd better be we're damn well not and I want Frank Black to make that good and damn clear to the press corps down there and anybody else that noses in hear me? Civil war breaks out seceding this Uaso province it's nobody's business but these damn Africans', we can't get in there and support secession don't mean we want some damn fool introducing a resolution on the floor supporting the established government either hear me . . . ? he hunched further getting the phone to his other hand, —what's that . . . ? getting it clenched to his other ear. —You do some arm twisting get that damn resolution tacked on there hear me? We're the ones that's building the damn smelter the government's not, we're the ones taking the chance they're not, you hear me . . . ? and the phone came tendered at arm's length where Miss Bulcke caught it. —You hear that Beaton?

—Excuse me sir General Blaufinger is still . . .

—Here I'll take it.

—Mister Moncrieff is on the line now, thank you for wait . . .

—Hello, General . . . ?

—Beaton you hear that? Resolution exempting private investment in a hazardous business climate you make damn sure that's cleared up before Monty signs, hear me?

—Rumors General, just rumors, we . . . three planeloads? No they couldn't be ours, the whole . . . but half the armies over there have U S stamped all over them there's no reason to be afraid the . . . no of course not General I didn't mean to imply . . . Yes I know you did General even our own history books treat it as a brilliant campai . . . I've never discussed it with General Box no, but . . . Yes I'm sure he would General but we want him out of there right after this groundbreaking, these reports have already jeopardized the contract and if you can't restrain Doctor Dé until we have the . . . now just a minute General, we . . .

—Damn brown nose here give me that . . . Blaufinger? if you can't sit on this thing till this damn contract's wrapped up we'll lose the whole shooting match, damn left wing . . . what? Not talking about a shooting match no damn it I'm talking about this contract, if . . . Couldn't sign it till these cobalt stockpile requirements were raised could we? What the devil you think Broos' Armed Services Committee's been . . . well that's the damn difference between this country and yours, don't think Pythian's mentioned in the damned contract do you? can't tell them where to buy the damn ore can we . . . ? That's the damn point where the devil else can they get it . . . don't know no wait a minute, Monty? Anything in this contract about management services . . . ? Hello? Not a damn thing no, what's . . . by God no put in something like that we'll have the Pythian interest in Typhon spread all over the damn front page . . . No and I want to be damn sure we don't, this Doctor Dé goes off half cocked again lets his black boys run around blowing up bridges before we settle this end of things you'll have this whole damn third world backing Nowunda leftwing press line up behind them leave us sitting with a wish in one hand and . . . well you sit on him, hear me . . . ? and the phone came up offered nowhere. —Squeezing out the last damn drop wants Pythian to get the contract for management services on this smelter like hiring your uncle to do your damn laundry . . .

—Nothing we can do about it I'd just like to see him off our board, this Doctor Dé they dug up for defense minister's the worst fraud you could . . .

—Damn it Monty don't own them you can't trust them, get out there you have to take what you can get . . .

——sit on, auf ihm sitzen . . . ?

—I know it that's what I don't like about the whole . . .

——mein Onkel soll meine Wäsche waschen . . . ?

—Here somebody hang this damn thing up! Beaton? Where's the notes on this hearing.

—Yes sir I think you have them right there sir.

—I do not have them right there sir! I have this damn Endo decree and a lot of fool nonsense on this alleged conspiracy to fix prices of materials supplied to the cable industry right there sir!

—Yes sir I, we thought Mister Moncrieff might want to review the material contained in the indictment in case any questions arise at his confirmation hearing relating to . . .

—Read the newspapers do you, Beaton?

—Yes sir.

—May even have come across a little piece tucked away in the Times when they dropped this criminal indictment against the company officers?

—Why of, of course yes sir but since the indictment against the company itself was left standing I . . .

—And as of close of today's business he's got no more connection with the company than Rin Tin Tin who's going to bring up this damn nonsense. Now what the devil's Endo doing here.

—Yes sir since this recent decree allowing the Diamond tender on condition of the divestiture of Endo Appliance Company just came through from the Justice Department, I thought any question relating to the family interest in Diamond Cable might prompt further . . .

—Don't mean they're going to pick over Endo does it? Want somebody to ask him under oath when this Endo spinoff was first contemplated? No damn use to anybody just make sure you've got those patents reassigned put Dick Cutler on it, only damn thing this bunch will have their minds on's conflict of interest, Broos going to lead him through it?

—Yes sir it shouldn't present any difficulties, all his security holdings have been placed in the foundation accounts the papers are right here sir, we . . .

—Right where! by God Beaton that's all I've been trying to get out of you here for the last hour.

—They're right here yes sir your niece has, excuse me Mrs Joubert . . . he hurried the papers from her lap where she opened her bag for a handkerchief, caught it up eyes unblinking over its lavender border crumpled in her hand.

—You look tired Daddy, she said to him paused half turned from her as he might have at a window if there'd been one there, looking down, fingers long like those crumpling the handkerchief coursing the bridge of his nose as he brought his gaze past hers down the long line of her throat, —and Daddy if you're leaving today I have to work things out more clearly for Francis, couldn't we try to . . .

—Yes I know . . . his hand came down, left his lips pursed with concern.

—Because you know all of you know, the only thing I've ever . . .

—Beaton? just a minute Amy . . . and her hand, edging back a black fall of hair from her temple, hung there empty behind him. —This last option here, the one I just picked up have you . . .

—It's yes sir it's all taken care of we, I don't think . . .

—What's that Beaton?

—Oh, oh nothing sir Mister Mon . . .

—Look pretty damn rattled over nothing, that what you're paid to talk about here? nothing?

—No sir no, I meant . . .

—What the devil did you mean, just said you've got all his stock distributed in these two foundations didn't you?

—Yes sir it's, we're still waiting for delivery on one certificate from Mister Crawley but there's no . . .

—Crawley? Probably got it listed in his street name down there out borrowing against it to buy another damn elephant gun why the devil'd you . . .

—No Uncle John? Excuse me we just left Mister Crawley, I think I happened to see it in his office a certificate made out to the Emily Cates Mon . . .

—Sounds like it how many shares.

—I don't recall, it did seem rather large but . . .

—Don't matter if it's one damn share Beaton you send somebody right down there and get it hear me? Leave Crawley sitting on a plugged nickel he'd . . .

—But he was really awfully kind to us I don't think you should make him sound . . .

—Didn't call him a thief Amy he's just not too damn bright, heard from Handler he thinks he's got jungle rot leave him sitting on these certificates go down there someday when you need them find nothing but a damn ant hill what's all this Beaton.

—Which the, yes sir yes since both foundations are being used as receptacles for these securities if any questions are addressed to Mister Moncrieff regarding their tax-exempt status I thought he would want to be familiar with the details of the . . .

—Seem to me one thing he don't want to be's too familiar with the damn details, no question on their status is there?

—No sir none, since the hospital is becoming sole recipient of any gifts and income accru . . .

—Any damn reason for him to say any more than that? Want more details they can go ask Infernal Revenue, Monty gets up there reciting all these damn details you'll have the damn leftwing press on the doorstep asking what bank holds the hospital's pension fund next damn thing they'll be combing over the directors of this nonprofit health insurance program coming up with some damn story what's insured's not the public that's paying the premiums but every doctor and surgeon in creation charging what he damn pleases hospital rates going through the roof because they all know they'll get every damn penny's that what you want?

—No sir no but, I thought . . .

—Didn't think Beaton damn it if you'd thought you wouldn't send him in there with every figure you can lay your damn hands on look at all this, think it's a damn Patman hearing on these two foundations? Simple damn hearing to confirm a simple damn appointment in a simple damn post last thing they want to do's embarrass the damn fool who appointed him, get him up there volunteering all this fill their mouths with a lot of irrelevant damn fool questions next thing they'll have me up as a witness on control of the foundation assets drag in this issue of Diamond preferred and we're back on the damn merrygoround with Infernal Revenue SEC and the whole damn leftwing press that what you want?

—No sir of course not but the, but of course the legal position regarding your original authorization of the preferred issue was carefully explored in terms of control of the foundations' assets, and the decision that it appeared advisable for tax purposes that the preferred remain without voting rights only if four div . . .

—Know that damn it made the decision myself didn't I? Think the fact it's legal means these papers won't be in there yapping about the public's right to know all my damn business? Tell them it appeared advisable for tax purposes this preferred pays six percent semiannually don't vote unless four dividends are missed any of their damn business why we've passed up the first three? Public that don't know the damn difference between tax avoidance and tax evasion tell them you've wiped out thirty damn years' capital gains tax with one unlimited gift to charity they'll think you're, what's that Amy?

—Oh nothing, nothing I've . . .

—Never heard so much nothing somebody pick up that damn phone, if it's Zona tell her I went to the toilet already throwing her weight around on this block of Boody's Diamond common she's sitting on, tender coming up might be just as damn easy to deal with Boody where the devil's she at, last time I saw her she had a dirty neck.

—Still in Nepal I had a call from the cons . . .

—Had her picture in the paper too damn good place for her, law spreading from one state to the next like the damn plague gives eighteen-year-olds every legal right you can think of want you to look into that Beaton, get hold of what's his name in the legislature see if there's any damn way to slow it down.

—No ma'am he's gone to, to the men's room . . .

—Yes sir I've alread . . .

—While you're at it some little wop up there just been named to head the state banking committee see where he stands on these bank charters in the damn suburbs might be able to bring him around, that her on the phone Bulcke?

—Yes sir that was Mrs Selk I told her you . . .

—Heard what you told her, wants you to get that girlhood home of hers made a national landmark once you're in position down there Monty have to move the whole damn river, you tell me the date on this third dividend's passed Beaton?

—Which the, yes sir I thought you were aware the . . .

—Can't clutter up my head with a lot of damn dates what you're paid for here isn't it? You just keep a damn sharp eye on the fourth one, Monty goes in and tells this hearing his stock's in a blind trust pass up this fourth dividend we'll have Zona in there chewing up Amy here voting this preferred with these other fool trustees blind leading the blind be the blindest damn trust since Samson got Delilah by the, what's that Amy?

—If you think I'm so stupid and, and childish why am I a trustee why do you keep . . .

—Damn law tells you how many trustees to have that's why, want us to go pick them off the subway?

—You might as well, they'd know as much about what's going on as a seven-year-old boy who's . . .

—Just the titular head damn it Amy, want a course in inheritance tax law go down and see Ude got that all straightened out Beaton?

—The, what sir the . . .

—This Francis Cates Joubert what sir!

—Yes well it's, the foundation ruling has been . . .

—What about the boy's father.

—Yes sir of course there's no need for him to know anything about it sir, Mrs Joubert's the boy's guardian in the matter duly appointed by the Surrogate and when this power is signed over she . . .

—When it's signed over? Why isn't it signed over!

—Yes sir it's, it's being prepared now sir we . . .

—Being pre, look out there! help her quick! help her . . . and Beaton stumbled for the falling papers, lurched back from Cates' hand stabbing toward Mrs Joubert sitting forward just then to pick up her handkerchief.

—But, but Uncle John I . . .

—I, I think she's all right sir she . . .

—You do do you Beaton? Had a little scare though didn't you suppose she wasn't, keeled over lying dead at your damn feet right now where would we be, damn Frenchman she married march in take over as the boy's trustee guardian every other damn thing rob us all blind if this power isn't prepared you get right out there and prepare it yourself don't you do another damn thing till it's signed sealed and delivered hear me?

—Yeh yes sir . . .

—And don't you ever bring in another halfbaked proposition like this again, don't you forget this Beaton.

—I, I won't sir . . .

—He won't either, Amy.

—And I, I won't either . . . she brought her eyes up as though from a glimpse of herself keeled over, lying dead at their feet —and he's, Lucien he's not a damn Frenchman he's, he's not even French I don't know why you always have to say that he's, he's Swiss you know Lulu is Swiss . . .

—He's a lulu all right, stunt this Italian drug outfit of his just pulled on these patents tell me that's not a lulu, any word on that Monty?

—On Nobili? I think he's ready to make a deal, have you cleared up anything with him yet Amy?

—Think he's in any damn hurry to clear things up? Long as they're still married he's got claims on the only damn things he married her for in the first place don't he?

—He'd never heard of Typhon Uncle John, he'd never heard of us or any of it when I met him, he was just . . .

—Didn't take him too damn long to find out, you don't cut him down now Amy you'll lose every damn thing you've got so will your boy, little stock deals of his we were damn lucky to get him out before he got us all put in jail.

—Oh he, he was just showing off he didn't know it was was wrong, he just thought it was smart business and he wanted to show Daddy and all of you that he wasn't just . . .

—Didn't know it was wrong, didn't know it was against the damn law you mean using his . . .

—But what does it matter! We're separated aren't we? and he's not even . . .

—Still see him don't you?

—When Francis comes down from school that's all he, we just do it for Francis . . .

—Do it for him damn it Amy can't do things like that for him, grows up the only damn thing he'll care about's what you are not what you did . . .

—Beaton? Come in . . .

—It's me Boss.

—What is it Dave.

—This press statement, I . . .

—Just hold it Dave, take that call Miss Bulcke. Beaton? he went on over Davidoff's shoulder, —those papers ready?

—They were all ready yes sir, we just need her signature . . .

—Monty told me he'd made the soccer team. Well? Proud of that aren't you?

She looked up to a gaze that seemed to end in his glasses where he sat hunched further, thumb plucking a nostril. —I'm just afraid he'll get hurt, he's so . . .

—Do him good.

—But he's, even for seven he's small and they have him playing against the . . .

—Let him get banged around a little now Amy he may not have to go out and bang himself up later to prove his family don't know what's good for him, eh? Teaching school for five dollars a week out in the damn woods someplace just to show everybody he don't even . . .

—Please! can't we ever just let, just let me sign whatever it is where should, how should I sign it Emily? Amy? isn't my legal . . .

—What do they call you at school, name that French lulu gave you?

—Jewbert they pronounce it like you do, now where . . .

—Right there yes Mrs ah, if you'll sign just the way it is there we won't need . . .

—Not Stamper on the phone there was it?

—No sir it was a Mister Duncan sir, he said he believed his wife had discussed their wish to retire with Mrs Selk and wanted to know when it would be convenient for you to . . .

—Wouldn't be, calls back tell him we'll make the bank trustee of the stock till he and Vida decide what the devil to do about it, went to school with Zona only damn thing they studied's lunching and the mandolin just make damn clear one business I'm not going broke in's the book business, always thought Vida was so ashamed of all the damn money his family'd made in cement this trade publishing looked like the fastest way to get rid of it get hold of their p and l Beaton, see if they've got a five year consolidated statement worst run business in the country can't run it right because there's no damn way to budget for it, had any calls from Stamper Monty?

—Not today no, Miss Bulcke that plane time have you checked it? And call that Pentagon number about my golf date Sunday . . .

—Yes sir, the . . .

—Get Stamper on the phone there Bulcke, said he'd call me here about this Dallas mortgage deal trying to pick up an outfit called JMI paid the big stockholders a few hundred thousand for options wants to borrow the whole damn seventeen million purchase price outright, thinks he can declare a twenty million cash dividend to his own outfit use it to pay the damn corporate dividend tax and pay off the loan want you to look into that outfit Beaton, may be buying himself a lawsuit . . .

—Yes sir . . .

—What is it now Dave.

—Just this press release and your okay on this picture Boss, before it goes out with your bio . . . he flapped the glossy likeness at Mrs Joubert, —pretty classy looking guy . . .

—Yes I, I wonder if I could have a glass of water.

—Coming right up.

—And Daddy I have to talk to you about Freddie isn't there some way you . . .

—They can't reach Mister Stamper at his office sir, he's . . .

—Spends half his damn time answering police calls try his car, may be out fighting Indians hear about that yet Monty? Probably get hold of you on it when you get things squared away down there, got the bank backing this pipeline consortium he's putting together says he's found a bunch of damn Indians camped out square in their path look into that too Beaton, here get my arm . . .

—I don't think your gal here feels too well Boss, if oop!

—Oh I'm sorry Mister Davidoff, I . . .

—Just water don't worry about it, I'm trying to get the Boss in to have a word with your, Boss? I think her gang in there would think it was pretty great if you could just take a minute to welcome them aboard, they . . .

—Wait what's all this, attributing the stock's activity to long overdue technical adjustments taking place in, what am I supposed to saying here.

—I thought we should make it as general as possible Boss, the . . .

—Who asked for a press statement on Diamond stock.

—The, the press did, they . . .

—Who's paying you, the damn press?

—No sir no, but . . .

—Happens the people that are paying you want a statement on nickel futures ever hear of that?

—Yes sir, we . . .

—Stockpile requirements ever hear of that?

—Yes yes sir the, we're work . . .

—Want to see it in the morning papers hear me? Where's my damn hat . . .

—Yes sir we, the government, I mean the Governor Boss, the Governor might like a look at our material for this book The Romance of Cobalt, we're lining up a topflight name writer who can handle the whole . . .

—Call me at the hospital after the hearings Monty, going in for these damn corneal transplants.

—Can Mister Stamper reach you tonight at home sir?

—Same train Bulcke haven't missed that game since my last operation, Amy? Take care of yourself hear me?

—Thank you Uncle John you, you do the same . . .

—The Governor may get a look at the new painting we have for the lobby, a real topflight name painter we, here let me get the door for you sir . . .

—Get out of the way.

—Right sir the, better get on deck about these lunches that gang looked pretty hungry and Boss, when you talk to them we're playing up the idea of them as new owners I think we can put together a nice feature for the next Annual Report . . . he came sidestepping up the corridor beside them as though selling something on the street until a flight of yellow cut a corner ahead —oh Carol, that photographer checked in for pictures in the board room?

———two edged sword which at one fell swoop has severed the . . .

—Oh Mister Davidoff . . . she'd reached the door, held it open, —Mister Eig . . .

—Boss is right behind me I want these pictures lined up before he comes in and those box lunches, we get the ham and cheese? That gang looks pretty hungry this thing about over? Where's Eigen tell him to turn off that projector where's the photographer . . .

———riddled with red herrings and blind alleys . . .

—Nobody's in there the projector's running by itself, Mis . . .

—Can you, here. Lights? Somebody get the ow! here get up, sit over there . . . he spilled the hunched tenant from the chair at the head of the long table as heads rose from balled sweaters, Annual Reports, gum wrappers, to follow Mrs Joubert to a corner chair against the drapes.

—Dave? We all set in here?

—Oh, right Boss we just, Carol? You've got the picture off but the sound's still on, that little white button . . .

———of industrial ingenuity rising like a glittering peak above the surface, for like the iceberg . . .

—Hey didn't we already see this movie someplace?

—We getting tested on this Mrs Joubert?

—Like remember where that tree's falling right on top of you like?

—All right boys and girls? or I should say Diamond shareowners, begging your pawdon . . . down the length of walnut his truckling glittered beneath expressions of intent vacancy. —The top man in your company has taken a minute to come in and welcome you aboard, this is Mister Moncrieff boys and girls reporting for work. That's right reporting to you, you're the owners aren't you? The rest of us only work here, we work for you and all the other shareowners running your company exactly the way you want it run . . .

———Today, the riches which belong to us all . . .

—that you and your other fellow Americans no longer play a passive part in our nation's great economy, Carol . . . ?

————we call knowhow, modern technological advances enabling the hand of man to . . .

—By your active ownership you participate directly in our great free enterprise system, giving jobs to thousands of, Carol . . . !

————two edged swor . . .

—One second, better turn that sound off myself . . .

————wedding of the grand alliance of technological knowhow and the free enterprise syssssrrrrp

Faces surfaced from sweater wads, balled gum wrappers, glazed illustrations of the earth's riches to turn to Mrs Joubert against the litter of shekels and denarii tentatively sitting her chair's edge, hands crossed over crossed knees. —Perhaps we . . .

—Could we ask some questions yet? a hand went up, —because I was just wondering . . .

—Perhaps we can hear Mister Moncrieff first, I know he's a very busy man . . . she raised her eyes the length of the table where he stood chin sunk on watered silk sequestering papers from the lounging thrust of a burst elbow.

—Thank you. I want to welcome you all as Diamond stockholders, as ah, as Mister Davidoff said the company's management and directors are your team. I see you all have copies of our Annual Report there so you know our earnings increased fifteen cents a share last year to a dollar ten. Our earnings this year and for the foreseeable future look even better and, yes since we're working for you and the other stockholders you'll see them reflected in your regular dividend checks I'm sure you all, I'm sure your teacher Mrs Joubert has explained all that to you . . . he cleared his throat as their faces turned to the cautious opening of the door —we're, as I say we're your team and this man, come in Beaton, you might not pick him for a lineman but when I'm carrying the ball there's nobody I'd rather have out there running interference for me. I want you all to meet our Secretary and General Counsel Mister Beaton . . . and he inclined for a whispered confidence. —Yes well thank you all for coming in, I'm sorry I can't spend more time with you now but . . . he saved his glasses from the hand abruptly thrust up at him, —if you have any more questions I'm sure Mister Davi . . .

—I just wondered down here where it says . . .

—All right everyone, we'll have to let Mister Moncrieff . . .

—The photographer? Davidoff reappeared, gaining speed.

—No but just down here where it says the figures in these columns show stock beneficially owned based on information furnished by nominees and do not include stock held by family members of these nom . . .

—What's he got hold of there.

—That's the, must be our last proxy statement Boss a little kit we put together for them on the, boys and girls? We can't get into too many details now, we just wanted you to meet the topflight managerial talent your directors have working here for you, we're all here to keep your profits rolling in and even if you just have one share right now any time you think we've stepped out of line don't forget that one share means you can haul us right up on the carpet and . . .

—Don't need to press that point Dave let's just get the . . .

—Is that what this here bylaws means where it says . . .

—What's, where'd they get that . . .

—Must have ah, just dropped it in the kit Boss give them a feeling of, like joining a club isn't it boys and girls that doesn't mean you have to try to read every word though does it, you'd need a lawyer like your friend Mister Beaton here to explain it let's just, one more second of Mister Moncrieff's time let's just ask him the secret of his success shall we?

—Well I'd just say boys and girls, as long as you're in the game you may as well play to win.

—I hoped he'd say hire smart people, Davidoff winked disappointment past his shoulder to them.

—That's right hire smart people . . . he paused folding away his glasses from a glance down at the pencil stub grinding on the yellow pad, —but run things yourself.

—Is that what you're going to do at Washington?

—What's, where'd she . . .

—Where this says here taking leave of his leading role in private industry to join the official family as undersec . . .

—Where did, that in this damn kit too Dave?

—Must have, one of the girls must have dropped it in we, boys and girls? That's just a, it's what we call a news release it's just a story about something that's going to happen and we write it to help out the newspapers so that when the . . .

—Like you get to write this here news which it didn't even happen yet?

—Well that's not exactly what, what I mean boys and girls a story like this we haven't told anybody yet because Mister Moncrieff's appointment hasn't really been made yet officially so let's, yes let's keep it like a club secret shall we? One for all and, and I think I smell those box lunches . . .

—All right everyone no more questions, let's . . .

—No but I just wanted to go to the boys' room.

—Here I'll take him while we see about these box lunches . . . Hands went up everywhere.

—Two at a time then, two at a time . . .

—Here, here this way . . . he caught the bowl of a cropped head in one hand, the sweater's gap at the narrow shoulder in the other steering an abrupt turn up the corridor, stopping to rattle keys.

—How come you lock up the toilets.

—It's the executive washroom now just hurry up in there, come back and join the others . . .

—Wait can we get out all right? Let's see hey . . .

—Try it see if it opens from inside.

—Okay it turns, they must be scared somebody's going to steal their toilets look at this hey.

—Push it, didn't you ever see one?

—All this hot air's coming out hey look out, somebody's in that one . . . they came up the row of metal doors stooped hands to calves, looking under. —These two . . .

—Somebody forgot to flush mine. Shhh . . .

—What.

—Shhh, somebody just came in . . .

—Damn fool don't have the sense to avoid taxable income like the plague what the devil'd he think would happen . . . black shod feet crowned by gray cuffs shuffled up the rank of doors, —obsession he's got about running low-cost operations didn't even look at the damn tax angle did he?

—I thought Wiles handled the whole thing for him . . . burnished bluchers followed, drawing heads down to rest on dropped wales of corduroy where they peered under the doors.

—Damn it Monty think Frank Wiles would have let that happen? Situation like that got out and spent something could have turned his whole damn tax picture around let the damn government's money work for him for a change how the devil's he think the damn phone company got where they are . . . a urinal flushed emphatically and one black shod foot rose in a brief glimpse of hornpipe. —Don't know the first simple damn rule there is buy for credit sell for cash now he wants the bank to step in and bail him out? Had any damn sense he would have taken what he could borrow against those assets when he had them, used that to build up their value where he could have borrowed enough to pick the whole damn thing up he'd have it to borrow against now . . . A toilet flushed. —That you in there Beaton?

—Yes sir.

—What's the latest on Diamond.

—Twenty sir.

—Get Wiles tell him to buy at nineteen.

A urinal flushed long and patiently. —I just don't want any repercussions when this tender comes up, if . . .

—Being sold on the open damn market isn't it? Company buying from its own assets no damn legal question till its capitalization's reduced by a third no need for any damn press statement on it either, make sure that what's his name knows it where the devil'd he come from Monty.

—Dave? He's all right, goes off half cocked sometimes but he works hard even puts in Saturdays . . .

—So do the damn cleaning women keep an eye on him hear me Beaton?

A restrained trickle of water sounded behind them. —Dave? that you in there?

Black, burnished, black, the shoes turned to point toward the ranked metal doors as one came slowly open, then the other, with a cinching of belts. —Well by, what the devil are they doing here, get an earful did you boys?

—No we didn't even . . .

—Why not . . . he tore off a paper towel and blew his nose, —hear more straight talk in the washroom than you will at twenty board meetings . . . and he held the paper towel off to look into it before he wadded it up. —Anything else we can tell you?

—Well I just wondered what you said about . . .

—Are you a millionaire?

—Millionaire? What would you do with a million dollars, you tell me that.

—Me? First I'd get this great big place with like these electric fences and . . .

—Be a damn fool too wouldn't you, he muttered as the carpeting swallowed their footsteps in the corridor. —You in this class of Mrs Joubert's are you? Mean she's never told you the only damn time you spend money's to make money?

—She did too hey I mean that's what we're having where she said your money should work for you or it's like this here lazy partner which you . . .

—Think she's pretty smart do you?

—Sure she's real smart, like . . .

—Real smart is she? She ever teach you what money is?

—Like anybody knows that I mean, wait, here like this here quarter is . . .

—What most damn fools think, next time you just tell her money is credit, get that?

—It's what?

—Tells you your money should work for you you tell her the trick's to get other people's money to work for you, get that?

—Sure but . . .

—There they are . . . Davidoff rounded a corner ahead, —oh and Carol . . .

—Dave, that press statement . . .

—All squared away Boss . . . Davidoff hurried the boys ahead of him, —we had to clear them out of the board room Boss I think a pipe in the ceiling went, oh Carol . . . they rounded the corner behind her, —that press release I want to see it before it goes out, just a few word changes . . .

—But it went out already, you said . . .

—You mean it really went out? Well get the, get them on the phone. Wait. Get a pad. Got a pad?

—Hey wait all my stuff in that room hey that stock we bought's in there wait . . .

—It's all right your teacher got it hurry up . . . he pulled a door and they broke out on the hard floor to round the corner on a massive panel of black on white stroked with a mad reserve, —Carol? In the first paragraph for attributing the stock's activity just read attributing the activity in nickel futures trading . . . he swerved them toward the elevators past a man balancing the huge canvas, —and in the second paragraph, for . . .

—Hey buddy where do you want this thing.

—Just, just lean it there don't drop it get into the, wait I'll have to show you where the board room is, Carol? he got the elevator button with a stab as one behind him ejected a figure hung with bags and cameras pursued by a cartload of white boxes —wait here's the pho, doesn't matter look Carol get these kids over to the automat with the others where's . . .

—I got the wrong subway.

—Never mind forget it just get me proofs of the pictures you got downtown here get those box, wait . . . he came on empty hands fighting his tie, —Gov . . .

—This it?

—This is yes sir this is the painting Governor, the one we . . .

—Don't match the carpet don't match the walls don't match a damn thing, what's all that.

—What sir the oh, the box lunches yes sir these are the box lunches but the class Mrs Joubert's youngsters had to leave because of the leak in the board room we'll have to throw them out, there's no . . .

—Throw them out? What's in them.

—Ham and cheese sandwich, banana, cupcake potato chips pickle wedge . . .

—Don't throw out good food, who ordered them.

—I did yes sir but . . .

—You ordered them you eat them . . . he bumped the surge of yellow where she backed the boys into the elevator, —hear me? Waste shows an undisciplined strain of mind, Mister what's your name . . .

They descended to Country Gardens, pressed out ahead of her —hey aren't we going to eat?

—You're going to the automat instead . . . she held the yellow skirt against a gust of wind, —see over in that next block?

—Hey look . . .

—Come on boys, don't stop . . .

—Boy but wouldn't you think the police wouldn't just let him lie there hey?

—You coming with us to eat?

—Did you see all that blood hey?

—No I have to go right back to work, there's your friends . . . she gained the glass, pointed in over beans mounting a withered frankfurter remnant charred en casserole. —Come see us again now . . .

—Who's that with Mrs Joubert hey . . . they burst from the revolving door.

—That guy Bast, she better have my stuff boy . . .

—Boys? No running . . . she called seated near bread and rolls, an elbow on the table and her fingers, curved as fingers curve on a violin's fingerboard back on the heel of her hand where her chin rested, quivered there as though bringing the tremolant tone to her voice. —Not at you no, no I was laughing at myself when I was young, at what I thought all composers were like I'd read something about Wagner somewhere, about how he couldn't stand books in a room where he was working and how he stroked soft folds of cloth and scent, he liked attar of roses and someone sent it to him from Paris, that's what I thought it was like all silk, silk and attar of roses . . .

—Is this here all my stuff Mrs Joubert?

—How we suppose to eat.

—Yes I think if we can borrow another dollar from, thank you Mister Bast just take it over there boys, she'll change it into nickels for you I'm sorry Mister Bast, I don't know what we would have done if we hadn't run into you again.

—Yes well I'd hoped . . .

—I don't know how I could have left without money, I'd barely enough for their train fare and their lunches were supposed to be . . .

—No it's all right . . . he'd brought his eyes up sharply from the loose collar of her blouseless suit, more the appeal of asking a favor than granting one in his tone —that was when he was old though, Wagner I mean, when Wagner was old and . . .

—Yes but that's what you meant isn't it, about creating an entirely different world when you write an opera, about asking the audience to suspend its belief in the . . .

—No not asking them making them, like that E flat chord that opens the Rhinegold goes on and on it goes on for a hundred and thirty-six bars until the idea that everything's happening under water is more real than sitting in a hot plush seat with tight shoes on and . . .

—Mrs Joubert could I have a dime?

—I think you've had enough to eat Debby, we're . . .

—It's Linda.

—Linda yes I'm sorry, where's your sweater.

—Over on the table, I don't want to eat they said it costs a dime to go to the toilet here, you have to put a dime in to get in the . . .

—Yes yes all right if, oh thank you again we must be taking every penny you . . .

—No no it's all right I've, I'd put some aside for the union and when they wouldn't take me, when you say you're a concert pianist they give you as hard a score as they can find there was a drummer there and all they asked for was give us a paradiddle . . .

—But why must you join at all, if you simply want to compose . . .

—No well since this teaching was, since it didn't really work out too well I thought if I could find some work playing I could keep on with my . . .

—Mrs Jou . . .

—Here . . . ! he thrust a dime at the figure shifting rapidly foot to foot beside her, —that I could keep working on my . . .

—But couldn't you earn something writing music for, I don't know but there must be somewhere you could . . .

—Yes well that's what I did, what I'm doing I mean somebody I met there, a bass player, he was on standby he's getting paid not to play at a Broadway show they say is a musical just because it . . .

—Mis . . .

—Excuse me, boys please! You've just had a dollar J R you don't need . . .

—No I know, I just wondered if Mister Bast wants me to change some nickels from a dollar for him.

—Not, no but if you'd like something?

—Some, just some tea I think, I don't feel awfully well . . .

—Yes wait, here . . . he peeled away a bill under the table.

—And he found you something? this bass player?

—No well yes sort of indirectly, he said he wanted to help me out and sent me to a place over on the West Side where they said they wanted some nothing music, three minutes of nothing music it's for television or something, they said they had three minutes of talk on a track or a tape they needed music behind it but it couldn't have any real form, anything distinctive about it any sound anything that would distract from this voice this, this message they called it, they . . .

—But of all things how absurd, paying a composer to . . .

—Yes well they didn't, I couldn't do it I mean, they were in a hurry they would have paid me three hundred dollars and I tried and all I could, everything I did they said was too . . .

—And that's hardly what I meant, someone being paid not to play who sends you somewhere to write nothing mus . . .

—Well what do you think I . . . ! he caught one hand back with the other, —I'm sorry I, three hundred dollars all I could think of was that concerto of Mozart's the D-minor, that's more than he got paid for the whole series and I couldn't even . . .

—But I think it's marvelous, that you couldn't write their nothing music? I mean just because you can't get paid to play Chopin or even write music that's . . .

—No but I am though, I didn't finish . . . he looked up from her fingertips touching his hands clenched there, —when I left somebody else there said he'd like to help me out and sent me downtown to see some dancers who want their own music for . . .

—Boys . . . ! her hand was gone, —settle down! she called after the collision at the marbled cashier's cage —I'm sorry, we . . .

—Do you like Chopin?

—Oh of course I do yes, that ballade the Ballade in G? it's simply the most roman . . .

—In G-minor yes that's on the program if I could get tickets would you, it's next week would you like to go if I can get the tickets it's a recital by . . .

—That's awfully sweet Mister Bast I . . .

—No well I guess I, I mean you're married I didn't think of that I just . . .

—That's hardly the reason no but, I'm just afraid I can't, I'm . . .

—No that's all right I just, I just thought you, you wanted some tea yes I'm sorry I'll get it . . .

—Thank you I'd, oh be careful! she'd seized his wrist.

—No I'm all right . . . he came up slowly as her hand fell away, —I'll get it . . . he righted the chair and stood looking, turned toward the figures huddled at a table near the telephone booths foreheads almost touching, hands churning coins.

—Boy did you see how she throws out twenty nickels without she doesn't even look at them? Like her fingers can count them like they're this here machine wait, let's see that one . . .

—Like these blind people which they see with their fingers did you know that hey? No wait here's one . . .

—That's crap let's see. It's got no D on it, like it's nineteen fifty only it needs this here little D on it that's, oh hi Mister Bast you need your nickels now?

—Yes and settle down, Mrs Jou . . .

—Excuse me sir . . . he turned at a tug on his jacket by a woman filling the phone booth behind him. —You Mister Slomin?

—I? No, what . . .

—Hello . . . ? she got the phone back to her ear, closing herself in with difficulty. —No Mister Slomin's away from his desk right now. Can he call you back when he comes in . . . ?

—Eight, nine, is twelve enough Mister Bast? I'll bring the rest over in a second we're just looking at them.

—Give them to me yes . . .

—And I had to lend two to Mister Gibbs okay?

—To what?

—Two nickels . . . a door clattered open behind him and a hand emerged to point, —or I mean three . . .

The hand withdrew into the booth, —Ben . . . ? No I've just been out there I've just seen her, she . . . her lawyer did? Well what does her lawyer . . . what do you mean he says I go to the track if I didn't go to the God damned track do you think I could keep up these payments? She . . . Well whose fault is that, the court order tells me to pay it directly to the Department of Probation if it takes them two weeks to get it to her what am I sup . . . Well God damn it she's the one who took it to court in the first place look, if there's some way to . . . what kind of a lump sum, where does she think I . . . the door started its clatter closed, —Christ what a thing to, that bitch that, stupid stale bitch . . .

—Boy is he pissed off at somebody, did you see him come in hey? Like he tried to go the wrong way in the revolving door.

—He's a pisser, give me some more of your water.

—What does it taste like.

—Like tomato juice what do you think.

—That old guy over there keeps looking over.

—So what.

—So he looks like the manager and he's going to come over and boot your ass for using up all the ketchup.

—It's on the table free isn't it?

—Okay but you didn't even buy a sandwich, you get fifty cents for lunch and you don't even buy your sandwich.

—So . . . ? A sodden paper bag came dragged from the battered portfolio —I'm buying one off myself so whose business is that.

—'Sixty-eight, 'seventy, 'forty-nine look hey here's an old Indian head one what's it worth.

—Five cents look I'm trying to read this thing hey, could you . . .

—What that crap they just gave us up there? You can't even understand it.

—So what I can ask somebody . . . the pencil stub ground down a margin —holy, you got a napkin?

—They're by the spoons over there. Like a club boys and girls I mean that's some club boy, you don't even get to . . .

—Look I'm trying to read hey . . . a handkerchief wad came up to smear the ketchup splash across the page —could you shut up a minute?

—Sure 'seventy, 'seventy-two here's another Indian head one you know why the Indian's nose is all squeezed up like this hey?

Doors clattered behind them. —Excuse me are you Mister Slomin?

—If I was I'd change my name.

—Hey wait Mister Gibbs? Could I just ask you wait a second, what does it mean where it says at the top here options exercised.

—Take them out walk them around the block, look where did you . . .

—No honest hey, what . . .

—Means you have the chance to buy something like stock at a certain price within a certain time, you exercise it you've bought it look what are you all doing here anyhow.

—It's this here field trip where's this other thing wait, divested here where it says he divested himself . . .

—Took off his clothes, what field trip . . .

—No honest, divested himself of his holdings in order to . . .

—Means he got rid of all his stock what field trip.

—Mrs Joubert she's over there, see? by where it says bread and rolls? And wait aggregate, what does aggregate . . .

Behind them the door clattered. —Mister Marks? Just a minute I'll see if he's in the office. Mister Marks . . . ? but his back had reared in an abrupt turn that the right bar of music just then might have claimed for a moment from a tango leaving him pitched and staring, steadied against a table before he moved avoiding the approach of age grazing with ruminant dignity in the retrieval of napkin wads from unmarked paths leading to where it said bread and rolls.

—Look out here he comes, hey.

—So what . . . the glass came down emptied, the sweater sleeve up to wipe away the ketchup tinge mustache —if that badge he's got says he's this here manager see why they don't put these napkin things on the tables.

—They're over by spoons get me one hey, what are you doing.

—Giving him back his nickels, watch my stuff . . . he swept them off the table turning for where it said beverages, coming up behind a renewed assault on the beverage gargoyle —hey Mister Bast? Here's the rest of your nickels . . .

—Just, careful just drop them in my pocket . . . and cup rattled on saucer recovering the course toward where it said bread and rolls to reach the table without accident until it was set down —I'm sorry I, I'll get a napkin . . .

—Why they can't simply put them on the tables . . .

—Cut down waste, same reason they make these chairs so God damned uncomfortable afraid you'll try to come in and dine. Napkins on the table people would use them if there's none in reach they use the back of their hand problem's manners take time why they won't let you have any, time is money money's the . . .

—Thank you Mister Bast, please don't bother to . . .

—Like a gas station come in feed get out they, Mister who . . . ?

—Oh I, I thought you must know each other, Mister Bast? She put the neatly folded napkin under the cup, —Mister Gibbs. We were terribly fortunate to run into him . . .

—Yes glad to help, what's . . .

—No no Mister Bast I meant, he's been . . .

—Mister Bast? Sorry didn't recognize you Mister Bast, I want to congratulate you on that music appreciation program. Real milestone wouldn't you say Miss, Mrs . . .

—No she she didn't see it, I . . .

—Real milestone shame she missed it, probably electrify your whole teaching career Mister Bast have you talked to Mis . . .

—No I'm, no, no I . . .

—But he's given up teaching haven't you Mister Bast, he's going to give his full time to composing. I think that's quite courageous, really.

—Certainly is. Those who can do, those who can't, teach. That it Mister Bast?

—Well I . . .

—Blessed is he who has found his work, let him ask no other sorry, that your knee Mister Bast?

—No I'm afraid it's mine Mister Gibbs if you'd, if you could sit up a little straighter you didn't finish Mister Bast, about these dancers you've been commissioned to write something for, is it ballet?

—Not no not exactly no, no there are only two of them they want something that's, something more Spanish they want something with some class this bass player told me who's a friend of theirs, I mean I guess he's a friend of hers that's why he sent me down there something like Bizet he said, they want something like Bizet only not Bizet, if you see what I . . .

—Certainly do yes, like Bizet was condemned for being something like Wagner but not Wagner by people who had never heard Wagner and couldn't understand Bizet, that it Mister Bast?

—Well I, yes all I meant was . . .

—Yes we, we were talking about Wagner earlier weren't we Mister Bast . . . she pressed one hand in the other as though to restrain her voice's tremor in her fingers —about his, the conditions he needed in order to work scents and, and silks to touch and . . .

—Women, and women . . .

—Oh and the garden path yes I forgot, that he couldn't concentrate if he looked out and let his eyes follow the garden paths because they led to an outside world, to the real . . .

—Led in.

—Pardon?

—They led the God damned outside world in.

—I, I see yes thank you, it's rather like your studio isn't it Mister Bast the one you were telling me about, where a vision can exist unfinished with a life of its own till the moment Mister Gibbs do be careful, tipping back like that these chairs are terribly untrustworthy, Mister Bast almost . . .

—Why our view of life's misleading, Mister Bast.

—What? I don't . . .

—I said our view of life's misleading but of course we have bad seats, not some relation to James Bast are you? the composer?

—Well, well yes I . . .

—What I meant, genius does what it must talent does what it can, that the line?

—Mister Gibbs please we, we were talking about Mister Bast's opera I don't think you . . .

—What I'm talking about that whining tenor part he gives Ulysses real stroke of genius, comes off as a real sneak the only man who's ever seen Ulysses clear whole opera's the God damndest thing I ever . . .

—I don't think we . . .

—No well that's, that's his opera Philoc . . .

—What I'm talking about Philoctetes real stroke of . . .

—No I'm afraid we're talking about something else Mister Gibbs, an opera this Mister Bast is working on that's quite . . .

—Like Bizet only not Bizet, thirty-seven years of failure get to die of a broken heart if you're luckier than the outside world pounding down the garden path on us here now, concentrating what's left of his dignity trying to keep his teeth in place . . .

—Mister Gibbs please . . .

—Spread the checked cloth over the rusty green table, if the lady and gentleman . . .

—And I thought, wasn't it just heart disease Bizet died of and Carmen, they produced Carmen before he died and it was a great success . . .

—Three whole months before he died veritable lifetime . . .

—Excuse me sir . . .

—Mister Urquhart? he straightened back from examining the penciled name pinned under the fraying of the false buttonhole, —what can we do for you sir.

—It's just the, these children, are you with them?

—Well let's say they're with us.

—Yes sir well they, the water glasses and the ketchup and, and the napkins if they could settle down at one or two tables, the other customers, to not disturb the other customers . . .

—Understand perfectly Mister Urquhart, refreshing to see a man in your position take his responsibilities seriously must be quite a task managing this establishment, wouldn't think of . . .

—Yes thank you, thank you . . . he backed away eyes down, went for a fork on the floor behind a pillar.

—If the lady and gentleman wish to take their tea in the . . .

—Please I, I think we should get them together and, oh . . . ! she'd turned the profile of her raised chin and, one finger delicately cocked, her hand risen with a white cracker to her parted lips where Bast abruptly thrust a lighted match.

—Oh I, I'm sorry I, I thought you were smoking, did I . . .

—No it's all right . . . she bit the cracker but her hand came away trembling, like his with the match. —It simply startled me . . .

—But I'm, I'm really ow!

—Oh here, here put the teabag on it it draws out the heat please could one of you, Mister Bast could you tell the children to get their things together . . .

—Oh the, yes . . . he was up, —yes of course . . .

—And Mister Gibbs I think if, if you can excuse us . . .

—No no it's all right haven't been this entertained since . . .

—Well would you mind sitting up! simply, simply trying to sit up straight the children have been looking over and they, I'm just afraid they'll think you've been drinking.

—Think I've been, listen they don't know what drinking is I could sit down over there shoot myself through the head they'd think I was dead and expect to see me in school tomorrow Christ they don't know what, look at them over there look like a God damned settlement house Mister Urquhart creeping around picking up napkin wads like something out of Dickens they . . .

—Is that any reason you should treat him like . . .

—What who Urquhart? I'm God damn it I didn't invent him look at him, think he hasn't got a skinful to get through the day in a place like this? That almost distinguished profile that authority in his face but it won't stay still afraid people will notice his teeth don't fit, afraid he'll lose them and we'll all laugh so he's telling that sloppy busboy to clean up a table he's almost finished anyhow keep his authority intact just those God damned teeth can't relax for an instant he's . . .

—Please stop it!

—But, but what . . .

She'd caught her lower lip to one side and she shook her head quickly. —I don't know I, I don't know . . .

—But . . .

—No please! she caught her hand away, opened the bag in her lap —if you'll just let me . . .

—Because Christ if you think I'm, you think I think he's funny out there trying to hang on . . .

—You all do, she said in a voice near a whisper over the handkerchief's faint edge of lavender —all of you that, that poor man this morning standing in a cradle he kept talking about standing in a cradle, we are now standing in the cradle he said trampling those sharp little leather heels of his who, who ever stood in a cradle no please!

But he held her fallen wrist there —listen! you can't, always somebody standing in your cradle somebody setting fire to your cracker you can't . . .

—Well why shouldn't he! he, even that even lighting my cracker he was trying it's, I think it was quite dear of him it's certainly nicer than, than the way you pick on people for trying especially on him when all he wants is to, why you can't simply, simply act like a grownup . . .

He'd recovered his hand, busied it now digging a matchbox from a pocket. —Never really expected to . . . he dug elsewhere, came up with a broken cigarette.

—To what, to grow up? she looked away from his hands, —do you think any of them do?

—Does. Any does.

—Pardon?

—Expect to die too, get to come to school next morning tell all their friends about it Christ, the thought of you herding them out across these filthy streets and the train that train, staring through dirty panes at the waste out there train creaking along the sun gone down leaves blowing and the wind, dead leaves blowing you and these kids along from behind . . .

—But I don't think they . . .

—Indian summer somebody says but I don't see it just the wind, sun gone down the God damned wind rising dead leaves you and these kids blowing along from behind . . .

—It's always a sad time of year but, but I don't think . . .

—Sad Christ it's, life draining out of the sky out of the world it's . . .

—But it's quite beautiful too, the fall colors the leaves changing you can't really say . . .

—See life draining out of everything in sight call that beautiful? End of the day alone on that train, lights coming on in those little Connecticut towns stop and stare out at an empty street corner dry cheese sandwich charge you a dollar wouldn't even put butter on it, finally pull into that desolate station scared to get off scared to stay on . . . he'd slid the matchbox open, picking out matches to arrange all their heads in one direction —school car waiting there like a, black Reo touring car waiting there like a God damned open hearse think anybody expect to grow up . . .

—But was, this was boarding school? did you . . .

—Telling you that's what we did there, got to bring these God damned colored leaves in to class try to copy them with crayons . . . he squeezed the matchbox closed —I, I watch you sometimes, he looked up abruptly —your lessons I mean, on television when I don't have a class and, or when I stay out . . .

—But, but why in the world, my lessons aren't . . .

—No with the sound off I, I just watch you . . .

—Oh I, I see yes well I think, I wish you wouldn't stare so I think he has the children together and we really should . . .

—Excuse me ma'am they found this sweater in the ladies' toilet, I think one of your kiddies . . .

—Yes yes thank you so much Mis, Mister Urquhart I think we're leaving in a moment yes, thank you . . . she pressed the handkerchief to the corner of an eye, snapped her bag closed —we must leave Mister Gibbs no please, you don't need to come with us I don't think it would be . . .

—Did you see my sweater Mrs Joubert? It's like red with . . .

—It's right here Linda just, here just put it on so you won't lose it again go over and tell, ask Mister Bast to get everyone together we're leaving in a moment . . . she pushed her chair back. —I'll just be a minute . . .

—Do you, wait . . . !

—No please I, I just felt faint . . .

—Yes well here let me . . .

—I'm all right no it's, it's just sitting so long . . . she steadied her hand on the back of a chair. —You might help Mister Bast . . .

—But . . . the hand he'd raised in support fell empty and he looked after her, after her legs lost among legs of tables and chairs as he gained his own with a wince, came lifting one foot along like a weight —say, Mister Bast . . . ?

—What? Oh, yes I think they're all ready what's the matter.

—Nothing foot went to sleep, listen . . .

—No I mean Mrs Joubert where is she, I don't think she feels well she's . . .

—What I'm trying to tell you she's out on her feet hardly knows it herself, look . . .

—No but do you know what she's . . .

—No and she doesn't either nobody does look Mister Bast something you should know, in spite of its appetizing symmetry woman's body's an absolute God damned chaos spend their lives at the mercy of their bodies, whatever it is she can't handle this bunch for the rest of the day I'd try to myself but I can't even count them so listen, I just told her you'd offered to take them over, get them home on the next train and . . .

—Yes well, well all right but what about her she's . . .

—Be fine look best authority there is says just get those breasts to stop shaking we may be able to collect some fragments of the afternoon I'll concentrate on that you just tell her you're taking this bunch over, she'll protest you insist don't be so God damned deferential just take over, women like that . . .

—Yes but . . .

—Where we going now hey . . .

—Where's everybody going hey where's Mrs Joubert . . .

—Over by where it says desserts come on . . .

—Look you're going with Mister Bast . . . he came trailing them across the floor kicking a foot out as though to shake them loose —go wait with Mister Bast . . . and he'd shed the last of them when he reached her sitting the edge of one of those chairs by where it said desserts rummaging her bag. —Are you all right?

—Yes but wait there was something I . . .

—All taken care of relax, Mister Bast just . . .

—That's it yes I, you don't have a piece of note paper . . .

—Plenty of it relax . . . out came bits of newspaper, cards, paper scraps —look Mister Bast just offered to, here how's this . . .

—I don't, no it says Clocker Lawton's Suggestions I don't think it quite, it's for a note to a broker you see, I . . .

—Wait here here's a piece look, Mister Bast just offered to take . . .

—Beware women who blow on knots is that, that's nothing you want to keep? It's written on the . . .

—No no I'll remember it look, Mister Bast is . . .

—Oh Mister Bast that note I said I'd give you to Mister Crawley, before I forget it . . .

—Yes well thank you but if . . .

—No go ahead plenty of time relax, Mister Bast kind enough to offer to take these kids off your hands get them home on the next train I'll just get a . . .

—Oh but no . . . the pen stopped, —the school bus is meeting the four seventeen they, they wouldn't be able to get home if you leave now they, we were going to a money museum . . .

—No trouble is it Bast turn them loose in the money mu . . .

—I had the address here it's a, in a bank somewhere . . .

—Know right where it is don't you Mister Bast let's get them together here two, three stay together there . . . !

—You're, you're sure it's all right Mister Bast it's awfully kind I, I just feel . . .

—It's yes it's fine it's, fine yes . . .

—And here's, dear it does look awfully shaky doesn't it I'm sure Mister Crawley will understand though and don't let him alarm you, he's rather a bear but I know he'll be glad to help with your aunts' stock you will get them home on the four seventeen?

—Yes and thank you, I . . .

—Wait yes six, seven there were twelve I think, Linda? you have your sweater? Nine where's, who's that man those boys are sitting with, there by the phones he looks . . .

—Businessman name of Slomin perfectly respectable, feel a little steadier now? This way . . .

—And Mister Bast thank you again . . .

—Hey Mister Bast where we going . . .

—Where's everybody going hey.

—Could I have a dime Mister Bast?

—All right stay together now, boys? Go over and get those two boys by the, never mind wait right here . . .

—Hey look there goes Mrs . . .

—I said wait there!

—Oh hi Mister Bast, where we . . .

—What are you doing in the phone booth come along . . .

—I just wanted to get the number off it wait, wait let me get my stuff . . .

—I said come along! Now where's, all right stop pushing, now where's . . .

—Bast look, sorry . . . his arm was seized from behind, —if you've got a couple of dollars for a cab . . .

—But, yes but wait what did she mean about a money museum she, here, she said a bank somewhere but . . .

—Look there's a bank out here every two blocks every God damned one of them's a money museum forget it, take them to a movie and Bast? Didn't mean to be that unpleasant look I've got to talk to you some time when I'm . . .

—Yes well, yes whenever you . . .

—We going with you Mister Bast?

—Like where's he going hey.

—The movies hey, we going to the movies?

—Come on look out, here comes the manager . . .

—One at a time in the revolving door, one at a . . . I said one!

—There's a movie hey. Over there.

—Is that it over there Mister Bast? Where it says playthings of what's that hey.

—A carte blanche invitation to ecstasy . . .

—Is that it Mister Bast?

But he stood staring in the other direction where the street's traffic stopped for a cab exchanging fares until its door slammed and their heads, inclining, showed through the rear window, and everything moved again, and the wind picked up a little from behind.

—Look. You can see her tits.

—You cannot they pasted something over them.

—So? peel it off, hey look at this. Relive the pulsating moment of climax . . .

—No subject is taboo! No act is forbidden! What's taboo hey. Hey. Look at this one. A generation in heat . . .

—Look at that pair of knockers!

—Excuse me . . .

—What?

—I thought, have we met somewhere? My name is Gall . . .

—I don't, not that I remember I . . .

—Hey! Women wrestling in a tub of eels hey.

—Look at this one what they're doing. What are they doing?

—Karate.

—Naked?

—They may not let you take them in.

—Here? Oh, no I wasn't, we were just looking for . . .

—There's a Western up in the next block, want to take them to that? I've got to kill some time till four o'clock anyhow, maybe I'll remember where I know you from . . .

—We're not seeing these women wrestling these eels?

—Wait for the light . . . !

—Where we going now? I thought we're going to the movies.

—That one Mister Bast? His soul seared by the flames of passion, his eyes scorched by the fires of hell . . .

—Seven, eight, nine, stay in line now.

—Seven eight nine, stay in line, it rhymes. Seven eight . . .

—Quietly!

—Didn't you pay for me? Gall pursued.

A child fired a derringer point blank in their faces. Flames climbed curtains and drapery.

—Quick her tit! Did you see it?

—That's her elbow dopey.

—Shhhh . . .

Unmade beds, plates, broken glasses, bottles, chairs tipped and candles flaming haphazard, underclothing and sequined smalls, feather boas, a bearskin blanket snatched away.

—Look!

—That's just her under of her arm.

—Shhhhhhh . . . !

Dawn, finally, and church bells faded under the hollow clop, clop, clop of horses entering the empty street. Dinner by frontier candlelight, moans and petting in the pea patch, gunfire, the fluttering pennon of the cavalry troop, sunlight, darkness, bonfires, gunfire, crowds filling the streets, milling toward the platform hung with flags and bunting in red, white, and blue.

——I'd shoot him down myself but I ain't carrying a gun.

—What time is it!

—Please, it's almost over . . .

—Mister Bast please just till he shoots him, please . . . ?

—Shhut up down there!

—Please . . . ?

They stumbled into each other looking back over their shoulders, erupted into the lobby in a crash of gunfire, the street on a gust of wind. —So when this one guy shot at this other guy this first guy thought he was shooting at him so he shot him.

—Who.

—Who shot him.

—Shot who.

—We should have went to see those women wrestling those eels.

—Wait for the light! Here stay together now, this way . . .

—Look out hey quit pushing . . .

—Straight ahead, watch those stairs . . . !

—Wait up hey my shoelace is . . .

—I said hurry!

—No but can I just get a newspa . . .

—Can I get a candy bar Mis . . .

—No! I said watch the stairs . . .

—But where we suppose to . . .

—Anywhere just get on the train! six, seven how many, I said stay together!

—Boy I almost lost my sneaker back there you sitting here Mister Bast?

—Look just find a seat anywhere and, there's one over . . .

—No that's okay just let me get my stuff up on my, could you move your foot a second? Just so I can get my knee, there. Who was that guy we took to the movies, is that some friend of yours?

—I've never seen him in my life no, now . . .

—Boy he squeezed right in like he's this real old friend of yours what did he . . .

—I said I don't know! He thought he knew me and wanted some help with a book or something, now . . .

—Okay don't get mad, I just . . .

—And look, haven't you got a handkerchief?

—Me? sure just a second . . . he wedged a sneaker into the seat ahead burrowing the sweater's burst elbow into the ribs beside him, coming up with a discolored wad —here.

—No I mean you. Use it.

—Oh. He blew his nose hard and then wiped the back of his hand across it. —Are you a college graduate Mister Bast?

—I went to a conservatory.

—Oh . . . he looked up from the handkerchief's contents and wadded it back. —What did you learn there, how to be this forest ranger?

—This what?

—I mean like now this is all you do is teach?

—No, no I have my own work.

—What, like you said before you're going in the city on business? I mean what business you in.

—Look I'm not in, what . . . ?

The conductor's punch tapped the rim of the seat ahead. —These kids all with you?

—Yes they, here get your tickets out . . .

—You got them.

—Didn't she give you them, Mrs Joubert? Like she kept them so we wouldn't lose them.

—But she, no, no you mean nobody has a ticket? But does, did any of you bring any money?

—Six, seven . . . the punch counted over their heads, —eight . . .

—That's all you've got hey? a dollar? Wait a second . . . the handkerchief wad surfaced again bringing with it a tangle of bills, paper scraps, a pencil stub —five, six, seven how much do you need hey . . . the bills came up damp and separate, —that's nine is that, no you take the change that makes it easier to figure when you pay me back, okay?

—Well thank you yes but, but is all that yours?

—What this money? Sure why, you want one more to make it ten even? A single came off freed in a wad of its own —I mean that makes it easier to figure up the interest and all, you know?

—Yes but, all what I . . .

—No I just mean the interest like, I mean that's what we're having now these percents could you move your knee a second? I mean this here portforlio the zipper never hardly worked right even when I first got it you know? he tugged at the battered thing —holy shit look at that it's already ripping, I mean that's why I need this here professional carrying case you know . . . ? he got it opened on his lap extended now with both feet dug into the hinge of the seat ahead, —see? I mean like here it costs thirty-four million dollars to equip this armored division and it costs like ten million dollars to equip this here infantry division see so what you have to find out is . . .

—Yes well look I don't know anything about armored div . . .

—No that's okay see it's just about equipping them like you're equipping anything just to figure up these different percents, I mean here's this Mister A with this here business which he owns thirty percent of it see it doesn't matter what business it's just this here business, see so anyway it says he sells this forty percent of his thirty percent for fifteen hun wait, thousand I mean, fifteen thousand one hundred twenty dollars so you have to find out how much is the whole thing worth see?

—Fine yes, now I . . .

—No but see I wanted to ask you . . .

—Look if you need help with this you should talk to, to Mrs Joubert or . . .

—No that's Glancy, I mean this is just our math homework where you wanted to know about these percents see but I got this other real stuff which wait a second . . . he tugged at the heap, —holy . . .

—Here be careful you're spilling the whole . . .

—I know boy this train it's like you're riding some rolycoaster how it stops could you pull that corner sticking out there?

—What this, fingerprint and identi . . .

—No that's just crap for trading see I had this thing about import export where you get to wait hey could you hold this stuff a second till

I, see this here proxy thing we got today I wanted to find out where it says what's that wait . . .

—Unretouched pages in swinging color, finger licking good look will you get all this off my . . .

—Wait no his crap's always getting mixed up with mine there's this thing where I wanted to ask you here, look.

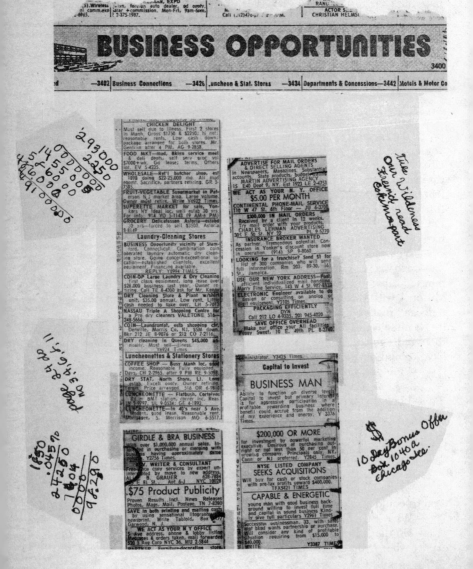

—Well what, what is it what's . . .

—No well see it's just these here opportunities I pasted up see where it says we act as your . . .

—Look will you just get all this off my lap? I just said I couldn't help you I don't . . .

—Okay don't get mad I was only . . .

—I'm not mad I'm, I'm just tired I've been . . .

—No but see I thought like where I just helped you out on these here tickets you'd maybe . . .

—All right! but, thank you look thank you for the loan I appreciate it but what makes you think I know anything about these, this girdle and bra business or a coin op laundry and dry cleaner I don't even . . .

—But you said before you have your own business.

—My work, I said I have my own work.

—I know. What is it.

—Composing.

—What?

—Music. Composing music.

—Oh. You mean teaching it like?

—Writing it.

—You mean like making it up?

—Yes.

—Oh. The train drained to another standstill and he came forward over the heap on his lap to add another to the succession of knots in the sneaker's lace. —Are those the only shoes you've got hey? Mister Bast?

The foot propped in the far hinge dropped from sight. —Why.

—Nothing I just wondered, see I got this thing where you send away for this here selling outfit which . . .

—Look J R would you mind I'm, I just want to close my eyes for a minute.

—What, like go to sleep . . . ? he wedged a sneaker more tightly into the seat ahead bringing the heap higher with his knees, sinking slowly until a nostril came in reach of his thumb, finally —I just wondered, I mean can you make much doing that? writing this here music I mean? he paused, his elbow grinding against the arm hung limp beside him. —I guess not or like why would you teach, right . . . ? and then he twisted abruptly bringing the burst elbow over the back of the seat —where's that magazine hey.

—Which.

—With all the tits, give it here a second.

—Here take it, you coming back to finish trading?

—Just a second . . . net stockings, parted lips, hams, breasts fled under his thumb —hey Mister Bast?

—Look I told you I . . .

—No but wait a second I just remembered something, it's back here someplace wait . . . his thumb stopped on Unusual Poses, ran its black crescent down Strange Pleasures, I Have What You're Looking For, Honeymoon Love Drops —here look, you want to send it in? Song writers wanted. Send no money now. Our master tunesmiths will put your song to music that will, hey . . . ? He turned to the profile riding severed down a cheekbone in the cracked pane beyond, —look I'll just stick it in your pocket then . . . it came out torn the length of the page —for if you want to send it in okay? and he crushed it with the back of the page out displaying a graveled nipple in the breast pocket beside him, freed his feet from the seat ahead for an ungainly step to the one behind. —Here.

—What did you rip out hey.

—Nothing something Mister Bast wanted and look, take this here fingerlooking good thing your crap's always getting into my stuff . . . he got the sneakers wedged into the seat ahead, brought his knees up under the heap.

—Crap boy look at yours I never saw such crap look, Investments Facts, A Glossy of Investment Terms who wants to trade that crap.

—Who said I'm trading it . . . the hand burrowed beneath him paused to scratch, came up with the pencil stub —look hey I'm trying to figure up some stuff okay?

—I thought you came back to finish trading but who wants that bunch of crap, I mean where's Break exciting cases Solve vicious crimes.

—Under here, you want it?

—Keep it, I can send for it too.

—Go ahead.

—You got it free.

—So? you got dinner invitation free.

—What do you want with it, you can't even go.

—Either can you. B . . . the pencil stub smudged down the glossary's margin —no wait d, it was d . . .

—What was.

—This here word I'm looking for where I'm sending away to find out what they are g, h, no wait d's before wait, c . . .

—How come you want them if you don't even know what it is.

—Because they're real cheap wait, d . . .

—Boy no wonder you get so much crap look, for fingerprint and identification plus bona fide reports of private investigators plus Green Book of Crime plus break exciting cases okay? For you're getting rare coins plus dear law student plus this here surplus book and three cosmetic samples plus gala dinner okay?

—Okay plus spot bid sales where's that.

—No well then I get powerful muscles plus rush me K'ung p'a in plain wrapper plus renowned Oriental doctors okay? You want this here defenders of wildlife or this cutting up these Jews thing?

—Who wants all that crap no look, just these whole six surplus books plus reference guide and spot bid sales plus gala dinner that's all, watch out for your foot . . .

—My foot! Boy I can't hardly move with all this crap what's that, you even stole that yellow pad off them?

—What do you mean stole . . . his dangling thumb moored at the nearest nostril, —we're this here owner aren't we?

—Owner shit, boy . . . the hand beside him brought up its crew of fingers for a siege of nailbiting, —go ask that old fart that caught us in the toilet you'll find out you don't own shit.

—Oh yeah . . . ? he said in a tone so low it was lost before it reached his image on the dirty pane where he stared now as though staring through at something far beyond. —That's what you think.

A lighted platform loomed past the windows and was gone.

—We went right past the station hey. Mister Bast? wake up . . . !

—Quick hey, hurry up . . .

—Look out for my stuff . . .

—Hurry up before it starts again . . .

—I can't get this, hey Mister Bast can you get this door open?

—One at a time now, one more car back don't push!

—Look out hey, it's full of teachers . . .

—Aggressive and action-oriented . . .

—to demand duty-free lunch periods, I didn't go to college to learn how to teach kids how to eat peanut butter and jelly sandwiches or . . .

—say career oriented, and making less than an average construction worker . . .

—with insurance for cars damaged in the school parking lots and . . .

—when the plumbing in the junior high gets stopped up with contraceptives, if you call that . . .

—creative tension, creating creative tension they call it . . .

—mass resignation, you call it mass resignation, with the antistrike law if you call it a strike you . . .

—call a spade a spade.

—Try that and they'll burn down the school.

They milled past Debbys cespool freshly annotated We kick ass yours too toward the stairs, crowding down, pairing off to seek parked cars in the rising wind that caught up leaves and bits of newspaper.

—Mister Bast did you see my sweater . . . ? The bus door shut in her face and he watched it bully its way into traffic before he turned back for the station, shook a locked door, finally swung open the one beside it.

—I want to report a lost sweater, he said at the grating. —Red. A girl's red sweater.

The agent looked up at the clock. Then he thrust a form under the sign on the grating Agent on Duty J Teets. —Fill out this, hey buddy! You want to bust that?

—Too God damned late, beat me to it . . . a crash came from the shadows.

—What do you think you're trying to do?

—Think? another crash, —know God damned well what I'm trying to do . . . and another, —get the cigarettes I paid for out of your God damned machine here.

—Kick it like that again you'll have trouble.

—Like that? another crash, —already got trouble what the hell do you think I'm kicking it for.

—You want me to call a cop?

—Police! Like that? the figure recovered balance from a final kick. —Police . . . ! he broke from the shadows waving a rolled newspaper —call them myself sue your God damned railroad for theft of services, witness right here saw the whole thing.

—But, but Mister Gibbs what . . .

—Who? he caught a hand at the window grating, —Bast! what the hell are you doing here.

—Well I, I just got off the train and . . .

—So did I God damned lucky we're alive.

—But I thought you were with Mrs Joubert was she, is she here?

—Where! where!

—No, no I meant . . .

—Better get him out of here buddy, came from behind the grating where the hand slid down to rest on the sign promptly followed by a sagging scrutiny.

—Teets. Want to give you a message for Agent Teets, Bast.

—Get him out of here buddy.

—Next time you see Agent Teets Bast God damned eavesdropper watch out for him, loyal friend but a cunning and dangerous enemy walk over his God damned grandmother why they got him behind bars here theft of service Bast, civilized conversation get over here where he can't hear us God damned eavesdropper, watch out for him . . .

—Yes but, Mrs Joubert is she all right?

—Momentary recovery Bast, got inhaled each momentary recovery thought I had a newspaper.

—It's under your arm yes but was she, what happened . . .

—Got lost in the dark caverns of her throat Bast, bruised by the ripple of unseen muscles ought to be ashamed of myself, told me I should apologize to you how's that.

—Well no but that's not what I . . .

—Told me you're talented sensitive purpose Bast sense of purpose need help and encouragement lock yourself in write nothing music, take defeat from any brazen throat get to be like Bizet only not Bizet where the God damned doors . . . he hunched as though with cold, hands buried in pockets —dum dum dedum . . .

—Over here yes, but . . .

—Don't spit upon the, garden path lead the whole God damned wait, Bast? Something I'm supposed to give you these right here she forgot to give me wait, forgot to give them to you here.

—But what are they, why . . .

—Kiddies' train tickets here.

—But, no but this one says combined number five, seventh race what . . .

—Call that train tickets?

—No that's what I . . .

—Eight to one broke at the God damned gate here, what are these.

—Wait you're dropping, they're train tickets but what . . .

—Just told you they're train tickets didn't I? Told you she said give them to you forgot to give them to you didn't I?

—Yes but, but you were on that same train with these tickets?

—What train.

—This train the one we just, the four seventeen the one we . . .

—Four seventeen what I just told you didn't I?

—Yes well yes but these tickets if you'd given them to me I . . .

—Four seven God damn it Bast four seventeen what she told me wasn't it? Told me get the God damned four seventeen give you these God damned tickets Bast need help andcouragement from any brazen throat? Got the four seventeen didn't I? Gave you the God damned tickets didn't I? All you stand here and complain?

—No but what I meant was . . .

—Go around tell everybody you need help andcouragement break their God damned neck for you try to set their cracker on fire any way to behave?

—No but, wait there's a key here Mister Gibbs it's mixed up with these tickets you, here . . .

—That's a key Bast.

—I know it yes, here.

—Place of stone Bast one flight up, how hard a path the going down and going up another's stair told me you need help andcourage-ment, sensitive purpose lock yourself in write nothing music how's that.

—No but it's your key, here . . .

—Sitting right there Bast heard her say you need a place to work give all your time to composing, heard her say that's quite outrageous really.

—No but she, I have a place Mister Gibbs I don't really . . .

—Told me you need help andcouragement place to work Bast God damndest person to help andcourage I ever met, give you those God damned tickets get the God damned four seventeen apologize to you give you place of stone supposed to be in there working all you stand here and complain, number on the tag right up on Ninety-sixth Street see the number? Place of stone supposed to get in there and exult even throw in a piano how's that, laughing fring whereon mad stringers told me Joan of Arc voices she heard? If not you, who. If not now, when, told me your talented sensitive purpose Bast take help andcouragement from any brazen throat here . . . he seized a shoulder for support, took the key by the tag strung to it to drop in the breast pocket where he sagged for closer scrutiny. —Clever idea Bast tell you make a clean breast? Of all things known . . .

—What's, oh that's no that's just . . . he jammed it into the pocket —if I can help you Mister Gibbs, if you'll just wait here a minute I want to cash in these tickets . . .

—When Bast! When . . . ! the door shuddered with a kick.

—No if you'll just wait for a minute Mister Gibbs I . . .

—If not you, when! and the door banged as he turned for the grating.

—Say ah, hello? I just want to turn in these tick . . .

—Closed.

—Yes but, but you're right here couldn't you just . . .

—Closed can't you see the clock?

—Yes well, well then when are you open.

—Can't you see the sign . . . ? Over penciled-in Os and 9s lipsticked lettering spelled suck and he turned at a sudden trot, hit the door hard and pulled it open.

—Oh hi Mister Bast. Was that Mister Gibbs yelling police just now?

—Yes but he, where is he did you see him?

—Around there, there's this bar around there where he goes . . . the load shifted, —you walking home?

—Yes but, but why didn't you get the bus.

—I just thought I'd wait up for you, how come you got more train tickets.

—I didn't, he just gave them to me and I tried to turn them in but that agent says he's closed so I can't pay you right back but . . .

—There's no big rush hey! did you see that?

—What.

—That lightning, boy it got real dark didn't it? You in a hurry?

—Yes.

—Mister Bast? Could you wait up a second? I just have to fix this here shoelace . . . he'd crouched jackknifed over his armload, a sneaker mounting the curb that checked the rampant advance of grassgrown cracks stemming from the empty concrete shell of the Marine Memorial Plaza where a disabled French machinegun and a vacant flagpole held off the sky. —Boy it looks like we both need shoes, right? he finished with an urgent tug —holy, shit . . .

—And look will you please stop . . .

—No but it broke again, you know what I was thinking on the train hey? he came on righting his load, hurrying alongside —like I have this thing which what it is is it's this selling outfit where what you do is you send in and they send you all these different shoes which you get to wear them around so people can see them, you know? See that's how you sell them, see? I mean not the ones you're wearing right off your feet but like you take their order and then you make this commission, you know? Like it says you can make a hundred dollars a week in your spare time and you get to wear these shoes around too, you want me to find it?

—No.

—Okay but I have this other thing about have your own import export business right from your own home, you know? Maybe you could do that . . . they crossed a rutted bog opening on a dirt road. —Would you want to do that? Mister Bast?

—Do what.

—This import export business right from your own home.

—Import and export what.

—How do I know but I mean that's not the thing anyway, you know? he kicked a can up the highway's unkempt shoulder kicking the weeds for some remnant of sidewalk, —I mean the thing is just where you get to sell something like, wait a second . . .

—Look I want to get home before it rains, I can't . . .

—No but anyway it's just this other selling thing I got where it says you'll never have to clean your toilet bowl again, see they send you this here . . .

—What makes you think I want to go around selling things! I don't even . . .

—To make some money just like anybody I mean that's what you wait up, I mean you're taking such long steps hey? Mister Bast? Did you ever hear that one about if you need any money just ask my father he's got piles?

—No.

—No but wait up hey, do you get it? Just ask my . . .

—I get it yes, look does your father know about all this sending away you're doing?

—What?

—I said does your father . . .

—No but that's just suppose to be this here joke see, where . . .

—I know it's supposed to be this here joke! it's the, it's one of the worst I ever heard, I said does your fa . . .

—No but hey Mister Bast . . . ? he came pushing shoulder high through Queen Anne's laces hemming him in behind, —like what business is your father in.

—Music.

—What he writes it? like you?

—He writes it and he's a prominent conductor look, music's not a business like shoes or . . .

—No I know, I mean that's why he's this here prominent conductor right . . . ? he came hurrying alongside for the brief stretch of sidewalk, —I mean where he makes some money being this conductor so he can go write this here music in his spare time he doesn't make much off, right?

—I suppose yes now look I'm in a hurry . . .

—No that's okay I can take bigger steps it's just all this here stuff I can't hardly. . .

—Well where are you going, where . . .

—No I'm just walking you home, see I . . .

—Well you don't have to it's practically dark, doesn't your mother expect you to . . .

—Her . . . ? the sidewalk ended abruptly —no she comes in all different ow! holy, boy I almost lost my . . .

—Different what.

—All these different times see she's like this here nurse could you wait up a second hey? My sneaker . . . he'd gone down to one knee where a pole of rust bore Doges Promenade in barely discernible letters over the rutted opening in the weeds. —Boy hey did you hear that? that thunder?

—Of course that's why I . . .

—No wait I'm coming . . . he got across the rutted mud, —hey?

—Well what!

—Nothing, I mean what do you want to talk about.

—I don't want to talk about anything I'm . . .

—How come. I mean are you thinking of a tune . . . ? he took advantage of the broken remnant of sidewalk to hurry alongside —have you still got that master tunesmith thing I gave you hey?

—Look I'm not trying to write tunes for money, I'm . . .

—I know, I mean how come you're writing it.

—It's just what I have to do! now will you . . .

—I know, that's what I mean. How come . . . the sidewalk remnant was gone and he plunged in behind —hey? I mean when you're writing this here music do you need to be someplace with a piano or a horn or something? or like can you make it up anyplace. Hey? Mister Bast . . . ?

—What.

—I mean when you make it up right inside your head do you hear it playing like? I mean if I think of some song I can like hear it playing only if you're making up this here music which nobody ever heard it before do you hear these here instruments playing like tee, boy I'm getting out of breath, like teedle leedle leedle right inside your head then you go write down these little notes? Or, or first do you think of all these little notes which you write them down then when you read them you get to hear . . .

—Look I can't stop now to explain it, I'm . . .

—Okay don't get mad, I mean I just thought where you're teaching it and all you'd . . .

—Well I'm not! I'm not teaching anything, now will you . . .

—No but how come, you quit hey? I mean how come you, boy I can't hardly see where wait up hey, Mister Bast? I mean this opera thing which I'm being this here little dwarf in it you're not teaching that anymore either hey?

—No!

—No but wait, see I thought we'd be . . .

—What difference is it, you're just being this here little dwarf in it to get out of gym aren't you?

—No well sure but I mean what are you going to do now hey . . .

—I just told you!

—No I know but like you just said you're not writing these here tunes for money I mean if you quit teaching see all these here business oppor, hey? Where are you wait . . . he burst from the weeds where another agony of rust signaled ruts running in toward the dark bank of trees —hey? this is where you turn in? I mean just a second I just wanted to . . .

—Look don't start to get these papers out again it's dark! I can't see them why do you want me to see them anyhow, why do you pick me to . . .

—No well I just thought maybe we can use each other you know? like I said that time? So I mean where I just gave you this here loan for these tickets I thought . . .

—All right! I thanked you didn't I? I'm paying you interest aren't I? I'll give it to you as soon as I can turn them in and the school still owes me money for . . .

—No wait a second, hey? you want me to turn them in for you?

—Fine yes, here, here and look I'll give you a dollar that should make us about even wait, here's another one . . .

—No but see the dollar is . . .

—All right here! here I still have some nickels from that cafeteria here, now goodnight goodbye!

—No well see we'll keep that separate because I have to like discount these here tickets, you know?

—No I don't know! look . . .

—No but see that's what you do hey, see because while you're loaning this here money off me it's not working for me while I'm waiting to get it back off these here tickets so I mean you just discount it like, you know? I mean like we had where this Mister Y goes in this here bank to loan this four thousand dollars off them for five years see? Only they like loan him five thousand which all he gets is this here four thousand he came for where they're loaning him this here other thousand to like pay them back this interest for this four thousand ahead of time so I mean he never even sees it, see I mean like he loaned it off them only all they do they just take it out of this one pocket and like put it right back in this here other one I mean that's what discounting is, see?

—Fine yes look just give them back to me, I'll . . .

—No that's okay hey I'll do it for you and I mean we'll make this here discount rate like ten percent okay? Like that makes it easier to figure up where you just move the dot, so that's . . .

—Fine yes you move it goodbye, it's starting to . . .

—No wait we have to figure it up hey seven, eight . . .

—There are twelve tickets they cost nine sixty, now goodni . . .

—Eleven, wait there's thirteen here so that means like if twelve cost . . .

—Wait there can't be, there were twelve of you on the train I bought twelve . . .

—There's thirteen go ahead and count them so like if twelve cost nine sixty then one, twelve into nine wait, ninety-six no wait, seven what's seven twelves wait seven tens is . . .

—Listen if there are thirteen then thirteen of you went in with Mrs Joubert and only twelve came back out now who . . .

—Wait eight, eighty cents each right? So eighty move the dot wait, seventy-two plus what am I giving you, plus eight seventy-four . . .

—Listen! who went in and didn't come back out, did you . . .

—Wait nine forty-six right? I mean I can barely see five, six . . .

—Look we must have lost somebody! Will you . . .

—And thirty-five, forty-five I can't hardly see I almost gave you a dime, wait, here's a penny forty-six, right?

—No listen who went in with you on that field trip and didn't come back out.

—Who Mrs Joubert?

—No! one of your . . .

—How do I know hey look out you're dropping . . .

—And look what are you giving me this for this money, I just gave you the tickets to turn in didn't I? You lent me the money to pay for them now turn them in and get it back and if you want me to pay you this int . . .

—What?

—I said you have the tick . . .

—No but it's these two separate deals you know? I mean there's this here loan which that's one then there's this where I bought these here discounted tickets off you so nobody gets screwed hey? Mister Bast? I mean like this here Mister Y which . . .

—I don't want to hear about Mister Y! Just, goodbye I'll . . .

—I mean there's no big rush to pay it back okay . . . ? the voice pursued over the high grass —because hey Bast . . . ? its harsh edge followed him down the weeded ruts where the trees closed overhead —didn't I tell you maybe we can use each other . . . ? He walked faster looking, listening as though something had moved that instant before his look stilled a torn branch, a tire nested with leaves, the porthole ajar in a foundered washing machine then abruptly the car filling the turn as though it had simply chanced upright there, windows framing limbs that might have been caught in some random climax of catastrophe as he passed silent, distinguishable only as movement till the road's end filled with illumination flinging his shadow suddenly forward in the headlights behind him and, at the gate there, as suddenly gone. He pulled it shut on the stubbled lawn infiltrating the terrace bricks fronting the studio where the screen door shook on the risen wind hung twisted on one hinge. Beyond it the door stood open. Next to it something, the handle of something, a shovel handle now he came closer, protruded through a broken pane, and thunder gently shook the space he left behind to crush glass underfoot, stepping inside. He stopped. Up, through the balcony rail, light cut across the door to the hayloft and was gone. A plate cracked under his step as he drew back and knocked the shovel to the stone floor, and there he crouched, clutching the shovel handle.

—Who's there! he rose slowly and pushed the light switch by the door. Nothing happened. —Who's up there! he called loudly, raising the shovel, crouching again as light danced past the door above, then through it to the stairhead to break down on him between the eaves.

—Yes? Who is it?

The shovel came down slowly. —Who . . . is that!

—Oh it's you Edward, watch where you step.

—You, who . . . who . . . The light caught his face square, then the smashed ink bottle flooding the carpeted stone toward the stairs.

—You look quite threatening with that shovel, I'm glad I . . .

—But the . . . Stella? What . . . She'd turned away with her light back into the hayloft as he mounted the stairs. —What's happened!

She sat on an end of the bed dangling a flashlight. —What you see, she said, moving the light now over drawers jammed open at angles, a lampshade crushed, a spoon, a dresser scarf and Piston's Harmony torn through the spine, sheet music and a player piano roll flung toward the opened window he walked past her to close and sink on the windowseat there, poking into its opened drawer.

—But what, what would anybody . . . he stared where her light fell on a Bach Wagner Program of Miss Isadora Duncan and Mister Walter

Damrosch at Carnegie Hall Wednesday Afternoon February 15, 1911, at 3 o'clock —why anybody would . . .

—No I opened that . . . her light swept over postal views of Cairo, —looking . . .

—But what looking for what! he was on his feet again —how did, where did you even come from!

—Just now? From the house, Edward . . . she sank back on an elbow, pulling her dress from a knee where the light caught it —those papers they want, a birth certificate just anything, Aunt Julia thought they must be there in the windowseat. Norman's having some business problems he's rather desperate to get things settled, we . . .

—Business look everything smashed broken the whole place torn up you're sitting here in the middle of it with a flashlight like a, talking about Norman's business problems all you want is some scrap of paper to prove I, that I'm . . .

—Oh Edward.

—What oh Edward what! you, you came out here once to make me look like I, I shouldn't have told you . . . he stood over her where she'd come up from her elbow, where the light fell now on a souvenir menu from the Hamburg America Line still as her fallen shoulders —I should never have told you about that day seeing you that day up at, at, seeing you . . . and the flash of lightning that filled the skylight over them arrested her rising hand, arrested in detail strands of her pinned hair fallen loose on the defenseless slope of her back where he'd bent closer, where perspiration beaded her neck, where the balance of near dark left his hand's tremble stilled in hers as Stella rose.

—It's stifling, almost hot she said, —why don't you open that again, that window . . . Again her light came up as if to search its casement out but held on him as he turned from it, opened, swept slowly down the desperate inquiry he posed, and then went out. Some sound of his come forward with him broke and left her sigh, so aspirate it seemed laid out there even when it was done, so heavy that it squared her shoulders turned from him so he ran on her elbow raised up against him in what light there was. —Can you undo this? little hook . . . ? Hands suddenly in collision there he sought it but —no, she said, —I've got it, and left his hands hung shaping indecision for the instant till he caught her waist and caught his parting lips against the damp hair fallen at her temple. She turned and stepped away, not even looking, her hand behind her coursed the zipper down. —You can save that till we're in bed, she said, inclined to draw the gray dress up and off, to steady a hand against a rafter and thrust one shoe away and then the other. —You don't have to try to seduce me, Edward.

—I, Stella I . . . from there the tremor ran right through his fingertips tearing at laces, at his belt, a button, buttons, her shape a white slip bending forth to bring the torn spread into line before she raised it over her, lay back, and stared into the shadow of the beam in the eave's drop above her head, unblinking for the flash that filled the skylight and as motionless for the thunder that came after.

—Well?

—I just . . . wanted to look he whispered, his voice like one long out of use gone in abrupt and shapeless fragments that might have framed apology or gratitude, or both, coming down, fighting a foot out of the spread's tear as his shoulders came down to hers and lips delayed at her throat brushed up the scar there, moistened quickly before they sought her own. The opened window beyond was still enough but she turned her face from his so sharply toward it there might have been a light, some sound, some sudden movement from outside to leave his lips lodged at her ear so, filling its convolutions with his gasp of shock at how unseen beneath the spread her hand, unhesitating and without surprise, caress, or brush of exploration found and closed on him swelled to bursting and, silent, motionless, knees fallen wide, led him left thicketed there in dry abrasion as he swarmed over her and clinging headlong wrenched her shoulder in a plunge that left her open eyes fixed on a gap between the rafters where, even in this light, the points of shingle nails showed through in irregular rows, her only sound one that she might have made out of impatience jostled in a crowd, her only movement that sharp turn of her head away from the quaking rise of his, catching the threat of his lips and protest stifled in a bleat against her throat.

There half withdrawn from ambush lightning froze him seeking kneehold, poised upon the thrust to come, the thunder to come, the ease of the screen door below hung shaken twisted on one hinge, as wind might have shaken it, and then the crush of glass underfoot and the voice still to come, and loudly, —Stella? And then the thunder, sounding far away.

—Up here, she called unblinking past his shoulder, —we're coming down . . . the instant's twinge of her knees gone, limp as her hands spread wide beside them there palms up as though listlessly waiting to be filled.

—You're what?

Her hands closed empty where he'd come down all weight and she gained an elbow bringing her shoulders up, dropping them with a sigh of movement no more than pushing a chair back leaving table. —Don't try to come up without a light, she called again, one foot out to the floor, and the other —it's quite a mess . . .

—But who is that!

—Just Norman . . . she stood steadying a hand to the rafter's slant as she pressed into one shoe, then the other, bent to pick up that gray dress from the floor.

—I've got the police, the voice came up to them again, —Stella?

She stood hands high for the dress to drop round her and pulled its shoulders into place walking the length of the bed to stand there, wait-

ing, till his hands left fighting buttons and rose to pull its zipper closed.
—Yes we're coming, she called back, dangling the flashlight lighted toward the door and pausing, one foot cocked on Miss Isadora Duncan and
Mister Walter Damrosch, to run its spot up on him full sitting on the
welter of the bed, staring at her. —Edward's here.

—Edward? Up there?

—He's trying to get a window closed.

—Up there?

—He'll be right down . . . and she turned for the stairs as the sound
of rain came, finally, scattered across the roof, a fall that now gave substance to the stilled beams of headlamps in the drive where those of
flashlights rose and fell to cadenced steps come back and round the range
of yew and up the terrace and through the door to fall on broken glass
and flee across the inkstained carpet, darting, climbing, caught fixed in
niches, they scaled the walls and leaped the beams to skirt the hayloft.

—Who found it like this?

—We did, officer, I did, an hour or so ago . . .

—And who are you?

—We're, I'm part of the family we came out visiting, my husband
and I.

—Visiting? Him?

—That's Mister Bast yes, she said as a light caught him on the stairs
and led him down before it leapt the fireplace for the kitchen. —Norman? You've never met Edward?

—Sorry, it's a hell of a way to meet you Edward . . . he took his hand
and shook it. —Be careful there, Stella. I guess you didn't find anything,
any papers? He took the light from her and splashed it over them, —be
like looking for a needle in a haystack. Even that waiver they couldn't
find that, your aunts, right over in the house there, Edward. The one
Coen just brought out for you to sign? The light came down like the cut
of a saber. —I couldn't get across to them in there at all. That ink, watch
your shoe there Stella . . .

She stepped aside. —I think they just want to wait until . . .

—Wait? Wait till the tax people step in and pull the whole company
out from under all of us? He put his empty hand on the shoulder sunk
before him and the light dwelled on the tie knotted out over the collar,
—I don't care who inherits what, you and Stella, you understand that
Edward? It's all in the family, that's just where we've got to keep it.

Light from behind caught his barbered neck. —You'd never even
know this place was back here. The policeman shot his light up the stairs,
—let me just take a look up there. They must have been throwing plates
around, watch where you step . . . he lit a way behind him. —What do
you do here, use it like a summer house? Who reads all the books, you?
he followed his light into the hayloft. —Anything taken? You miss anything?

—I don't know I, I don't know what they wanted.

—A place for a little fancy screwing . . . the light swept over the tumbled bed. —The first chilly day and that's what they look for, a dry place to screw where they won't freeze their nuts . . . He pulled away the spread and paused his light along the sheet. —You ever find any drugs in this place? any joints? needles? empty bottles of glue? Underfoot Miss Isadora Duncan and Mister Walter Damrosch grated in his turn for the door. —You better try to get the whole place boarded up.

—Edward? came from below. —We're going to have to leave . . .

And there Norman's arm sank his shoulders hunching the man to do so, gesturing the light with his free hand as he went on with —what that's got to do with the price of apples here anyway Stella, his father James there going out and adopting that Jewish boy out of that Jewish orphan asylum don't mean he thought Edward here was . . .

—The boy had talent, you've heard him play Edward?

—He, Reuben you mean? he, he plays like an acrobat it's all technique he, like a stunt like asking somebody to . . .

—Why you'd want to bring that up right now for anyway Stella, if James wanted to take the boy in he just must have thought . . .

—For his talent yes that's what you just said Stella his talent, for his talent . . .

—But wasn't it? She was gone behind the light, —just the talent he loved? not the boy?

—Well sure and with Edward here it was the boy, like you'd expect a . . .

—That's what she said! Just the boy not the talent, that's what you meant isn't it Stella? Because there wasn't any talent that's what you meant isn't it? He ducked from the weight of the arm on his shoulder into the beam of light —isn't it? The talent yes that he had it and I didn't that's what you meant when I, when you came out here and wouldn't even listen to what I'd . . .

—Edward please . . .

—What please what! you can't even, just now it's what you meant up there just now too isn't it when you knew all the time . . . he caught balance backed against the piano as overhead in the beams, from the kitchen, through the bull's eyed door to the garage lights came on all together, and a policeman through it brushing his hands.

—Want to get this place boarded up, lucky these kids didn't burn it down for you.

He was staring down at the label of a record underfoot as though its label were in a language he did not understand and looked up slowly at the fragments of plates, glass, records and more records flung among books split, ink splattered pages of music some still untorn, with a sound of trying to clear his throat. —Kids . . .?

—Kids . . . the policeman nodded past his elbow, —who else would shit in your piano.

—You, you never can tell . . . he stared for an instant at the staved and unfinished notes on paper crumpled and smeared in the strings there before he turned with one step, and another as vague, to reach and tap a high C, and then far enough to fit his hand to an octave and falter a dissonant chord, again, and again, before he corrected it and looked up, —right? Believing and shitting are two very different things?

—Edward . . .

—Never have to clean your toilet bowl again . . . he recovered the dissonant chord, —right?

—Well yeah you, you want to get the place boarded up, some kid gets hurt in here you could be in real trouble . . . straightening jackets, belts, pocketing pads, flashlights in departing scurries to the lighted eaves, toward the door abruptly choreographed, Sousa in chords of play by ear, a glissando descending to a dull thump.

—Kids that's all! a generation in heat that's all . . . he pounded two chords against each other's unrest —no subject is taboo, no act is forbidden that's all . . .! and he struck into the sailors' chorus from Dido and Aeneas, —you'll never, no never, have to clean your . . .

—Look Edward we, we have to get back in to New York Stella's got some dinner to get to and, watch that glass Stella . . .

—Rift the hills and roll the waters! flash the lightnings . . . he pounded chords, —the pulsating moment of climax playing teedle leedle leedle right inside your head . . . he found a tremolo far up the keyboard.

—Edward that's enough please, we're leaving . . .

—Wait wait trust me cousin! you wanted to hear this part . . . he banged C, hit F-sharp and bracketed C two octaves down —how she turned her bosom shaken in the dark of . . .

—Stella you think maybe we should wait and . . .

—I think we should leave yes, Edward . . . ?

—Now for me the woods may wither, now for me the rooftree wait here's Norman's part, it may be my lord is weary, that his brain is overwrought . . . he hunched over the keys to echo the Ring motif in sinister pianissimo, —he will hold thee something better than his dog, a little dearer than . . .

—All right yes maybe we just better go along, Edward?

—Rain or hail! or fire . . . he slammed another chord, stood there, and tapped C. —Master tunesmith wait . . . he dug in his pocket, —make a clean breast of the whole . . .

—Once you get things straightened out maybe you can call us up Edward? I'd like to get this waiv . . .

—Oh please! she caught his arm closing his suit jacket and his coat, hat on now tucking ends of his muffler and seeming all clothes beside her, —Edward? goodnight . . .

—We'll call you up Edward, you'll just be right here will you?

—I don't know! he was getting a foot up now —I've had some offers, I've . . .

—But where would you . . .

His foot came down on the cluster at middle C —to, yes to Tribsterill go into the shoe business there . . . he bent to tie the lace —get to wear them around of course, where the muck runs down to . . .

—Please!

—Or wait yes that other place what was it, go into import export there in the privacy of my own . . .

—Well you just let us yes I'm coming Stella, watch that shovel there . . . and he got her arm past curtains stirred through the broken pane and the screen door hanging there on one hinge, neither open nor closed. —Kind of hate to just leave him there like that but I couldn't see where there was anything we, watch that puddle . . . he caught her elbow as they gained the lawn.

—A laughing place . . . stabbed after them making their way round the yew, and then a sprinkling of piano notes, as beams of the police car swept them in an officious turn and sought the opening in the hedge.

—You think maybe we ought to stop in there again? He nodded over her head to the lighted windows where streak mounted streak down clapboards and glass from the gutter dangling at the corner of the house and branches thrashed where the trees rode high losing sight of each other as though readying to hurl their fruit in all directions and make a real night of it, one to emerge from with old wounds reopened and new ones inviting attention. —Or just to tell them goodnight . . . ? but he was already holding opened for her the door of the car, and nothing turned her to look out or back as their lights caught the opening in the hedge, and then moved through it.

She leaned forward to turn on the radio, fleeing one wad of sound for another there as he swung the curve past the pepperidge tree. —Uh? She'd snapped the radio off. —I kind of liked that, he said as she rested back with that aspirate sigh leaving no sound but the regular rhythm of the windshield wipers. Passing the firehouse he began to hum and, passing the dark cavity of the Marine Memorial Plaza, she turned the radio on and sat back abandoning it to a novelty group playing Phil the Fluter's Ball with vocal accompaniment that could only be described as suitable.

—Kind of hated to go off and leave him like that . . . they stopped for a light, —the way he was acting, you think he'll be all right? The car moved ahead. —Stella?

—What is it.

—I said do you think Edward will be all right.

—Whatever all right means.

—Well does he always go around with his necktie tied out over his neck and his hair like that? and his shirttail out under his jacket in the back? Just seeing his face, the look on it . . .

—I'm sure you'd have a look on your face if we came home and found the place ransacked.

—That isn't just what I meant though, he . . .

—You're driving too fast with this rain.

—It was you that was in such a hurry.

—I just, I thought we should leave.

—Do you think he's going to press a claim? to your father's estate I mean.

—If you force him to.

—Me? Why would I want to do that?

—Just by going on about it the way you do.

—Well hell Stella what am I supposed to do then, it's all got to be settled he could just as well give you that waiver even if he wants to claim your father for his instead of James like you said he . . .

—That's not what I said. Can't we go more slowly?

—All right, but you said . . .

—I said maybe Edward's suddenly afraid he's not Uncle James' son. There's quite a difference.

—Why. What's James got to leave him? The car slowed somewhat. —Stella? What's . . .

—I heard you! You just can't understand anything you can't get your hands on, anything you can't feel or see or, or count . . .

—Well I just meant . . .

—Be careful . . . !

—It's all right I saw him coming, the way they build these little foreign cars they don't give you room to move your . . .

—Obviously it wasn't built for someone your size I don't know why you insisted on buying it, but you can't drive so fast on these wet roads.

—It's all right, he said, —I saw him coming . . . and he leaned forward and turned the radio off, and stayed that way, leaning forward over the wheel as though searching for landfall on a horizon far out ahead. —Why hell, I'm just trying to hold things together here, everything your father and I built up there. All this time every penny's gone right back into the business so there's just no cash, there's no excess cash around to pay off these death taxes and they come in, the tax people come right in and take their bite before anybody else even gets to taste, you see what I mean? There's two, three million dollars tied up here, maybe closer to four altogether but there's no way to know what value the tax people will put on your father's forty-five percent because it's a family company and the shares have never been traded. They can just get some shyster appointed to administrate forcing us to go public and sell shares to raise cash for these taxes, they all end up with a nice cut and we end up with a crowd of stockholders squabbling for dividends and bankers who know as much about punch cards and continuous forms as a hog does about holy water in there telling us . . .

—Yes, all right.

—You see what I mean? And we've already borrowed against assets, we borrowed for that last big expansion and now the tax people are even

trying to deny us interest on that loan as a deduction like we been taking
it the last six years, can you beat that? And they're trying to force us to
settle that claim right now, too, can you beat that?

—No.

—What?

—I can't beat it, no. I can't even understand it. I simply wish we
could stop constantly talking about it.

—Stella how can we just not talk about it if you're going to be the
administrator? You come right down to it after all, it hasn't been too bad
to you.

—What are you talking about.

—Just these concerts and benefits of yours and these artists and
people you collect . . .

—What people do I collect.

—Just these artists and these musicians and . . .

—But who.

—Well you take this Reuben we were talking about, he . . .

—If you could simply see something more there than, what was it
you said, a little sissified . . .

—I didn't mean anything Stella I just, I said there was people that
might think he was kind of effeminate, he seemed like a nice enough
little fellow that time you introduced me. But I just mean you add up
these concerts and benefits and like this hundred dollar a plate dinner
you've got tonight for this art museum, you add it all up and . . .

—I thought you added it all up and took it off taxes and were just
delighted.

—Well all right Stella, all right. It's just . . .

—What.

—I guess nothing.

She turned on the radio and hardly searching found something of
Delius that lasted all the way until, about to be identified, it silenced as
they entered the tunnel.

—What time is your dinner? he said as they emerged. —You want
me to drop you off somewhere?

—Home.

—You have time to go home first? I could . . .

—Just home.

Lights approaching, passing, splashing wet surfaces in reflections
suborned the reality of streets and distance. —Can't hardly see where
you're going, he said never stopping, scarcely slowing until out of thousands, of hundreds, tens of brownstone steps, brownstone entrances, he
drew up at one. —You're in a hurry you go ahead up, I'll park the car.
You got your key? He reached across to open her door. —Watch where
you step. He reached across to close her door. —You want to take your
book?

—What?

—This Wagner Man and Artist, it's been in the car . . .

—All right, give it to me . . . and, watching where she stepped, she sought the entrance, head down until she reached it, fumbling for keys and then among them for one to fit the door, shaking them out under the light at the mailboxes, turning and saying suddenly —Oh! The man standing beside her wore the kind of small-billed cap with earmuffs tied over the top that boys wear, and one hand raised more in restraint than threat he put a shopping bag down with the other and straightened up, his clothes already open at the front scarcely demanding her attention there, pressed closer as her key trembled at the lock that moment wet down the side of her skirt and stockings, turned it and the door opened, tracking a wet print across the small lobby without a look back to rise in the empty elevator swallowing a sound in her throat and repeat the ritual of the keys, cross carpeting silently to light a single lamp and drop her bag and her book in a chair, into the bathroom hands fighting the zipper open at the back of her neck, stepping out of her shoes and pausing about to draw that gray dress up over her head, and then forcing it down over her shoulders rending a seam, her slip likewise, turning water on in the basin as she sat to strip off her stockings and drop them in with the slip, leaning naked over to turn on the bath and then holding there to the tub, coming back up, finally, with a towel she held up to her into the bedroom where the light caught her from behind as she reached to get a robe and then, more slowly, sat down. The telephone rang beside the bed. It rang again, and she sat, one hand covering her eyes, until it stopped ringing.

—Stella . . . ? Stella, you left the front door here open. Left your keys right in the door. She got up and went back into the bathroom. —Who was that on the phone?

—Wrong number, she called over the sound of the tumbling water, and closed the door.

She came out holding her robe closed lighting lamps barely brightening the living room under their opaque shades, down a corridor to the kitchen where he'd hung his jacket over a chair and had out a box of eggs. —You're not ready yet?

—I'm not going anywhere.

—But the, you already got the ticket didn't you? It ought to be quite a meal for . . .

—I'm not hungry.

—Oh. He looked back to what he was doing. —I didn't mean anything against you going to these benefits and something like this dinner tonight Stella . . . he cracked an egg on the edge of a bowl, and she watched him scrape out the shell. —You sure you don't want to go?

—I just want some milk, she said reaching to a high shelf for a glass, turning him for that moment to look into the gape of her robe.

—I was going to have some eggs, can I fix you some? It's no hundred-dollar dinner maybe, but . . .

—I'm going to bed, she said waiting to pour milk, watching him unwrap a stick of butter and scrape the flecks of it that remained on the paper into a pan.

—You're not going to sleep right off are you?

—I'm going to take a pill, she said, and he turned to look down the line of her that took shape in the robe as she took her glass and left him staring there a moment longer. Moving more slowly he put his pan off the stove, got out ice and a glass and poured it half filled with bourbon. He sipped it and then suddenly came out through the living room for the hall, tapped on the door. —Stella . . . ?

Her robe lay in a heap on the foot of her bed and he sat on the edge of his, —I just had a good idea Stella, he rattled the ice in his glass at her back. —If I got Edward and your aunts there in for a tour of the place, take them around the plant and give them a real look at the whole operation, I'll bet they've never even . . .

—Why, she said without turning from the book she sheltered.

—Why? To show them their stake in the General Roll Company is something pretty impressive, more than just a few pieces of paper that say they own, what do they own with James about thirty-five out of that original hundred shares?

—It would . . . she cleared her throat. —It would be ridiculous.

—What? Well but why, if they really saw what they've got there they might not be so ready to see a lot of outsiders coming in and . . .

—Simply getting them in to a desolate place like Astoria, it wouldn't impress them they'd be horrified.

—Well but . . . he stood up rattling the ice in his glass as he raised it. —Wait, you come to think of it now they must have nearer thirty, maybe twenty-seven shares altogether, that Jack Gibbs he took five shares with him when he quit didn't he?

—Took? And she did half turn, more to pull the blanket back to her shoulder as his weight sank the edge of the bed.

—I don't mean to sound like he stole it Stella, your father wanted to give it to him for all the help he'd been with those ideas he had I went right along with it, but that was just the thing with him you know? How he'd work out some crackerjack idea right to the point you could do something with it then he'd just leave it there, like it wasn't worth just getting down and doing it . . . he brought the glass down shaking nothing but ice in it. —A while after he left there I'd look in book stores when I passed one to see if there was a book with his name on it, he said that's what he was doing writing a book. If you ever heard him talk about these ideas he had about random patterns and mechanizing you name it but if he ever wrote that book, I sure never saw it . . . he rattled the ice again staring into the glass. —I used to think he must be the smartest man I ever met, why he'd . . .

—He probably was. Is that what you came in to tell me?

—Well no Stella I just got off on it talking about those five shares, you figure if these death taxes take maybe up toward half this forty-five percent of the company your father had that leaves maybe twenty-five coming to you, with my twenty-three we're still on top of things and if anything comes out of this old lawsuit that just came back to life with that jukebox company there's no telling where it will take us. You see but now if you have to split what comes down from your father with Edward there and he takes up with what your aunts and your Uncle James hold, well that could give them a maybe four percent margin for control so where these five shares that Jack Gibbs had fit in that could turn the whole, Stella . . . ?

—What is it.

—I just wasn't sure you were listening to me Stella, I mean I thought going out there to see them like we just did we'd at least get a clearer line on things even if we didn't dig up these papers but your aunts, I just couldn't get across to them, your Aunt Anne there talking about somebody called the young planter whose father was an undertaker part of the time I don't think they even knew who I was. And Edward there, I can see how he'd be that upset coming into the place like he did but standing up there singing like that, talking about going into the shoe business someplace nobody's heard of . . . he swirled the ice in the glass, drank off the bit of water to rattle it again. —Stella? I mean I just don't know what you meant saying maybe he's suddenly scared James isn't his father, did he say if . . .

—I just mean he's a rather selfish boy, that's all.

—Yes well that's what I mean he certainly looks like he can use the money, that's . . .

—Well it's not what I mean! her sudden turn lost her the sheet from her shoulders, —he's a boy with a lot of romantic ideas about himself and everything else I tried to help him get rid of that's all, now please . . .

—Well but Stel . . .

—And please stop calling me Stella! she pulled the sheet up as though it was the force of his stare that had abruptly bared her breast spilled toward him there, turned on her back to reach the light.

—But, but that's . . .

—Oh I just mean stop saying it . . . the light went out and the mass of her thighs rose again under the blanket as she turned away.

Back in the kitchen half tending his eggs he poured some more bourbon finally settling down to eat with his left hand, a blunt pencil in his right sketching, adding, subtracting, crossing out on a kitchen pad he brought with him into the living room when he was finished, moving among the furniture like a stranger looking for a chair large enough, a lamp bright enough, moving Spring in Derby biscuit and Brassaï Retrospective to make space enough for his forms and papers and the latest catalog of Ardo Heavy Duty Stamping Equipment and Parts List, squeezing off his shoes and working on a larger yellow pad until the telephone rang. He looked down the hall as he crossed the room to answer it to what appeared to be light under the bedroom door, but it continued to ring until he answered it, and then went dead in his hand.

In the bathroom he lifted her things dripping from the basin across to the tub and washed, in the bedroom stepped on Wagner as Man and Artist broken open on the floor between their beds looking, as he got into his own, at the shadow of her thighs' descent there just beyond reach and unchanged it seemed in any detail next morning as he paused again up on one elbow to look, and then stepping on Wagner as Man and Artist got to the bathroom and shaved, lifted her things from the tub to the basin and picked up his shoes dressing half in the hall, restoring Spring and Brassaï, gathering papers and locking the door after him humming, out into the day and as he steered through streets and over the bridge and down rows of false fronts desperately simulating brick and fieldstone, stray fretful bars of Phil the Fluter's Ball.

—Leo? he called barely inside over the clatter of machinery, —come over here a minute. Look . . . he spread yellow pad pages on a filing cabinet. —This problem we been having over there with number three, if we just go get this wall knocked out right here and move this whole setup right over around this way we've got the line running right through with nothing to hinder, you see what I mean?

—Run into money.

—Well hell I know that. It'll double this whole production run just about too.

—You might double your run all right, but it will run you into money.

—Well let's see how much. You get onto those people we had to do those shipping platforms, that little Eyetalian, get them in here for a cost estimate.

—Mister Angel? If you got a minute there's something here I think you'd ought to know about, we'd maybe ought to go over here out of the path . . . Leading the way to the shelter of filing cabinets he dug in the inside pocket of a suit curled round its collar down the length of its lapels coming up with a soiled envelope, —I figured you . . .

—Mister Angel . . . ?

—Wait a second, that's Terry calling me.

—Mister Angel? Oh, I didn't see you back there. Mister Coen's on the telephone from the hospital.

—Coming. I'll see you later Leo, get hold of that Eyetalian . . . He followed her down a hall of plastic flats and cement block painted a green, eyes held on the practiced rise and fall of her step one foot crossing the path of the other before her and a tight turn at the door where she pushed red hair away from her face and held up the phone. —Gee they hung up on us . . .

—That's all right he'll call back.

—Gee I wouldn't have picked him for reckless driving, you know Mister Angel? Like he's always so shy and quiet when he comes in, you know?

—Well it wasn't reckless, he'd broke his glasses, been out in Long Island and couldn't see where he was going.

—Gee, she said turning back to her typewriter, and he leaned back hands clasped behind his head, looking across to how the fullness curbed in her simulated leather skirt spilled from the sides of the orthopedic typist's chair, abruptly bringing his eyes up to the hair pushed back at each return of the carriage.

—Terry? What would you think of a little redecorating in here, maybe getting some of that paneling up on the walls and covering over those pipes up there.

—Gee, I think that would be real nice.

—We even ought to get some carpet in here and plants, we could get some plants in here and get a new leather sofa instead of that old chair over there, and a coffee table.

—That would be real nice Mister Angel.

—And we ought to get some pictures up on the walls here.

—I saw one downtown of the ocean that was real nice, you could like almost hear the waves looking at it.

—We have pictures back in the files here, historical pictures of some famous musicians autographed to old Mister Bast back from the days when the business was piano rolls we could even, there's an old Welte-Mignon down there in the basement we could get working, shine it up and put it out in the front there where you come in, you know what I mean?

—Yes I, that would be real nice.

—For, you know, when we have visitors to come in, somebody coming in that didn't know anything about the business, I think they'd be pretty impressed . . .

She turned to answer a buzz. —They want you out on the floor, Leo. That would be real nice Mister Angel, she said as he got up and hung his jacket on the coat rack, going out.

—You get that Eyetalian in this quick, Leo?

—What? Oh. No, it's this what I was going to show you before.

—What's that Leo, he said following him to the shelter of the filing cabinets.

—I figured you better have a look at these. The soiled envelope came out and he closed a frayed buttonhole behind it, —see what goes on here.

—Where did these come from?

—Boys in the shipping room had them.

—But the, this, is this Terry here?

—Don't know who else it is, with a ass like that on her.

—But who's the, the man here, that's not one of our men.

—Might be one of the soldiers from over to the base there.

—And, this one? these?

—More soldiers I guess. What you going to do.

—Well hell I, I don't exactly know right off. You can't just go and be that sure from these they're none of them real sharp and . . .

—You mean you think they maybe ain't her? They used that kind of camera that develops itself but just because you can't see the color of every hair, you don't see tits like that come down the street every day. I don't know who else it could be with a ass like that.

—Why hell you never saw her naked like this neither did I Leo, hell. She might, it might be just somebody's trying to get her in trouble, she . . .

—Like she didn't know they was being taken? Look at this, no this here one with the three of them in it she's twisted around him looking right in the camera having a whale of a time, look at that.

—Well you can't just, unless it's a hundred percent certain you can't just go around and, hell there's things they can do now with doctoring pictures that you can't hardly tell it.

—That's some doctor then is all I could say. You mean like pasting on somebody's different face? Look at this here, you'd have to have a picture of her eating a cucumber to paste onto this one, that's some doctor.

—Well just right now let's just . . .

—Wait, wait, that there one spread-eagled over the chair look at it, don't that look like that old leather chair right there in your office? all them little brass studs showing out of under her knees?

—Well, it . . .

—And the corner of this here curtain showing you can almost make out the little design, see it?

—Well it, it sure as hell does but we're just going to wait and don't say anything till . . .

—You think them boys in the shipping room ain't saying . . .

—You just tell them to do what they're paid to around here and any that don't understand that get out, that's the first God damn rule right down the line produce or get out and something else, you know that big old Welte piano down there in the basement? Go down and take a look at it, see what shape it's in.

—I used to play on that Mister Angel, the old man had it right up in the . . .

—Well go down and see what shape it's in, we might clean it up and set it up out here in the front.

—All right but all them tubes and bellows, that's all probably cracked and . . .

—Just do what I'm asking will you Leo? and he turned down the wall

of porous green tapping the soiled envelope against his leg out of sight
as he came in behind his desk.

—Oh Mister Angel Kenny just called from Dayton on that order and
those people in Chicago called again they said they're up against the wall
on these specifications, it's that letter I put right on top there . . .

He looked down where an ellipse had already taken shape under his
blunt pencil in the margin. —Same story isn't it, want something done
right you have to do it yourself.

—You have to go out there again? I'll call about your tick . . .

—That's all right no I'll just pick it up at the airport, just call them
up and tell them I'll be out there this afternoon . . . but all that moved
about him was his hand laboriously blacking in the shape in the margin
there until she pushed her chair back from the typewriter.

—I'm just going for coffee. You want your regular?

—I don't want any, no.

—Gee I never heard you turn down coffee, you okay Mister Angel?

—I'm fine Terry . . . he watched her turn for the door and then sat
back staring at the worn leather chair near the coat rack, and then he
came forward to open the soiled envelope down in the shelter of his desk,
looking up from its contents to the chair, working his mouth and swallowing with apparent difficulty, finally pulling open the desk drawer and
thrusting the envelope to the back of it, reaching forward to dial the
phone and sit staring as it buzzed at his ear. When she came through the
door balancing a cup he was sitting back as though studying the curtains.

—You going home and pack first Mister Angel? or . . .

—I'll just buy a shirt and a toothbrush when I get out there . . . he
stood tightening the knot at his wilted collar, brought a wallet up from
a hip pocket to thumb through bills and double it back, reaching his
jacket and pulling it on. —When Coen calls tell him if he gets out before
I get back tell him to go ahead and get me everything he can on that old
lawsuit over holes with that jukebox company tell him I heard they're
changing hands, tell him I couldn't make any more sense than he did out
there with this estate situation you got that number for them I gave you?
Try and get hold of this Edward Bast out there try and get him and Coen
together yes and wait, tell Coen the boy's just not quite, just say he's kind
of hard to get to I couldn't get to first base with him myself . . . by now
he was in his coat, reached up for his hat —and see if you can get hold
of my wife Terry, just tell her I'll try to call her tonight.

—I can't usually reach her Mister Angel, should I say how long you
think you'll be gone?

—I know I just called there just keep trying, shouldn't be more than
a couple of days unless I stop off there in Dayton to give Kenny a push
I tell you, when I was on the road here if old Mister Bast would have had
to come in and check my territory I would have been out on the street
the next morning, used to be all you'd think about's your commissions

now all these salesmen think about's their expense accounts, his wife
called here lately?

—No sir only that nurse where she's . . .

—I'd just hate to be the one footing those bills that's all . . . he was
standing in hat and coat over his desk turning up the pile of letters there,
—if that finance company he got himself mixed up with calls again just
have to tell them we've gone as far as we can now here's these Triangle
paper people again, just hold up on this payment you tell them it's the
third time they've come up short on their shipments, they keep up that
way we'll all be out of business here and look at this Terry . . . he pulled
a page from the pile he was stuffing in a manila envelope,—this last letter
you typed to Ardo looks like you left off the s there, see right here
. . . she was up, thrust her hair back brushing against him —where it's
supposed to say metal scrap see it looks like . . .

—Gee! she snatched it up, pressed against him there —wouldn't that
have been awful if it went out like that? I'm sorry . . .

—No well that's, no harm done . . . he cleared his throat in the wave
of unconcealing scent, swallowed —I already signed it, you just, just
squeeze a little s in there and no harm done . . . he stood as though
waiting for her to move, and then came after her.

—No but I could type it over, gee it's very embarrass . . .

—No harm done Terry, one more thing . . . he'd turned abruptly
back to his desk, —I told Leo to get me some cost estimates you keep
after him on it, I want them waiting here when I get back.

—Okay but, Mister Angel if you got a second, it was just about
Leo . . .

—No go ahead Terry . . . he straightened up from locking the drawer.

—That day I stayed late typing up all those tax forms? Well anyway,
wait excuse me . . . hello? Oh hi look I'll call you back the boss is just
leaving . . .

—Well go ahead . . . he stood over her.

—No that's just my friend Myrna out in the order department, is it
okay if I take my typing out there sometimes while you're gone? It gets
sort of lone . . .

—Fine sure but . . . he cleared his throat again, —what's that about
Leo.

—No that's okay Mister Angel I don't want to keep you, I mean when
you get back . . .

—You suit yourself Terry . . . he stood there for a moment, —second
thought Leo he can be a funny old geezer maybe better just leave him
be, I'll talk to him on the way out here.

—Have a nice trip Mister Angel don't worry about anything, gee I
wish you had one of those nice cases like they carry instead of these old
envelopes you use . . .

—What's in it that counts, keep an eye on things Terry . . .

—So long have a nice trip Mister Angel, don't do nothing I wouldn't do . . . she looked up at the clock, down at her watch, studied her nails the length of her hand and then turned them in on her palm and studied them that way, picked up the phone and dialed —hi, he just went yeah bring in your coffee, you got any Nail Mender . . . ? Bring it yeah I just broke one . . . she hung up, dialed again, —hello? Mister Mullins' office . . . ? Hello? Yeah this is Mister Angel's office in New . . . oh hi, yeah would you tell Mister Mullins he's on his way out there? He just left . . . this afternoon sometime yeah, he's . . . okay yeah, goodbye now . . . she hung up. —Wait put your coffee here, drag his chair over.

—You tell him about Leo?

—I started to no, maybe when he gets back, you want your sugar?

—Here. I swear if Leo tries that with me he'll go out with a hole in his belly. So how long's he gone for.

—A couple of days he said, he's stopping in Dayton I think he's after Kenny's ass.

—That Kenny he gives me a big pain you know where, you got an emery?

—Here . . . a drawer rolled open between their crossed knees, —you want the radio? No just move your coffee . . .

—You still using his apartment?

—No his kid's still home sick we been using this friend of his, Kenny said he's a musician someplace I think he's a fag the way the place is decorated, you know? It's real nice.

—I can't make it like that, like that time with Ronnie I'm always scared somebody's going to walk in right when you're wait is that all the pink polish?

—We made it four times up there Monday before he went, I'll get more at lunch you want to go shopping? I saw this like silky yellow blouse over on Steinway it would go real nice with your coloring turn it up a little . . .

———and save four dollars on genuine leath . . . your gospel station. And ye shall . . . motion to dismiss a class action suit by . . . viernes sabado y domingo, el . . . market is down sixteen cents. The . . . for tomorrow, partly sunny windy and coo . . .

The voices met, parted, rose over the scratch of emery boards, dropped for the sound of the phone—no he went out of town for a couple of days Mister Shapiro, could I do something for you . . . ? no come on now don't get fresh . . . paused to dial, —yes I'm calling Mis . . . no ma'am no I'm not the lady selling the free dance less . . . no for Mister Bast, is he . . . he's where . . . ? answered again —that last order I got the order right in front of me it says twenty pound stock yeah . . . and silence, finally, with —wait out here for me, I forgot to turn off the lights . . .

———inbound traffic on the Gowanus Exp . . . favor, send your mouth on a vaca . . . and rain, the present tem . . . no tiene nada . . .

—Turn it off I swear, if he wasn't so cheap we'd have Muzak. How come you came in so late this morning.

—I got the worst cramps I been, wait. Hello . . . ? No he's out of town, he went yesterday Mis . . . tomorrow I think, I'll tell him to call you okay? Goodbye now . . .

—I got to get back out there, those new forms Mrs Krauer's having a hemorrhage.

—Wait lend me a Tampax, I thought I had some here. Kenny didn't call?

—Him? I told you he's bullshitting you I swear, he's a worse bullshitter even than Ronnie you going shopping at lunch? I'm taking back that yellow blouse I got yesterday my mother said it will shrink.

—I thought maybe I'll get a plant.

—For here?

—One yeah mainly just leaves, I mean I'm spending half my life here you know . . . ? the drawer rolled open —how the days go by you can't tell one from the next one sometimes . . . she studied her nails turned in on her palm and then studied them the length of her hand. —I mean sometimes I get real bored . . . and the emery board took up, the phone, the typewriter, voices meeting and parting.

—Yeah I know, he's supposed to be back yesterday he had to stop off at Dayton . . . no I told him you called Mister Shapiro, he . . . thank you that's very nice but I can't, no, my sister's having a . . .

——active issues. I T and T thirteen, up one eighth. Diamond Cable, seventee . . . revised forecast continued rain and . . . join the biggest savings bank fam . . . do your mouth a favor, send . . . four dollars on genuine leather work boots, come in now and . . .

—How come you go out this way now, it's so dark.

—Just not to pass the shipping room, you know? Those boys with their cracks.

—That one Jimmy's nice.

—Nice yeah, he's hard up like all of them in there . . .

——were killed when a taxi went out of con . . . sunny and colder, with temp . . . in next year's pennant race. The . . . of famous maker sheets and . . . to be expected.

—Hello . . . ? It's me yeah who did you think it . . . yeah what are you doing up so early I been trying to call you every night since . . . big order I bet yeah, I bet you're sacked out with this big order right now you . . . Yeah I bet listen you think I never saw you talk on the phone while you're in the saddle? don't . . . I heard it yeah don't tell me it's the television like that time you came back from Cleveland for two days you couldn't even . . . When yesterday? No . . . no he just called in he didn't say . . . Okay I kept telling you didn't I? What did he . . . yeah okay what am I sup . . . by talking to him yeah about what, you think I can save your ass now by telling him you . . . I bet . . . yeah I bet . . . I bet yeah, you . . . yeah okay you do that Kenny you can kiss my . . . you can kiss that too yeah, good . . . I bet you would, goodbye.

—He's fired?

—Yeah now he's telling, he's telling me will I ask the boss if, wait hello . . . ? Oh hi Mister Co, Coen they let you out . . . ? No he, he said sometime today, he's . . . no I, I guess I got a cold . . .

—Use my, wait here's a napkin . . .

—Yes I'm, okay go ahead Mister Coen I got my pad . . .

—I swear, didn't I tell you?

———revised forecast, partly cloudy with . . .

—Like I was saying in his car that time where he already had about ten daiquaris so I finally just tell him look, I don't go down unless I really like somebody, you going shopping at lunch? I saw this black wig . . .

—Okay just move his chair back so if he comes in wait, hello . . . ? Gee no he still didn't come back yet we . . . Sure yeah I'll tell him you wait, wait hold on a second, he's just walking in the office, Mister Angel? It's your wife calling . . .

—Well just, here. Hello, Stel . . . just walked in this minute yes, what . . . yes well fine you go ahead then I'll just fix something when I come in, are there any eggs . . . ? Don't do that no I'll find something, you didn't hear from our boy Edward while I was gone did you . . . ? No wait a minute, Terry? did you ever get hold of that Mister Bast at that Long Island number I gave you?

—No I called but they said he went abroad someplace accepting some award so . . .

—I guess not no unless Coen . . . that's all right you go ahead yes, goodbye . . . he dropped the large envelopes under his arm to his desk, took off his hat —you girls just going out to lunch?

—If that's okay Mister Angel, we just waited till late because it makes the afternoon shorter you know? Here's all your phone calls, this Mister Shapiro called about ten times and Mister Coen called this morning about this whole tax thing I wrote it all down . . .

—That's fine Terry . . . he came round behind his desk getting out of his coat, —ought to keep me busy till you get back.

When she did he was pouring bourbon into a paper cup. —Gee we didn't expect you to be gone so long Mister Angel, I mean even being gone the whole weekend and all, you notice any changes?

He put the bottle back into the file cabinet drawer. —I guess that looks like a new . . .

—No not about me I mean, that. The plant.

—Yes well, where'd that come from.

—I got it a couple of days ago gee it looks like it's wilting already, they had big ones too only they were a lot more, you know?

—Yes well it's, it's just fine Terry but you shouldn't spend your own money like that on something for the office.

—No that's okay, I mean like you said once we spend half our life in here . . . she was squaring papers on her typewriter, turned thrusting red hair back. —This letter to Dayton, you want carbons to anybody Mister Angel?

—One for the file's all it's just confirming that order, I just scribbled it on the plane can you read it?

—Sure . . . she squared them in the typewriter, —so everything went okay?

—Wouldn't have if I hadn't stopped off there, it looks like I have to replace Kenny.

—Really? gee that's, that's too bad Mister Angel . . . she typed a word, —maybe he's, maybe he just had an off day this time I mean that big Cleveland order he got that time, he can . . .

—No way you'd have known it Terry I spent three nights on the phone clearing that one up too . . . he put the paper cup down emptied. —I don't like to fire somebody any better than the next man but I can't do his job and mine too, some things about Kenny I picked up you'd as well just not hear but, something wrong?

—No, no . . . the drawer rolled closed at her knee and she brought up a tissue, —I just must have caught cold . . .

—I heard you had rain here . . . he picked up the empty cup and put it down sitting back slowly, looking, dug for a key and pulled open the drawer reaching to the back of it for the soiled envelope opened down at his waist's level, looking up from one to the next of the pictures as though to catch, in that moment of moistening his lips and swallowing, an evanescent matching tilt of nose or fall of hair, a turn of wrist or cheapringed crook of finger or grasp of hand regardless what it grasped or crooked or turned about coming up straight as her typing stopped and she stood suddenly crossing to a filing cabinet, sinking back in his chair as she stooped for a folder in a bottom drawer there turning up the next picture and the next, and next, as though to seize the moment of that simulated leather expanse to match in one of them its crevassed counterpart in white.

—Excuse me Mist . . .

—Oh . . . ? he came up straight keeping his lap composed, in toward his desk where she stood over him, —what . . .

—No just, I'm sorry I just, in, just in this letter these specifications you put in if they should match their last order in the file here where we say sixteen . . .

—Yes well yes, yes that's, don't have to ask me that that's the, says it right here doesn't it to specifications contained in your order of June the . . .

—No no yes sir I just wanted to check I didn't . . .

—Yes well that's the, that's all right Terry I guess I'm just tired from all this running around haven't even had lunch myself yet I'm, you couldn't stay a little late could you?

—Well if you, I didn't know it's so late already Mister Angel my friend Myrna in the order room, you know? She waits for me to ride in on the subway together so we don't have to ride it alone and my sister's having this . . .

—Yes well that's all right Terry you're, you can leave that till tomorrow you got a cold too and . . .

—No that's okay but I mean you should get something to eat Mister Angel if you didn't even eat yet, you . . .

—Might as well I guess yes . . . he snapped the desk's drawer closed, turned the key —not much choice around here though where . . .

—There's this place Joe's where we go over by Thirty-third it's not bad.

—Near that Army post?

—Right acrost it's not so bad, this special they have of . . .

—Terry?

—Yes what sir . . . she came up straight at the typewriter.

—Leo did he bring in this cost estimate?

—No sir I didn't even hardly see him all the time you were . . .

—What's that you wanted to tell me about him there . . . he was up pulling on his coat, —just when I was leaving, you . . .

—No that's nothing Mister Angel you better get something to eat while you, I'll just put this on your desk if you're coming back . . .

He stood there with his hat. —Yes well, yes just finish that up and go ahead home then.

—Thanks Mister Angel you, it's nice you're back . . .

—Yes thanks Terry it's, I'm glad to be back you, you take care of that cold now . . . and he stood there a moment longer with his hat before he put it on and turned down the length of porous green. —Leo . . . ?

—Didn't know you're back I got that Italian for you, he'll be here next Thursday he's . . .

—Thursday hell he can be here tomorrow morning or he don't need to come at all you tell him that and wait, you got that plan I drew?

—I got it right here . . . the frayed buttonhole came open, with it a folded yellow sheet and a picture that flew up between them, to reach the floor face up.

—What's, looks like you been holding out the best one on me Leo . . .

—Must have, must have fell out . . .

—Sure as hell did fall out didn't it.

—Must have fell out in my pocket out of that envelope . . .

—Yes well just, here just better keep them all together . . . he faced it inside his shirt pocket —now . . . he flattened the yellow page against that green with the heel of his hand, —just give me your pencil there now look, I forgot to mark this in we're going to need vents all down here if we change it around like this see what I mean? Now you get that Eyetalian in here tomorrow on it or he don't need to come at all.

—I'll try to do that for you Mister Angel but wait, these here pictures what . . .

—Don't do it for me Leo you just do it and these pictures, you just let me take care of it . . . and he pulled the door hard behind him against the day that seemed to dim as he entered it, gray dimmed overhead to vindicate small shams of housefronts' glassed porches boxing retirement in undervests no longer anywhere for sale behind aluminum doors bearing aluminum initials, yards parceled behind chain link not even his waist high toward an American flag flown high and bleak some blocks ahead down one curb, up the next, shoulders down hands fallen to the depths of pockets, when a rubber ball hit him on the leg. He stooped and caught it, and looked up, around, into a drive squeezed along the fence to a man poised there in a gray patterned suit and wearing a shirt and a tie, and he threw the ball and stopped dead. —Wait is, Jack . . . ?

The man turned as the ball bounced past him toward a child who rounded the corner of the house and stopped it, half running toward her with the sudden and grotesque effort of the limp that dragged one foot behind him. —Jack? Gibbs? is that you Jack . . . ? But with one twisted turn the figure was gone behind the house. He stood there until a curtain stirred at the window, and then he turned and went on toward the flag, and the glass front just across where he went in and sat at the counter eating a western sandwich, looking from one face to the next of the sprawled soldiers, glancing repeatedly back at one more erect under a major's clusters until he finished and left, the flag behind him, up one curb and down the next. The child was in the driveway with the ball, and he hurried toward her. —Wait, little girl? Wait a minute, I just want to ask you something . . . she backed down the fence a step or two. —That man you were just playing ball with, is he here?

—He just went, she said half pointing up the block.

—He, see I thought I knew him, he . . .

—That's my father.

—Oh. When will he be back.

—Every week today, he comes to see me every week just about.

—You mean, where does he live then.

—Someplace else, he just comes here to see me and you know what?

—He'd ah, he hurt his leg did he?

—He always had that, he got it in the war and you know what?

—He always had it?

—He got that fighting the Germans in his tank, his tank broke and when he got out they shot him like that and he almost froze, it was in winter and you know what?

—Rose! came a woman's voice from the house, or behind it.

—Wait, what's you name?

—Rose.

—Rose you get in here . . . !

—What, Rose what . . .

—Rose get in here!

He stood there looking after her for a moment and then up the empty block where she'd pointed, breaking that way suddenly in a near trot and looking, down every curb, in both directions, dropping finally to a walk where the elevated limb of subway loomed ahead off one curb, up the next to stop off balance there and turn abruptly as though sheltering from the wind in the drugstore's entrance, apparently absorbed in Surgical Appliances for the Whole Family as cadenced heels stabbed the pavement passing behind him.

—So what happened.

—So I'm bringing this file folder over to his desk to check this specification, I guess he didn't see me because I look down and he's sitting there with all these dirty pictures in his lap, honest.

—Him?

—Honest, so he sits forward real quick and . . .

—No if you hardly saw them then maybe they weren't . . .

—Are you kidding? This one on top where she's going down I mean he's hung like Kenny you couldn't, wait you got a token? They stopped at the foot of the steps rummaging in purses, bumped by a man escaping a bar gleaming red behind them who muttered —sorry passing up the stairs where they followed, rummaging, through the turnstile and out to the platform pausing sheltered by a billboard loaf of bread surcharged Astoria Gents. —You want to come up that way? So I can be up front for when I change, don't look back he's really checking you out.

—Who.

—He's got on this gray suit with these big checks on his tie . . . they stopped toward the end of the platform. —Him.

—He just bumped us down at the bottom, he looks . . . the train roared in against the platform. —I swear, they're like animals . . . and they settled back to a gentle rocking motion —with all these rhinestones down the shoulder but I'm scared to wear it . . . lights dimmed, came up, halts became more frequent filling the aisle with feet kicking aside torn newspaper, flattening candy wrappers, —sitting right acrost yeah, your stop's next?

—Yeah good night, I'll see you . . .

—I'll see you Terry . . . and she settled back appearing to seek a gap between trouser seats and shifting bulks from cloth coat sales across the aisle to where arms folded over the tie's bold check he sat eyes fixed above her on a car card burgeoning the Statue of Liberty garnished with appropriate verse and the train stopped, and started, stopped as though exchanging refuse from one teeming shore to carry to the next.

—Watch out you stupid fuck you.

—Watch the doors there . . .

—Is this the Penn Station?

—Who you calling stupid you dumb fuck, you want me to bust your fucking ass?

—Let them out there, let them out . . . resonant, unrelated, syllables blared from a loudspeaker, purse clutched her glance over a shoulder swept ahead ready when he turned square in his path steadied against a vending machine.

THE LORD'S PRAYER
Use it as a
Lucky Charm Medal
25¢

OUT OF ORDER scrawled across it —sorry . . . he caught her elbow, —are you all right?

—I think I hurt my ankle, they're like animals I swear.

—Can't get you a lucky charm how about a drink . . . elbows found ribs and shoulders backs —place is like the dawn of the world here, this way . . . countless hands and unattached eyes, faces looking in different directions, rolled newspapers clutched and their wives' umbrellas, frankfurters redolent, a muffled explosion and falling glass.

—Here, I'm over here . . .

—My God a bomb . . .

—Five thirty-eight to Babylon . . . ?

—To Jericho . . .

—Over here . . . !

—What are you standing here shouting for. I was over there.

—What? Oh, Ann I didn't see you I didn't even know you were, I just thought I saw Mister Gibbs over there with a young . . .

—What are you doing here in the first place.

—Getting the five thirty-eight, I had an appointment I didn't even know you came in.

—You're the only one that can have an appointment?

—No I just, are you getting the train?

—What do you think I'm here for, the fresh air? I'm getting the train if we're not all killed first.

—So am I . . .

—If you don't push me down the stairs first.

—I just thought we should hurry . . .

—Then maybe you could have offered to carry something.

—Oh here . . .

—Well not now we're practically there . . . Elbowed, stabbed by folded umbrellas, they got two together staring at backs of necks as the procession shuddered into motion and the lights went out. After a wavering try they came on again. The conductor stood tapping his punch.

—Shall I pay for yours?

—Is that too much to expect? She looked back to her book.

—No no I, I just thought maybe you'd bought a round trip . . .

The lights went out and stayed out until the train emerged in what was left of the day. His head nodded slightly. He was staring over her shoulder.

El hedouli: hands and feet brought together so that her vulva stands out like a dome, the woman is raised by means of a pulley until the lingam is . . .

—Haven't you got something of your own to read?

—I, I meant to get a paper.

—Why didn't you get a paper? Everybody else has a paper. The train settled to a gentle swaying motion and suggestions of buildings fled past the filthy pane. —What are you doing?

—Me?

—You're making faces at yourself in the glass.

—No I'm, it's called role playing industrial consultants are beginning to . . .

—Well stop it.

The train was seized with a series of spasms, came to a halt to moan outside a bottling works and moved again. His head nodded.

Lebeuss er djoureb: seated between her legs, the lips of the vulva are fitted over the lingam with the thumb and first finger, so that . . .

—Haven't you got something to . . . but his eyes were closed and remained so until she dug his ribs. —Come on, we're here. He walked behind her, out and down the platform past Debbys cespool and We kick ass yours too down the steps and ranged rumps of cars to one that finally started with a tremor right through his livid grip on the wheel out in a whirl of gravel disputing passage only for the time it took his foot to reach the brake —unless we're both killed first . . . into Burgoyne Street menaced by kerosene flares toward a corner invitingly lighted, —Straight! Go straight! and the car righted narrowly missed from another direction.

—He almost, almost ran right into me!

—Well turn on your lights, my God.

Past ships' lanterns lighted now and sentry carriage lamps, they mounted the curb and fell to silence. —We're home.

—Home!

The frame door slammed with the sound of a shot.

—Mama we made a puppet show Mama, me and Donny.

—My God. Did you eat?

The door slammed with the sound of a shot.

—Daddy me and Donny made a puppet show.

The elderly dog eyed him from under a table as he leaned a shopping bag against the room divider, peering through the display of preColumbia erect to the flaccid saxophone, stilled fingers halted up its length to the mouthpiece hung between dentures left ajar. —Hello Dad . . .

—He's asleep and Daddy you want to see the puppet show me and Donny made? See it's this clown and this mouse and the clown says hey Donny! Come here, we're going to show the puppet show.

—Where's Donny?

—He's with his bed. Hey Donny?

—After supper Nora, he said starting the round of turning off lights, foyer, hall, bathroom, foyer, snap, snap, snap, —Nora?

—What are you doing now.

—We don't need lights on in rooms nobody's in.

—Rooms nobody's in, put them out in the kitchen too we can all eat in the dark. Nora get Donny for supper.

—He's with his bed. Hey Don-ny . . . !

—Don't scream! I said go get him.

—Shall I wake Dad?

—My God no, why.

—For supper?

—He ate already Daddy.

—Ate already? Ate what already.

—I don't know Mama, he just made something and . . .

—I said will you get Donny.

—Daddy will you help me get Donny? When he gets all those wires around everything with his bed he gets stuck.

—My God . . . a door banged, there was a sound of something falling, of dragging up the hall. —Nora let Donny sit there, you sit here.

—But Mama he has to sit by where the plug is so he can plug in.

—And I have to get through here without tripping on a cord every time I turn around.

—But he can't eat nothing if he's not plugged in. I need a fork.

—Use your spoon.

—Daddy can I use your fork?

—There must be more forks, I'll get you a . . .

—She can use her spoon. There aren't any clean forks.

—But we had plenty of forks, that whole set that . . .

—Ick, tunafish casserole.

—Sit up and eat.

—Yes we, we don't have meat very often we . . .

—Don't have meat very often! You think they give it away?

—No but there should be enough in the household money for just . . .

—Household money, Nora sit up and eat. You said Dad already ate, none of the casserole was gone what did he eat?

—Out of the blue dish with the cover, he . . .

—Oh God. He got in the dog's food again.

—Would it make him sick Mama?

—Does it make the dog sick?

—Then what's the matter.

—The way the bathroom smells afterward that's what's the matter, now sit up and finish.

—Then will you watch me and Donny's puppet show?

—Yes, just eat. If you, Donny!

—He couldn't help it Mama, the wire got caught around his milk glass and . . .

—My God, all over my skirt. Just stay at the table!

—But you're . . .

—Stay right there till you're finished! she got past them, rounded the corner and down the hall. —Dad! Are you in there? A rude sound responded promptly beyond the bathroom door and here she came again. —All of you! she whispered, getting her skirt off at the kitchen sink.

—We're done. We're done. Get ready for the puppet show.

—All of you . . .

—In here Daddy, in the living room. Donny you get the mouse. I'll be the clown and the cat and you be the mouse. Daddy you sit here, Daddy sits here and Mama sits here. Donny you're being the mouse. Mama? You sit here. This is where we live. I'm being the clown and I say let's get a cat. Come on Donny, you're being the mouse and you say you don't want us to get a cat because you're scared he would eat you, come on, so then you go out. So then the clown goes over and opens the door so the cat can come in and tells him to come in. So then the mouse, come on Donny you're being the mouse and you hear us, so then the mouse hears us and he comes in where the clown didn't see him and closes the door on the cat. Come on Donny, come on! You're being the . . .

—Nora? it's close to bed time.

—But just let us . . .

—Get undressed Nora. Both of you.

—Mama Donny always ruins everything, he was supposed to be practicing and he was always going back to work on his old bed while he was supposed to be practicing the puppet show. He's always ruining everything . . .

Somewhere a clock made a try at striking the hour. A door banged, a toilet flushed, a door banged. Tape measure, linen counter, calibrated pencil, perforation gauge, —what are you doing with all that stuff? she came in behind him.

—Just, just getting it out of my pockets . . .

—Would you mind dumping it somewhere else? I need the mirror.

Calibrated pencil, linen counter, tape measure, perforation gauge, —Aren't you afraid the children will see you like that? he said, picking them up.

—See me like what.

—Just, I mean, walking around naked . . .

—Why should they be afraid to see me walking around naked?

—No I mean you, aren't you afraid . . .

—Well say what you mean . . . leaning into the mirror she removed an eyelash. —Afraid! she removed the other eyelash, —because you're afraid you think everybody else should be afraid?

—Well no, he brought his eyes up from the smutch of hair she'd turned on him —I only meant . . .

—You only meant, you're even afraid to say what you mean . . . she padded past him and bent over to pick up something, a hairpin? behind the radiator, —afraid it will devour you, that anything alive will devour you.

He stared at it gone upside down, lips parting, cleared his throat. —Are you using the typewriter?

—Am I using the typewriter. She straightened round, an arm akimbo and a breath that briefly exalted things to the disposition of calendar art. —Do I look like I'm using the typewriter?

—There's something in it, he hastened round himself to turn the roller —I just didn't know . . .

—Well take it out that's right, throw it away, she came on, dispelling breath in a gesture that restored her homey disproportion fully dressed, —it's probably just something of mine for the Foundation grant.

—They were dead on foot. They were helpless too, because they were dead on foot. Probably had an earthquake. When you come to red brick dust you know you're coming to a house where the people are standing and the people died on foot . . .

—All right, I've read it.

—But what is it?

—What is it. What do you think it is, something of mine? It's a composition of Nora's what do you, don't you dare throw that away.

—I wasn't going to, I just . . .

—Just because you think it doesn't show talent? You probably wonder how she can be your own daughter she has more talent in, where are you going?

—Finger, he muttered crossing the room.

—What?

—Are you done at the mirror?

—I can tell you what you'll see there.

—It's in, something in connection with my work.

—Your work. What, Whiteback told you to take a good look at yourself?

—No this job, the people I talked to in New York today about . . .

—Job. What job, you're going to model?

—No it's in the area of, in the management area, he said to the reflection over the droop of his own shoulder where she was blowing up the inflatable belt that now bridled her thighs. —Executive decision making in the . . .

—Before and after, you could model before.

—De, decision making, he said to one side, and the other, catching reflections of her exercise over each shoulder. —Role playing, the use of role playing in teaching de, de, the decision making . . .

—So you're going to stand there all night and make faces at yourself in the mirror? she said, and dropped from sight.

—Mama what's the matter!

—Go to bed Nora.

—Daddy what's Mama doing on the floor with that . . .

—I said go to bed! She sat up. —It's like Grand Central station. Can't you go in and use the bathroom mirror?

—It stinks in there Mama. Daddy can you come plug Donny in?

—Go to bed I said! My God, roll play . . . She got the belt off and mounted her bed. —Roll play.

He stared into the mirror and then turned slowly to her seated bolt upright, knees yawning as she brought her feet up soles together. —But you, you see what I mean about them seeing things, they . . .

—Seeing things! She nested her heels, —it's about time they saw things, you and your roll playing it's about time they saw some of that. She thinks sex is bumblebees spraying dandelines . . .

—But she's only . . .

—Only going to grow up as dumb as I was when I met you about things you're even dumber about, where do you want her to learn on the bathroom wall? And do you think you could stop that for a while? I can't do my breathing with you making faces out of the corner of my eye.

On another face, his grimace might have signaled the decision to raze Carthage, turning from the mirror to find under her emptied brassiere Role Therapy and the Decision Making Process, huddled marking a margin and erasing that to mark one elsewhere already roughened by erasure, sheltering, once undressed, covert expressions of command, disdain, appeal and magnanimity by turn behind a knee raised underneath the blanket, with now and then among them one of quite candid stealth to where in hard-nippled profile she sat bolt upright with no sign of breathing whatsoever, as she was next morning when he sprawled for the alarm, no sign she'd closed her eyes or moved at all but the pillowslip smudged freely with mascara, disdain, command and magnanimity freed to flee cheaply framed above the spattered basin where he coursed them, shaved and wiped them fresh in the bathroom mirror to pursue their shuddering fragments in the rear view oval while he warmed the car and abandon them there with its halt at the Post Office, where the door banged behind him.

—Hi Mister di look out hey, holy . . .

—He didn't even see me boy did you see that hey?

—What you spilled both of ours? holy . . .

—What do you mean I spilled them he smashed right into me.

—Okay quick help pick them up before he walks all over them here he comes again, I mean holy shit I can't hardly tell what I'm sending from what I'm getting wait pile it in the middle hey, like how am I supposed to mail this . . . he blew at the footprint and then smudged it permanently with the heel of his hand across Defense LOgistics S eRvices Center, Battle Creek Mich, did the same with Dow Thoery Forecast as nailbitten fingers tore open a plain wrapper beside him. —Look out hey be careful, I'm suppose to have this check in here someplace . . .

—Wait that what's that, give it here.

—Hello, it's Mary Lou honey, here to say hello and bring you a sample cause I know you've shown an interest in ordering fotos of chicks posing in the buff . . .

—Okay come on give it here hey what's that, with the Canadian stamp give me it for the stamp hey?

—What do you mean give you it.

—You got it free didn't you? It's just this paper in here anyway.

—That's how much you know boy, it's this here debenture.

—Debenture shit, you don't even know what that is.

—What do you mean it says right on it look, Alberta and Western Power Company Series B Debenture . . .

—Okay so what's that supposed to be.

—That's this word I couldn't think of it that time I'm getting this whole bunch of them look out, what are you ripping.

—I'm just ripping the stamp off it.

—What's so great about some dumb Canadian stamp.

—You collect them for a stamp collection what do you think, like some day they're really worth something boy they're worth more than this crap what's this one, Ace Development Corporation where'd you send for this crap anyway.

—What do you think I got it off some broker, this Mister Wall like in Wall Street only he's at California there's this here ad someplace wait, it said aggressive growth opportun . . .

—Wall like at Wall Street boy I never heard such . . .

—Okay what's so funny about that, I mean there's this here big broker called Kidder something and this one Hornblower and somebody boy I mean if people would go buy stock off somebody called Hornblow . . .

—No but look this says a thousand shares like how could you buy a thousand shares . . .

—Because it's real cheap what do you think.

—Okay if it's so cheap so what good is it.

—Because they didn't find these here virgin minerals yet that's all, there's this here free booklet they . . .

—Wait that's mine that National Rifle Associa . . .

—So is this, the New Look in an Artificial Penis! No harness! No straps! Exciting sizes boy you talk about me sending away for crap, regulations and good taste prohibit vivid and detailed . . .

—Okay give it here, who said I sent away they just sent it to me here, here's your dumb booklet Frozen Fresh Boneless Beef Futures you don't even know what that is.

—So why do you think I sent for it that's . . .

—Wait there's something stuck in it what . . .

—Hi Hon, Ops pardon my back but I couldn't think of a better way to introduce myself, 'course this sample doesn't do me justice but I've got a jumbo set posed to show off my thirty-eights, twenty-threes and . . .

—Okay keep it wait what's . . .

—What do you mean keep it it says Hyde right on the envelope look, only five dollars sugar course you gotta be twenty-one years old or over okay!!! Boy what a, hey wait that little package give it here.

—How do you know whose . . .

—Because look it says right here to Mister J R . . .

—Okay but it says class six J, it just says your name sec open it.

—What do you think I'm doing.

—What's wait, what's it a clock? Who wants to send us a clock from let's see hey, from this bank at Nevada? How come they send us a clock.

—You get to pick this here free gift when you start this bank account there, what's wrong with that.

—No but how come it says class six J then it's all of ours, I mean does Mrs Joubert know you're doing this hey?

—Why shouldn't I, I mean she's out sick half the time now anyway what . . .

—No but how can you just go start some bank account at Nevada without . . .

—You just cut out this little coupon in the newspaper and send it in with . . .

—No but I mean you're supposed to be twenty . . .

—What like with this here Mary Lou honey you're suppose to be twenty-one and over? I mean how does she know any more than this dumb bank at Nevada all she knows she gets this five dollars off you for her jumbo set so you're twenty-one and over, what's the difference of her and this here bank someplace. I mean where Glancy gave us about modern banking would be impossible without the wonders of the computer see all these electric numbers down here? I mean like this here Mary Lou gets your five dollars why should they give a shit if you're a hundred wait give me that, boy I been looking for that . . .

—It's mine it's probably my . . .

—What do you mean yours give me it.

—It says Department of the Army what would you be doing with

Dep, wait let me see what it's, boy, boy are you going to get in trouble.

—Why should I get in trouble it's this here deal, give me it.

—I mean who cares about this other crap these boneless futures and debuntures and all that crap but you better not shit around with the Army boy.

—That's how much you know, move your . . .

—You don't call picnic forks shitting around with the U S Army boy they get some wise guy that writes to them about picnic forks you think that's what they do at the Army go for picnics?

—How do I know what they do at the Army look move your elbow, I got it right out of that spot bid catalogue I traded off you to send in for where the Navy got all these new plastic ones so they like spot bid these here wooden surplus ones real cheap for anybody that wants, so this here business opportunities thing the Army's putting out all these here contracts where one of them's picnic forks so . . .

—What a bunch of crap boy, if the Army wants them so much why don't they just go buy them off the Navy why should they want you in the middle of it.

—How do I know that's just how you do it move your elbow will you? Let me get this here envelope out . . .

—Yeah well you better watch out boy they'll the both of them boot your ass when they find out I mean look at this, this here Major Sheets Procurement Officer you think he's going to believe some letter he gets with a footprint all over it? Forks, picnic, wooden, nine thousand gr I never saw such crap, what's gr supposed to be.

—How do I know it's probably green, you just copy off how the Navy says it and say that to the Army is it my fault if they all talk backwards there . . . ? he blew at the envelope and then wiped at Defense SurplUs SAles Of fice, Fleet Station SanD iego Cal with his sleeve.

—Look at that boy even if it gets there you think they're even going to open it?

—They have to, what do you think they just open what they want? Besides what do they care what it looks like, I mean you think Mary Lou honey gives a shit if there's this footmark on the envelope if money's in it?

—Okay but how come you got enough to buy nine thousand wooden gr forks off them anyway, you . . .

—Because that's not what you do you just send this here percent, you make this here bid and send them this here percent of . . .

—Okay where you getting the rest of it then.

—Off the bank . . . he licked and pounded an envelope, —where do you think.

—What like you walk in and say Mister Whiteback I just need some money to buy this bunch of wooden gr pic . . .

—I wouldn't borrow off him boy you know what they do there? Like they say they pay this lousy four and a half percent on savings what those cheap shits never tell you they pay it on your lowest balance the whole quarter so you put like this thousand dollars in for awhile then you take out like nine fifty so you get like a fourth of this lousy four and a half percent of like fifty dollars while they been out loaning around this here thousand all the time it was . . .

—So what you think they're going to loan it to you? Just because you get a free clock off some bank at Nevada boy you walk in there they won't loan you shit wait what's that hey, give it here . . .

—Deluxe portable vibrator can be taken anywhere in pocket or purse for portable pleasure, a perfect gift for . . .

—Can I help it if they just sent me it?

—They just sent you this too then, here. Here comes another first in the marital relations field, the vibropenis . . .

—Okay come on hey . . .

—Look I'm trying to put all your crap over here and you keep getting it mixed up with mine again that eagle thing, right under there with the eagle on give it here . . .

—What this? What's . . .

—Give it here.

—What is it some more debunture crap? What's this here thousand in the corner shares?

—Dollars boy that's how much you know, it's this here bond.

—What you paid a thousand dollars for a bond? I bet boy . . .

—That's the whole thing you get them real cheap because they owe all this here interest.

—Who does, they owe who.

—Me, this here Eagle Mills they owe me.

—A thousand dollars?

—Plus all this here interest.

—I bet boy let's see, look, look they don't owe you shit look, it says right here Eagle Mills hereinafter called the Company, a corporation of the states of New York and . . .

—Come on give it here.

—No look it says it right here look, for value received hereby promises to pay to Selma Krupskaya or registered assigns at its office in Union Falls there, see? They owe it to this here Selma crap whatever her name is they don't owe you shit.

—That's how much you know look on the back, no down here where it's stamped, there's my name where I'm this here registered assign see? So what they owed this here Selma now they owe it to me.

—Try and get it look it's stamped all over the place, somebody just wrote your name on so you're this here registered asshole you mean who's going to believe you paid any thousand dollars for it.

—Who said I did, like that's the whole thing where they didn't pay this here interest all this time so you get to buy them for like seven or eight cents for the dollar I'm getting this whole bunch of them boy, then you'll . . .

—With what.

—With this here picnic forks deal what do you think . . . he was jamming papers into the torn zipper.

—You already got one don't you? Why should you get a whole bunch of them hey look what time it is . . .

—Because they're real cheap what do you think!

—Boy I never saw such a, I mean this here Major Sheets suppose he even buys all these forks off you so you've got all this money to buy stuff, who wants to buy this crap all these pieces of paper when you could buy . . .

—Because that's what you do! he brought a sweater sleeve up across his nose, —what do you think it means money working for you to . . .

—Working shit, all this . . .

—Wait a second wait, this here booklet I was looking for look. Prospectus one million shares, Ace Development Company look.

—At what. It's a bunch of trees.

—Yeah well they have all these mineral rights to explore for these here virgin minerals see that? where it says stretching as far as the eye can see boy when they find these here virgin min . . .

—They won't find shit, how can they find anything with all these here trees in the way hurry up hey, it's time. They have to knock all these here trees down before they even can . . .

—Hold the door a second . . .

—I mean all this crap you're getting you keep saying because it's real cheap so why should it be worth anything, I mean if it's worth anything why should somebody want to give it to you real cheap boy what a stink, I thought they finished all this asphalt Friday. I mean you better find somebody that knows about all this crap before you get in trouble.

—Okay who said I wasn't.

—Who, like Mrs Joubert? You just said you . . .

—How am I suppose to ask her, you go ask some broker that's what they do.

—Like who Mister Wall at Wall Street? He sells you crap so you expect him to tell you it's crap?

—Look quit saying it's crap will you? I mean that's how much you know besides he's at California anyway, didn't you ever hear of these ads like on the radio and all where they say come in and let us review the contents of your portforlio?

—Who like that guy we saw with all the heads? so you're walking in there and saying good morning sir I would like you to review the contents of my portforlio then you dump out this bunch of crap? hey . . . ? Wait up what's the matter . . .

—Because that's not what you do! You get somebody to help you out, like some business representative . . .

—Who, why should he help you out anyway who . . .

—Like you get somebody to do anything you pay them! what do you think . . .

—Okay who. You got somebody? hey? Because boy you're going to get in trouble going around loaning money for these here forks and all, just because you been reading up all these here little books since we went to that dumb field trip before that we used to have this neat time trading boy but now everything's . . .

—Okay so what am I suppose to do! he kicked up a burst of leaves before him, stopped there to shift his armload —go around selling like those free cosmetic samples with those matchbooks in these here shoes which they're a mile too big? or like that thing I got train at home for this exciting motel career or do import export at the privacy of your own home? I mean these funny hours my mother's always working how do I know when she's going to walk in, like I mean this here bond and stock stuff you don't see anybody you don't know anybody only in the mail and the telephone because that's how they do it nobody has to see anybody, you can be this here funny lookingest person that lives in a toilet some- place how do they know, I mean like all those guys at the Stock Exchange where they're selling all this stock to each other? They don't give a shit whose it is they're just selling it back and forth for some voice that told them on the phone why should they give a shit if you're a hundred and fifty all they . . .

—Look out hey you're dropping . . .

—Wait the clock quick, get the clock, just till we get to my locker okay?

—You turning it in?

—Why should I turn it in, I got it didn't I?

—Okay but it says class six J right on it boy wait till Mrs Joubert finds out, she'll boot your . . .

—How's she supposed to find out anything, you think she's going to be over at Nevada?

—Okay but if it says class six J on this here account you started over there boy you better . . .

—What's the difference if it says that they got my signature off this here little coupon where it said signature on it didn't they?

—Okay boy but if this here bank finds out the class puts money in some account where you take it out to piss away on this debunture crap and they find out you kept this here clock boy you're in . . .

—We got a clock! We already got a clock right up by the door in the classroom and I mean holy shit who said I'm taking any money that's not what you do! I mean didn't you ever see these things where they say come right in and borrow up to a hundred percent of your passbook balance while it goes right on earning these top dividends and all? So whose business is it if I just start this other account and loan against this here first one where they already have my signature so they know it's me, I mean it's just different electric numbers on these checks and all which this computer reads them it doesn't give a shit if you're three years old just if the money's there, I mean that's all Mary Lou honey that's all this Mister Wall that's all these here forks that's all any of it is don't tell me I did something against the law boy, that's just what you do! I mean this here class account I just loan against it and get through this here forks deal I never even touched it right?

—Okay okay! but I mean you're yelling about this here class account the class doesn't have shit you can't loan shit off it, I mean you're yelling about some check what check, this here fifteen cents that guy said you will see our earnings reflected in your dividend on this here one lousy share of . . .

—Yeah well that's how much you know boy, I mean what do you think that guy meant with the glasses where you get to make them give you these here damages if you catch them screwing up these by-laws someplace even with this here one lousy share and besides . . .

—You think Mrs Joubert's going to let you do that boy? I mean I never heard such a bunch of . . .

—Why should she know about it, I mean she never put in any money to buy this here share did she? Besides . . .

—No but I mean are you going to get in trouble boy, and this here Major Sheets I mean if he finds out how you're doing this dumb forks deal he's really going to boot your ass boy you better . . .

—What's the difference! he came on kicking up bursts of leaves from the gutter —what does he care, I mean like you go in some shoestore someplace do you go around asking the manager and everybody where'd they get all these shoes? did they have to loan money off some bank to start up their store and how old are they? I mean what's the difference if it's me that loans money off some bank on this forks deal they get their lousy forks don't they?

—Okay boy but you better . . .

—Wait duck hey there's Coach, I'm going in by east seven . . .

—So what, he's full of . . .

—No for later I don't want him looking for me, I'm taking off at gym for when that late mail comes boy if this here check isn't . . .

—Okay but you better watch out hey . . . came blown after him, —I mean is Mrs Joubert going to be pissed off if she finds out you been shitting around with our share of America . . . and the leaves came on, swirling for the doors, trampled into the corridor. —Hey you guys . . . !

—Where's Buzzie hey, they said he has some of the little red ones for a quarter . . .

—Somebody said the boys' room after math, is Mrs Joubert here today hey?

—How do I know, what's the difference . . .

—This here report we're suppose to do did you do it? Where we went to see that big guy with all the heads that shot that pig and all?

—What pig boy, the best one was that impala with those long skinny horns like.

—Impala shit. Impala's a car.

—So? it's named after the car, what's so great about that.

—It's name's a kudu anyway it said right on it.

—Kudu shit, who'd buy a car called a kudu . . .

A bell rang, lockers banged, clocks clipped away identical minutes out of each other's sight round corners, down corridors where the tide of sweat rose as lockers banged, bells rang, the door marked Boys slammed, slammed. —Come on back by the mops, you got those little red ones?

—No I got these green ones, they're the same only you need three.

—How much.

—Half a buck all three.

—What's the yellow one.

The door slammed. —Shhh, that's like Buzzie had they really . . .

—Shhh . . .

The door slammed.

—Come to join me in a leak, Whiteback? I'm treating.

—Oh Coach, I've been ahm, looking for you . . .

—Doing business right here at the same old stand . . . there was a prolonged flush.

—Yes that ahm, I wanted to ask you about that new curricular material you were developing for us in terms of the ahm . . .

—Just finishing it I'll drop it off on your desk, sort of a preliminary sketch, give these youngsters a picture of how the old box really works.

—Yes well of course you wouldn't need to describe things quite so ahm, crudely, to help them see things at the ahm, at the visual level that is to . . .

—That's right, the scanning process, that's the heart of the whole thing, Whiteback. How the old box operates.

—Yes developed along the lines of your ahm, your body engine concept utilizing the ahm, the utilization potential of ahm . . . there was a succession of quick flushes —old parts that is to say . . . he raised his eyes, —structuring the material in terms of . . .

—Just need to get across the way this complicated circuit of horizontal and vertical deflection coils makes the old box operate.

—Yes well of course that should ahm, that approach should help eliminate the offensive human element in this ahm, in this area of ahm, Dan's wife, I just talked to Dan's wife about it that is to say and you might develop something with her when he's felt her ahm, her out . . .

—Kind of you to think of me Whiteback but I won't count on it . . . the door slammed behind them, —once he's felt her out he'll probably start wondering who's kissing her now.

—Yes well I don't quite ahm, he's right here in my office if you want to discuss her ahm, her now that is to say . . . the door marked Principal quavered, —Coach . . . ? it bunged hollow behind him. —Dan? I thought Coach was right behind me here he wants to discuss your wife's ahm, yes well he'd better explain it himself you've met Mister Stye? Dan runs all our testing Mister Stye he's our resident psycho ahm, keeps an eye on tangibilitating the full utilization potential of our student ahm, body yes student body Major you've met Mister Major Hyde yes, Major Hyde . . . and the flurry of pastels subsided as hands seized hands at arms' lengths, —we thought Mister Stye might look alike at the ahm, like a look at your drivers' ed tapes Dan . . .

—I didn't know they were on they're, what class would be watching them now I thought they . . .

—Elementary Dan the, help motivate the elementary youngsters' potential carwise that is to say, potentiate them for a real meaningful driving experience when they're big enough to get out and hit the, hit our nation's highways yes of course that's what Mister Stye here . . .

—Mister Stye is connected with one of our prominent insurance companies, Dan. Hyde massed against the desk weighting its corner with a discreetly herringboned web of creases where his legs met, and knocked a telephone from its cradle. —Get another phone, Whiteback?

—I had a line put in to the bank, for calls I get at the bank . . . catching light from nowhere, his lenses went blank as he retrieved it —keeping the fish and fowl separate you might say, separate the sheep and the ahm . . .

—Mister Whiteback heads up the bank here you know Mister Stye, sort of doubles in brass, gives him a real surefooted grasp of community affairs, kind of a grandstand view of both sides of the coin I'm sure Mister Stye knows what I'm talking about Whiteback, probably sees it at the corporate level all the time just like I do.

—Yes he's ahm, Mister Stye that is to say Dan, he's shown an interest in running for the school board.

—That can be a pretty thankless proposition, I guess you're aware of that Mister Stye but you take a company like mine, they're glad to see their people in working for community and civic betterment right at the decision making level I'm on company time right now in fact, trying to help Whiteback here solve a little space problem with this new equipment coming in.

—We thought we could use your advice on it Dan, the . . .

—Language labs? His lips broke their silent concert with those on the silent screen recalling the emergency brake, how and when employed. —The language labs have come?

—Not quite Dan more the enrichment ahm, in the motivational resources area where's that list, marriage, potentiate these girls to make marriage a more meaningful experience when they get out and hit the, I had that list a minute ago . . .

—But that's still in the decision mamaking stage, equipment for the sex education program we haven't even . . .

—Right Dan I just talked to Vogel about it, he's working up something on his body engine concept as soon as he's out of electrical circuitry said he'd drop a copy on my desk yes, structuring the material in terms of, out of old parts, he ahm, here, here it is. Washing machine, dryer, stove electric, stove gas, dishwasher, vacuum cleaner . . .

—We're talking about appliances Dan, home appliances.

—Hair dryer . . .

—Home ec Mister Stye, give these little future homemakers a shot at . . .

—Implementing unplanlessness in the . . .

—Day they step out of school they'll know what they want, Mister Stye here knows what I'm talking about. That ad your company runs with the empty chair at the head of the dinner table? One look at that and your little homemaker really puts on the clamps, take that what was his name that shot the president over a washing machine . . .

—But this equipment, I don't remember this equipment in the budget.

—Matter of fact Dan it's all coming to us, all this modern equipment is coming to us courtesy of a subsiderary of the company Major Hyde here is connected with.

—But where's all this equipment going?

—Resource materials Dan, we can set this home ec motivational center you might call it, set it up in the south annex there . . .

—But adult ed is there, the Great Books program and . . .

—Adult ed, where is it, adult ed, I just saw it . . . he tugged under the web of wrinkles, —here. Home catering and slipcover making, that's it. We can put it all in east seven, east seven, where is it, to implement the, fit a whole washing machine in the space the Great Books take here it is, east seven, we've got the, it looks like we've got the retreads in there now, the . . .

—Retards that's supposed to be, that's the . . .

—Retards, right. A little trouble with your machine printout here Dan. Retards.

—Dan's been having a lot of trouble with his holes, an old story to you and me of course Stye, the minute you hook the corporate process into a computer, testing, evaluating these, look. Set your little retreads up in business over here in north seven and then . . .

—But that's where the equipment's stored, the teaching equipment we bought last year we can't just . . .

—Fine, it can all go right down to the . . .

—Wait though you can't store delicate equipment like that just anywhere, it needs controlled temperature and humidity till we unpack it and use it.

—Utilize it, right, and . . .

—Not quite Dan, open one case of that equipment of yours, unpack one teaching machine you'll have every teacher in the district in here with a sledgehammer, Mister Stye here knows what I'm talking about. Anything to dramatize the issue, that's all your teachers are looking for here Whiteback, something to pounce on.

—As a matter of fact it's already ahm, I thought Dan might be some help to us on this as a matter of fact. She, his wife, your wife that is to say Dan, orientationwise that is, I understand she's ahm motivating factor there activationwise, she's probably talked to you about it.

—To me? About what.

—This strike threat over firing that young Best was his name? With the Mozart . . .

—That's what I'm talking about Whiteback, dramatize the issue. Fire him and you'll have the whole outfield behind you running interference, there's too much milksop management sitting back in the defense zone while the opposition marches up to the basket and drops one in. Let us carry the ball for a change, I know Vern's with me on this one. Put the ball over in their court for a change.

—If he doesn't have tenure he . . .

—Tenure? He doesn't even have a certificate, but the . . .

—A little problem with one of these artistic types Stye, he got up on our open-circuit system here and passed out his foulmouthed opinions on some of our great classic musicians, came in on a Foundation gravy train, Stye knows what I mean.

—He was a composer yes, writes music you might say we ahm, we tried to integrate him into, tie him in that is to say, into a grant request as part of a cultural resource pilot program aimed at deepening the cultural aspects of the arts in ahm, in depth yes . . .

—Composer in residence he called himself.

—Yes well he didn't, he didn't actually live here of course, he's right under here somewhere I just signed it, under the Foundation grant that is, Bast. Here it is, that's his name, Bast. A hundred fifty-two fifteen and he hasn't shown up to collect it, call his house even his mother doesn't know where he is, Dan? This Bast, have you seen him?

—He was, I heard there was a field trip to New York he helped out on yes but my wife . . .

—Horned in on probably, my boy's had trouble with him.

—That field trip, yes, six J. There was something about train tickets, one of the youngsters turned in a lot of train tickets for refund, they're right here somewhere . . .

—Quite the little musician, Stye, trumpet, nothing pansy, said he wouldn't let him play the Call to the Colors. Just let one of your patriotic groups get hold of that, Whiteback.

—Yes they've, one of them's been in touch with Pecci, Assemblyman

Pecci that is to say some Defamation League I think it is, he departed from the curriculum quite severely, some reference to superstitious Italians yes you may know Mister, Assemblyman Pecci, running for Senator Mister Stye?

—He's a good man to know Stye, very close to the community here I expected him this morning in fact Whiteback, clear up a few points on that proposition thirteen he's introducing . . .

—He's busy with the, out activating his SOS campaign, the SOS for Mario campaign that is to . . .

—SOS? Sounds a little negative PRwise, SOS . . .

—Stamp Out Smut.

—Smut, let me tell you what my boy got in the mail Stye, sent away for a ball glove and wait, wait turn that up will you Dan? The sound, turn up the sound.

———of our share in America, it says this is to certify that class six J is the owner of one share of no par common stock of . . .

—Sixth grade Mister Stye, they . . .

—Look. Look what they're holding up, look. A stock certificate, see? Diamond Cable, that's my parent company Stye, youngsters pitched in and bought a share of Diamond Cable as a share in America that's my boy there, the one back there by the flag want to turn that sound down a little Dan? As I was saying, this man Pecci is a good man to know, he's a good friend of this district what part of the district is Mister Stye in, Whiteback?

—Right there on the border with district thirteen, out past the Dunkin Donuts location . . .

—A smart move Stye, really smart. That's where they're talking about locating the new Cultural Center, right out in that area, a new shopping center ready to go up right there where the highways cross nothing there now but a couple of empty old houses and woods, I drove by there this morning, have you seen that new sign Coming Soon, Mister Custard? That highway's next on the list to be widened when they clean up Burgoyne Street here, you can see why it's a natural for a Cultural Center.

—This is Gottlieb's daughter, remind me to call him.

———America. Mongst the giants of money and finance gainst the sky so high, kneels the little church so shy, it whispers I am . . .

—You want to turn that sound down a little Dan? He knows what we're talking about, Whiteback, somebody connected with wait, turn that sound up a little Dan?

———We had a trip which was very interesting for our share of America to a man which mainly collects animals he having killed them his gun is manlicker the noted sports rifle, muzzle velocity two thousand eight hundred feet a second this noted sports rifle can kill up to the elephant, the hearty beast having killed his dogs all animals looking very lifelike which he stuffed having killed them . . .

—Sixth grade Mister Stye, orientationwise . . .

—Yes, well, gets right to the facts and that visual, nothing pansy about that, the, want to turn that sound down just a little now Dan? The ah, as I was saying . . .

——I am the song the Brahmin sings and when he flies man, I am the . . .

—Yes that ahm, visual might be misinterpreted . . .

—As I was saying Stye, this whole Cultural Center project, we're thinking of tying it right in with the school Spring Arts Festival in the spring, expanding it a little with a few remote specials on the itv that will get across the remote capabilities of microwave transmission with a good dependable cable system, get the patriotic theme in there. Whiteback?

—Yes the ahm, this boy who turned in all the train tickets where are they yes, something about a lost child . . .

——the thing of our company share in America is not just to own but to use, that is the thing of a share as investment capital money works for you all the time by other people do the work of the company you are not even there you just own, how you own is that you . . .

—As Whiteback was saying, he's suggested doing a remote special on my shelter, tying it right in with the whole theme, what America's all about, wall thickness, food storage, waste, what we have to protect. I guess you know what I'm talking about in your business, right Stye? That empty chair at the head of the dinner table, protect what you have, am I right? And you can get your cameras right in there now Whiteback, that pile of dirt out in front of it is gone. I don't know where the hell it went but it's gone. Arms cradled, he sank back on the desk's litter, staring at the screen. —This project seems to have sparked real interest in these youngsters, turn that down a little more Dan?

——Our trip our trip was to buy this share of America it is this company that makes things they are baskets. Why nobody buys this baskets is there is this law the law of supply and decline passed by Congress consisting of three branches judicial executory and legislature which . . .

A telephone rang. —What? Whiteback cupped a hand over the mouthpiece. —Ganganelli.

—Who?

—Of Ganganelli, Pecci and Peretti, they're handling the, hello?

——baskets, so instead of you're trying to get everybody to buy them, if you could get it where you don't have to be trying to sell all these baskets in the first place . . .

A telephone rang. Hyde shifted a hampacked web of creases and got hold of it. —Parentucelli . . .

—Tell him, just a minute . . .

—He just wants to know if you want the French doors in the dining room to open out or in.

—Tell him, tell him out. Wait, in.

—Hello? In.

—No wait, tell him . . .

—He says he's got to raise his quote for blacktopping from thirty cents a square foot, he says the Flo-Jan Corp wants twenty cents for every yard of asphalt landed over the town dock with a seven fifty a month minimum, he wants to offer them fifteen with a five hundred minimum.

—Tell him to tell them, wait . . . hello? Parentucelli's on the other phone here, he's offering fifteen cents a yard on the Flo-Jan contract with . . . what?

—They're on the other phone here with, here you talk to them. Loud. Give me your phone there Whiteback, get them together and let them straighten it out.

—Did you tell him out or in?

————little girl who read us the charming poem about Trinity Church kneeling among the world's financial giants, that shy little church of yours could probably buy and sell Wall Street without turning a . . .

—Who the, who's that, that Gibbs? I thought this class was supposed to be Mrs, Mrs . . .

—Joubert, yes, Mrs Joubert . . . Whiteback's hands clasped over the nested telephones ranting at each other in the small under his tented sleeves, —she's taking a few days' sick leave she . . .

—Do you hear what he's saying? Like putting the fox to guard the henhouse, right? Sounds like every crazy radical in town got in on that field trip.

————that shy little church squatting on millions of tax-free dollars' worth of real estate from a land grant made by . . .

—Mister Gibbs usually teaches physics Mister Stye, he's ahm, just filling in here that is to say . . .

—Squatting, what's he want to do, offend the religious sensibilities of every parent in the district? He shifted, waved off by a flurry intent over the telephones nested mouth- to ear-piece in the desk. —A church, squatting . . . ?

————to go piss in her hat, that car she was in pulled out right in front of one of my trucks, she wants to sue me for losing her laugh you can tell her for me I'd rather hear a fat boy fart . . .

Uncoupling the phones, Whiteback raised one to his ear reflecting its vacancy in a rimless gaze. —Hung up, he said finally, restoring it to its cradle as the other continued to rant into his sleeve. —Apparently

Miss Flesch is suing the Catania Paving Company too I, I happened to overhear Mister Parentucelli discussing it with his attorneys here he ahm, seems rather upset . . .

—Why shouldn't he be? Creases intact, the herringbone massed to standing —thinks she can sue the school and anybody else for getting her smile knocked sideways and ruining a promising career in television, she was employed here as a teacher she wasn't hired as an entertainer, the only people who thought she was a star were all your jobless, old, retired, shut-in, welfare, Stye here sees plenty of it in his . . .

—As a matter of fact he, that's why Mister Stye is here yes, the insurance aspect of the ahm, insurance that is to say . . .

—This ah, yes he shouldn't have any trouble smoothing this over, probably sees little lawsuits like this all the time at his level Whiteback, suing the school because she was on school property, is that about it?

—She's ahm, yes suing the school, the Catania Paving Company, the Ford Motor Company, and Skinner. Catania, Parentucelli that is to say, he's suing her, Skinner, and the school, and Skinner is suing . . .

—Who the hell is this Skinner?

—The textbook salesman who was riding her over, he's su . . .

—Yes well I'm sure Mister Stye here is a busy man Whiteback, we've taken up a lot of his time, his company's time that is, he'll ah, as soon as he gets this situation smoothed out we should get together again and kick around this school board idea Mister Stye. It can be a pretty rewarding experience, see it pay off at the community level and the corporate level and these little headaches that come up now and then, helps you get a consensus, see things our way . . .

————like, so that means like if we paid twenty-two dollars and ninety cents for this share of America then we already lost over four dollars so what good is . . .

Billowing to a rise, blue fought blue to free a cuff of the ranting telephone and seek mid-air for a handshake —when you have some more time Mister Stye, we're always on the lookout for ahm, for experienced knowhow in terms of implementing our efforts activitywise down to the bank that is to say, housing, small business applications, potentiating some of our ahm unadvantaged citizens here . . .

—Out this way Mister Stye, I have to stick around a little longer stop off over at the Holy Name of, Holy Name school there see how they're coming setting up their closed-circuit facility, they ought to stop lifting your lessons off the air for free any day now Whiteback, worth stopping in there sometime just to see Sister Agnes cut up a frog . . . His energy pitted against the apparent weight of the door as though for the first time almost flung it off its hinges, —and I mentioned our Assemblyman Pecci to Mister Stye here, a good man for him to know, we ought to get them together as soon as he's straightened this little situation out so nobody's embarrassed. Pecci's a good friend of the district of course, we wouldn't want to see him embarrassed right now, Mister Stye knows what I mean . . .

——by what you call a paper loss, boys and girls. On paper you've lost four dollars, but . . .

—If you can stay with us a minute longer Dan, we just want to discuss, you awake, Dan?

—I don't like it. Hyde massed against the door as though it were being assaulted from the other side. —Notice the way he just sat here and took everything in? And what's this about him running for the school board.

—He ahm, before you came in, he mentioned it before you came in, he ahm, I think he said Vern had sugges . . .

—One thing I don't trust it's a sullen black, not a word out of him just sitting there taking it all in, look at their face and you don't know what's going on inside if he's on the line past Dunkin Donuts there Whiteback I'd just let district thirteen have him, you've already got two other black families pulling into that area. Blockbusting . . .

—Yes well the, in terms of the ongoing situation integrationwise, that is to say, we have some Koreans, a Korean family out by Jack's Discount Appliance . . .

—Your Koreans aren't white blackbite.

—No the, yes, nonwhite you might say the directive is right here somewhere, in terms of structuring our district integrationwise, it refers to nonwhite, integrating them in that is to say, before we start getting busloads shipped from Queens yes which phone is ahm, hello . . . ? No he's here yes but . . .

—That my office?

—No it's for him . . . Whiteback gestured the phone at the face on the screen which continued unperturbed to address a vacant confine near the door. —Hello? Not exactly here that is to say he . . . I'll give him the message, I'll give him the message as soon as he . . . goodbye. Some friend of Mister Gibbs, an accident, put his eye out with a pencil it sounded like.

—Accident? Like that painter of his cutting off his ear, just listen to him . . .

——how your share in America relates to your country's history with a little background on the famous man you met, Governor John Cates, better known as Black Jack Cates back when he helped open the industrial frontiers of . . .

—Do you hear this, Whiteback?

——by his private army in the great Bitterroot strike in Montana where ninety-seven miners were killed . . .

—Do you hear this Whiteback? Is he getting this out of a textbook, this strike talk?

—Yes, this strike talk, threat that is to say, Dan was going to feel his wife's ahm, feel her out on this teacher strike threat activationwise that is to . . .

——to remember his famous line on politics. If they don't own you, they can't trust you . . .

A bell sounded silencing motion where anything moved, hurling motionlessness into activity, books gathered at a sweep, papers to the floor, a glove through the air. —Just a minute, you in the third row there.

—Me Mister Gibbs?

—No you, you read the lines about the song the Brahmin sings?

—And when he flies I am the . . .

—Yes, what was it all about?

—My trip, they said read a report on your trip.

—Were you on this six J field trip?

—The whose?

—What grade are you in? What class are you in?

—Isn't this Communications Skills?

—You'd better go down to see Miss Waddams.

—Your telephone Mister Gibbs.

—Thanks. Get him down to the school nurse, will you? Gibbs . . . for me? Be right there . . .

—Mister Gibbs could you just look at . . .

—Not now I'm sorry, I'm in a hurry . . . he came through the door, down an up stairway two at a time.

—Oh Mister, yes Gibbs, you had a call, an emergency I just wrote it down somewhere, somebody . . .

—Yes Schramm you said, what happened?

—Here somewhere, he . . .

—Put out his eye with a pencil look Gibbs, I want to know where you got your material for this lesson on . . .

—Wait what's, what is all this.

—This lesson of yours on Governor Cates, I want to know . . .

—Yes here it is, Schramm, a Mister Eigen called . . .

—And where you get the material to justify telling these youngsters about a church squatting on . . .

—Just a minute, this is important.

—Well so is this important, Gibbs. I want to know if you're using regular textbooks for your sources of . . .

—Listen this is an emergency I've got to . . .

—And while we're at it I want to know how much truth there is in reports you're starting class without the proscribed openings, the Pledge of Allegiance or the Star Spangle . . .

—Listen I, Whiteback if this idiot will shut his mouth for a minute I, this is an emergency I've got to get to New York . . .

—Yes well of course if you ahm, if you're taking the train that is to say I have some tickets here one of the youngsters turned in yes they're right here somewhere, if you could ahm . . .

—He can really pick them can't he . . . came from the arm of the sofa where Hyde had sunk slowly restraining his chest by folded arms, his collar ridden up hollow behind —his friend here with the pencil . . .

—Here they are yes if you could turn them in for us Mister Gibbs, on your way to the . . .

—Sounds like that painter that cut off his ear, what did he do Gibbs? sent it to somebody in a . . .

—Wait wait . . . !

—Mister Gibbs! here, now . . .

—Don't try that again Gibbs.

—No come with me Major come see him! Schramm come see him you'd be a real tonic Major you know why, Major? Because he feeds on outrage that's what keeps Schramm alive, just his rage over the mean insensitive stupid you, you'd be the biggest God damned inspiration I could bring him with your proscribed op . . .

—Just, just stay away from me after this Gibbs just, just keep away . . .

—Yes well let's ahm ahm let's all ahm, these tickets yes here Mister Gibbs if you'd turn them in on your way to the train yes ten forty, not the train no the ten forty that is to say you've missed that of course yes the ten dollars and forty cents we reimbursed the boy who turned them in from a field trip of Mrs ahm ahm, Bast yes I was told Mister Bast helped out but no one's been able to ahm, seen hide nor ahm . . .

—Can't waste any more company time like this Whiteback, I'm due over at . . .

—Of course yes after you Major ahm, hair that is to say hair nor hide you were going to see Sister Agnes cut up a frog I think you said we all have somewhere to go, Dan? Let's ahm, have somewhere to go I think Coach wanted to discuss your wife's ahm of course he can't discuss anything like that now he has a gym period yes I have to get to the nurse's office, the fourth graders there they seem to be conducting a sitdown or ahm, in is it . . .

—Mister Gibbs you, are you all right?

—What? oh Dan, fine yes I . . .

—You look white your, here . . .

—Fine I said! I just, just mad as hell at myself losing my temper at that God damned . . .

—Yes well you shouldn't have tried to pull his . . .

—First God damned rule never hit somebody you don't like, you coming out?

—Yes, yes I . . . he stood there tugging at the glass door that never yet had opened in, and then stepped through the one held wide beside it —I could ride you to the station . . .

—Thanks no I'll walk, I have to stop at the Post Office . . .

—That's yes that's where I'm going I'm expecting something from an executive placement ah, place I hoped I could talk to you about this sometime, I thought I saw you in the station in New York I thought I could ride out with you but you were meeting a, a young lady I guess you were going to ride her someplace so I didn't want to wait where's my car . . . he sought down the row of stares leveled in chromed grimaces for the familiar ptosis left from a jump up a curb into a fire hydrant, —down there yes where those boys, where are they going . . .

—Choir practice, that's Hyde's share in America the urchin with the head like a toothbrush, nothing pansy about him is there looks like something from a God damned German vintage orphanage . . .

—But they shouldn't be going off the, boys . . . ! Oh but wait aren't you . . .

—Thanks no I'm in a hurry Dan, I'll walk . . .

—Yes but, but, well, boys . . . ! Where are you going . . . !

—Come on don't stop hey, this way . . . they made for the reek of asphalt clouding Burgoyne Street, —so then what happened . . .

—Nothing he just said if they catch me in there again using the telephone they'll have to resort to these here disciplinary measures, I mean what am I sup . . .

—Okay but if you do what you said boy are you going to get in trouble, I mean that's forgery boy.

—What do you mean forgery I just scribbled this here name which it's nobody's down at the bottom where it says arthurized by, I mean you think the telephone company goes around asking everybody is this here your signature? All they care it says requisition order right across the top so they come stick in this here telephone booth.

—You'll find out boy you think Whiteback won't be pissed off when the school gets this bill for . . .

—That's how much you know they don't pay them they pay the school, the telephone company pays the school like this here commission to have this phone booth in there so I'm like helping the school out, I mean like the more calls . . .

—How do you know, I mean boy what a bunch of . . .

—I called them up what do you think, I mean what am I suppose to do run over to the candy store all the time? Or like home I mean suppose I get some deal going where they call me up so they get some lady that says yes this is J R's mother could I help you? I mean what kind of . . .

—Look out you want to break the door? That's U S government property boy . . .

—So what they got plenty of money.

—You'll find out boy look, didn't you ever see this little sign? Penalty for theft is five hundred dollars fine or one year in prison that's for stealing this shitty little ballpoint pen boy you bust a door and they'll . . .

—That's a bunch of crap they're like nineteen cents, I mean who wants to steal it anyway move your elbow, I just want to use it . . . he bent to the minuscule effort of lettering Investors Fullfilment Corp on a money order blank.

—You'll find out boy, what did you get let's see hey, I mean where's this big check you been yelling about.

—That's my business, come on you're dropping all the . . .

—Inventors Information Kit boy what a, record of invention look. Be it known that I residing at state of have invented certain new and useful I mean you couldn't invent shit, you want to trade it hey?

—For what, move will you? I'm trying to . . .

—I mean what a bunch of, look. To the individual inventor the world is his oyster, what good is that I mean somebody already invented one. You want to trade it?

—Okay for what! The silent defender, made of lightweight aluminum look hey your crap's even getting mixed up in the stuff in my portforlio here, coitus splint made of finest spring steel will you . . .

—Give it here then I mean go ahead invent an oyster if you think you're so, wait hey look you got a package, if it's this clock I get it this time okay? I mean if it says class six J and all why shouldn't . . .

—Okay! How do I know what it is look I'm trying to do something!

—Go ahead and do it, you want me to get the pack . . .

—Go ahead . . . ! he dug among paper scraps and envelopes for a letter four lines long of skips and smudged erasures, licked the ballpoint to grind in initials, pounded a stamp on US SAVings and loan Ass R eno Nev and came in a turn for the Money Order window digging for the wad of bills with a sudden stoop after a penny rolling toward Parcel Post.

—Look out!

—Holy . . .

—It's not my fault look, the box was already bust . . .

—Okay! just help pick them up . . .

—Look the whole end's busted, what's, what are they sup . . .

—Nothing! just these here little cards will you help pick them up before somebody . . .

—No but what do they, wait a second is . . .

—Look you don't need to read them! just, just pick them up!

—No but, him . . . ?

—What's so funny!

—He's your business representative, Edwerd Bast?

—What's so funny about that!

—I mean he doesn't know shit look he can't even spell his own name Edwerd look, e d . . .

—I said quit laughing! How do you know so much anyway and I mean he didn't even spell it, he . . .

—Because I got this here Uncle Edward that's why, it's w a what do you mean he didn't spell it, I bet he doesn't even know it . . .

—So what! boy if you don't quit laugh . . .

—Then how do you know he'll even do it, he doesn't know : . .

—Because he will that's why!

—He doesn't know shit about business how can . . .

—So what! I'll give him these here same little books to read up come on just pick them up . . .

—Then how come you even put this little telephone number he's not even around anyplace, he . . .

—That's my business look shut up will you, Mister Gibbs just came in you think I want to broadcast the whole . . .

—Okay but he's not even around anyplace, my father said . . .

—That's how much you know boy he has to come by the school to pick up this here check they owe him doesn't he?

—Yeah well my father said he said s, h, i t on the tv he better not show his face . . .

—Yeah well your father he's full of . . .

—Yeah well you better watch out boy, if he ever finds who got that whole mountain of dirt out front of our house hauled away you're going to be in . . .

—So what you said he's always yelling he wants to get rid of it practically since you're born didn't you? I mean it already had these little trees growing in it look be careful how you're picking them up will you? I mean you can't give somebody this dirty business card when you go in some office and . . .

—So throw away the dirty ones who needs all these, I mean it looks like there's a thousand . . .

—So what you had to order a thousand if you want this here free wallet gift so . . .

—Look there's a couple over there hey, he's stepping on . . .

—Holy . . . he came on at knee level, —excuse me could you move your foot Mis, oh hi Mister Gibbs . . .

—What?

—Hi . . . came from down there, —I just wanted to ask you . . .

—Wait a minute, what . . . ? he ground a foot turning back to the window, —probation, it's made out to the Department of Probation p, r, o . . . well God damn it I didn't name it, here. Twenty, forty, ninety, one ten, one sixty, one eighty yes I do use an old-fashioned fountain pen is there a regulation against that too? Two thirty, two forty, five, seven, eight wait I've still got some change nine, nine fifty, seventy-five, eighty-five Christ wait, ninety-five, six, there . . .

—Hey Mister Gibbs?

—What is it!

—No I just wondered, did you see Mister Bast around anyplace?

—Bast? he licked the envelope in a turn for the Out of Town slot, —you had him last . . .

—I, what?

—Thought your gang took him to the money museum, he said in a turn for the door —most popular man in town . . . and it banged closed behind him where smoke and flame escaping the black spread up Burgoyne Street found purchase on a descending bloat of Chloe as he dodged the car mounting the curb in arrival, digging in pockets at a half trot through the reek of asphalt to come up with a crushed cigarette package, matches with a half fare ticket stuck in the cleft, still digging as the door banged behind him and he reached the grilled window emptying a pocket —just turning in some tickets . . .

—Wrong window, buddy.

—What do you mean, it's the only window here.

—Maybe you got the wrong track then . . . the heap was pushed back under the grill. —Next?

—No wait, sorry . . . he recovered a torn half of Jack's Little Green Card, squares bearing Place ten number three sixth race, Win —sorry there, I think I get ten dollars and forty cents back.

—For what.

—The refund for these tickets.

—Fill out this and send them to this address.

—What for, can't you . . .

—Look buddy I had enough of you the other time, start getting wise again and . . .

—What other time what are you talking about? I simply want to turn in these tickets . . .

—For the refund you want, right? So you fill out this and mail them where it says.

—But I need the money now, I'm . . .

—You want to take them in yourself, go ahead.

—In where.

—In Brooklyn where it says. Next?

—Brooklyn?

—One way?

—Wait a minute . . .

—That's one seventy-eight.

—But I didn't say I was going to Brooklyn, I'm . . .

—You buying a ticket or not. Next?

—Wait. Look. There isn't any next. There's nobody behind me, he said loudly over the sound shaking the station from above. —Is that the train?

—What else would it be, wise guy?

—I mean the train to New York, when's the next train to New York.

—Make up your mind, here . . .

—But, no but this timetable's, these are trains for the whole East Coast, can't you just tell me if that's the next train to New York? I have to get to New York . . .

—New York?

—Yes, I . . .

—That's one eighty-four.

—But that's the point I don't have one eighty-four, I . . .

—You buying a ticket or just trying to make more trouble?

—More? All I want is, all I have is thirty-one cents Mister, Mister Teets I can't give you one eighty-four that's why I need the refund, don't you . . .

—Fill this out and mail it in. Next?

—Teets look behind me! There's nobody there Teets! Nobody next! Nobody! He clung to the bars a moment longer and then grabbed up the tickets and ran toward the stairs and up them two, three at a time, out to the platform and the train to slump in the first seat he found with a newspaper jammed in the hinge which proved, when unfurled, to be the Staats Zeitung und Herold.

A conductor with a wisp mustache stood tapping his punch. —Ticket?

—Ja? He looked up from the paper with a great smile.

—Your ticket?

—Ahh, Sie wollen meine, meine . . . He rummaged in pockets, to come up with a cardboard square and offer it with a beaming smile.

—This is a half fare ticket, Mister.

—Bitte?

—I said this ticket, this is half fare ticket.

—Ja ja . . . he beamed, nodding, his eyes beginning to cross.

—Half fare, half. Kiddie. Child.

—Ja, wissen Sie . . .

—Look. You, man. Ticket, child ticket. Get it?

—In dem Bahnhof, ja, he commenced still beaming, eyes now firmly crossed, —in dem Bahnhof habe ich die . . .

—For Christ sake look. Where you buy ticket?

—Herr Teets, verstehen Sie? In dem Bahnhof, Herr Bahnhofmeister Teets, Gott-trunkener Mensch, verstehen Sie? Mit der Dummheit kämpfen Götter selbst vergebens, he beamed, eyes abruptly straightened, —nicht?

—Oh for Christ sake.

—Bitte? The smile gone, his mouth hung open.

—Forget it. The conductor punched the ticket emphatically and turned up the aisle, abruptly snagged by a hand on his arm.

—Ja danke, danke schön, he beamed shaking the conductor's hand up and down, raising his great smile from the Staats Zeitung each time the conductor passed the entire trip in and trapping him with a final vigorous handshake upon arrival, where he sought a telephone and sat in the booth wiping his face before he dug out his coins and dialed. —Hello? Mister Eigen please . . . Hello? Mister . . . oh, would you ask him to call me right back? It's an emergency. My name is, God damn it

. . . No, somebody's scraped the number off this phone, I'll have to call back. He banged it down and ducked out, into the next booth studying the three coins in his hand before he raised one and dialed again. —Hello? Ben? No I'll hold on . . .

Syllables resonant and unrelated fused arrivals and departures on the loudspeaker as he sat with the door pushed open, staring out, —Ben? Yes, hello, listen. Has her lawyer come up with any final offer? I can't keep living by my wits this way much longer I'm . . . No I just mailed a God damned payment, if they come up with some kind of a final . . . I don't know! I know it yes, I don't . . . What property and securities Christ I don't even, I had five percent of some brokendown family held company I used to work for probably still got it someplace but that's the . . . they said what . . . ? No now listen God damn it I'm not trying to get out of support for the girl Ben you know that God damned well it's this other, this God damned alimony part that's . . . I know it I know you set it up that way but listen what God damned good is a tax position if I can't even . . . when, now? I can't take a cab over no I can't even take a bus over, I've got exactly eleven . . . all right yes all right, late in the week . . .

He pulled the door open studying the two coins in his hand before he raised one to the phone and dialed again. —Mister Eigen please . . . Hello? I just called . . . Eigen? I just got into town. Where's Schramm . . . he wedged the phone against a shoulder digging in a pocket to come up with the cigarette pack, hesitate over the last one there and take it. —Christ how, who got him into Bellevue? What? All right, I agree, but Christ it couldn't have happened to anybody else, it was an accident that could only have happened to Schramm . . . Who? If they want to keep him there overnight for observation let them . . . Well he could too you know God damned well he could, especially after this, the last time I talked him out of it he . . . I know it . . . Right now I'll walk down there right now, it should take me about . . . Because I have exactly one cent, that's why! What . . . ? Nothing. Fine, great, sitting in the railroad station with a God damned penny in my pocket looking for a familiar face been like this since I was seven, come down from school for the weekend or being put on the Sunday night train it never leaves, Schramm's right you can't just kill part of it you, wait, wait I see somebody I, I know, wait hold on . . .

He came out of the booth pulling his tie closed at the throat, his voice constricted in the call —Amy . . . ? as though that had constricted it, knotted his voice and his face in consternation as hers filled with her smile, her arms extended open passing him where he sank back against the booth and then into it watching her come half to her knees to embrace the boy who stood away quickly in embarrassment to pick up a suitcase, straighten the school blazer, as he caught the dangling phone —like, like one of those old Shirley Temple movies, Jack Haley goes in one side of the revolving door and she comes out the other but Christ, Tom? Imagine having her, having anybody that glad to see you? Eigen? hello . . . ?

And the glass of the shuddering door caught her eyes and her profile framing the boy's stooping close as they passed with her arm to his shoulders to catch —I can recite The Charge of the Light Brigade.

—Let's hurry, Francis.

—Half a league, half a league, half a league onward why are we hurrying?

—Let's just hurry.

—Into the valley of death rode the . . .

—Did you eat something on the train, Francis?

—A cheese sandwich, it was a whole dollar just cheese and bread. Cannon to the right of them, cannon to the left of them, cannon in front of them volleyed . . .

—Let's go this way for a cab.

—Volleyed and thundered. Where are we going, home first?

—Yes.

—Is Papa there?

—He'll be home late tonight. He's been away.

—At Geneva?

—Why Geneva?

—He asked me if I'd like to live at Geneva. Into the jaws of death, into the mouth of hell . . .

—Here's a cab.

—Can he take me to the hockey game tomorrow?

—I thought we might go to the Cloisters.

—What's that.

—A sort of museum, she said, and got his bag in pausing, before she followed, for a look back.

—Mister Merton hates me Mama.

—Who's Mister Merton?

—My math teacher, he hates me.

—I'm sure he doesn't hate you Francis.

—He does too. Look at that movie, can we go to that?

—We'll see.

—Would you want to live at Geneva Mama?

—I don't know, Francis.

—If you could live anywhere you wanted in the whole world where would you live?

—I don't know, she said, staring at his back, at the back of his head where he sat at the edge of the seat looking out the window, until they stopped and doormen of different sizes in interchangeable livery opened doors.

—Where am I going to sleep? he dropped his bag in the foyer.

—In your cubby I suppose, where you always do.

—Everything here's always so neat and shiny it never looks like anybody lives here.

She'd put her bag down on the sofa and there, from half under one of its white leather cushions, picked up a black lace brassiere, and her bag again. —I'm just going to put on some lipstick, then we can go out . . . In the bedroom she pulled open the first drawer she came to, one filled with shirts evenly stacked, and laying some of them back to stuff the brassiere away from sight stared at a studio portrait theatrically highlighted and shadowed and, as she pulled it forth, lavishly inscribed.

—Mama . . . ?

—Just a moment Francis. She opened her lipstick.

—Half a league, half a league, half a league onward . . .

When he came in she was finishing her eyes. —Don't you want to wash before we go out Francis?

—I did once already. Can we go to that movie?

—We'll see.

At the first museum he said —Is that really worth a million dollars? At the next, —I guess he didn't have time to finish it . . . and at dinner —can I have steak? Later, —You know what I used to think Mama? if I didn't talk now, if I kind of saved it up and didn't talk, that then I'd be able to talk after I'm dead.

She leaned toward him abruptly in the dark cab. —Francis? You don't want to live in Geneva do you?

—Would you be there?

—I, I should think you'd want to stay where you are, in school where, where your friends are . . .

—I haven't got any friends, he said without turning from the window, sitting that way at the edge of the seat looking out until they stopped, and a doorman opened the door. —Is Papa home yet?

—We'll see.

He pushed the door in as soon as she'd turned the key, ran into the dark foyer and stopped. —When will he be here?

—Probably not till after you're asleep. You'll see him in the morning.

—Can I watch television till he comes?

—It's late, you'd better get to bed. You'll see him in the morning.

—Can I read before I turn the light off?

—For a few minutes . . . she came down for his quick embrace, standing, watching him go, till a bathroom door closed and she turned for the bedroom to undress in the dark, and lie awake, half awake in the dark, and then awake at the sound of the bedroom door, opening in the dark.

—Francis?

—Amie?

—Lucien?

193

—He is here? Francis?

—In the cubby, he's asleep. Don't wake him now.

—I? I don't wake him.

—I told him he'd see you in the morning. I hope you can do something with him, take him somewhere tomorrow. There's a hockey game he wants you to take him to.

—Hockey game . . . a shoe dropped to the floor, then coins spilling, rolling off the carpet. —Hockey game, eh?

—He says he hasn't any friends.

—He has what?

—No friends, at school. He says he has no friends . . . bedsprings strained in the dark, and were still. —Lucien?

—Eh?

—He said you talked to him about moving to Geneva, living in Geneva . . . Lucien?

—Eh?

—Well what have you told him, what are you . . .

—Perhaps he goes there to school some day, in Geneva.

—Yes but you can't, someday maybe but you can't simply take him . . .

—Look Amie . . . Bedsprings strained abruptly under weight coming up in the dark, —you are always afraid. So he went to Genève with no friend? He must not also be always afraid Amie, until something is settled . . .

—Well why won't you then! Why won't you settle things?

—I? Yes, I wait for the lawyer, this one of your father, tell him. The Nobili settlement? I still wait, tell him.

—I've never heard of it it doesn't . . .

—Yes, I still wait, tell him.

—I don't know what you're talking about Lucien.

—The boy, yes?

She lay awake, half awake in the dark, then awake at the sound of the bedroom door opening, the rustle across the carpet, the faint figure paused between the beds and then, as she started to one elbow and caught her breath, and sank back, the strain of the springs across the gap, and the toss of covers on the bed there.

When she waked it was empty. She'd sat up and looked over in the cut of sunlight, and said —Francis? But it was only a swirl of blankets, and she got up slowly and went into the bathroom to dress. A man's shirt hung from the shower rod, a boy's lay crumpled on the floor and she reached to hang them on the hook on the bathroom door where, when she swung it closed, a douche dangled. She washed quickly and dressed, threw the shirts on a bed, and leaned across the high chest of drawers to follow the line of her lips in the mirror with a barely discernible lipstick, of her lids with black eyeliner, looked at herself for a moment and abruptly pulled open the shirt drawer and took out the portrait, paused the eyeliner over the opulent décolletage, and then drew a huge mustache over the pouting lips and thrust it back under the shirts. There was a note on the table in the foyer. It was signed love, F. and she read it three times in the cab downtown. The doors opened silently. She pushed 15 and ascended alone to The Light Cavalry Overture as far as 3, where the doors opened silently on youth unbuttoned to the waist shifting packages to enter and press 5 and stare into the top of her dress until they opened silently and he ran a hand up 6 7 8 9 10 11 12 14 before they closed behind him, to open silently on her alone at 6, and close, and open silently at 7, and close, and then at 8, at 9, at 10 she suddenly got out, pressed the up button and stood there waiting till, behind her now, doors opened on him waiting, and closed as she recovered her quick step forward to turn and press the up button again, and then again behind her doors opened silently on youth here white buttoned to the throat and black above it wheeling a cart of interoffice mail back for her entrance, staring at black backs of hands the bar or two mounting a Spanish rhythm for his exit at 11, the door closing silently behind him suddenly seized and held and now, as it closed, she caught her breath and her eyes away from the glistening chest and buttons flung loosely undone down it for those on the wall panel orderly numbered but for one reading simply, Doors, another Alarm, The Peanut Vendor seething through the palm sized screen above, an idly scratching hand thrust down the front of denims burnished where it moved hidden as the other, empty, rose behind her gasped against the waist high rail there for —You like to give head? posed in a tone as vacant as the face she fled for the lobby length explosion of blacks streaked with mad reserve on white doors opening silently on a coatless figure askew there as though he'd just burst free from the painting's restless labyrinth like a demented Virgil for the amorphous Dante surfacing behind him, dropping a briefcase of Gladstone bag design square before her in collision to stare, with apologetic fixity blurred by rimless lenses, into the top of her dress.

—Ma-dame . . .

—Oh, Mister Davidoff . . .

—Mister Skinner, you've just met Mrs Joubert . . .

—Gosh.

—No damage done? Recovering full stature from his version of a bow, Davidoff came up closing his tie full throttle at the throat with a punch for the down button and —get us some figures, just get us some figures on it. Mrs Joubert ought to be interested in this little project too, she . . . he turned to see her already out of reach. —Oh Mrs Joubert? Oh and Skinner . . . The doors had opened silently on youth lounging unbuttoned, empty handed along the waist high rail at the back of the car, motionless for the amorphous entrance pursued through the closing doors by —that writer you're digging up for us Skinner, a name, we want a name. Mrs Joubert . . . ? he came cornering like a vehicle to get past her for the doorknob. —Glad you could get in today . . . he held the door just far enough opened to obstruct her passage, —I'm up to my ears since your dad left but you'll . . .

—I don't need to bother you at all Mister Davidoff, I just . . .

—Don't worry about it, no bother at all . . . he'd got the door opened far enough now to bar her way with a look at his wristwatch. —Pretty tough sticking to a schedule, it just took me an hour to teach that fellow Skinner the facts of life, he's just . . .

—But please don't let me keep you.

—Don't worry about it that's what I'm here for, he's just joined Duncan and Co in their top sales slot doesn't even know the difference between perfect binding and Carol? Oh Carol, Mrs Joubert wants a look at those picture proofs for the Annual Report, oh and Carol? Get the ones in Mister Eigen's office too they're in there for captioning, I want to get a set of these right off to your dad, he came on a half step ahead.

—I'm sorry I'm in rather a hurry Mister Davidoff, I have to see Mister Beaton and . . .

—Beaton? Beaton can wait, he's used to it. Now I see this whole thing as, sorry . . . he'd stopped abruptly to frame nothing in a square of fingers up before her, —whole feature on your youngsters buying their share in America built around the concept of corporate responsibility present and future tense, and . . . he recovered his half step ahead to emphasize —and giving the stockholders and the security analyst boys a sneak preview imagewise of our entry into the fastest growing market in the economy, once this new corporate restructuring is nailed down I guess you saw the site of the new parent world headquarters building up the street, you saw the sign? Nothing but a big hole there now but the next time you talk to your dad, I think I've got him pretty steamed up about getting a foot in the door with this Romance of Cobalt we're sponsoring, it's what I had this Skinner in here for just now, good solid background in the textbook field and of course you know Duncan and Company, really solid old line prestige publishers this Skinner's digging up a top-flight name writer for the project right up in the class of this name painter with the lobby mural out here. I even had to fight getting hold of that for us till even the Beatons around here got the picture we could subsidize name art and get a tax break at the same here, this way, I'm down this way . . .

—But Mister Beaton is . . .

—Probably something I can help you clear up in half the time Beaton would . . .

—No it's a, something legal.

—Meant to tell you yes, we've got this minority suit all squared away, it came across my desk last week and . . .

—This what?

—I put an authorization right into the works don't worry about it, corporate democracy in action and all the rest of it, I saw what you're getting across to your youngsters right off the bat you get Beaton in on something like that he . . .

—I don't think I quite . . .

—Don't worry about it. Bring Beaton in on something he'll pick it to pieces till you don't recognize it, just hasn't got what it takes to make an on the spot decision I've heard the Governor himself tell him, trouble with you lawyers, all you do is tell me why I can't do something instead of how I can and Beaton . . .

—Oh how is he? She'd paused where the carpeting started.

—Beaton? He's . . .

—Uncle John, I meant to . . .

—Oh the Governor, don't worry about him they don't make them like him anymore, they won't match those steel gray eyes of his with all the corneal transplants in the world right now all he's burned up about are those bridge games he's missing on the train down this way, I'm down this way . . .

—I, thank you Mister Davidoff, I do think Mister Beaton has some papers for me to sign, it's just a family matter . . .

He caught his balance and plunged into the stream of carpet beside her, regaining that half step ahead as though to avoid a confrontation of heights as his, no longer buoyed by the sharp punctuation of his heels, seemed to drop in consonance with the confidential lowering of his tone. —Of course you won't have to get into these other details with Beaton, means well but he hasn't got what it takes for an on the spot decision like your dad or the Governor glad I was on deck when you came in, of course I know your dad could use me in that Washington spot but he probably needs me here to keep an eye on the store while this corporate reorganization goes through things coasting along without the top man for these on the spot decisions . . . He rounded the corner in a side step, —next time you talk to your dad you might want to suggest . . .

—I'll tell him you've been awfully helpful Mister Davidoff, and now . . .

—Yes you might want to put in a word . . . he got in ahead of her with an arm out for the phone. —Better grab Crawley while I have a minute, straighten him out on this oh Miss Bulcke, straighten him out on this brush fire in Gandia tell Beaton Mrs Joubert is here . . . he dialed, —tell him she's in a hurry.

—Yes he's expecting you Mrs Joubert. How nice to see you.

—Hello Shirl? Hold on. I'll be rounding up these proofs while you kill some time with Beaton. Shirl? Put Crawley on, I . . .

—Mister Beaton was in Mister Cutler's office, Mrs Joubert. I think he expects . . .

—Shirl just tell him I've got Mrs Joubert here on the, Shirl? Hold on. Cutler's back?

—He'll be with you in just a moment Mrs Joubert.

—What's Cutler doing back.

—Mister Cutler is still away, Mister Davidoff.

—Well what's Beaton doing in Shirl? Hello? Crawley?

Buttons blossomed with light at the telephone's base and Miss Bulcke pushed one. —Oh I meant to press hold . . .

—Hello?

—Hello . . .?

—Hello? Hello? Shirley what the hell is going on here.

—I think it's Mister Davidoff calling you Mister Crawley, he . . .

—Well I can't waste the, just tell him I've got someone with me . . . and the phone disappeared under a massive hunch of tweed. —Now sir. This is your aunts' telephone stock is it? twenty, thirty, joint tenants all the way are they? fifty . . .

, —My aunts? yes well they, no they live together yes but they've owned the house for a long time in fact it's been in the fam . . .

—No no in this stock ownership I mean seventy, eighty joint tenants with rights of survival just means if one of them should ninety, expire, five . . .

—Well, well yes I mean Aunt Julia had some trouble with her colon once but . . .

—I see yes, yes we don't need to turn this into a medical discussion Mister, Mister . . . a slip of paper came crushed from his hand —Bast yes, Mister Bast, rather elderly ladies I take it?

—Oh yes yes they're both quite, but does that make a diff . . .

—No difference at all no just occurred to me, don't see these very often any more you know picture of the globe here with wires running round it ten, twenty . . .

—But they're not, there's nothing wrong with them is there? I mean I think it's about all my aunts have for . . .

—Nothing wrong with them at all no forty, fifty just a good many years since they issued certificates in these separate denominations isn't it sixty, seventy like currency yes five, six, didn't sign them though did they, eight . . .

—Sign them?

—Wise enough precaution yes considering the ah . . . he paused to raise his sight across the blotter's green as he might have over some desolate savanna, —the circumstances yes just pick up a handful of stock powers from Shirley out there as you leave let them sign those and mail them in no problem at all now, do we have an asking price?

—Well, well no I guess whatever you . . .

—Just want to sell them at the market then, do they?

—The, yes the Stock Market yes if somebody . . .

—The market price Mister Bast . . . his hand stalked the black box beyond the confines of the green, —when we say at the market we mean at the market price . . . his hand leaped, —going at forty-four and an eighth yes I'll try to get you a quarter . . .

—A quarter? but . . .

—Want to sit still and wait for a half you can try it but I look for it to close off two or three points, already a little overbought at forty-four . . .

—Oh well forty-four yes forty-four dollars that's fine yes they'll be very pleased, I think they said once it cost about twenty-three . . .

—Had a couple of splits in there too haven't they, come off quite nicely yes . . .

—Splits? but . . .

—Three for one when was it, 'fifty-nine? Selling around seventy when it split two for one in 'sixty-four yes come off quite nicely, now what's this.

—What? Oh that yes that's some other stock another aunt of mine got a long time ago, it says nineteen eleven down in the corner there it was just in the drawer with this telephone stock and they thought I might as well . . .

—Norma Mining Company? Pretty thing isn't it.

—Yes right there under the eagle it says par value ten cents per share so a thousand shares would be worth a hun . . .

—Pretty thing yes, take my advice Mister Bast. Frame it.

—Frame it?

—Or just use it to, don't mean to be indelicate just use it for toilet paper.

—The, but it says right there . . .

—Nothing better to do write to the Attorney General in Montana, probably tell you this Norma Mining Company defaulted on its taxes the year this was issued never even lived to see nineteen twelve. Mining schemes Mister Bast, mining schemes, that all of it then? Good of you to drop by Mister Bast, like to chat with you but I'm a busy man can't be too, wait now wait what's all this . . .

—No well you see this is just the portfolio of a, of an associate of mine who . . .

—A what . . . ? the end of the battered thing came off with a tug at the zipper, —portfolio?

—Yes well you see he understood that brokers offer to review the contents of a, of one's portfolio and when I mentioned I was coming in to sell this telephone stock he . . .

—But the, what in the hell is all this?

—Yes well it's the ah, I hadn't really looked in it myself it's the contents of his portfolio you see he's not very . . .

—But it's, my God Mister Bast nothing here but a lot of trash . . . his hand pawed ribbons of newspaper and smeared envelopes, prospectuses, the Dines Letter, Moody's Midyear, Value Line Survey —having a little joke, are you?

—Oh no no he's very serious he, you see I just offered to help him

I'd stopped to pick up a check he was going to cash for me but the computer had made a mistake on it and since he was, since I was a little short of cash I . . .

—Mister Bast I am a busy man, I think . . .

—No no wait just that, what's that . . .

—This?

—Yes it's a thousand shares of a . . .

—Fine, yes, serve the same purpose as your Norma Mining there.

—No but you see here's their little booklet that . . .

—Look here Mister Bast, a mining company incorporated under the rules of Delaware, capitalization limited to three hundred thousand a year you don't know what that means?

—Well I suppose it just , . . .

—Means their disclosure papers don't have to be audited by the SEC. I don't deal in penny stock Mister Bast.

—But you see their little booklet here shows . . .

—Trees! nothing but trees! Doesn't even say they own it, probably just filed an exploration claim and . . .

—But these pictures of all their equipment are . . .

—Who says it's their equipment! Anything here say this equipment belongs to this what is it? Ace Development Company? Pretty pictures Mister Bast, pretty pictures. Anybody can print pretty pictures.

—But isn't the . . .

—W Decker, Underwriter, who in the hell is W Decker? Know him? No, nobody does. Probably put out a million of these shares and has another million tucked away just in case a virgin mineral should turn up, posing as the underwriter here to disguise his ownership. Childish nonsense Mister Bast, your associate must be . . .

—No but, just one more moment, there's something else, right under there . . .

—This? Hi Tiger. That's me in the photo hon, I put it on my letter as a sorta sample of a set I posed for with each and every one of you guys in mind, posed the way you like to see a, what in the, just what is this sir!

—But it, I don't know I, I meant that red thing there that, that red . . .

—This? Here comes another first in the marital relations field, my, my God sir! Perfectly barbaric! He tipped back and the mass of the chair tipped with him, cornering with a dulled blucher a delicately striped and more delicately shaded hindquarter remnant of one of the lives lost to the walls beyond now covering the wastebasket where he dropped these solicitations coming forward with a reach that commanded the entire expanse of teak and blotter stretched before him to seize a small bottle beside an opened book there and get its cap off. —Get out very much do you, Mister Bast?

—Out, where . . .

—Outdoors sir! Out of doors! Just what is it you do Mister Bast? Outside of being a ah, business representative as your card here has it.

—I'm a composer I, I compose . . .

—Music?

—Yes, you see I . . .

—Ought to get some outdoor interests Mister Bast, these ah, these indoor pastimes breed a sort of a, not the healthiest state of mind . . . he popped a small pill into his mouth and snapped the cap back on the bottle. —Best medicine there is.

—Oh, what, what is it . . .

—No no, not this, this is just nitroglycerine . . . He pushed the bottle to a distant teak expanse, —the outdoors sir, the outdoors. Now if we've cleared up our business . . .

—Yes well there was just one more thing there if you could, it's a bond, that red thing, I think it's a bond . . .

—You understand I'm a very busy man Mister Bast, if you hadn't come so highly recommended I don't know what I'd . . .

—Yes well I, I did appreciate her writing that note to you for me, she . . .

—Says anything I can do for you will be a kindness to her, yes. Just how do you come to know Amy Joubert, Mister Bast?

—Well you see we both . . .

—Always had a kind of weakness for the arts though didn't she, probably why she refers to you here as such a dear person. Charming girl yes, lovely girl, almost say generous to a fault.

—Did she . . . did she, really say that?

—Say what.

—That, that dear person, that I was such a . . .

—Don't sound like my words do they, Mister Bast? Now, you want to clear up this . . .

—Yes well you see I've been carrying her note around for quite a while and then yesterday when I went out to pick up this check I . . .

—No no no this, this red thing as you call it. What do you want to know.

—Well I just wanted, I mean I think my associate wants . . .

—Looks perfectly clear to me, bond issue that defaulted ten, let's see there, thirteen years ago, company still losing money faster than they can write the figures. Wallpaper Mister Bast, wallpaper. Know what wallpaper is?

—Well I thought I . . .

—Good goat country, happened to know a little about this Eagle Mills myself, used to go up there for goat. Nobody else ever heard of them, they went to sleep up there before you were born and nobody woke them up. Did they get out of woollens and into synthetics after the war, no. Did they move south to a cheap labor pool where some red union wouldn't run them down? No, they sat up at Union Falls and put out a million dollar bond issue.

—But if they haven't got any money how do they . . .

—Didn't say they didn't have any money did I? Net worth's probably around a million, most of it probably in their net property account, may even be sitting on a fat pension fund they've forgotten exists . . . he came forward again to paw at the heap. —Pick these up a few cents on the dollar, this the only one you, your associate has, is it?

—Well no, no he said he's getting a whole bunch, he . . .

—A what?

—A lot. He says he . . .

—One lot? Nothing to cry about, client of mine got stuck with twenty lots of Boston and Maine interest been due on it for ten or fifteen years, pick one up for you for ten any time you like.

—Dollars?

—When we say ten we mean hundred, Mister Bast . . . and he sank back from the heap before him, eyes taking on the glassine vacancy of the rest of the audience.

—Yes well there was just one more thing here I, that I think you might . . .

—That? My God, haven't seen one in years.

—No this isn't what I . . . what is it.

—Russian Imperial Bond.

—You mean it isn't worth any, worth very . . .

—Mister Bast, anything is worth whatever some damn fool will pay for it, only reason somebody can make a market in Russian Imperials is because some damn, somebody like your associate will buy them. Happen to know how he, how this associate of yours got into all this?

—By, well buying and selling at first I think and then he had some stock in a company and was going to bring some kind of legal suit for, for his class, I mean he . . .

—A class action? What was the company, another Ace Development outfit?

—No it was a, Diamond, the Diamond Cable Company he, well maybe I should just tell you the whole story, you see he's only . . .

—No please Mister Bast, for the love of God please! You don't mind if I give you both a bit of advice?

—No, no well of course that's why I came in to . . .

—Stay in music Mister Bast. Stay in music and advise your, your associate here to stay in whatever in the name of God he's in, where neither of you will ever have to know the value of anything.

—Well but, well yes thank you then but if I could just ask you why this company of, this Eagle Mills, if they have a million dollars why they don't . . .

—Mister Bast I, I didn't say they had a million dollars, I said their net worth . . .

—Yes but what does net . . .

—Mister Bast . . . he loomed slowly forward toward the heap on the blotter, —Mister Bast I, I've just had a thought.

—Yes what does net . . .

—I take it a composer's life is no easier than it ever was, Mister Bast.

—Yes well that's true of course but I, that's the reason I . . .

—Suppose I was able to throw something your way Mister Bast, something a little more in your line.

—In, do you mean in music?

—Commissioning you to write a bit of music, what would you say to that sir?

—Oh well that of course yes, yes that's what I . . .

—Think you could write me some zebra music, Mister Bast?

—Yes I, some, some what?

—Zebra music Mister Bast, zebra music. Just take a minute to fill you in here, friend of mine and I have gone to no damned little expense to put together a little film, fellows you see up here mainly . . . and he herded the stares of the wall gallery indiscriminately together with a sweep of his arm, —and zebras, damned lot of zebras in fact, whole idea is to wake up some people down in Washington to the idea of stocking our public lands with something more suitable than a lot of trailers and beer cans.

—With, with zebras . . . ?

—For a start, for a start yes, and all these fellows of course, all antelopes, don't look related do they but they're all antelopes. Now the whole . . .

—It sounds very, yes it sounds very interesting but first could I ask one question about . . .

—Him over by the door yes, didn't mean him of course, certainly no antelope is he but we'd want to bring him along pretty quickly too. Nothing like wild pig to liven things up a little, and then of course you begin to bring in your beasts of prey . . .

—No I meant what would happen . . .

—What do you think would happen, can't just throw your balance of nature off and leave it off now, can you.

—No I just meant about these bonds, I mean what's going to happen to . . .

—What, this Eagle outfit? Don't ask me sir, why their creditors haven't thrown them into bankruptcy and picked up whatever they could on the dollar before this, now as I say we've got this whole . . .

—Yes but what would happen then, would they . . .

—To this Eagle outfit? Courts would probably just wash out their whole common and preferred equity and hand it over to a receiver to reorganize, as I say we've got this whole film put together now, not quite the finished thing of course but pretty close to it, a jump cut I think they call it, runs about two hours and twenty minutes and we think a little . . .

—Of, of zebras?

—Plenty of movement yes, last trip over Stamper found a nigger boy right there in Malindi who knew how to run a camera and we packed him up country with us, couldn't get him near lion though, brought down a nice Cape Buffalo but we couldn't get him near that either so we're pretty heavy on the zebra side, beautiful things, great sense of freedom and dignity you see in all these fellows . . . and, as he gestured again, the entire mass of tweed and chair rolled back and a drawer came open.
—Give you an idea have a look at him, yes hold it up to the light there, of course you don't get the sense of movement you get in the film and that's where Stamper and I think a little music would make it look a little more professional but that gives you an idea. Fine looking fellow isn't he?

—Yes he's, is this Mister Stamper?

—No no on the left there, the zebra, that's just one of our nigger boys with it, the zebra there, hole hardly shows does it. Got him right behind the head there at four hundred yards, gives you some idea of this grace and dignity you'd want to capture in your music . . . his fingers were drumming on the teak, —plenty of movement . . .

—Well two hours and, it might get a little repetitive if . . .

—Good point Bast, good point . . . and the contents of the box of slide transparencies cascaded between them, —got some film we haven't even used in this, we just had a few shots from it printed up here to keep track of things, give you an idea, antelope mainly, kudu over there and hartebeest, fellow right behind me here. We didn't use this film though because this nigger boy forgot to turn something on the camera and we got some damned odd colors but a little of it here and there might give it all a little more artistic feeling, use your music to tie it in and it would look like we'd done it on purpose, all these damned colors, what do you think.

—Yes it sounds interesting it, but could I ask you one more thing about . . .

—Of course, yes, probably be able to add another good forty minutes or so and give your music a chance to change the pace a little, see what you mean yes, take the dik-dik here, might have a little fun with the dik-dik . . .

—No what I mean was what would happen if that happened and a receiver took over the company, what . . .

—Company? What company.

—This, this Eagle Mills, if you had a bond would it . . .

—What, this Eagle outfit? Just reorganize it if they want to keep things running, probably put out a new issue of common and convertible preferred hand out a few shares of each for every bond, the rate they've been losing money up there they must have generated one hell of a tax loss carry-forward position but that's no damned use all by itself is it, now here he is, little fellow running out ahead there, see him? Of course you'll never see a purple dik-dik but there's no damned law against a little artistic license is there.

—Yes, no I mean no but then if you did have some of these bonds would you be able to get any money from . . .

—What, these? Eagle? Just depends if the man who came off with the biggest bite had the sense to convert all his preferred to common and pick up some more common if he needed it to step in and take over certainly shouldn't be hard, local people up there sitting on most of this paper would probably hold onto their preferred because of the dividend position wouldn't care a damn that they couldn't vote it, what got them into trouble in the first place of course sooner or later you'll want to see the whole film itself but you might take these along for what you'd call inspiration I suppose?

—Yes I do have to leave, I just had one more question about . . .

—No no no sit still, sit still, we've already gone to a good deal of expense on this and a little more won't hurt, of course it's not hurting Stamper anyway because it all comes right off taxes as an educational expense project, educate these Parks people and a few of these big conservationist lobbies and environmentalists and clean up this tourist glut that's turning these great public lands and wilderness areas into rubbish heaps and outdoor latrines like camping in a lot of damned parking lots, turn a few wild pigs loose in these National Parks we'll clear things up in no time.

—Yes I, yes I did just want to ask if . . .

—Just told you Bast, can't throw your balance of nature off and leave it off now can you, get these zebras and the rest of these fellows in there without something to hunt them and they'd all go berserk. Ever see zebras grazing with lion in the grass a few hundred yards away? Know damned well they're there and know damned well why they're there but you don't see them pack up and run do you? Don't see an apple tree pack up and run when you come to pick an apple do you?

—Well no, no I never . . .

—Know damned well you don't, whole problem facing us now is the rate Africa's developing it's going to be nothing but a lot of niggers driving around in hats and neckties no place left for the game at all, pushing these fellows right off their own land like a lot of damned Indians if we don't set them up over here pretty quick there won't be any place left to hunt them at all. That answer your question?

—Yes well, no not exactly you see I just wondered if when you say someone would come in and take over, how they . . .

—You still on this Eagle outfit? Just walk in and take over.

—But then what would they, I mean would the people who had these bonds be able to . . .

—Loosen up their cash position a little, lease-back arrangements and that kind of thing, and clean up their net properties accounts, probably things in it they've forgotten they own. Grandeur Bast, that's the quality you want to get across in your music here, restore these great public lands to their natural grandeur, stock the National Parks with some of these fellows we'll clean out all these trailers and tin cans and these damned filthy kids with their hair and drugs and beads and motorcycles of course Stamper's idea is a damned site simpler, says why not just go in and hunt them. Use tranquillizers and pellet guns but they don't have the instinct for survival that a good healthy animal's got, lie down in the dirt and sing you a song and there's no damned challenge in that . . .

—Yes well, your phone yes maybe I'd better . . .

—Just sit still a minute yes . . . Shirley? If this is Davidoff again just tell him to . . . who? Better put him on yes just hold on a minute Bast, start turning down calls from the press you see your credibility go right down the, hello . . . ? he recovered from a gesture apparently intended to direct attention to the litter of slide transparencies which got no further than a book on the desk there, A Moveable Feast left opened to page 190. —Talking about the piece in Forbes this morning I saw it yes, got the whole thing blown out of proportion this talk about fabled mineral wealth and outside interests the whole thing's tribal, want the key to this Gandia situation it's right there in Gandia this Doctor Dé's an Idi . . . no no just Idi, i, d . . . first three letters yes, hill tribe up there in Uaso province been at the Blakus' throats for a thousand years and this Nowunda's Blaku, Dé sees his chance to get up in the world and starts these secession rumors probably find him floating face down in the river the whole thing will die down, I know Afri . . . any time yes, goodbye . . . he came forward again to rid himself of the phone —now, sir. Where were we.

—Oh. Yes there was one more thing I said I'd ask about it's a, I think it's under the portfolio there . . .

—This? Looks like a, what the hell is it. Coronal extension measuring tape, fit tape in groove behind head of organ and measure distance around . . .

—No what I meant was, it's a, I forget exactly what you call it it's, there it is . . .

—Don't need this I suppose do you . . . the calibrated length of paper dropped to the wastebasket. —Now, this . . . ?

—Yes where it says Alberta and Western . . .

—Debenture, series B debenture didn't know they'd even brought out a series A. Never see a nickel on this one, wouldn't fool with these people they're worse off than your Eagle outfit there, now of course you understand I wouldn't ask you to do something like this for nothing Bast.

—Something like . . .

—This music you're doing for us yes, gives me a little chance to do my part for the arts too doesn't it, might even be worth five . . . and he paused, gaining his feet with a look from collar to heel down the figure bent over the split portfolio jamming in papers, —might even be worth two hundred dollars to you, what would you say to that sir.

—Well I . . .

—Glad to be able to do it, help along a struggling artist you'll want to take these along with you too . . . He freed both hands to scoop the slide transparencies into their box and reached for a button, —Shirley? Give Mister Bast a handful of stock powers on his way out here and, yes, you want me to open a discretionary account for your aunts here then, Bast? Just keep it in the street name save them a lot of bother . . .

—Yes well however it's done, I . . .

—Put it out of your mind then Bast, get right down to your music, eh?

—Yes I, I'd certainly like . . .

—Might hear a sample in a day or two do you think? Yes and as you go out take a look at the dik-dik, little fellow right up there over Shirley's head, give you an idea . . . He sank back to the chair and his fingers galloped across the teak, cleared the blotter's green and sprang. —Shirley get me Doctor Handler on the phone here . . . his other hand dropped to the wastebasket, —yes and look in the Directory of Directors for somebody named Decker, W Decker, sounds familiar. And then get me Beaton up at Typhon will you? His hand came up trailing the calibrated length of paper and hung there till he settled it as a bookmark. —Larry? Is, yes hello is the doctor in? Tell him Mister Craw . . . what? What do you mean call Tuesday, this is . . . No damn it I certainly am not a patient! Tell him this is his broker calling . . . yes! Yes hello Larry? Say, I think I can unload those old Eagle Mills bonds for you at eight or nine cents, pick up your tax loss for any . . . oh you did? Yes in that case I might be able to unload your Boston and Maines, probably get you twelve or fifteen on them, got somebody who seems to be looking around for those things yes, I'll let you know . . . and again his empty hand stalked the green, —Beaton? Got me, Shirley? Got me Beaton? While you're there Shirley see what the pink sheet has on Alberta and Western Power, thought they'd thrown in the towel, they . . . oh, Beaton? no but what the hell is this I hear about somebody bringing a class action against Diamond? Shirley . . . ? You still on?

—I have Mister Beaton for you Mister Crawley.

—Well so do I, get off the line.

—Hello?

—Hello . . . ?

—This is Beaton yes I'm still on, what . . . certainly not no where did you hear . . . Of course I am yes obviously an action like that against the company would have come to my immediate atten . . . No no grounds imaginable it's . . . definitely not no issuing a public denial would simply spread the rumor further and if it should reach Gov . . . yes especially at this particular moment oh and Mister Craw . . . in terms of issuing a denial yes I think it might be inadvisable to bring up the matter with Mister Davi . . . Exactly yes I think that's precisely what we want to avoid, now . . . the Forbes piece? I did yes but I can't get into it right now I'm . . . I will yes, goodbye . . . he pressed a button moving no more than the finger it took to do so, —Miss Bulcke? Will you please hold any calls unless they're . . . thank you. I'm sorry Mrs Joubert I know you're in a hurry and . . .

—It's all right no, I have to meet Francis, she said into her handkerchief —I . . .

—Pardon?

—I'm meeting Francis to take him to the Cloisters, she said suddenly loudly.

—But, are you all right? has something happened?

—Nothing no, nothing an unpleasantness in the elevator it's not important . . . she sat forward, knees clenched —Mister Beaton could, could Lucien Francis' father, could he simply take Francis to Switzerland?

—Take him?

—Take him there, to live.

—Why, has he threat . . .

—Could he!

—Well as, as things stand of course Mrs Joubert if your, if he took the boy with any such intentions we would immediately apply for a court order to . . .

—Court order! can't you, can't anything simply be settled! she'd opened her bag, thrust the handkerchief in and snapped it closed —I'm sorry Mister Beaton, I know it's not your fault . . .

—Yes unfortunately the complica . . .

—I just asked him, Lucien, why he couldn't simply clear things up . . . she had her bag opened again coming up with dark glasses, thrusting those back to bring out a pair rimmed with tortoise shell —all he could talk about was this business settlement, are these the papers . . .

—Yes but, but when was this Mrs Joubert, have you seen Mis, I'm sorry . . . he got the phone, —hello, Bea . . . oh, yes sir . . . Yes go ahead yes sir . . .

—Must I read all this? she'd brushed her hair back putting on the glasses and as quickly it fell again over the murmur of her voice. —Please be advised of the possibility of highly damaging litigation involving our ethical product currently marketed in the class of monoamine-oxidase inhibitors whose chief active ingredient, tranylcypromine sulphate, recent confidential medical reports associate directly with fatality if taken inadvertently in combination with such strong cheeses as Stilton, Brie, Camem . . .

—Ex excuse me just a moment sir, I'm sorry Mrs Joubert those are the wrong papers you needn't read . . . pardon? Yes sir she's here now, she just stopped in to sign the . . . if that's all yes sir I'll take care of it with Frank Black . . . I will yes sir, goodbye. I'm terribly sorry Mrs Joubert, I went through the Nobili file in a hurry and, is something funny?

—The word ethical there, it's just so utterly grotesque. . . .

—No well of course that's a, it's only a term they use to distinguish prescription drugs . . . he recovered the papers from her, —and this really has nothing to do with . . .

—It has nothing to do with anything why am I reading it! Every time I come in I'm given something to read I don't understand something to sign I don't even . . .

—Yes well you see, Mrs Joubert, excuse me for interrupting you but some time ago, you see, a small company we had acquired because of its attractive patent position in the pharmaceutical field was negotiating a very substantial contract with the military due to the steady upsurge in demand by veterans' hospitals and ah, at any rate these negotiations were suddenly broken off when an Italian firm came in with a far lower bid, since Italy is not a party to our patent agreements you see, and this Italian drug firm had simply pirated the patents on which our entire . . .

—Oh you do! pick things apart till no one can recognize them, I ask you about Francis and you talk about patents, I ask Lucien and he . . .

—Yes but don't you see, Mrs Joubert, I simply wanted to give you the background because under the circumstances your father's position in the government makes it a rather awkward moment to consider bringing suit since the validity of the patents themselves is, I won't go into those details but these papers, you see, simply involve you in your capacity as a trustee of the foundations into which your father's various holdings were placed when he joined the government, in order to allow us to handle this particular situation by making some accommodation with this Nobili firm, this Italian drug firm, in which as you probably know your former, Mister Joubert, is a principal. As an Italian firm, actually it's Swiss based of course, Nobili is . . .

—In Geneva? It's in Geneva?

—Yes but simply in terms of . . .

—Going to school in Geneva, that's what he was talking about isn't it, putting Francis in school in Geneva.

—Did he say that? When did you see him.

—Last night. She'd opened her purse again, getting her handkerchief. —I didn't see him really, we just talked for a moment.

—He called you?

—No not on the phone, no, I just meant it was dark. I was in bed when he came in and we . . .

—He, when he came, into your bedroom?

—It's his really, of course. She blew her nose. —His apartment, the only times I . . .

—But, I don't quite understand . . . he turned in his chair to face her, drawing his small dulled black shoes close as he might have done placing them empty away in his closet. —You don't still live together?

—Of course not.

—I don't mean to be, to be indelicate Mrs Joubert but, in bed, you were in bed in his apartment?

—Why yes I'd, when Francis is down, it's our arrangement when Francis is down from school.

—I'm afraid I still don't quite understand.

—Simply we haven't wanted to upset him. We simply, until everything's definite there's no reason Francis should be upset prematurely and so we simply, we simply want him to have a feeling of security as long as he can that we, that his parents live together like any parents that, that he has a home . . .

—I see. The ah, you must realize the ah . . .

—The what, the impropriety?

—I meant the ah . . .

—Oh nothing happens, in the bedroom? Nothing happens if that's what you mean Mister Beaton.

—Ah. But you see Mrs Joubert it isn't, it's not simply a question of your actual ah, any actual . . .

—They're separate beds after all Mister Beaton, last night in fact, she cleared her throat without looking up, —last night Francis slipped into bed with him and, and slept there all night with him . . .

—No but you see . . . he cleared his throat, —I'm afraid you still don't understand Mrs Joubert, simply by returning voluntarily to his ah, I take it it is voluntarily, to his . . .

—I've just finished saying it's, yes the arrangement we've . . .

—Yes but you must realize that if he, if Mister Joubert wished to make it appear that he, that you ah . . .

—He can't make it appear anything Mister Beaton! he, he wants it cleared up as much as I do he's mixed up with some, you probably saw her picture in the papers when she was still dancing not the one I saw this morning of course with a, an inscription his coq rouge in an inscription no, but . . .

—Yes I, I see yes incidentally does, is your father aware of this arrangement you have with Mis, with Francis' father?

—Daddy? I don't know, I haven't the faintest idea what he's aware of, it might embarrass him is that what you mean? if something unpleasant got in the papers? The way he's aware of Freddie when Freddie gets out and the rest of the time he's . . .

—No please Mrs Joubert I didn't mean he, that was he on the phone just now I meant to tell you yes . . .

—Oh?

—He asked me to give you his best wishes yes, he . . .

—He knew I was here?

—Yes I told him you'd come in to, excuse me. Hello . . . ? It's Mrs Selk I'd better, yes hello? Good morn . . . pardon? Yes sir, ma'am yes ma'am . . . I see yes ma'am have you talked with Boody hersel . . . no ma'am I . . . Yes ma'am have you talked with Mis . . . yes ma'am possibly if Mister Moncrieff himself called the Greek Emba . . . the Greek Embassy yes ma'am he might be in a better position to . . . Yes ma'am I . . . yes ma, hello? hello . . . ?

—Boody?

—Yes she ah, apparently she's been arrested again . . . he replaced the phone, —she was stopped at the Greek frontier and charged with carrying I'm sorry, hello? Bea oh yes ma'am I . . . no ma'am no I . . . No I didn't no ma'am no sometimes the switchboard just cuts in and discon . . . no ma'am no I don't know anyone on the switch . . . but yes but all of them ma'am? It's quite difficult to find experienced op . . . yes ma'am . . . yes ma'am immed . . . Yes ma'am but of course the police themselves should . . . yes ma'am but of course the insurance company has its own investiga . . . Yes ma'am but I might suggest if Deleserea has been missing only since last evening there may be a possib . . . yes ma'am . . . yes ma'am immed . . . hello? hello . . . ? he held it away, brought it back to his ear —hello . . . ? and hung it up slowly —she, now she thinks Deleserea has disappeared with a diamond brooch . . .

—I wouldn't blame her at all, I can't even blame Boody for carting drugs into Greece she's . . .

—Not this time no they've charged her with carrying incendiaries, incendiary bombs, we just got her out of Nepal and I think your father is beginning to . . .

—Be aware of Boody?

—Mrs Joubert please I, I think your father has been quite patient, he . . .

—Patient . . . ! she turned pages, —now where am I to sign.

—On the last page where it says, yes down there . . .

—He's been patient with Freddie for what, ten years? as long as Freddie's where he can't bother him.

—But under the circumstances Mrs Joubert, I think your brother is prob . . .

—Does Daddy ever visit him? she pulled off her glasses looking up, —ever?

—Well I . . . he cleared his throat, reached for the papers —are you able to visit him often?

She got her handkerchief again, but simply held it tight in her hand. —Once I, I went once and they had a concert he was learning to play the, played the cymbals I just couldn't ever go again . . .

—But, but perhaps your father finds it just as pain . . .

—Freddie's his son! she used the handkerchief and then, stilled, her eyes over its lavender edge looked even larger —sends his, he sends his best wishes he knows I'm sitting a foot away but he couldn't . . .

—Mrs Joubert he had an important meeting and just took a moment to call with something quite urgent regarding the situation in Gan . . .

—A moment yes he couldn't take a moment to speak to me to, even to ask how I am there's always a meeting an important meeting he hides in meetings even that day, the day I brought the children in I was in his office to, waiting to sign something like I always am he was standing beside me there molding his nose like he always does looking down at me and he said, he said you look tired Amy he looked so concerned so, so concerned I thought he wanted to talk to me to tell me something to say something he, and then he turned with all that concern he turned to you and asked about his last option . . .

—I, I understand yes but I think you should consid . . .

—I'm sorry, is this all you want me to sign?

—Yes and, oh the changes yes if you'll just initial the changes, they're marked in the margins Mrs Joubert it's not my, I just mean to say your father has been under a good deal of pressure recently I don't think you should take that to mean he's not extremely concerned about you, when you mentioned earlier the trusts your mother had set up for yourself and your brother, your income . . .

—Oh honestly . . . she initialed, initialed, —how can you call it my income it's . . .

—No but you see I understand your impatience but I think in expressing his concern under the provision that the income may be reinvested by the guardian until . . .

—By Daddy yes till he thinks I've stopped drifting? till I stop wasting my, stop teaching school out in the woods somewhere just to have something to do, something alive to do even if it's, even if I hardly know what I'm teaching them just following the lesson guide but it's something it's, something . . .

—I didn't mean . . .

—And don't say the trusts Mama had set up for me and Freddie no, no Daddy and your father and Uncle John set them up and old Judge Ude in the Surrogate Court where Uncle John put him they set them up, it was Mama's money and they set them up with all these provisions and she signed the papers just like I'm signing these without even knowing what she, why they . . .

—Please no wait a moment, no I should make it clear of course I have no way of knowing the conditions surrounding these trusts of your mother's Mrs Joubert but, but in signing these papers in your capacity with these foundations the implication that you're being taken advantage of beyond . . .

—A convenience . . .

—Well in a, perhaps in a manner of spea . . .

—A convenience yes, it saves Uncle John the trouble of finding trustees on the subway.

—Yes well, perhaps yes but certainly you do understand his wish to secure his financial position? You see in eight of ten previous years, his taxes plus charitable contributions had taken ninety percent of his net income enabling him to make a charity gift of some nineteen million dollars to . . .

—Oh honestly, charity just the word . . .

—Yes well I use it in its tax law connotation and of course since his bank holds the pension fund of the hospital where he's a trustee, and his position as a director of this leading nonprofit health insurance program assures the hospital against nonpayment of . . .

—The idea of him ever giving away nineteen cents nineteen, nineteen peanuts nineteen anything if he had them he'd . . .

—No you see Mrs Joubert the point is that this particular nineteen million represented the market value of the securities constituting his gift he'd originally paid something like, something under half a million as an original investor and this approach merely enables him to avoid the substantial capital gains tax he would have been liable for if he'd sold them, and made his income for the following very prosperous year entirely tax free, you see the high personal tax rate, in setting up these foundations in view of the high personal tax rate he was subject to on the dividends from these securities it was decided that since a dividend in the form of stock was not considered income, he might authorize and receive a new issue of preferred at one hundred dollars par redeemable by the company at one hundred two which of course would not affect his control of, Mrs Joubert? you, you did want to know . . .

—Preferred stock doesn't vote, yes. We had it in class, preferred stock doesn't . . .

—Yes in this case however it appeared advisable for tax purp . . .

—Doesn't sing doesn't dance doesn't smoke or drink or run around with women, doesn't even . . .

—Pardon?

—Oh nothing Mister Beaton it's all so, just so absurd so, lifeless, I can't . . .

—Please I, Mrs Joubert I didn't mean to make an emotional issue of it, the . . .

—Well it is! It is an emotional issue it simply is! because, because there aren't any, there aren't any emotions it's all just reinvested dividends and tax avoidance that's what all of it is, avoidance the way it's always been it always will be there's no earthly reason it should change is there? that it ever could change?

—Only, well, in this particular case as I was going to say it appeared advisable for tax purposes that this preferred issue paying six percent semiannually would have no voting rights unless four consecutive dividends were missed and of course in that case, the trustees would vote the stock, install new directors if they wished to and assume control of the extensive assets which . . .

—I think that's your phone again, if this is all you want me to . . .

—I'm sorry yes, hello? Beaton . . . yes, yes just hold on a moment Dick, you did initial the second set Mrs Joubert?

—Oh dear . . . she opened her bag again digging for glasses, coming up with the wrong pair —I'm already . . .

—I'm sorry I thought you'd, these right here yes. Dick . . . ? I did yes but I think this Endo divestiture has priority, he's getting quite impatient about the Diamond tender and of course nothing can be . . . for you specifically to handle it as soon as you're finished there yes, Frank Black's doing most of the spadework and as soon as you . . . Yes originally yes, but they informed us the substantial tax write-off we proposed could be jeopardized by a suit with an original stockholder over sequestering the patents, that would probably drag the goodwill write-off down with it and the most sensible thing seems to be straight divestiture in connection with the Diamond tender once this decree has been . . . I know it yes but the sooner you can clear it up and get to Washington the better, we . . . you did yes she's right here . . . I will yes, goodbye . . . I will, yes. That was Mister Cutler, he sends . . .

—Sends me kindest regards . . . she initialed, turned a page.

—He's in Rome yes he, I'm terribly sorry Mrs Joubert did you want to speak with him? I didn't even . . .

—What on earth about . . . she initialed, initialed.

—Well I, I don't know of course I, he did ask me to tell you he hoped to be back in time to take you to the horse show and I think if your father is . . .

—Mister Beaton that's what we've been talking about! he, Daddy still wants it all to be like it was when I rode at the Garden myself with that ghastly Ude girl, when her brother came down with Dick Cutler from Choate and, if he could see if Daddy could just see the only men I've met I can imagine getting into, into anything with them he'd die, one's probably Freddie's age he drinks and plays the horses his face is like the, he laughs and his face is just torment and, and his hands and the other's a boy, a composer and he's just a boy just all, all radiant desolation and he's dear . . .

—Then I think you realize the . . .

—And they wouldn't mind the money either of them honestly, I'd almost marry them both just for that . . .

—Exactly yes I think you can understand your father's, that as guardian under your mother's will you realize he has certain obligations to what would have been your mother's wishes to see that the trust doesn't become an attraction to, leading to another unfortunate marriage and so naturally he . . .

—Asks Dick Cutler to take me to the horse show . . . she'd folded her glasses again —that would be like, like marrying your issue of six percent preferreds . . . she opened her bag to thrust them back in, —avoidance payable semiannually . . . she snapped it closed. —I'm sorry Mister Beaton I, I shouldn't talk to you like this but there's simply been no one else . . . her hand fell empty, only half closed on the desk between them to close suddenly seized there in one even whiter —what . . .

—You, you must understand that I, that your father that, that for anything to happen to you would be, because you're such a a stunning woman a stunning young woman I I, I . . .

Her hand turned that sharply on the tremor enclosing it —please there's, Mister Beaton there's nothing you can . . .

—No no I, all I can do honestly . . . he stared there where his hand lay hidden, and then it fled hers for the phone —hello Bea, Beaton . . . he cleared his throat. —It's Senator Broos I'd better, hello . . . ? Yes sir yes I . . . he called a few minutes ago yes sir if you could hold on for one moment I . . . he no sir his daughter is here she . . .

—No please Mister Beaton go ahead, there's nothing else is there?

—Yes wait no there's a form, there yes if you'd just sign it and, yes just one moment sir where it says age last birthday it's just a formality, you can write over twenty-one if you, sir . . . ?

—Right here? Twenty-seven, it's still just a formality and thank you Mister Beaton . . .

—Sir . . . ? Yes no sir no I believe it's cleared up, General Blaufinger's statement in the foreign press urging intervention was apparently made on the assumption that we would support the secessionists but when it was made clear to him that Washington sediment sed, sentiment favored the joint resolution backing the Nowunda regime the General immed . . . not a no sir not a retraction no a clarifying statement simply saying that the press had distorted his pos . . . his position yes sir exac . . . yes exactly sir your position on Chile regarding Kennecott during the . . . yes sir sir? If you could excuse me one moment Mrs Joubert? Thank you for coming in, please call me if there are any sir . . . ? Yes sir she's . . . yes sir Mrs Joubert? Senator Broos sends his . . . on which matter sir . . . ? No sir I'm drafting the legislation on the banking bill now for him to . . . Oh I see yes sir no I don't think you need to be concerned, it's the state senate he's running for sir, not your . . . just the state yes sir I'm certain he . . . I've never met him no sir but . . . no sir it's c, c, i an Italian name not, not peachy no sir . . .

The door closed behind her, freeing one hand from the other she turned —oh . . . !

—I think we're all set and, oh Miss Bulcke we're going to camp out in the chief's office here so Mrs Joubert can run through these proofs, we . . .

215

—But Mister Davidoff I . . .

—No trouble oh and Miss Bulcke tell Carol to put my calls through here, tell her to screen them I'm waiting for one from Washington and the, call Florence and tell her to tell Mister Eigen I want him on this speech draft for General Box ask him where the captions are for this Annual Report feature that we, sorry . . . ! he'd made an abrupt end to a glide from a lost dance step. —One of us has an electric personality lady, he steered her —right in here, we can lay them all out. Static electricity, it piles up in the carpet you touch a doorknob and, you want to sit right here? he came on rounding the clear expanse of the desk still settling the acrylic sheen on his shoulders, put down the pictures and shot his cuffs to display gold simile coins of the Austro-Hungarian Empire. —You can sit down right there if you . . .

—But I am in a hurry Mister Davidoff, I . . .

—Right, this will save you a trip to my office.

—But, there must be a hundred of them.

—Two eighty-six, I know how important this project is to you that's why we want you to make the picture selection yourself, now I thought we'd lead off with that one on top there, one second . . . He stabbed the button-studded console and picked up the phone as he sat, his feet parting from the floor. —Pretty classy looking guy, am I right? Your Dad really, oh Miss Bulcke get the Waldorf, tell them the General won't be back till the twentieth and I'll be using his suite . . . he came forward hanging up the phone, feet treading air. —Your dad really comes across doesn't he, a real statesman of ind . . .

—This looks like a picture of a, a nun cutting up a frog.

—What? What's that. There's no caption on it? I gave this top priority . . . he stabbed at the console, —make it clear we're backing your educational effort with these youngsters getting a foot in the door of this whole field of visual literacy and they send up pictures with no captions as though Eigen? Hello? Where's Mister Eigen . . . At lunch? now? What man from Thailand . . . no just tell him to call me, is somebody typing the captions for this Annual Report story . . . ? can't find what . . . ? No, just tell Mister Eigen to call me.

—All your pictures look very nice Mister Davidoff, I'm sure you can select . . .

—Now this one here, we have to have Crawley of course but we're angling your story more along the lines of the share itself, corporate responsibility to this one, must have been when Crawley was picking up the coins one second, I'm expecting a call from Washington, Senator Broos hello . . . ? No tell him I'll call him back now there, that one's not bad, not bad of Crawley but it looks like that pig is climbing in the window over his shoulder wait, here's my call now, hello? Senator? Mollenhoff? What does Mollenhoff want? . . . No that was his memo to me not my memo to him . . . what? Wait a minute . . . He was pushing buttons as though playing an instrument —who? No this isn't the maintenance department . . . Hello? Where's that call I had in to Senator Broos? Miss Bulcke? Who's this? Eigen? What's this about somebody from Thailand . . . Taiwan? No, that's a Chinese medical relief group he was supposed to come over for the fifty cent tour before lunch, did you check his hotel? . . . No a donation, just take him out to lunch and tie, one, on, I said tie . . . never mind, look. This Box speech for Gandia you've got a delicate situation, you've got the defense minister Doctor Dé and President Nowunda both up there on the platform, work them both in but so one of them can come out at the last minute . . . Yes it's top priority the General's in Bonn waiting for it now, one of us may have to go over there and spoon feed it to him we can't have him pull another one of those Plato rhymes with tomato . . . Oh Mrs Joubert? Wait you don't need to leave, just a couple of brush fires but you can tell your dad when you see him what it's like tending the store here with no executive officer on board. They're typing those captions up now, if we run out for a little lunch we could look over the whole package when we got back there's a little place . . .

—Oh I'm afraid not Mister Davidoff I, that's why I must leave now in fact, I have to . . .

—Don't worry about it I'm too busy to leave the shop myself, we'll just get something sent in . . . he had the phone again. —Oh Miss Bulcke send out for a couple of, what would you like? The ham, cheese . . .

—Honestly I haven't time Mister Davidoff, and I'm . . .

—Just cancel that Miss Bulcke and oh Miss Bulcke, while you're on there get hold of Colonel Moyst, he can begin cutting orders for me for a week, make it a ten day TDY for Germany and, just make it Europe and Africa, CIPAP, they'll have to give me a field grade equivalency rating, Colonel, probably a GS sixteen I've got to have CIPAP or I might as well stay home. Now . . . Empty-handed, he stood knuckled under at the desk, —that one's better, a little less of Crawley and we can touch it up to get that pair of horns out of his here, this one's better, you've got your stock certificate right up front and center the kid though, too bad we didn't get a kid up there with a haircut and a sweater that wasn't ripped down the, let's see this one. Same kid. Same kid seems to have pushed himself into all of them with the stock certificate, he . . .

—He has been sort of, this boy's been sort of acting as a class secretary on our . . .

—Wait, wait! Up came his hands framing nothing —look. It fits right in. A share in America, right? And these kids, this kid here, that must be a pretty what you'd call culturally deprived area where you're teaching? Well anyhow we can play up the wait . . . His hands dropped scattering pictures —looking for, no blacks? I don't see any blacks in any of these, don't you have any blacks in your class? he swept them together again —don't worry about it, we'll make do one second, this must be my Washington call. Hello? . . . ? No it's not. He stabbed buttons. —What happened to my Washington call, Senator . . . what? he stabbed again and

began to pace —hello? Senator . . . ? Oh he's not? When will he . . . At
the end of the cord he paused, his back on the room —well just get him
this message then, confidential. Background for handling the press on
this Gandia thing playing up the angle of the U S getting in bed with the
U S S R, China, Albania and the rest of them on it, he can talk to Frank
Black at that end on the canned editorial content side, capture a what?
Me? Davidoff . . . Davidoff, d, a, v, i . . . well tell him I called for Mister
. . . hello? Hello? . . . He walked back to the desk, cleared his throat as
he hung up the phone. —Yes, we'll want this boy's name for the captioning . . . he looked up, and then stabbed at the console. —Miss Bulcke?
Is Mrs Joubert out there? has she . . . probably just went to the ladies'
room, the . . . who? Who's this, Carol? Hyde who . . . Well what does he
want with . . . what appliances . . . Oh. Well tell him to talk to Mollenhoff
about it . . . Oh, well if he works for Mollenhoff why did Mollenhoff tell
him to talk to me about it . . . Oh. Well tell him I'll talk to Mollenhoff about
it, is he right there? Put him on the blower Carol and stay on yourself,
I've got a couple of brush fires that . . . Carol?

—Yes sir he's right here . . . she leaned across the litter to cradle the
telephone and reach a button on the far side of the desk, drawing the
figure looming behind her forward till her skirt stopped just short of
revelation. —Mister Hyde this is Mister Davidoff, she recovered, pointing at the speaker beside the spilling out basket.

————Yes hello Mister, Carol? turn it down, you've got some feedback in there
that's bursting my . . .

—Hello, Mister Davidoff . . . ? He followed the course of the stocking
seam again and remained sagged over the litter toward the speaker as
though seeking recognition in its face. —I'm . . .

————Hyde? Get further back from that speaker we're running into some feedback,
I'm topside in the chief's office tending store here can't get away right now, you're
in sales? over in Mollenhoff's stable? Good thing I got hold of you I just had him on
Carol while you're on deck, you still on deck there? Pull Mister Eigen off those
captions tell him I've just come out of conference on it, rethinking the whole feature
in inner city terms culturally deprived black slice of the corporate pie probably
need an airbrush on some of those pix too Hyde? still with me? Mollenhoff can't
keep his communications lines straight good thing I got hold of you on this, Justice
Department on our tails this vertical integration policy's the big must right down
the line, bending over backwards keeping our skirts clean if he's handing out that
appliance inventory on a tax write-off tell him our legal boys switched the game
plan clearing the whole thing out through sales till we get the loud and clear from
Justice on Carol? While you're on deck get hold of Miss Bulcke on this TDY she's
lining up tell her to make sure CIPAP includes commercial travel authorized means
I'll need a field grade equivalency that's colonel or better get this other call, the
Senator call me back on that line? Must be on this other line, heeep . . .

—I guess he signed off Mister Hyde, is there anything else?
—Ahhh . . . he got upright, —better see if you can get Mister Mollenhoff for me.

—Yes sir. She found a company directory in the litter, —is that Herbert B? or is that . . .

—Herbert B.

—That's the only Mollenhoff anyway . . . she dialed. —Did you want to, hello? Mister Mollenhoff? Yeah this is Carol, Ginny? He did? Thanks. You want to go shopping at lunch . . . ? By the cooler, yeah. She hung up. —He went to Akron, Mister Mollenhoff. Is there anything else?

—When will he be back?

—She didn't say, you want me to ask? She had the phone again.

—No, no, don't, don't bother, he turned for the door —oh, while I think of it tell Mister ah, Mister Davidoff, tell him that major is field grade too.

—Major what? I better get a pencil.

—Field grade includes major, not just colonels.

—Field grade includes major, yes sir, she said from her pad, —you know the way out? I'm going down toward the elevators you can just follow me okay? He did, eyes lowered till she turned. —We can just go through this way and, here. Here they are.

—That's some painting you've got on this floor.

—It's real big isn't it.

—I wouldn't cut off my ear for it.

—Your, gee no she said as the doors opened silently and he stepped in, closing as silently on her —come see us again, and the figure rounding the corner behind her fighting loose a tie with —Oh Carol . . . descending to Don't Fence Me In and a lobby filled with policemen which he got through and as far as the city ambulance at the curb before his —What happened? provoked response, a dulled obscenity from a lounger against the granite sill unbuttoned to the waist in the cool air where Don't Walk flashed as he crossed at a lope, down the block, down the ramp into the garage.

—Kinda car?

He handed over the ticket folded in bills. —A brown . . .

—You not suppose to get this car till five o'clock. We got it all blocked in down there, you say you don't want it till five o'clock.

—Look I'm in a hurry, here's an extra buck. Can you get it out?

—Can't just get it like that . . .

He watched the dollar stuffed among greased folds in a turn toward a group lunching on the hood of a distant Cadillac where, as he began to pace under the roar of an exhaust fan, he glanced with each about face to look at his watch in a heavyweight's gesture, and back, paused to study racing cars on end, in mid-air, in flames, taped to the wall, the distant picnickers again, his watch in an awkward left cross, and back; pitted navel, graveled nipple, calendar for July simmering under the exhaust fan, his watch, that lunch, dimpled cheeks bared on a diving board for August, racing car in flames, one in mid-air, on end, he sat, stood, paced, returned to gauge the cleft in August's cheeks yawned at him from the diving board, and back, muttered, called out, sat, stood, at last himself descended, ramps, caverned ranks of cars and his, free-standing, as the third inning began, feet dislodged from the dashboard, loud words dulled to muttering as he drove up the ramp, two men on, one out, and a called strike nearing the bridge stopped for a light, window rolled down where his arm rested from a thrust for a look at his watch and from its face up to one in the car stopped close beside him for the light, black, black in the driver's seat, black behind,

——and it's . . . a hit, a line drive toward third . . .

and a roar as the light changed, the watch was ripped from his wrist and the car beside him swerved across oncoming traffic, horns sounded around him and the cry —Wake up buddy! from a cab wheeling past as he pitched his car forward with the gasped —I . . . don't believe it, over the bridge on a double play and well along the expressway ribbon of filth, battered hubcaps, rusted twists of tailpipe, curls of tire tread before the engine missed once, twice, and he pulled off to the side in the seventh inning stretch, got out, opened the hood, lifted out the air filter and was reaching in to free the butterfly valve when the whole car shook to a wrench of twisting metal. He came round it holding his head where he'd just hit it on the hood straightening up, another tearing wrench and the car's trunk flapped open. —What the, hell are you doing!

—At's all right, you here first, you take the front.

—You, what do you . . .

—You got the front, ain' that fair? Even gettin the battry just leave me the back, ain' that fair? I ain' . . .

—You you crazy son of a bitch you you, you . . . get out of here!

—What you want to hog it all, got everything in the front can't just leave me the back?

—Youg, it's mine, get out of here it's mine!

—You the meanest shit I ever . . .

—Youc . . . come back here you . . . he advanced on the car pulled up behind as its door slammed, a duplicate of his own but for dents and color —my car, you come back here you son of a bitch look what you did to my car . . . !

—You just a real mean shit, came back to him from the dented car pulling away, into the stream of traffic.

—You come back here you, you son of, you . . . He stood there panting, staring, sagged, finally found a wire coathanger in the trunk to secure its twisted lid down and got round to replace the air filter, slammed the hood, the door, pitched back into traffic still muttering —I don't believe it . . . when he pulled up at the school in the top of the ninth and down the corridor for a futile try at slamming the hollow core marked Principal behind him.

—No we're looking in the ahm, come in Major yes the budget that is to say we're going through the budget right now I don't see any mention of . . . no well of course they may be part of the federally subsidized cafeteria lunch program if the freight office says the shipper is the ahm, some branch of government they . . . No of course that's why the children are prohibited from bringing their lunch to school in the first place, we can't . . . class six J? Yes well we can ask Mrs ahm of course we can't ask Mrs Joubert no she's still out on sick . . . how many? No well look at it again Leroy there can't be a hundred and sixty-eight thou . . . from a total shipment of what . . . ? Gross yes that means gross no that's impossible you'd better go down there and ahm, in terms of the ongoing situation enrollmentwise yes you'd better go down there and ahm, and count them that is to say . . .

—Hello Hyde, been in a gang fight?

—Now listen Vern, don't . . .

—Yes sit down Major you look ahm, Vern just dropped in to excuse me a minute, hello . . . ? Oh for yes the District Superintendent he's right here yes, Vern . . . ?

—Hello? Who is it . . .

—Yes well I was just telling Vern we ahm . . .

—Other phone here Whiteback I'll get it, hello . . . ?

—And who gave you that information.

—Just Parentucelli, wants to know if Vern wants the blacktop running around to the back of the house.

—No comment right now, no. Tell him all the way around except the breezeway . . . What . . . ?

—He says everything except the breezeway . . .

—We're making a full investigation yes, goodbye. Here I'll talk to him.

—He hung up, who was that.

—That was the newspaper Whiteback, they had a report on a sit-down strike in your fourth grade.

—Yes well that was ahm, those fourth graders yes Vogel had them making models of ahm, the glue that is to say smelling the glue the little ahm, youngsters some of them went to the nurse's office and couldn't stand up so they ahm, sat down that is to say yes I'd better call the paper back and . . .

—Don't you dare touch that phone, haven't you ever learned not to volunteer information to the papers?

—Yes well of course we ahm, communityrelationswise that is to say Vern you don't get popular support without the ahm, how did that Flesch woman put it yes without the support of the community of course she had a gift for expressing ideas and my job is ahm . . .

—Your job Whiteback? look . . . and where they did a roll of cigar ash bounded down worn folds of tweed and burst on the floor. —Your job is to make the District Superintendent look good, and you're not making me look good with this thimble theater you're running here. You're not doing it by calling up a paper to take a story about a fourth grade sitdown strike away from them with one hand while you're giving them one about a fourth grade drug trip with the other. And get that damn bear off the screen.

—Yes we use it as sort of ahm, can you reach that knob Major?

———useful to make the distinction between a given concept, the number, and the symbol which represents it, the numeral . . .

—Downright brilliant, know what he's talking about?

—Yes well of course this is simply enahm, richment that knob on the left yes, the on off that is to . . .

———define the number in terms of the equivalence class of ordered pairs of the equivalence classes of ordered pairs . . .

—Anybody know what he's talking about?

—Yes well I think what Vern means is ahm, Glancy's been having some financial difficulties that may have affected his approach to ahm, in terms of educational content that is to . . .

—That's not what I meant at all and don't try to describe what flows through these tubes as educational content, equivalence classes of ordered pairs when I said plumbing I meant plumbing, doesn't matter who pulls the chain.

—Yes well I'm afraid Major Hyde doesn't ahm, Vern just dropped in to discuss this next budget referendum Major he thought there might be a few soft spots we could ahm, I just had it yes is that it? that pile right under your . . .

—This? Report to the police any stranger who tries to join you in your play or offers to take you for a ride or walk. Do not play near public toilets . . .

—Oh no that's something the police ahm, like those don't pick up a stranger matches that were handed out in the vd campaign last year and those junior high girls burned down the ahm, it's right here somewhere under here if you'll just move your ahm, I was just looking through it for . . .

—Glue, per quart, three fifty-nine, masking tape each, two forty-seven, chalk per box, three eighty, ladders, each, thirty-six, toilet paper, per case . . .

—Remind me to call Gottlieb yes that's his brother-in-law that is to say but what they do with all that toilet paper, is there anything there about picnic forks? Something Leroy just called about the first part of a shipment of wooden picnic forks . . .

—Here's something from Leroy, glass, sixty-nine panes . . .

—Oh yes well the glass that's in the budget, that was just sixty-nine panes on the weekend but of course with glass running a dollar a square foot and the unbreakable runs three times that . . .

—Bulletproof?

—No that's just the, what they call strengthened glass but . . .

—I'd check out the price differential on the bulletproof while you're at it Whiteback, sooner or later we're going to have to face the facts.

—Well yes but of course right now all we have to do is comply with the ahm, the insurance company recommendations and that man Stye of theirs who was in here hasn't made things any easier since ahm, of course I don't think Vern . . .

—Vern wants solutions, all right, this Stye, colored fellow Vern in here for the insurance company, if he was on our team maybe he'd see things a little more our way, I'm talking about that empty slot coming up on the school board. He lives out there past the new Dunkin Donuts location and Whiteback here seems to think he may be over the district line, but nobody's going out there with a tape measure. Quiet type, tight lipped, doesn't talk much but his eye's on the ball every second, Whiteback here knows what I mean. He probably doesn't make beans with that insurance outfit and wants to get ahead, some of them have a streak of that am I right Whiteback?

—Yes well I didn't think you ahm . . .

—Didn't recall you as such a champion of the race myself Major, even heard somebody say once it made you mad to see a car like yours with a black face behind the wheel, how . . .

—Just let me finish here Vern, if he has a shot at the school board maybe he can clean up this insurance mess the way we want it cleaned up and after that I can probably find him something in our organization, something in sales he'd consider pretty attractive . . .

—All sounds a little like Saul on the road to Damascus Major, something blind you on the drive out here today?

—Listen Vern don't, just don't push me too far. Before I came out here I had a gut session with one of our company's top brass and our big must there right now is vertical integration right down the line, black slice of the corporate pie and all the rest we've got the Justice Department on our tail and we're bending over backwards to keep our skirts clean. Bring this man Stye in it won't hurt us right here in the district integrationwise Whiteback come to think of it he's probably got some white . . .

—Yes well of course the, we just lost that family of ahm, Hawaiians were they? Out by Chick's Auto Body yes sending their little ahm, their youngsters to the parochial school they're not even Catholic, nonwhite of course yes but they're not ahm . . .

—Do you know why? Discipline, that's what they've got to sell and we haven't let me finish Vern, Catholics I met have a kid there in art class the sister tells them color inside the lines, color outside the lines and whap! ruler right across the knuckles, the kid comes home black and blue every night. Discipline and a decent respect for the flag, you blame these Chinamen for sending their kids there? get them away from the kind of inflammatory material a teacher like this Gibbs is handing out, you talked to Vern about this Whiteback? and the kind of friends he has? somebody that goes around putting out his eye with a pencil?

—Yes well no we ahm, Vern stopped by to discuss the new budget referendum that is to say and we ahm . . .

—That's what I'm talking about isn't it? Expect any yes votes with this Citizens Union bunch sending out questionnaires having parents tell their kids to report any teacher that starts his class without the proscribed openings? This budget will bring the tax rate up over nine dollars and we need every vote we can get Catholic and white while they're paying to send their own kids to parochial school, you know how much they've sunk into this new closed-circuit facility over here at Holy Name? Getting all the mileage out of it they can too, I just sent in some pictures of Sister Agnes cutting up a frog to the parent company may give them a boost in our Annual Report, they've got an archbishop coming out to bless it and Father Haight's putting this brokendown two-star General brother of his right up there on the stand with him why should they vote a tax increase to educate our kids. Mention anything else they'll vote for it, roads, they all use roads take this how many million dollar referendum of Pecci's for widening the state roads will go through without a whisper have you seen up there where the highways cross? where that new shopping center's going to go up? I just drove past it coming off the expressway they've got both shoulders cleared all the way up past the Catholic church you think Parentucelli's sitting waiting for a referendum? He knows he'll get paid, by the time this referendum goes through he'll have every state road in sight ten lanes wide but just mention education and they grab for their wallets.

—Yes well of course if ahm, if they keep rejecting the budget that is to say every cutback we submit is ahm, an austerity budg . . .

—We can't cut it back, submit a nickel and dime budget once that's all they'll ever vote for see it at the corporate level all the time, what you don't ask for you don't get and if we keep trimming it to just let me finish Vern, these Catholics want to send their kids to private school let them but they're not going to shortchange the rest of our youngsters on anything from a box of chalk to the appliances for this new what did you call it Whiteback? The home ec motivational center?

—Yes well but I thought that was ahm, this equipment from Major Hyde's company Vern a subsiderary that is to say stoves, washers, dryers, hair ahm, dryers we're getting them all for home ec as a . . .

—Good thing I got hold of you on this Vern, Whiteback can't keep his communications lines straight sometimes I thought we could check out the budget for the door there, somebody . . .

—Yes well Dan come in yes, what . . .

—No I didn't want to interrupt, it's not really school business I . . .

—No come in Dan sit down, just talking to Whiteback and Vern here about your teaching equipment looking for a soft spot in the budget to fit all this into, goes right along with Dan's sorry didn't see your foot there Vern, supplements it you might say. Take this Edsel Responsive Envirement runs around thirty-five thousand a unit, that about right Dan? Now you take some of these youngsters, maybe the equipment can respond but they can't, not fair to shortchange them because of that is it? Bring in these appliances where a washing machine's a responsive envirement to some youngster for a hundredth the price and we key the human being to, how did you put it once Dan? Key the . . .

—The individual yes, key the technology to the individ . . .

—Dan knows what I'm talking about, key the individual to the technology find the soft spots in this budget and we're in business, take for a start . . .

—I just saw this shelter item in there Major, how about taking that for a start.

—I don't think we want to jump right into these controversial areas Vern, still waiting for Whiteback here to get his mobile unit over so these taxpayers can have a good looksee at what's possible before they make a rash decision they might not live to regret, I'm talking about the frills. Take these telephone booths, how many phone booths are you putting in Whiteback?

—Phone booths? Yes I don't ahm, we're not yes . . .

—They're installing one right now down past the boys' room I saw it when I came in, may not look like much but bring in a whole fleet of them you've got a pretty substantial item like these, what was it you just found tucked away in the budget here Whiteback? forks . . . ?

—Wooden yes wooden picnic forks no that's the problem, I can't find them, nine thousand gross wooden pic . . .

—See what I mean? Wooden picnic fork it doesn't sound like much but bring in nine thou, gross? you said gross? Well that's, nine thousand gross that's over a million! See what I mean about things adding up now? Wrong time for picnics anyhow, trim a few more items like that we can set these future young homemakers right up in business over in, setting them up in the south annex Whiteback?

—Yes well we've ahm, they've run into some problems shifting adult ed because the gym's being cleared for the hobby show so the classes in prenatal care had to be ahm, I had it right here somewhere yes driver training was ahm . . .

—Just a little space problem Vern, over in east seven trying to fit the retreads into the space the Great Books were . . .

—I don't want to hear about it.

—Yes well I think what Vern means is ahm . . .

—I just said what I mean Whiteback. Don't tell me things I don't want to know and I won't bother you. If I can stand two more years of this I'll be able to retire, and if you can keep me looking good that long I won't bother you.

—Yes well of course we ahm, Dan that is to say, Dan here has been ahm . . .

—It's your job to make me look good and it's Dan's job to make you look good, if he's just going to sit here making faces I don't know who can make him look good but . . .

—Yes well of course his wife is ahm, if we ask her to come in as curriculum specialist of course we hoped she might be a little less active activationwise in terms of this ongoing strike threat yes is that what you stopped in for Dan? You were going to ahm, feel . . .

—No I can come back later, it's not really school bus . . .

—I don't want to hear about it.

—You'll hear about it Vern they're just looking for an excuse, trying to make an issue over firing that young music what was his name, bastard probably cost us half our tv budget with the show he put on for that Foundation team. Had any calls from them on him yet Whiteback?

—Yes on ahm, Bast you said Mister Bast yes not from the Foundation no the Senior Citizens of course have ahm, are quite put out but . . .

—What did you expect with this open-circuit setup, you'll see them down at that referendum in wheelchairs they . . .

—Yes well apparently they were looking forward to a lesson on Edward MacDowell in connection with their therapy cutting ahm, he seems to have mentioned cutting out paper dolls and of course a music union called threatening legal action against us because he played a note on the piano and he's not ahm, not a member that is to say of course he has a right to ahm, in fact I believe some civil liberties union is preparing to defend his right to free speech but . . .

—If he dares to show his face after that performance I'd just like to get hold of him and . . .

—I've been trying to yes, get hold of him that is to say call his home again to tell him we're preparing a new check, I understand he stopped by for it late yesterday but the computer had misplaced the decimal and made it out for fifteen dollars and ahm, fif . . .

—Fifteen dollars more than he's worth but if you don't get that straightened out Whiteback the whole community's going to blow up, this trouble Dan's been having with his holes Vern . . .

—That's really something I don't want to hear about.

—Yes well of course if that's what you stopped in to talk about Dan maybe some other ahm, of course I thought you might have some word for us about this strike threat in terms of your wife's ahm, I think you were going to feel your wife's ahm . . .

—He doesn't have to feel her anything, if they want to strike let them strike.

—Yes well I think what Vern means is ahm, in terms of the ongoing situation at the curricular level Dan's wife is . . .

—I just finished telling you what I mean Whiteback, it has nothing to do with curricular anything. The function of this school is custodial. It's here to keep these kids off the streets until the girls are big enough to get pregnant and the boys are old enough to go out and hold up a gas station, it's strictly custodial and the rest is plumbing. If these teachers of yours strike just sit still and keep the doors open, by the time these kids have been lying around the house for a week their parents will march the teachers back in at gunpoint.

—Yes well of course I don't think the police would excuse me, hello . . . ? Oh, yes send him down to my office in fact you better have someone bring him down yes he . . . yes thank you. One of our drug ahm, our pupils that is to say I understand his older brother was severely wounded in the ahm, that he's a veteran yes so this boy seems to have access to a variety of ahm, in fact I think he was sent down in this condition yesterday but of course since he's ahm ahm, in terms of the enrollment integrationwise that is to say we've made every effort to encourage his attendance of course his record is somewhat ahm, Dan? That's not what you, you had some school business you said yes is that letter something you, something we . . .

—No no it's my, it's not school business no it's just my mortgage, my application to refinance my mortgage, I didn't mean to take school time just for . . .

—Yes well I don't think Vern would . . .

—No go ahead Dan, go ahead. You sit here picking your nose on school time why shouldn't you talk about your mortgage on school time.

—Yes well of course Dan the ahm, let me see the letter yes I think in terms of the ahm, nothing personal in this of course Dan but down to the bank that is to say we operate under certain regulations ahm, restrictions on mortgage outlays dictated by what you might call the actual construction of the house and the ahm, standards, the standard spacing of the wall studs of course is sixteen inches and yours appear to be ahm, twenty-four, inches apart that is to say . . .

—But I didn't know . . .

—Yes no nobody's blaming you Dan, we know you didn't build it yourself it was, of course it was the builder who ahm, who built it of course but the, since the term of a mortgage is related to, dictated by the number of years the house is reasonably expected to stand depending on its, directly related to the way it's built, constructed you might say, the wall studs having a direct bearing on the part, you might even say actually part of the structure so that of course the farther apart they are in a given space the fewer there are of them because the fewer there are of them the farther apart they have to be placed so that under certain conditions such as a, even the passage of time which is directly related to the term of the mortgage and the reasonable life of the dwelling, if the wall studs were closer together of course there would be more of them which in turn could be reasonably expected to provide a more substantial structure timewise over the time period the, the period of time the mortgage is being amortized and the bank of course, banks that is to say, in order to protect their borrowers in granting these mortgage applications because you understand there's nothing personal in this Dan, the same thing comes up with other applicants, the banks usel, utilize the safeguards set forth in the building code stating the safe legal minimums for materials and construction in terms of course that's what building codes are for such specifications as the spacing of wall studs in the ahm, the Hyde house yes I think you have your mortgage with us Major but of course it was built back in ahm, a Cape Cod ranch type split when they were still building those fine old homes back in the fifties yes the sort of home you pass on to your ahm, to his children that is to say his son when he grows up of course if he, if you see what I mean Dan?

—Yes that's why I was surprised he was moving, the . . .

—Who was moving Dan, what . . .

—No I thought you were, aren't you? That moving van at your house right after lunch I . . .

—Probably just parked on the street there, nobody around us moving that I know of.

—No, no it was backed up to your house they were carrying things out, a stereo . . .

—Now wait a minute Dan let's yes let's just get this clear you saw a moving van at my look, those houses aren't all that different even the streets they, probably the same house a street or two over mine has the . . .

—The eagle yes and that chimney sticking up out of your . . .

—Ventilator Dan part of the shelter's generator-driven forced air system that what the hell do you mean carrying things out!

—And a big console television and, is something wrong? I could ride you over, my car's . . .

—No no mine's right out front here I'm, I don't believe it but what's happened already today I'm, where my keys . . . looming, slapping pockets like a man infested —must have left them in the car . . . and the inside door threatened its hinges.

—Ow . . . !

—Well get out of the way!

—Yes well what ahm, sorry Vern here, what are you doing out here.

—Me? Nothing Mister Whiteback I'm . . .

—And what's all this trash on the floor pick it up, is it yours? And you, what do you . . .

—I just came to ask when's rehears . . .

—There aren't any, there are no opera rehearsals they've been postponed you've been told that, even when there are you're not supposed to wear your costume to school you've been told that too, now . . .

—This ain' a costume Mister Whiteback it's my clothes.

—You call tails and horns and, and those reflectors you call that clothes? Your mother know you come to school like this?

—Who?

—Your mother, your mother!

—She's ugually asleep.

—If you come to school like this again you'll be sent home to wake her up. Now you, what are you doing here they weren't supposed to send you down, they said they were sending down that what's that boy's name, Percival . . .

—I don't know all I saw was Buzzie.

—That's the one yes the one you call Buzzie, where is he.

—I don't know, he sat here a second when they brought him in then he ran up the hall there.

—Well why didn't you, what were you sent down for.

—Well see Mister Whiteback I needed this here typewri . . .

—Playing with a school typewriter? do you know how much they cost?

—No I wasn't playing with it see I just had this here thing which I had to type it so . . .

—You'll take typing when you get to ninth grade, until then don't touch one again. Have you picked up all this trash you dropped?

—I couldn't help it I was just . . .

—Look ow, sorry Whiteback damn, Dan? still here? Can you give me that ride?

—I'm coming yes . . .

—My car, somebody stole my car right out front there. You out this way . . . ? they came down the corridor, pulled, pushed the doors —get over there fast but I still don't believe it . . . and behind them a hand severed a minute's remnant on the clock beyond the shelter of the lockers.

—Holy, look what time it is the bell's going to ring, didn't they finish that telephone booth yet?

—There's still this one guy there, boy did you just see my father hey?

—Did I see him he almost knocked me down, here . . .

—What's he so pissed off at.

—How do I know he said somebody stole his car here, hold this stuff a second while I, wait quick lend me a dime.

—What do you mean a dime look at all the quarters you . . .

—I need to make this call what do you think, I'm giving them fifteen cents extra free?

—Who you calling up, your buddy Major Sheets to tell him you got his forks stuck in the freight office which you're scared to go get them? Boy if Whiteback finds out . . .

—Why should he, I mean this deal's all fixed up and paid why should he find out anything unless the freight office calls them about all this here ammunition boy I never heard anything so dumb, I mean you get this rifle association to send you this here free ammunition which you haven't even got something to shoot it off with boy I never . . .

—Okay how did I know they'll send it by freight hey look, there goes the phone guy . . .

—Give me the dime then will you? he came up the range of lockers juggling his armload wrapped in a battered newspaper, dredging the handkerchief wad from his pocket —hurry up . . . he got in with the heap on his lap thumbing the pages of Alaska Our Wilderness Friend for a torn envelope with a telephone number, jammed the wad into the mouthpiece and dialed. —Hello . . . ? the door clattered closed —is Mister Bast there . . . ? Who me? I'm his, I'm this here business friend of his is he still at the city? See I have this urgent matter which I have to discuss my portforlio with him to . . . No I said I have this here urgent mat . . . he went where . . . ? No but look lady, he . . . no but holy . . . no but how could he be someplace accepting some reward see we have this here ouch, boy hello . . . ?

The line rang with three more piercing notes. —Mercy! they could burst an eardrum, hello? I said Mister Bast is abroad somewhere just a minute, Julia? The card that came yesterday with a picture of a mountain, where, hello . . . ?

—Who in heaven's name . . .

—Well I never! The oddest voice, it sounded like someone talking under a pillow. I thought he said he was a business friend of James, the most awful shrill sounds on the telephone line and then it sounded like a loud bell ringing and he simply hung up. I thought we asked Edward to have them take it out.

—No the stock Anne, the stock, we asked him to sell our telephone stock. Once that's done I may take it out myself.

—I hope he can find someone who wants to buy it though I must say, I'd feel a little bit guilty. It's like selling some poor soul shares in a plague, my ear is still ringing. Who was it that called here this morning.

—Some wretched woman who had a wrong number. She asked me to name the second president of the United States, when I told her Abraham Lincoln she congratulated me.

—Oh I think Lincoln came later, didn't he? When Uncle Dick came back from Andersonville prison . . .

—I'm certainly quite aware of that, I simply said Lincoln for a little joke but it didn't disturb her in the least. She told me I'd won a free dance lesson.

—It sounds like that woman who's called for Edward with an accent like the grocery boy's. Tell him Ann called about the strike, that's all she says and Ann, if you please. Tell him to look in this week's paper . . .

—It's probably someone from the union, they called last week sounding quite put out.

—Well I'm not surprised, they've been put out at James since the Chicago theater strike after the war.

—I certainly never blamed James for that, and after he had that tooth replaced he never did play quite the same.

—Now that was just something Thomas said, Julia, getting back at James for his remark about all those years Thomas practiced clarinet, that the reed had loosened something in his head. James' teeth never were right once Doctor Teakell weakened them.

—But Father thought he was an excellent dentist, what . . .

—I know he weakened my teeth Julia, it's almost a wonder I still have them he was doing it all in exchange, you know, for the lessons Father gave his son. He was Father's only student who appeared every week without two quarters, of course learning to play violin he couldn't very well . . .

—He could never have learned to play the kazoo, I remember Father saying that boy couldn't carry a tune in a bushel basket.

—Yes and Doctor Teakell put the blame all on Father, I have a lower here in back that's bothered me on and off for years. Whenever I feel it everything stops, I can hear that scraping on the violin and I wonder what's, what's become of them all sometimes I hear so many things, I hear Father's step out on the veranda when it gets dark and, like it is now and then I recall this house doesn't even have a veranda . . . and from far the wail of a siren rose as though brought into being by that concentration, rose and was lost until, unsought and unheard, it passed again close toward the break of another day.

—Julia! Come quickly!

—I wouldn't peer through the curtain that way, Anne. It puts me in mind of that awful woman who spread that gossip about Nellie and James, how the curtain would move when you passed her house and you knew she . . .

—But look! our hedge is gone!

—Why, it can't be! It can't be gone. I remember when Charlotte had it planted.

—See for yourself, it's just not there you can look right out across the road on that field of dahlias and, that car going by! Just staring in at us as though, it's like standing out in the yard stark naked we should call the police.

—What would we say. That they came at night and stole three hundred feet of privet hedge? so they'd have a place to park their cars for their bingo parties Wednesday nights?

—I'm afraid to think what James will say.

—James will say what he's always said, that money buys privacy and that's all it's good for.

—I think he just meant the hedge kept noise out, it certainly didn't stop those two dreadful women from the sisters of heaven knows what they called themselves. Marching right up here to the front door to say they'd heard the place was for sale.

—I don't think they dreamed of paying a penny, the stout one said she thought it was vacant. She stood there with one foot in the door just gaping right in over my shoulder and said what a nice room this would make for their teenage dances, of all things.

—Yes that's the way Father always put it, let them get one foot in the door . . .

—And the rooms upstairs could be used for games. They take such pride in being prolific, I imagine the sort of games they'd be. When I told her we had no notion of selling, she had the gall to go on and ask if we knew of any other old rundown houses they might fix up as a community project. I found it difficult even to be civil, it was all I could do to keep from asking how they'd like a troop of strangers prancing through their houses.

—I'm sure they'd like nothing better, Julia. From the pictures one sees of these pasteboard interiors they try to make every inch they own look as much like a public place as can be.

—Own! they don't own the shirts to their backs. They make a down payment and stay just long enough to vote in every desecration they can think of before they move on to do the same thing elsewhere, to leave behind the mess they've made for the people here who've been paying taxes for fifty years. There's hardly a tree left standing.

—I even miss the smell of cabbages there used to be this time of the year.

—I meant to order one yesterday, I thought we'd have that nice pork butt.

—It's a shame that we can't save it for Edward.

—We can't simply save it forever Anne, I'll just put it on. He might even appear, I think I heard a train just a minute ago . . . and clear the mile away the wind might bring its sound from the tracks when the wind lay right, blowing off the day and finally letting the darkness settle, and damp, for day to return like a rumor of day and lurk in the sky unable to break.

—Those acres of flowers, all of them black. Did you see what the frost did last night Julia?

—Well I wouldn't peer out through the curtain that way, we're naked enough as it is with the hedge gone.

—I still think it wouldn't hurt to call the police.

—After the mess they left things in right back here in James' studio? that night Stella's what's his name, Stella's husband went in and turned everything upside down for a scrap of paper he never found? Edward said things were flung every which way.

—Yes I meant to tell you, he called again.

—Edward?

—No that, Stella's husband, he sounded more confused than ever and finally put his little friend Mister Cohen on to say he'd heard nothing yet from Mister Lemp.

—I scarcely know what he expects to hear, he's the one who's making the difficulties with his prying questions about our shares, and all that talk about going public. Is that what they tried to start again?

—Selling some of Thomas' shares yes, just selling them to total strangers. I'm sure Thomas is turning in his grave right now.

—Well I shouldn't blame him a bit if he were, when that's all they'd been waiting for. Simply sitting there waiting for him to die so they could sell it right out from under us, to people we wouldn't even know in the street.

—I'm sure they'd know one another Julia. You never saw them in the trenches Father used to say, just let them have one foot in the door and . . .

—That name was changed from Engels somewhere along the way.

—Julia you don't think, those stock powers we signed and mailed back to these Crawley and Bro people Edward found? that they might use them to sell our shares and James'? They were blank after all, and there were so many . . .

—I'm sure they don't even know we have it. It's right out there in the kitchen drawer, I don't see how they could possibly sell it so long as it's in the kitchen drawer, Anne? If you're going out there you might turn the fire down under those beans. We'll just let them simmer overnight . . . from there, and then from room into room their aroma moved slowly, taking on a near tangible presence, finally mounting the stairs with the ease of the night and remaining, long after it had descended and gone.

—Anne? I thought perhaps the mail had come.

—It's on the shelf over the kitchen sink, I left it there when I tasted the beans. They do seem a trifle overdone but that was the way Father always . . .

—I thought I saw the newspaper somewhere.

—Yes that's the only thing I opened, I put it right under the, here it is. Did you see this picture of the old Lemp home? It looks like they've torn off the porte cochere to put up a monstrous kind of chute that's meant to serve as a fire escape now it's become a nursing home. Here, it says it's to speed the evacuation of residents who have trouble with stairs.

—Old Mrs Lemp walked with a stick of course, but I can't see her leaving like a bundle of laundry.

—And I don't see a word in here about Edward or the strike that woman called about, the one who calls herself Ann and told us to look in this week's paper.

—She called again yes wanting to speak with him, I suppose those are the chances one takes, going to teach in a place like that. It puts me in mind of James and his asylums, she seemed quite eager to find Edward something right in music as she put it, music therapy to rehabilitate criminals and handicaps, of all things.

—From the way she sounds on the telephone I'm sure she knows a number of both. Is that who called while I was sewing?

—No, no that was Stella, asking for Edward. She said she'd just called to see how he was getting along, and not a word about anything else.

—It's the things she doesn't say that disturb me.

—Yes I don't quite know why it is, I find even the sound of her voice disturbing, that almost languid, uncurious manner . . .

—I'm sure it's just that languorous way that makes her seem attractive to men, I recall her as such a high-strung child but after her marriage to this what's his name, he struck me as quite slow that first time I met him . . .

—And that scar of hers yes, now you speak of it someone said she'd had that thyroid operation simply in order to subdue, one might better say to match her pace to his . . .

—That does seem a lot of trouble to go to, why she wanted to marry him in the first place . . .

—I think it's perfectly obvious Anne, if there was any doubt it's quite clear now the reason he married her plain and simple was to gain this foothold in the company. Once he got those twenty-three shares out of Thomas he was in a position to step right in about the time Thomas became less active. Now with Thomas gone and no one to look after things we and James have only twenty-seven among us, and if Stella's to have all twenty-five or so from the estate they can bring this gang of strangers in and run it all however they please. Why else would she and that husband of hers have come out here turning things upside down, hounding Edward to kingdom come. He's just afraid that if Edward claims half they'll end up with something like thirty-five shares, we'd have almost forty with Edward's half and keep things in the family as Thomas intended.

—But Julia I don't think Edward . . .

—Let's not drag it all up again, I think we'd be wise just to keep our own counsel until we hear what James has to say.

—Well I'm not at all sure that Stella doesn't know more than she tells. The way she questioned us about Nellie's death . . .

—I'm afraid for one I've never doubted it, those stories about Nellie and James that woman spread right after the fair that summer up in Tannersville, the one with the tip of one finger missing there was only one way she could have learned them. I certainly don't want to see it dragged up again even if it costs us what's rightfully ours, though I must say I can't picture selling to strangers. It would be like selling the telephone stock, if these Crawley and Bro people find someone to buy them.

—Yes I think there was something in the mail from them Julia, I'll get it now when I look at the beans. There's enough of that nice pork butt left for dinner.

—It would be nice to get back what we paid, but heaven knows how likely that is the way the telephone behaves. Do you recall that half-witted boy who always drove the honey wagon? that rather alarming laugh he had? I hadn't thought of him all these years until I answered it this morning, someone sounding exactly like him who asked me to sing a Campbell's Soup jingle . . .

—Yes here it is Julia. I don't see a check, they've just sent us some sort of statement.

—It was just over four thousand dollars I think, I seem to recall that figure because . . .

—This just seems to say you sold, you bought spelled b o t. You sold, one thousand sixty-eight A T and . . .

—That can't mean shares Anne that's absurd. We sat right here with Edward and counted them out, I think there were a hundred and seventy some.

—At forty-four, it says it right here Julia and not a word about that mining stock. And then over here where it says you bot, five hundred Quaker Oats at twenty-nine, two hundred Ampex at twenty-two and an eighth, five hundred Diamond Cable at eighteen and a quarter, five hundred Detroit Edison at seventeen and three, Julia? Where are you going . . .

—It all just sounds like nonsense Anne I don't know where Edward finds these people, bought spelled b o t indeed. I'm just going up to the landing while it's still light, I want to make certain our trees are still out there. I'm sure I heard something . . .

—No I heard it too, it's just the branch outside my window. When the wind blows and whenever it rains . . .

—I think it's starting to rain right now . . . and streak mounted streak down clapboard and glass from gutters filled and sodden with leaves thrashed down in the dark from what apple limbs remained.

—Anne? was that you at the side door just now?

—At the back door Julia, the side doesn't open. I thought we might pick up some of those nice apples the wind brought down in the storm last night. Did I hear you on the phone just now?

—A lady called yes, asking for Edward. I can't imagine who it might have been.

—Not the one who calls herself Ann?

—Heavens no, this was a lovely contralto. I was certain I'd heard it somewhere before but the voice I was thinking of was Homer, Louise Homer when she did Gluck's Orfeo, she said she'd just called to thank him for something.

—She must be getting along in years, I wasn't even aware he knew her. I thought he might be out this weekend and ordered two nice chickens, they're here on the drainboard.

—I thought the mail might have come.

—Yes I'm bringing it in. This is all that came, perhaps you can make sense of it . . .

—Well, I never! It's a tax assessment for new sidewalk, three hundred feet of concrete sidewalk . . .

—I don't think we asked for a sidewalk, Julia.

—We most certainly did not but you know who did, to march to their Wednesday night bingo games, to parade right past our front door Sundays the women like housemaids in cheap new clothes and the little boys they dress like midgets with elastic neckties and fedoras, did you leave something on the stove Anne?

The curtain stirred. —I've never seen such heavy mist, I think the sun is breaking through but I never will get used to it, this feeling of everything out in the open, of everything out there coming in, over where frost killed those acres of flowers now it all just looks blacker than ever . . .

—I do smell something, I'm going to look.

—I think it's coming from outside, Julia. It's odd how even the faintest smell can suddenly bring the past to life, but we'd just been talking about James hadn't we, that summer up near Tannersville? when they tarred the roads . . . ?

—These two chickens out here you ordered, they've got one heart and three gizzards between them. It makes one wonder when even a chicken can't, Anne? did I hear you say Edward was coming?

—Julia . . . ? the sound of a siren rose closer, —Julia? I didn't hear you . . .

—I said is Edward coming?

—No . . . the curtain quivered, —all I see is the sun that makes a haze, and the grass looking wet . . . and the curtain fell still on the soaking lawns where apples laced in the grass hard as stones snared in seaweed imperiled passage toward the road stretching slick as a breakwater before the burst of the siren toward the highway, swept up the rutted shoulders flowing with rivulets into the flattened weeds forming a pool round the extinct washing machine gone to earth in the sanctuary of Primitive Baptist Church where woodbine renewed its attack on the locusts in the next lot, penetrating to the mangled saplings and torn trunks at the forward edge of the battleline fronting a hill of mud naked but for the protruding legs of a chair and the fluke of a toilet seat pointing on toward Burgoyne Street where the sky opened wide for the siren's shriek that

would have flung birds broadcast in the air when there were limbs to
fling them from, now merely added a note of cheer to White Christmas
already spilling from the bank, of adventure to the elderly venturing
from curbs and indoor hostages to Alaska Our Wilderness Friend alike,
even of fugitive relief from hopeless combat.

—Pardon . . . ? No I didn't hear what you . . . yes I couldn't hear you
a police siren just went by and ahm . . . oh you did? Yes well of course
they probably have more than one ahm . . . and yes doing a very fine job
that is to . . . I see yes no I'm not calling about your hedge no, no I called
once before to . . . sound like who . . . ? Yes well that must have been
someone else I . . . no I'm no, no I don't want you to sing the Campbell's
sou . . . pardon? No well yes of course I didn't mean to dist . . . I see yes
but I'm calling Mist . . . no no Mister Bast yes is he . . . Bast yes, b a
. . . no I'm sorry yes I'm sure you can spell it I didn't mean . . . Mister
Bast yes, is . . . oh he has? I see yes when do you expect him to . . . yes
well of course he . . . yes well I'm sure he deserves it of course he . . . yes
no this is a check yes I called to tell him we're putting through a new one
for the correct amount, I'm afraid he's been inconvenienced twice now
by our . . . No because yes we wouldn't want the Foundation to ahm, we
wouldn't want him to give the Foundation the impression we were
withholding funds provided by them for our . . . yes it's no no not another
award no this is in connection with his ahm, his services as composer in
. . . on Mozart's ahm, a very fine job that is to say yes his Mozart presentation created quite ahm, drew quite a response that is to say from ahm,
from other senior citizens that is to say regarding his ahm, regarding him
yes as our ahm, our Peter Pan of . . . Pan yes, Peter he . . . pardon? Maude
yes no I'm afraid I don't know a Maude Adams of course our present
enrollment is . . . that's very interesting yes, I . . . Yes I see but . . . it is
yes but I'm afraid I have someone at the door I . . . very fine job I'm sure
yes well goodbye, thank . . . Goodbye yes I'm sure they do excuse me,
come in . . . ? Yes well no I assure you I have a good many other things
to do here I'm . . .

—I'm sorry I didn't mean to inter . . .

—No no sit down Mrs Joubert I'm . . . pardon? Hello? yes goodbye
thank . . . good yes, bye . . .

—I don't want to interrupt you Mister Whiteback, I . . .

—Yes no it's a great pleasure to see your ahm, to see you that is to
say looking ahm, to see you back looking of course you always look quite
ahm, feeling as well as you look that is to . . .

—I'm quite well thank you I'm just still a little tired, I'm sorry I had
to be out but . . .

—Yes well no sit down we all have our ahm, Mister Gibbs conducted
your class that is to say doing a, did a very fine job of course he ahm, some
of his . . .

—I'm sure he did yes I must thank him, I just stopped in now about
this eighth grade field trip tomorrow. If it's . . .

—Saturday yes well of course there seem to have been some scheduling difficulties involving the transportation since your basketball game takes place on a Saturday and this trip to the ahm, the schedule's right here somewhere a museum I think it was yes the date was set for a Wednesday but apparently Mrs diahm, someone looked at last month's calendar and the ahm, this month Wednesday falls on a Saturday that is to . . .

—No that's perfectly all right Mister Whiteback I don't mind the Saturday, all I wanted to ask you see I'm going into town now, and I hoped rather than coming back out I might simply . . .

—Yes well no that should ahm, now? No no I don't think they can ahm, here's the schedule yes they can't ahm . . .

—No I meant if I might simply meet them somewhere in town tomorrow, when they get into town? Unless the problem of taking them in on the train is a . . .

—Yes well of course they're not taking the ahm, they're taking buses that is to say the last time we used the train there seems to have been one less youngster coming back out than ahm, yes well that was your trip wasn't it you don't happen to remember the number of youngsters that ahm, of tickets that is to . . .

—I don't offhand no but, but you don't mean a child may have been . . .

—Yes well no we probably would have heard from a parent by now but of course these days you can't always excuse me, hello . . . ? Yes just a minute Leroy where's, yes here if you just take this schedule Mrs Joubert you can ahm, I can tell them you'll meet them at ahm, whatever it says there yes . . .

—Thank you I do appreciate . . .

—Yes well thank you for ahm, for coming in Mrs Joubert excuse me, hello . . . ? Yes excuse me I have someone on the other phone here, hello Leroy . . . ? But what happened to them that many, even that many picnic forks can't just disap . . . yes but where transshipped where, who auth . . . I know it said six J yes she just left I meant to ask her what . . . no well then do they know where the rest of the shipment went that never got here in the first pla . . . No I know it, I know we never found them in the budget that's why they must have something to do with the cafeteria lunch program, if it looks like we're turning down a federal subsidy they might withhold funds like they're threatening on the milk if this Coke machine's installed in the . . . What . . . ? No now wait a minute just tell him to wait a minute Leroy, we . . . no there's nothing in the curriculum that calls for brake linings unless Vogel of course ahm, how many . . . How many? No well even Vogel couldn't use that many bra . . . No I'm not coming down to the freight office no, you . . . no well that can't . . . no now wait a minute, what caliber . . . ? No well that's no, no we don't even have a rifle club unless of course the government is ahm, yes well just tell them to . . . no no I don't want to talk to Agent Teets no just tell him to . . . no I have someone waiting on the other phone here just tell him to, to hold everything there I have somebody at the door, yes . . . ?

—Is this here rehears . . .

—There is no rehearsal no! I said you'd hear it announced in home-room, close the door behind you. And wash your face, hello . . . ? Oh yes no I'm sorry Father I didn't mean . . . I saw it yes I was just ahm, just going to call you about it myself could you hold on just a moment? I have another call here I'm, hello . . . ? Gottlieb? just hold on a minute I have Father Haight on the other phone here about the . . . yes. Hello, Father? Yes about all that fine publicity you had on the blessing ceremonies for your new plumbing facilities of course we . . . pardon? Yes yes no your new tv facilities of course that's what I . . . yes of course I'm aware you have plumb . . . Yes yes I realize your brother and the Archbishop would have made the front page if it hadn't been for the accident but of course we didn't arrange . . . one of yes well of course the boy was one of our ahm, our youngsters yes but of course the condition he was in when he ran out of the building here was ahm, we . . . no yes of course we didn't no he wasn't ahm, wasn't in our driver training program that is to say I think one of his classmates said he'd learned from a comic book but of course Major Hyde didn't . . . he is on our school board yes Father but I'm sure that had nothing to do with . . . that he was instrumental in installing your cable facilities yes I'm sure if he promised it would be on the front page he had every intention of ahm, no intention at all that is to say of taking over the front page himsel . . . as soon as he gets out of the hospital yes Father I'm sure he . . . I'm sorry your brother feels that way Father, I'm sure Maj . . . that he's a retiring general yes I'm sure Major Hyde is aware of that Fa . . . I will yes Fa . . . yes yes thank you for calling Father. Hello? Gottlieb? Yes that was Haight on the other line he . . . no no Father Haight down to the parochial school, he said his brother who's leaving the Army had made a great effort to attend their dedication and deserved something better than being tucked back on page seven because the whole front page was taken over by . . . his statement about wanting to continue to serve in however humble a position yes that he's ahm, looking for a job that is to say yes he . . . Yes no I wouldn't call Vern about it no I'm sure he wouldn't want to ahm, he's so upset about all the blacktopping he's liable to . . . just the lawns yes, all . . . yes well all the trees too that is to say Parentucelli said he couldn't get his equipment in unless they were out of the way and so of course he . . . to get the whole job done in that one afternoon that is to say yes so of course when Vern got home he . . . yes well of course it's just one of those little misunderstandings like our French doors opening the wrong . . . yes who Ganganelli? The town board meeting on this Flo-Jan hearing for leasing the town dock yes, they . . . twelve hundred a year with a five-year lease and option to, someone at the door here, yes?

—Sorry, I didn't mean to . . .

—No that's all right yes come in Gibbs I'm just ahm, this phone line to the bank that is to say hello . . . ? Yes I haven't heard anything on it no, no Dan was going to feel his wife out but of course he's in no position to ahm, to feel anyone up right now that is to . . . no but of course we can't embarrass Fedders he has the union ahm, war chest down to the bank in deposit certificates and of course he's directed the purchase of mortgages through the bank in their pension fund so that ahm, ahm yes I'd better talk to you about this later down to the bank if . . . yes if there's any question of Ace Transport defaulting on that loan of course we . . . what? Glancy did . . . ? Yes but of course right now Glancy's credit is ahm, how did he finance the . . . yes well of course if you sold him a new Cadillac they must have looked into his ahm, if he's driven it out of the showroom that is to . . . down to the bank yes, come down to the bank. Yes now, Gibbs?

—Sorry to bother you with this Whiteback, just a small matter of money I . . .

—That yes I'm glad you remembered it ten ahm, yes ten dollars and forty cents? I wrote it down somewhere yes the money we disahm, reimbursed the boy who turned in those train tickets just a matter of bookkeeping of course but I'm glad you ahm, you have it there?

—Matter of fact . . . digging in pockets he'd come up with a crumpled cigarette, —that's not . . .

—Yes well of course excuse me, hello . . . ? Oh Mister Stye yes I . . . no I'm not at the bank now no, no I . . . oh I see you're at the bank yes could you hold a minute? I have another, hello . . . ? Well what are you doing still at the freight office, I said just to tell them to . . . you mean just now? It all arrived just now . . . ? Yes well no they'll just have to find a place to store them until we . . . because we can't set up all these appliances there without moving all the teaching equipment that's already . . . no because Dan's still out from the accident and I can't do anything without his, hold on a minute Leroy I've got Mister Stye on the other line about the stolen baseballs just . . . I know it's your dime yes just, just say we'll call Monday and hang up then. Yes hello Mister Stye? yes, yes about the stolen baseballs but Mister, Major Hyde you remember Major Hyde wanted to talk with you sometime too about this empty ahm, empty slot coming up on the school board, he . . . no not his empty slot, no he should be out of the hospital in another day or so, yes . . . yes he was sitting in the death seat I think you call it in the insur, the phrase they used in the paper that is to say beside the driver, sitting beside Mister diahmCephalis when the car hit them and . . . oh you do? Yes, yes I do too I have another call waiting, thank you for ahm . . . Hello? Oh. Yes well when I gave your newspaper the statement after it happened of course we weren't aware that the boy who was ahm, who was killed that is to say stealing the car, that he was ahm . . . pardon? Oh yes now of course we've ahm, Miss Waddams, our school nurse Miss Waddams has instituted urine tests right down the, down through the third grade that is to say for the detection of ahm, of drugs, any sort of drugs down through the . . . pardon? They hung up. Yes now what was it you were talking about? those ahm, railroad tickets yes . . .

—No what I stopped in for Whiteback was ah, I just wanted to ask you how I'd go about getting a small advance.

—Oh well ahm, oh, on your ahm . . .

—Salary, yes.

—Oh well of course ahm, well the state that is to say Mister Gibbs the ahm, teachers' salaries are ahm, of course if you came down to the bank we might work something out on your car in terms of ahm, of a loan, a car loan that is to . . .

—I don't have one.

—No that's what I mean, yes, we could probably arrange one, a loan that is to . . .

—No a car. An automobile that is to say, I don't have one.

—A car? You don't have a car? Yes well of course no one can ahm, I'm sure we can arrange something for you down to the bank so you can get one Glancy, Glancy after all, did you hear that? On the telephone, that was Gottlieb down to the Cadillac agency he just sold one to Glancy, of course if you . . .

—Listen, no, I don't want a Cadillac, I don't want a car, I don't want to buy a car I just, all I need is a small advance on my salary, just . . .

—Yes well the ahm, with a car of course you could excuse me, hello? Oh. Yes it is . . . Yes we do, he . . . yes and doing a very fine job, he . . . he what? Oh, I see . . . Oh . . . I see. Yes well the, yes someone from the school of course, as soon as we . . . yes tell him as soon as we can yes, goodbye.

—Never mind it Whiteback, I . . .

—Yes that was the ahm, have you got a few minutes Gibbs?

—What is it, I've got a train I . . .

—Yes that was the police they ahm, Coach, Vogel, Coach Vogel that is to say, you know him, you know him? I mean of course you could identify him that is to ahm, that police flyer telling the youngsters to, I have one right here somewhere yes, report any stranger who tries to join you in your play, do not play near public ahm, Coach was passing that field down near Hyde's ahm, Major Hyde's shelter this policeman thought looked like a public ahm, convenience I think he said and Coach stopped to join in their, throw the ball around with them that is to say and one of them, youngsters who don't know him of course one of them called the police and they ahm, you know him of course? Coach? They just want someone to identify him so they can ahm, have you got a few minutes?

—Be glad to yes, can you drive me over?

—Yes well I was just ahm, I have to get over to the bank that is to say there was something I ahm, I'll come out with you yes these complaints that is to say Gibbs, opening class without the ahm, the proscribed openings we've had some complaints through this new citizens' group you probably know them yes let me lock this door, after those baseballs of course you probably . . .

—Certainly do yes who are they, the Ku Klux Klan?

—Who this ahm, this citizens' group yes no they, it's the Citizens Union on Neighborhood Teaching yes they . . .

—All women?

—Yes well no I don't know of course I wouldn't laugh no, no they're quite serious about their ahm . . .

—Their proscribed openings yes never knew one that wasn't, how about the Constitution. Next time I have homeroom I'll start things off reading the Constitution how's that.

—Yes well that sounds ahm, of the United States that is to say yes that certainly sounds like a proscribed ahm, of course the last thing we want right now is any cause for dissension that is to say all you've done for the ahm, taking on Mrs Joubert's class in addition to your own in terms of ahm . . .

—She's back yes, she's back isn't she?

—Yes but of course she doesn't look, quite a striking looking woman but of course these doors open out don't they yes, of course in terms of her health that is to say if we had to let her go it wouldn't cause a problem because she hasn't got her certificate none of the right credits in ahm, she studied in some foreign country where they don't have it yes I think she has a master's in French civilization which of course doesn't ahm, educationwise for teaching sixth grade social studies doesn't really do the ahm, doing a fine job of course there she is now yes quite a striking looking . . .

—There? Christ no that's . . .

—Yes no that's Mrs ahm, Dan's wife yes I think I'll go this way, my car's right around the ahm, you were going to the police station?

—I have an idea, Whiteback. Why don't you just stop in and identify Vogel yourself, save you the trouble of driving me all the way over.

—Yes well ahm, yes of course that does make things simpler . . .

—Just get my train then . . . and he turned a heel in the gravel, —sorry . . .

—Oh Mister, Mister Gibbs? I'm . . .

—Dan's wife yes . . . he sidestepped, —I was sorry to hear about it.

—About what, oh his accident you mean . . . she came on beside him —Jack? Don't people call you Jack?

—Yes occasionally they . . .

—I thought you might have seen Mister Bast Jack, the young composer we had here he doesn't seem to be anywhere.

—Maybe after that rather, that remarkable lesson on Mozart he may have arranged some sort of hasty sabbatical.

—I'll tell you who arranged a hasty sabbatical for him, the same ones who sabotaged his lesson they . . .

—Did you see it?

—Jack I didn't have to see it, the minute they see talent and sensitivity they sabotage it and call it technical it's not just him they're after it's all of us, anybody creative scares them Jack, maybe you don't know it but they're after you too because you're talented and creative I can tell by your hands . . . she seized the one nearest her leaving the curb —just your fingers, the strength of character in your thumb look . . .

—Yes I, I've seen it . . . but he did look down, slipping its length from her peristaltic grasp as though relieved to see it again —I'm sorry I, I have to get the train Mrs di . . .

—No Ann, Ann. Jack? because I know, because I'm a talented woman who's never been allowed to do anything Jack? I'll be home later, maybe we could get together and talk?

—Yes but I'll be, I may not be back out at all I . . .

—As late as you want yes Dad, Dan's Dad lives with us but they're in bed by nine Jack . . . ? pursued him round the turn, —maybe we can talk . . . ? digging in pockets to come up with a cigarette packet, empty, crumpled and flung as he made the steps to burst out on the platform above where a length of train moaned and fell still and then, in total silence as he ran toward it, moved. The platform narrowed with his pursuit, rapping on the glass in the door at what might have been a face through the encrusted filth when all at once the door, all the doors flew open, and he staggered on as though the train's momentum had become his own in the squeal of its halt, searching a clean handhold slipping past the serge shine of the conductor's back and up an aisle through planes of smoke grabbing, as the train lurched forward, at the corner of a seat, disturbing, enough only to bring her eyes half up from vacancy and limn her profile the woman seated there as he fell back, ducked to retrieve a rolled newspaper jammed in a seat hinge and sidled with it raised before his face toward the door and the car beyond.

—Your ticket?

—Ah? He lowered New York's picture newspaper.

—Oh Jesus.

—Ah! Wie geht's!

—Okay look, just give me your ticket.

—Ja, ich bin es, beide Hälften, nicht? He was digging in pockets with enthusiasm. —Für den Kopf, ja? und . . . he thrust out a battered cardboard square, —und . . .

—Look, if you can't speak English how come you're reading American newspaper?

—Ah, die Zeitung? He flourished it, digging with his free hand,

—amerikanische Kunst, ja? Schwarze Kunst, grausig . . . he came abruptly forward with a lurch of the train, aiming an index finger at his temple, thumb cocked, —das Blut! der Krieg! And he straightened back, rolling eyes settled in a leer, plumbing a closed hand with the length of a finger, —geschlechtlicher Umgang! Scheisserei . . . !

—For Christ sake just give me the other ticket.

—Für den Unterkörper . . . he was digging again, —ja . . .

—And let the lady get by.

—Oh I, ja die ah . . . he came up with another battered cardboard, —das Hinterteil nicht vergessen eh? he leered cupping from behind the curve of Mrs Joubert's skirt as she got past and through the door to the next car, where he turned and threatened a handshake, —danke, danke . . . and got it closed after them before he spoke again. —Hello I, I didn't ah, see you . . .

—What in the world was all that? she asked, down the aisle of empty seats.

—Oh the ah, the conductor, yes . . . he sank into the seat beside her. —A young German boy, hasn't been over here very long and I've sort of befriended him, sort of try to encourage him. It's his first job over here and he's sort of ah, gets sort of discouraged sometimes.

—Oh I see.

—Yes you can't really blame him can you, passing a scene like that day after day . . . he gestured across her where broken fence enclosing a fleet of rusting bus hulks fled past the dirty pane, tried to cross a knee and gave it up. —How any normally constructed human being can get comfortable in these . . .

—Here, let me move my bag, she said and, doing so, —oh, you've torn your pocket.

—Well I . . . he straightened up piecing it together, pulled the flap over the tear —damn it, did it on that door trying to make this God damned train.

—It's late, we sat there at the platform for hours, she said. —Every time the train started all the doors opened and we stopped again. I thought I saw you on the platform, running.

—Oh?

—And you came into that car up ahead?

—Oh well the, oh, oh yes the smoker, yes I got in there and found I didn't have any cigarettes. He slumped further in the seat beside her, his elbow over the back of it and his hand that close to her shoulder. —You don't smoke?

—I do sometimes.

—I meant, you don't happen to have any cigarettes with you now, do you?

—I'm afraid not . . . She'd opened the bag on her lap, bending over it, thrust back her hair and he stared along the line of her cheekbone as though seizing this sudden opportunity to study this close the meticulous care in her makeup. —No . . . she looked up square at him and he dropped his eyes to his own hand, and a nail that might have been cleaner. —I'm sorry, I don't . . . she had out a pair of tinted glasses and he dropped his eyes again, from her long fingers there putting them on, to her knee, and cleared his throat. —You come into New York quite often, don't you, she said.

—To get away from that place? I certainly do.

—Is that all? just, to get away?

—Well I, no, no today I'm coming in to, I have an appointment to, coming in to see a publisher yes . . .

—You're writing a book? she turned sharply, caught her glasses against his dangling hand.

—Yes but it's still, it's not finished I'm . . .

—A novel?

—Not a, no no it's more of a book about order and disorder more of a, sort of a social history of mechanization and the arts, the destructive element . . .

—It sounds a little difficult, is it?

—Difficult as I can make it.

—Oh? she drew her knees close as he tried again to cross a leg, —you do have trouble with seats don't you.

—Seats?

—The day in that cafeteria after that field trip when you . . .

—Had trouble with more than seats yes, wasn't really one of my better days . . .

—I hope not.

—No but listen when we left there in the cab I didn't mean . . .

—It's all right no, I got where I was going but you know you really were quite unkind to that young man Mister Bast, talent doing what it can? and those who can't, teach? and turning everything upside down he tried to say about, who was it Bizet? All he wanted from you was encouragement, he . . .

—Bast? from me? All he talked about was . . .

—Himself of course, the things he's doing because I'd asked him, that was all. He's so young and earnest so, just such a romantic I suppose, he's really quite dear I hope you've seen him and told him you were sorry?

—Well I, matter of fact . . .

—I've felt badly about it, I've tried to call him once or twice to thank him for bringing the class back out. I felt so foolish when I found those tickets in my bag I, you did give them to him didn't you?

—Matter of fact . . . he'd finally got one knee wedged over the other looking deliberately slumped, a foot dangling in the aisle, as flags, pennants and used cars, beer by the case, hero sandwiches, Dunkin Donuts fled past the window opposite —I meant to yes I, somehow I thought I had but things got a little confused . . .

—But you did get the right train didn't you? You told me you would . . .

—Thought I had yes, but . . . he was unlimbering his leg, digging in pockets to come up with an assortment of battered cardboard —keep finding them in my . . .

—Oh honestly, now I feel simply terrible about it he must have had to pay all those fares himself, I know he couldn't afford it and whatever's become of him . . .

—Just coming to that, yes . . . he separated a soiled square of white from Win Third Race, half fare, —found it on the floor in the Post Office.

—But, what in the world. Business representa, representive? It must be a, some sort of . . .

—Lackawanna four phone number must be somewhere in midtown but . . .

—But is he, have you called? do you know . . .

—Haven't needed a business representive no, what . . .

—But how, how odd I thought he, he was going to spend all his time composing I thought he was working on a, music for some dancers a ballet or something, that that's why he left teaching . . .

—You didn't see his maiden venture on the, his little presentation on Mozart did you.

—No, no someone mentioned it but . . .

—Strayed a little from the curriculum you might say, rather White-back might say, that probably had a little more to do with his leaving teaching the minute they see talent and sensitivity they sabotage it and call it tech . . .

—Oh honestly you're not going to start that again that, just taunting him as though he . . .

—Look no Christ I'm just, don't you know when I, when someone takes a ridiculous situation and just tries to . . .

—But that's all you do . . . she snapped her skirt tight at the knee straightening against the seat's discomfort. —Isn't it? without turning —well? isn't it?

—All right look I, all I meant was the whole thing's ridic, out of proportion that appalling diCephalis woman, do you know her?

—I don't think so but . . .

—Ann, she's sort of you in a cheap edition, twentieth printing of the paperback when things begin to smear . . .

—No I think I did get something from her in my box, about a strike?

—Because they're after all of us yes, sabotaging your friend Mister Bast because anything creative scares them. They're after me too because I'm talented and creative, she could tell by my hands almost took my thumb with her, she . . .

—You do have marvelous hands though.

—What? I . . . he stared at hers resting half opened on her knee, hitched himself higher in the seat —doubt if that's the reason they're after me though.

—Well of course they're not, why should they be.

—A little scuffle I had with that Major Hyde idiot on the school board, friend of mine had an accident and he was there when they called he, he said something stupid and I lost my temper that's all.

—But how could, what sort of accident would . . .

—You don't want to hear about it.

—I only meant . . .

—You don't want to hear it! he slumped again, his hand on the seat's back just touching her hair —I'm sorry I, it's just something you don't have to hear, somebody who goes through some bad periods I guess we all know somebody like him, talk him out of suicide till the day one of you finally dies in bed like talking to yourself most of the time . . .

—But he, is he all right now?

—In the hospital coming out of it, out of this last one as all right as he ever is he's one of these, one of those men who wanted to write and had a father who thought writing was for sissies, made a million dollars in timber and Schramm's spent the last twenty years just waiting for him to die, when he finally did well, there's Schramm. The only time he was ever really alive was the war, he was a tank commander in the Ardennes and when it was all over he just never could quite, he has some bad periods that's all and coming up against the insensitive stupidity of somebody like Hyde I just, just let go . . .

Bent over her bag again, —I think I have a Hyde boy in my class, she said slipping off the glasses, —is he . . .

—Same military caste yes, he's your class fire marshal in fact, about the most unpromising human being that size I've ever come across keep stumbling over him with that grubby boy he hangs out with over in the Post Office, they're moving in.

—Oh that's J R probably, I think they send for things in the mail together. Cosmetic samples if you can imagine . . . and all the smile that lit her eyes was as suddenly gone again behind the tinted glass. —There's something a little touching about him, I think.

—About as touching as a bull shark.

—No this other little boy I meant, J R he's so, he always looks as though he lives in a home without, I don't know. Without grownups I suppose, like he simply lives in those clothes of his.

—Probably does, have you ever seen him when he wasn't scratching himself somewhere?

—Oh I know yes, I have felt he doesn't bathe often but, no there's something, something else, when you talk to him he doesn't look at you but it's not as though, not like he's hiding something. He looks like he's trying to fit what you're saying into some utterly different, some world you don't know anything about he's such an eager little boy but, there's something quite desolate, like a hunger . . . she turned to him abruptly —you, you must have been awfully small . . .

—Small? I, what these half fare tickets? just told you they . . .

—Don't be silly no, no I meant young, when you went away to that boarding school you must have been awfully young, coloring leaves and . . .

—I was five.

—Five that's, that is terribly young isn't it, were you . . .

—In the way, that's all.

—But I'm sure that's not . . .

—Not what, kids are in the way that's how they're all brought up now, do a good enough job on them it can last for life just look at the, what's the matter . . .

—Nothing.

—But I don't . . .

—Please! she'd turned away, pressed the tinted glasses closer —I'd just, I remembered you talking about going away to school in the fall and, and bringing in leaves to color . . .

—I always found brown ones . . . he sank lower in the corner of the seat, —been in the way since the day I could walk.

A train passed from the opposite direction with an enveloping shock and was gone, the door up ahead banged half open, half closed to the sway of the car past billboards, unfinished apartments Now Renting, another vacant platform, diaper service trucks marshaled against the day to come. —Do you stay in? she asked finally, —in town I mean? for the weekend?

—Will if I can get through Friday.

—But it's almost over isn't it.

—Friday? No it's, I mean this is . . .

—It's Friday, we had our Friday morning quiz on . . .

—Can't be . . . he came up straight —can't be, wait . . . he was twisting, digging the newspaper from the seat hinge —look.

—But it's yesterday's.

—But wait, wait, he was tearing through back pages, —if the, here. Christ. T'd Off and Marry Me God damn it, yes, that was yesterday's double.

—It what?

—The daily double at Aqueduct yesterday, God damn it how could I have . . .

—And that's why you're upset? you missed betting on a race?

—No! it's . . . he flung the newspaper to the floor and as abruptly caught his hand in air as though, too late to have it back, he realized that with it he'd flung the cool of hers which had enclosed it just that instant.

—God damn it. Her hands lay lightly folded on her lap. —You're sure you
don't have a cigarette? maybe a loose one in the bottom of your bag?

And she snapped it open, bent over it again. —No I'm sorry, but
wait . . .

—You do?

—No but here's a pin. For where your coat's torn. You shouldn't be
so upset about this appointment, she went on, pulling the tear together,
—but I'm glad it's so important to you. There, she straightened the
pocket flap and sat away, —but I wish it were a novel.

—Why would you say that, he muttered.

—The way you look, she said not looking.

—Like a novelist? Only problem is a novelist has to understand
women.

—You don't?

—Apparently not, from all the . . . turned full to share her smile he
found it gone, only her eyes wide through the lenses. —What's the matter.

—I wish you hadn't said that, she said looking away as quickly.

—What?

—I hope it's not true.

—But, but what . . . And he stared a moment longer, but with such
concentration he might have been, given this final opportunity, trying to
commit to memory for all time each delicate convolution of her ear, the
lobe barely large enough to support the whirl of gold that pierced it.
—There, you see? he slumped further, brought his hands up to draw
them down his face and got that knee wedged over the other again
—if I wrote a novel it would end where most novels begin.

—But this book you're working on, is it . . .

—Is it what it's, it's like living with an invalid real God damned
terminal case, keep hoping he'll pick up his bed and walk like the good
book says.

—If you feel that way maybe you should just, can't you put it aside
until . . .

—Till what! till I come out like Schramm? he brought his foot in,
wedging it into the hinge of the seat ahead —marching around the room
quoting Tolstoy's something terribly lacking between what I felt and
what I could do suddenly throws his pencil, sharp pencil with an eraser
on it bounces back and goes right into his eye . . . there was a pull at his
side, her arm coming up, —is that . . .

—Why did you tell me that.

—What, I . . .

—No please, never mind . . .

—But . . .

—Please . . . ! she'd snapped her bag open for her handkerchief,
brought it up turned toward apartments Fully Rented, a laundry displaying a stopped clock, cars queued at a traffic light.

—I, Amy? he freed his foot, hitched himself up in the seat again —I wanted to ask you something I, one day when I was in Penn station, I was in a phone booth and you brushed right past me and a boy . . .

—I'd just rather not talk for a few minutes . . . she snapped the bag closed on her handkerchief, squared the tinted glasses on her face again as the train drained to a halt at another platform and he sank in the seat beside her getting a knee crossed and that foot back in the aisle brushed by a passing trouser leg black serge all the way up to the round collar, easing into the seat in front of them.

—Well Christ.

—What . . .

—Why in the, why do people do this? Look, the whole front end of the car is empty, the whole God damned car is practically empty and he comes and sits right . . .

—Shhh . . .

—No why do people do it! Go into a lunchroom and sit at an empty counter some idiot comes in and sits one stool away, what is it? Twenty empty stools and he'll sit right down beside you, what . . .

—Please . . .

He wiped a hand down his face and sank lower, knee thrust more sharply into the seat ahead and eyes on the serge elbow draped over it close enough to bite, it shook, ruffling a newspaper, and the buildings on both sides began to swarm with fire escapes, rising from sight as they dropped in a culvert, dropping back as they rose, until the tunnel enclosed them like a blow. Lights came on, and ahead the door clattered open on the young conductor and closed behind him, down the aisle calming the mustache wisp with a finger tip, brushing the protruding shoe, eliciting a muttered —heil!

—He doesn't seem awfully friendly, she said, —after all your efforts.

—Well my, my German isn't too good, he may . . .

—I'm sure it's much better than his.

He got his knee out of the seat, straightening up. —What do you mean.

—That I know he isn't a poor German boy, over here with his first job.

—Then why did you . . .

—I talked to him last week about train times.

—When I told you that then, why didn't you . . .

—I don't know. Why did you?

—I just, sometimes . . . he ground one hand in the other, suddenly brought it up to seize her shoulder —listen could we, later can I see you later, for dinner if you're free for dinner . . . and he stood, stepped aside for her, caught her elbow as the train lurched at the platform —when you've done your errands I mean, if you're free . . .

—I, I don't know . . .

—Listen because there are some things I, if you could meet me

. . . he came on up the aisle behind her —we could, that awful cafeteria around seven I'll wait there for you there's a place, a French place where we could have dinner it's not far . . . he caught her arm again on the platform, —look I'll wait there for you anyhow if you don't come I'll just, just get the next train . . .

—You'd better hurry and make your call, she said already a step away, —I'm sure they won't mind about the appointment . . .

—Yes but, around seven . . . ?

—I, I'll try . . . she was already far from reach —and Jack . . . ? beyond the vacant wonder of a woman lost with a suitcase, —your book? and beyond the weaving approaches of a sailor lost in uniform —I hope it's true . . . ?

—Excuse me, sir?

—Look sailor I'm in a hurry . . . he brushed past sorting bits of cardboard for the coin he found there making for a wall phone niched in plastic, thrust it in and dialed.

—But sir . . .

—Look beat it, will you? Hello . . . ? Yes listen I just got off the train I . . . Yes I know it is! I . . . because I thought this was Thursday till a minute ago I . . . but couldn't you just call and change her dentist appointment? wouldn't she . . . No, no I'm not asking you to make your plans to suit my convenience but just this . . . Well listen if she's standing right out there at the bus stop waiting for you could you call her in for just a . . . Yes I know she wanted to show it to me herself, that's why I'm trying to . . . all right. All right! I'm sorry it didn't fit, I saw it in a window and thought it was something she'd . . . what? Well then get them for her, if she needs them get them and send me the . . . Well what the hell happens to the money I do send you . . . All right! It comes to you through welfare because that's the way the court set it up who took it to the God damned court! Do you think it's any less humiliating for me to . . . I don't either but listen. Just let me ask you this. What time will you get her back from the dentist? I could still come out and . . . All right then listen, could you call her in from the bus stop for just a . . . what? No but maybe just once, just once in your life just once in your selfish, miserable God damned life you could . . .

—Hey, sir?

He smashed it down on the hook. —What the hell do you, look if you need money I haven't got it, I've got one God damned dollar left here and . . .

—No sir I got my whole pay here, I just need some change to call up my . . .

—So do I that's where I'm going, now . . .

—Hey sir . . . ? came after him bursting through doors to the pavement —could I go with you then . . . ?

—Don't give a God damn where you go, he came on down one curb, up the next bumped left, right by elbows, muzzled umbrellas, a yellow fender, finally through the whirl of a revolving door toward where it said desserts to thrust the crumpled bill under the glass and recover a spray of nickels bumping chairs, tables, coming up with a handful of cardboards for the one soiled white as he sank into the booth and dialed, a foot braced up against its open door eyed across an empty coffee cup drummed by a finger sporting a cat's eye ring, shaken by the abrupt departure of an expanse of print dress for the next booth with the hasty removal of an earring, the clatter of the door. —Hello . . . ? I'm calling a Mister Bast, is this his . . .

—Just a minute . . . came at his ear, —I'll see if Mister Bast got back yet . . . echoed somewhere beyond his foot as the door of the next booth shuddered open. —Mister Bast? Is Mister Bast here . . . ?

—Hello, Miss . . . ? he came slowly forward lowering the phone.

—Hello? No Mister Bast didn't get back to the office yet. You want me to say who called?

—It's just a, a personal call . . . by now he was half out of the booth, —do you . . .

—He went away on this business trip but he should be back any time now, do you . . .

—Miss . . . ? he reached round to tap the floral prospect bulging from the next booth —you wouldn't happen to . . .

—Did you want to leave him a message?

—Say, Madam . . . ? he reached in —look I'm standing right here . . . and he pulled his arm back as the doors crashed closed.

—Look buddy . . . the cat's eye tapped him from behind, —can't you see she's on the phone?

—What? Thanks a lot . . . he grabbed the phone left dangling behind him —hello . . . ? Sorry yes, I was calling Mist . . . yes but do you expect him back today? This is a pers . . . No look frankly I called to see if he could advance me ten dol . . . I don't expect to bump into him no, that's why I'm call . . . Fine yes, he should call in for an urgent message about an appointment with his boss tomorrow look why the hell do you think I'm calling him if I . . . hello?

—Hey sir . . . ?

—Now look sailor I'm about at the end of my, wait got a cigarette? The next booth clattered open on its floral emergency —thanks I can light it! he came up with two more nickels to dial again —now beat it will you sailor? Things are getting, hello? Mister Eigen please, in . . . no Eigen, Thomas Eig . . .

—Hey sir?

—God damn it will you, hello? No, no in public relations, Eigen, e, i . . .

—But hey sir? Your shoelace is on fire.

—I said beat it! bugger, what the . . . he had a foot up, slapping it —bugger off! God damn it what, Eigen? Tom . . . ?

Silence came summoned in the snap of a button to suffuse the line.

—You have a call on two nine, Mister Eigen.

—Tell them I can't, no never mind. Hello . . . ? Oh, Gibbs? Jack? I thought you'd call yesterday when you . . . oh. I can't, I can let you have ten though, if you . . . your shoelace what . . . ? Look Jack I'll have to call you back, things here are . . . What key, to Ninety-sixth Street? No if you've lost yours . . . well borrow mine then come down after work, down . . . no down to the apartment I'll go straight home, I have to pack for . . . What? No I have to go to Germany tomorrow, one of these damned . . . No but come down for a drink, I have to talk to you about Schramm anyhow before I leave, he's . . . I can't go into it now, he's been giving them a rough time and they may release him before I get back, so you've got to . . . No he knows he's lost the eye, they told him . . .

—Mister Eigen? Mister Davidoff is on two seven.

—Jack? I've got another call, I've got to . . . hold on then, give Florence your number and I'll call you right back . . . Hello? Yes this is . . . Miss Bulcke? Is Mister Davidoff calling me on . . .

—Mister Eigen! Mister Eigen, quickly!

—What . . .

—Mister Eigen there's this man out here you've got to come out, he says he wants to see you he's shouting at Carol and he's, there's this dirty bandage all over his face and he can hardly . . .

—Yes yes wait Christ, excuse me Miss Bulcke just a moment, Florence? What's the, call back the man who was on two nine and . . .

—He went off Mister Eigen, he said something about his shoelace but quickly, this man's going to . . .

—Yes yes I'll be right there, let me just . . . hello? Miss Bulcke, will you tell Mister . . .

—Hello. Hello? Mister . . .

—Eigen?

—Mister Eigen? Mister Davidoff is . . .

—Eigen you on deck there? I want, oh and Miss Bulcke call Colonel Moyst and tell him we'll send a messenger down to hand carry Mister Eigen's orders, he needs them tonight and oh and tell Carol to put my calls through here, Eigen? I'm topside in Beaton's office small brush fire but before you leave I want to run through this speech again, we can't have another Plato rhymes with Miss Bulcke? While you're still on deck tell Moyst to make sure we have CIPAP in Mister Eigen's orders, if he doesn't go CIPAP he might as well stay at Miss Bulcke? Are you on? Where did she, Eigen? Before you leave I . . . what? Who's out there look if it's the man from this Taiwan medical relief outfit just give him the red carpet treatment, take him out and tie one on yes but before you leave I want to give this speech one more . . . oh he's right there now? No go ahead go out and tie one on with him and when you're back in the office we'll give this . . . no, then I'll call you at home, oh and Eigen . . . ? He stood intent on the phone's silence and then reached it across the desk toward its cradle. —Another brush fire, this Taiwan . . .

—I know all about it but we can't go into it now . . . the phone was caught before it came to rest, a button came to light, —Governor Cates is out in the, oh Miss Bulcke, please don't put any more calls through here until Mister Davidoff and I are finished, unless Mister Cutler . . . yes of course. Now. Governor Cates is out in the board room, and before I go in there I need every detail of the settlement you authorized on this threat of a minority stockholder . . .

—Look Beaton, before you go in there and shoot off your mouth you'd better have all the angles or you'll walk out of that board room without a pot to piss in.

—Precisely. And I don't think we have to conduct this discussion in the gutter. Now . . .

—And don't precisely me. Go in there trying to dig my grave with your preciselys and you'll be lucky to walk out with your hat and your ass.

The papers rattled in Beaton's hands on the desk before him, and he cleared his throat. —All right. Now apparently on the basis of this rather, amateurish letter to say the least, if you look at the spelling, let alone the typing, you authorized payment to settle this threatened minority stockholder's suit by the class of . . .

—Out of the PR budget, right, and any . . .

—I think the point here is . . .

—The point here is the PR budget is my budget Beaton, and any interference from you or . . .

—Yes all right, all right. Let's simply try to take one thing at a time then. Here is our check, drawn on your authorization, in the amount of one thousand eight hundred sixty-two dollars and fifty cents, returned to us paid by a bank somewhere in Nevada over an endorsement that appears . . .

—Will you tell me why you've got your balls in an uproar over eighteen hundred dollars? I've paid that much for one speech, Beaton. One speech. Do you know what I'm paying the name writer we're getting to do the . . .

—Yes all right, can you simply tell me how you came up with the figure one thousand eight hundred six . . .

—Damages based on one hundred times holdings, Diamond was selling at eighteen and five-eighths, simple enough. Do you . . .

—But my God, one hundred times . . . !

—Probably because it was easy to multiply by so that's why they claimed it. Do you know what I'm going to pay the name writer we're commissioning to do this cobalt book? If I told you you'd cream your drawers, the point is the PR budget is my budget to make the best use of for the company I see fit while you pussyfoot around with your preciselys, I had a gal in here this morning with a topflight track record in curriculum management for the spot of project director the minute things get off the ground because this cobalt book is just a door opener and if you're worried about another lousy eighteen hundred dollars, any time we can tie in with an old prestige publisher like Duncan and Company through this man Skinner I brought in to take us one step closer to what's waiting out there for us in a field growing faster than . . .

—What's waiting out there right now, Beaton said raising neither his voice nor his eyes to the calisthenic hazards beyond his desk —is Governor Cates, and if you think that he can be convinced that opening us up to hundred-times damage suits by every stockholder in sight is great PR, you'd better explain it to him yourself.

—You want me to tell you the reason you're crapping your pants Beaton? It's because you're the one who left the barn door open on Monty picking up that stock option before he pulled out for Washington, and then liquidating everything to keep out of a conflict of interest, right? Without serving out the rest of the time with the company spelled out in the by-laws, just like they've got it right there in the letter. They're a pretty savvy little bunch and you . . .

—And who ran around handing out proxy statements and copies of the by-laws, like joining a club boys and girls. This is Mister Moncrieff reporting to you for work, you're the owners the rest of us only work here, your one share of Diamond stock means you can haul us on the carpet any time you think we've stepped out of line and the rest of that show you put on for them, if Mrs Joubert . . .

—Try to shoot her down with this Beaton and you'll really come out with your ass in a sling, she's got a pretty savvy bunch of kids there and she's not far off base herself. I talked to her about it the last time she was in here and she . . .

—This suit? You've talked to her about this? His eyes came up as sharply as his fingers abruptly squaring the papers before him, to fix on the emergence of what at this, or any distance, appeared as gold carriage bolts holding the white cuffs to.

—It's going to be the feature spread in the Annual Report isn't it? Even finished the layout, just remember it's her pet project and if you want to go in there and blow everything to the old man it's your ass. There's nothing there about any of this, just the kids buying the share but if she tells Cates with those eyes of hers about trying to give these kids a looksee at the system with a few corporate dollars to play with, he'll nail you for pulling the rug out from under her and all the rest of us by leaving the door open, you'll be lucky to get out of here with your . . .

—Don't be, don't be ridiculous a suit like this would never come to court. Leaving the door open, I won't try to explain the technicalities the point now is simply that the precedent set by your, this authorization and payment might be construed as tacit admission of irregularities that could jeopardize our entire, excuse me. A button glowed. —Yes sir . . . He squared the papers again, standing, —and I think I can clear this up without bothering the Governor.

—And I think you better consider it cleared up right now, go after her with all your preciselys and if she thinks she's made a booboo she'll lay it all right in Uncle John's lap. Beaton? he came on in the silent wake cutting across the carpet toward the door, —if it lands in his lap you'll come flying out of that board room ass over teakettle . . . The carriage bolts shot unaimed from the acrylic barrels of his sleeves and, poised for the moment, he seemed to seek something vulnerable, as abruptly recovering a swift turn in stabs at the telephone. —Oh Carol I'm tied up here in Beaton's office just want to know if there were any calls, oh and get me the name of that name writer Skinner was digging up . . . he'd reached the end of the cord and, turning to pace it back, raised his eyes toward the door, —give us a rundown of . . . what?

—Mister Davidoff did you want me to . . .

—What are you doing here I'm talking to you on the, never mind . . . he put down the phone forcefully —oh and Carol while you're right here, he came on after her pulling the door closed behind them with an unfinished nod to the empty desk outside, —tell personnel to put a rush on processing the gal who was in here this morning for the project specialist spot in our shop, make sure they've got that recommendation on her in their folder the one I got from Mister Skinner . . .

—That got mugged in the elevator? We're all scared to . . .

—Skinner yes, the publisher who was in here, he's dug up a name writer for us who's coming in this afternoon to touch base on this cobalt book and I want Eigen to check out his credits before he . . .

—Mister Eigen already left for the day, he went out with this man that . . .

—That Taiwan medical relief that's right, took him out to tie one on.

—This man with these bandages on his eye and all, yes sir, they just went . . .

—Bandages and all what.

—No I meant like he was just kind of loud and walked funny, we were all scared to . . .

—Sounds like he tied one on before he got here, he passed her on the turn unlimbering his jacket —you can't ever tell about these oh and Carol, the Annual Report feature on that field trip get the layout and captions together and that new set of pix we had airbrushed in to get across this whole inner city concept of wait what's that . . .

—Oh that's Mister Eigen's I forget what you call them, from Mister Moyst Mister Davidoff, it came in around lunch.

—Eigen's orders where have they been all this, oh Carol, he paused fighting out of his jacket to assail the manila envelope with the same vigor, sundering it across its face with —better be getting Moyst on the phone to stand by while I check out the, CIPAP they've got that in, Mister Eigen will rept McGuire AFB Wrightstown NJ NLT one thousand hours wait, here it ought to be, for air movement to Frankfurt, Germany on Flt K eight one one AMD WRI-FRF sounds like, get Moyst on the phone and that's Colonel Carol not Mister Moyst or we'll all be, make sure we have approval for commercial air here if they've stuck him with military air we might as well just get Miss Bulcke too will you? Beaton's been trying to horn in as usual got her phoning Moyst to get these orders up here on the double try to flag her down before he and his buddy Cutler put us all up the, wait let me get through this, TC two hundred Indiv placed on TDY as indic RPSCTDY Eigen, Thomas, GS twelve Equiv they wouldn't give him a thirteen Distribution: fifty Indiv Concerned he won't need all those, five CG AMC, Attn: AMCAD-AO, Washington but where the, CIC: two XX four nine nine where did they put the, TDY to: West Germany, thence to where did they put Eigen will rept McGuire AFB Wrightstown just read that, the hiring of special conveyance here it is, special conveyance auth IAW Para three three c for use in, around and this is it, in, around and between TDY stations got Moyst on the phone there yet? Check out this term special conveyance when you get him if it doesn't include commercial air he's liable to end up riding in on a, oh and before you get Moyst just try Eigen at home, he may have just tell him I'll give him a call as soon as I've put out these brush fires . . . and they looked from his receding back, fighting his tie loose up the hall, to the still face of the clock.

—I broke another nail.

—I'm glad at least it's Friday.

—I know, I'm supposed to go out tomorrow and I just broke another nail. My girlfriend's giving me this shower.

—I didn't see the coffee wagon.

—I know, I think it just went when I was looking for him . . . A telephone rang. —Hello . . . ? No he just stepped away from his desk Mister Mollenhoff, he . . . Yes I'll have him return your call. I can't hardly drink the coffee here anyway.

—I think it's the same ones who run the cafeteria.

—I had that chop-suey sandwich today, it wasn't so bad.

—I can't eat things like that. They give me gas.

For time unbroken by looks to the clock the only sound was the chafing of an emery board, and the clock itself, as though seizing the advantage, seemed to accomplish its round with surreptitious leaps forward, knocking whole wedges at once from what remained of the hour.

—I wonder who he wants to stay late.

—I was so tired last night I almost went up the stairs on my hands and knees.

—I know, my girlfriend's giving this shower for me tomorrow and I already broke a nail, can you tell now looking at it . . . and the clock suddenly appeared to have reached a good stopping place.

—Oh Carol see if you can get me wait, Florence get me Mister Beaton just sit down here Mister, can you move these things Carol? Sit down here Mister Malinovsky till I find out who's authorized this, if it's all on the up and up we haven't lost a thing but coming in after hours like this with your crew starting to pull down a painting as big as that one in the lobby, Carol get Mister Eigen for me at home while I think of it and . . .

—Mister Beaton is at a meeting sir, he . . .

—Well try Cutler, Dick Cutler's office he might be at the bottom of this or know who is a painting that size by a name painter doesn't grow on trees the only person who could authorize removing it is that Eigen Carol? Just sit tight a minute Mister Malinovsky, you get Cutler Florence?

—No sir, Miss Bulcke said they're all at a meeting in the board room. Did you want me to stay or . . .

—Get Miss Bulcke back and I'll, just tell her this is urgent I've got a man sitting here and a crew out there on double time and a half waiting to, you get Eigen yet?

—He's waiting on three four Mister Davidoff.

—Oh and Carol . . . he stabbed at a button. —Hello? And Florence while you're at it hello? Eigen? he stabbed again. —Look in the files for the name of the painter that did the big lobby mural out there Florence, that big color spread we got on business and the arts in, hello . . . ? He stabbed again, again. —Hello? Eigen . . . ?

The line was dead.

—Tom? was that the phone?

—Idiot cut himself off, he called slumped on the sofa's arm reaching the phone back, prodding a heap of laundry for space to sit —always hope he'll forget who he called but . . .

—Who?

—David don't climb . . . it rang again and he reached for it, a piece of toast clinging to his sleeve. —Yes? Eigen . . .

—Tom? Who, oh. David get down, don't bother Papa when he's on the telephone . . .

—Yes I am, go ahead . . . he'd dropped the toast crust into an ashtray and was wetting a random corner of sheet from the laundry heap with his tongue —go ahead yes, I'm writing it down . . . he bent scrubbing the grape jelly stain into his sleeve —right yes, tomorrow mor . . . but the . . . ci what . . . ? if General Box leaves directly . . . from Bonn I wouldn't need . . . yes, they . . . but . . . but which one is . . . yes if . . . got it all down yes, if that's . . . Did what . . . ? that painting yes, his name's Schep . . . no I . . . no idea no, I haven't seen him for . . . right . . . right . . .

—Papa can you . . .

—Just a minute David, get down.

—Carry me.

—No now get down, I'm just going to the kitchen for a minute. And you know you're not supposed to bring toast and jelly to the living room.

—Papa Mama said you'd play a game after Mister Schramm went.

—I just want to get a drink David, he said down the dim hall.
—David? What are all these shoes doing out here, come pick them up.
Marian . . . ? he rounded the corner —what are all those shoes in the hall.

—Who was on the phone.

—Just Davidoff, last minute nonsense can't stand the idea of somebody finding a moment's peace . . . he was stooped over a low cabinet,
—got a brush fire going about that lobby painting now he wants me to
go out and find Schepperman, Christ. I thought we had some scotch.

—There's some vodka.

—Hardly half a bottle . . . he held it up, —where . . .

—How much scotch do you think we had! she turned from the sink,
—when you bring people home that way why don't you stop and pick
some up if you . . .

—Stop with Schramm the shape he was in?

—Well I didn't know you were bringing him. She'd turned away
again, staring through the window above the sink. —When you don't call
there's no way I can . . .

—How the hell could I call? I just had to get him out of there, this,
God damned . . . He had the refrigerator door opened, pounding the
blade of a table knife under an ice tray, this . . . he pounded, —God
damned thing, it's got to be defrosted.

—Will you make me one?

He wrenched it out. —By the time I got him here I could hardly get
him up the stairs, they'd packed him so full of morphine and belladonna
at Bellevue he said he couldn't feel his feet touch the ground. Then we
got here and the God damned elevator's broken.

—Every time it breaks down I climb those three flights carrying
groceries.

—Do you want water in this?

—I usually have to carry David that last flight too, she said straight
armed at the sink staring down at movement in a recessed fire exit across
the paper blown street.

—You want water?

—I said just ice. Could I have a cigarette?

—Don't we have any?

—I thought you'd bring some. And we need milk when you go down
too.

—David's in there waiting for his game, he came up behind her to
reach his glass under the tap, reaching round her for it as he would have
a piece of furniture —and what the hell's happened to Jack . . .

—You know what the hell's happened to Jack, she said moving no
more than to reach her glass where he placed it, and they raised them
in opposite directions. —He's in a bar somewhere letting someone he's
never seen in his life buy him another drink . . .

—Listen Marian . . .

—So he can cheer up his good friend Schramm when he finally gets here.

—God damn it listen, when Jack called I didn't even know Schramm had got out. Jack lost his key to Ninety-sixth Street and he wants to borrow ten dollars, that's why he's coming down here. He doesn't even know Schramm's out loose in that shape.

She raised her glass again, then lowered it repeating —in that shape . . . tossing the loose cubes, —the way you and Jack talk about him but you just let him walk out the door alone, in that shape, that filthy bandage, and Jack, all Jack has on his mind is a key to Ninety-sixth Street to take some woman up to that . . .

—Marian God damn it you're always ready with half the God damned facts whenever somebody else is trying to, Schramm left because Jack's coming, that's why he left. He was scared, God damn it Marian I've been through this, I know what he, I've talked him out of it before and so has Jack, so has Jack, he was afraid if he waited here Jack and I would try to get him back into Bellevue. That's why he left, that's why he was suddenly in such a God damned hurry to leave when he knew Jack was coming.

—I see. She held her glass out where he tipped the bottle over his own. —Did he know where he was going? in that shape?

—Yes Marian . . . Paused stooped there in the doorway he drank deliberately. —He was going to get laid.

—That's pretty.

—You asked me. She moved in with him down the hall there at Ninety-sixth Street a couple of months ago, one of these kids with bare feet and dirty hair but she can do more for him in bed than Gibbs and I can over a bottle. That's why he didn't want me to go with him, best sublimation there is for blowing out his brains.

—Pretty.

—How the hell would you know . . . he stood looking into his glass for a moment before he emptied it and reached for the bottle.

—Papa?

With the tug at his jacket he appeared to shrug. —I'm coming David.

—Papa has Mister Schramm only got one eye left now?

—We hope the doctors can make Mister Schramm's eye better David but if . . .

—But he could still live if he only has one can't he, because is that why you have two when you start and then if . . .

—That's enough David, get your book and maybe Papa will read to you before bed.

—But you said he'd play a game when Mister Schramm went.

—I played four games with you this afternoon David and . . .

—But when you play I always win, I want Papa to play.

—I'll play with you David. Go get it ready.

—I did.

—Did you pick up all those shoes in the hall?

—No.

—Go put them away and I'll be in in a minute. Marian?

—When do you want dinner, she said turned again to the window, the breadth of her shoulders gone in the rise of her weight to her arms spread embracing the sink from end to end.

—I'm not hungry. He raised his glass, and from a plate there lined with a ketchup spatter of beans selected as from an hors d'oeuvres tray hot dog in wrinkled remnant. —David finished his supper? He paused, found another. —That God damned Davidoff handed me an Oriental for lunch whose doctor has him on rare beef, tells me to take him out and tie one on, Christ. I thought I could pick up something on the expense sheet until I saw our bill at The Palm.

—If you want bread with dinner get some when you go down.

—Cigarettes, milk, bread. Butter?

—I don't know, you'll have to look.

—Marian I, why don't you ever make lists? And when you go shopping, milk, you know we'll need milk . . . He had the refrigerator open pushing things aside, looking, —and why are you keeping this gravy left from the veal, we . . .

—Well just look at it! She'd turned behind him for the ketchup spattered plate. —How much food can I stock in that refrigerator? How can I make lists and shop a week ahead with a refrigerator that size?

—All right, with the one in the new house you can shop for a month, he went on stooped, pushing things aside, looking, —don't see any butter.

—Get some when you go down then, she said scraping clots of bean over the scotch bottle upended in the trash.

—I didn't know there was more asparagus at dinner last night, I would have . . . what's this, lamb chops?

—I got them for dinner.

—Three ninety-six for three lamb chops?

—I can only eat one, I thought . . .

—But three ninety-six, what would . . .

—I thought they looked good, I was hungry when I went shopping and . . .

—If you go shopping when you're hungry you always spend . . .

—Well what should I do! Come up for rare beef at The Palm? instead of sharing David's chicken noodle soup and finishing his peanut butter sandwich?

—All right! Would you like to have been there today like I was? Making stupid conversation with a grinning Chinese who's chewing up slices of his nine dollar steak and blowing them out on his plate? tells me his doctor says he can't digest the meat but he needs its juices so he patiently chews the whole God damned thing bite by bite and blows every one of them out, now what the hell kind of a lunch do you think that was, the whole place staring at us and the waiter coming over to ask if anything is unsatisfactory. Do you think I wouldn't rather be right here? in my workroom with noodle soup and a peanut butter sandwich trying to clear up the second act of that play?

—David's waiting for you, she said streaming away the ketchup smears under hot water, gazing down through the window. —How early will you leave in the morning.

—On a trip I may never take? if you don't go CIPAP you might as well stay home, paying a grown man a good salary to watch a Chinaman blow food across the room and fly three thousand miles to spoon feed a speech to another grown man so he won't say Plato rhymes with tomato?

She put down the plate, motionless. —If you do go will you leave me some cash?

He put down his glass. —Forty? he dug deep in a pocket and opened a roll of bills behind her, twenty upon twenty, tens, tens, —I'll only be gone a few days.

—Those suits you have at the cleaners will be more than ten, I don't have . . .

—Well just ask, he said, pulling another ten. —Here.

—Just put it down, she said without turning. —I always have to ask.

And he had the ice tray again, scooping cubes into his glass and staring at them there, swirling them around and simply staring at them. —Davidoff had a woman in this morning, a gal he calls her, bringing her in to help jazz up our PR operation as project director with her topflight track record in curriculum management, as he calls it. Then he got me aside and . . . He gazed at the swirling cubes a moment longer and then reached for the bottle, —he asked me how I'd like working for a woman. And I told him.

She turned with her own emptied glass for the ice tray, and took the bottle where he put it down. —Why don't you just quit then, instead of, instead of all this, your book's being published again and when you get this award . . .

—And how long could we live on that? Just David's nursery school, and the moving, the house up there, splitting a five percent royalty with those stupid God damned, that won't even pay for David's nursery school and that award, it wouldn't even be just giving up the salary, these companies are so damned paternalistic with their deferred stock options retirement plans insurance medical benefits they finally have you tied hand and foot, just stop and remember when David was born and we could hardly . . .

—You know what I stop and remember Tom? She'd turned abruptly, resting elbows back on the sink's edge, facing him. —I remember Doctor Brill telling us David needed his operation for double hernia when you first went to work there and you put it off, and put it off. There was that baby and we didn't know what was going to happen but you kept putting it off till your company medical benefits took effect, so you wouldn't have to . . .

—Marian you . . . you have a real instinct don't you Marian, a real God damn instinct . . .

—And you didn't want him. Did you, you didn't want him in the first place.

—What, Marian what the hell do you think you're saying?

—David. You didn't want him in the first place.

—Marian you, you've said some rotten things but you, that's the rottenest thing you could say isn't it, so completely . . . dishonest and rotten.

—Well it's . . .

—I wanted to wait to have children, didn't I, I wanted to wait till we got on our feet, that wasn't David I didn't want, there was no David and if you ever dare to, you know God damn well that when he was born when he was David you know God damn well he's everything I . . . he stopped and got breath. —You've got a real instinct for the jugular haven't you Marian.

—Well it's true she said, elbows back on the sink's edge, facing him.

—You're like a, sometimes you're like an illness Marian, you're like a God damned long illness I picked up somewhere . . .

—You're your own God damned illness Tom, she said coming past him with her glass for the hall and there, over a shoulder, —what are you going to do with these newspapers.

—I haven't been through them yet, he came after her empty-handed —haven't had the . . .

—You've got papers and clippings piled everywhere, I can't even find a place to . . .

—All right Marian, I'll . . .

—Take them into your workroom or, somewhere, you said you were going to store them uptown.

—All right! He got past her in the hall carrying them, got the door opened at the end of it and the light switch with his elbow. —What are all these curtain rods doing here?

—I had to put them someplace, she said past the door and he stood there turned one way, the other, finally put the newspapers on the chair drawn up to the typewriter, leaning toward it to move the curtain rods and turn the unfinished lines up on the roller.

And there, coming over the foot of that rise, three cock pheasants burst up from the ground with the terrible slowness of things in a dream. They wheeled, I fired, and they were gone. But there on the ground with a broken wing one of them struggled across the stones, I fired

again, and it kept on, struggling till it reached a wall where it fought
its head in amongst the stones . . .

—Papa? Which do you want to be, Piglet or Pooh.

—Yes I'm coming David . . . he snapped off the light and pulled the
door closed, and came up the hall slowly. —Wait David, we can't play
there, here get your feet out of the laundry.

—I'm being Rabbit, I beat Mama four times being Rabbit.

—Here let's, wait, there's never any place to sit down.

—Mama was Piglet, do you want to be him or Pooh Papa.

—I just haven't had time to sort it, she said holding her glass high,
gathering the laundry to an end of the sofa with her free hand. —Did I
tell you the Bartletts are separating?

—No. Here David just, here, just put the board on the floor. We'll
play here on the floor, he said spreading the board between his feet,
looking up. —Maybe he finally had enough of that grinning pear she's
painted on everything they own. What about the children.

—I won Mama four times today Papa. I always win.

—You don't always win David. Nobody does.

—She said he's agreed to move out and get a room in town, he'll
come up to see them weekends, she says she just can't live with someone
she doesn't respect. He lost his job, you must have heard that.

—Better to go down dignified, watch your foot David. Provide, provide here, sit over here.

—I want to sit beside you.

—All right but don't climb. Now, shake the bag, really shake it.

—She said she just can't respect a man who doesn't respect himself
. . . and she stood over them a moment longer swirling the cubes loose
in her glass before she turned. —I'll start dinner, you can eat when you
want to.

—Papa are you being Pooh?

—Yes. What did you get.

—I got blue. I go all the way here.

—You skipped one David.

—What?

—You skipped this blue back here. You're back here.

—Oh.

—And I got green. Here. Now really shake the bag.

—I did. I got red, Papa if you got black you'd go all the way there.

—That's why there are only two blacks in the whole bag.

—Why.

—To make it harder to get. And I have . . . green again.

—You only go here. Shall I move you?

—Yes now, wait, now wait David.

—I got yellow, I go all the way to . . .

—No, no you can't take two out of the bag and then decide which one you want and put the other one back.

—I didn't take two out. They just came out.

—All right, then put them both back in and shake the bag again, and when you reach in just take one.

—I got yellow anyway, see? I don't even have to close my eyes, do the rules say you have to close your eyes?

—Yes, so nobody will be able to . . .

—Who made the rules?

—The people who made the game. That's what a game is, if there weren't any rules there wouldn't be any game, now sit up.

—If you get yellow the next time you'll get in the Heffalump trap. Papa do I have to close my eyes even if I hold the bag way over here and look over here?

—Yes now sit up David, it's my turn.

—Papa?

—What.

—Papa was Jesus a regular person?

—Well he, he was a person yes but, he . . .

—Did he grow up to be an Indian?

—Did he what?

—Did Jesus grow up to be an Indian?

—What makes you think that.

Twisted away from the bag at his arm's length, he faced the wall opposite where as art an ikon hung unapproachable behind a chair.

—He has no shirt and he has those red marks on him.

—Those are blood David, you know that.

—Then why is he wearing that hat?

—That's not a hat, it's a crown of thorns, you know the, you must know the story about Jesus being crucified when they mocked him about being a king? and made him a crown out of thorns to . . .

—Then where did he get that blood on him.

—Well he, when he was crucified. You've seen the crucifix and the pictures of Jesus on the cross with the nails through his hands and feet, so his blood . . .

—Papa do those nails go right through his hands?

—They, yes, yes, they . . .

—I always thought he was holding on up there. Papa?

—Let's, sit up now, if you . . .

—Is it my turn?

—No it's my turn, David if you're not careful of your feet you're going to kick the pieces off the board and we won't know where we're supposed to be.

—I know, I'm here and you're way back here, if you'd get black you'd get way up there.

—Blue.

—You only go three. Red. I got red. Look. Look Papa look where I am now and look where you are.

—Yes all right let's . . . yellow.

—You got in the Heffalump's trap. Mama Papa got in the Heffalump trap. Mama?

—She can't hear you David. Don't shout.

—If I get red now I'll, yellow. I got yellow too look, I always win look, now look where I am and . . .

—David you don't always win, nobody . . .

—I won Mama four times today. Mama?

—Stop shouting David . . . He held the bag down, —and I . . . got . . .

—Black! You peeked. Papa you peeked!

—Peeked?

—You peeked in the bag Papa I saw you. You peeked.

—Come on David, you . . .

—You peeked in the bag, I saw you.

—Look David you, nobody always wins, every time you play you can't expect . . .

—No but you peeked.

—There's the doorbell, listen. Do you want to answer it?

—No.

—Maybe it's Jack, don't you want to go open the door for Jack?

—No.

—Tom . . . ?

—Come on help me up, then we'll come back and finish the game.

—No. You peeked.

—Tom it's a policeman, she came on ahead —David . . . and she held him aside in a stare that dropped from the height of the badge peaked on the cap to the holstered gun swept past his face toward the windows.

—We're just checking your building.

—Yes but what . . .

—Nobody here went out a window?

—Out a, what? What do you mean.

—David come along now.

—Out a, David go with your mother. What do you mean out a window.

—We got a call somebody might have fell or jumped.

—Here? But who, but wait a man? Was it a man?

—That's what we're trying to find out Mister, why. You know a man here that might have went out a window?

—He, but no, no I know . . . no. No what makes you think . . .

—Look down there, see where the pipes of that awning frame's all bent down there? We got a call there's somebody on the sidewalk out front here, see the blood on the sidewalk down there? by where that car fender's dented there? We get here but there's no body down there, just that awning frame bent like that and where that car fender's . . .

—No, no but listen a friend of mine, a friend of mine was here and he's, he just left, he just got out of Bellevue and he's, he left a few minutes ago but I'd talked him out of it, I'd just talked him out of it.

—Out of what.

—Out . . . out of this.

—He lives in the building here?

—No he lives uptown he, that's where he was going and I'd . . .

—After you and him talked you didn't leave him alone here?

—No I went to the, Christ look do you think I wouldn't know it if he'd . . .

—Okay don't get excited, he went out the door? What about out by the elevator in the hall there, there's a window there?

—Yes but he . . .

—You saw him go down the elevator?

—No but, no the God damned thing's broken he . . .

—You know where he lives, we'll take a ride up there.

—That's where he was going yes but, yes so he couldn't have done this, he'd be, still be down there on the sidewalk . . . He came crowding the uniform down the hall before him, —Marian when Jack gets here tell him . . .

—Yes I heard, she came after them.

—We'll ride up and have a look. People can do some funny things.

—And Tom . . . ?

The door slammed and she turned, more slowly, to the kitchen, to the ice floating in the ice tray, and rinsed a milk glass.

—Mama?

—I'm coming, she called, unscrewing a cap, shaking a pill into her hand.

—Mama hurry . . .

—Yes I'm coming David. She poured the drink and came back up the hall with it. —David come away from the window.

—Mama Papa's getting in the police car. Look!

—Yes, come get your pajamas David. He'll be back.

—Where are they taking him. Mama where are they taking him.

—He'll be back in a little while David, come get your pajamas.

—Can I stay up till he comes back?

—We'll see now, get your pajamas, if you hurry I'll finish the game Papa started with you.

—I don't want to.

—David don't climb in the laundry, what do you want to do then.

—Read.

—All right, if you promise to get into pajamas right afterward. Now where's your book.

—Here . . . he surfaced thrashing from the sheets —we were here, he said holding it open.

—Right here?

—Here, he burrowed in beside her, the delicate black crescent of a nail on Nana.

—Nana had filmy eyes, David be careful of my glass. Nana had filmy eyes, but all she could do was to put her paw gently on her mistress's lap. They were sitting thus when Mister Darling came home from the office. He was tired. Won't you play me to sleep on the nursery piano? he asked. And as Mrs Darling was . . .

—Why does he want to sleep on the nursery piano?

—No, he just wants her to play him something that will make him feel . . .

—Mama?

—What is it.

—Mama if God called you doesn't that mean he would have to kill you first?

—David I explained that to you. That was just your teacher's way of trying to explain to the class why the little Priftis girl's seat is always empty now. You know she was a very sick little girl, and Miss Duffy used to teach in the parochial school so she . . .

—Mama?

—What David.

—I hope he doesn't call me.

—David he's not going to call any of us . . . Suddenly she had him close. —Do you love me?

—Yes.

—How much?

—Some money . . . ? She was holding him so when the doorbell sounded. —Is it Papa?

—Or Jack.

—Jack! he broke free, and down the hall to work at the door lock. —Mama? Mama it's Jack Mama. It's Jack.

—David, she came after him —don't climb David, don't . . .

—It's all right Marian . . . up! Watch your head David.

—David, Jack be careful, you . . .

—It's all right Marian just a, a little problem with a shoelace, he came steadying himself, dragging one foot slightly.

—And you've torn your pocket, David if you hold Jack's throat like that he can't breathe. Jack? Can you have a drink?

—Yes I've, don't mind, not so tight David, just been the guest of Seaman Third Class Stepnik, prefers vodka . . .

—Good, that's all we have. David that's enough now, get down and go get your pajamas.

—You said after we read, Mama you said . . .

—After you get into pajamas and pick up those shoes in the hall, she said dropping ice. —Jack and I want to talk for a minute.

—I just stopped down to pick up a key, isn't Tom here yet? key to Ninety-sixth Street, I have to go up there and look for that manuscript I . . .

—I'm sure, she said handing him the glass —hurry David, if you hurry you can come out and talk to Jack for a minute. She turned in the door. —I hope you brought cigarettes?

—I was going to ask you the same thing, he said following her up the hall. —What happened to Tom I thought he'd be . . .

—That's what I want to talk to you about, she said rounding the sofa. She pulled the heap of laundry to the floor there, pushed the book aside and sat, at that end of it. —Jack. I'm going to leave Tom.

—Oh? He'd reached the windows, about to raise his glass, and he lowered it. —What's Tom's ah, what does Tom . . .

—I don't know.

—I mean have you told him?

—No.

He brought his glass up and drank half of it off. —Last I heard you were going to move, I thought he'd just rented a house for you up near the . . .

—For me? She raised her own glass and drank. —There's nothing I can do to help Tom anymore. Jack I'm doing this for him.

—And David?

—David?

—What about David.

—David will be with me of course, he'll be fine. Jack I can't live with someone I don't respect.

He stood looking into his glass for a moment and then finished it and put it on the sill and stood there looking down to the street and the sidewalk below. —Well, what do you want me to say, Marian.

—I thought you might . . .

—After a few drinks you used to work me over with your instant psychiatry, growing up without a father guilt feelings about my mother now you're going to do David the same favor?

—That's ridiculous, Tom will always be his father.

—Marian you don't know what the hell a father is.

—I'm not going to . . .

—A father is someone who's there, someone who . . .

—Jack I won't have him live that boy's life for him!

—Oh come on Marian, he turned, hands dropped into his pockets —you don't really know what you're, listen. I just had another round with that stale bitch who's got my daughter penned up out there in Astoria, destroying her inch by inch just, making sure nothing grows, biggest event in that kid's life is a trip to the dentist, Marian you don't know what a Christ awful mess everything turns into when these things happen, and it never . . .

—I think Tom and I . . .

—And it doesn't end. It doesn't end.

—I think Tom and I will be able to work things out in a more civilized way than you and . . .

—Marian listen! You don't commit murder in a civilized way! He picked up his glass and looked into it and put it down again. —Sure there are no cigarettes?

—No, Tom was getting some.

—Where is he, I thought he'd . . .

—Jack he goes into that room, he goes into that workroom of his every night and nothing ever comes out.

—You've hung on this long haven't you? aren't things just starting to break for him again? He's got this award coming his book's out again in paperback, he's got . . .

—Do you think that helps? All he does is swear about splitting a five percent royalty with the publishers, he says the only reason they let somebody reprint it is so they can hang onto the rights themselves he doesn't even . . .

—Well what the hell Marian, that publisher's a fatuous bastard you know that, he's been sitting on that book for how many years? blubbering about his loyalty to it pretending it was what did he tell Tom? very much in print? when the only God damned place you could find it was a rare book dealer's for twenty dollars a copy after they'd remaindered practically the whole first edition? He didn't know anything about this new reprint till he saw one in a window and now it's bringing him some attention he . . .

—He what Jack, he what! He gets letters from Who's Who and invitations to read from his work, letters from editors and college girls and he just fights them off, he won't even . . .

—I know that, I know all that but he's going through a, just trying to readjust after nine years of . . .

—And what about me! What do you think those nine years have been like for me? You won't give me anything though, will you Jack. That Ninety-sixth Street tenement when you used to come up there for dinner and we had to wait for him to get his typewriter and papers off the card table so we could eat Jack he's still working on that play, he's still rewriting it and changing it and rewriting it he won't let go of it, he won't finish it because he's afraid to compete with himself, it's himself he's . . .

—Well look Marian what, as Freud said what the hell is it you want.

—Just a man who, who's happy with what he's doing.

—You're not asking much are you.

—Jack I can't respect a man who doesn't respect himself, do you know what he's like about this job? Do you think we ever talk about anything else? from the minute he comes in the door . . .

—How many husbands do you think come home from work all smiles come on Marian, it's the oldest God damned story there is putting up with the same crap day after day trying to make a living and then coming home to I've been slaving all day over a hot stove while you've been down in a nice cool sewer, he's just trying to pull this play together and make a decent living at the same time for you and . . .

—Yes you won't give me a thing will you! None of you will! How do you think it makes me feel, why do you think we don't go to parties anymore, because I have too much to drink? Yes why because all of you, you and his friends and these editors asking about his next great book shaking their heads admiring how hard he works to support us, me and David but what a tragedy for American literature how do you think that makes me feel! The great Thomas Eigen's talent being thrown away in a stupid job because he has to make a decent living for his wife and son he resents every bill he pays, the rent, nursery school he even resents that, paying David's nursery school and food, three lamb chops Jack, three lamb chops! A decent living standing in that kitchen looking down at that man with no hands and, no face, just a burn scar with holes in it and that coat to his ankles hiding from the wind in that fire exit screwing the cap off a bottle with his mouth and holding it up between his wrists to . . .

—Marian listen! Listen you've talked about that man before it's, you just use him to, I don't know put up curtains or pull down the God damned shade you don't have to stand and stare at him but you, you use him to bring things down, like you talked about Schramm's accident as though he'd done it on purpose just to . . .

—Because all of you, all three of you the way you and Tom and, and Schramm the way you find excuses for each other's failures and I can't stand being one anymore I might have done something, nobody thinks of that do they I might have . . .

—There's your doorbell.

—Everybody's idea that I've kept Tom from his work by being a burden maybe he's kept me from mine, all these years I might have done something myself I might still if . . .

—Marian Christ, I just met a talented woman who's never been allowed to do anything and, is there any more vodka?

—Mama? Mama it's a man . . .

—I'll be right back, give me your glass.

His hands abruptly searched pockets as he turned back to the window, one to come up with matches, the other empty, and he returned the matches and stood there staring down at the sidewalk.

—Jack?

—David, oh. He turned to the somersault off the sofa's arm into the laundry heap. —I thought you were getting pajamas.

—Jack when the Chinese people look at television, are the people they see on television Chinese?

—Why of course, and the . . .

—Lift me up.

—Hold on.

—Higher, hi . . . what are you doing?

—Trying to see how you'd look on Chinese television.

—Would I be upside down? Why would I be upside down.

—Because you'd be on the other side of the world wouldn't you? Get into your pajamas I'll finish that game with you, were you playing with Mama?

—No. Don't drop me.

—Oh, she was playing by herself.

—No with Papa, before the policeman came.

—What policeman.

—The one that came and got him when he peeked. Jack?

—When he, what policeman, Marian . . . ?

—Do you know what I'd like to do Jack?

—What . . . he reached up to free his throat from an embrace suddenly so close he faltered.

—I'd like to go right up to the sky and disappear, and then come down like the rain. Jack?

—What, Marian what . . .

—That was Tom's orders arriving by special messenger. She held out a glass. —Tomorrow he . . .

—But where is he? David just said a policeman came and . . .

—I was just going to tell you yes, David I told you to go get your pajamas now get down, go to your room and find your pajamas, now hurry . . . Then she turned. —It's Schramm, she said, —something about your friend Schramm . . .

—Well what, what about him?

—I don't know, Tom was talking to him and he . . .

—Tom's at Bellevue now? Why didn't you . . .

—No that was, that was it, Schramm got out and came to Tom's office and Tom brought him down here and then the, I don't know, the police came, they thought he'd, maybe he'd jumped, they thought somebody'd jumped and they wanted Tom to . . .

—But where is he! Where are they!

—Tom went with them, they took him up to Ninety-sixth Street to see if . . .

—Why didn't you tell me! he turned for the hall, —why the hell didn't you tell me when I got here?

—I thought, she said following him —I just wanted . . .

—You just wanted the God damned spotlight a minute longer didn't you, looked like Schramm was grabbing it with the last thing he's ever done but you . . .

—But Jack if it . . . they'd reached the door and he pulled it open. —Jack if Schramm's dead? And, I'm here . . . ?

—I, Christ I, you've got to have soap opera, Jack I'm going to leave Tom, Ginger I'm going to leave Tony the minute something real happens you have to star in your own God damned soap opera . . . The door slammed, and she'd scarcely turned from it when it shook with his pounding on the other side. —Marian?

She got it open. —What.

—Tom was going to lend me twenty I've got to get a cab up there, did he leave it for me?

—No.

—Well he, could you . . .

She turned to the kitchen, put down her glass and opened a cupboard there. —I have ten.

—Fine and, fine thanks, he took it, holding the door, —and Marian one last thing if you think you're going through with this, you can pull that on anybody else just don't ever try to tell me again you're doing it for him, you can lie to Tom, lie to yourself lie to David but don't ever try to . . . the door came closed flat in his face and he turned sliding one foot toward the elevator, slipped and made for the stairs, down them and out hailing traffic before he reached the curb.

—I'm off duty buddy, see the lights? Where you going.

—Straight uptown, look I'm in a hurry I . . .

—Do you a favor. Get in.

—To Ninety-sixth Street, he fell back as they started, —near Third . . . they moved into the traffic and came to a halt. The meter was silent. Another half block, firmly embedded between trucks, the driver tilted the rearview mirror to embrace his own immediate vacancy, plugged a cord into the cigarette lighter opening on the dashboard, and watched his hand course ineffectively up and down one cheek with an electric razor. —Listen I'm in a hurry, can't you . . .

—Look at the traffic, what am I supposed to do.

—You know what Third's like, why didn't you take Park.

—Same shit over there.

—Like hell it is, you got trucks and buses on Park? He was thrown against the arm rest. —Now where the hell are you going.

—Try First . . . Up one cheek and down the other, each nostril flared with a heavy thumb, this earlobe, tragus and antitragus, that one, down one cheek and up the other, finally looking back unchanged, —which building.

—Up there right past Second, there, where those police cars are . . . and he was out holding the ten. —How much?

—That's right.

—Wait . . . it was gone, —wait a minute, you . . .

—Look buddy you didn't have no meter, I did you a favor right?

—Stop! Wait, you . . . God damn you! He kicked, it swept away, window open, and he stood there for a moment with one stockinged foot on the street before turning to push through backs and elbows toward the door.

—Wait a minute buddy, where you going.

—Listen officer I have to, I live here, second floor front right up there he pointed, —Eigen? he shouted past the uniform up the dark stairs, —you up there? Tom . . . ? Tell them to let me come up there!

—Go ahead.

—Thanks . . . he pushed by, his one shoe reaching three steps at a time —where's . . .

—Jack I'd talked him out of it! I'd just talked him out of it Jack!

—Where is he.

—No they just cut him down Jack, don't . . .

—Don't what! the door gave already splintered, —let me . . . oh Christ. Oh Christ.

The sprawl flung there on the linoleum gathered shape as the uniform rose slowly and the policeman turned toward them, stood there wiping his mouth. —We didn't make it . . . he started to button his tunic, and then he looked around and took his hat from the policeman standing near the sink, put it on and squared it. —You be around for a few minutes?

—Yes, yes we'll, Jack listen . . .

—You a friend of his too Mister?

—Me? Yes I'm a friend of his too Mister I'm, we're both friends of his too Mister what the hell do we look like? Like we'd let this happen to him? What the hell do we look like we'd let him . . . who's she?

—Jack listen . . .

—Wait, wait who's she? Who are you?

—You better get your friend out of here.

—Who the hell are you! he pushed toward her pressed back against the sink there, back behind the policeman now opening a pad, raising it to bar his way.

—Look try and get hold of yourself Mister, you . . .

—Jack wait she's just a, just his girl Rhoda, her name's Rhoda.

The policeman with the pad looked at his watch, and turned to her. —How old are you, Rhoda? She just looked at him.

—Kind of a funny guy anyway, wasn't he.

—Funny . . . !

—Hanging up pictures of dead kids on his wall like this, the policeman went on across the room straightening up from photographs taped up over a card table and looking over the clutter there, papers, books, a scarred typewriter, soiled bandages, a box of teabags, some loose change.

—Funny! He's the, he was the funniest . . .

—Jack listen let's, we can go next door and . . .

—The funniest guy you could, look at his feet could you do that? Something that funny with your God damned feet, look at them!

—Okay Mister, just go next door with your friend here and . . .

—No wait I want to tell you those pictures, those were children killed in Belgium he put them up there because he, he, he . . . Christ can't you, here . . . he pulled a robe from a hook behind the door and flung it —just . . . cover him up?

Caught by a sleeve, the robe spread between the policeman's hands. —What's all the blood on it.

—It's mine.

—Know something about this, Rhoda?

—I said it's mine.

—I heard you. What else happened here Rhoda? She just looked at him. —You want to tell us what happened?

—You live here Rhoda? said the policeman beside her. —Keep your things here? Your clothes, your robe, your . . .

—It's not my robe.

—You just said . . .

—It's my blood.

—You want to tell us what happened Rhoda?

—I was supposed to meet him here but, her voice caught, —like I was late that's all, man.

—You were here at the door when we got here, weren't you Rhoda? You want to tell us about this blood?

—Like I came to get some things of mine, I mean just let me get them okay?

—You can get them later, you want to tell us about this blood?

—We were screwing, okay? I had my period and I put the robe on after, okay?

—You live here with him Rhoda?

—Officer for the love of Christ what are you trying to, of course she lives here look at the, you think a man puts dishes in the dish rack backwards like that? collects all the dirty ashtrays and then leaves them in the sink? leaves the cap off the toothpaste? the cap off everything? And the, that coat hanger look at that God damned coat hanger, you ever know a man who'd do that to a coat hanger? Go look in the toilet you'll see the paper's on the roller backwards too, one will get you five the paper's . . .

—Look Mister the both of you better wait next door. Rhoda, you want to tell us . . .

—I just want to get my things, man.

—You can get them when . . .

—Get them when shit, when you get through cleaning the place out? There was thirty-seven cents on that table there you just put in your pocket you prick, I saw you you . . .

—How do you know it was thirty-seven cents Rhoda?

—Because it was my thirty-seven cents you . . .

—We're taking his wallet and his watch too, they can be claimed at the office of the chief property clerk, everything else here gets locked up. How old are you Rhoda?

—Officer for, what God damned business is it of anybody's how old she is, she . . .

—Because if this keeps up she's on her way to the juvenile shelter where they'll give her a bath, now just take it easy . . .

—Easy! what do you, stand here asking stupid questions while . . .

—Look Mister we're waiting for the medical examiner, just go next door with your friend here we might want an identification on him.

—All right but look, that cabinet over the dishes . . .

—I said you can't take nothing out of here.

—Well can you just open the God damned thing and look? There, bottle back there says Old Struggler see it?

—It's that scotch bottle officer, the Old Smug . . .

—Take it, here. Now go with your friend will you?

—And wait, wait on the floor there by his, that pack of cigarettes must be mine because he didn't, doesn't smoke . . .

—Here take them, can you handle him Mister?

—Yes he's, wait Jack let me carry that . . .

—Okay Rhoda, now you want to tell us . . .

—Hardly see where I . . .

—Here get the railing let me get the door open what's, no wait, wait Jack there's mail all over the floor out here just let me get in and get the light, this damn door's falling off its . . .

—Sound like the torrents of spring in there what's . . .

—Light a match will you? I, no I got it damn it look don't just kick that mail in can't you pick it up and . . .

—Got a misplaced reverence for mail Tom, think Grynszpan's getting invitations to birthday parties? Edison Company look, A Piscator Attorney at Law ever hear good news from an attorney at law? Lighthouse for the Blind, Crawley and . . .

—All right just get up and bring it in, who the hell left the hot water in the sink running like this . . .

—Better turn it off before we . . .

—What do you think I'm trying to, damn it look at that the handle's broken right off the faucet.

—Where's Old Struggler.

—Right there on that pile of film cans Jack who the hell broke this fauc . . .

—Find any glasses? came from behind 36 Boxes 200 2-Ply where he threaded his way through the stacks of cartons for an opening ahead —where the, what happened to the lamp in here . . . He rested the bottle on an H-O carton to find a match, held it high along a further reach of cartons rising to a plateau of bound volumes heaped toward the wall and then came on for the windows ahead where an askew blind caught flashes of light from below.

—Jack? When were you up here last, turn that light on will you?

—Hell do you think I'm . . . he poised the stockinged foot on Wise Potato Chips Hoppin' With Flavor! —how it got over here . . . and he reached under the punctured shade, —there . . .

——treasured heirlooms, many were from the finest homes in . . .

—God damned radio still alive, find a glass? Better get, ow!

—No is that all the scotch we . . .

—Wait don't sit down, place is boobytrapped with sharp pencils . . . he pulled the soiled blanket from the armless sofa, sank back with the bottle. —Who the hell's reading Moody's Industrials . . .

—That's what I, wait if that's all the scotch damn it Jack you're drinking the whole . . .

—Couldn't wait, where's your glass.

—There aren't any glasses! do you, you think I don't need one too Christ I, I'd just talked him out of it Jack I . . .

—Did a great job.

—What? Look don't, don't say anything like that to me again Jack don't . . .

—Well how the hell could you let him leave like that! just, just let him go out alone even if you'd . . .

—He wouldn't let me go with him! I told him you were coming down he thought we'd try to put him back into Bellevue he had this, this girl this God damn girl if she'd been here waiting for him like she said she would she, he'd be . . .

—Need some more scotch, I'd go myself but Hardy Suggs stole my shoe.

—I'm going yes, look Jack I'll hurry if the police come in just don't start, just tell them I'll be right back will you?

—New liquor store right on the corner can't miss it, I saw it from the cab, Tom? Can't miss it, big sign in the window Back to School Sale can't miss it . . . he put down the empty bottle, got up and dug for a match favoring his shod foot toward the window where he parted the blind to peer down at the flashing lights in a puff of smoke, reached to drop the burned match behind 2-Ply Facial Tissue Yellow sagging closer to it, picking a page up —what the, Tom . . . ? he came down on 1 Doz 59¢ Wise Potato Chips Hoppin' With Flavor! to bring the score under the light —pom pompom, pom . . . escaping him till he sang out abruptly —halte là!

—Hello . . . ?

—Qui va là! That you Tom? Got back God damned fast what, wait who are you . . .

—I, Mister Gibbs . . . ?

—Yes but who the, no. No. Bast? What in, what the hell are you doing here . . .

—Well I just, I've been away I just got back . . . he dropped a soiled manila envelope and a paper sack on the armless sofa and stood there —I, I've just been working here I, I mean what, is everything all right?

—Everything's great, look . . .

—No but what are those police cars down there they . . .

—Those are police cars Bast now look, will you just tell me how you ever got here?

—Yes well the bus came in downtown and I walked across and took the subway up to . . .

—Bast?

—What, did I . . .

—Listen. Can you just tell me how the hell you found this place to begin with?

—Yes well the tag, the number was right on the tag on that key you gave me and the name Gryns . . .

—I gave you?

—Yes and the name Grynszp . . .

—No wait, wait. I gave you the key?

—Well, well yes you, that night at the train station when you remember don't you Mister Gibbs? I mean I, I think you'd had something to drink but you gave me the key and said I could work up here if I, I mean is it all right?

—Fine great look just sit down will you? Don't just stand there like a . . .

—Because I mean if it's not I could . . .

—Said it's fine didn't I? Few details I didn't follow find that card here someplace I, will you sit down!

—Yes well I, I was just going to fix something to eat . . . he'd picked up the paper sack again, —I've been on the bus all day I haven't had anything since . . .

—Fine go fix it, just . . .

—I'll be right back . . . he got past 36 Boxes 200 2-Ply, —Mister Gibbs? Would you like a cup of tea?

—Hate a cup of tea listen . . .

—Yes well I could only find one cup, he called over the torrent at the sink, —Mister Gibbs? I've tried not to disturb things I just put all the lampshades back here in one place and moved some of the boxes so it would be easier to . . .

—Bast?

—And the sink yes, yes I'm sorry . . . he came through with a cup dangling the string of a teabag —one day I turned on the hot water and when I tried to turn it off the handle on the faucet broke off in my hand and I couldn't . . .

—Look don't worry about the God damned sink just, listen . . .

—Would you like one of these Mister Gibbs . . . ? he was tearing a cellophane wrapping —I just got them because it's all I could . . .

—Christ no now look . . .

—Mister Gibbs are you, you've only got one shoe on are you . . .

—I know it! now, now listen . . .

—And your coat's torn there by the pocket I mean are you, is everything . . .

—Listen! everything's, I mean what are you doing here!

—Well I, I just thought when you said I could come up here and work you said, you were talking about a place of stone in that cafeteria about writing an opera and . . .

—Cafeteria thought you're writing an opera call up they tell me you're on a business trip, woman looks like a God damned carnival tent tells me . . .

—But, but how did you . . .

—Jack . . . ?

—Tells me to bump into you have you call in for an appointment with your . . .

—I, I just did yes when I got off the bus but, but how did . . .

—Jack? Have they been here to, who . . .

—Like you to meet Edward Bast Tom, meant to tell you I said he could work up here he's a composer, here pass the bottle . . .

—Yes well I, I'm glad to meet you Mister Grynszpan I've sort of expected you any day there's a lot of mail for you, I put it in the oven to . . .

—No wait, look . . .

—Thought we needed a composer in residence cheer things up here, busy composing somebody else's opera needed a piano, found the piano yet Bast?

—Yes well I, I mean I got about two octaves uncovered but then some books slid down when I was trying to find a, it sounds like a radio under there somewhere but I can't . . .

—Tell you about that later Bast, he's a little sensitive this was his honeymoon apartment, Tom? Tell Mister Bast how you used to clear your typewriter and papers off the card table when your charming bride invited . . .

—Look be quiet Jack, I'm not Mister Grynszpan no sit down Mister Bast go ahead with your, your supper look Jack . . .

—Come on Tom be Mister Grynszpan just for tonight? Backward turn backward oh time in thy flight, make Tom Mister Grynszpan just for Christ wait what time is it!

—There's a clock right under you Mister Gibbs, under the sofa there but it . . .

—Look out Jack damn it you're spilling that will you . . .

—Fine only two thirty plenty of time, have to meet a lady Bast great admirer of yours have to talk to you sometime, got a lot of great admirers you . . .

—Jack listen you're not going anyplace like this will you just sit, here bring that bottle back!

—What the hell's keeping them over there! he was past the fleet of cartons and over the film cans, up 24-One Pint Mazola New Improved across bales of the Morning Telegraph toppling a peak of lampshades to mount Appletons' Cyclopaedia of American Biography at the sill of the window to the rear where light squared the window across the airshaft, —Christ . . .

—Jack? What's . . .

—Like a, like a sack of potatoes . . .

—Just come back in here and sit down will you? Not a damn thing we can do yet, you didn't find any glasses here did you Mister, Mister Bast?

—No but I'm finished with this cup and there's a . . .

—Wait give me the bottle Jack here, take this cup in and rinse the, what . . .

—Just brought the mail see what Grynszpan's up to.

—Well don't just dump it on the . . .

—And Mister Gibbs could you save that teabag? I've only used it twice oh and there's a tomato soup can in there if you . . .

—Where the hell all this mail's coming from, Jack?

—Yes well I was just going to say Mister, Mis . . .

—Eigen sorry, my name's . . .

—His name's Eigen Bast, Thomas Eigen wrote an important novel once I think you're sitting on it he . . .

—Look just sit down Jack give me the cup no here, let me pour it you're . . .

—No no here you take the cup Tom, I'll . . .

—Well damn it give it to me then!

—Sorry Bast here, like some Old Strug . . .

—No, no no thank you but the mail I was just going to say maybe some of it's . . .

—Mail yes see what's, good Christ looks like Grynszpan's enrolled in Dale Carnegie poor bastard no God damned friends he, wait get that one Tom says on it important open immediately, better open it immediately . . .

—Mister Eigen I was just going to say this mail I think maybe some of it's . . .

—Looks like a, El Paso Natural Gas looks like a stock certificate how the . . .

—God damned shrewd Grynszpan take a flyer in El Pas . . .

—What do you mean a flyer it's one share what's, wait I'm sorry let me see the envelope it's made out to, here I'm sorry Mister Bast. I didn't even look at the envelope . . .

—No well that's all right I, I mean I've been getting some mail here if it's all right but I don't know what this . . .

—God damned shrewd Bast move in on El Paso gas, lone star bastards get the hell out of the United States set up their own God damned country real lone star democracy, million dollars get a million votes thousand dollars gets . . .

—Jack be quiet, look . . .

—Fifty cents skin the wrong color gets half a . . .

—Shut up! Look if Mister Bast wants to buy a share of . . .

—But I didn't Mister Eigen, I don't even know what it's . . .

—Look Mister Bast you don't have to explain anything sit down Jack, if you said he could come up here and work he wants to get mail here what the hell's the . . .

—Try to help andcourage him Tom shows up here on a business trip writing somebody else's opera what . . .

—Watch that lamp!

—Halte là . . . ! pages came swept down from 2-Ply Facial Tissue Yellow —qui va là! Tavern where Carmen's hiding with the smugglers old Don José comes marching up, how's that.

—Well yes but that passage I was just, I mean this is just music I wrote for those dancers but now she wants to sing too, I scored the instruments for the key of C but she can only sing in the key of G so I have to score it all over again tonight to take in tomorrow and get paid so I can . . .

—Look Jack stand that lamp back up straight and sit down!

—Wait I can reach it Mister Eigen, if . . .

—Just helping him with his libretto Tom, need a libretto don't you Bast?

—Well I, for what I'm working on myself I've sort of started with Locksley Hall and tried to . . .

—Locksley Hall Christ, next thing you'll shock us with a novel call it the Sorrows of Young Werther.

—Well I, if you could just move your foot Mister Gibbs I could reach the . . .

—Wait what's he stepping on damn it, pick that up will you Bast? before he . . .

—Get to wed some savage what's, where'd that come from . . .

—It's mine I just brought it from Schramm's, look put it up on that box before it gets . . .

—Ever see this Bast? Schramm's girl Irma rendered in the altogether by Lucas Cranach where . . .

—Look it's not Cranach it's a sorceress by Baldung, now just give it to me will you?

—Surprised they didn't confiscate it God damned indecent, little bush there ever meet her Bast?

—Who no I, I mean there was a girl I, I saw a girl once with Mister Schramm but . . .

—Nothing to be embarrassed about Bast, stand her up here all enjoy her how's that. Book I read once the girl had breasts like warm duck eggs Cranach must have read the same God damned book, missed the spirit here with what's her name, Irma? More like ostrich eggs up front.

—Rhoda.

—That's it Rhoda, should have brought her back with you Tom have a little wake.

—They were getting ready to take her away why the hell would I bring her back, she look out! Damn it Jack what are you . . .

—See out the God damned window that's all, Christ what, never seen so many flashing lights real mixed media show down there really got their hands full with her, ought to get yourself one Tom wed some savage woman let her rear your dusky . . .

—Look just sit down and be quiet will you Jack? She's, if she'd been here when he came back that's why he came back here God damn her, if she'd been here it wouldn't have happened she . . .

—Kept him at your house till I got there wouldn't have happened either, he . . .

—Jack God damn you! you, where have you been, all this time where the hell have you been!

—But, what happened has something happened? to Mister Schramm I mean?

—Two or three things Bast didn't even know you knew him.

—No well I really don't, I mean he comes in sometimes and talks about things like writing and my, this work I've been trying to do helping me with some of the . . .

—Schramm? Never knew a God damned thing about music.

—But he really does, he . . .

—Never could read a God damned note, tone deaf too couldn't even tell the . . .

—Jack look you're spilling that all over the . . .

—I'm not spilling, it's spilling. I'm not . . .

—Damn it just let me pour it will you!

—But about Mister Schramm is he, he's all right isn't he? I mean, where is he . . .

—Down the hall there look, he had an accident Bast he . . .

—I know it yes I was, you mean another one?

—Yes he, wait listen don't go in there now!

—I'm just going back here . . . he was already through and past the torrent at the sink, over the Morning Telegraphs —but that, on the bed is that . . .

—Will you come away from that God damn window!

—Yes but he, they've got a canvas bag they . . . the shade tore down in his face, footprints on it ascending from sill to molding.

—God damn it just, just let them do what they have to do . . .

—Tom? Leave him alone, come back in have a drink Bast.

—I don't want one.

—Sit down then don't have one. I'll have one . . .

—But what, what happened . . . he came through brushing dirt down his front —if I'd, if I'd been here . . . he caught at the tipped lamp coming down on Wise Potato Chips Hoppin' With Flavor! —if I'd . . .

—Look it wouldn't have helped, you couldn't have done a damn thing this time it wouldn't have helped . . .

—No but if he knocked, I know he knocked at the door he must have! and if I, if I'd been here . . .

—Course it would have helped Tom, cheered Schramm up takes his mind off this mess look at it, young composer running out of barakē sitting in this Christ awful mess eating a cupcake enough to cheer up anybody, pulls Schramm in sort of emergency barakē can't read a God damned word of music's helping him write an opera?

—No but he, Mister Gibbs he talked about the Ring he didn't have to read music to understand the, I mean he talked about the Kalevala about Freya and Brisingamen he . . .

—Well Christ I could have told you about that Bast I told him about Brisingamen, seen the necklace around her throat I know every God damned link in it have to talk to you about her Bast, she . . .

—Damn it Jack get down, where the hell are you trying to . . .

—Helped Mister Eigen here too Bast, helped him with his play didn't he Tom, told him to drop the first act it wouldn't change a God damned thing, told him it was undigested Plato, told him he didn't leave the actors or director an inch to move in because he didn't trust them told him the ending was too neat he can tell you Bast, writer who's run out of agapē same God damned thing tell him Tom, squeeze the universe into a ball and . . .

—God damn it Jack shut up and get down, you're going to knock that whole pile of boxes over what the hell are you doing up there.

—Hell do you think I'm doing looking for that manuscript, only reason I came up here in the first place seen it Bast?

—No well I, all I found was something by Mister Grynszpan it's in a blue cover, something agape I think it was I put it in the oven with all of his . . .

—That's it yes where the hell is it, said you'd read it?

—No well just the first part it was a little hard to . . .

—Hard what do you mean hard! Read it to you tell me what's so God damned hard where is it, hand me that can . . .

—I'll go get it if you . . .

—No sit still leave it where it is, Jack? If you want this drink come down off that pile of books and . . .

—Said I'll read it to him Tom . . . he pulled up the board cover of the bound volume of Musical Couriers for 1901 —tell me what's so God damned hard . . . he slapped pages over in a heap —here. The music of the world is free to all. Is that hard?

—Well no but . . .

—The Pianola is the universal means of playing the piano. Universal, because there is no one in all the world, having the use of hands and feet, who could not learn to use it that so God damned hard? Use of hands and feet . . . he got one of each on 12–38 Oz Btls Won't Burn, Smoke or Smell coming down. —Problem Schramm's having use of hands and feet he said Tolstoy told him, something terribly lacking between what he felt and what I could do Bast anything hard about that?

—Well I, no but I still don't know what happened to him he . . .

—Problem what happened he always woke up the same person went to bed the night before only way he knew it these God damned words going through his head, go to bed knew he'd wake up the same God damned person finally couldn't take it anymore, same God damned words waiting for him only thing to do get rid of the God damned container for the thing contained, God damned words come around next morning God damned container smashed on the sidewalk no place for them to . . .

—Look get his arm will you Bast? Listen Jack . . .

—Container for the . . .

—Damn it listen you don't know what you're talking about, think he was going around quoting Tolstoy the last thing he told me when he left a man goes into a hardware store asks for a can of blue paint a can of orange paint, a paintbrush and a hammer, the clerk thinks that's a funny selection he tells him I'm going home and paint one ball blue the other one orange and when I see my new girl tonight damn it Jack he was jealous that's all, dimwitted little piece Rhoda if she'd been here when he . . .

—Ought to get one Tom, having use of hands and feet ought to get yourself one . . .

—Mister Gibbs are you . . .

—Just trying to get to the God damned window see what's . . .

—Know what I think Jack? You're jealous.

—Got one Tom, ought to get yourself God damned people down there think they'd bought tickets even brought the children, half fare little bastards whole God damned mezzanine's full too, every God damned window across the street somebody hanging out . . . he jerked the blind further askew catching the flashes of light from below —five God damned Jones boys right in the middle of it with their here it is, here he comes canvas bag with handles Christ why aren't we, three cops pallbearers three cops somebody in white pajamas stowing him in the back of a, looks like a bakery truck City of New York Department of Hospitals looks like a God damned bakery truck Christ what a, God damn it Tom if you'd . . .

—Finally stole your act didn't he, Jack.

—I, I think somebody's at the door I'd better . . .

—Didn't finish your joke Tom, if she says what funny looking balls I'm going to hit her with the hammer think you're jealous Tom.

—Stole your act and left you here didn't he Jack, look out . . . !

—Halte là! Qui . . .

—Look sit down and shut up, it's the police.

—Come in officer we, we have trouble with this door but . . .

—Somebody break in on you?

—No it's just, like this . . . he got it open on one hinge.

—Nobody lives here like this they'll break in on you. Who walked up your shade.

—Officer! I can explain that, officer . . .

—You still with us?

—That was Lazarus officer, having use of hands and feet Lazarus come back to tell us all. I am Lazarus, come from the dead, come back to tell you all. Believing and shitting are two very different . . .

—Jack damn it shut up!

—But turn your eyes from Lazarus that cannot find a tomb, took one look around saw what he'd come back to and did it all over again . . .

—Bast get hold of his, no, no just let him sit on the floor.

—You know any next of kin Mister, what's your name?

—Eigen, Thomas Eigen, e, i . . .

—You want to come down and make the identification then?

—Make way, make way for Lazarus that must go search among the desert places where wait, his eye, his eye . . .

—Okay, let's go.

—Left his eyes to the eye bank, still got one good one if we hurry quick, need a shoe . . .

—Look Mister don't make it hard for yourself, take another drink and sleep it off. Your friend here can handle things.

—Sleep it off? We're friends of his too Mister what the hell do we, Bast quick a shoe, officer? Want you to arrest a cab driver named Hardy Suggs no the right one Bast quick, stole my right shoe officer . . . he tore at the laces and pulled it off —get him with the evidence, riding around with it in the back of his cab right now thought I didn't see his name on the hack license Hardy Suggs, and his picture before he shaved I can point him out in the lineup . . .

—But I'll need it in the morning Mister Gibbs I have to . . .

—He won't get this one Bast it's all right, he won't get it . . .

—Jack listen . . .

—Suggs his name officer wait, I'm coming with you . . . The film cans crashed to the floor as he reached the door —still got one good one if we hurry . . .

The policeman turned in the doorway. —You got your water running there, he said to Bast and left him fitting the door back into place and then standing there with his back against it, staring at the footprints on the shade and appearing to listen, finally to make his way through film cans and lampshades back, over the Morning Telegraph, to reach the shade and send it up with a snap, and stare through the window beyond, motionless, staring, till a knock on the door brought him round.

—Who is it?

—Hello? came from the other side. —Could I talk to you?

—Who is it?

—One minute could I ask you Mister?

He got the door opened enough for the shaft from the bare bulb to catch an old face in the hall there. —What is it?

—I came to ask the apartment Mister?

—It's not mine I just sort of, work here.

—No by the end of the hall Mister, it's empty now? the apartment? My vife Mister . . .

—But, what do you . . .

—We live upstairs Mister, five flights stairs up, my vife Mister, her legs, she couldn't go up and down, I see them take him away in the bag Mister, I ask, maybe . . .

—But you you, miserable . . .

—My vife, Mister . . . ?

—Go away! He stood backed against the door, pulled a shirt from the dishtowel rack and wiped his face with it, waiting, and then he suddenly started picking up film cans and stacking them, lampshades and stacking them, scores, papers, pencils, in to the armless sofa where he pounded shape back into the punctured lampshade and sat putting down notes, drawing lines, curves, sitting back to wipe his face, up to find the cup, trip on the bottle, shake the empty teabag box, pick up the bottle and empty what little was left into the cup, drink it, stare at Baldung's sorceress propped sideways against 24/One Pound H-O, grab it up and examine it and finally return it, upright, and stare at the ceiling. On his feet again and halt with his shod step forward, he scaled The Musical Courier and, strung out atop it, put his ear to a crevice between the volumes.

————a country the size of California has the fourth largest army in the world, thanks to . . .

He raised himself, reached a mop protruding over the edge of the submerged piano, forced its handle down into the crevice between the volumes and pounded, brought it back out and put his ear to the crevice again.

——timely food tips, brought to you by . . .

Over cartons and lampshades the mop flew to lodge behind Appletons'
and he hitched himself back to the edge of the plateau steadying one foot
on Won't Burn, Smoke or Smell, looking into it, digging among undeveloped film rolls, string, an odd glove, defunct cigarette lighters,
coming up with a straw beach slipper he fitted descending, paused again
to brush another layer of dirt down his front before he sat on the sofa's
edge staring down at a fresh lined page, up at the ceiling, at the Baldung,
at 24–7 Oz Pkgs Flavored Loops, appearing to listen as shreds of sound
escaped sporadic partings of his lips, scribbling a clef, notes, a word, a
curve, still reaching fresh pages as light chilled the skewed leaves of the
blind, lapsed motionless as it warmed the punctured shade and finally
cast it into shadow, coming to abruptly and through to the torrent at the
sink with the slap, slap of the straw slipper back to set the cup dangling
the teabag string on Moody's and reach a sharper pencil, a fresh page,
pages as shadows rose, crossed, fell, hunched as though listening to bring
sounds into being, up in a sudden turn that might have been a pose for
the mirrorless wall as though holding them off.

——time to join the biggest savings bank fam . . .

—Wait who is it . . . ! he was through to catch the door as it came
in at him —oh it's, it's you Mister Gibbs wait let me . . .

—Bring in the mail see who's in the package . . .

—No no wait I'll pick it up don't, wait here's your newspaper . . . he
held up the Turf Guide, —just let me . . .

—Good, today's? Where'd you get it . . .

—You just dropped it no be careful . . . !

—Christ . . .

—Yes well I wouldn't try to sit on those film cans they're not very,
just let me get the door here . . . he heaped the mail up on 24-One Pint
Mazola New Improved, —can you . . .

—Keep tripping on this God damned . . .

—Wait yes let me pick up this music's scattered around in here
. . . he came sliding the slippered foot ahead past 36 Boxes 200 2-Ply
—I mean I've been working all night and . . .

—Left my cigarettes here, who took my cigarettes.

—They're under you, on the floor right under your . . .

—Call that cigarettes? A hand worked blindly under the sofa —that's
a bottle, tell a bottle by its shape Bast take my cigarettes left an empty
bottle.

—Well but, I can make you a cup of tea I have to shave anyway
because I have to go . . .

—Saw your car waiting outside why I broke my neck to get here
Bast, said I'd . . .

—My what?

—Car waiting downstairs take you on your business trip, why I broke my . . .

—That, no that black limousine down there? he let the blind fall back —that's not, I mean that couldn't be . . .

—Said you're going on a God damned business trip didn't you?

—No but that's, I mean I've already been Mister Gibbs just somebody who asked me to help him out this one time it was just a, just sort of an errand he couldn't really handle himself just to earn some money till these dancers pay me if you could move your knee, just let me get these pages before they . . .

—Problem Bast you don't trust them, God damned performers sit up here write music for them you don't trust them to . . .

—No well they wouldn't even play it till I rescored it I mean I don't really know what it sounds like myself yet but . . .

—Why I just told you broke my neck to get here didn't I? Help you dig out that God damned piano promised I'd . . .

—No but right now I, I mean maybe you should just rest for a while Mister Gibbs you don't look, you look like you haven't had any sleep and your . . .

—Better take a look at yourself Bast, call the God damned kettle back better go take a . . .

—No that's why I have to go clean up and shave before I . . .

—Can't compose without a piano Bast promise to help you dig the God damned thing out didn't I? What Beethoven told Cipriani Potter can't compose without a piano may be tempted to consult it, Bast? Talking to you where the hell . . .

—Yes I can hear you Mister Gibbs I just have to shave, he called over the sink's torrent pulling his shirt off, working his face with the cracked bar of yellow laundry soap from the rusted shelf there —Mister Gibbs? It's all right if I use this razor I found here isn't it?

—Never compose in a room where there's a God damned piano Beethoven told Cipriani Potter because you may be tempted to consult it, Bast? you hear me?

—Yes but I'm . . .

—Problem Bast there's too God damned much leakage around here, can't compose anything with all this energy spilling you've got entropy going everywhere. Radio leaking under there hot water pouring out so God damned much entropy going on think you can hold all these notes together know what it sounds like? Bast?

—What . . . he drew the rusted razor down his cheek, tipped a cookie tin top on the shelf to catch its reflection.

—Not listening.

—Yes but . . . he drew blood and paused, reached for the shirt dangling from the dishtowel rack. —I mean there are some things you can't really write down especially simple things, they just have to be left for the performer and till the music's actually performed it doesn't really exist at all so the only . . .

—Problem writing an opera Bast you're up against the worst God damned instrument ever invented, asked me to tell you about Johannes Müller didn't you?

—Well I, I don't think so but . . .

—Just told Mister Eigen his play doesn't exist at all didn't you? Doesn't trust actors doesn't trust directors he ties up the end with a knot because he doesn't trust the God damned audience told you Schramm had a tin ear didn't I? Problem how to get rid of the God damned artist why he kept coming in here and bothering you didn't he?

—No who, Mister Schramm? No but he . . .

—Asked me to tell you about Johannes Müller didn't you? Told you you're not listening I'm talking about Johannes Müller, nineteenth-century German anatomist Johannes Müller took a human larynx fitted it up with strings and weights to replace the muscles tried to get a melody by blowing through it how's that. Bast?

—Yes it sounds quite . . .

—Thought opera companies could buy dead singers' larynxes fix them up to sing arias save fees that way get the God damned artist out of the arts all at once, long as he's there destroy everything in their God damned path what the arts are all about, Bast? that's why you hid it?

—What . . . he came pulling on one shirt, holding a sleeve of the other to his throat spreading with red —hid what, I . . .

—Manuscript you told me's so hard why you hid it didn't you?

—Which the, no the one in the blue cover? No I just put it in the wait, wait sit down I'll . . .

—Found it! the oven door crashed closed. —Promise to read it to you hide it in the God damned oven . . .

—No I just put it in there so it wouldn't get any dirtier but . . .

—Read it to you tell me what's so God damned hard.

—Yes but I haven't time right now Mister Gibbs I have to go somewhere could I, could I have my shoe?

—Says quarter of seven under there Bast got plenty of time sit down.

—No but for the right time you have to subtract that from ten because wait wait don't sit on my . . .

—Opening kind of epigraph here please do not shoot the, listening?

—The opening epitaph yes but I need my . . . he sank down on Hoppin' With Flavor! —my shoe what, what happened to it . . .

—Told you been tripping on the God damned sole's loose, now listening?

—But it's almost, how did you . . .

—Told you I broke my neck to get back here wanted me to read this to you didn't you? Please do not shoot the pianist. He is doing his best. There, anything hard about that?

—No it's, it's fine . . . he got the inert foot propped on Moody's and bent forward to work on the knotted lace.

—Posted in a Leadville saloon, this appeal caught the eye of art in its ripe procession of one through the new frontier of the 'eighties where the frail human element still abounded even in the arts as Oscar Wilde alone, observing the mortality in that place is marvelous, passed on unranked by that phrase doing his best, redolent of chance and the very immanence of human failure that century of progress was consecrated to wiping out once for all; for if, as another mother country throwback had it, all art does constantly aspire to the condition of music, there in a Colorado mining town saloon all art's essential predicament threatened to be laid bare with the clap of a pistol shot just as deliverance was at hand, born of the beast with two backs called arts and sciences whose rambunctious coupling came crashing the jealous enclosures of class, taste, and talent, to open the arts to Americans for democratic action and leave history to bunk. Now God damn it Bast anything hard about that?

—Well, well no . . . he eased the shoe off.

—Good, nothing so God damned hard about this, anything hard about this? A remarkable characteristic of the Americans is the manner in which they have applied science to modern life Wilde marveled on, struck by the noisiest country that ever existed. One is waked up in the morning, not by the singing of the nightingale, but by the steam whistle . . . All art depends upon exquisite and delicate sensibility, and such constant turmoil must ultimately be destructive of the musical faculty and thus, though the flute is not an instrument which is expressive of moral . . . what's the matter.

—Nothing I'm, I just have to get this envelope you're sitting on and this, these newspapers . . .

—Good yes, yes though the flute is not an instrument which is expressive of moral character, it is too exciting, it had not taken this particular rebuke of Aristotle's to check young Frank Woolworth's rash ambitions on the instrument. He was becomingly tone deaf, and by eighteen seventy-nine had already crowned a decade of insolvency with the failure of his five-cent store in Utica, New York, where the rewards of leisure were then being advertised in the hapless passage of George Jones through McGuffey's Fourth Eclectic Reader, last glimpsed as a poor wanderer, without money and without friends. Such are the wages of idleness. I hope every reader will, Bast God damn it keep complaining about how hard it is and then wander around the room while I'm trying to . . .

—No but I have to leave Mister Gibbs, I told you I . . .

—Good. I hope every reader will, from this history, take warning, and stamp improvement on the wings of time problem most God damned readers rather be at the movies. Pay attention here bring something to it take something away problem most God damned writing's written for readers perfectly happy who they are rather be at the movies, come in empty-handed go out the same God damned way what I told him Bast. Ask them to bring one God damned bit of effort want everything done for them they get up and go to the movies I mean I'm the one who told him about agapē Bast, formulated the law of common foci did I tell you that? Promised to tell you about Grynszpan I tell you that?

—No but I have to leave now Mister Gibbs I . . .

—Bast? Listen the better among us, said I'd tell you what Beethoven listen . . .

—You did Mister Gibbs now I really wait no don't try to get up just, I really have to leave . . . his armload of papers bumped 36 Boxes 200 2-Ply backing past —I'll be . . .

—What he wrote the countess of, the better among us Bast?

—Yes . . . ? he got the door poised on one hinge.

—God damn it listen! Bast? The, the better among us bear one another in mind . . .

For a moment he hesitated there and then put down his papers on the descending stair behind him taking both hands to fit the door closed silent as the dim hall till he made for the stairs, the separating sole of his shoe lending a percussive effect to his haste down them broken only for his pause on the pavement where he stared at the vacant limousine double parked there, abruptly recovering a rhythm double time past a fleet of garbage cans, another, down a curb, curbs, declining at last to a flapping cadence up the wide range of museum steps to find brief echo through the rotunda and recover silence in a sudden glide toward the sculpture gallery, as a horde emerged from the armor collection.

—Bast?

—What? I . . .

—Not you back there is it? Mister Bast?

—No I, I think so yes . . . he peered round the marble buttock of a marble Hermes —I mean I, I didn't expect to see you here Mister Crawley I . . .

—Can't say I expected to see you here either no, might have looked for you in the Museum of Natural what the devil's happened to you, you look . . .

—Nothing no I'm, I think I cut myself shaving a few times shaving I haven't had much sleep because I've been . . .

—Good good yes, been working hard have you? Looks like you've got something there about ready for me to listen to?

—Yes well not quite no, no you see I . . .

—Expected to hear something from you before this you know, called your office and your girl said you were out of town on business. Want to get yourself back to your music Mister Bast.

—Yes there's nothing I'd rather . . .

—Didn't want to press you on that of course, reason I called was just to let that associate of yours know I think I can unload that, what was it? wallpaper you brought in?

—Yes Eagle Mills, yes, well that's where I've just . . .

—Might get him twelve or thirteen cents on the dollar, kind of a favor of course, how many lots you say he has?

—Well he doesn't have it anymore, they gave him some stock in place of it and now . . .

—Oh, heard about that have you? Yes, you're well out of it Mister Bast, and now back to the music, eh? That's the right spirit, want to see you have a little more room there to exercise your talents.

—Yes well I certainly . . .

—Good, yes, now the idea is, Bast, they're having one hell of a problem there in the Uganda with elephant damage, overgrazing and all the rest of it, don't do a damned thing for sixteen hours a day but stand around and eat you know . . .

—Yes I, I see . . . Bast sidled toward a marble raised in the contorted grace of sport as the cafeteria horde reappeared.

—Talking about cropping around four thousand of them to preserve the habitat, of course Stamper and I want to get in there and do our part but it's a damned nuisance when they could ship them right over set them up a habitat right down in the Everglades is Stamper's idea, give us all the hunting we could ask for preserving a habitat like that one, he came on stalking Bast beyond the athlete's flanks, —think we can work in a little elephant music, Bast?

—A, little elephant . . . ?

—Big fellows Bast, big fellows, eat five or six hundred pounds of rubbish a day you know, grass and tree bark, a good bull runs up over ten feet and damned smart too, see all eight tons of him coming down on you and he's the most dangerous game you could ask for. Of course this time we'll bring along our own boy to run the camera but don't let that hold you up, got a good imagination have you?

—I, I think so, I . . . Bast retreated round sarcophagi edging deeper among the marbles as the dispersing horde spreading down the gallery toward the splash of fountains shed an unkempt fragment knelt knotting a knotted lace at the foot of the Sardis column.

—Want to leave yes, I won't keep you from your work but take your time to it Bast, don't want to hurry you, Bast? Exit's out that way . . .

—Yes I, I was just going to stop in the men's room.

—You all right there Bast?

—Fine yes I, I'm fine.

—Don't look fine to me. Outdoors, when you've cleaned up this work of course. Have something for me to hear in a day or two will you?

And his —I'll try, was lost to the cadenced flap of his shoe taking up toward the splash of water, round the column's base, where he tripped.

—Hey look out you . . . oh hi, boy am I glad to see you Bast!

—Well get up off the floor.

—Okay just a, shit . . . no but this lousy lace broke again, what do you expect me to do . . . With a final yank he straightened up and hurried alongside, the attaché case he carried barely clearing the floor between them. —Where shall we go hey.

—Anyplace, I just want to give you these papers and . . .

—Because I just had this neat idea. See I could just sneak away for like an hour and we could go up to the office. Okay?

—What office.

—This here new office you said you just got to do your work at, okay?

—No.

—How come? See they're all going down to this here snack bar anyway so . . .

—I said no! now, now just . . .

—Okay don't get mad, I only thought . . .

—I'm not mad I, I'm just tired and I don't feel very well.

—You don't look very good, did you look like this up there hey? Hey Bast? Did something happen to your foot?

—Nothing happened to my foot, no. Now . . .

—No it's just your shoe, I think I got this big rubber band hey wait. We can't go down there, that's where they all went to this here snack bar. You ever been here before hey Bast?

—Of course, now will you hurry up?

—You know where the Egypt exhibit is at?

—Yes but why do you . . .

—No I just wondered, wait I can't hurry or my sneaker will come off . . . and side by side, left foot, right foot, they got through the door marked men. —Back here hey . . . he mounted the attaché case on the first flat surface he found and lifted out the battered portfolio mended, now, down one end with black friction tape. —See? he stepped back, —isn't it neat?

—Well why don't you throw the old one away.

—No see I got this one for you. Doesn't it look like real leather hey?

—Well it's, it's a little shiny but . . .

—No but I mean if you don't get real close, you know? So you won't have to carry these papers and stuff around in this here dirty envelope for like when you go to these meetings, and when they see you on the train and all, you know?

—When who sees me on the train.

—I mean like these other businessmen and see I even got your initials on in gold, even if they . . .

—But, those aren't my initials.

—No I know see that's what I was going to say, see when I sent away they must have thought this here B I made looked like a D but I was thinking maybe you could just change your . . .

—Look it doesn't matter now, just let me . . .

—And anyway if some wiseass says something you can just say it says like E D for Edward, so what happened up there anyway I mean did everything . . .

—I brought you the newspaper you can read about the whole thing later, now . . .

—No but I mean didn't they get mad when you just walked in and said we're taking over? Let's see hey what, holy look hey! I mean it's the whole front page almost! Is this you?

—Yes, it . . .

—Who you shaking hands with?

—That's Mister Hopper, he runs the bank that took over the receivership and . . .

—I didn't know he looked like that, I mean like I've talked to him on the telephone and all but I didn't know he's this nigro.

—Well he's not, what makes you . . .

—Because doesn't he look like it in this here picture? No but I guess you do too wait let me read it hey. One of the oldest textile mills in the region and mainstay of the Union Falls economy for more than a century, Eagle Mills changed hands this week following a shrewd move by downstate financial interests headquartered in the New York area where hey that's us right? I mean shrewd financial interests what are they trying to say we screwed them?

—No, it just means . . .

—Rumors of bankruptcy which have circulated here for many years were confirmed in an exclusive statement to the Union Falls Weekly Messenger by bank president Fred Hopper, who has also served on Eagle Mills Board of Directors since nineteen twenty-eight. In his exclusive statement Mister Hopper outlined the procedure by which outstanding stock of Eagle Mills, which has paid no dividends since nineteen thirty-four, was dissolved and the company assets handed over to bondholders in a court action presided over by Judge R V Begg, whose marriage to Mister Hopper's younger sister Adeline in nineteen twenty-seven will be remembered by older Union Falls residents as the leading social what's all this crap hey.

—I told you to read it later, if you'll just . . .

—Okay wait a second, generally, it had been generally understood that wait where does it tell about us, that it came as a surprise to many that the bond issue, which had been selling at a discount in recent years, had been snapped up in a lightning like stroke by outside interests here it is, since it had been generally understood that the majority of Eagle bonds were held in this area. The recent rumor that the mills were to be closed and the extensive site converted to a public park and speedway had already been denied in an exclusive statement to the Union Falls Weekly Messenger by Park Commissioner Edgar Begg, reached at his home on North Main Street where he has been confined since returning from the service with injuries sustained in the Mouse Argonne. Again disclaiming these and sim continued on page five . . .

—Look don't read it all now, I just brought it so you could . . .

—No that's okay, came through the flurry of paper, —page five, end of the baseball season approaches the hometown Eagles have racked up another wait, here it is, ilar rumors in an exclusive statement to the Union Falls Weekly Messenger, the youthful representative of the downstate financial interests Mister Edwerd Bast asserted hey see? how they spelled it? See so you can just . . .

—They got hold of one of those idiotic cards before I . . .

—And like how come everybody's always giving them these exclusive statements hey.

—Because there's nobody else to give them to, now . . .

—Bast asserted that although present plans remain somewhat indefinite, he knew of no park or speedway being contemplated for the area at this time boy that's no shit, a public park boy. Mister Bast, whose associate was unable to accompany him on his whirlwind visit due to is that me hey?

—Who else would it be? Now will you just read that later and . . .

—Okay but just let me finish this part hey, press of urgent demands in the New York city area, appeared somewhat surprised himself at the swift turn of events. Declining to discuss financial details related to the takeover, Mister Bast stressed the investment nature of his associate's interest in Eagle Mills, hastening to reassure the many Eagle employees among loyal Weekly Messenger readers that he saw no reason for apprehension at this time. Hardly fitting the description of the hard driving financial interests he represents, Mister Bast's modest and courteous manner won him many friends on his short visit. When not occupied with the demands of business he enjoys cultural and artistic pursuits, and music being the hobby Mister Bast enjoys most his visit fortunately coincided with the long awaited fall concert of no wait a second . . .

—I said you could read that later! now . . .

—No but see I have to see what you said up there. Following a repast of fruit cup . . .

—That's all I said! now will you . . .

—No I'm almost to the bottom hey, roast turkey with giblet gravy accompanied by candle salad, the famed Union House specialty of pineapple ring with standing banana stuffed with peanut butter topped by marshmallow whip, Mister Bast accompanied by his hosts Mister and Mrs Hopper and son Bunky repaired to the basement of the former Masonic Temple to how come you repaired the basement of the . . .

—Will you give me that!

—Temple to enjoy selections rendered by the Eagle Mills Employees' Glee Club including Stout Hearted Men, their famed colored light rendition of God Bless America and the perennial favorite Okla hey!

—Well I said put it down! Now . . .

—Okay but you didn't need to rip it, I mean it ripped right through this picture of this here big brick boy it looks like a prison hey, what's this over here.

—That's where the offices are.

—How come if the mill's over here the office is way over here?

—Look I wasn't there when they built it, I don't . . .

—And like what's this here long thing with all these doors and hey is this a train track? they've got a train there?

—They're just rusty tracks, and that's a garage.

—What do they need this tremendous garage for.

—They don't, they let the town keep all its trucks and snowplows there and . . .

—What's this big place over here where it says Eagles Visitors.

—It's where they play softball, now look . . .

—Who.

—The company softball team, they . . .

—That's these hometown Eagles? What does the company need a softball team for.

—Because they like softball! I had to sit through three games of softball, now look. These papers from Mister Hopper . . .

—But why should they get paid to play softball?

—Who said they got paid! They just play weekends and after work, now . . .

—Okay but it's on company property isn't it?

—Well what's wrong with . . .

—No but see that's the whole thing of when we sell everything off on this here leaseback deal, you know?

—No, I don't know! All I know is I told those people up there they didn't have to worry, you saw it right there in the paper, and now if you think you can . . .

—No but see all you do is you sell it then you lease it right back like, see that's why they call it leaseback.

—Well then why sell it in the first place, if you . . .

—Because that's what you do. See I read in this thing where you sell everything and lease it right back off the people you sold it to on this like ninety-nine years lease because I mean who cares what's going to happen in ninety-nine years, see so then you stay right in business and get to keep losing money just like before only now you have all this here cash. But see what I was just thinking was like why should we lease back this here ballfield and these garages and this whole building of all these here offices if we . . .

—Look if you sell people's offices how do you expect them to . . .

—No but see look . . . he pieced the paper together on the radiator top, —see instead of they're probably like running back and forth from the mills to the offices all the time and calling each other up on the telephone if we just move all their desks and stuff over here in the mills someplace then the office building and this here ballfield makes like this one parcel which then you . . .

—Look this is, this is ridiculous even if you really could do things like this, I just told you how they feel up there and . . .

—What, like they'd get pissed off if we sold their ballfield? So if we sell it to the bank let the bank let them play softball and like with these here garages, why should we pay taxes and leases and all so the town can keep some broken down trucks there, I mean let somebody else let them. Like I mean selling something doesn't change it into something else and like if the bank won't let them play softball or park their trucks let them get pissed off at the bank, you know? he got a sneaker up on the radiator and started to work on a knot. —So anyway when we get all this here cash . . .

—And what makes you think anybody's going to give you all this cash you keep talking about is just as . . .

—No but see that's the thing because like even if they buy it off you for way under this book value of what it's worth see then they get this here real bargain and you get to subtract what they pay you from that and you get this whole other bunch of tax credits see which then you can . . .

—Look can't you understand? Just because you read about these things it doesn't mean you can just step in there and do them even if you could, you can't even if you could, you . . .

—How come?

—Because these are real people up there that's how come! A lot of them who owned the stock still can't believe it's not worth anything and even the ones who owned bonds, a lot of them are old and when they first bought the bonds it was almost like they were lending money to, to someone in the family. And the ones who work there, even if you could sell their ballfield and put their offices in the mills how long do you think they'd . . .

—No but look hey I mean holy, I mean this isn't any popularity contest hey. Besides what could they do?

—Well they could, they could quit they could . . .

—Okay well then see we wouldn't have to fire anybody because that's mostly what costs so much anyway is all these here people, you know? See because if we could like get them out of there and get this here new machinery I read this thing where you get this new machinery which then you divide how long will it take to wear out into how much did it cost you which then you get to take that off taxes too see? Only the neat thing is see they let you like pretend it's going to wear out two or three times as fast so you're getting this big bunch of tax credits right off, they call it depreciated acceleration or something only the thing is you can't do it with people see so . . .

—Depreciated acceleration, you don't know what it means it doesn't mean anything, you . . .

—So why should I have to know exactly what it means? The contents of the portfolio came dumped abruptly to the radiator top —I mean why should we pay this here lawyer to know something if we already know it? and he stooped to the floor for an envelope smudged with penciled notes.

—Did you send away for him too?

—Didn't I tell you how we got him hey? See when I thought we might get screwed on . . .

—And will you stop saying we? I wasn't even . . .

—I know, I forgot to tell you how we got him, see I just read all these job ads in the Times till I found one of this company which sounded real professional see so I copied it and put in my box number instead, this here Mister Piscator didn't you get this letter from him? Because this is just this here carbon copy he sent me of it when I told him on the telephone he should write all this stuff to you at the office because you were handling it there for me like this branch, you know? So when he says he can get all these figures on Eagle Mills off their accountants for those ideas you got me off that smartass broker with all the heads which hey I meant to tell you, you know he said I'd never see a nickel on this Alberta and Western debenture? Well right after they put out another one called series C I got this here interest payment on series B if he's so smart. And like he told you Ace was like toilet paper the price of it just doubled right after this progress report that said they expect to pay this dividend and they offered me twenty cents a share which I only paid like ten for so I got this whole bunch more, I mean I'd like to know how many stocks he's got which their price doubles that quick boy. Anyway you didn't bring this here letter from Piscator?

—No I didn't even . . .

—Okay that's okay because I got this here copy, see so anyway remember where he says all this stuff about generating cash and lease-backs and hey look, see? Where it says accelerated depreciation? When I just said that you said it didn't mean anything?

—Well that's not what you said, you said . . .

—I did too, I said . . .

—No you didn't, you said something like . . .

—I did too.

—You . . . Somewhere behind him a toilet flushed. —Look, all of this is just . . .

—No no okay don't get mad, I mean look remember here where he says from premil, preliminary figures their net worth is in the neighborhood of eight hundred twenty-six mil, wait where's the dot, thousand rather, thousand dollars of which an estimated six hundred forty thousand dollars is in the net property account which once he sees these tax assessments and stuff you were supposed to get off Hopper . . .

—This is what I've been trying to give you for the last five minutes, here. Now will you . . .

—Hey is this stuff about this pension fund in here too hey? He tore open the soiled manila envelope —see because if Eagle Mills is so old this here pension fund ought to be real old too see so . . .

—Wait till you see your employees.

—What do you mean?

—I mean did it ever occur to you that a lot of them might be getting real old along with everything else?

—So what.

—So instead of accelerated depreciation and a whole bunch of tax credits they're almost ready to retire and draw their pensions, what do you think a pension fund is for.

—Oh yeah . . . he wedged a sneaker into the radiator to shape a precarious lap where he shook out the papers, —I didn't think of that, see because we have to work something to like pry loose some cash like Piscator says here so we can . . .

—Stop it look what kind of a lawyer do you expect to get in the mail anyhow, these people who've worked all their lives for miserable wages so they can finally retire on a miserable pension and this, this Piscator thinks you can take that too?

—No wait hey, see that's not the . . .

—I don't want to hear it, just let me settle these expenses and get out of the whole idiotic . . .

—No but wait a second hey, I mean who's taking it off them? Because like what good is this here pension fund doing just sitting there if we can like put it to work for them to get this here acquisition, you know?

—No and I don't . . .

—Right here on the next page where he says about getting this acquisition of this here brewery.

—There's no brewery it's a textile mill, now look here's the list of expenses I . . .

—No it's this acquisition of it off these two old brothers in wait a second, Wisconsin or Minneapolis or someplace . . .

—No now stop, just stop for a minute! This, this whole thing has to stop somewhere don't you understand that?

—No but holy, I mean that's the whole thing Bast otherwise what good is this neat tax loss carryforward and all these here tax credits and all, I mean that's all Eagle is and see where Piscator says here Eagle probably has this here limited charter so they can't buy this brewery but if the pension fund could like buy the brewery stock and the dividends could go right in it and cut down what the company has to put in see then we . . .

—Stop it! Look aren't things in enough of a mess with a broken down textile mill without getting into a broken down brewery?

—What do you mean broken down! I mean holy, I mean you sound like you didn't hardly read this at all I mean they have these earnings of like a million dollars a year look, and where it says two million dollars in excess working capital see? where the asking price is five, seven two six, one three . . .

—But five that's, look that's five million, that's five million dollars! It's just, even if it wasn't just numbers on paper do you think there's five million dollars in the whole town of Union Falls?

—I know see that's why we have to work some deal where it isn't all cash because like if we . . .

—All right look, look if somebody had something with two dollars already in it and it earned a dollar a week why would he want to sell it for five dollars? In three weeks you . . .

—No but see that's earnings before taxes that's the whole thing, I mean didn't you read this part Bast? See because like if you can put it all together and write off all these here losses of Eagle against all these profits of like this here brewery then you get to keep them, I mean like otherwise you get screwed out of everything by these taxes like these two old brothers see they had all these profits which they didn't collect them on account of this here tax so now when they do collect them they'd have this tremendous tax which is this undistributed profits tax, see? See so now they're scared if one of them dies the other would really get screwed, but if they just sell the whole thing then all they have to pay is this here capital gains tax which is only like a half of a half, I mean don't you even remember this part hey?

—No.

—But how come because holy, I mean this is the whole . . .

—Because I didn't read it, I didn't read any of it. I didn't even open it. Now if you'll just . . .

—But, but holy, but I mean how come you didn't even open it?

—Because when I came back from that trip last night there was mail everywhere letters, magazines, books I haven't even . . .

—Wait what about one from X-L Lithograph Company, I mean was there this letter from . . .

—I told you I don't know! I don't know what any of it is I, do you think I came in and sat right down over that pile of trash in the middle of look, a friend of mine had just had an accident when I came in if I'd been there, if I'd been there when he . . .

—No but holy shit Bast this is serious, I mean like I'm sorry about your friend and all but holy shit this is like five million dollars and I mean where I'm paying your expenses for like this here trip and helping you out so you can . . .

—I did what I said I'd do didn't I! I went up there and settled this thing to help you out just this once didn't I?

—Okay sure but . . .

—Like this trash I took in and showed Mister Crawley to help you out just this once didn't I?

—No but you said you had to go see him anyway and besides, I mean I paid half your train and subway and all or you couldn't even have went in and . . .

—All right yes but just because something's gone wrong every time I've come out for that school check so I could pay you back the ten dollars from that field trip you . . .

—Okay but like is it my fault if they keep screwing up your check and all? And I mean like I'm advancing you these expenses like this here whole fifty dollars to help out for your . . .

—All right! Look that's all I want to get straightened out here, I've got exactly ninety-four cents that money wasn't to help out for my anything, it was expenses for this trip, I've got them all written down I mean I'm the one who's been doing everything while you sit here picking your nose talking about five million dollars now . . .

—No but holy, I mean listen I'm the one that has to figure things up and like make these here decisions with these risks and all like I mean I barely made it boy, getting this here stockholder suit money in this one account to borrow against in this here other one to get all these forks shipped to pay for all these here bonds which I'd already sent away for them where these here brokers start . . .

—That's what I'm talking about! You send away for this, send away for that, you send away for a lawyer you get into one mess and ask me to help you out just this once and while I'm up there trying to straighten it out you're sending away for a brewery and I don't know what, I'm trying to get you out of trouble and you're just making it bigger with all this, this paper, these numbers on paper and this nonsense about lease-backs and depreciated whatever it is, you ask me to help you out just this once and . . .

—But what am I suppose to do! his foot came to the floor and he got the other one free of the radiator, —I mean who asked them for their lousy mills? All I did was buy these bonds for this here investment and mind my own business and then they turn around and dump all these wrecked up buildings and people and stuff on me and what do they expect me to do, build them a park? I mean holy shit . . . he ripped a paper towel down and worked it at his nose, —I have this here investment which I have to protect it don't I? And I mean you're so sorry for all these old people with this here stock they got in exchange for their bonds which they'd bought them for this investment just like I did so what about them? I mean this broker says convert my preferred stock to common and buy more common so I can do something to protect my thing there let them have the preferred because all they give a shit about is will they get their dividends anyway, so like how are they going to get them if we just keep paying everybody to play softball and sing Stout Hearted Men and then some smartass comes along and screws us with a stockholder's suit, I mean holy shit Bast . . . He took the paper towel away from his nose and stared into it, —I mean I'm just trying to protect their investment too, you know?

—But it has to stop somewhere! can't you understand that? Can't you just let your mail order lawyer straighten out this Eagle Mills without talking about buying breweries and . . .

—No but that's the thing! he wadded the towel and dropped it. —You can't . . . and he kicked it toward the radiator, —I mean like when we went on that field trip where that Diamond Cable Company the president of it said if you're playing you might as well play to win but you can't just might as well, he came on skating the towel wad across the floor, gave it a slap shot with his instep. —You can't just play to play because the rules are only for if you're playing to win which that's the only rules there are.

—All right then look. I said I'd help you out just this once and I did, now you can go ahead with this Mister Piscator you've got. You and Mister Piscator can get out there and play to win.

—No but I can't just go out there and meet him hey!

—Out where . . .

—Out by the Egyptian stuff see we had in school where they have this Egyptian tomb and all here so I told Piscator you're like real interested in Egypt and I thought after we went over all this Eagle stuff from your trip you could just bump into him there like, see and then you and him could go up to the office and, and what's the matter hey. Hey Bast?

—What.

—Well see I thought if you'll help me out again just this once till things get going like with Piscator and wait wait don't get mad hey because see like I've only talked to him on the telephone which that doesn't work so good because when I stuff this handkerchief in it to make me sound bigger he says he can't hardly understand me, so see like I wrote all this stuff down . . . he had the attaché case open and snapped down a flap in its cover where pages of coarse composition paper lay filled margin to margin in thick lead pencil. —See it won't take you long because it's just all these little things only you have to have a lawyer to do them, like if we want to open a business account at the bank he has to get us this here business certificate off the state of New York, and then this here is I was thinking of if we want to get incorporated on the side like what do we have to do. See and then here's this stuff about this X-L Lithograph thing we were just talking about see we can figure out these expenses now and like how much you still owe me and if you still need more for expenses ahead of time if you can help me out again just this once? I mean like all I've done for you like getting to take this trip and staying at this here hotel and this banquet you went to and all those softball games and getting your picture in the paper and all . . .

—No no stop, stop I . . .

—And like this here attaché case I got you with these gold initials on and that neat alarm clock and I mean I go get all these here business cards printed up for you and I call up that Virginia and fix it up where you get her to take telephone calls at that cafet . . .

—Look these aren't my initials! and that, that clock it runs backwards I have to stop and do arithmetic whenever I want to know what time it is look I hate softball, don't you understand that? I don't want my picture on the front page of the Weekly Messenger can't you understand that? Getting to stay at that broken down Union House the rug was so filthy you couldn't even, you had to put a quarter in the radio to make it play and that banquet! Sitting across from that Bunky eating a banana stuffed with, he spent three years in eighth grade the newspaper didn't mention that did it I mean getting to take this trip, do you know how long the bus takes to Union Falls? Because you wouldn't pay for a plane ticket you wouldn't even pay for the train who asked you to get a thousand business cards printed, business representive with footmarks on them who asked you to subscribe to Textile World and . . .

—No but wait a second hey I mean, I mean where we were going to like try and help each other out and I'm advancing these expenses and figuring up paying you without . . .

—Paying me what! Look if we can just settle these expense . . .

—No but I mean where I'm getting you all this different stock see? Only you get this here mail which you don't even open it up I mean what am I supposed to do! I mean where I'm trying to help you out and you don't even . . .

—All right look there was, what was it a share of some gas company one share what's that supposed to . . .

—No but that's one of them hey I mean that's what I been trying to tell you! This El Paso Natural Gas I got you it cost like twelve fifty see that's the . . .

—You mean you spent, why didn't you just give me the money! What good one share of . . .

—No but then you get taxed like this regular income and I mean it's not just this here one share, I mean I'm getting you this bunch of different ones like this here bonus see so . . .

—But why! If I just have to turn around and sell them what . . .

—No but you can't Bast I mean that's what I'm trying to tell you! I mean if you'd read up these here booklets where I find out all this stuff see if you go right and sell it you get taxed like this salary where you're some dumb teacher or bus driver or something you know? Only with this stock this here whole first hundred dollars of dividends is excludable see like El Paso, they pay twenty-five cents a quarter wait . . . he was sifting the heap on the radiator —look, International Paper they pay fifty cents, U S Steel sixty cents see you get to add these all up to this hundred dollars that's excludable, see like Disney pays . . .

—But from what! excludable from what! Fifty cents sixty cents what are you buying one share of this one share of that what . . .

—No but look hey listen, I mean like if we went and got one bunch of shares like U S Steel see then you just get this here literture off U S Steel like this one annual report and quarterly report and proxy statements and like where they're in some law thing and all, see but if you own this here one share of all different places they still have to send you all this here literture see so I was thinking, I mean see you could read up so if one of them was like screwing up someplace maybe we could get this here stockholder suit going like at Diamond Cable I mean like Disney boy wouldn't that be neat hey? I mean if we could get them by the short hair and . . .

—Look I don't want to get them by the short hair! can't you understand that? And reading all these things I couldn't understand them anyhow don't you understand that? I'm just . . .

—No but look Bast I mean that's why I been sending away for these books and all for you, like Understanding Financial Statements I mean it tells how to read a balance sheet and all didn't you get that? and like Statistican something of the United States and this here Moody's something, didn't you get them?

—I got them yes! What do you think I . . .

—No but I mean they really cost plenty, like you didn't even read them hey? Like this here Moody's something manual I mean it cost like . . .

—Of course I haven't read it it would take a month just to, look that's what I just said who asked you to! The Statistical Abstract of the United States Moody's Industrials who asked you to buy them! What . . .

—No but look hey I mean holy, I mean where we said we'll help each other out like and I mean all I said is will you read up this here literture and . . .

—Will you stop saying literture! Look I said I'd help you out once just this once, and you . . .

—No but I can't help if that's what they call it! and, and I mean holy shit like you're getting to keep all these here dividends which they're excludable and all I mean I just thought you could like read up this here, this here stuff in your spare time like where you said once you can compose this music where you're doing something else like you're going for a walk or on the train and all see so I just thought where you have all this here spare time to do your own work like you're always . . .

—To do what work! what spare time! watching a bunch of idiots play softball listening to them bray God Bless America do you think I look, look these expenses let's just clear up these expenses and whatever you owe me and . . .

—Okay don't get mad I mean see that's what I mean about this here operating cash on this here loan you know? See we . . .

—I don't know no! I don't want to I just . . .

—No but see it's all wrote out there from Mister Piscator this here loan off Hopper's bank to Eagle management see so we have some operat . . .

—Look will you look at this? Just . . .

—And I mean this here whole fifty dollars I gave you at the boys' room at school for like expenses and . . .

—Well that's what this is! You wanted me to write it all down didn't you? every nickel I spent so I wouldn't cheat you out of . . .

—No but wait hey wait! Who said you'll cheat anybody, I mean see what it is it's this whole thing where you get to deduct all these here business expenses like riding around and eating you get to deduct them off taxes and all see that's the whole thing of it hey, I mean see I was reading in this little booklet I got where this here corporation tax it's like fifty-two percent after you take off these expense deductions and all, see so that means for every dollar you spend it's only costing like forty-eight cents see? I mean that's the whole thing of how it all works see so where I said will you write down . . .

—All right! look, bus fare nineteen eighty, hotel three nights seventeen sixteen, three breakfasts one twenty, two lun . . .

—I mean you didn't charge that turkey dinner and all did you hey? Because like it said in the paper where they're the host and all see like if they're deducting it too we'd be . . .

—No! and I, look I didn't charge the quarter I put in the radio either will you just . . .

—No I mean I just wondered . . . he had one leg up on the radiator working with the pencil stub —because, I mean how come it has like two lunches a dollar forty then there's this here sandwich a whole dollar I mean how come . . .

—Because lunch in Union Falls is cheap and this bus stop sandwich was two pieces of dry bread with a piece of dry cheese . . .

—No that's okay I just wondered twenty, three, four, carry two and one is three, four, forty-four twenty-one then you still have this here ninety-four cents so that's eight, five . . . somewhere a urinal flushed —wait, four from nought borrow ten, five, I mean then you already spent like your pay you already spent five dollars forty-two cents from it so I mean even with what I still owe you minus that and like minus this here ten dollars from that field trip I mean that doesn't hardly leave . . .

—Look it doesn't matter! Just give me whatever you . . .

—No but see how it comes out there's still most of this ten dollars from that field trip I loaned you and I mean you'll need more for bus fare and all later anyway where you're taking this guy to dinner see so . . .

—Look I'm not taking your Mister Piscator to dinner don't . . .

—No not him hey it's one of these here old brothers this Mister Wonder, see . . .

—No.

—No but wait a second see he's only here this once see and . . .

—No!

—And I mean you have to eat anyway see so I just thought wait, wait where you going hey! What's all that stuff wait . . . !

—It's music what does it look like, I'm . . .

—No but you wrote all this here music hey?

—Of course I did, now . . .

—No but I mean how come you're just yelling about you don't get a chance to do your own work and you write this whole pile of . . .

—It's not my own work! I just wrote it for some dancers to make enough money to . . .

—No but hey Bast? I mean, I mean where I said maybe we can use each other so you can do this here work you're always yelling about you can't get it done holy, I mean is it my fault you go write all this music for these here dancers instead? I mean . . .

—Look I just told you I did this to earn some money so I can do my own work. I'm taking it down there now to get paid and I can settle things with you and get that check the school owes me and get out of this mess that's all, now . . .

—No well, well okay. I mean go ahead I, see I just thought I was helping you out and I mean now you . . .

—All right look, look. I'll stop on my way out and see this Piscator for you and give him these papers and then whatever you . . .

—Okay wait a second . . . he got a leg down, digging in pockets —I mean where you only got like this ninety-four cents . . . he had out a glistening black wallet secured by a heavy elastic —wait you want this for your shoe hey? I mean where the bottom's coming off like you can put this rubber band around it.

—Yes well, if you don't need it yes I . . .

—Okay and look, I mean you might need some expenses see . . . he had a wad out of the wallet, tugged out the corner of a ten and thrust it back, untangled a single, another —and I mean we can just settle up when you get all these payments okay?

—Yes well I, as soon as . . .

—Okay look here's four dollars, okay? And see I was just thinking, I mean later if you got nothing to do if you want to take this here old Mister Wonder to dinner see it wouldn't cost you anything because I already got you this invitation to this here gala banquet which here's the delicious full course menu of it, see? And where it says you get to see this here movie Golden Evenings which will cast a haunting glow over this festive occasion, may we make reservations for yourself and your spouse see so I made these reservations where you can pretend he's this spouse because he's real old anyway and you and him can talk about this brewery deal which I wrote it all down while you're having this here festive occasion and wait, wait that real smooth quarter I just gave you it looks real old, hey? If it's nineteen sixteen it's worth like a hundred dollars

. . . he called after Bast pursuing it now in a long curve brought up short against a fine blucher, where a length of tweed shook and the urinal flushed.

—My God Bast, you all right there? In here being sick, are you? Good thing I caught you before you got back to work though, forgot to mention these hippos. Same damned thing along the Nile River there, overgrazing, talk about killing six or seven thousand of them to preserve the habitat, but what about our own bayou country down here, eh? Great fellow the hippo, give you the chance to change pace a little, get in a little hippo music? Liven things up down here in the Everglades maybe, preserving that from him eh? And take care of yourself there Bast, came back over the mass of shoulder thrust against the door, —don't look well at all, no . . . he repeated as the door closed behind him, —didn't look well at all . . . up the marble toward the Sardis column where he was hit knee, waist and elbow. —Here here! What in . . .

—Look out for the man hey!

—Children stop running! Now where are the, why Mister Crawley! what . . .

—What? What? Amy? What the devil are you doing here?

—We've just come in on a field trip.

—Oh. Thought you were still off teaching somewhere.

—Well yes I am, that's what these children . . .

—Oh I see, all these little ruffians yours, are they?

—No it's really an eighth grade trip, I'm just helping out. But I wouldn't have expected to see you here.

—Oh? Yes, well, little change of scene of course, he muttered looking down as from the height of a shoal at the heads bobbing past, —came up for a chat with that young fellow you sent around to me in fact, young composer fellow . . .

—Not Edward, Bast? Here now? in the museum?

—A bit inaccessible right now I'm afraid yes, got him doing something for me you know.

—Edward? for you? But what in the world would he . . .

—Doing something in music for me yes, composing a little something you know.

—But I never would have, you don't mean you've commissioned him to compose something? I think that's simply marvelous of you Mister Crawley, I know he . . .

—Glad to help him along Amy, not every day there's the chance to patronize the arts this way is it. Help the starving young composer along in his garret? Looks the part too doesn't he, shame he can't stick to it.

—To music? But that's the only thing he really . . .

—Yes, problem is I try to talk to him about art and all he seems to talk about is money.

—But, Edward? Bast? I'd heard something yes, but . . .

—This business association he's tied himself up in yes, pretty shrewd outfit of course but it would be a damn shame to see him sit back and let this fine talent of his go to pot, eh? Anybody can be a millionaire but a young fellow with a talent like that owes the world something, don't you think? Ought to take better care of himself. Looking a little peaked yourself Amy.

—Well I'm just, just waiting until things are . . .

—Always said I admired your spirit a good deal more than your judgment you know, think you'd have proved whatever it is you want to prove by this time.

—There's nothing I can do until all this with Lucien is settled and I can . . .

—This Joubert you mean, yes. Shouldn't be long though, get that Nobili business straightened out and you're rid of him, better get back to your charges though hadn't you, don't think they should be sailing cups in the fountain there . . .

—Boys! Come away from there . . . !

—Nice to see you Amy, I'll give Beaton a call and try to move things along.

—If you could, I know Mister Beaton means well but all he seems to do is complicate things . . .

—Can't blame him, just doing what he's told you know and of course he's had to stall things a little hasn't he, give your Uncle John a chance to pick up enough of the stock to give this Joubert of yours a run for his money.

—What? What stock.

—What? This Nobili of course, takes time to pick it up a bit here, bit there without running the price up, even with the bank in there doing all the . . .

—But I thought they were buying it from Lucien, I thought the whole point was simply that he wanted the money and they wanted his controlling stock interest, Mister Beaton said . . .

—Was until he tried to hold them up, yes, little bit of an opportunist isn't he, this Joubert of yours.

—He's, and please don't keep saying of mine he's, if he already has the controlling interest what good is Uncle John running around buying it up in bits and pieces if he can never . . .

—No no, just until he has enough to start dumping it and drive down the price you know, thought Beaton had probably tried to explain it to you.

—But even if the price goes down and Lucien still won't sell I don't see what good . . .

—Won't have much choice of course though will he, looks like he's borrowed against it all over the lot and when the price drops and he runs out of collateral the banks will sell it for him, all a damn nuisance for your Uncle John of course but . . .

—But what will happen to . . .

—This Joubert of, Joubert? Might ruin him of course but I wouldn't . . .

—No to Francis, to Francis.

—Who?

—Francis! My little boy Francis, they said Lucien would try to use him as a weapon, that he . . .

—Wouldn't get mixed up in this Amy, too many compli . . .

—Mixed up in it! But I am mixed up in it, he's my son! Francis is my son! If Lucien took him to Geneva I don't know what I . . . boys! I'm sorry, I'd better go after them . . .

—Yes take care of yourself Amy, wouldn't get mixed up in all this right now you know. Take care of yourself.

—But, goodbye then, I hope . . . boys! Here, give me these cups. Where's everyone else?

—They went all over, could we just go back and look at the . . .

—Well where's Mister Vogel?

—He went to the toilet Mrs Joubert, could we just . . .

—No here he comes, I think we're leaving, Mister Vogel? We're over here. But where did you . . .

—Found one of the lost tribes camped out in the gents'.

—But where did you come from? she said bent down to the figure being weighed toward her by his shifting armload and the hand heavy on each shoulder.

—Me?

—Yes what on earth are you doing here?

—I'm on this here field trip.

—But you're, this is an eighth grade trip and you're not even . . . she straightened away from the trespass in the gaze fixed fallen over the boy's head. —You've been with us all this time?

—Sure I was in the back of the bus, didn't you see me? See I got this here special permission off Mrs diCephalis when I first heard about it, you know?

—No I don't, what did you . . .

—See because like I'm real interested in art and all.

—You?

—Well like in all that Egyptian stuff and, you know, like these here broken statues and all. You know?

—I certainly didn't, but I'm glad to hear it. And please find a handkerchief. Mister Vogel I'm awfully sorry but I have to leave, I really hadn't counted on doing this today and something's just come up . . .

—No I didn't either, I thought I was taking them to the basketball game.

—Yes I'm afraid some of them did too but these mixups happen, and I'm sure no one will blame you, now how many were we. Three, four, boys over this way . . . They surged for the doors, —I'll help you get them

down to the bus and then if I can find a telephone, it's a sort of family
problem that I simply must, seven, eight, let's all use the same door so
we can keep, eleven, twelve, try to keep a line going down the steps,
there's a wind isn't there . . . she excused the hand brushed behind her,
and stepped away from it, —I hope you understand Mister Vogel and I'm
sure you can explain things . . . She stepped away again but now it
followed, lingered down the crevice. —I, I'm sure you can explain . . . she
said, half a turn to him.

—I could feel its whiteness.

—I, pardon?

—I could feel its whiteness, underneath. I hoped you wouldn't mind.

—Well I, I have to hurry, I . . .

—But just, Niadu Airgetlam Mrs Joubert, have you heard of him?
Niadu of the Silver Hand?

—No I'm afraid I . . .

—Or Nodens, under the name Nodens?

—No I'm afraid not I . . .

—Or of the Fisher King? the Fisher King?

—No I can't say that I, I think you'd better see to the children . . .

—It's not that they don't notice, at first they stare and then it's just
another fact, disfigurement is just a fact in the wasteland kids live in.

—Yes well I, I must hurry, I . . .

—Let me once, just, let me reach . . .

—Mister . . . Vogel please I . . .

—Just once . . .

—Mister . . . Vogel please you, you must see to the children . . . she
got a step back toward the doors straightening her collar, —they're
waiting down there for you . . .

Down there the bus roared.

—Come on quit pushing . . .

—Hey Mister Vogel . . . ?

—I know you can explain things to Mrs diCephalis when you get
back out there, do be careful . . . It roared. The door clattered. —She may
even have enjoyed the basketball . . .

And the cargo heaved, shifted, through lights, blocking intersec-
tions, —I'm sure no one will blame you . . . The bus wallowed through
traffic, seethed through the tunnel where light caught his lips moving in
the glass, —I know you can explain things . . . Lights passing in both
directions, —She may even have enjoyed the basketball . . . He licked his
lips. —Just once . . . the seats bounced, lights from both directions, —you
can explain things . . . Lights, minutes, the hand on the illuminated dial
pointing 50, 40, 55, the hand —She may even have enjoyed the basketball . . . the hand retreating at last, dropped to 20, 5, the cargo shifted,
heaved, cheered from behind, —just another fact . . . mounted a curb

crushing leaves, candy wrappers, —they're waiting for you down there . . . And the lights came on, caught his lips again, the door clattered, —down there waiting for you . . . and he came through the still clash of headlights. —Just get back? crushing leaves, —enjoy the basketball?

—Enjoy the basketball! Are you . . .

—No way of knowing one bus from the other was there.

—Enjoy the basketball, my God! What are you talking about, one bus from the other.

—Never mind. I was afraid you'd understand.

—Afraid I'd, Vogel you're crazy you know that? You're crazy.

—Daisies won't tell.

—Vogel you . . . wait, you're not going to leave me to sort these kids out, come back here! I'm the one that's leaving. All of you give your permission slips to Mister Vogel, she got back over a shoulder and then, past post and rail treated to appear old and frilled ironwork made of aluminum to appear new, wagon wheels at threatening angles and post lights bright in bilious greeting, —Daisies won't tell, my God . . . up past the cast iron stove still stranded short of the door, —enjoy the basketball! and the door closed like a shot.

Foyer, hall, bathroom, foyer, snap, snap, snap, she started the round of turning on lights. —Nora? Donny? My God it's like a morgue in here . . . and she rounded the corner where light now alerted the residents of the room divider in erect silhouette against the flaccid shadows beyond. —My God. What are you doing home.

—I thought you knew they were going to release me from the hospital today, I looked for you there and then I remembered . . .

—Released you, they thought you were a lion? So where did you think I was, dancing on the Starlight Roof?

—No I remembered this was the day you planned the trip to the Metropolitan Art . . .

—So you thought I was finally getting a chance to commute with the arts, do you think they didn't sabotage that too? I spend a month planning something cultural and you think they didn't grab it? Miss Moneybags and that crazy Vogel pretending he didn't know one bus from the other, you think he went there for the art? The way she waves them in his face looking down her front like all the rest of you, with that face he's got like Custer's Last Stand you think he wasn't grabbing one in the back of the bus while I'm watching a lot of smelly men play basketball?

—Basketball?

—That's right you start it too, ask me did I enjoy the basketball. Daisies won't tell, my God you're all crazy. How long are you going around in that getup?

—The doctor thinks I should keep this arm in a sling until he thinks I'm strong enough to . . .

—The day he thinks you're strong enough to remind me I'm still a woman tell him to send me a telegram, what about your friend.

—Friend? Who . . .

—Friend, that's right, just repeat what I say, don't you know what a figure of speech is? Did you think I thought you had any friends? I mean that bonehead on the school board who hides in that underground toilet he's got in his back yard and calls himself a major you didn't manage to kill, anybody that rides with you they should give them Purple Hearts.

—He's still in the hospital, he . . .

—He'll stay there if he knows what's good for him. That dope fiend Buzzie you killed in the accident his whole black family is getting him a surprise party ready in court.

—Hyde? they're suing Mister Hyde? Because I thought they'd sue us but . . .

—Us? What do you mean sue us.

—No me I meant, me.

—Don't worry, they're suing you too. Now what are you looking for.

—I thought some mail might have come while I was in the hospital, I've been waiting to hear from . . .

—The mail should stop because you're in the hospital? Three weeks I've been waiting to hear from that Foundation. Did Dad eat yet?

—I don't know, he's been asleep there since I . . .

—Just from the smell in here he probably did. Where's Nora. Nora . . . ?

The elderly dog eyed their passage from under a table but did not move.

—I think she's helping Donny with his bed, he . . .

—His bed, are you going to do something about it? Nora . . . ? Bring Donny for supper. He's going to spend his life in it, the way he goes around trailing those wires looking for a place to, Nora? I said bring Donny for supper!

—Well I, I, I think he should see someone, I've said I think he should see someone, we should take him to . . .

—See someone, what do you mean see someone, he can see someone on the BMT. To see a psychiatrist? that's what you mean? Then say it, to see a psychiatrist . . . The lid of a saucepan fell to the floor and rolled toward him. —You think I want everybody saying my son's crazy, I had to send him to the psychiatrist? They should have sent you, that's who they should have sent, before you got loose in this house with your ideas about controlled envirement and everything else, Nora what are you coming in here like that for. Pick up that lid, will you? You think it's funny dressing up in bandages like your father? Can't you show him some respect? Now what are you crying about.

—I'm a bride.

—Dressed up in toilet paper you're a bride?

—It's a bride dress. Daddy don't I look like a bride?

—Maybe it's something she saw on television, she . . .

—Saw what, Nora I said get Donny for supper and take off that mess, you're trailing it all over the floor. Here, sit Donny here and you . . .

—But Mama Donny has to sit by where the plug is so he . . .

—All right, my God it's probably too late for a psychiatrist anyhow, we should take him to the electrician. Here, put down that spoon till I finish serving.

—Daddy I got fourteen Brownie points, while you were at the hospital I got fourteen Brownie points.

—That's fine Nora, that's . . .

—Fine? She got twice as many as anybody, is that all you can say, fine?

—And I still didn't spend any allowance, you know how much I saved already Daddy? I've saved two dollars and six cents already except Mama . . .

—All right Nora stop talking and eat.

—Except Mama borrowed two dollars so I only got . . .

—I said stop talking and eat.

—What is it.

—What do you mean what is it, it's your supper. What does it look like.

—It looks like lingam.

—Like what?

—Like a lingam.

—Like a lingam! How do you know what a lingam looks like.

—Because it looks just like this.

—Maybe she, maybe she saw that book you had . . .

—I can't hear you, will you stop whispering?

—That book you had about, about India, things they do in India.

—Things they do in India! My God! You sound like, I don't know what. You think they aren't doing them right this minute someplace a block away?

—No what I meant was, just the book, I put it up on the bathroom shelf so Nora . . .

—So Nora what. So she couldn't read at home what they want me to teach them at school?

—No I, I thought Mister Whiteback wanted Mister Vogel to try to, to work up some visual aids that would . . .

—Vogel! What's he going to do, build a model? Did you hear he had the whole fourth grade out sniffing glue? What do you think the police picked him up for, with those scars on his face, my God. Daisies won't tell. He ought to be locked up. So what did Whiteback tell you.

—Well just before I had my, before I went to the hospital, he wanted me to feel you out on this job of curriculum specialist . . .

—Feel me out, I'll tell you what he wants with his dirty mouth Nora come back to the table, where are you going.

—Just in the bathroom to vomit.

—Well clean up when you're finished and come back to the table, I'll tell you what he wants. He wants me to forget about this strike, he wants to give me that stinking Ring that that bag in the car with that book salesman was rubbing everybody's face in so I'll forget about this strike. They know him all over, that's the way he made his commissions, getting the textbook orders from bags like her in the back seat of his car, the kids saw them right up in those woods where we dumped that old washing machine going at it like, what's the matter you're not hungry?

—Not very I, what is it . . .

—It's tongue what does it look like. The only reason Whiteback wants you to feel me up is this greasy little dago politician with the wife that was Miss Rheingold so it's her Ring they're rubbing everybody's face in for the Spring Arts Festival in this Cultural Center he's getting put here.

—Oh.

—Oh. What do you mean oh.

—No I meant the strike, when is the strike . . .

—When is what strike. How can we strike if Fedders put the whole of the union war chest in buying deposit certificates at the bank now we can't get the money out for two years, and mortgages, so he buys mortgages with it. Now they're trying to fire the one teacher left in the place that knows what it's all about so what does Fedders do he buys mortgages, and you talk about a strike.

—Who? Who are they firing?

—Don't worry it's not you, I said the one man who knows what it's all about, he opens the day without singing them the Star Spangle Banner so they start a loyalty day parade. You never heard of the Citizens Union of whatever it is? Nora go wash out your mouth and get ready for bed, I can smell it way over here, and take Donny. Of Neighborhood Teaching or whatever it is with this mother going around to classes spying dressed like a kid, where were you keeping yourself.

—Yes well I, I've been in the hospital but who . . .

—Who? I just told you, it's some kid's mother when the kid stays home sick she dresses up like her and comes to school, can you pick up your dish and put it in the sink instead of leaving it there for somebody else to clean up? Where are you going now.

—I thought some mail might have come for me while I was . . .

—What do you think that pile on the bread box is, Mister Coded Anonymity.

—Oh, oh yes this is what I've been . . .

—They want you to be president of General Motors? Wait till they get a look at you . . . a fork dropped, a spoon followed it.

Somewhere a clock made a try at striking the hour. A door banged; a toilet flushed; a door banged. —Dad . . . ? are you in there? A rude sound responded promptly from within. —My God . . . rounding a corner shedding one shoe, the other. —Now what are you looking for.

—I had some money put away here, in the back of this drawer. It's gone.

—What do you put money in the back of a drawer for?

—There was almost fifty dollars it, it's gone.

—Nora? Come in here.

—What Mama?

—I said come in here. Daddy says he put some money in that drawer and it's gone. Do you know . . .

—Donny found it.

—Well where is it, get it.

—He sold it.

—What do you mean he sold it.

—He sold it to some boys.

—He sold it?

—He didn't know, he thought the coins were better because the other's only paper. He sold the fives for a nickel and the ones for ten cents.

—Well why did he, my God, why did he . . .

—He thought the ones were better because they had George Washington.

—My God.

—But, but Nora what boys. Why didn't you stop him.

—I don't know Daddy just these boys, I wasn't even here. He got eighty-five cents, I helped him count, after. Mama . . .

—All right Nora that's enough, I told you to get ready for bed and pick up that toilet paper, it's all over the house. So what are you going to do now Mister Morgenthau.

—Well I, I don't know, I . . .

—You better get back to making faces at yourself in the mirror. When are we going to see your nose again?

—The doctor said I should leave this bandage on until he thinks I'm . . .

—Does he think you can get up here and do a little roll playing? A skirt went to the floor, hose peeled down to a wad and followed. —What's all this stuff.

Calibrated pencil, linen counter, tape measure, string, —things they took out of my pockets at the hospital, they put them in a . . .

—Well can you get them off the bed? My God, like doing it on the counter in Woolworth's, here's another of your pieces of paper.

—Oh I've been looking for . . .

—General Electric Credit Corporation? If you have made your past payments regularly, you have established a valuable saving habit.

—No that's from the payment on the washing machine, I didn't mean . . .

—Don't break this worthwhile habit. Your dealer will deliver the appliance of your choice today my God no wonder you're in such a mess, you hide money in drawers and save it by spending it, now they want you to save some more by buying something else, you're all crazy . . . Elastic snapped, something shapeless black flew toward a chair. —Nora can sit there and Donny can sit over there.

—What for.

—What do you mean what for, so they can see.

—See what.

—See what. What do you mean see what. See us.

—See us, what . . .

—See us what! My God what do you think what! Unless you're going to keep on those pants with the rip all the way down the crotch, what do you think what!

—No that, happened in the accident but . . .

—All right just forget it.

—But did you really mean . . .

—I said forget it! where pearled nails suddenly bit deep, —if that was Miss Moneybags you'd have your face in it! You'd have your, get away from me!

—But . . .

—I said forget it! If I ever thought we could show these kids something beautiful I should have my head examined . . . and up, heels drawn abruptly nestled in the rough as though preparing el modakheli, —the things they do in India! My God look at you . . . where the struggle rose between shirt and sling, a shoe dropped and —you don't even wear underpants like other men do, they come to your knees . . . an end of the inflated belt encircling her where she drew breath deep and held it as around her movement slowed to the tearing of envelopes, rustle of paper, silence, tap, tap, tap . . . Cinched upright, nipples standing pebble hard, she turned slowly. —What are you doing!

—Oh nothing, nothing I just . . .

—Nothing! What do you mean nothing! You're crawling around on your hands and knees tapping the wall and listening! You're crazy! Or you're trying to make me crazy aren't you. Aren't you! I'm going to call the police.

—No you don't understand, I'm just . . .

—Don't understand! I understand you're crazy, what are you doing down there! You think there's somebody in the wall?

—Mama what's the matter.

—Shut up and go back to bed Nora, ask your father what's the matter!

—Daddy what's the matter.

—He's crawling around on the floor with his measuring tape making little pencil marks and tapping, that's what's the matter! Tap, tap, tap and he listens, look at him. Go ahead do it again, show her, drive us all crazy.

—No but I just . . .

—Don't tell me that's not what you were doing, I was watching you.

—Can we call the police Mama?

—Shut up and go back to bed Nora. And you, just stay on your side of the room . . . she slid upright and disencumbered herself, —my God, and you talk about the things they do in India. And leave that light on! You think I'm going to lie here in the dark when you start in again? And I thought it was bad when you just made faces at yourself, you're probably doing it right now under the bandage where I can't see aren't you. Will you turn off that light? You think anyone can sleep with the whole place lit up like Coney Island . . . ? and somewhere the clock took up its occasional tries at striking the hour till morning made a tentative approach as though uncertain what it might discover. —My God, can't you get up and make them something to eat? do I have to do everything in this house . . . ? doors banged, the toilet held a round of flushing, smoke rising from the toaster lay a blue pall down the hall and the morning still lingering outside appeared to have decided to stay there, dwindling to the gray of afternoon. —Now what is it Nora, my God can't Mama spend a day resting without everybody going crazy? Go tell Daddy to make you a peanut butter if he can do it without burning the house down, close the door and turn down that television . . . ! and finally the gray yielded to dark, the clock made another try at striking the hour, missed, waited, tried again unheard, again, until the alarm stung the silence into another sunless day. —You're making faces again aren't you.

—What? oh I . . .

—Well what are you doing hiding in the closet.

—No I'm looking for some clothes, I just . . .

—Why don't you put the closet light on then.

—I didn't know you were awake, I didn't want to . . .

—Awake? Could anybody sleep with you banging into doors like that? What are you doing at that end with all my dresses.

—I'm looking for something to wear, I can't . . .

—Pull up your underpants and you'll look nice in the green one.

—No a suit, I can't find a suit, if you sent them all to the cleaners I can't get one out before school and . . .

—Who said they went to the cleaners.

—But where are they then.

—Nora took them to the Thrift Shop.

—The Thrift Shop? My suits?

—How do you think she got her Brownie points? If you think . . .

—No but my suits she, how could you let her just take both my suits and . . .

—Because you were supposed to go right down and buy them back.

—Buy back my own suits?

—Yes buy back your own suits, who else would buy them. For two dollars each you couldn't help your own daughter earn six Brownie points? She thought you could go down and buy them right back, was it her fault you went to the hospital instead?

—No but one was, one cost sixty dollars, the gray one with checks and the brown one, the brown one was only a year old, suppose they've sold them.

—So don't tell me tell your daughter, tell her the first time she goes out and shows some initiative that just because you . . .

—But what am I going to wear!

—I just told you, pull up your underpants and you'd look . . .

—But even my slacks, there were some blue slacks back here and they . . .

—Those you could have had for a quarter. So where's the suit you wore for your joyride, wear that.

—You saw the tear down the front of the pants, and there's blood down the . . .

—Then wear Dad's. He's not going anyplace.

Doors banged, water flushed, splashed, shook the pipes, desultory notes of the saxophone rode out through the room divider on shifting planes of smoke from the burned toast.

—It's too big and it smells.

—So roll up the pants and don't go close to anybody, they'll think it's the Duke of Windsor coming back Nora get that wire away from Donny's juice.

—Nora, that eighty-five cents you said Donny got for the . . .

—There! my God I told you, well don't just sit there Nora get Daddy a rag. So now you want Donny's eighty-five cents?

—No but it's really . . .

—Really what. Really the first time he ever Nora not that rag, my God look what you're doing to the pants, that's the one you just cleaned the jelly off the floor with. The first time he ever shows some initiative to do something you want to take that away from him too?

—But I don't even have . . .

—And just stand still a minute so she can get it off your shoes, my God . . . through the planes of smoke swirled by his passage toward the source of the sudden spurts of music, an angular catastrophe of liver spots escaping one piece underwear beyond the room divider, and his initials in aluminum carried the door closed behind him like a shot in the back, billowing past the potbellied stove and up the walk trousers hiked high by his free hand in an empty pocket to keep them from dragging which lent him the raffish air of shore leave the morning after, and had even imparted a kind of glazed shine to one shoe where the juice had spilled by the time he rounded a corner to tug at a glass door that never yet had opened out.

—Stick 'em up!

Sling and trousers went in different directions, recovered as the door swung in for him. —Oh Coach, Coach wait . . .

—What? Who did you . . . Dan? Why, why Danny, I hardly knew ye.

—Yes I, I was in a . . .

—In a road crash, we read about it in the newspaper, but come in . . . and the boy between them holstered arms and wheeled with a savage stamp of heels, —quick before there's more killing Dan. Why look at ye, ye'll have to be put in a bowl to beg.

—No, no I'm all right but I, I thought I was in north seven, that boy's class is supposed to be in east . . .

—Been demobbed Dan, make room for the equipment.

—Yes but that's what I, where is it? all the equipment that was here, the teaching equipment and all the, what's this? all this?

—Stoves, washing machines, brake linings, hair dryers . . .

—But what happened to all the equipment that was still . . .

—Ask the C O Dan, it's too many for me . . . and they rounded the corner in full collision, backed against a racked firehose as the shock of bangs lost to the toss of blonde hair receded repeated in the thighs. —Look at that rise and fall, just look at that! they came on up the corridor, —look at that reciprocating beam motion and you can see what got Newcomen started on the steam engine can't you.

—Well I, I hadn't thought of . . .

—Never pictured him with Mrs Newcomen out together dancing cheek to cheek?

—No, I guess I . . .

—Frightening thing how machinery can give you ideas like that about a simple schoolgirl. Start off with that steady reciprocating movement and the next thing you know you've got a bottom, round and droops a little but still good, nothing wrong with it at all. It's when you add that socalled párallel motion James Watt introduced that you've got ass, push pull, push pull, quite an improvement, always sorry I never got a look at Mrs. Watt.

—Yes well I, I think I'd . . .

—It's rump you want to steer clear of Dan, that sort of mononate you get with a girdle and goodbye nates, goodbye Rock of Ages and goodbye Augustus Montague Toplady, he never would have come out singing if she hadn't dropped her corset that day back in eighteen thirty-two.

—Yes well I think I'd . . .

—Rock of ages cleft for me, let me hide my . . .

—I think I'd better get over to . . .

—The song is ended but the malady lingers on, we forgot derrière didn't we, kind of a euphemism? euphuism? You know Mrs Joubert, Dan?

—Well I, yes but not . . . and he ran up against a shoulder on the turn.

—Trying to see where the horse bit me? Here, come a little closer and . . .

—No no I, I was just looking at your suit.

—Almost looks like it might have fit me once doesn't it, if I stand still? kind of slump and drop the crotch?

—Well it, could I ask where you got it?

—I don't usually give out the name of my tailor Dan, but you look like you need it. There's a little thrift shop down . . .

—Yes that, that's what I . . .

—I usually go for the Scottish worsteds, but for two dollars . . . he pinched up a pleat of the nondescript leaning closer, —it keeps me decent. Just between us I needed something in a hurry after a little run in with the local constabulary, I even found a free premium in the back pocket, there. How's that . . . he held out a circle squared in foil on the flat of his palm, —not sure I'd trust it though, it looks like the poor bastard sat on it for ten years waiting for the chance that never came. Augustus Toplady waiting for the whalebone curtain to part but it was another hundred years before you could lean out of a tank turret and yell hey Shotsie, you want to sit on my face? Spend any time overseas, Dan?

—No, no but I think I'd better stop in the . . .

—It's that hide my face, that's the part that always got me, you wonder how Mister Toplady stayed out of jail in those days.

—Yes, well I . . .

—Everybody singing about it you wonder how Mrs Toplady felt Sundays at church don't you.

—Yes but I, I meant to ask you, was there another suit there at the thrift shop? a brown . . .

—Tweed, and I came off better than Glancy, I'll tell you that.

—Glancy?

—He got in there ahead of me and grabbed it, he couldn't get into it with a shoe horn.

—Oh then he, he didn't buy it?

—No, he split the seat getting it on so he had to buy it . . . and paused at the door marked Boys, —you treating?

—Well I, I thought I'd just . . .

—I'll join you in a quick one . . . and that door banged on their entrance and the clatter of a seat behind a door secured further down the line near the mops against whispers escaping top and bottom.

—Shhh, somebody just came in.

—Okay look hey, just piss up to this line here.

—How much.

—A dime?

—It's a quarter.

—Okay go ahead, Miss Waddams is waiting.

—First give me the quarter.

—Okay . . . here, now go ahead. Come on, go ahead.

—Okay I'm trying, can't you see?

—Well come on hurry up, she's waiting.

—I can't, I must be out, like you're the fifth . . .

—Well come on, try. Drink some water then.

—I drank this whole quart before I came to school, I can't . . .

—Okay well drink some more.

—Out of what.

—This, use this.

—This? You must be crazy, anyway it don't work that fast.

—Okay then just try, try once more, squeeze . . .

There was a crash of glass.

—There's a market for everything Dan, you look like you're good for a dollar's worth yourself there and if you don't mind my saying, I'd spend it on a new suit. There was a checked number on the rack they wouldn't dare ask more than a dollar for and the one you've got on looks like a dog pissed right down your leg.

—Yes well that, that was just something that spilled but . . .

—If anybody mentions it just tell them you're from Cleveland.

—What?

The door banged.

—Whiteback, step up and join us. Dan's treating.

—Dan? Oh, oh Dan, came down the line a safe two stalls away, —glad to see you back Dan, but you don't look . . .

—Just a small accident Whiteback, he ran into a neighbor from Cleveland. Rabbi Goldstein out there cuts on the bias.

—Yes well the ahm, the bandages that is to say Dan . . .

—Next one's on the house gentlemen, sorry I can't stay. Want to line up your teacher's guide on this new circuitry lesson Dan, I tossed a copy on Whiteback's desk. Compliments to the chef. Dum de dum, dum, cleft for me . . . and the door banged.

—You're ahm, sure you should have come in this soon Dan, I mean it looks like you're having some trouble there with ahm . . .

—No I'm all right I'm, it's just this sling and these . . .

—Wait, wait let me get the door. Can you see where you're going?

—Yes I'm all right I'm, I wanted to ask you what Coach meant when he . . .

—Yes well Coach is getting a little bit ahm, I mean I certainly wouldn't say it was a small accident in terms of the ahm, the person you ran into wasn't from, yes who ran into you that is to say wasn't ahm . . . he led on past a clock as it severed what remained of a minute and a bell sounded, —from Cleveland of course . . .

—No what I, wait, wait why is everything so, all the halls are empty. Wasn't that bell homeroom?

—Yes well things are a little off this morning Dan the ahm, Mister Gibbs is taking homeroom and it seems to be, he seems to be reading the entire declaration of the United ahm, United States Constitution that is to say . . . and the door marked Principal swung open lightly, bunged hollowly closed behind them —and of course classes can't start moving until he ahm, my telephone . . .

———shall, without the consent of the other, adjourn for more than three days, nor to any other . . .

—Hello . . . ? No he just walked out, who . . . What mystery what are you wait, he just walked in, Whiteback? Student librarian calling you about some wait a minute what is this, a joke?

—No no it's ahm, come in Dan let me get the . . . hello? Yes this is Mister Whiteback, have you . . . The Constitution yes, the U S Constitution, I told you to look in . . . who? What's Charlie Chan got to do with . . . no no no I said history, a history book, with an h . . . Yes it's c, o, n, s . . . all right look for a pencil . . .

———except treason, felony, and breach of the peace, be privileged from arrest during . . .

—Didn't know they'd let you out of the hospital Dan, it looked like somebody trying to make a fool of me with that sling and the bandages over your . . .

—t, i, t . . . tution yes, I want to know how long it is so we'll know when classes can start to . . . American yes, American history . . .

———Article one section seven. One. All bills . . .

—Yes I thought you were still in the hospital too, I . . .

—Mister Hyde stopped in to discuss the school budget defeat Dan, we just excuse me . . . hello? Yes this is . . . what? Oh Mister Stye yes, about the stolen baseballs yes and the . . . one adding machine and three typewriters over the weekend yes . . . Yes well that's not really a school ahm . . . he paused for the muslin wing flapping before him, —I think Mister Hyde wants to speak to you himself, he . . . yes he's right here that is to say . . . and the phone cord swept papers heaped to the floor.

—Hello, Stye? Say I just found out my insurance policy is, wait a minute. Can you reach the button with your good hand there Dan? turn off the sound on that crazy, yes hello? My policy yes . . . Yes with your company, keeping things all in the family, the . . . automobile yes, the . . . Oh you have? Yes the accident with diCephalis and . . . oh you do? I just got out this morning and . . . fine, if you call one arm in a cast and bandages all over my . . . Of course he's still alive, he's sitting right . . . Right, head on, that's right, they . . . no I was in his car when my car came around the . . . no I wasn't in my car, I was in his car when my car came around the . . . right, and hit my car, I mean his car head on, right, the whole . . . how the back of my car got damaged too? No that was something else, driving out here I stopped by the side of the . . . Well of course I was in my car when I drove it out here, how do you . . . Now wait, wait, let me start at the beginning. My car was stolen right here in

front of the school and when I . . . What keys . . . No, before I drove out
here my car was in a garage where they . . . in New York, yes, where they
must have taken my address off my license and made duplicate keys for
every . . . What do you mean? Because they walked right in the front door
and carried out all three televisions, the washer, dryer, stereo, sauna,
both slide projectors, the short wave . . . No, the reason the watch is on
a separate claim is because it was a separate incident, I was driving up
the . . . yes in my car, yes! I know it's hard to . . . Well all right I know
it all sounds . . . ! No, when the claims adjuster from your company came
up to see me in the hospital I gave him all this information and he
. . . Well how could I give him complete descriptions without saying that
every one of them was . . . what? What do you mean I . . . Well what do
you mean it sounds like my testimony has racial overtones, how could
. . . All right racial undertones, could I help it if every . . . All right could
I help it if . . . what? What if they did find my keys in the ignition, it's
my car isn't it? wasn't it? Look you're supposed to be my . . . No but your
company is supposed to be my . . . No, I told him that happened when
I was driving out here, I stopped for a light and a car pulled up beside
me full of . . . what? Ripped it right off my wrist yes, before I could even
. . . Trying to make the whole thing sound like a what? Look I'm not
shouting but could I help it if . . .

—Get the phone, it's sliding off the . . .

—Could I help it if every one of them was a . . . hello?

—Hurt your head Dan?

—No it's, it's all right I'm, I was just trying to pick up all these papers . . .

—Hello? Are you . . . who?

—I'm sorry, I squeezed the button when I caught it and . . .

—Who the, how did that happen. Somebody calling you here, Whiteback. He must have hung right up in my face.

—Yes excuse me, hello? This is Mister . . . Pecci?

—He tells me I'm imagining a conspiracy and then hangs up in my
face, how do you like that.

—Yes no Mister Pecci isn't here no, no he should be here in a . . .
in the newspaper this morning yes, the smear story that is to say, of
course the . . . no your name wasn't mentioned, it just said the Town
Board yes, the . . . yes Ganganelli, call Ganganelli, he . . . who? No, no
Glancy hasn't shown up, no we thought he was out sick but they said his
car isn't standing in his drive where he usually . . . oh he did? Yes well
we've had some inquiries about it down to the bank, all bills he was sure
that he'd paid yes, he showed me the stubs but the checks have never
come in for payment, of course his wife had withdrawn nine hundred
and eighty-three . . . Mrs Glancy yes, she . . . yes well of course I should
be talking about this on the other telephone here, the line to the bank
that is to . . . yes no don't call back, no, call Ganganelli . . .

—Did you hear that Whiteback? Tells me I'm accusing them of a conspiracy and then hangs up in my face, what did I tell you that day he was in here. Not a word out of him, he just sat there taking it all in, am I right? Look at their face and you don't know what's going on inside, am I right? Talking about racial overtones, whose insurance company does he think he's working for, am I right Dan?

—Maybe he meant, when they take you to court maybe he meant you should . . .

—Take me to court? Who's taking me to court.

—Well I heard, I think I heard Buzzie's family was . . .

—Taking me to court? I'll take them to court, what do they think they, you saw that kid Whiteback, one look at his face and you could see he was so hopped up before he ran out of here . . .

—Yes well of course the ahm, communityrelationswise that is to say we ahm, excuse me . . . hello? Oh, yes Gottlieb just called, yes, I told him to call you, he . . . Yes no simply because he was sitting on the Town Board when you presented the Flo-Jan offer to lease the town dock and he thinks they're trying to make some connection between him and ahm, the loan, the connection between the bank's directors and the unsecured loan to ahm, to embarrass us down to the bank that is to say, he . . . what? No not that loan no, yes no of course that suggestion of seizing the assets if his Ace Transportation defaults on its loan is just an attempt to embarrass me as ahm, seizing the school buses that is to say, as a . . . to Pecci yes, Mister Pecci, of course as he said in his statement anyone who tries to serve the public must expect smear stories but . . . in public office yes but of course the attempt to embarrass me as . . . yes no I'm not running for anything, no . . .

—Hello? No he's on the other phone here, he . . . wait here he is.

—Yes hello . . . ? Yes well classes should start at any ahm, as soon as homeroom is over that is to ahm . . . yes I heard the bell too but of course the . . . no it's the Constitution, the United States Constitution yes, yes do you happen to know how long it . . . hung up yes, Dan? Can you tell how many pages he still has to go there? look like you're following it pretty closely that is to . . .

—No I was, I was looking at his suit.

—Yes well it's a nice enough suit of course but the sleeves don't seem to ahm, when I saw him come in this morning his pants hardly reached his ankles that is to say, yes which is all right of course but it made the old straw slipper he was wearing on one foot look like he'd ahm, more like he'd ahm . . .

—Been on a bender, look at him! Do you need color tv to see how red his eyes are? And the muslin wing flapped heavily in the direction of the image just then paused to preen a crease and raise the dirt line on the pocket handkerchief square into view, —been on a bender with that friend of his that cut off his ear with a pencil, look at him! If there's one thing I'm going to see while I'm still on this school board Whiteback, it's to see him fired.

—Yes well of course we ahm, can you turn that up just a little Dan? see what Article he's up to? Of course if we tried to fire him now we ahm, in terms of the ongoing situation anything that might touch off the ahm, precipitate a strike that is to say, Dan you were going to feel out your ahm, your wife's ahm . . .

—Touch it off then, why not! The budget was just voted down wasn't it? Let them strike. Lock the doors, turn off the heat and save some money, see it at the corporate level all the time. What do you think U S Steel does when a new contract's coming up? Goes into full production, builds a big inventory, no contract no work and they're out on strike, would have had to fire half of them anyway. By the time they've sold out their inventory these red unions are banging down the gates to get back in, just like these parents will eat up your budget and march their kids back in just like Vern said they would. Somebody at the door there.

————or engage in war, unless actually invaded, or in such imminent danger as will not admit of delay. Article two section one. One. The Executive . . .

—Did he say two? He can't only be up to, come in? How many do you think there, oh come in come in Senator . . . and the door fell ajar on the flurry of cloth, introducing silk in the muted iridescence of a famous name suit, —we were just discussing the United States ahm, Hyde, you remember Major Hyde on the school board and, yes no this is Major Hyde here Senator, that's Dan our ahm, Dan diCephalis, our psycho . . . and the flurry subsided. —Maybe you read about their accident in the papers?

—Smear stories, the papers . . . and the flurry renewed in newspaper streamers from an inside pocket —I say it myself right here in my statement, smear stories, they find the Cultural Center is a rider to my highway bill so they smear me because they stoop to nothing to smear Parentucelli. Look, right here they try to tie his state contracts to my highway bill through Flo-Jan Corp but right down here they admit Catania Paving pays Flo-Jan Corp eighteen cents every yard of asphalt landed at the town dock, minimum five hundred dollars monthly, you see? They stoop to nothing.

—Yes well of course in terms of the ongoing situation down to the bank we ahm, excuse me . . . hello?

————United States. Six. In case . . .

—Because he is represented by Ganganelli, Pecci and Peretti? Because he is Italian American he should not have the best legal counsel?

—Yes well of course I know it doesn't make you look good Vern but of course we ahm . . .

—This teacher woman from your television sues him for a million dollars, he is not entitled to defend himself?

—Yes well of course she's suing the school too, she . . . what? Oh yes, Vern? Yes I'm sorry I was listening to something else, we ahm . . . yes to bring you solutions of course but in terms of the ahm . . . that you didn't want to hear about it yes, but of course we . . . Yes no Mister Pecci is right . . . No no right here that is to say, he dropped in to discuss the ahm . . . want to hear about it, no I . . . no I'll tell him, yes . . .

—That Vern, Whiteback? Here, I'd better just speak to him about the . . .

—Yes well he ahm, he hung up.

—Well what was that he wanted you to tell me.

—Yes well it was not you, no, no he wanted me to tell Mister ahm, tell the Senator here to ahm, of course I can't repeat it but he seemed quite put out at the reference in the newspaper story to what Mister Parentucelli did to his yard as ahm, as a gift.

—What I said? they stoop to nothing? Because Parentucelli tries to make a gift they smear him with the District Superintendent?

—Yes well of course I don't think it was a gift that Vern especially ahm . . .

—So to say there is no gift he sues Parentucelli for damages? Parentucelli comes to do a nice job, maybe too much enthusiasm, all his work to do the nice job, all the trees out, all the blacktop, how does he offer to settle? Free, no bills, nothing. You take out one tree, one elm tree, one oak tree seventy feet, eighty feet high, how much it costs to take out one tree? Two-inch pressed blacktop the best, indestructible, no grass to mow, nine thousand square feet no more grass to mow, no leaves to rake all the time, he parks the car anywhere, no trees to smash the fenders, no birds shitting the Simoniz . . .

—Yes well of course Vern ahm, since all Vern had in mind was a small driveway I think that seeing the newspaper refer to all the ahm, all Mister Parentucelli's fine work that is to say as ahm, of course he did a fine job on the addition he put on over to our place that is to say even though the French doors don't open exactly the way we'd ahm, don't open yes but of course that has no connection with his bid for thirty-two thousand dollars for blacktopping the studio parking lot and replacing the ahm, the stone lintel over the main door for twelve ahm, it's right here somewhere in those papers you just picked up Dan? Something the Citizens Union people circulated just before the budget referendum in an attempt to embarrass right under there yes, The Citizens Union on Neighborhood Teaching wishes to call your attention to no, no this was something about an example of the smut circulating in the junior high they said they sent me but I haven't seen anything that might be ahm, anything supporting the Senator's campaign that is to say, Stamp Out Smut for . . .

—Quart of glue two fifty-one for which the school pays three fifty-seven, masking tape one forty-nine for which the school pays two . . .

—Yes that's it Dan, just a, Dan? The Senator's handing you an SOS button to ahm, yes thank you Senator it's ahm, it's a catchy design, the SOS against the background of stars and be careful Dan you're spilling all those checks.

—These? I thought it was just . . .

—Yes well of course they're wadded up and dirty because the youngsters seem to have carried them around in their ahm, their attempt to embarrass the school by paying for lunch with a thirty cent check, but of course if we permit them to bring lunch to school we lose the federally subsidized cafeteria lunch program and in terms of the ongoing budget sit . . .

—Mention education and they grab for their wallets, was I right Whiteback?

—Yes well of course the figures Dan has there are ahm . . .

—Ladder eleven ninety-eight for which the school pays twenty-three . . .

—Yes sending their people out to ahm, sending them out dressed like spies that is to say making one shot purchases at Jack's Discount Appliance to discredit the school's policy of dealing with ahm, utilizing dependable, reputable sources of supply like Mister ahm, Gottlieb's brother-in-law is hardly fair to excuse me . . . hello?

———from office on impeachment for and conviction of treason, bribery, or other high crimes and . . .

—I think the school phone is ringing there Senator, could you reach the . . .

—Oh yes. Yes hello . . . ?

—Yes this is Mister Whi . . . what? Yes no not at the bank right now no, no I . . . No no yes it is the bank telephone line yes but . . . yes I have another call that, just a minute . . .

—He says it is urgent, he says to tell you the Constitution is two hundred and four feet long.

—Two . . . just a minute. What?

—Hundred and four. He says do you want the beam too? Forty-four feet eight . . .

—No no no just, hello? Yes just hold on a minute, let me . . .

—Built of live oak and red cedar . . .

—No just hang up yes, tell him never mind, thank no no not you, hello? Yes hello? Yes . . . yes well of course we saw it in the paper too but digging up a minor building variance he got three or four years ago just to make the point that he was represented before the town board by Gangan . . . and Peretti yes, his attorneys, yes they just seem to have dug it up in an attempt to . . . Yes but of course the variance itself is so minor that . . . yes a matter of eight inches one way or the other can't be that . . . what? Oh. Oh yes no I didn't quite get your ahm . . . Yes I never heard that one, it's quite funny yes . . . Yes well as a matter of fact Mister ahm,

Assemblyman Pecci happens to be right here, I think he . . . Pecci, yes, his law form, his former law firm that is to say represents the builder who . . . yes I think he wants to say something . . .

———crimes, except in cases of . . .

—Hello? You're calling about this smear story in the paper look, these lies they print to smear me because they try to smear somebody higher up, you understand what I mean? This little variance they say the builder saved six hundred dollars every house, that's a lie. Twelve hundred houses they say, that's a lie, they print them to smear me because they try to . . . what? No, ask Whiteback the correct figures, Mister Whiteback. Here.

———them aid and comfort. No . . .

—Hello yes? Yes I just wanted to say that . . . what? Oh those yes, yes those figures are right here somewhere I just, Dan could you look under those ahm . . . Yes no but of course in terms of the ongoing situation down to the bank the inferences of a story like this one are ahm . . . Yes the suggestion of ahm, of an overabundance of bad home improvement loans and mortgage risks calculated to undermine confidence in terms of the ahm, investment confidence on the part of investors that is to say which is hardly fair to . . . and yes well in the case of home mortgages like these which are insured by County Land and Title there should be no . . . no yes I know the premiums are high but of course the element of ahm . . . Yes no I wasn't going to say risk of course but County Land and here, here are these figures and apparently the builder saved only ahm, yes only saved five hundred and seventy-two dollars on each of one thousand one ahm, eleven hundred thirty-six houses that ahm, homes that is to say that ahm . . . Yes well no, no I would have called you of course if you . . . yes well no we wouldn't want anything like that to . . . no, no, yes thank you for calling, yes . . .

—Who's that?

—Yes well that was ahm, that was Mister Fedders Senator he just ahm, he just needed reassurance on this home mortgage situation because of course if anything suddenly precipitated a ahm, touched off a strike that is to say and forced the union to raise a strike fund by liquidating its ahm, trying to retire its home mortgage investments right after this ahm, this smear, this smear to use your phrase about this minor stud variance of course the ongoing situation down to the bank could become quite ahm, Dan, I think Dan was going to look into this, Dan? did you get a chance to feel out your ahm, feel things out?

—Yes by tapping, I couldn't really feel anything but by tapping along the baseboard I could hear where the studs were and then I measured between them last night, they were twenty-four inches apart but maybe the . . .

—Yes well of course your house is ahm, is your home that is to say but your wife ahm, I think you were going to feel her out in terms of her position activationwise in the ongoing strike situation and the ahm, with the idea that she might be a little less active activationwise that is to say if she had the opportunity to expand her, to use her ahm, utilize her talents in more constructive school programs in terms of her own interests that is to say, her ahm, yes I think you mentioned B'hai and some artistic Kashmiri ahm, India I think that is, yes, things they do in . . .

—Well she, she she has been working on that yes but she, but I thought Mister Vogel was going to . . .

—Yes well of course Coach Vogel is ahm, we don't want to improach on his preserve even though I understand she just took a group of youngsters to a basketball game but of course if she enjoys basketball I'm sure that Coach wouldn't ahm, that no one would object to her taking over as curriculum specialist and implementing the program to ahm, to help actualize the cultural aspects of the arts in depth for our, if we can find a place for our Spring Arts Festival in our ahm . . .

————against domestic violence. Article five . . .

—Yes well no he what did he say? Twenty-five . . . ?

—Meant to ask you about that Senator, when you start looking around for a site to put up this Cultural Center of yours there's a nice location out there past the Dunkin Donuts, right there on the border with District thirteen. Nothing but some scrub pine and a couple of new little ranch houses would have to go and we had some blockbusting out there so the acreage ought to come cheap if you can get your condemnation proceedings . . .

—What do we want that, we already got condemnation proceedings, you don't read the legal notices? right in the paper? Plenty of parking, they just blacktopped it up there right across the street for the new shopping center fourteen acres, Sundays the Catholic church, nights the Cultural Center parks, plenty of people you need plenty of parking.

—Yes well of course I didn't mean a place to ahm, I meant a place in the budget that is to say without a continuing grant from the State Arts Committee the Festival can hardly ahm, when the Committee learns that our composer in residence is no longer in ahm, in residence, the grant that's been helping with our little Ring presentation would ahm, could . . .

—Look Whiteback what do you want to rip your knickers on him again for. If nobody can find him there goes their excuse for a strike, am I right?

—Yes well the pressures to fire anyone of course are ahm, of course if someone as active activationwise as Dan's wife here was busy with ahm, Dan?

—Yes but I think she thinks Mrs, Mister Pecci's wife is interested in doing it.

—Doing it?

—Yes well of course I believe Janice Pecci was in the original production Senator? of this Rhinegold that is to say this Ring, yes, but it probably doesn't really matter exactly whose Ring we see because there can't be that much difference, we've all seen Miss Flesch's that is to say and if Dan's wife wanted to do it for us I thought ahm, I thought that was probably why you stopped in, Dan?

—No it was, I wanted to ask about the equipment, all the teaching equipment that I . . .

—Yes well those were major budget items of course and in terms of ahm, of resubmitting the budget to the voters some of them may have to ahm, that paper the Citizens Union people sent around in an effort to embarrass the ahm, we just had it here somewhere and I think some of your equipment is ahm, your talking typewriter yes I think they found thirty-five thousand dollars for the Edsel Responsive Environment a little, what did he say there?

————Pinckney, Charles Pinckney, Pierce Butler, William . . .

—Wait that can't still be the . . .

—Yes well no, no I think he's finished and ahm, he must be calling roll yes you can turn that sound off but leave it on to see what's happened to our scheduling, is that it right there Dan? Of course some of the equipment they question is ahm, the burglar alarm at two thousand six hundred dollars for example but of course at the rate typewriters and adding machines are disappearing it probably comes out to about the same ahm, they've even put the telephone booth down there I suppose one of their ahm, their spy saw the new one down near the boys' lockers but of course the telephone company itself is ahm, yes what's this coming on now?

—Arithmetic, all the little pluses and minus.

—No it's, I think it's electricity, it must be Coach . . .

—Vogel's new ahm, yes but of course if they started the tape at homeroom bell without knowing Mister Gibbs was ahm, yes well then the youngsters will have missed most of the lesson Dan so your testing might not be ahm . . .

—He said he put an outline on your desk, maybe I can find the place where it . . .

—Yes well in those papers you picked up it might ahm, that yellow sheet there might . . .

—Micro Farad yes that's, farad's an electrical unit, his resistance at a minimum and his field fully excited, laid Millie Amp on the ground potential, raised her frequency and lowered her capacitance, pulled out his high voltage probe and inserted it into her socket connecting them in parallel, and short circuited her shunt . . .

—Yes well that's ahm, he said circuitry didn't he and that sounds ahm, excuse me . . . hello?

—bar magnet had lost all its field strength, Millie Amp tried self induction and damaged her solenoid . . .

—No Leroy, he's been trying to find out what happened to a shipment from the government in connection with the cafeteria lunch program subsidy, the . . . picnic forks yes, they seem to have ahm . . . well tell him to call me back, yes . . .

—fully discharged, was unable to excite his generator, so they reversed polarity and blew each other's fuses . . .

—Yes well I think you'll just have to take a look at the whole tape yourself Dan, all that electrical language is a little bit ahm, here just let me initial it and send it back to him we don't want to take any more of the Senator's time and we can clear up your ahm, look into your equipment requests later in terms of ahm, of budgetary terms that is to . . .

—No but it wasn't that equipment that I, I meant the equipment we already have that was stored in north seven, I came in that way this morning and . . .

—I think I can straighten Dan out on this Whiteback, with the equipment coming in for this home ec center in east seven you were going to set your little retreads up in business over in north seven, am I right? And then all Dan's equipment here would be . . .

—Yes well no we ahm, when the home ec equipment came into north seven we had Dan's moved over to east seven where we were going to set up the retard ahm . . .

—Set them up in business in east seven, that's what I just . . .

—Yes well we've ahm, put them out of business that is to say, in terms of the ongoing situation spacewise the skill builders and the ahm, the reading accelerators ran over two thousand dollars I think didn't they Dan, in budgetary terms of course damage to equipment like that if we put it in the ahm, out in the cold that is to say the taxpayers would probably ahm . . .

—You say this new home ec equipment's in north seven? I'd like to take a look at it Whiteback, matter of fact I thought I might take a couple of pieces, a couple of the appliances maybe, take them off your hands at cost, might help you out a little on your space problem.

—Yes well at cost of course I ahm, I thought they were gift from your subsiderary, a subsiderary of your ahm . . .

—Matter of fact that's what I meant yes, after the way they cleaned us out in that robbery . . .

—If you're going to look at it now I'll go with you, we can make sure the . . .

—You go ahead Dan, one of us going around bandaged up with an arm in a sling is one thing but the two of us these kids would think was a comedy team. Anyhow I want to talk to the Senator here for a minute about your proposition thirteen, Senator? Your bill to get the schools out of the entertainment business, make closed-circuit systems . . .

—That bill, we tabled that bill.

—What do you, what do you mean you tabled it, you . . .

—When the Foundation announced it's dropping support for the school televisions we tabled it, too much . . .

—The Foun, what? What do you, what the hell do you, what's he talking about Whiteback?

—Yes well the ahm, of course I forgot you'd been in the ahm, out of circulation that is to say Major but the Foundation has apparently decided to put its support into educational broadcasting ahm, community stations as opposed to school, educational television as opposed to instructional television that is to . . .

—But what do they think they, they stick you with a million dollar setup like this and then pull out? Put us in the entertainment business where every brokendown jobless retired radical welfare freeloading Tom Dick and, and, and that writer they sent out here, you remember him? Messy looking kind of a, I gave him a whole armload of research material he never returned, what kind of a write-up do you think he gave the whole thing after that lesson by that, that Bast, that, that's what did it, that, owww . . . !

—Yes be careful Major that desk corner is ahm, no I'll pick up the papers Dan why don't you just go ahead and check on your ahm, excuse me . . . hello? Oh, oh yes Mister Parentu . . . yes he's right ahm . . . A flash of nails and the blue stone intervened. —Right, right yes well of course he just said you're right but he just ahm, unfortunately Mister Pecci just left, he . . . yes well of course I can give him your message about the story in the . . . yes, yes go ahead, yes . . . the phone dangled.

—And that Gibbs that, that what do they expect when you've got somebody like that up there representing the school to every jobless old retired welfare watch your, your pants there Dan, looks like they're going to . . .

—Listen, at the door there somebody? listening . . . ?

——to go shit in their hats . . .

On the screen was Smokey Bear.

—Here, what are you doing there!

—What, me . . . ? The door opened far enough to admit a torn sneaker toe.

—You, yes, there's no one else there is there? What are you doing at the door there.

—Nothing. I got sent.

—For what was it now, typewriters again?

—No it was, I was using this here adding machine up in the . . .

—Using it? You didn't happen to ahm, take it home with you?

—What? What like, steal it?

—Three typewriters and one adding machine disappeared over the weekend, do you know anything about it?

—Me? No I mean holy, I mean if I stole one why would I get caught using this here one up in the . . .

—What makes you think you have a right to play with expensive school equipment like typewriters and adding machines? Do you know how much one of them . . .

—No but I was real careful Mister Whiteback but see I had all these here big numbers to add up which I had to be sure it came out right see so I . . .

—This is the last time, do you understand? This is the last time I want to see you sent to my office for something like this, do you understand?

—Me too but I, yes sir but I just wondered, see this list of all these numbers I was adding up in this here adding machine I wondered if I could just get it back because like I thought maybe then Mister Glancy could . . .

—Mister Glancy's not in today and you can do your homework the way everyone else does it, with a pencil, now get to class or wherever you're supposed to be and, and look out there, you're dropping that whole pile of ahm, Dan if you're going you might ahm, if you see Mister Gibbs in the halls anywhere you might tell him I'd like to see him as soon as he ahm, he can . . .

And out under the benign reproof in the fixed gaze from the wall they moved at home through crowd and noise, the one pursued by admiring gasps toward east seven, the other abruptly submerged half down the range of lockers to tuck a shoelace and surface to a stride that brought the coins bulging one pocket to a heavy clank each step toward the telephone booth as a clock beyond disposed of the hour with a click and the doors clattered closed on him with the second ring. —Hullo . . . ? chin sunk deep as though seeking cords down toward the spleen somewhere, hand mounting handkerchief wad, pencil stub, tugging the torn zipper on the portfolio balanced as a lap desk —this is him speaking . . . handkerchief wad firmly in the mouthpiece, —is this here Mister Wiles . . . ? Yes how much could you get me . . . at what? Holy . . . no that's okay go ahead and get it, I just wondered why this Eagle stock is so . . . no just the common I already got rid of the other, hey I wanted to ask you about this stuff you sent me on these here nursing homes, this . . . what? No, no I can hear you fine, wait . . . he loosened the handkerchief wad, —now can you hear me better? We're always having trouble on these lines, I know, listen I . . . what? What paper, today's? No I . . . No just these Series B and Series C debentures, they already . . . what? What . . . ? No but what do you mean the whole thing, the whole thing? But holy . . . no but holy . . . What? No but wait a second you just said Alberta and . . . no I know it but what's Ace Development got to do with Al . . . What do you mean, the both of them? But holy . . . No but holy

. . . No but this here Mister Decker which was the underwriter, he
. . . What, like when the interest was due on this here Series B he put
out the Series C and used that money to pay off the . . . No but like the
price of the Ace stock just went up so how come he wanted to merge it
with Alberta and Western if they were like already losing ten thousand
dollars a . . . oh you mean that's why it went up? No but first I have to
talk to this here lawyer, I . . . what? No I know it's a bad connection, I
said I have to talk to our attorney first but see if you could look up this
company called X-L Lithography at Ohio or someplace, find what their
. . . No I said Ohio, find their book value and their dividends and all, I've
got somebody waiting to see me . . . and the door cracked with the
cropped head pressed against the outside glass, —the what? Oh that
nursing home thing, is that how you pronounce it? No I said I got the stuff
you sent me that is to say but I'll call you later . . . and the door clattered
as far open as the lap desk allowed.

—What are you doing?

—What does it look like, I'm talking on the telephone.

—You better hurry up, Mrs Joubert's going to . . .

—Look hey tell her I had to go see the nurse okay?

—Okay, you going to the Post Office after? Boy wait till you see what
I'm getting hey.

—We can go over at gym, hey and tell Mrs Joubert I went to see Miss
Waddams okay . . . ? and the door shuddered closed on him writhing for
the depths of a pocket, stacking coins to size, the black nail crescent in
the dial, the coin drop and chin dropped deep, —Hullo? Virginia? This
is . . . J R yes I just called to see who called, is Mister Bast there . . . ? and
a fitful silence, hunched for a thumb to reach a nostril. —He's not? Okay
then who . . . which one . . . ? No see there's this one named Bunky which
I don't want to talk to him but the . . . yes the old one, no I know the
number, it . . . No I know it's long distance, who else? Who . . . ? Moon
like in moon you mean? e, y, h, Mooneyham? holy . . . no just what's the
number . . . and the pencil stub worked . . . —okay and who . . . ? Yeah
Mister Crawley, what did he just have some wisecrack to make about
Alberta and . . . no sure tell him I already knew it, he thinks he's so
. . . Of what? n, o, b, what is it Italian? No I'll have Mister Bast look into
it, at thirty-eight he said . . . ? No but tell Mister Bast to call me at this
here new branch number collect at two fifty . . . no that means ten of
three exactly tell him it's urgent, he . . . Okay I know so when he comes
in tell him I said he should pay you . . . no sure in cash I know, sure
. . . no sure I know what it's like, sure . . . and a sharp crack at the glass
shot a line down it. The door clattered open. —Holy shit hey what are
you trying to do, you cracked the glass.

—Come on hey help me out . . . the jar that had cracked the glass
was thrust inside. —A quarter hey, Miss Waddams is waiting, I even had
to snitch another bottle.

—What do you mean, right in here? Go find . . .

—No come on, there's nobody hey, look I'll stand right . . .

—Look I already went, find Anthony.

—I already found him, he's all out. Thirty cents hey?

—I told you I already went . . . and the door clattered closed on the turning dial, the succession of quarters raised to the slot, sneaker wedged high against a hinge, finally —Mister Hopper please, this . . . No not him, the old one . . . Hullo? Mister Hopper? This is . . . yes, you recondized my voice . . . ? No my secretary just told me you called, is there . . . No sure I can hear you okay, we been having trouble with the connections from this . . . what? No our mail didn't come in yet today, what . . . No well that's too bad, I . . . Yeah well that's too bad but . . . No well I mean I'm sorry these hometown Eagles lost this here game but when the . . . No but when the Weekly Messenger says it's because they lost their home field see I think that's just this attempt to embarrass you Mister Hopper since the bank's taking it over in this here leaseback deal we . . . No but see in terms of this here loan to Eagle management, we . . . senior management yes see we . . . Yes me and Mister Bast that is to say, see we . . . the what? No well like the status like you call it of this Eagle pension fund buying this here stock in Wonder is . . . this here brewery yes, they make . . . Yes no I'm sorry Mrs Begg doesn't think that's exactly the kind of investment we . . . no I know she's this stockholder but . . . No but like me and Mister Bast we're neither of us a drinking man so why she thought he looked like he . . . what . . . ? No but like being this here banker Mister Hopper you can look at it better in terms of the profit picture instead of just what they make at this here brewery that is to say, am I right? Oh and hey I meant to ask you . . . what? I said say I meant to ask you you know that there big track of land with the rail-road tracks which we just found Eagle owns this big right of way around that big cemetery so I was talking to our attorney about . . . no about the cemetery see we . . . What, the cemetery? belongs to what . . . ? The Ancient and Loyal Order of what . . . ? Honest? of which you're the Grand what . . . ? Honest? Sure no but I mean what would we do with a cem . . . No but what . . . No but sure I mean we don't want this law-suit with this here Ancient and Loyal Order and all, like if we . . . How many . . . ? Holy, I mean this here Order must be tremendous, do they all come there to . . . No I said like are they mostly old . . . ? Oh you mean like from the whole countryside up there who . . . No so okay so while we're waiting for this loan to management maybe we can just settle this here lawsuit, you understand what I mean . . . ? No I mean like on a friendly basis once this here loan is . . . No I know you can't hear me very good so anyway what I'll do I'll talk to our attorney and have him write you the whole deal so we can . . . No that's our accountant, our lawyer is this Mister Piscator, he already wrote you about all the . . . no Pis cator, pis . . . That's him yes, Arnold, so anyway I'll discuss it like

with Mister Bast and then he'll write you the whole . . . who, Bast? No I
don't think he'll be up there again that quick, see he's been real busy with
. . . No I know, you really wouldn't think so because he's . . . I know we're
real lucky to have him with us because like everybody always seems to
like him because he's . . . Yes and he told me all about this neat time he
had up there and . . . what? I said he told me how you arranged this here
banquet and took him to these baseball games and all and he really . . .
Sure well I'd like to once we get some of these hard driving demands of
business done but, yes I have to go now . . . A sling paused at the glass,
flapped dispiritedly, eyes peered over gauze and were gone. —No I said
I'd like to sure but I . . . No I have this meeting yes . . . and one hand scooping the stacked coins into the other, the foot down from the hinge and
the pile of books, papers and that battered portfolio pulled together, the
door came open slowly and he looked one way up the corridor and back
before the silent tread of his sneakers got him to the culvert of the door
marked Boys to watch sling and billowing step reappear, pause again
at the booth to shake it open on the first ring and get the phone with a
free hand on the second.

—Hello . . . ? It's what operator . . . ? No but I haven't talked any
overtime, I haven't even . . . No I didn't even, I don't even know anybody
in Union Falls and I . . . But I don't have sixty cents, even wait wait wait,
operator? Operator I wanted to call New York and I just happened to
pick up the . . . but I can't dial again I just, I don't have the right change,
since you're right there could you . . . No it's collect, yes . . . and the door
clattered closed on the number, —Yes say it's Mister diCephalis calling
in answer to . . . yes, d, i, capital C, e . . . no small d, it's . . . what? No
wait, wait, then let me give you a number they'll . . . my number yes,
it's zero, zero, six dash . . . No it's not a telephone number no, it's my
coded . . . No they'll understand, it's my coded . . . hello? Operator?
hello . . . ? hello . . . ? and the door struggled slowly open, to clatter closed
a minute later on the pile gripped tottering on a knee and that hand
rising to drop coins, stack them, knot the handkerchief as the other
dialed and dropped to distribute office requisites.

—Hullo? Let me talk to Mister Piscator please, this . . . yeah this is
J . . . Yeah this is him, I sound like I'm where . . . ? Tell him that yes tell
him that's why I'm in a hurry because I . . . hello? Nonny? look, I just
talked to this broker Mister Wiles about this whole Ace and Alberta
. . . what? No didn't she just tell you . . . ? No well some of these overseas
connections are real good but . . . no I can hear you fine, look I called you
to . . . No well that's what I called about, I just heard the whole thing went
. . . Okay but where does that leave me? I mean if I was the biggest holder
they had in both . . . what? I already told you because it was real cheap,
now so where does this . . . possible what . . . ? But what good are leases
on mineral exploration rights if I . . . okay but what good are tax write-offs
for mineral exploration if like what am I supposed to do, go out there

with a hat and a shovel looking . . . not a hatful of no I said a shovel and
go looking for these here virgin . . . what? No I mean these minerals
what's the difference of that and you said probably all Alberta and Western has left is this bunch of rights of way and leases to . . . No I know I
can't so look, when you find it all out you can . . . no now can you hear
me? I said tell Mister Bast. Did he call you yet about . . . No I know it
but see he's been doing a lot of reading up on all this and he . . . No, sure
I know it's inconvenient but see we're changing that office up there over
to these picturephones which the telephone company says they take
longer to . . . No I know he doesn't but see we're still a little shorthanded
down there too so Virginia's been . . . Not down in Virginia, no I said
Virginia the secre . . . no I know she's not the brightest secre . . . No from
Mister Bast, he was supposed to call you once him and Mister Wonder
got together and got this whole deal all . . . No I know this other brother
did but see I just got this call from this Mister Mooneyham at . . . he did?
What did you tell him . . . ? No but look see instead of just trying to get
back that Wonder stock this brother loaned him as collateral for X-L
suppose we just take over the whole . . . No but I just told this broker to
get me the book value on it and all so see if we . . . Okay can you hear
me? look, once the pension fund buys out Wonder it could just sell the
stock right back and it would be overrefunded so . . . what? Overfunded
I said yes so we'd never have to put anything in it again, see and then
the . . . no back to the Wonder employees, see then the pension fund
would be all set and these here Wonder employees would like own this
stock of their own company and we get to keep this almost three million
dollars of these unpaid dividends against Eagle's tax loss credit carryforward understand what I mean? Which then instead of just trying to clear
up that X-L thing we could move in and . . . what do you mean lose the
brewery, we . . . Oh. Okay I didn't think of that but look, if you think they
might buy this stock and vote it to put up these new officers that would
declare this big dividend and the whole thing would collapse, is that what
you said? Okay then look, if we set them up this employees' stock option
plan where they buy this here stock but see we keep the voting rights
so we can . . . What do you mean go to jail? why should . . . no now
. . . no now look . . . No now look Nonny, see I'm not asking you what
I can do, I'm telling you what I want to do and paying you to find out
how I can do it, understand what I . . . what? No didn't you get it
yet . . . ? No it's coming to you from Eagle, I just talked to Mister Hopper
up there and he said the check's in the mail and look, he's got this here
old lawsuit up there about this cemetery which it's right in the middle
of this right of way, you can get the whole story on it later from Mister
Bast see but the thing is settle it, see but . . . for anything just settle it,
see but not till we have this okay on this here loan to management, I
mean don't make it sound like we're holding out see but like it's just this
like regular thing you happened to . . . Sure I think you know your

business or why would I . . . No there's just a couple of things like this new issue on this string of these nursing homes that this broker sent me all the . . . No because it's real cheap and then there's some Italian drug company this other broker says is . . . no I didn't look into them yet but look . . . A figure loomed in the glass panel over his shoulder, —look . . . he hunched lower, —I have this meeting I have to . . . what? Back in what country . . . Oh, oh sure tomorrow this was just this short . . . for this meeting yes, I . . . to incorporate what? Just a second . . . he cracked the door open, and over a shoulder —You need this here phone Mister Gibbs . . . ? and at a nod, —okay just a second . . . and the crack closed, —sure go ahead then if you think that's . . . In Jamaica? how come you . . . no I said go ahead, you can tell all this to Mister Bast when you and him . . . no well I just think he's been too busy lately to get a new suit he . . . okay . . . and the door shuddered open. —Just a second Mister Gibbs, let me just get this stuff . . .

—No wait, wait looks like you might have change of a dollar there, I . . .

—Sure, quarters? Or no you need a dime here, three quarters and wait a second let me look at that nickel a second, I just . . . no it's okay, here.

—Thanks . . . funny, I don't seem to have a loose dollar.

—How come? you put on the wrong suit today?

—I suppose that's a way of putting it yes, here . . .

—No that's okay Mister Gibbs keep it, you can owe it to me okay? And he got upright with his armload, out of the booth. —Hey what happened to your shoe though, you hurt your foot?

—Gout.

—Honest? What's that.

—Catch it from horses . . . he sagged into the booth, —and thanks for the loan.

—No that's okay but, you okay Mister Gibbs?

—I don't know why you'd think otherwise . . . and the door started closing —here wait, is this something of yours?

—What, I . . .

—It may even once have been a handkerchief, it . . .

—I forgot I, yes it's . . .

—Just out of curiosity, could I ask why you have it knotted like this over the . . .

—Oh well sure see it's, well see I always do that because like especially right now in the cold season Miss Waddams is always talking about you know? he bent in, freeing it. —There are all these germs probably on the telephone from everybody talking with their mouth right up to it see so . . .

—And that indescribable wad of, of cloth protects you from contamination?

—Yes well, see like it's the only one I have see so . . .

—Then let me make you a gift . . . and the initialed square came unfurling from the breast pocket of the jacket, —on condition you drop that one in the first wastebasket you see.

—Well sure I, I mean that's neat thank you, that's neat . . .

—It's certainly not neat but it's a little neater than the one you're giving up, so you don't have to thank me.

—No but, but I mean people don't usually give me things, you know?

Gibbs stopped the door, staring at him there, and then he cleared his throat —well, well then, you're welcome . . .

—And hey Mister Gibbs? came back as the door shuddered, —Mister Whiteback wants to see you when you can he said, I just heard him tell . . .

—Thanks, Gibbs muttered, a hand already on the phone as it rang. —Hello . . . ? But the . . . now wait a minute operator, I can't owe you twenty cents overtime I haven't even dialed yet, how can . . . No listen, I have an important call to make and I . . . well all right God damn it here's your twenty cents, will you . . . Well why not, is . . . All right all right listen, you've got your twenty cents, now will you just give me a dial . . . to where? Listen operator don't . . . no but listen don't press your good fortune, I did not make a call to Union Falls earlier, I've never made a call to Union Falls, operator you may find this difficult to believe but I've never heard of Union . . . no now look operator if you'll just give me a dial tone so I can . . . Jesus . . . ! his hand rose to dial, to drop coins —yes, is Ben . . . Ben? Yes listen, I . . . no listen that's what I called about, this God damned comic strip out here's getting closer to the last episode and I've got to have that thing settled before I . . . well I know she does God damn it that's the whole point a lump settlement like she says she . . . No I've already done it that's what I called to tell you, I sent her all I . . . Cash? forget who you're talking to? it's stock in a broken down company I used to work for, five shares of General . . . Christ no it may not be worth anything but it's the only God damned thing I had that might be worth anything and I . . . No in a drawer under some shirts, it's an old family owned company that used to make piano rolls now they . . . because there's no way to find out, the whole thing is tangled up in an estate squabble I'm not going to waste time trying to . . . No I knew you'd say that and that's why I did it before I called you, because I've been waiting for advice getting advice listening to advice for, for how God damned long and I'm right where I started . . . with her? No, no the last time I tried she said they had to go to the dentist, she wouldn't even let me talk to her on the phone and when I . . . I don't know, that broken down book salesman probably still hanging around but . . . Look Ben the son of a bitch looks like he came out from under a rock, do you think I relish the thought of him answering the door when I come to see my . . . No Christ no they deserve each other but my daughter, to see my own daughter do you think I . . . Yes and this has nothing to do with that, do you think she spends that support on the girl? God damn it Ben if I hadn't just bought her a ninety dollar winter coat she wouldn't have one and I'm sitting here in a suit I paid two dollars for, now what do you . . . at a thrift shop where the hell do you think! now what do you . . . Of course I do, I wrote something on the back of the stock certificate subject to visiting rights and that's the only . . . No but I want to be the one to decide, can't you understand that? I want to be the one to decide! can't you . . . Well it's too late for that now, I just . . . no just being led around like that with a God damned ring in my nose, goodbye. Let me know when you hear from her lawyer . . . and half a minute, a minute passed silent before the door shuddered open and he came up the bank of lockers with hardly a glance for the casualty emerging from the door marked Principal which he banged again as he entered.

—Oh is that ahm, Leroy is that you out there? Yes come in I ahm, oh it's you Gibbs yes come in . . .

—You're sure I'm safe?

—Yes well of course ahm, safe?

—Apparition going out the door there bandaged from head to foot, I thought it might have been an applicant for one of your car loans.

—Yes well I suppose he ahm, yes well I hadn't thought of that of course but since his car was totally ahm, I suppose Mister Hyde will be looking around for a new one that is to say . . .

—Hyde? That was Hyde?

—Well yes he ahm, yes I thought you might have heard he was in ahm, excuse me, hello . . . ? Oh yes well Mister Pecci left yes . . . yes well no he was but he left . . . the bank? Oh well yes this is the bank ahm, telephone that is to say, yes . . . ? Oh it is? Yes well of course I have no way of knowing Mister Pecci's connection with ahm, any arrangement he may have with County Land and Title that is to say he ahm . . . and Peretti yes but of course Mister Pecci is . . . yes I'm sure you can yes, yes goodbye . . . Yes I'm sorry Mister Gibbs that was ahm, you were talking about a car loan yes but of course your salary is ahm, of course we know your salary that is to ahm . . .

———to all go shit in your hats . . .

—Look let's not go into it, your other phone's off the hook there I can see you're busy, if there's nothing else . . .

—Oh, oh yes that's Mister ahm, yes just leaving a message and I think he's made himself quite clear so it really isn't ahm . . . and he restored the phone, —but while you're right here there was something I meant to ahm . . .

—Probably our proscribed opening this morning, next time I thought we could get through the Amendments.

—Yes well of course how many ahm, in terms of length that is to say because our scheduling situation is somewhat ahm, two hundred and four feet I think someone said this morning and of course in terms of, yes excuse me, hello . . . ? The newspaper, yes we saw the . . . oh you mean this is the newspaper calling?

—Mind if I turn this sound up a little? Hear what's happening to our share in America . . .

———accept the tender offer of twenty-four dollars? If we do, we simply sign here and send this with our share to the City National Bank which is acting as . . . yes? Yes, the transfer agent. Of course nothing forces us to accept the . . .

—Yes well of course implementing the new drug detection program is providing a meaningful insight into the students ahm, body, the student body's ahm . . . urine yes, urine tests under the school nurse who, yes no by the school nurse that is to . . . yes yes very successful, no cases have been reported at all since the detection program went into ahm . . . Yes of course because without popular support we don't have the ahm, the support of the community that is to, yes I have another call yes, goodbye . . . Yes, hello . . . ? Oh yes, no he . . . no no Mister Glancy's out today yes he . . . No we haven't, no we . . . Yes I'll tell him, yes . . . Yes that's what it was Gibbs Mister ahm, Glancy seems to be out today and I wondered if you . . .

—Can't help you Whiteback, I wouldn't know where he . . .

—No that wasn't what I ahm, yes just a minute excuse me, hello?

———goes through, it would be worth one third of a share of Typhon International, the company making the tender, so we . . .

—I'll stop by later Whiteback, I . . .

—No no just a minute, yes . . . ? No I heard you yes, yes the bank examiner just called but all he . . . no well simply because the name Janice ahm, her name appears in a list of the bank's stockholders is no reason to ahm . . . Yes well no, no they may not even be aware that he's sponsoring the legislation to protect suburban banks in this ahm, in the suburbs that is to say, no they simply asked about his position with ahm, any interest he might have in County Land and . . . Yes well the mortgage insurance of course after the allegahm, inferences in today's paper but ahm, yes I have someone with me right now that is to say and . . . yes, later yes . . .

—Could I ask you something, Whiteback?

—Yes well of course I ahm . . .

—I worry about you sometimes, doesn't it ever occur to you to give up one or the other? the bank or the school? When you stop and . . .

—Yes well of course the ahm, when I know which one of them is going to survive that is to say of course I can ahm, yes all I wanted was to ask you if you could take Mister Glancy's classes today, he doesn't seem to ahm, he seems to be out . . .

—Yes I don't know his schedule, my day to monitor cafeteria and then I . . .

—Of course if you wanted to take some time right now to look around for ahm, to stop at the cleaner's and pick up a suit you might have ahm, might have left there yes, another suit and of course your ahm, if you've hurt your foot you might excuse me, hello . . . ? Oh! Oh well yes he ahm, yes send him in . . . and the rimless lenses came away for a hand to rise and rub the vacancies beneath as the phone clattered down, —the Internal Revenue Service man to look into our programming but of course you might ahm, yes turn that down it's a little ahm . . .

—Incidentally she's in today isn't she? that isn't just last week's tape or . . .

—Glancy? Oh no yes Mrs Joubert you mean to say, no this is just a monitor from her class so she must be ahm, of course you wouldn't know she'd been ill because she looks well doesn't she but then she always looks quite ahm, yes you might want to stop and see if Miss Waddams can do something to ahm, she might have an ace bandage or Vogel, yes Coach Vogel might have an ace bandage so you could get your shoe on that is to say even ahm, yes even a tennis shoe I think someone's . . . Yes? Come in . . . ? I think the lesson guide's right here somewhere, yes he might like ahm . . .

————the Eskimo who is no longer segregated in the wilderness, but encouraged to take his rightful place at the side of his American countrymen in the cities, in the factories, on the farm . . .

And Nanook's losing battle against the blizzard of scratched remnants of film finally gave over to the barrage of flying milk cartons that daily signaled lunch and the furtive departure of the monitor whose back could be seen through the A blazing red in B A R a step beyond the legal distance off by anyone on the way to the Post Office or even, some time later, returning from it. —Was that Mister Gibbs in there hey?

—Who else would it be, he's . . .

—Shhh he just came out he's right behind us, come on around by the parking lot . . .

—So what, he doesn't give a . . .

—Quick look out hey! there's Coach . . . !

—Coach? Say Coach? Wait . . .

—Why, it's like the morning after Blenheim Mister Gibbs, walking wounded everywhere. Come into the locker room and we'll fit you to a crutch.

—Have to walk this way or the God damned slipper will fall off listen, have to take a glass of, class of Glancy's tell you what I need though, a shoe.

—For want of a nail wasn't it, watch the door here. We'll have a look in the lost and found box I think there's a pair of ice skates that might fit you.

—Didn't lose ice skates, listen . . .

—Just a flight of fancy Gibbs, skating down a slope of Tchaikowski's Eighteen Twelve Overture it's been on my mind since the time you told me Venice was frozen music, but what was the name of the tune they used? Steady, steady now, remember Howard's sacred gore? Here it comes now . . .

—But that's, wait. He's shrunk!

—Shrunk? He never was a towering figure but to say . . .

—Saw him this morning coming out of Whiteback's office look where's your locker room, I don't want to see the bastard again . . .

—Dan? a bastard? Why the poor . . .

—What do you mean Dan, coming toward us? Saw him this morning it's that God damned Major in his bandages and his arm in a, God damn it he's shrinking look at him jacket's down to his, look where his sleeve is look at his pants, can't walk without hiking up his pants he's . . .

—Just enjoying a strolling game of pocket billiards, do you happen to know the wife? Mrs Carlyle, wasn't it? waked up in the middle of the night by the bed shaking? Dan we're over here discussing Sartor Resartus, Mister Gibbs and I seem to have the same tailor. Here comes Dan with all the news, got the boxback coat and the . . .

—Oh I, I'm sorry I didn't see you, I . . . he broke off looking from one to the other, finally settling on Gibbs' vacant breast pocket.

—Sorry Dan, for a minute there I thought you were . . .

—You gave Mister Gibbs quite a turn here, I've got to get him tended to he's . . .

—But, but wait Coach I just wanted to ask you, this morning when I saw your . . .

—Not only saw it Gibbs look at his pants there, he told Whiteback I was an old neighbor from Cleveland. That's a new touch isn't it Dan? the SOS button?

—Oh I, I forgot I had it on, no what I meant was your lesson on circuitry I couldn't quite match the script to the . . .

—Got to get this man tended to first Dan, he has to get down for a glass at Clancy's. Spend any time overseas yourself, Gibbs?

—None I want to discuss right now, look, just . . .

—When you could lean out the tank turret and, steady . . . they matched step up the corridor. —You happen to know Mrs Joubert, Gibbs?

He watched their backs for a moment, one already splitting at the shoulder, and then freed his hand to remove the SOS button before turning down the range of lockers to leave the only hand in sight that coursing out the hour, ten minutes short of its goal when the phone rang, twice, three times, caught with a crash of the doors in a nailbitten clench.

—Yeah hello? Yeah hey wait a second operator he's coming, he just . . . yeah hey just wait a second he's coming, can you wait a second. . . ? the doors parted for the cropped head to peer up the corridor. —Yeah here he is operator wait, he's coming . . . hurry up hey, they're waiting . . .

—Okay get out of the, hello? Get out of the way hey so I can, hello? Yes I'll accept the call yes, hello . . . ? the doors clattered closed. —Hello Bast? Boy I almost didn't . . . no I'm out of breath, I had to stay in at . . . No but first hey how come you didn't call Piscator about this here whole Wonder . . . what? No but where are you at then, you . . . What? What do you . . . No but how come you're at this here hospital . . . Holy . . . no but holy . . . no but you mean right at that there gala banquet you and him were . . . No but how was I supposed to know that? I mean I knew the both of them were old but holy . . . No but if he had his arm around you singing how come you . . . You mean right in the middle of the movie? Holy . . . No but like if, like I mean he's not going to die or something is he? Because if him and his brother don't sign that stuff Piscator was supposed to get ready we're really up the . . . What his brother's there right now you mean? Can you . . . What, they already did? Why didn't you tell me, I mean if they both signed it everything's okay we don't have anything to . . . No hey I didn't just mean that Bast, I mean sure I hope he gets better real soon tell him but . . . No but wait tell him he can't do that hey, it's . . . No but if he sold the company it isn't even his trade secret anymore it's ours hey, I'll . . . No I'll bet you a quarter hey, ask Piscator, he . . . that cobalt in the water puts such a great head on their beer? did he tell . . . No but see even if this here nurse he's whispering it to doesn't get it see she might just tell somebody which . . . No but tell him to quit it anyway okay? So what else did . . . No wait a second, who . . . ? Did he say that, he's coming there . . . ? No but see he's been calling me and Piscator because he's scared this here bunch of Wonder stock this other brother gave him this loan of to use it like for collateral when this company of his was getting in this trouble because they used to both play football at some college, see so now Mooneyham's scared that if we give him a hard time over this here stock this whole X-L Lithography Comp . . . No but how was I supposed to know this here other brother had . . . No but what do they expect me to . . . No okay, okay but . . . Sure I know you don't but . . . No sure Piscator will do all of it anyway see so you don't even have to be . . . just for like if he checks in with you but . . . Sure I know you don't but just tell me one thing hey, what's lithography . . . ? Honest . . . ? and then they what . . . ? No but like putting some picture on these stones with this grease no wonder they're losing all this money, I mean like you can buy a camera for . . . No okay, okay, I didn't . . . No there's just this one other thing, did you see the paper yet . . . ? No not that, I mean about you remember that Ace Development Company which I bought all that stock of? Well see what just happened was this underwriter Mister Decker what he did was when he set it up all it had was these claims to explore for these virgin minerals see so to bring the stock up he found this here Alberta and Western Power Company to merge them by exchanging their stock but see this Alberta and Western was already losing like ten thousand dollars a month so he hires this shit Mister Wall see for . . . No but he is because listen, they give him this big expense allowance and like this twenty-five percent sales commission to handle their financing so like remember I got those debentures which I was getting this interest on the Series B right after they put out the Series C? Well see like what he did was first he put out this Series A which then when the interest on it was due he put out this here Series B and used that money to pay it see, see then when the interest on the Series B was due he just put out this . . . No but so what if he goes to jail, I mean I'm the one that . . . No like Piscator just said maybe we have this lousy bunch of mineral rights and like drilling rights or something on these old Alberta right of ways so wait have you got a map there hey . . . ? No I forgot where you are, don't . . . No don't get mad I forgot where you . . . What do you mean did I learn a lesson, it's this shit Mister Wall who . . . No no but wait, hey Bast . . . ? Wait no I know but . . . No but you don't have to call Hopper see because I already called him this morning, see he . . . I know see he sent me all this same crap in the mail too but I just told him like if the bank owns their ballfield now and they get pissed off at . . . No okay but . . . sure but . . . no but see I told him you're not coming back up there that quick anyway so . . . No no sure I know you don't but I couldn't hardly tell him that or . . . No well that, see that's just this little thing about this here cemetery right in the middle of where those train tracks go on that big right of way, see it's owned by this Ancient Order of some kind of animal where Hopper's this here Grand . . . No I didn't either but that's what he said, so anyway there's this here old lawsuit which . . . No wait I know that's what Piscator's for hey, see so I already told him to settle it any way they . . . No but what am I supposed to do! I mean who wants to buy all these like Hopper kept saying these here departed loved ones and who wants . . . no wait don't . . . okay okay but don't get . . . The what? Crawley sent you all that stuff too? I thought you were still talking about . . . no look hey it's nothing you have to even . . . No it's just this here drug company at Italy or someplace which he says their stock is this good deal so I called this here other broker which said it just went from thirty-eight to thirty-four and three eighths see so . . . No I know you don't, see I just . . . No well that, no well see that's just this other thing Crawley said was . . . No but see it's just this here spinoff where this Endo Appliance Company is getting spinned off this here other company which got this consent order see so they . . . No but . . . no but wait hey

I . . . No sure Bast I know I said just till this here Wonder deal is straightened out see but . . . sure I know I said Piscator would see but . . . No
I mean I'm not crazy about him either but like right now he's all we
. . . no no but wait hey I never said you should dress like him either with
all those flaps and belts and that thing tied around his neck and those like
sideburns and all but . . . No see I think all he meant about your clothes
was maybe like where the back of your coat was . . . no I know he thinks
that too but see I told him you're reading up on all this stuff see and
. . . no but . . . no but wait hey, I . . . No sure I think he should do something
about it too, it sounds . . . No you mean the Nonny part that's just from
what he called himself when he was little no I mean Piscator, I mean I'm
always having to yell it to somebody over the phone they think . . . what?
No but . . . no I know but . . . no but see that's what I mean like just for
right now if you can like keep things straight with him see once this thing
gets incorporated we . . . No but wait hey wait . . . hey? Bast . . . ? No
I know I said that but . . . no but see getting incorporated all it is is then
you don't get screwed on taxes like everybody else and like for this here
limited reliability and all if something happens they can't . . . No but
. . . no but listen hey . . . no I know it but see first there's this here
accountant up at Piscator's office which he's working up this best arrangement for you taxwise where you don't get screwed on this here
salary I'm saving you from see so . . . No but . . . no I know but look hey
Bast, I mean is it my fault if you went down there and now this here band
wouldn't even play your music because you're not in some union so they
still didn't pay you yet? I mean holy . . . No well okay then but I mean
like what would of happened if you didn't finally take that whole seventeen dollars expenses up at the museum after we . . . Okay but look I
mean you won't even have to see because Piscator said he thinks maybe
he can find us some public relations company which that's this here
deductible business expense where a dollar's only worth forty . . . no I
know I did but . . . no but that's why I wrote it all out for you see once
you see this here Mooneyham and get this X-L thing fixed up I mean then
you can what . . . ? No I know but . . . okay but I mean if you said you
need this money to join this here copier union so this band will even play
what you . . . how much? He did hey . . . ? No but that's neat I mean
. . . no but look hey Bast I mean if Mister Wonder wants to help you out
where he'll pay you like fifty dollars to write this jingle for his beer I mean
that will pay to . . . no but I mean like he says making fifty dollars on the
side, you . . . what? No I just mean on the side like, you know . . . ? No
well sure but . . . no I know but I mean see when you get to do your own
work you're always . . . No okay okay! I mean holy, I mean where I'm just
trying to help you out it's . . . no I know but I mean it's like with me all
this here homework which I'm already getting this D in math and Mrs
Joubert says I'm heading for one in social studies and even . . . Who, Mrs
Joubert? Sure she's okay, she . . . No like she was out a few days but hey

there she is, isn't that funny just when we're talking about her she walks down the . . . No she looks real healthy sure, she just a second . . . Do you want to use this here phone Mister Gibbs? Okay just a second . . . Just this one thing hey you know you said it would take you like a month to read that statistician thing of the United States book I got you? See well I sent in and had you enrolled in this here rapid reading course which all you . . . hey? Hello hey? hello . . . ? And the door clattered fully open.

—Hey where'd you get those Mister Gibbs?

—Those what.

—No I just meant those sneakers, I mean like I never saw you wear . . .

—My mother got them for me, where else do you get sneakers. Don't you like them?

—Honest? No sure I mean they're real neat with those red stars and all, he said getting his armload. —I always wanted them since, you know Buzzie? He had them . . .

And the door clattered closed, silent for a moment before the receiver came down, the dial spun, —Mister Rich? Jack. I want fifty on Sam's Pet tomorrow in the second at . . . what? Well then how the hell do you expect me to . . . Well look, give me twenty on the double, Sam's Pet and Belle Amie and I'm in for an even eight hundred . . . the last time, yes . . . the receiver clattered down and the door, more slowly, opened, —bastard.

—Jack . . . ?

—Oh! he started up, half out of the booth, —didn't see you . . .

—I wasn't sure, when suddenly I saw your foot . . .

—These? He sank back to extend them, —I'm just ah, a favor I'm doing for Coach, tie-in he has with a sneaker company and he asked me to . . .

—No please, please I don't want you to explain . . .

—Have to explain Amy . . . he was getting to his feet, —lot of things I, things I wanted to straighten out first . . .

—I've just felt you've been avoiding me, that you, where have you been? I've hardly . . .

—Been? Been, straying from the curriculum, you miss my home-room this morning? Doing it all to please Whiteback . . . he stopped at the clock there and drew a hand over his face, —going to be a long day. Now what was, Glancy's class straying from the curriculum yes, people on other worlds, the chance of running into one and two dimensional people out there . . .

—Jack . . .

—Run into a two dimensional people sideways you couldn't even see him . . .

—Jack please, she put a hand on his arm turning back down the corridor, —you don't look . . .

—Just so damned many things from so many directions Amy, trying to straighten them out before I, when I didn't get down to that cafeteria to meet you for dinner that night because . . .

—No it's all right I, I couldn't get there either . . .

—Well I'm, God I'm glad of that . . . and he turned abruptly where they'd stopped just short of the outside doors to stare with that intentness of committing some detail to memory, loft of brow or curve of throat, —few things I have to go in and straighten out . . .

—Into town? I'm going in later I think . . .

—Are you? are you? Look . . . he took her arm to move her away from the glass door being pushed vainly from the other side, without a glance up till it came open on a sweep of fur, —what time do you . . .

—Jack . . . ?

—Why what . . .

—I had to drive out here and I thought I'd stop in. Is school over?

—Well yes it's, yes it, excuse me this is, this is Mrs Grynszpan, Mrs, Mrs diCephalis . . . he stepped back for the gloved hand to brush the other's tapered fingers, —just wouldn't have expected you here, I . . .

—I don't want to interrupt anything, I know you're . . .

—No please it's all right, I have a class to prepare for tomorrow. I enjoyed meeting you.

—Wait . . . he fled his image on the dark glasses, —Stella wait here, be right back . . .

She watched them as far as the clock, and then stepped away from the draft of the door.

—Excuse me, are you looking for somebody?

—Pardon? Oh, no no I'm just waiting for someone . . . cornered, she caught her breath, —thank you . . . and she watched that back up the corridor, saw it through the salutation returning now from the other direction.

—Stella what are you doing here.

—I told you, she said stepping through the door he held for her. —Who was that.

—Who.

—That man who just went in with the, with the scars . . .

—Oh Coach, that's our Coach, why.

—He just, just startled me.

—But what the hell are you doing here anyhow!

—I told you, I came out to see my aunts and I thought I'd stop and, I thought you might want to come into town with me.

—What for.

—But you're not in the nicest mood are you, and that suit Jack, she led on into the parking lot, looking down, —and those sneakers you're wearing . . .

—Helping Coach out on the, trying the youngsters out on floor hockey.

—You?

—They love it, get to hit each other with sticks and . . .

—You can't have been drinking?

—Think I stay in here at noon and eat carrot sticks?

She stopped by a car. —Shall I wait for you to get your shoes and, and a coat?

—Have to ride me in like this Stella, he got the opposite door, —or shall I ride you in.

—Please stop it, she said, in behind the wheel, and as they started to move —was there any particular reason to introduce me as Mrs whatever you . . .

—Grynszpan yes, sorry I didn't give the full name did I, Mrs Hyman Grynszpan. College chum.

—And I suppose some day I may even learn the name of your lovely Mrs, whatever that ridiculous name you made up . . .

—No no diCephalis, here let me stop and introduce you, this figure going out the gate ahead of us, you can see he's accident prone go slowly, thinks of himself as a vehicle sometimes and he might try to . . .

—That? she swept the wheel in a turn, —that's her husband?

—That's Dan diCephalis our ah, our resident psycho . . .

—It's quite an assortment you work with isn't it, except for your Miss, Mrs, turned out by Patou even three or four seasons old she's quite elegant . . . and they turned into open highway. —What's someone like her doing there.

—Same thing someone like I is. Am. Like I am is, there, something like I am is, is that what I said?

—Will you please take your feet down?

—These? Pardon?

—Those terrible sneakers, will you get them off the dashboard.

—When suddenly I saw your foot, know that poem?

—Isn't she a little young?

—For what, teaching?

—For you.

—Listen Stella what . . . he was getting knees around, getting an arm over the seat, —what did you come there for anyhow, you don't like my friends, you don't like my sneakers, you . . .

—I told you.

—I don't believe you. I don't believe you got into furs and dark glasses to come out and see your aunts, what are the shades for anyhow? Day's so gray I can hardly see without them.

Without turning from the road she raised a glove from the wheel to lift the glasses away, and drop them back. —Now do you?

—But my, good lord what . . .

—Norman.

—Gave you that? He must have hit you with, must have hit you with a hammer what happened, he got a can of blue paint and a can of orange paint and . . .

—Please Jack, stop it. It wasn't nice and it, it certainly wasn't funny.

He sagged somewhat, dug out a cigarette and came forward, trying buttons, —there . . .

—Do we need the radio?

—Looking for the God damned lighter.

—It's that one, at the end. Can you turn that down a little?

—Little, thought it was Moonglow but it's that damned Tchaikowski thing . . . he settled back in smoke as they veered to an open lane, waved to the glimpse of age clinging to the wheel of the car they passed.

—Jack I wish you could just . . .

—Wait let's hear the commercial, thought it was Tchaikowski but it's that God damned . . .

—I thought maybe you could . . .

—Well what the hell did happen if that's what you came out for, not the wasn't funny part the wasn't nice . . .

—Look in my bag.

—Never liked to look in ladies' bags, found something once in one that, while I think of it, he rummaged among bills, —if you hate my sneakers so much you might lend me ten toward a pair of . . .

—Take it.

—Only find twenties here, and ones . . .

—Well take one of the . . .

—Good, good lord is this, this what you were talking about?

She glanced down. —Yes.

—Right into the eye of the hurricane, almost see out the other end can't you.

—Jack please, you don't have to start . . .

—Ought to borrow it to show to our principal, he's a great one for proscribed openings. Got both of them here in fact haven't you, takes me back to my boyhood in Burmesquik . . .

—Jack that's enough, will you just put it . . .

—Well what do you want me to say, that she has nice eyes? that I'd like an introduction? I mean is it somebody I'm supposed to know or is she just . . .

—No but I thought, it just looks like his secretary, I've only seen her once but . . .

—Norman's passing these out, you mean?

—No please stop being, it was in his shirt pocket. I was getting laundry together and . . .

—And what, you mean you think the lucky man here is . . .

—Jack please stop it, if you can't simply . . .

—Doesn't really look like Norman's ah, knee though, does it, of course you'd know better than . . .

—I said please! The car swerved as she reached to thrust it into her bag.

—All right but I don't follow your story, he said rearranging knees, —you found it in his pocket and he hit you? I mean why didn't you hit him.

A horn sounded and she looked up to the mirror and slowed to the right, and a horn sounded. —Well you know him, she said quietly, —can't you imagine?

—Not because I know him though Stella, he turned to open the vent window and drop out his cigarette, —but I know you.

—Jack if you're going to start . . .

—Because I know what you said to him when you found it. You just moved in and finished the job didn't you, couldn't have done it better if you'd sat down with the girl there and planned it.

—Jack I don't want to hear . . .

—I know damned well you don't, last twist of the knife and he's out of business for good, why the hell did you ever marry him Stella.

Her gloved hand came up to press the glasses closer and they veered out, passing cars. —Have you got a cigarette?

He came up with one and lit it for her with a match, shook the pack and crumpled it. —Why.

—When you and I were, when you started behaving just the way you are now and I started seeing him he sat down one night and told me he'd added up what he'd spent so far taking me out. It came to ninety-four dollars and a half, and he wanted to know if I was serious before he went on. Does that answer you?

—Poor bastard . . . he slumped further beside the glass, —you know, I believe that part Stella . . . and his knees came up again.

—Jack can't you settle down, it's like driving with a ten-year-old.

—Just these damned little expensive foreign cars, must mean the piano roll business is still pretty good though.

—I think business is but the rest of it's quite confused apparently, taxes and the shares in Father's estate. And didn't he give you some when you left?

—Shares? Gave me five, mustering out pay, and I just . . . he broke off, glancing up at her and trying to wedge an arm behind the head rest, —for whatever they're worth, what the hell are they worth?

—I don't know, I don't think even Norman knows really.

—He must have a nice wad of them put away himself.

—Twenty-three I think, but my aunts and uncle have something like twenty-seven.

—But with what you come into from your father . . .

—Probably not more than twenty-five Norman says, when the estate taxes are paid.

—Well, twenty-five and what did you say he had? twenty-three? Makes forty-eight, I don't see what you're . . .

—Assuming we keep them together, she said without looking up from the road, where the banks had narrowed and the screen of trees thinned before the rise of buildings. —And you still have your, five you said?

—Had them in a shirt drawer, he said, and then he half turned to look at her for a moment before he sank back beside the glass again as the screen of trees lost to concrete before a fall of birds from the bridge overhead, thinned to anchor fence penning a battered fleet of empty cabs, finally he turned to her bag between them on the seat and opened it, bent over it, a hand in it.

—Please don't start that again.

—Start what. I was looking for a cigarette . . . he came up with a package and a bill he twisted to get into a pocket before he lit the cigarette and opened the bag to put the package back in. —Start this again, you mean?

She glanced down. —Yes, will you put it . . .

—Off with that weary coronet and show, the hairy diadem which on you doth grow. Now off with . . . The car slowed sharply and he threw up his arm. —Just a little poetry, John Donne the prominent churchman little tribute to his . . .

—Jack this is enough, if you . . .

—Will you let me out here then?

—Don't be ridiculous but stop . . .

—But what's the matter? I quote a prominent churchman on hairy diadems when you bring out a snapshot of one, nicest name for it I could think of offhand and you almost throw me through the . . . a horn sounded, —look out!

—Well what are you doing this for!

—Because I don't believe this is the reason Norman hit you.

—What do you mean now.

—I mean you've been saying twenty-three I think and didn't Father give you some shares and you know God damned well it was five, you know twenty-five plus five is thirty which is more than twenty-three and more than twenty-seven . . .

—Jack you . . .

—But Norman's twenty-three plus five would be twenty-eight which is more than your aunts' twenty-seven and more than your twenty-five well you didn't have to bother Stella, I haven't got the God damned five shares.

—But you said . . .

—I said it was in a shirt drawer and I took it out of the shirt drawer and right now I don't know who the hell has it, can you just pull over up here and let me out?

—Jack please, please stop being ridiculous you . . .

—No I mean it, Stella for you lying is just a practical way of handling things, remember how cheerfully you used to lie to your father when we, when there wasn't even any real reason to? You just need somebody to lie to.

A horn sounded behind as the car slowed sharply and bumped over a low curb onto grass. —I don't know where you think you're going.

—I'll get over the fence there and find a subway try to make the last race, that's why you married Norman isn't it, find somebody that God damned decent he deserves to be lied to Stella I'll bet you haven't been really laid since the day I met you again on that train platform . . .

Horns sounded as the door slammed and the wheels dropped to the pavement where she turned without a look back, pressing the dark glasses close against her face, over rises and down, through the tunnel and up the dim arcade along the river, dim as the rooms she moved among lighting lamps under opaque shades, dropping the bag on An Informal Evening at the Juilliard Theater, the glasses beside it, down the hall thrusting away one shoe, the other, a hand behind her coursing down the zipper as the other sought among robes for the robe fallen open from her where she bent over the basin to bring her eye close to the mirror when the doorbell rang and she caught it closed, caught up the dark glasses passing the table and had them on when she reached up to put the chain in place before she opened the chain's hand's breadth, —Oh! . . . and she closed it to slip the chain off again, and draw it wide. —But you should be in Palma . . .

—Oh I know darling, they ran out of electricity or something and the whole thing was canceled. Like here, you always have it so dark I don't know how you find your way.

—I know it by heart, she led in, paused at a sofa, —do you want anything? before she sank down.

—Nothing, no, a cigarette? Oh, in your bag? Let me . . .

—No I'll get it, she started up, arched over the sofa's arm to reach for it.

—Oh and you heard his concert, did you like it?

—Yes all but the Berg, she said getting the package out, and a lipstick rolled to the carpet where she left it, snapped the bag closed and dropped it over the sofa's back.

—Yes I can't stand Berg too. But how nice to find you, I called and of course you didn't answer, I was sure you are entertaining. Is this an ashtray?

—Yes, but how mean.

—Not mean at all darling, would you lie to me? The one Wednesday night at Elaine's with all the marvelous chains . . .

—No please . . . She pressed the glasses back to her face.

—But I only wanted to see, it's almost gone?

—I don't want you to see . . . she moved her head for the finger tracing a strand fallen loose on the slope of her shoulder. —I don't want anyone to.

—But you should know better darling, you read all the statistics of accidents in the bath, I can't look?

—No no one, it's too ugly.

—How can something about you be ugly?

—Even this . . . ? and the robe fell open where she raised her throat to the light.

—Even this, this is precious! There is never such a necklace, how many times do I tell you? Wait let me show you, in pale rubies how precious . . .

—No . . . her hand came up to the pendant already half fashioned there in lipstick, —no I don't like it touched.

—I might steal it? like Brin, what did you tell me, the name your terrible friend told you for it once?

—Bris . . . she caught breath as breath stirred a strand at her ear, —Brisingamen . . . as the lipstick lingered along her breast.

—But a goddess of love and beauty he told you? Then he was not so terrible to say that.

—He was terrible, she said, the lipstick mounting in slow circles to fleck quick as lashes where its color gathered in the pebbling peak.

—Wait be still or I spoil my work, no don't look yet.

—Always terrible, she said near a whisper, robe fallen away now where the lipstick came down in a flourish to slow and shade a heart on the clear rise and fall of the soft swell, suddenly shot through with an arrow down, and she started.

—Now, you must see how gay, look! You must come next time like this, they will be enchanted, would you?

—Don't be . . . she broke off, looking down her, —of course not, how silly you are.

—You don't see, is it not like a cat with one large eye?

—How silly.

—No, silly no. Look, how he aims to hide deep in the bush, may I seek him?

—Silly.

—It is nice too, the lipstick. Is it Lanvin?

—Oh . . . ? The telephone rang. —Do Lanvin make lipstick . . . ? and she lay a hand over her darkened eyes.

It rang again, and then again, a long ring.

—They don't answer Mister Angel.

—Hell I told you she wouldn't Coen, even if she's there, just forget it Myrna. I don't know what help you think she'd be if she did answer.

—I would like to clarify her position on . . .

—Well she's sure as hell not going to help you, anything you come up with she's got so many positions she could go get a job in the carnival, Myrna why don't you just go take a coffee break or something, I can buzz for you on the buzzer when I need you back. Mister Coen and me have to sit down to these figures for a while . . . he loomed behind her, pent by her short steps as far as a cabinet just inside the door. —Little bourbon here to clear our heads before we dive in.

—Oh no not for me.

—Just got these put in . . . he was bent over pulling at the cabinet door —pretty shoddy job too, he yanked at it, —supposed to look like this modern paneling so there's no place you can hardly get a grip . . .

—Be careful the whole thing's tipping . . .

—Might be better if it did, I wouldn't have to . . . go through this every time I . . . now, where'd she do with those Dixie cups.

—You've changed your scenery since I . . .

—Well you can see we didn't but just get started, those new drapes instead of the old curtains we had over there, I put that big old chair and that old coat rack down in the basement . . . he paused, bent over pouring into two paper cups, —but you know what they want now for a sofa out of leather?

—Oh, no what I meant was . . .

—Even thought of getting that music they play in banks and elevators piped in, he turned walking carefully and set one of the paper cups on the corner of the desk. —But you know what they want for that?

—Oh but I didn't want any.

—What did you mean though, you don't like those drapes?

—No I meant the young lady, you had a secretary with red . . .

—Terry you mean, yes, well she . . . He raised his cup and drank half of it off, —she got a little lonely in here I guess you'd say, I changed her around with Myrna out there in the order room. Softest berth in the place right in here but I guess sometimes they, they get a little lonely with just me to look at . . . and he finished off the cup. —This Myrna's good though, you know who she almost reminds me of sometimes? You remember Joan Bennett when she dyed her hair black? I always thought it was terrible when she did that, he said back at the cabinet, bent down shaking its door again, —think a man that calls himself a big contractor could put a little cupboard door on straight now wouldn't you, look at that. Same little Eyetalian that just gave us that sky high estimate on this new production layout, he thinks he's doing you a favor by walking in the door. Sooner we can get that going though the sooner we . . .

—No but wait Mister Angel you, excuse me for interrupting you but you can't. You can't commit that kind of money right now. You don't know when this estate will be settled and the government may step in any minute with a lien on the property and tie your hands. With their back tax claim against the company I don't know why they haven't already done it, and these estate taxes are going to . . .

—What's all this then . . . his hand came across to sweep the neatly piled papers toward him, —is this it?

—Rough preliminary figures yes, now I think we discussed three million dollars as a conservative figure in evaluating the company which would bring the decedent's share, the value of the decedent's forty-five percent to one million, three hundred fifty thousand. Now anticipating the government taking four hundred twenty-three thousand on the first million, and forty-two percent on anything over that, forty-two percent of three fifty is one hundred forty thousand, add the state's flat eight percent and you have six hundred seventy-one thousand dollars.

—I have? What do you mean I have, they have, and I have a handful of . . .

—Just preliminary figures yes, of course we can't put a precise evaluation on the company until recapitalization goes through and the underwriter makes the . . .

—Look, God damn it now look, don't get me started on this going public again Coen you know what I . . . he paused there pulling off his jacket, the shirt he tucked in behind coming back out with his hand, and he turned to drape it over the back of the chair at his desk where he sat down heavily.

—But I don't know how else you plan to raise six hundred-odd thousand dollars Mister Angel.

—Well for one thing I told you to look into what we can get for our interest in Nathan Wise there, no reason to hang onto an outfit like that and I never did like the . . .

—I've looked into it yes, I think some of the correspondence is right there on the bottom, apparently your lack of ah, enthusiasm is widely shared. From a look at their consolidated statements recently it's not hard to see why no one's interested in acquiring it of course, a chronic money loser though considering the nature of their product it's hardly surprising. I would have thought demand would have evaporated some time ago.

—Well sure, the pill hit them real hard, they just never expected something like that.

—The, pardon?

—The pill all these girls are taking, you read about even twelve-year-old girls on these pills, I read where one of them's own mother had her own doctor prescribe them.

—Oh I, I see, yes I'm aware this entire pill situation has assumed quite alarming proportions among the ah, the young, though I'm afraid I fail to see precisely how its deleterious effects could extend to something as . . .

—See that's a good example there at Nathan Wise of old-fashioned management, one quality product that pretty much took over the top of the market so they just stayed with it.

—Yes, I understood they . . .

—Never used rubber or anything coarse like that you know, just these strong real thin sheep membranes.

—Yes I recall Miss ah, the decedent's sisters mentioning . . .

—The, you mean those two old ladies out there talked to you about this? He drew his hand over his mouth and his cup closer on the desk. —Well. I'd never have thought it.

—Our conversation was, I think I've mentioned that it was not the most logical, they seemed to have the impression I was trying to pry into family matters but . . .

—I have to hand it to you Coen, I sure never would have . . .

—As I recall this matter though they appeared to take a good deal of pride in it, the quality aspect you speak of, I remember them mentioning the sheep membranes yes and a senator I believe, from a sheep producing state in the west . . . ?

—Yes Billikin or Millikin or something, some old goat that got quite friendly there for a while, but it sure does beat . . . and he brought his paper cup up, and put it down empty. —But this isn't selling any apples, now look . . . He pulled over a pad and found a blunt pencil, —one way or the other you see twenty of the old man's shares going for these estate taxes, now where the hell are they going?

—Well, in the very nature of making a public off . . .

—I mean that would be one hell of a big foot for those Jubilee Musical people to get in our door here.

—Unless they did it through a third party though I think it would be possible to get an injunction to prevent it, in view of the longstanding litigation between them and your ah, the decedent over these punched forms and the entire concept as it might be held to apply to . . .

—Holes is what it is, a lawsuit over a lot of God damn holes.

—Precisely but of course in the event of an eventual decision supporting the position of the decedent, the ramifications could very well extend far beyond the immediate . . .

—All right but that's eventual, I want to get back here to right now, I want . . .

—Yes once we've resolved the financing I think we can . . .

—And that's not what's on my mind right now either, it's not just the money it's who the hell's going to end up running the show here.

—Well as I say, I think any immediate threat by the Jubilee Musical Instrument Company can be effectively dealt with by . . .

—All right then what about the rest of it, now look. He recovered the pad, where a large ellipse had begun to take shape. —Here's my twenty-three shares here. Here's this twenty of Stella's aunts and this seven of her Uncle James, then over here . . .

—Five, yes I find five listed in the name Gibbs, someone named Gibbs, I'd intended to ask you if you . . .

—Wait we'll get to him, now look, down here is this twenty-five there in the estate after taxes, now . . .

—Speaking frankly Mister Angel I think you can put your mind at rest there, from my dealings to date with this rather ah, this artistic branch of the family, I doubt if there will be much difficulty in establishing your wife as sole heir and with those twenty-five shares and your own twenty-three there should be no . . .

—Well just wait though, just suppose it did come to her and Edward splitting up this twenty-five shares, I'd like to . . .

—That would seem, excuse me for interrupting but that seems extremely remote. This nephew, this nephew Edward has never sent me the signed waiver I requested, I've never received the particulars on his birth, I've never heard anything from him in fact or even a call from an attorney representing his interests and I can only assume he doesn't find it worth bothering with, though this rather lofty indifference to money on his part does seem rather ah, exceptional. Of course I did understand from his aunts that his consuming interest is music and artists in these matters are rather notoriously impractical, if I recall the case of . . .

—Yes well I don't know about all that Coen . . . he sat tapping the empty cup for a moment, and then stood pushing the chair back and the jacket off to the floor. —You see you got to remember he was pretty upset by all this, I just met him that once out there that night and I've tried to call him since but I never can get him at home, his one aunt there even told me one time he was off on a business trip but . . . he paused, pouring, and turned, —there's just something about him you like, something you kind of like and trust about him that you want to help out. Now right now he's maybe a little mixed up but I think I could talk some sense to him and maybe . . .

—That may all be quite true Mister Angel but I don't quite see the precise relevance to . . .

—Well put it this way then. I don't exactly want to go into details here but put it this way. If instead of Stella holding twenty-five shares against my twenty-three it turned out that her and Edward split that twenty-five I'd, well I guess you see what I mean . . . and he raised the cup again before he came down behind the desk.

—Oh. I see.

—Yes you see it's not hardly the question of the money here it's, it might even sound to you like I'm just trying to step in and grab all I can but . . .

—No you make your position quite clear Mister Angel but, excuse me, there is a point regarding this nephew you may have overlooked. Now even assuming that half the residue of the estate should fall to him and that he is as ah, as appealing a young man as you find him, it is still not established whether or not he is a minor and should that prove the case of course, his aunts or his father, or rather his Uncle James it would be if his claim on the decedent's estate proved valid, one of them at any rate would in all likelihood be named his guardian in this matter with the right to exercise the rights of his twelve and a half shares added to their aggregate of twenty-seven. Now . . .

—Well but I wouldn't mean to . . .

—No but please let me finish because I shouldn't want you to mis-understand me. While his aunts did express a rather impatient interest in seeing some return on their investment in the form of dividends I don't for a moment wish to accuse them of being particularly venal, in fact it seems quite a normal attitude for anyone apparently living in somewhat straitened circumstances. But even on my brief visit with them I did feel that their grasp on reality seemed somewhat ah, tenuous at times, they do appear to have occupied that Long Island residence for some time yet what they refer to as the local paper is a weekly they have mailed to them from the Indiana town the whole family apparently left a good generation ago. The attorney they referred me to there has never answered any of my correspondence and I almost feel his very existence may be open to question, and very frankly the figure of James Bast himself seems so ephemeral that when they tell me he is abroad some-where accepting an award there is the sense that they may be referring to the Paris Exposition of nineteen eleven. The only point I wish to make is that if these ah, if they exercised anything approaching control in an enterprise I was trying to conduct in a rational, businesslike manner, I believe I would be rather uneasy.

—Well that makes enough sense but . . .

—Now and so, excuse me, from your point of view even though you may have reason to regard the prospect of your, of the decedent's daugh-ter holding this larger number of shares as a threat to your position, it still might be somewhat safer than the alternative I just outlined if you can explore the possibility of these five remaining shares, added to yours of course they would give you the bare majority you . . .

—Yes well I can add Coen, he said looking up from the long narrow ellipse constricting Gibbs 5 that had taken shape under the blunt pencil, —the problem is so can she, so can Stella.

—But I oh, oh I see, I wasn't aware this Gibbs person might be someone you both had access to, in that case of course the sooner you can . . .

—Well I don't know who in hell she has access to as you put it, Jack Gibbs, I lost track of him a few years ago but, this may sound funny but I thought I saw him not too long ago right out here a few blocks away, that first minute I saw him it couldn't have been anybody else but him and then I just wasn't sure, playing ball with a little girl there and he had a bad limp that Gibbs never had and what the hell he'd be doing out here next to nowhere in the first place. And then he was gone and when I asked the little girl after she said that was her father, I'd heard someplace he'd got married that didn't last but just a few months, right after him and Stella stopped seeing each other and he got to drinking there for a while . . .

—Yes, well of course the sooner you . . .

—See he worked here for a while just before I came, just real brilliant but, I don't know but just to give you an idea, one time when we'd all three had lunch and he'd taken a few drinks a bum came up to us on the street with his hand out and the wind blowing his torn coat, a whole wreck of a man that couldn't hardly see us anyway but Jack all of a sudden reached out and gave him a dollar and that really, well you know a long time after that I said something about it once to Stella and all she said was, she said he did it because what he saw coming toward him was himself. And I just always remember the way she said that . . . he broke off, returned to the figure before him to fringe its edge with heavy strokes and stand abruptly, reaching his cup as he passed toward the cabinet.

—See Stella, he said from over there bent to tug at the door again, —sometimes she's just got no real understanding of just how the way things are, that this idea you can fail will just build up inside a man . . . he tugged it, —or you know maybe she does, he tugged sharply, —better than anybody can guess . . .

—No be careful!

—There . . . ! He stood with half the door off in his hand, —now look at this thing, look at it! That's a wood cabinet I had put in here, did that split like wood with no grain to split along? There isn't any. They press sawdust and glue together and paint on a grain . . .

—Yes I, I see it is Mister Angel but I wouldn't let it upset me this much, after all it's only a . . .

—Coen God damn it can't you see what I mean? Can't you see this is what's going to happen right here, after all it took to put all this together? Can't you see you go public and all these people owning you want is dividends and running their stock up, you don't give them that and they sell you out, you do and some bunch of vice presidents some place you never heard of like the ones that turned this out, this wood product they call it, they spot you and launch an offer and all of a sudden you're working for them trimming and cutting and finally bringing in people to turn something out they don't care what the hell it is, there's no pride in their work because what you've got them turning out nobody could be proud of in the first place . . . He broke the piece over his knee and stood up with the bottle, —if they'd just understand I'm not just trying to grab this whole show for myself but to keep it doing something that's, that's worth doing . . .

—Yes and of course the sooner you can . . .

—You know it's funny, I look back sometimes and I think if it hadn't of been for Stella in there, sometimes I think we could have done something here, me and Gibbs, really done something.

—Yes of course the sooner you can reach him . . . the unemptied cup was placed carefully aside for a sharp squaring of papers on the corner of the desk, —the sooner the status of these five shares can be clarified and . . .

—I know, I've been keeping my eye on the time here, I thought I'd just walk over about now where I saw him playing with that little girl if it was him, if it really could have been him I saw . . . He'd put the bottle down on the desk and stooped behind it to pick up his jacket from the floor and shake it, and he dropped it over the back of the chair again.

—I thought you might want to ride back into Manhattan with me, the day's practically over . . . and the briefcase came up for papers squared smartly on the desk, —I could wait for you if you . . .

—No you go ahead, he said without looking up from the pad on the desk before him as though reading something in the heavy shadings of pencil for the first time, tore off the page and crumpled it as he sat down again, —I wanted to try to get a word with Terry later anyhow, don't want to bother her now but I thought I'd get her aside after we close up shop here, just something I want to clear up . . . he reached for the blunt pencil and sat back picking it clean with a thumbnail. —That's her plant over there, she was helping out on the decorating, I thought she might have some ideas for bringing it back to life a little.

—Oh yes, well we've given up on them in our offices, all bamboo now, a Japanese miniature bamboo, of course the initial outlay for these plastic varieties runs somewhat high but eventually . . . the briefcase snapped closed and then paused in its swing toward the door. —I'm just leaving this to be typed out and, Mister Angel if you don't mind my, if you just got your mind off all this for a little while and did something to, went somewhere and had a good time . . .

—That's funny you'd say that right now Coen, you know when I was a boy we were brought up pretty strict, I had a kind of asthma problem that made it kind of rough sometimes. You see we grew apples up there and my brother and I had to work packing crates, and we'd get a chance to read the funnies down there in the papers we used packing apples because funny papers just weren't allowed in our house. We weren't real close at all but in a way you look back maybe we were, we used to hunt rabbit together with twenty-twos and I still have that old octagonal barrel Winchester in a closet somewhere. I remember it seemed strange to me then, before he got killed in the war what he always wanted to be was a geologist.

—I, I see yes, well I've left those papers there to be typed and as soon as you . . .

—I'll get Myrna to knock them right out . . . he leaned forward, hand searching the button under the desk, and reached the unemptied paper cup. —Anyhow every year in the spring the circus would show up, but with the animals and all the hay they'd have around I never could go to it with that asthma I had, I couldn't even go near the parade. So the night it would come to town, there was a hill right up outside the town you could look down from and my father would take me up there in the old open Reo we had, and we'd sit up there and watch the whole thing, just the two of us up there. You couldn't see everything too clear because it wasn't all that close and the evening was coming on, but you could see the wagons and horses and the elephants and hear the band playing, you'd get a sudden little breeze that was almost warm and bring the music right up with it, and the lights coming on all along the way, I don't think we hardly talked at all, and you know? he said, chair tilting back and the jacket gone to the floor again. —Maybe those were the best times I ever had . . .

—Excuse me Mister Angel did, did you buzz? She paused there behind the figure backed to the door, briefcase shifting from hand to hand.

—I think he just wants you to type up that material there Myrna, and send me a copy?

—Sure okay Mister Coen . . . she came across for the papers neatly squared on the desk. —Is it okay if I type these out front Mister Angel? where we just got coffee . . . ? pausing, for what might have been a permissive shrug under the clinging shirt, before she retreated to the door and down the cement block green where her discrete walk rose and fell to the eyes fixed discreetly upon it as far as a rail of golden oak, flattened there with no intent apparent but to let him pass, pursued with a wave and —Goodbye Mister Coen, come see us again now . . .

—I just broke a nail.

—I got this Nu-Nail back in my desk but I don't want to go back in and get it, you know?

—I know, did he say anything?

—I don't mean that, he just seems sort of far out, you know?

—I know see what I meant? like you have this feeling he's looking up you only you look up and he's looking off someplace like he's not even there.

—I know, anyway I have to type this up before we go, wait for me?

—I want to go to this sale on sweaters maybe, okay? and the emery board took up briskly, —what, you meeting somebody? and the emery board stopped as she looked up with no answer. —I still didn't get used to your hair black, she said pushing back red, —he still like it?

Paper rolled into the typewriter. —Are you kidding?

—He sounds like a real character . . . and typewriter and emery board paced time unbroken by looks to the clock where a good portion had fallen away when they stopped, paper pulled from the typewriter carried down the empty hall to the empty office, left on the empty desk.

—He's not even in there Terry, did you see him go out?

—Maybe he went out by the shop, come on . . .

—Did you see my comb . . . ? Drawers slammed, coathangers rattled on the rack, they came out arm in arm, down one curb and up another, rounding a corner in step past brick and fieldstone sham, down that curb and —Terry look!

—What's the . . .

—Didn't you see him? The Boss, didn't you see him up there running? chasing somebody?

—Are you crazy? What would he . . .

—No I swear it, right around that corner up there . . . and they moved on again, past fence penning aprons of dead grass and on around that corner up there toward the elevated limb of subway, rummaging in purses as they reached its steps, looking behind them and both ways on the elevated platform waiting pressed against a telescoping loaf of bread surcharged Astoria Gents Suck until the train came. —Don't look now, he just got in the next car . . .

—Did he see us?

The seats filled, so did the aisle, feet kicking aside torn newspaper, flattening candy wrappers and they sat closer, faces lowered from that hung over them agape through rimless glasses down into their tops, knees nuzzling theirs confining a briefcase of Gladstone bag design upright on the filthy floor. Lights dimmed, came up, and they roared underground.

—He's up the other end now, right past that woman with the green, it's like he's following us you know?

—Why should he do that, wait, wait I'm getting off here with you and change for the express . . .

—Don't look back, is he getting off too . . . ?

Elbows found ribs, heels unprotected ankles, —ay coño . . . where strange hand cupped briefly strange skirt, —hold the door . . . and the lady in the green raincoat dug an elbow hard. —Sorry . . . he got by her to the platform, the flaunt of red hair gone that moment behind a post, newspapers streaming Mata a sus niños, shopping bags and wives' umbrellas clutched like staves in a relay race with no course and no finish as the scream of steel wheels on steel rails left the teeming concrete shore opposite where suddenly he stared arrested, waved and shouted —Edward . . . ? Bast! Edward . . . ! off balance as the flaunt of red reappeared alone from behind stairs, sheltering to draw breath for the cry —Ed . . . ! smashed on the roar of a train from the other direction leaving Bast halted there on the far platform hit before and behind like an invalid in a hotel fire, looking, one way, the other, finally dropping his shoulders and his eyes to dead rivulets leading toward stairs, up them catching breath at the top against uneaten frankfurters turning with venemous patience on a counter grill, more stairs and the street, where the sole of his shoe took up its flapping cadence windblown past ranked garbage cans capped at merry angles down the hill to a doorway lighted, like the rest, by a bulb so dim he cast no shadow as he entered, pursuing a broken refrain up the stairs and down linoleum worn through by fatigue, pausing to move mail with his foot before fitting the long iron key and lifting the door on the sound of running water.

—Hi.

—What . . . ? he held the door, turning to the shadows in the stairs rising behind him. —You, you startled me I didn't see you there.

—You live here?

—Yes I, well I mean I've been staying . . .

—Like what's going on with that back apartment.

—I don't know it's, no one lives there right now but . . .

—Look man I know nobody lives there right now, there's some stuff of mine in there I want to get out, okay?

—Oh, yes, yes but I don't have a key . . .

—I mean I've been sitting up here in the dark just waiting for somebody to show up, you know?

—Yes well I, I'm sorry I can't help you, I don't have a key but . . . he lifted his door open and held it balanced there, —if you want to come in here and wait for, for whoever you're waiting for . . .

—Look man I just told you I'm not waiting for anybody, okay? Like I just want to get my stuff out of that back apartment. What's all this, mail?

—Yes that's all right, I'll get it as soon as I lean this door . . .

—What were you like away for a month? You want me to bring it all in?

—It's just today's I'm afraid, if you would yes . . .

—Except the package, I mean you don't expect me to lift that.

—No no I'll get it, if you can get the door here, it just hangs on one hinge and . . .

—I mean like somebody sent you a box of bricks, like man I mean you really get mail.

—Yes if . . . you can just . . . he got the box in over the sill, —put it in there on that sofa . . .

—You left the water on.

—Yes I can't turn it off, he said fitting the door back into place behind her, —something's wrong with the . . .

—Man I never saw such a, like I mean what's in all the boxes, mail?

—No just, I don't know just papers, books and papers I think, he said following her in past 24-One Pint Mazola New Improved, 36 Boxes 200 2-Ply as she dumped the mail on the armless sofa and stood to pull off the long raincoat.

—Hyman Grynszpan, that's you? she said sitting beside the heap, picking up the Bulletin of the Atomic Scientists.

—No I'm, my name is Bast, Edward Bast. Are you, I mean . . .

—Am I what.

—No your name, I just meant your name . . .

—Rhoda, okay?

—Oh yes you were Mister Schramm's, a friend of Mister Schramm's weren't you, the night he . . .

—Look, I mean let's just cool it with the Mister Schramm okay? She got a denimed leg up to rest a foot on Wise Potato Chips Hoppin' With Flavor! —like I mean what do you expect me to owww . . . !

—Oh I'm sorry that's one of my . . .

—Wait here's another one and, look at them . . . she'd come forward to pull the pencil from the stretch of denim —I mean I never saw so many fucking sharp pencils.

—Yes well I was working there and I . . .

—What, like you write?

—Music yes I, I write music . . .

—Like you just come here to work? I mean why don't you sit down, you're standing there holding that little suitcase like you're selling something, like I mean you don't really live here, right?

—Well I've been staying here while I worked on, something I've been working on, he said cornering on Hoppin' With Flavor! beside her moccasin, —just to be alone so I could work on . . .

—What, you sit up here with all these boxes and write this music? Like I mean where do you sleep.

—Well right there where I, where you're sitting, I . . .

—With all these fucking pencils sticking in you like some Indian faker man, I mean you must be stoned before you dare to lie down on it.

—Well, no, no I usually . . .

—I mean like those footprints going right up the shade back there man.

—Yes I've, I've wondered how those . . .

—Man like right up the wall really stoned . . . she came down to one elbow on the sofa, gaping her denim front between the white buttons. —You eat out?

—No here I, I usually eat here, I . . .

—Where. I mean the kitchen in there is so full of boxes and lampshades and everything you can't even find the stove.

—No it's right under there but there's no gas, so I just use the oven to . . .

—Like I didn't even eat lunch.

—Oh, oh well I could make you a cup of tea if you . . .

—No I mean eat man, like that's all you've got a cup of tea?

—Right now yes but I thought I'd go out and get some cup . . .

—Have you got any bread?

—No but I thought I'd go out and get some cupca . . .

—Like even two dollars . . . she came upright, —there's that A and P up at the corner like we could get a pizza.

—Well, two dollars, he said standing, digging into a pocket, —here's one and I . . .

—Like I mean just to get me through the checkout, okay? She stood to pull on the long raincoat. —What do you carry money in your sock?

—No it's, I have a hole in my pocket and the coins drop down my trouser leg . . .

—Man, I mean . . .

He fitted the door back into place behind her and stood, swallowed, went over and tried the hot water tap till his hand went white against it, finally stood back from the rush of water to look into the rusting cookie tin propped above it for a moment, swallowed and cleared his throat past 24-One Pint Mazola New Improved to pull the aging blanket loose and gather pencils, thrust points up in the tomato soup can, before he smoothed it carefully and sat to comb the mail heaping Grynszpan separate, stood to straighten the askew blind, to turn on the light in the punctured lampshade and try to round its creases, stare at the Baldung and finally stand it atop 2-Ply Facial Tissue Yellow with a deep swallow. When the door shuddered again he was by it tearing open the package from the hall. —Rhoda? is, wait . . .

She stepped in over it. —Like what did you get for Christmas.

—Oh it's just ah . . . he squared round the green volumes, —it's Thomas' Register of American Manufacturers, I . . .

—Of what? She put a bag on the floor, balanced the flat box from under her arm on a pile of film cans, —I mean you must be kidding.

—No it's really just, I think they were just sent to me by someone I've been doing some work for for, for reference . . .

—I thought you said you write music, she said holding the raincoat wide to come up with small tins and jars from depths of pockets.

—Yes I do yes, yes this business is, this business work is just something I've been doing to help pay . . .

—Hey the sink, quick!

—What . . .

—I mean its coming over the side quick . . . The raincoat dropped to the floor, —like we both could drownd in here man . . .

—No I'll get it, he hesitated, grabbed a coathanger from the dishrack and thrust it in, —just something got, stopping the drain . . .

—Like what about the floor . . .

—Yes there's a, a mop back there by the window behind those shades and things I, I think I threw it there one night, he said working the coathanger, watching her tight denims breach the lampshades, mount the bank of Morning Telegraphs and scale Appletons' —right near the window, I . . .

—Wait look there's somebody over there in, oh wow.

—What? did you . . .

—Oh wow . . .

—What? He came up with a sodden wad on the end of the coathanger and stood looking at her spilled toward the sill there under the shade. —Did you . . .

—Man like his underpants come down and it's standing up like this poker . . .

—The, the . . . what? and the wad dropped back into the water and sank as the coathanger followed.

—Like now he just drops them on it like it's this big coathook and, wow . . .

—But . . . lampshades went down in a heap as he cleared the Morning Telegraphs. —But what . . . he reached Vol III GRIN-LOC beside her, —who . . . staring into the dark maw yawned at them across the airshaft, —who . . .

—Like man I thought by now these chicks that go down were all in the movies you know?

—I, I no I . . .

—But like I mean what beautiful ass.

—Yes I . . . he cleared his throat, —it . . .

—Like how her cheeks hang where they part how high and round, you know? I mean like I have these bulges in here . . . she brought up a knee to squeeze a full roll of denim —you know? Like I'd give anything for her ass, you know?

—Yes well no I . . . his hand brushed a closing knee and he cleared his throat, —but I'm sure your . . .

—I mean like with that ass she could really model you know? Like I was trying this modeling a while when I thought if I could get like on the cover of like Vogue I'd really have it made, I mean like before I got my nose done they always had to shade it in here see? See? Along here?

—Oh, oh yes, yes . . .

—And photograph me from just this certain angle on account of like shadow, you know?

—I see yes, yes your, but your nose is certainly . . .

—And then like they're always telling me my tits were too big for how tall I am, you know?

—Yes but I'm sure they didn't mean to be uncompli, that just because skinny fashion models were, were in fashion . . . he was half over on Vol II CRA-GRIM looking abruptly down from the window to the denim gaps straining her white buttons, —because your, you're certainly well proportioned for . . .

—I mean like did you just see hers? they're like just little and round?

—No I, I saw she had long black hair but . . .

—Like I mean they don't hang like mine, and these very pointy like clear nipples but mine spread all out like, you know?

—No but, but I'm sure your . . .

—What are you doing.

—Oh, oh nothing I . . .

—So like I thought I had this big chance when I got hit in this revolving door of this big office building and I told them I'm this model, okay? So I get enough out of them to like settle so I can go get my nose fixed by, come on what do you think you . . .

—No no I just, I was just going to say I think you're . . . he straightened up, —I think your, your breast . . .

—Like I mean just don't fuck around, okay?

—Yes I, I'm sorry, I . . .

—No come off it, I mean like don't be sorry man just don't fuck
around.

—Yes well I, I . . .

—Like I mean I just don't feel like screwing, okay?

—Well, well yes okay . . .

—And like you better go back and look at your sink, I mean it's
coming over the side again . . .

—Oh, yes okay . . . he slid off the volumes, over the bank of papers
to push past lampshades and pull back a sleeve.

—Wow like too much, he just put her . . . wait man you know who
that is over there?

—No I, I didn't see her face and . . .

—No come on not the chick man him, he's the one that night the
cops were here he was running around stoned with one shoe on giving
them a hard time . . . She crossed Vol III GRIN-LOC descending, —like
he just sat up and put her panties on his head rocking around like he's
pretending he's some aviator and down he goes in a nosedive, man is this
place really dirty . . . she came on over the Morning Telegraphs to pause
behind 36 Boxes 200 2-Ply and flap a hand against her front before she
came in to pick up her raincoat and shake it, —like I mean really dirty
. . . she threw it in to the armless sofa, pushing past film cans for the box
she'd brought in. —Where . . . she looked up, ripping it open, —are you
back there again?

—Yes I, I forgot to get the mop . . .

—Well like don't you want to eat? I mean I got this pizza.

—Yes I, I just wanted to see if she was somebody I . . .

—Man you must be kidding, I mean look at this.

—What . . . he plied through lampshades with the mop.

—I mean like what's all this in the oven.

—Oh that's mail yes, I put Mister . . .

—Well like take it out so we can make this pizza okay?

—Yes but, no but the oven doesn't work, they turned off the . . .

—Like what do you mean it doesn't work, I mean when I went out
you said you use the oven to . . .

—No I was going to say the gas is turned off so I just use it to keep
Mister Grynszpan's mail separate I, I didn't know you meant a frozen
pizza why did you . . .

—Look man I get a frozen pizza so I can slip a couple of records in,
okay? So like now what are we going to . . .

—I don't know I, I mean there's no place here to play them but if
you . . .

—Like I just mean eating okay? She was squeezing past cartons along a chipped porcelained edge toward a handle once chromed, —like I'll put this in the refrigerator till you get your . . . the door came open to her tug. —Man I don't believe it. I mean I don't believe it man.

—Yes well, well that's where I keep some scores and, and business mail to keep it clean, he said looking up from mopping, —because there's no other . . .

—Like it doesn't work too?

—Yes well, I don't know but I haven't had anything else to put in it, he said wringing out the mop as she reached high to shelve the pizza on FLAKES 24–8 Oz Pkgs and squeezed her way back, —but these other things you got . . .

—Well like turn on the light so we can see them.

—No this bulb burned out but . . .

—So like bring them in there, and that bag on the floor, it's got grape drink. Like now where can we put it.

—Yes well just a . . . he let the things go on the sofa beside her —here's an opener and, wait . . . he pulled Moody's Industrials over between them and sat down on Hoppin' With Flavor! —there . . . he reached.

—Like this is mushrooms in oil, what's that one.

—Well it, it says yeast extract but . . .

—Wait this is pate of anchovies . . .

—Don't cut yourself, I . . .

—I mean I didn't see a can opener like this since my grandmother.

—Wait let me . . .

—What's that one.

—It says smoked frog legs in cottonseed oil, I don't think I've ever taste . . .

—Like what's marinade, lemon pepper marinade.

—I don't know, I think it's something you . . .

—And like napkins, I mean you don't have any?

—Well no I, there's an old shirt I use . . .

—Like these frogs' legs are weird man.

—Yes I, I wondered why you chose them and these cocktail onions and, and capers . . .

—Are you kidding? I mean you think I'm going to drop a roast beef in my pocket?

—Oh . . . he handed over the shirt, reached for a frog leg from the tin she'd placed on Moody's in a pool of cottonseed oil.

—Like you've got these dumb clerks wandering around all over the place you think I'm going to stop and read every fucking label? She caught up the sleeve of the shirt for her lips and the mail slid toward her weight on the sofa. —I mean like you really read these magazines? Textile World, Forest Industries, I mean Supervisory Management like does somebody really read that?

—Yes well those are just, they're in connection with some business I've been, I mean I think they just entered these subscriptions so I could, read up . . .

—And like this . . . cottonseed oil ran down the diploma from her thumb —I mean like it says you graduated from the Alabama College of Business?

—Well I, no not exactly, I mean that came in the mail too and I haven't found out what . . .

—Man like you keep saying you write this music but like everything I see you say it's some business you're in.

—No I do, all that over there is, wait don't touch it . . . ! she dropped a cherry wood smoked oyster. —No I'm sorry it's just, those are scores I've copied over and if spots get on them these musicians can be so temperamental that . . .

—Look man like don't keep being sorry you know? She poured grape drink. —And like then who's this Hyman Grynszpan? She tore open the top one, —Dear WHO'S WHO IN AMERICA Biographee your generous cooperation, I mean like he's in Who's Who?

—I don't know but he . . .

—I mean like he's just going to walk in here?

—Oh no, no I don't think so no in fact I've never . . .

—Man look at that, like he owes Consolidated Edison twelve hundred sixty-seven dollars and nine cents, like no wonder he split . . . she took the last frog's leg, put the tin back in its puddle on Moody's. —And like what are these?

—Oh those are just, just slides, pictures of . . .

—I mean like what's this supposed to be?

He held it to the light looking through her cottonseed oil thumbprint. —Yes that's, a dik-dik I think, a little . . .

—Like a what?

—It's a small breed of antelope someone I, I'm writing some music for a film and those slides are just . . .

—Man you must write some music . . . she came down to one elbow as he took the last smoked oyster.

—Oh I'm sorry did you, I mean did you want that? or, or anything else?

—Like if you have something to smoke man.

—No, no I'm afraid I, wait right under you . . . he came forward over Moody's —no I meant under the sofa, there's an old package of Chesterfields that . . .

—Of what? Like I mean are you kidding?

—No I, I don't . . . he sank back on Hoppin' With Flavor!

—Like to turn on man. I mean I have this stash right over there he didn't even know about if I could get in there and get it.

—Oh in the, over in the other apartment? maybe you could . . .

—What like just walk in while they're balling and ask the chick move your ass please while I reach under you? Like they'd think I came in for a double bill, I mean like if I knew them that's something else.

—No I just meant . . .

—But like man you must be kidding, I mean I never knew a musician that doesn't turn on. Like you must write some music.

—Yes well recently I haven't had much chance to do what I . . .

—I mean some music. I mean like that's what everybody I know is in, music. Like I mean you ought to talk to Al.

—Oh, oh yes well, well who's Al.

—Like he's just Al, okay? Like some time he could bring up his guitar.

—Oh, yes well that might be . . .

—Because like I mean he really can talk about it, you know?

—Yes well I'd . . .

—I mean he can really talk about it.

—Yes well I've missed talking to, having Mister Schramm to talk to, he had insights in music that I've never . . .

—Look like will you just do me this favor and . . .

—No I'm, I was just going to say when I was working on an opera . . . he turned to get a knee on H-O, reach up to 12–38 Oz Btls Won't Burn, Smoke or Smell, —the problem was I didn't have a very clear picture of the libretto I didn't really have a libretto . . . he opened the manila folder, —and so when I . . .

She stared at it. —Like that's an opera?

—No well this is, I'm working on this cantata now and, do you read music?

—Like read that?

—Yes it's still very rough but . . .

—Man like nobody could read that, I mean like that's supposed to mean something right there?

—Yes well this is, you see these are the strings that come in behind the soprano and . . . pages turned —here, the woodwinds come in here behind the tenor and then when the brass . . .

—Like you said a what?

—The brass, it comes in behind the . . .

—No like what did you call it?

—Oh a cantata yes that's, it's a choral work voices and a large chorus with an orchestra, it's a sort of dramatic arrangement of a musical idea that . . .

—I mean it's all this messy?

—Yes well this is just the, it's like a sketch a painter does before he starts painting, to work out the form and structure so every note and measure will . . .

—So like you never heard this, right? I mean how do you know what it even sounds like.

—You don't yes that's one of the, you don't really know till you hear it performed that's one of the . . .

—Man like you really better talk to Al some time he can really, what was that . . . ! she was over Moody's past him, parting the blind —oh wow, I mean like three, five of them, like these five Porto Ricans down there pushing this car across the street this bus almost wiped them out.

—I've seen them before yes I don't think the car runs at all, they have to push it back and forth for the alternate side of the street parking it's kind of their clubhouse, they sit in it with a portable radio and . . .

—Man like I don't care if it's their fucking clubhouse I mean who wants to walk past it down there in the dark, man.

—Well you, you can stay here if you . . .

—Like where, in the sink?

—No I meant right, right there you can sleep right there . . .

—Here? So where are you supposed to be on the bottom or on top I mean look man, I didn't sleep any last night I'm really beat I mean if you think you're going to grab a handful of . . .

—No no I just meant, I mean you can sleep there I won't even, I have to stay up and work anyhow if the light won't bother you . . .

—What, on your cantata?

—Well not, no not yet I'm working on a long piece of music some-body wants for a film, the one those slides are for, you see once I get paid for that finished music up there I can get this done and have enough money to . . .

—Man like I just don't want to walk past that clubhouse down there that's all, like I mean I even hate to go down to this cold can in the hall here . . .

—I know yes it's, be careful of the door . . .

When she came back the blanket was clear, mail stacked on H-O and the diploma protruding from the volume of the Musical Courier for 1903, Moody's wiped in a stack with Thomas Register of American Manufactur-ers under the front blind and Hoppin' With Flavor! drawn up to it.
—Like you're going to work right there?

—Well yes if the light won't bother you, I have to have it right over me because . . .

—I mean this place is really dirty you know? she brought one foot up, the other, pulling off the moccasins. —Like I don't want to get my feet black . . . and she stood on the blanket to zip down the denims, a shoulder against the wall as she bent to pull them off leaving nothing behind, pausing up there opposite 2-Ply Facial Tissue Yellow —like wasn't that picture over in the other place?

—Yes it . . . he coughed staring up, —I, I think Mister . . .

—Like see those are these kind of little bubs they want you for modeling you know? And like where you can see her ass in the mirror with those like dimples like that chick in the back but like look at her belly, I mean it's this real pot, like I mean mine's real flat compared to that . . . she drew breath parting the shirt —but like see . . . ? she flexed closer reaching below for —this like bulge here? how it . . . listen!

The knock sounded again harder, the voice fainter behind it, —Hello Mister . . . ?

—But like who . . .

—No it's just, it's just an old man who . . .

—What like Grynszpan? I mean how do you . . .

—No no it's just, wait he'll go away . . .

—Hello Mister?

—Beat it, she called out.

—Hello Missus . . . ?

—I mean . . . she was down at a bound toward the door, —I said beat it, screw . . .

—My vife Missus, could I . . .

—Just fuck off okay? she pushed the door hard and came back, paused against 24-One Pint Mazola New Improved to raise a foot behind and look back down at it —I mean now look at my feet, she came on to the sofa to cross ankle on knee, looking.

—Yes I . . . he cleared his throat, looking.

—Like man this isn't dirt it's like just black . . . and her knees came up and met with a pull at the blanket, Forest Industries to the floor and her face to the crevice where back joined seat, silent until —listen . . . ! Her head came up without turning, —like I hear somebody talking, listen . . .

—————information on adopting a foster child, call the special dial a child number at Plaza five . . .

—No that's just, there's a radio somewhere over under all those books, I can't find it to turn it off and . . .

She came up sharp on an elbow. —Like you're staying up?

—Well yes I, as long as I can work on . . .

—Because like watch that sink in there man . . . her head went back down, —I mean if that happens again we might both wake up drownded and nobody would ever know it okay?

—Yes o, okay . . . and he drew a hand over his face and went back to the page, another, cleared his throat muffled.

—Bast?

He started. —Yes I, I . . .

—I mean like can you move that light? she said into the crevice —so it's not like shining right on me?

Once, twice nearing the bottom of a page he looked back to see a whole bar missing, stopped a hand raised to crumple it and stared at the slow rise and fall on the sofa, standing to slide a foot silently toward the kitchen and past the rush of water over the bank of paper to Appletons' to stare under the shade into darkness and as silently back, standing over the sofa licking his own lip against a mucous whisper in the crevice bending, once as though to loosen his belt and then as abruptly standing away to blow off a clean scored sheet back under the punctured shade of the lamp, pausing as though to listen, shreds of sound escaping sporadic partings of his lips and he was up, mounting the Musical Couriers, pulling their gap wider with his ear to it.

———just heard the first movement of Anton Dvořák's sev . . .

He tried to jam the volumes spine to fore edge back together and half lay up there for a moment, to come down blowing at the front of his shirt, looking up abruptly as though fearful to find that sofa empty of its sullen heave as he blew off a fresh sheet under the punctured shade, itself chilled and finally cast into shadow by light separating the slats of the blind that caught him head rested motionless against 24–7 Oz Pkgs Flavored Loops where abruptly he coughed, started, came slowly to his feet to where, now, elbow thrust against the confines of the blanket, a white button had given way.

—Oh wow . . .

—Oh good, good morning, he caught breath from it, standing.

—I mean it's like camping out at Niagara Falls . . . no effort but in turning on her back to draw the shirt over that red brown diffusion all spread out like on the white mound that quickly gone from sight, —I mean listen . . .

—Did, did you sleep well, enough?

—Are you kidding? I mean . . . knees fallen wide under the blanket a hand plunged down there, —something's been sticking me like, I mean like one of your fucking pencils . . . she came up with a square of glass, —like wow . . .

—Oh I'm sorry it's just, it's just my . . .

—Like man quit being sorry, it's your picture of your dick dick . . . and her knees came down in a bounce. It was the first time she'd laughed. —Like is there more grape drink?

—Oh, oh yes wait . . .

—I mean look at my feet . . . she reached up for the cup, —like I mean that's a bathtub in there under all that stuff isn't it?

—Yes I think so but, we'd have to move all the . . .

—So like move it . . . Knee followed knee from a fling of the blanket, —like let me get . . . she had a foot up to the porcelained edge, —get up here and, wait give me your shoulder . . .

—I don't know where we . . . her weight came on him, —where we can put it . . . a shirttail brushed his face, hung there, he caught breath and blew gently.

—No come on, like over in that corner there's still room up to the ceiling, she turned abruptly, shirt drawn up in her reach for 12–2 lb 10 oz Round Pkgs QUICK QUAKER —like I mean what's in all these, books?

—I . . . I don't know, he reached up for it.

—Like I mean . . . down came 24–12 Oz Btls Fragile! —like I never saw anything so heavy . . .

—Yes they . . . he said getting breath between trips, —they . . . they are . . . finally, —is that the last one . . . ?

—Yes but . . . I mean like I never . . . it came down with a crash. —Like what's in them!

—Oh these are, these are film cans cans of film, he pursued one rolled toward the sink —I'll, I'll just stack them here . . .

—Man I, I don't believe it . . . she was down knees and one elbow on half the tub's porcelained cover lifting the other half. —I mean I don't believe it man.

—But what, what's . . .

—Like paper bags. Like I mean the whole fucking bathtub is full of these paper grocery bags.

—Well I, I guess they can go over there with the . . .

—I mean are you kidding? she came up glistening, rivulets coursing toward the undone button —like I mean you're really going to save them?

—Yes well I, I mean none of this is really mine to throw away and someone might, Mister Grynszpan might want . . .

—Okay but like just don't explain it okay? I mean here, she came up with an armload and then off to the floor —and here . . . feet planted apart bent over the side of the tub, —here . . .

—I'll just, just squeeze them over by . . . he cleared his throat stooping close to pick them up two, three at a time, eyes on a trickle gaining momentum, —over there . . .

—There, she stood, —like I mean now I can't turn the . . .

—Oh here wait . . . the five or six bags dropped, —it's, it's probably just, there.

—Like you think I'm getting in that? Man I'd come out looking like some rusty nail I mean . . .

—No, no if you let it run, he was down embracing an armload of paper bags.

—Till like when, I mean I'm supposed to stand here cooling my ass like till Christmas?

—No it shouldn't take . . . he was forcing bags behind the Morning Telegraphs, back for the last of them —it shouldn't take that long no, he said jamming them down with his foot, getting his shirt off coming back to the sink where he tilted the cookie tin top, reached down the razor and held the cracked yellow soap bar in the dwindled torrent.

—Like you're going someplace? she said from the edge of the tub, looked in it and leaned in to press down the plug, —finally . . .

—Yes I, I have a business appointment with a Mister, Mister something, he drew blood —is that towel any, that old shirt I mean, he came after it past her, back blotting red.

—But like when's your appointment, I mean like how can you have appointments when you don't even know like what time it is here.

—No there's . . . the razor raked down, —there's a clock on the floor right there under the . . .

—Are you kidding? I mean I just saw it it says like one o'clock.

—Yes it's . . . electric and it runs backwards, someone . . .

—Man like don't try to explain it to me okay?

—No it's very simple it . . . there's a little conversion chart I made beside it you add whatever number to what it says to get ten except when it says . . .

—Man like I just don't want to know! I mean are you done with the soap?

—Oh I'm, yes, yes . . . he turned to her shirt suddenly empty dangling from the dishcloth rack and she reached from the short tub knees drawn up failing to cover the circles gone pink from the edges somewhere the wrong way down the spectrum toward hollyhock.

—Like, man like this is laundry soap.

—I know but it's the only . . .

—I mean like this will take the skin right off my, like I didn't see this since my grandmother.

—Yes I've been meaning to get some but . . .

—I mean you're not wearing that shirt are you?

—Yes well I, it's the only clean . . .

—Clean? Like man look at the front of it where you were climbing around back there, like that should be some business appointment.

—Yes well, but there's nothing I . . .

—Like just turn it inside out, I mean like then where the collar's dirty it's inside the collar you know?

—Oh, oh I never thought of that, he came out of it pulling its sleeves through.

—And like where's there a mirror here.

—Well I, there isn't really one but I've been using this . . .

—Man . . . she dropped a knee to reach for the cookie tin top, —like it looks it. I mean you're leaving right now?

He paused there swallowing —I, I have to yes, yes I'd hoped I could wait for the mail but . . .

—Oh wow.

—No there's something I'm waiting for . . .

—Like what, she had an arm up soaping under it, —the new issue of Forest Industries? I mean it already came didn't you hear it? she called over the water tumbling at her feet, —like there was this tremendous thud out in the hall like it's the next fifty volumes of . . . he came past her without even looking up, got the door open and balanced with a heel against it dragging a box over the sill and then envelopes, envelopes, grabbing one up addressed Edwerd B ast and tearing it open to pocket the crumpled bills inside before he stood. —Like you're not opening your present?

—Oh, oh no I'll look at it later, he dragged it under the sink, picked up his case and a soiled manila envelope.

—Wait like before you go, like right over the sink there's some pins there, like I saw these rusty pins in a crack there.

—You, want one? he dug one out with a thumbnail.

—Just one like and I mean like turn around . . . she reached up for the hem of his jacket, folding it in working the pin —and then like where's a towel when I'm done.

—I thought you, I mean all there is is this shirt, I . . .

—Like man if I use that I'll be worse than when I got in here.

—I'm sorry I thought you, I didn't think of it . . . he stood over her knees drawn up again there, looking slightly off balance. —When you, if you leave I don't know how you'll lock up, I only have this one key and if I lock the door now you . . .

—Are you kidding man? I mean like you think I'm going to get locked in this place? Like I mean I could drownd and nobody would know it, she said, the tumbling water still rising around her.

—Yes well, but if you leave can you fix the door so it . . .

—Look man like don't worry, okay?

—Yes well, yes well, well it was nice to meet you maybe I'll get back before you go if you, I mean, I mean you're welcome to stay if you . . . he cleared his throat as her head went down, knees went down, hand seeking deep for the soap.

—Man like all I want is to get in over there and get my stuff okay?

—Well, well yes okay and, goodbye then . . . he hesitated, and then the door came into place behind him, shuddered once or twice and was still, leaving only the rush of water at her feet. She spread her elbows up to the tub's sides and came back slowly to rest against its slope, one foot then the other rising prehensile at the opposite end as the water slowly climbed pink to hollyhock, closed over deep magenta at the tips and mounted to her armpits before her feet came down and she forward to reach the tap. Her knuckles went white. Her other hand came up, did the same, and she held there long enough to whisper —oh wow . . . before she grabbed the sides and stood over the rush of water at her knees in a pose broken only by a sharp knock on the door.

—Come in, is that you? Like quick . . . !

—Telephone company . . .

—I said come in will you!

—Telepho . . .

—And like watch the door but quick . . . ! The door shuddered open, came to abrupt rest at an angle —man like quick, turn this thing off or we'll drownd . . . He was there in the step it took, no strain discoloring the rich dark of his hand as he reached the tap and broke it off. —Oh wow . . .

—Wow.

—Well like do something quick man or we'll . . .

—Maybe first just pull out the plug . . . his arm plunged past her knees, she reached the shirt and stood there holding it pendant, watching the water slowly reveal her calves. —Going out faster than it's coming in, no problem just leave it run.

—I mean that was close man, like where'd you come from.

—Telephone company, I . . .

—Are you kidding? Like I mean there's no telephone here so don't give me . . .

—No I came to install one if, this is, Bast? I mean are, you're the lady of the house?

—Like what do I look like the fucking butler? She started to dry a shoulder with the shirt, and stopped. —Look man if you came to install a telephone install a telephone.

—If you just ah, he looked around, —just tell me where you'd . . .

—Come off it man, I mean like you're this telephone man okay? Like how am I supposed to know where you install a telephone, I mean just install it like they taught you how to install a telephone in telephone man school okay? And she got a foot up on the side of the tub to dry a knee as he turned to hurry a box through the door and knelt beside the film cans opposite her to tear it open. —Man like wait a minute, she paused on a dry knee, —I mean like that's supposed to be a telephone?

—Call that a picturephone . . . he raised his eyes slightly to her face.

—Are you kidding? She got the other knee up.

—Talk to somebody you see their face right there . . . and he stood as though seeking a vantage point. —Somebody walking the walls here, must have been some great grass.

—Like man there's nothing here but like Chesterfields, I mean like I have this stash next door but I can't get in there.

—Why not.

—Like I don't have the key man.

—Old place like this what do you need a key? He picked up a coathanger.

—Oh wow . . . she stood, reached down her shirt from the dishcloth rack —like I mean could you get in there and get it for me? Wait, like right in past those boxes throw me these shoes, they're these moccasins like, she said getting into the shirt, buttoning it —I mean like I don't want to get my feet black again you know? And she stood away from the tumbling water to put them on, stepped out and closed the tops of the tub. —Like go get it man, I mean I don't want to go in there.

—But you have to show me where . . .

—Man like I just said I don't want to go in there okay? I mean there's like this big bed you just reach way in under the mattress and I'm not going in there okay? And like knock, I mean there was this chick in there last night balling somebody you know . . . ? And she turned back past the sink to step carefully up the Morning Telegraphs to Appletons' and blow off Vol III GRIN-LOC before getting to her knees on it motionless there peering under the shade till where she looked nothing moved, and she came down to fit the door closed behind him with —I mean like now I don't have any papers man.

He followed her through opening a shirt pocket, settled high on Moody's Industrials tapping the envelope over a paper. —Looks real good.

—Man I mean like the best, like I mean from Guatemala man I got it from . . . listen! She stood, grabbed up her raincoat —I mean no way, she said getting to the door. —What do you want?

—Is, is Mister . . . Mister Bast in? The door came open no wider than the dim hall showed of the gap in her raincoat. —I just stopped to see if he'd like to go to a Bible breakfast but . . .

—Oh wow.

—No no I have a business lunch appointment with him but I, I thought I'd stop by early to see if he wanted . . .

—Like go to a what, man?

—It's a, a businessmen's Bible breakfast but . . .

—Oh wow.

—Yes but I must have the, have the wrong . . . he took a step back from the smile suddenly looming behind her —wrong Mister Bast yes I, I must have the wrong address yes . . .

—I mean like you must man.

—Sorry to, to disturb you . . . he backed into the rail in the hall gone abruptly dark with the door closed in his face, trampling the latest issue of Industrial Marketing overlooked in the morning's haul and still there when Bast, climbing from dark to dark, trampled and picked it up before groping for the knob and lifting the door on its hinge.

—Hello? Rhoda? are you . . . he stood there and sniffed, listened, felt his way past film cans, Mazola New Improved, 36 Boxes 200 2-Ply to the punctured shade to turn on the light, stood there and sniffed again before he put down his case and Industrial Marketing on Hoppin' With Flavor! and returned carrying a paper sack, listening, turning abruptly to lift a cover on the tub and look in, reach in, and then stand more slowly letting it close. He had dropped a bouillon cube in the cup and held that under the dwindled torrent at the sink, carried it in with pâté of anchovies, cocktail onions and Hostess Twinkies from the paper sack and arranged them on Moody's Industrials, and was bent recovering the blanket gone in a tempestuous heap to the floor when the sound of a bell brought him upright like a spring. By the third ring he crested 12 2 lb 10 oz Round Pkgs QUICK QUAKER, by the fourth found the receiver and lifted it. —Hel, hello . . . ? What in the . . . Yes but what in, what do you mean you had it installed here, what . . . What do you mean can I see you . . . yes there's

a little screen on it but . . . no listen if you're calling from a candy store how would you expect it to . . . No wait a minute, just wait a minute I . . . no I said wait a minute! now there's somebody at the door . . . and he tipped in that direction, a foot braced against 24–12 Oz Btls Fragile!
—Rhoda . . . ?
  —Hello Mister?
  —No, no go away . . .
  —Hello Mister could I . . .
  —Go away! Will you just, go away . . . ! Now hello? No I don't know, it's just some old . . . No but listen how could you just have this thing put in here without even letting me . . . Yes I know I said I couldn't go down to that cafeteria twice a day for messages but this . . . what? What noise . . . oh that's, that's just a hydrant they opened down in the street it's . . . did what come . . . ? Yes and so did somebody's register of American manufacturers look even with a rapid reading course what do you . . . Yes that came too but . . . because I didn't go to the free sample session, now . . . because I don't want to learn how to sell myself and develop into a more poised confident forceful person that's why! Look if you want to take a Dale Carnegie course go take it, I'm . . . Well that's not the way I want to be helped out! and listen, what makes you think I'd want anybody to think I graduated from the Alabama College of Business what kind of a . . . why should it sound better than a conservationist school that's not what I told you anyhow, I said I'd gone to a conservatory, a place where . . . what? I haven't been through all the mail yet I don't know how many stock certificates have come no but why you send away for Forest Industries and Supervisory Management if you think . . . all to impress who . . . ? Yes yes all right but why a picturephone look, I'm glad you think the office must look pretty neat by now but that's not . . . Because I don't want a lot of visitors! there's too much . . . Well why did you give Mooneyham the address in the first place, you knew I was meeting him for lunch and . . . naked? What did he say she . . . No he told me that too look he's, he's from out of town he must have got lost and gone to the wrong . . . Well if you've just called him at his hotel what do you want me to . . . All right look you didn't tell me you were taking his company away from him! what would . . . All right but he doesn't think you're doing him this big favor, he's been . . . I told him that and look, it's subsidiary with an i, I said we wanted him to stay on and manage it as . . . Listen you can sit there in that candy store and say you're bailing him out and the whole deal's just something these here lawyers fixed up for taxes and all what do you think it's like sitting across from Mooneyham in that awful cafeteria with tears running off his cheeks into his Spanish omelet, telling me how he went to a Bible breakfast seeking guidance and . . . Yes I told him that, I said we couldn't just carry that loan of the brewery stock to X-L on our books with stockholders like Mrs Begg starting to . . . what? Yes well he, he said he'd had a drink after the

Bible breakfast but . . . a drink or two yes but he . . . one on the way to the Bible breakfast too yes but when you'd said a thing to him like . . . all right wait a minute I've got what you wrote down right here, wait a minute . . . he braced an elbow on QUICK QUAKER to raise himself and probe a pocket —here, two hundred thousand cash from that loan to Eagle management, and then to pay him the rest in promissory notes over the next five years so it will be the same thing as coming from future earnings but . . . No but listen did you have to tell him we had him by the short hair on that stock loan and that big debt X-L is being pressed for by some paper company? What do you . . . that I told you lithography was this greasy what . . . ? No but . . . listen I didn't know all X-L did was print matchbook covers so how would . . . No but wait a minute, what's exploring for virgin minerals got to do with it? Look I've told you this whole thing is . . . All right, for X-L to make the matchbook covers too but what's exploring for . . . what trees . . . Yes you make paper from wood pulp but look, you can't just go in and strip off all this lumber to make matchbook covers and say you're really exploring for virgin minerals just because you got stuck with some old mining claims on those penny stock . . . and get tax write-offs for it too? Listen J R listen don't try to explain it to me just . . . no but listen just talk to your friend Piscator with ideas like this because I don't even . . . Oh he did, yes well I might have known he'd . . . No when I returned his call they said he'd gone to Jamaica but . . . I don't know, something you told him to do about getting incorporated but . . . yes that's what I told you yes and if you can't just stop all this you and Piscator can go out there and play to win and just let me . . . No because wait a minute just listen, when I got down to that cafeteria today to meet Mooneyham Virginia had telephone messages for me from all kinds of . . . wait, just wait a minute there's somebody at the door, just . . . look can you just wait a minute? He slid for the floor. —Yes is . . . Rhoda?

—Delivery for Grynszpan.

—Oh, oh just a, just a minute . . . the door shuddered.

—Where do you want them.

—But, but what are they, it just looks like . . .

—Look I don't ask questions buddy, to me they look like bundles of old newspapers but I don't ask questions, where do you want them.

—Well, well I, but where did they come from.

—Here, you want to sign here? Party named Eigen downtown.

—Oh, yes well, yes and you can put them, put them right up there on the tub.

—You got your water running in there.

—Yes I know it's, it's all right just, here let me help you . . . With the last of them he stood and brushed his shirt front.

—Got your water running in the sink there too.

—Yes I, I know . . . He fitted the door closed and turned, a foot up on 24–12 Oz Btls Fragile! and paused to draw a hand over his face before he reached up for the receiver. —Now hel, what . . . ? No it was just, just a delivery, it . . . No it's not, it's . . . No a heavy box came this morning and I haven't opened it yet but . . . you had a what sent here . . . ? No but look what do we need an electric letter opener for? You keep talking about running a low-cost operation what . . . No but if you send away for every . . . No I know you want it to look like an up-to-date operation but I keep telling you I . . . No all right, all right! But listen this list of telephone messages Virginia had waiting for me about all kinds of . . . no that broker Crawley about some drug company with an Italian name and something called Endo whatever it is, somebody named Wiles had been trying to reach me about a string of nursing homes and a lawyer named wait a minute, here it is Beaton who wants to discuss drilling rights on those Alberta and Western right of . . . what? No but listen he's a lawyer and Piscator's a lawyer, let him discuss it with . . . well when he gets back then and you and Piscator can get out there and play to . . . to see who . . . ? No, no I haven't been up to the hospital today and I . . . look I don't know if he's still whispering his trade secret to the nurse and I can't sit beside his bed day and night to . . . no I don't have a map right here! and I . . . Well of course the brewery is on a river but I don't know where it is in relation to these Ace mining claims or the Alberta and . . . what? You meant to tell me about what Indian reservation right in between what . . . No listen I don't . . . I said no! And now listen, four calls from Pomerance Associates who the, who the hell are Pomerance Associates and Hopper, she said old man Hopper up at Eagle kept calling very upset about some big plans you have for a cemetery and salary cuts at Eagle I didn't know anything ab . . . what? No now wait a minute what do you mean take a salary cut, I don't even have a salary in the first place you . . . No what do you mean set this here example by not taking one yourself, I . . . No look, look don't try to tell me you're just doing this so we can tell them the truth up at Eagle that we're not taking salaries until we get everything on its feet, you don't even . . . Listen I don't want to hear about stock options and tax benefits! I just want to get . . . get what? Yes I did, I got it this morning but it wasn't twenty dollars it was eighteen and I had to give Virginia . . . Yes I am sure, two fives and . . . yes all right go ahead and look at your accounts but I'm telling you it . . . Well of course I need it! why do you think I'm . . . No, no I know I told you that but I can't settle everything up with you right now I, when I took the music down to their rehearsal today they said come back Friday when everybody else gets paid so I . . . Yes I paid Virginia four thirty-five out of it and bought her the ninety cent blueplate, and then . . . because you have to do things like that sometimes they're just forty-eight cent dollars aren't they! Of course we paid for Mooneyham's too, his and mine came to three twenty and ninety cents carfare for . . . yes I did go to the nightclub on the same trip so . . . Yes all right then! All right! Forty-five

cents! so it all comes to . . . to make three copies of all this? Look of course
Virginia doesn't itemize everything, what do you . . . what rent, this rent?
I don't know, I . . . as a business expense? Well fine yes if you . . . Yes I
know you think you're trying to help me out but . . . No it's a cantata,
I've just . . . Well maybe I did say it was an opera but now it's a cantata
and I've . . . to look up what . . . ? Well I've already told you yes I did
get the eighteen dollars not twenty and I . . . Yes of course I appreciated
it but after all what do you think I'm . . . look up what mortality figures,
the whole United States . . . ? Yes all right! all . . . Statistical not statistican,
the Statistical Abstract of . . . No I can't do it right now no, no and look
there's somebody at the door, I have to hang up . . . No, and I . . . Me?
No I don't know how to play golf and . . . No and I don't . . . No I said
no! Look goodbye, I have to get to the . . . Mister who . . . ? Look I
don't know who's at the door no and listen you don't have to give this
address out to everybody you . . . Printed on what letterhead . . . What
telephone number, this one? with this telephone number? what . . .
No I can't no, goodbye . . . no, goodbye yes, goodbye . . . ! and he sat
up there and drew a hand down his face watching the door shudder
in.

—Bast . . . ?

—Mister Gibbs? Is, that you Mister Gibbs?

—Bast . . . ? A bottle appeared thrust through the opening, and then
—where is everybody?

—No there's no one here but me, I . . .

—Thought I heard you in animated discussion Bast, he said briefly
forming the side of an isosceles triangle there with the door —didn't
want to intrude . . .

—No that was, just talking to myself I, let me get the door . . .

—Don't want to intrude Bast thought you might like some company,
meeting a man named Beamish here we thought you might like some
. . . he stopped abruptly. —Listen . . . !

—What the, the water? Yes well . . .

—Through caverns measureless to, where the hell . . .

—Yes well the, I had the tub running and the handle broke off
the . . .

—Bosom where the bright waters meet, like living in Pittsburgh Bast
. . . he was under way again, —confluence of the Mongahela and the vale
in whose bosom the bright waters meet to form the mighty Ohio . . . and
he stopped short of Moody's Industrials. —Bast never seen anybody with
quite such fastidious tastes . . .

—Yes well that's just . . . Bast got by him for the cup, —just eating
what was here . . . he went on, back to the sink to rinse out the discolored
water, wipe away bouillon clots with the shirt sleeve —I've been trying
to . . .

—Don't want to intrude Bast looks God damned epicurean, sorry
wait . . . he brought the bottle up to the cup wavering before him,

—there, meat in the hall, a bin of wine, a living river by the door what the hell more would you . . .

—No no I, I brought the cup for you Mister Gibbs, I don't . . .

—Problem Bast you're too God damned considerate, God damned people take advantage . . . he got the cup in both hands, —have to meet Mister Eigen here Bast, don't want to disturb you . . . he drank, put the cup down on —Thomas Register of American Manufacturers, haven't read that in a long time if then, mind if I try one?

—Oh yes please . . .

—Have to meet Eigen . . . he speared at the cocktail onions with a pencil point, —said he'd meet me here what the hell time is it . . .

—Yes the clock's right under you there but . . .

—Clock . . . ? and two, three cocktail onions rolled merrily down Forest Industries —fine only three o'clock, got all afternoon Bast have to do some research, came up here to check out Raindance and Mister Fred . . .

—No but the clock is, it isn't really quarter of three it's, wait, the clock runs backwards but I made a little table there beside it to figure out the right time and it's, it's about seven fifteen, you subtract what the clock says from ten unless it says ten eleven or twelve and then you have to . . .

—This . . . ? Onions danced down Forest Industries, —Pom, pom pom pom, sounds like an elephant running between the raindrops Bast . . .

—Oh not that, no . . . he came forward on Hoppin' With Flavor! to reach under the sofa —that's just something I've been working on for, for something, here's the table I . . .

—Opera, must be your opera, sure as hell not Bizet only not Bizet problem Bast you don't finish things, jump from one thing to the other don't finish anything.

—No I did finish that, in fact I just came from that nightclub rehearsal where they, after all that copying I did that accordionist didn't even look at his part, he just said he always played off the first violin's and then all he played was oompah oompah writhing around and grinning at the empty tables and they still haven't paid me, they . . .

—Bast that reminds me, family matter . . . the cup came up, emptied, the bottle followed, —company Stella's father had . . .

—Stella?

—Stella, Bast. Stella Bast, what is she's your cousin? Your father James was her father's brother so . . .

—But how would . . . how would you know Stella?

—Worked for her father once, little company he had Bast what the hell is happening to that little company he had.

—Oh that I, I don't know. He just died and we were never, he and my father were never on good terms so I . . . I don't know but, but did you know Stella very well?

—Knew Stella very well Bast . . . and the cup came up and went down half emptied as he got to his feet again waving a paper, —problem here you're working with a base of ten instead twelve, got twelve hours in the day problem is the God damned clock never is right.

—Yes I, what happened was I plugged it in and set it at six o'clock and then the electricity went off for four hours but, but I mean have you seen her? Stella I mean?

—Bast got to be God damned careful . . . he nipped the cocktail onion from the pencil point, —look set the God damned thing right at noon then it has to be right twice a day, pass itself at midnight again going backwards at noon all the rest of the time you've got a nice base twelve, six and six, eight and four, five fifteen it's quarter of seven got to find Raindance and Mister Fred . . . and he got through past Mazola New Improved, —never heard of them did you Bast know why? Holding them back, last time they ran they took the field and then they're gone, dropped out of sight, been holding them back till everybody forgets them and then bring them in at long odds God damn it both running tomorrow one in the first one in the second where the hell's the light in here . . .

—Oh the, the bulb burned out yes I . . .

—Can't see a God damned . . . a match flared, —you saving paper bags Bast?

—Oh, yes no those were . . .

—Need any more there's plenty in the tub, Bast? Package here for you.

—Oh that's just, yes never mind it it's just . . .

—Better open it might be food . . . he came wielding it in collision with 36 Boxes 2-Ply, —more cocktail onions, too God damned heavy for Hostess Twinkies . . . and the carton sundered on the floor. —What the hell is it.

—It's ah, it might be an electric letter opener, it . . .

—Bast God damned stroke of genius Bast, one thing we need here where'd I put that cup . . . he brought it up and finished it, —looked like some mail in there under the tub.

—Yes that's, that's just today's I haven't sorted it yet, sorted out Mister Grynszpan's I mean oh and Mister Gibbs I meant to tell you. A man came to the door a day or two ago and said he was from the Treasury Department looking for Mister Grynszpan, he . . .

—Treasury agent Bast, got to be God damned careful . . . he reappeared trailing envelopes, —say what it was?

—He said race track winnings yes and, yes he wasn't very nice about it he thought I was Mister Grynszpan and he wasn't nice about it at all, I thought he was going to take me with him. If he comes again what do you think I should . . .

—Problem better call Grynszpan's lawyer . . . and envelopes cascaded to the floor as he got a perch on some film cans and dug in the carton, —want to just plug this in over there . . .

—Yes I'd, but I'd better sort out Mister . . .

—Open yours too Bast glad to do it, here just plug this in under there and . . .

—Maybe you should take it out of the box first, it . . .

—Always have an answer don't you Bast, must just put them in this end and . . . Jesus!

—Maybe there are some directions with it that . . .

—Working fine, working fine just so God damned fast shoots them into the kitchen though . . .

—Wait, wait there's someone at the door I'd better . . .

—Must be, Eigen? Tom? that you?

The door came open upright. —Jack . . . ?

—Tom come in stand right there will you? No little closer, stop these when they . . .

—Christ Jack what . . . look out!

—Just opening the mail, Mister Bast here got us a . . .

—Stop, stop it look it's slicing most of it in half . . .

—Must be some God damned little adjustment here . . .

—Bast pull the plug will you? before he loses a finger? Damn it Jack look at this mess, what do you . . .

—Just have to match them up God damn it what do you think technology is for, have to open them all by hand? Just match bottoms to tops, here, anybody got a top half from the Internal Revenue Service? Tell you one thing from the bottom half here somebody's in one hell of a mess . . .

—Jack listen this lawyer's going to be here any . . .

—Enclosed, your sample Value Line report on A T and . . .

—Oh that might be something of, of mine I . . .

—The case for a bull market in, somebody getting into pork bellies?

—Well that, that might be . . .

—Know somebody named Pomerance Bast? Bottom half of somebody named Pomerance . . .

—Jack damn it listen . . .

—No wait wait something came through in one piece here look, came for Grynszpan called Taxing and Giving better look into it Tom listen. In no case does your gift to the Harvard Fund cost you as much as its real value listening? Gifts of Securities listen. We welcome and encourage gifts of securities that have risen in value how's that. God damned white of them isn't it, had a wife welcomes gifts of securities risen in value God damned white of her she . . .

—Damn it Jack . . .

—No wait look got a little table here tells you how it works look, income's fifty thousand net cost to Grynszpan per hundred dollar gift's forty-one dollars, fifty-nine percent of gift borne by government God damned white of them look. Get his income up to a hundred thousand gift costs him twenty-eight dollars a hundred, seventy-two percent borne by the taxpayers God damned white of them, black meter reader down there poking past ashcans made it all the way through ninth grade gets to use a real flashlight wear a uniform read electric meters all day pays two thousand a year withholding gets to help buy lacrosse rackets for Harvard God damned white of him what's this . . .

—Mister Gibbs that might . . .

—Executive's Complete Portfolio of Letters look, letters you might have to struggle over for just the right phrase completely written for you guarantee save you hours of work, no more struggling over the right way to phrase letters to Christ glad we got this aren't you Tom? Have to write to Mister where the hell's the bottom half of this, as a newcomer to the textile trades it gives us great pleasure to invite you to serve on this panel. Your topic will be Import Quotas and the Case for American, know Grynszpan was a newcomer to the textile trades Tom?

—Mister Gibbs I, some of that mail may be . . .

—That the validity of these claims has been subjected to repeated litigation, to proceed with caution in this direction. Top half of the U S Bureau of Mines there anywhere?

—Jack listen get up off the floor, this lawyer's on his way and I want to get . . .

—No wait, wait, can't miss this wait, Bloody Mary Volleyball Game at ten thirty a m, free bloody marys to all players. Golf tournament at the beautiful Wianno course, Tom must be Grynszpan's twenty-fifth reunion. Registration at Kirkland House, a mixed bag of old friends and classmates you never, got to see he gets there Tom where the hell's the other half of . . .

—Bast look will you help me clean this up before he . . .

—To extend these timber-cutting operations to adjoining federal lands in conformance with the Multiple Use-Sustained Yield Act of nineteen sixty stretching the working circle concept as far as is legally, that's not it where the hell . . .

—Mister Gibbs I, some of this mail may be . . .

—Morning symposium, opportunity to heckle allegedly distinguished classmates here it is, the traditional parade to Soldiers Field at two p m, costumes for all damn it Tom got to get him there . . .

—Wait listen what . . . what's that noise.

—It's, it's just the tub Mister . . .

—Bosom where bright waters meet Tom, confluence of the mighty Mongahela and Mister Bast and I were just discussing what the hell conflues with the Mon, Monongahela form the mighty Ohio at Pittsburgh's bosom where . . .

—It's just the tub Mister Eigen, I . . .

—God damned clever if you ask me, couldn't shut off the sink so he turned on the tub to distribute all this God damned entropy a little better, hand me that bottle will you Bast?

—And Mister Gibbs I meant to say, I meant to say Mister Eigen since I'm using this place and Mister Grynszpan only seems to get his mail here maybe I could pay the rent and . . .

—How's that Tom ideal tenant, saves paper bags and keeps all this God damned entropy in balance . . . he tipped the bottle over the cup, —provides an electric letter opener and offers to pay the rent, what's the rent . . .

—Sixty-one something, it went up, sixty-one forty, is that the only cup?

—God damned thoughtless of me, here. Now what was I looking for top half of . . .

—Mister Gibbs I think some of that mail is . . .

—Here. Now get up Jack, I want to get next door and look over Schramm's things before . . .

—Tom no God damned hurry pull up Thomas Register and sit down . . . he reached up for the emptied cup, tipped the bottle, —who the hell's taking a rapid reading course . . .

—Mister Gibbs I think some of that mail's mine, I . . .

—Bast taking a rapid reading course Bast? What . . .

—Yes well, no not exactly, I mean it's something I . . .

—Most Reading Dynamics graduates can read between fifteen hundred and three thousand words per minute Bast got to hear it, Tom quick get him a book . . .

—Jack listen I'm going next door, when the lawyer gets here I'll call you and . . .

—Still have to find Raindance and Mister Fred God damn it got all afternoon, we're Schramm's executors know that Bast? Named us joint executors handing out millions, even threw in little something for the kids . . .

—Yes I, I think someone's at the door now . . .

—Be right there Tom . . . he picked up the cup carefully, —got to understand the shape he's in Bast, just came back from Germany found his wife walked out, most cases that's a God damned blessing but this one it's all nine God damned beatitudes except she took the boy, understand the shape he's in Bast she took the boy . . .

—I'm sorry to, wait you're stepping . . .

—What? looks like a share of, got half a share of U S Steel here Bast where the hell's the bottom half . . .

—No that's all right Mister Gibbs I'll pick all that up, just . . .

—Have to find a book . . . he had a knee on 24–7 Oz Pkgs Flavored Loops up digging into 2-Ply Facial Tissue Yellow —how the hell'd she get up there what's her, Irma? girl of Schramm's?

—It's, I think it's Rhoda I just put that up there to, be careful!

—Rhoda, Rhoda with the burning bush ought to get one Bast . . . he caught a book in the abrupt cascade, —Traité de mécanique, God damned French not fair wait . . . he was down flapping pages, —Bess the landlord's daughter, plaiting a dark red loveknot into her long black hair try that.

—Yes I, I just wondered Mister Gibbs have you seen Mrs Joubert?

—Unbelievable Bast, black cascade of perfume came tumbling over his breast unbelievable wait, here's one nice short one . . .

—But she, did she come with you up to the back apar . . .

—Twelve, thirteen fourteen . . .

—Jack? He's here, will you come out and . . .

—Twenty-three, four, bring him in seven, eight, thirty-one . . .

—He's waiting for us, damn it Jack will you . . .

—Nine, sixty, sixty-one . . .

—Mister Gibbs I think Mister Eig . . .

—Bring him in Tom, count deep-brow'd one word? Eighty-eight, -nine . . .

—Jack get up damn it, he's out there waiting for us.

—Hundred twelve words On First Looking into Chapman's Homer, three thousand a minute ought to make it in two point o two seconds ready? MuchhaveItravelldin . . .

—Jack!

—God damn it I'm coming . . . he got past 200 2-Ply, —just thought he'd like to hear . . .

—Mister Beamish, this is Mister Gibbs the other executor, I'm afraid he . . .

—Glad you got here Mister Beamish settle a dispute, call that arbitrage Tom, buy low sell high . . .

—Jack just wait there till I get in and get the light . . .

—Mister Beamish is an attorney Tom, settle this dispute about the confluence of Mister Beamish what's the confluence of the Mongahela and what form the mighty Ohio in whose bosom, sorry I spill that on you?

—Jack this door's already open, it's not locked what . . .

—Got one question at a time, got Mister Beamish catching them faster than he can string them . . .

—Yes I, I believe it's the Allegheny Mister Gibbs but I'm not absolutely . . .

—Allegheny Tom hear that?

—Right in here Mister Beamish it's, I'm afraid it's not exactly what you . . .

—No that's quite all right . . .

—Don't need to apologize Tom he's not moving in, not moving in are you Beamish? Ceiling's ready to come down.

—Oh no, no I . . .

—Sit down Mister Beamish, nice bed over there sit down watch the ceiling.

—Well thank you I don't think I, I don't think this will take very long, there doesn't seem to be anything here of ah, of any great value and I don't think we . . .

—Good let's get started, Mister Beamish as the kindly Schramm family lawyer how do we price this shoe? May even be another one somewhere . . .

—Jack damn it get up off the floor, you're the one who insisted Mister Beamish meet us here instead of his office what in hell are you trying to do.

—Trying to help the kindly fam schrammly lawyer evaluate the God damned estate, legal obligation as executors right Mister Beamish? Get a little percentage too right Beamish?

—Well yes Mister Gibbs but ah, I don't think we need include such personal effects as ah, shoes, and I . . .

—Looks like a damned fine shoe to me sir, late King George V, Bootmakers, Peal and Company Limited can't get the damned thing on though . . .

—And I should add Mister Gibbs I'm not really the Schramm family's lawyer. I have handled occasional personal matters for them but my work is generally confined to the company and since the bulk of the ah, of your friend Mister Schramm's estate appears to consist of his holdings in Triangle Products we face the problem of . . .

—Problem is Beamish . . . he was getting to his feet again, —problem isn't anything here of any great value . . .

—Jack never mind it look, just sit down again and . . .

—Got to understand my co-executor Mister Beamish, problem is he wrote a very important novel a few years ago just won a modest award, comes out in paperback gets letters from college girls and little magazines ask him something for nothing but he hasn't got anything to . . .

—Jack shut up.

—Problem was Beamish we all knew each other too long, whole God damned problem Schramm thought the very important novel was about Schramm . . .

—Jack God damn it listen . . .

—Please Mister Eigen I think, Mister Gibbs I don't think you need go into . . .

—Ought to know what did Schramm in though Beamish, problem was the self who could do more problem was somebody ran off with it, read all about it in Mister Eigen's very important . . .

—Jack! God, God damn you shut up!

—Yes I, I think if we can get on to more relevant matters Mister Gibbs . . .

—Well God damn it can't you see that's what I'm trying to do? Problem where's that cup, problem isn't anything here of any great value God damn it what do you think this is!

—I, I'm sorry Mister Gibbs I don't follow your point, an old type-writer scarcely . . .

—No he means the papers Mister Beamish but it's just something Schramm, the manuscript of a book Schramm was . . .

—I see yes of, of course but establishing a monetary value for the manuscript of a published work is still a gray area and in this case would merely complicate . . .

—Point is Beamish God damn it Tom explain it to him will you Tom? Point is it isn't published Beamish, point is it isn't even finished, point what the hell do you think the point was Schramm comes back here one eyed comes back to tell us all comes back and takes one look see that God damned pipe up there Beamish . . . ?

—Yes but, that isn't what I meant . . .

—Jack just sit down and, here damn it give me that cup.

—Empty Tom, have to go next door and get Old Struggler.

—Give it to me I'll go next door and . . .

—No no hurry Tom have to tell Beamish . . .

—Well I want another one myself damn it . . .

—Have to explain to Beamish Tom, you go next door and fill it while I explain something to Beamish Tom . . .

—But Mister Eigen . . .

—I'll be right back Mister Beamish and we'll clear this right up.

—Point is Beamish you have to know the facts, I can't read this manuscript to you till you know the facts, see that in his will about Arlington but you have to know the facts, point is the war was the only time Schramm was ever really Schramm, that right Tom? Where the hell did he go. Little town called Beamish Mister, Saint Fiacre Mister Beamish, Belgian town snuggled up against the Ardennes where they broke through in that last big offensive and there's Schramm out there with a few tanks holding the point. God damned general pulling his armor back as fast as he can there's Schramm out there holding the point of the whole God damned defense perimeter with a few tanks against a whole God damned Panzer army coming down out of the Ardennes. Second night Schramm's out there holding the point gets ready to fall back to his own lines there aren't any God damned lines, general's got himself and his whole God damned division what's left of it pulled back twenty miles says later he radioed Schramm to pull back the end of the first day was a God damned lie, whole God damned Panzer army coming down on them finally knock out Schramm's tank he damned near froze, hit in the leg and they take him prisoner damned near froze, ever see his limp? So God damned ashamed being taken prisoner he always tried to hide it, walked without showing it except when he was tired always drag a foot when he was tired, God damned general shelling his own front lines while he's pulling out recommends Schramm for a medal for calling in shells on his own position holding that point God damned general still going around calling this the classic use of armor in defense, tells the history books how he stalled Blaufinger's whole God damned Panzer army at Saint Fiacre long enough to break the back of the whole God damned Ardennes offensive there's Schramm out there waiting for orders that never, Tom? Just filling Mister Beamish in on, thanks . . . wanted to know why in hell Schramm wants to be buried at Arlington out there holding the point waiting for orders while General Box wins the war, didn't offer Mister Beamish any Tom. Here you go Mister Beamish . . .

—Oh no, no thank you . . .

—Sorry any of that get on you?

—It's quite all right but, perhaps now we could . . .

—Trying to hurry Beamish . . . the cup came up for a long pull and he reached for the papers, —point is Schramm wasn't just trying to write another God damned war book, whole God damned point in Faust the Lord has everything laid out for Faust to win but he won't tell Faust, what the hell do you expect Faust to do? Lord staying above the God damned battle letting him break his God damned neck fighting for what was planned for him all the time what the hell do you . . .

—Jack shut up! We've got to . . .

—Look how the hell do you expect me to read this whole God damned thing to Mister Beamish without filling him in on the facts, ever see Schramm's Western Beamish? Wrote a movie Western didn't even have his name on it, point is he's out there hanging on waiting for orders to fall back that never came from the Lord and this God damned general radioed him was a God damned lie, comes out saying he won the bet and . . . wait what the hell are you doing, expect me to read this whole thing to Mister . . .

—I don't Jack! Damn it I don't expect you to read anything to anybody now put . . . put it, down . . . !

—Mister Eigen perhaps we should wait and meet at my . . .

—Tom you're spilling everything all over the God damned wait, wait that red book . . . and he was down among papers and dried teabags, dried squares of bandage —lent it to him five years ago never knew what happened to it wait, just read you this part Beamish give you a real insight into . . .

—Jack that's enough God damn it! Here, give me . . .

—Wait you're ripping it, what do you . . .

—Well then put it down damn it and . . . he caught a picture falling from its pages —who the, look at this, who's this.

—Never saw Schramm's mother Tom?

—Schramm's, her? No, but who . . .

—Ask fam's schrammly lawyer Tom, that Mrs Schramm Beamish?

—Yes I, I believe it is but not Mister Schramm's ah, mother of course, his father's second wife yes, I believe she married him just a few years before he died . . .

—Real number Tom, really see how she made the old man's mickey stand for him can't you Beamish . . .

—Well she, she was a good many years his junior yes, even younger than your friend Mister Schramm himself but . . .

—See why Schramm felt like Hippolytus turned backwards can't you, get a hand on that raw lung see how Schramm felt can't you.

—Yes I, I understand their relations were never entirely cordial but at this stage of course matters involving his estate will make it necessary to, I have some papers right here for her to sign in fact, I'd expected to drop them off but I'll be out of town for a few days and . . .

—Where is she.

—Right there in the east Sixties somewhere but it's getting rather late and I . . .

—Here I'll take them, I can drop them off.

—Be very helpful if you would Mister Eigen, the address is right on it and it might help expedite matters, I know she is anxious to see things settled . . .

—Don't blame her, get her hands on all that God damned money see how long she's been waiting for it there where her crupper's beginning to sag can't you, hand that cup down will you? Probably more God damned surprised than anybody the way Schramm pulled out and left the whole God damned thing in her lap.

—Well she, of course she was shocked at the manner in which he met his death Mister Gibbs but ah, after all she's quite comfortably off even without this trust portion in the estate reverting to her and I hardly think . . .

—She's the one in such a God damned hurry to convert everything into cash isn't she?

—I wouldn't really put it that way Mister Gibbs no, in fact if a sale can be arranged I'm the one who suggested it as the most expedient way of settling the estate. There are a number of modest bequests to be taken care of like these to your and Mister Eigen's children but quite aside from that the company's profit picture has been steadily on the loss side and I wouldn't say Mrs Schramm really had a, has a head for business she's not really . . .

—Tell you what she's got a head for Tom, where's that picture.

—Shut up Jack, while we're on it Mister Beamish these bequests, if they're made directly to the children how do we . . .

—Yes unfortunately Mister Eigen, Mister Schramm drew up his will without the help of an attorney and since the children are minors the bequests can't go to them directly without . . .

—Point is Beamish . . . came from the floor now near a battered chest of drawers, —three shirts here never been worn, point is Mister Eigen's afraid his wife will step in to help and the boy will never see a nickel, what's your neck size?

—Yes unfortunately if Mister Schramm had simply left the bequests
to you in trust to be spent at your discretion on the children's education
it wouldn't be necessary to . . .

—Point is I'm afraid of the same God damned thing, says it's to be
used for the kid's education she'd buy a swimming pool and say it's to
teach swimming . . .

—No I don't think you need fear . . .

—Buy a fur coat say the kid's learning to be a trapper . . .

—Jack shut up, what . . .

—Yes well since the shares in question would probably not qualify
under the prudent man rule, once you've obtained letters of guardianship and been bonded in order to take possession and furnished the
judicial accounting required to sell them, the proceeds . . .

—But wait how long does, how do you furnish a judicial accounting
if you don't even . . .

—Get a lawyer Tom, right Beamish? Always find a lawyer glad to
oblige for a small consideration, only talking about a couple of thousand
dollars for each kid anyway aren't we Beamish?

—Yes I, I believe it's something in that neighborhood . . .

—Neighborhood everybody lives there's lawyers right Beamish? Go
to court with your judicial accounting, get your letters, get bonded,
finally aren't any God damned proceeds point the whole God damned
problem's the decline from status to contract right Beamish? Whole God
damned problem right?

—Well there are ah, of course certain legal expenses are involved
but ah, once you and Mister Eigen have yourselves declared your children's legal guardians and the proceeds are deposited in a court approved bank account administered jointly by yourselves and the Surrogate . . .

—Bank president's the Surrogate's brother-in-law and you can't get
the God damned money out right Beamish?

—Wait shut up Jack, what do you mean have myself declared my
son's legal guardian he's my son, David's my son . . .

—In these matters of course Mister Eigen the interests of the child
are . . .

—Point is in these matters Mister Eigen's a God damned good father
Beamish, kind of a father wants his son to have everything he didn't have.

—Shut up Jack . . .

—Courage, integrity, perseverance . . .

—Jack God damn it shut up!

—God damned good man Beamish don't worry about him, just having a touch of the Türschluss syndrome beginning to see the doors closing, all sad words of tongue or pen the same God damned doors Schramm
saw closing . . .

—Jack I can't . . .

—Schluss die Tür, der kommen in der vindows . . .

—God damn you . . .

—Schluss der vindows, der kommen . . .

—Mister Eigen . . . !

—Didn't need to do that, Tom.

—Well then damn it what do you think you . . .

—No sit down Beamish, point is look at us Beamish, God damned point is life is what happens to us while we're busy making other plans, read that in a dentist office once and look at us, eighteen neck built like a God damned bull. What's your neck size.

—The point is Mister Beamish, if you want to know the point of this whole performance Mister Gibbs here wasn't in the war and Schramm was . . . he kicked the red covered book across the floor toward the chest of drawers, —Schramm was and he wasn't and he's never forgiven him for it . . .

—Yes I, I see Mister Eigen I, I don't think I'll have to keep you both any longer right now, of course I'll let you know when we have any expressions of interest as far as disposing of Triangle goes, though the prospects look extremely dim . . .

—What looks dim, Beamish sit down what looks so God damned dim?

—Simply our preliminary inquiries Mister Gibbs, apparently the asking price has discouraged several prospective . . .

—How much, wait need any socks?

—No thank you I ah, twelve million Mister Gibbs, as I say I'll let you know when any . . .

—Cash?

—Jack shut up and let him go, Mister Beamish thanks for . . .

—God damn it got a right to know these details God damn it Tom, got a legal obligation as Schramm's executor protect his widow's mite right Beamish? How's that for a fit.

—Take it off, Jack look you don't know a damn thing about . . .

—Twelve million what's the book value Beamish, here want to slip this on?

—No thank you I, I really don't need one Mister Gibbs, twelve million is substantially under book value in my opinion but in light of the declining profit picture I mentioned, rising costs in the paper industry and several very substantial accounts receivable that may simply have to be written off as bad debts, I have some of the figures right here but of course . . .

—I see those papers Beamish?

—Oh, yes of course but . . .

—Thanks. How you fixed for ties.

—Oh I'm ah, fine thank you yes, I don't think you'll want to take time to go into all those figures Mister Gibbs . . .

—Love figures Beamish, rather read a consolidated financial statement than where the hell's that book, don't want to forget this book, ones I like to read best where they're losing money hand over fist looks like a good one . . .

—Yes as I say certain situations that had been allowed to develop before I joined the company have contributed to . . .

—Tobacco, wait what the hell's this about tobacco, I thought you said paper industry . . .

—That was one of them yes it ah, through some family connection of Mrs Schramm's apparently Triangle acquired certain tobacco interests at what now appears to have been precisely the wrong . . .

—Nice string of accounts receivable Beamish, what the hell's Duncan and Co.

—Yes they ah, they make wallpaper yes, continuing their credit seems to have been among the unwise decisions made at a time when Triangle was also indulging such extravagances as purchasing the company plane and . . .

—Fixed assets seven and a half, got a pencil? Wait, how's that for a fit . . .

—Jack damn it look take that off will you? and just let Mister Beamish leave if he . . .

—Wait shut up Tom look, twelve million only get about nine after capital gains though right Beamish? Fixed assets seven and a half million look, somebody gives you two million one hundred thousand on that and you get eighty percent of the difference what you ask and what they pay back from taxes, two, three, four hundred wait, God damned many zeroes, million, four million three hundred twenty thousand, wait let me got a pencil?

—Jack God damn it will you just take that off and let Mister Beamish get . . .

—No this ah, this sounds interesting Mister Eigen, I . . .

—Getting all this down Beamish? Wait damn it . . .

—Look now you've split it, what the hell did you . . .

—Three million Beamish can't be right, inventory three million Beamish?

—Yes I'm afraid inventory control had been rather poor until . . .

—Poor must have been God damned nonexistent, all right you take ninety percent of that two point seven million get eighty percent of the difference back on taxes for two hundred forty thousand add it up . . . here Tom, drop in on Mrs Schramm give her these . . . he'd reached under the bed, —still plenty of good wear in them . . .

—What in hell is . . .

—Add it up your asking price is four and a half million and four and a half back on taxes you've got nine all you'd get anyhow, write off some of those accounts receivable as bad debts and you might cut off another half a million, how's that.

—Yes in fact it ah, it looks very interesting Mister Gibbs . . .

—Damned strong elastic too, God damned out of fashion hardly see them anymore right Beamish? Where the hell they came from must have been . . .

—You know God damned well where they came from, that dimwitted little piece Rhoda what do you . . .

—Wait forgot good will Beamish have to get paid for good will, problem Tom you've got no God damned good will, little good will for Rhoda ought to get yourself one . . .

—What the hell do you mean good will for Rhoda, if she'd been here waiting for him like she was supposed to that night we wouldn't be here now.

—Been here that night he probably would have painted one ball orange and hung her up there instead all just God damned revenge, I'm his friend wasn't here God damned revenge, you let him leave alone God damned revenge, wants to be buried in Arlington National Cemetery more God damned revenge right Beamish? Decline from status to contract, right?

—Well ah, it's simply a wish Mister Gibbs, not legally binding on the family or executors and if . . .

—No God damn it wants to be buried there that's where he goes, out there holding the point of the whole God damned defense perimeter that's where he goes, wait turn that light back on get that cup . . .

—Hurry up then, what . . .

—Get this God damned manuscript wait a minute, Beamish ever see Schramm's movie Beamish? One God damned thing he ever wrote a Western didn't even have his name on it, movie Dirty Tricks didn't even have his name on it . . .

—I'm afraid not Mister Gibbs I, I don't usually go to . . .

—Jack damn it will you . . .

—Same God damned thing as all this but a Western, God damned general in there above the battle taking bets just like the Lord, Schramm out there holding the point while everybody praised the Duke who this great fight did win, want to get these shirts wait a minute . . .

—Damn it Jack will you hurry up?

—But what good came of it at last quoth little Peterkin, wait get that book quick little God damned red book on the floor can't lose it again, why that I cannot tell said he but 'twas a famous victory know who wrote that? Same man Southey, same man who wait . . .

—Well what the hell are you bringing one shoe for.

—Got a friend needs one shoe, same man who wrote my name is Death, the last best friend am I, how's that. Put that on Schramm's stone, how's that . . .

—Just move so I can lock the door will you? Watch your step here in the dark Mister Beamish . . .

—Thank you yes I, I want to thank you both, Mister Gibbs for your interesting approach on Triangle and . . .

—What? Oh that's you Beamish, haven't got a free hand listen, stone in Arlington cemetery here's what it says, es ruht im Feindesland how's that Beamish.

—And I'd watch that throat Mister Gibbs, it sounds . . .

—Never see a German military cemetery Beamish? Got them all over the God damned place, bury them where they fall same God damned thing revenge, es ruht im Feindesland point is who asked the bastard there in the first place . . .

—Yes I'm ah, afraid I don't understand German but of course . . .

—Means forgot those panties Tom, means he rests in the land of the enemy, thought you wanted to take them up to Mrs . . .

—Jack look out, can you see the stairs there Mister Beamish? I'm on my way downtown and I'd be glad to drop you off if you . . .

—Wait I'm coming too Tom, just have to stop and pick up some research material, Beamish? Es ruht im Feindesland how's that. Name rank serial number es ruht im Feindesland how's that.

—Well it ah, I think we'd have to discuss it Mister Gibbs, the cemetery authorities might consider the sentiment somewhat inappro . . .

—God damn what I'm trying to do discuss it, Tom can't discuss a God damned thing standing around out here in the dark let him in, got this book here Beamish wants to discuss the Malleus Maleficarum, Hexenhammer Beamish fifteenth-century legal mind at work questions and answers Tom said he wants to discuss the questions and answers how can I read him the God damned thing out here in the dark . . .

—Jack damn it you're dropping everything will you just wait here till I . . .

—Listen . . . hear that? Sound like a telephone hear that?

—Just wait here till I get that door . . .

—Sound like a telephone . . .

—Just . . . the door shuddered, —wait . . .

—No I can't now goodbye . . . !

—Bast . . . ? Oh, I didn't see you up there, sorry to bother you again but there's something Jack wants to . . .

—No come in it's all right I . . . he eased down to 24–12 Oz Btls Fragile! —I was just, looking for something . . .

—Little like Pittsburgh isn't it Beamish, pull up Moody's Industrials and sit down, gentleman wants to discuss something Bast, Bast? Manuscript in a blue cover where the hell is it, promised to give me an expert opinion you think it's so God damned difficult here's an expert opinion, man who reads legalese where the hell is he?

—Yes it's, it's up on top of those boxes Mister Gibbs, the one that says Flakes up by the refrigerator, I put it up there so it wouldn't get . . .

—Jack will you just put that stuff down and get what you came for?

—Here brought you a shoe Bast, go around flapping that sole's ready to come off so I brought you a shoe.

—Yes it, in fact it came off this afternoon but, one shoe?

—Left one's all right isn't it? Thought you just needed a right one, damn fine shoe belonged to the late King George V where's that bottle Bast, hold these a minute . . . ?

—Look Jack you're not going to take all that stuff downtown, what did you stop to get.

—Bottle Tom, just have to do a little research Raindance and Mister Fred . . .

—Well look I can't wait for you, I . . .

—No wait wait coming down with you God damn it, stay here with Bast and we'd both end up where the God damned bright waters meet like Paul and Virginia, just one thing . . . he got past Mazola New Improved, —asked me about Stella Bast got the book here tells all about it . . . and he came down heavily on the armless sofa. —Listen, got it marked right here listen, it may be asked, as to illusions in respect of the male organ, whether, granted that the devil cannot impose this illusion on those in a state of grace in a passive way, he cannot still do so in an active sense, the argument being that the man in a state of grace is deluded because he ought to see the member in its right place, when he who thinks it has been taken away from him, as well as other bystanders, does not see it in its place . . .

—Mister Gibbs I, I think Mister Eigen is ready to . . .

—Like those other bystanders don't you? Listen, and what, then, is to be thought of those witches who in this way sometimes collect male organs in great numbers, as many as twenty or thirty members together, and put them in a bird's nest, or shut them up in a box, where they move themselves like living members, and eat oats and corn, as has been seen by many and is a matter of common report, ever see that Tom?

—No and I'm . . .

—Make a nice musical listen, for a certain man tells that, when he had lost his member, he approached a known witch to ask her to restore it to him. She told the afflicted man to climb a certain tree, and that he might take which he liked out of a nest in which there were several members. And when he tried to take a big one, the witch said you must not take that one, adding, because it belonged to a parish priest. Make a God damned lively musical wouldn't it?

—Bast look I'm going to have to leave him here, I have to get down to . . .

—Wait God damn it Tom leave poor Bast here alone trying to write his opera needs a God damned libretto, stringer whereon mad thingers said I'd help him dig out the piano just trying to help him out with Schramm gone right Bast? All those God damned bystanders there's your chorus . . .

—Well it, it's not an opera any more Mister Gibbs it, I'm not working on an opera any more I've made it a cantata and . . .

—God damn it see that Tom God damn it see that? God damned

wise man pulls out nobody to tell him what to do next right Bast? Write a cantata you don't need a plot, problem everybody running around wants to be told what happens next don't need a plot, looking for the wise man tell them what am I supposed to do now God damned wise man find out he's doing the same God damned thing walks up the shade and he's gone, rest of us sitting here looking at his footprints think he took it with him and he's gone . . .

—Mister Eigen while you're here I, I wanted to ask what I should do about the electri . . .

—Abraham Lincoln walks at midnight rest of us sitting here staring at his God damned footprints right up the, where the hell did he go, got footprints all over the mail never saw so God damned much mail Bast where . . .

—Yes well that, that one I put on top for Mister Grynszpan from Consolidated Edison about a bill for twelve hundred . . .

—Simple God damned misunderstanding Bast . . .

—Yes but I can't understand why they've turned off the gas but left the electricity on if he owes them twelve . . .

—Turned off everything Bast, Grynszpan just trying to avoid unpleasantness tapped these lines in bypassed the meter save everybody a lot of trouble, whole God damned billing system save Consolided Edison trouble with their God damned billing system, save them postage legal fees all the God damned heartache goes with it, poor God damned meter reader poking around ashcans with his flashlight save him the trouble . . .

—Bast look I have to get downtown, if you're staying here tonight maybe we can put him back in the other apartment and just let him get some . . .

—Right with you Tom just want to look at this mail, somebody Bast must have stacked up tried to match tops and bottoms Bast know any Indians? Something from some Indians Grynszpan know any Indians Tom?

—Yes that I, I haven't found the top half of that yet so I don't know whether . . .

—Nice invitation Bast all go out and see them, got some rocks they want us to see sounds like they're selling something God damned bunch of Indians always selling something, says mineral exploration claims and drilling leases they're really out on the back porch making a lot of God damned baskets nobody wants to, who the hell is Eunice Begg, know Eunice Begg Bast? God damned mad about something I'll tell you that from the bottom half, she . . .

—Look just get his arm maybe we can . . .

—Wait what, wait, bottom half of a senator office of Senator Milliken Grynszpan know any senators Tom? Always ready to discuss matters pertaining to the welfare and prosperity of my constituents wants money, only time the bastards write form letters want money, half two tickets to Five Thousand Years of Egyptian History at Hunter College Auditorium with our compliments where's the other halfs, I go with you Bast? Sounds God damned interesting . . .

—Mister Gibbs I, if Mister Eigen takes one arm and I . . .

—One more second Bast right with you, somebody God damned annoyed all the looms being removed to be sent to South America going to strike wait, got a cemetery, Ancient and Loyal Order of wait some God damned cemetery might need one Tom, trouble Schramm getting into Arlington already got a hundred fifty-seven thousand packed in there like fish might need one God, damn it all right I'm coming, sounds like a God damn good opportunity though whole God damned cemetery . . . he steadied against 24–7 Oz Pkgs Flavored Loops, —not taking your Baldung with you Tom? Rhoda with the hairy diadem nicest God damned name I could think offhand ought to get yourself one, sounds like a God damned good opportunity . . . and he got past the armless sofa toward Mazola New Improved, —whole cemetery sell real estate plots six by eight instead of sixty by eighty lot more tenants don't complain no heating problems all the God damned heartache right with you Tom, just get my research material back here bring it along . . .

—Jack wait damn it, wait what the hell do you . . .

—Just need these top bundles Bast can you shove those lampshades over the . . .

—I said wait! Look damn it you can't take those downtown I just sent a load of newspapers up here, they get here yet Bast?

—Yes they, I meant to tell you yes I piled them in there on the tub and . . .

—Damn it Jack look at that, I haven't had a chance to read and clip those yet so I sent them up here and now you want to . . .

—It's all right Tom different thing, Morning Telegraph here and that's the God damned Times calls itself the newspaper of record, think you find Mister Fred past performance in the God damned newspaper of record?

—Look if you bring those downtown they're going out on the . . .

—Raindance with Melindez up, things are in the saddle Tom just pull that pile out under there Bast will you? No trouble Bast be glad to help us . . .

—All right but listen damn it tomorrow they go out on the street whatever you, watch the door there . . .

—Watch the wait, wait tell Bast what time it is get him back on base twelve, God damned things in the saddle and ride mankind Bast can't set it till midnight, Bast? Hear me over the bosom of shining . . .

—Just get the, it's all right Bast we can manage, just get the door closed . . .

—Can't see a God damned thing, like leaving Pittsburgh . . .

—Look Jack just, wait give me that pile and watch your . . .

—God damned stairs can't see a God damned, listen. Listen hear that? God damned telephone ringing someplace can't see a . . .

—Hello Mister?

—Tom somebody on the stairs here don't step on him . . .

—Mister you came in the apartment by the end of the hall? Is empty now he went away in the bag Mister?

—What, what the hell do you . . .

—Mister my vife, five flights her legs she couldn't go up and down anymore Mister . . .

—Went away in a bag God damn it I'll put you in a . . .

—Jack shut up leave him alone, just get the door . . .

—Put him in a God damned bag . . .

—Hurry up there's a cab . . .

—Come the five Jones boys pushing their God damned clubhouse across the . . .

—Look just wait here at the curb, if he sees you with those bundles of paper he won't stop, just wait here . . .

—Watch out Tom, cinco Jones run over you with their God damned club . . .

—Que dice?

—Dice sin cojones, coño . . .

—Madre, coño . . .

—Look out you crazy God damned bunch of . . .

Lights veered, drew up. —Jack! here . . . !

—Not taking him anyplace buddy.

—You're God damn well taking both of us right where I told you to, get those in here Jack . . .

—Hijo de . . .

—Crazy God damned . . .

—Coño mira el coche coño . . . !

—Get in here get the door, what the hell's going . . . what was that!

—God damned clubhouse, cinco Jones boys let go of it smashed right into a lamp post, jumped me for no God damned . . .

—Lock your door, driver if you're not out of here God damn fast you're going to have five crazy Puerto Ricans ripping your . . . he was flung back against the seat as they swerved in a wide arc, slammed to a halt at a light.

—Crazy God damned, put them in a bag too how's that. Cinco Jones put them in a bag how's that.

—Look can you just be quiet till we get there?

—Forgot Old Struggler, Tom.

—I've got something down there.

—Forgot the God damned shirts . . . and they slumped staring out opposite windows through jarring halts, abrupt snatches at velocity.

—This side driver last on the right, Jack? Get out, I'll push these out to you . . .

—Second want to look in there for a shoe, might be Hardy . . .

—Damn it just get this bundle will you . . . ? The door slammed, he handed bills in the window. —Get up Jack, what did you drop.

—Schramm.

—God damn it get up off the sidewalk and, look these papers are just going to stay right here if you can't . . .

—No no no got things in the saddle . . .

—All right get them in here then . . . he sorted keys, —I'll hold the door, damn good thing they fixed the elevator . . . and he sorted keys as they rose. —Hold the door there so I can see . . . He got the key in, kneed the door open —just drag them in the hall here, I'll get the light in the kitchen.

—Got to move out of here Tom, find a cheery little furnished room with print curtains and a hot plate move the hell out.

—Look I've hardly unpacked, I got off the plane and looked around even thought maybe she'd brought David out to meet me at the airport, see how damn stupid . . . he had the refrigerator door opened pounding the blade of a table knife under the icetray, —God damn thing hasn't been defrosted since, what are you looking for.

—Bottle, nothing down here but Mister . . .

—It's right behind you, I thought maybe she didn't get my cable but I took one look when I got here and called her friend Joan, then I called the office and got your message about meeting Beamish, get some glasses.

—Just says Liqueur Deluxe, what the hell is it.

—I don't know what the hell it is, I just grabbed it at the airport before I left Frankfurt but there's nothing else here. She went through every bottle in the house before she took off.

—Shame she missed the Mister Clean, where the glasses . . .

—Look in the sink. So Joan Bartlett said yes she told me you'd call, how the hell did she know? Got my cable and got the next train damn it Jack rinse them out, there's still milk in them. Who else would I call? The Bartletts are separating Tom, Joan says she can't live with a man she doesn't respect, always used the Bartletts when she was really talking about us, bright young couple who painted pears on every damn thing they owned until he lost his job. Joan says she can't respect a man who doesn't respect himself so the poor bastard agrees to move out and come visit the kids on weekends, finds your cheery little furnished room with the hot plate and now she's got him up for abandonment.

—Nice God damned thing about Marian so God damned fair, doing it for your sake Tom even told me can't get much more God damned fair, bring some cigarettes?

—Just going to ask you, he led up the dark hall, kicked a small red worn, laceless sneaker the length of it, picked it up and found the light before he reached a chair and sat down heavily. —Look under that pile of mail there, see how carefully she laid it out for me every damn one of them's a bill except that card I sent David, told him I was racing it home . . . he leaned forward and put the sneaker down, back and drank leaving only ice cubes. —So damn fair she believes it, took Kurt Weill left me Mahler, took the top half of the double boiler left me the bottom half so God damn fair she's doing it for my sake what about David's sake, how many damn times I've told her we could hold things together for David's sake . . .

—God damned worst thing you could have told her, God damned mother in Solomon's ready to cut the kid in half give you the bottom half time like that worst God damned thing you could tell her, time like that starring in her own soap opera worst God damned thing you could tell her.

—Well God damn it she, let her go star in her own damn soap opera is that any reason she has to drag David away from every damn thing he ever . . .

—Point is whole God damned point is she wants to be taken seriously needs a supporting cast, talented woman never been allowed to do anything sits here all day drinking Mister Clean works up a whole God damned drama has a part for everybody. Arabs Israelis Irish same God damned thing scared maybe nobody takes them seriously, God damned Irish know everybody knows they're a God damned joke so the worse they get, God damned self-righteous Israelis same God damned thing take the top half of the double boiler leave the Arabs the bottom half everybody so God damned sick of all of them all they do is run around shouting for an audience somewhere to take them seriously same God damned thing, fill this up? Whole God damned problem tastes like apricots, whole God damned problem listen whole God damned problem read Wiener on communication, more complicated the message more God damned chance for errors, take a few years of marriage such a God damned complex of messages going both ways can't get a God damned thing across, God damned much entropy going on say good morning she's got a God damned headache thinks you don't give a God damn how she feels, ask her how she feels she thinks you just want to get laid, try that she says it's the only God damn thing you take seriously about her puts you out of business and goes running around like the God damned Israelis waving the top half of the double boiler have to tell everybody they're right. God damned Arabs mad as hell sitting there with the bottom half pretend you take them seriously only thing you want is their God damned oil . . .

—Jack listen you could get damn sick on this stuff if you . . .

—Want their God damned oil have to respect them for themself, always find some God damned slob around ready to listen respect her for herself nods gravely looking up her skirt, talented woman never been allowed to do anything just listens doesn't make any God damned difference to her who he is takes her seriously, finally sure he's not just after her double boiler spreads the bottom half for him same God damned thing starts all over again, tastes like apricots what the hell is it.

—Why the hell I, why I ever even met her, some agency party I went to at the last minute never even would have met her, she damn near didn't go to it herself. Why the hell just one of us didn't go . . .

—Problem can't do that God damned problem can't hypothesize backwards Tom, never met her never would have married her keep going you hypothesize the kid right out of existence one God damned thing you can't imagine not existing, one thing I ever did in the world . . . he blew ice back into his empty glass, —only God damned thing I've got . . .

—Hypothesize any damn way I want to listen, that selective memory she's got takes the whole God damn past and reconstructs it, told me before he was born I didn't want David real instinct for the jugular. Takes the whole damn past and reconstructs it all the facts are there but you can't recognize a damn thing, here give me that bottle. Told me before he was born I said I didn't want David God damn it wasn't David there wasn't any David, got any sense what in hell do you want to bring one more helpless, one more whole capacity for suffering doesn't exist yet doesn't even have a name what in hell do you want to bring that into a God damn world like this one for, damn it Jack will you get your feet off the sofa out of those shirts? Haven't been able to find a clean shirt for three months find those eighteen dirty ones stuffed in the back of a closet she . . .

—Problem worst God damned thing you could have said Tom, hold things together for David worst God damned insult you could hand her, point whole God damned point wouldn't take her seriously her way she'll find another way, hand her a weapon like that she'll find a way to make you God damned stuff need ice. Can't get it down without ice just have to get used to it, God damned Irish won't have it with the mouse won't have it without the mouse same God damned thing just get used to it Tom . . .

—Damn it listen get used to, have to ask permission to see my own son if you think I'll get used to . . .

—Worst God damned thing never get used to the worst God damned thing leaving, stand there on the God damned street corner two hours visitation rights is up pretend you have to leave, no place to go God damned wind blowing pretend you have to leave she knows God damned well I don't have to leave thinks I want to, can't explain a God damned family court order two hours is up stands there waving thinks I want to leave her on that God damned street corner drugstore sign in the God damned window Surgical Appliances for the Whole Family . . . he was almost to his feet, steadied against the door frame, —no God damned place to go stands there waving pretend you have to leave, always wanted to get a look at that family . . .

—Wait damn it Jack you've got a shirt caught on your . . .

—Just got to get ice . . . he kicked, got into the hall, —can't get it down without ice . . . and he made the corner to the kitchen, banging the ice tray against the sink when the doorbell rang, —minute God damn it . . . He got there and pulled it open, looked down —what . . .

—Hi is Mrs Eigen here?

—All out of them.

—Oh, then would, would you like to buy some greeting cards then?

—Tom got a boy here selling greeting cards, what grade are you in.

—Six M, Mrs Manzinel . . .

—Tom boy out here working his way through six N selling greeting cards. What's the greetings.

—Well see these are all occasion cards, like for all different occasions they're all . . .

—All occasion cards Tom, got them for all different occasions.

—Like birthday, anniversary, you know all these different occasions like . . .

—Got a friend jumped out a window, got a card for that?

—Well gee I, maybe get well . . .

—Can't get well, went home and hung himself got a card for that?

—Well gee I, I don't think so but maybe you could . . .

—Got a woman on alimony sleeping with a book salesman hell of an occasion, got a card for that?

—Well gee I, like here's sympathy maybe you could . . .

—Jack God damn it what are you, hello Chris what is it.

—Oh hi Mister Eigen I, I was just selling these greeting cards . . .

—Says they're for all occasions Tom but every God damned occasion I can think of is . . .

—Jack shut up will you? Chris lives upstairs he's, how much Chris.

—Well see they're two dollars a box but like for five dollars you get three and you get this free premium of these flower seeds . . .

—All right I, I'll take the five dollar one Chris . . .

—Let him finish Tom wants to earn his . . .

—Here Chris and, wait look . . .

—Gee Mister Eigen thank . . .

—God damn it didn't let him finish Tom, didn't tell us what kind of flower seeds he . . .

—I just don't really need the cards or the seeds right now though Chris I, maybe you can take them along and sell them again, come back to see me . . . he got the door closed, —God damn it Jack talk like that to a poor kid who . . .

—Hell do you mean poor know what the markup on those God damned cards is? Making more money than I am but God damn it Tom wants to think he's earning it, do that you're taking away his whole God damned professional pride undermine the whole God damned free enter . . .

—Just forget it! Will you, get your ice?

—Got ice Tom can't forget it listen, God damned problem you see David every God damned boy you look at see David can't do that Tom, give him five dollars think you're helping birthday anniversary some real God damned occasion hits him he doesn't know where the hell he . . .

—Look damn it you're dropping ice all over the . . .

—Tripped on these God damned newspapers thought you were sending them all up to . . .

—Damn it they're the ones you just brought down here! What the hell do you think I . . .

—Wait, wait damned near forgot wait, Raindance and need a pencil, wait get this one . . .

—Get you a pencil . . . he dragged a bundle ahead, —some in my workroom . . . he reached in, got the light.

—Can't spread them out in here Tom, need room to spread them out.

—Jack damn it you can't spread them out in here, I'm just trying to find a pencil . . . he rummaged around the typewriter among papers and paperclips, a sheep with one leg gone, a red mitten, a broken music box, marionette in a tangle of strings, car with no wheels, Piglet torn from his base, a clock with one hand pointing the minute and an arm from a stuffed bear, an arm lofting a bugle, an armless headless soldier, marching, —never find one God damn pencil . . .

—Got to move the hell out Tom little furnished room with a hot plate, looks like the God damned dawn of the world in here necks without heads arms seeking shoulders, only God damned person live here's Empedocles . . .

—Well damn it I, don't you think I . . . he came down against the chair drawn up to the typewriter, —writer who can't even find a pencil, God damn instinct for the jugular told me the reason I don't finish it I'm afraid to compete with myself, terrible slowness of things in a dream . . . and he tore the page from the typewriter. —They wheeled, I fired, and they were gone, but there on the ground with a broken damn it Jack do you know how many times I've written that? rewritten that? Marries a writer like a politician wants him to win, she thinks you're in some God damn competition running for something, one God damn person take your doubts to lay them in her lap and she . . .

—Just told you Tom worst God damned thing you can do, bunch of God damned open wounds lay them in her lap what the hell do you expect. First time she has to get the God damned knives out she can't resist them, laid them all out for her she knows right where they are can't resist them, in here think you're writing a play characters come out of your typewriter what the hell you expect them to look like all those God damned knives going on around you, bunch of God damned arms wandering around bereft of shoulders right out of Empedocles hell do you expect. God damned knives going around she's standing at the sink in the kitchen man down there no hands no ears no God damned face drinks pints easier to hold between his wrist stumps, she's standing at the sink has to get the God damned knives out knows right where they go what the hell do you expect . . .

—All right but, look damn it don't untie those papers in here . . .

—Point God damned point only audience sit through it's Empedocles, shambling creatures with countless hands eyes wandering around looking for a God damned forehead parts joining up all wrong make a hell of a musical just telling Bast, nice operetta twenty or thirty up there in the God damned nest eating oats and corn everything down below joining up all wrong God damned commotion, heads swell up out of the nest give us a few bars from Traviata little opening chorus cinco Jones in there how's that, little Hexenritt from Hansel and Gretel God damned witch comes on . . .

—Jack listen damn it just, help me get these papers into David's room . . . he'd dragged a bundle to a door pushed open on darkness, got the light, —go through them in here . . .

—God damned witch comes on gives them a little Che volo d'augelli from Pagliacci God damned heads really rear up at that all pile out come down and dance around her hell of a thing to choreograph how's that, parish priest swells into a big God damned tumescent baritone gives us Se vuol ballare from Figaro breaks into a tap dance rest of them get the God damned Anvil Chorus banging away in the background how's that. Didn't want to tell Bast whole plot cousin's a God damned witch take you right off at the roots . . .

—Look just get that last bundle in here, you can sleep in here . . .

—God damned truth Tom real God damned witch lies there spread open for you really somewhere else, lies there takes it like a God damned cow really someplace else all the time didn't want to tell Bast, witches can't weep ever know that Tom? Tell Bast God damned cousin put you right out of business . . .

—In here, where are you going . . .

—God damned bottle, lost the God damned ice just get used to it . . .

—Wait you're dragging a shirt on your foot damn it, wait . . .

—Told you worst God damned get to the point shirts follow you around right in here, nice little furnished room needs curtains Tom can't take this room, discommode anybody . . .

—What the hell are you talking about it's . . .

—Suitcase open here thought you're taking in transients . . .

—Jack God damn it the room's empty can't you, it's David's room can't you see how God damned empty it is! He lifted the bag open from the low bed to the only chair, —just a bag I haven't unpacked, here move your foot . . .

—Hillbilly's wife says Zeb move yer foot yer astandin on a hot coal Zeb says . . .

—Jack damn it just move your foot will you? You're standing on a book you've already broken the . . .

—Good thought I forgot it, part in there about God damned witch takes this virgin up to a room where she, wait what the hell is this? Said you'd brought my book what the hell is this?

—I didn't say I'd brought your book here, give it to me, something I picked up to read on the plane . . .

—Heart of Darkness, God damned cheerful reading Heart of Darkness, part at the end he takes her picture and letters back to her . . .

—Jack be careful you, sit down or you're going to . . .

—God damned stuff make you sick, part she says you were his friend, part she says you knew what great plans he had something must remain wants his last word to live with, part you knock on the mahogany door take the papers up to Mrs Schramm wants his last words to live with believing and shitting are two very different things Mrs Schramm always remember that part . . .

—Jack shut up I, I don't want to talk about it tonight just, look I'm going to bed, just try to wipe the whole God damn thing out till tomorrow I'm so, so damn sick of all of it . . .

—Stuff make you God damned sick lost the ice, here . . .

—I don't want any more no, I tell you I just saw his God damn general? Hasn't changed a bit since he got his first star leaving Schramm out there still thinks he's wearing four stars, walk on the wrong side of him he thinks you've disappeared.

—Who.

—Box, General Box, he's a director of the company, made him one because he still has a few broken down connections at the Pentagon and he's great to send to a ground breaking in a broken down country where you've started a civil war to secede the one province where the whole God damn country's mineral wealth is, I had to fly three thousand miles to spoon feed him a speech so he wouldn't say Plato rhymes with tomato damn it Jack I can't take this anymore, little bastard Davidoff every damn speech I write we go over twenty times till he gets human betterment and a two edged sword at one fell swoop and his God damn iceberg into it, has me take a Chinaman out to tie one on and sit there while he blows chewed up meat across the table at me I can't take it anymore, the whole thing is just, the whole place there's nothing real about any of it, one thing that's real in that whole God damn place is that painting of Schepperman's, see it when you come in it's so God damn real you . . .

—Hell are we talking about painting of Schepperman's thought we're talking about Plato.

—That tremendous painting of his they've got in the lobby I told you about it . . .

—Tell me about any painting of Schepperman's Tom what . . .

—But I, I never told you? I never told you what happened? Met Schepperman coming out of a White Rose bar really looked like hell didn't I tell you? a few months ago didn't I tell you?

—Tom always meet him coming out of a White Rose bar lend him ten don't see him again till you meet him coming out of a White . . .

—No no that's the point it wasn't money, he had a wealthy patroness giving him some every month he'd been working like hell, giving him enough to buy paints and live on the way he lives in that loft he didn't give a damn for the money it was the paintings, he was giving them to her and never saw them again nobody saw them. She was just locking them away somewhere probably never looked at them herself, nobody saw them and there's Schepperman thrown out of one White Rose bar we went into the next one pounding the bar about making a statement, dirty flannel shirt hadn't shaved for a week and he put his face in his hands, he's bigger than I am and you see that whole back of his shake, pounds the bar again and shouts about making a statement locked up in the dark nobody to see it. One God damn statement after another where nobody could see it and he didn't give a damn for the money, just his statements shut up where nobody could see them only God damn reason he'd painted them, grabs somebody by the collar shouting is true? is true? and we're thrown out of that White Rose too . . .

—Schepperman God damned statements still got one of his God damned statements carved in stone over the God damned front door, God damned school board find it's Karl Marx I tried to help him out worst God damned thing you can do, try to help him out worst God damned . . .

—What the hell do you mean it's the best thing I've done since I've been with that God damn company, it's the only thing, little bastard Davidoff running around looking for a name painter when they decided to get in on this phony business honeymoon with the arts, a big mural for the lobby and this little bastard Davidoff running around looking for a name painter right after I saw Schepperman I thought I'll give you a name you little bastard. I called up a few people and talked up Schepperman, got together a few of his old grants and honors and let Davidoff take all the credit for discovering him just kept them from meeting each other and they bought this staggering thing of his must be ten by twenty feet, all shattering blacks and whites I don't know how the God damn company officers keep the jelly in their heads together when it hits them in the morning. I got him twelve thousand dollars for it he didn't give a God damn but I had to, paid any less that little bastard Davidoff wouldn't have thought he was a name painter but all Schepperman was excited about was having it hung up there where people can see it . . .

—Tom worst God damn thing you can do help out the God damned artist, comes back bites the nose that spite your face, stuff make you God damned sick Tom better off when he was selling blood to the Red Cross to buy paints stuff really make you sick . . .

—Just give me that bottle then will you? Damn it just give it to me . . . ! Jack listen you're in worse shape than I ever, never seen you in worse shape how the hell do you expect to walk into a classroom with a throat sounds like . . .

—Don't Tom.

—Well how the hell do you keep this teaching job? Show up there like this and they . . .

—Don't show up Tom only God damned thing tomorrow Raindance and Mister Fred have to show up, said you'd get me a pencil . . .

—All right just, wait see what the hell she left . . . he pulled open a closet, suddenly sniffed deeply and cleared his throat dragging a shoe box out with his foot, —crayon, give you a purple crayon . . .

—Don't want a God damned purple crayon want a God damned pencil.

—Give you pink, God damn it how did she leave that, left his crèche here how did she leave that.

—Don't want a God damned crèche just want a God damned pencil.

—Look you can have a God damn purple crayon or a God damn pink crayon, if you . . .

—Take God damned purple.

—Here . . . he came down next to a foot on the end of the low bed, caught a hand over his eyes —God, damn it Jack how do you, how do you get through Christmas . . .

—Kindly God damned family court judge fix it up for you Tom best God damned thing fool him, be Jewish get through Hanukkah fool him.

—No but how do you, Jack he used to set this up by the window there the whole damn thing he called it, he, he thought it was called Baby Jeeter and the Three Wide Men he . . .

—Can't get through it Tom just get through it worst God damned thing just get through it, kindly family court judge gives you visiting privilege deliver whole God damned bag of presents have to leave, God damned street corner waving goodbye God damned wind blowing knows God damned well no God damned place to go stands there waving God damned street corner drugstore surgical appliances for the whole God damned family . . .

—God damn instinct for the jugular she told me I . . .

—Wait wait listen Tom listen, idea make a million dollars God damn it listen. Invent a God damned parlor game where's the bottle listen, game about divorce sweep the God damned country parlor game call it Divorce how's that. Every God damned married couple young and old alike sublimate their God damned can't stand each other can't afford to split buy the God damned game for ten dollars sublimate their God damned divorce game call it Split make a million dollars how's that.

—I ever tell you David asked me once if Jesus ever, wait damn it be careful . . .

—No no just want to show you look, throw the dice little figure moves around the board take your choice pay your money just like real life look . . . a tall figure from the crèche pranced over The Morning Telegraph between his fingers —look, land on little God damned squares tell you what to do go to court, have to draw a God damned card tells you pay orthodontist two thousand dollars just like real life look . . . and the remaining members of the crèche joined in pursuit across Aztec Queen $19.40 Scores by 3 Lengths at Hialeah, —God damned support alimony cash, house, cars boat dog kids wife tries to get everything just like real life how's that . . .

—Jack damn it I don't want those broken, I ever tell you David asked me once if Jesus grew up to be an Indian?

—Wait God damn it goes here . . . the smallest figure was thrust swaddled from Big A to Yonkers Entries, —land here get custody of the kid one turn just like real life whole now generation God damned young couples sweep the God damned country, go to court draw God damned card says pay wife's back psychiatrist bills twelve hundred dollars wife passes go collects alimony . . . the only seated, only female figure was shoved arms spread in wild surmise to join a lofty black on Cocky Jane Runs Second on Coast, —lands here caught in motel getting laid loses custody two turns, game for two to four couples play just like real life sweep the God damned country how's that.

—Damn it Jack let me put these away before you . . .

—Didn't finish the God damned game my turn land here have to draw God damned card . . . paper tore, RAPH streamed through the air —says pay wife's lawyer two thousand dollars just like real wait what the hell are you doing . . .

—Put them back in the box Jack I don't want anything to . . .

—No no your turn wait God damn it Tom, can't play the God damned game have to invent it first sweep the God damned country look, land on this square says Bar . . . a figure bearing myrrh was swept to Results at Pimlico, —says buy drinks all round pay fifty dollars just like real God damn looks like Schepperman . . .

—Damn it just give it to me . . .

—God damned game just like real life stop on White Rose bar there's Schepperman can't help him Tom, woke up sitting on a God damned bench in Central Park one morning God damned lady's shoe in his hand didn't know where he'd been can't help him Tom . . .

—Just give me it Jack and, and damn it where's the little one.

—Sorry my turn? Draw a God damned card . . . paper tore, —buy surgical appliances for the whole God damned family pay one thousand dollars go to jail just like real life how's that.

—Look just shut up and help me find the other piece, the little Baby Jesus piece damn it.

—Thought you said Baby Jetter Tom stuff really make you sick, game call it Baby Jetter whole God damned family in surgical appliances make a million dollars sweep the country really make you God damned sick, your turn. Where the hell all the pieces go.

—I put them away God damn it look move your leg, where's the little one . . .

—Where's the little one got away Tom thought you just said Baby Jetter . . .

—Jeeter God damn it I said Jeeter, David used to call them Baby Jeeter and the Three Wide Men now God damn it will you get up so I can find it?

—Try to Tom, thought you said he grew up to be an Indian.

—No damn it that was just, I was just trying to explain once to David about the cruci, look Jack if you want to stand up get your feet down first, crucifixion, he asked me if Jesus was a regular person and damn it look out, you're going to . . .

—God damned profound question regular person Tom, whole God damned Council of Nicaea taste like apricots make you . . .

—Jack look if you're going to be sick don't, look get away from the bed, bathroom's end of the hall . . .

—God damned heresy Tom regular person hell do you think they banished Arius to Illyricum for . . . he was getting down the hall at an angle to the wall, —whole God damned problem Council of Nicaea give Baby Jeeter like substance taste like apricots . . . the light came on as his shoulder caught it struggling upright, —thanks, glass of water . . . he made the basin, pulled the medicine cabinet open to sweep the mirrored image away, —Tom . . . ?

—What.

—God damned drugstore Tom, Mrs Eigen two every four hours, Mrs Eigen one every two hours if headache persists, Mrs Eigen one every three hours but no more than God damned drugstore in here, Tom?

—What.

—Regular God damned drugstore in here caps off toothpaste every God damned coathanger, hell she did to that coathanger . . . and he caught himself steadied at the water closet in a dry heave, staring down. —Tom . . . ?

—What.

—Got to see this Tom.

—What.

—Said she didn't leave any message for you got to see this.

—What.

—Message for you can't bring it have to come read it yourself, Tom? God damned message for you left it where you couldn't miss it kiss goodbye.

—What?

—Kiss God damned goodbye I said . . . ! he lurched, caught the handle and the water swirled the imprint of thin lips slightly parted in a lipstick blot on the square of tissue and drew it down, a hand of his came up to touch his lips and fell, —hell I come in here for . . . he made the hall, —Tom . . . ?

—Went to bed Jack.

—Hell did he go . . . he reached the lighted door, reached for the low bed. —Tom?

—I went to bed, just want to wipe the whole damn thing out till tomorrow.

—Hell did he go, he muttered coming down carefully, pulling a bundle close and the string off it, —Raindance where the hell did he go . . . turning pages, gradually subsiding in fragments of chorus —kommen in der vindows . . . he turned pages, pulled more from the heap, —God damned purple crayon, schluss die vindows . . . and more pages, —Tom? have some music in here, God damned tumescent purple baritone container smashed on the God damned sidewalk . . . more pages, he invaded the next bundle, —schluss die God damned words waiting for him in the morning didn't know if the girl was alive and he was dead if they both were alive or both were dead . . . his foot began to tap, —he was alive then the milkman wasn't . . . and he hunched abruptly, turning pages, foot tapping heavily, —when, you're alone, in the middle of the bed, and you wake, like some, one hit you on the . . .

—Jack what the hell is going on in there.

—God damned thing Tom find Raindance and Mister Fred . . . he turned pages, foot starting again and his free hand thumping the offbeat, —cream, of a nightmare dream, and you've got, the hoo ha's, coming to you. Hoo hoo . . .

—Well God damn it can you shut up so I can sleep?

—Right with you Tom, Tom? Remembered get Grynszpan to that God damned parade Soldiers Field costumes for all . . . and he hunched to a whisper, pages sweeping under his hand until, —Hoo ha how's that, God damn it how's that. Raindance by seven lengths God damn it how's that, Tom? Raindance by seven lengths how's that . . . He tore at the next bundle, —stuff make you God damned sick . . . turning pages, sweeping papers aside, —Tom? hell did he go . . . pulling more from the heap, —hell did he go Mister Fred taste like apricots . . . until, abruptly, he came forward, gained his feet teeming in one direction and back grabbing the chair —God damned sick, Tom . . . ? God damned profound question regular person, Tom? Schramm God damned regular person get him in Arlington name rank serial number biggest God damned tombstone in Arlington how's that, name rank serial number carve in granite believing and shitting two very different things how's that . . . He tipped toward the door held back by his hand gripping the chair, tipped to a crunch underfoot and kicked aside the sea of paper, —Tom? Found

Baby Jeeter . . . and he caught the back of the chair with both hands,
—Tom know what I'd like to do Tom . . . ? Go right up to the God
damned sky disappear, come down like the, like the . . . and he pitched
abruptly over the open suitcase in a rush that left him heaving, another,
clinging there until he could free a hand to find a dry sock and wipe his
mouth, another, bringing the sock up again, clinging there till he could
drop the sock in and free both hands to bring the suitcase closed, snap
one of its locks and, as intently, the other before he fell back on the low
bed, flung out there still as a man cast up by the sea when light caught the
window and slowly gave it definition, finally filled it leaving the overhead
a yellowed pall and the buildings wide across the way in the sunlight un-
dulant through the cheap glass pane like a part of a submarine landscape.

—Jack . . . !

—What . . . ?

—I just woke up I'm late, I've got to get up to God what a mess, look
clean up these newspapers before you go will you? I've got to get right
up to the office.

—No wait, wait . . .

—I can't I have to get to the office, look clean up these papers before
you leave will you? he said in the door there pulling a tie under his collar,
—and Jack do something about your throat before you . . .

—Wait just wait a minute what time is it, look I have to get out to
the track Tom leave me ten can you? twenty?

—Ten . . . he came down the hall pulling on a jacket, —leaving it here
by the dishrack and Jack? He pulled the door open, —make sure this
locks when you leave?

—Wait wait twenty, can't leave twenty? Listen this double today's
the surest thing I ever had wait, damn it need a shirt, where the shirts
I brought down from Schramm's . . .

—You didn't bring them . . . he held the door with his foot to reach
in and drop another ten by the dishrack, —shirts in that suitcase right
there on the chair Jack, haven't even unpacked it . . . and he pulled the
door closed behind him, paused in a turn for the elevator and then made
for the stairs and down them two, three at a time and out, fingers parting
his teeth in a shrill whistle, and he slumped in the back of the cab tying
his tie, finally got the last of his shirt buttoned as their swoop to the curb
threatened to pin the dapper haste of a chauffeur against the Z S number
tag on the limousine throbbing ahead, and his own leap to the sidewalk
ended abruptly against a policeman.

—Just slow down buddy.

—That's not him.

—Okay buddy move along.

—What do you mean move along, I want to get into the building and
you're standing right in the . . .

—Just slow down buddy, slow down . . .

Beyond them a furred croup of ursine magnitude emerged from the cavernous shelter of the limousine. —Look what the hell is . . .

—Just move along I said.

He caught the glass weight of the outside door without a look back, caught a rise and fall of yellow skirting another stolid mass of blue toward the elevators, called —Carol . . . ?

—Oh Mister Eigen good morning . . . arms full, she stayed the elevator door with a hip, —you back?

Reaching across her for the button he muttered —Yes don't tell anybody, rising to Begin the Beguine.

—Oh Mister Eigen you're always so satirical.

—Listen just tell me what's all the . . .

—It's all this plant food, she said breasting the bundles as the door slid open, —Miss Flesch sent me out for all this plant food. Coming? She had the door with a hip.

—Wait it's the wrong floor it, wait . . . he stepped out behind her, —that painting, the big painting that was there . . .

—Oh you missed all the excitement Mister Eigen, right after you left they took it down, you know? And this crazy man came in yelling at everybody where was it? He was bigger than you, we had the police here and everything, they even said he threw a typewriter at Mister Beaton.

—Is that what all those police are down there for now? he came up beside her down the corridor.

—And they even have these private detectives that come in every day, like that one with the hat by the elevators? I think they have this board meeting this morning and they're scared he'll come back, he looked like he didn't shave for a month. Miss Flesch said he's psychiatrically unbalanced but he really acted crazy, you know?

—Yes just, Carol wait listen this woman this, this Miss Flesch, is she here? I mean, she's been hired?

—Yes didn't you meet her Mister Eigen? When she first . . .

—Yes I met her, I . . . he'd paused at an opened door, —where's Mister Davidoff.

—I don't know he didn't come in today Mister Eigen, like he didn't come in almost since you left, oh and Miss Flesch wants to see you but there's somebody in there with her now, this same man that got mugged in the . . .

—Yes all right Carol, thanks . . . He'd reached his own door and paused outside it, staring at the dirt rowed in conical heaps the length of the desk there. —Good morning Florence, what . . .

—Oh good morning Mister Eigen, are you back? She half turned, over a shoulder —Miss Flesch just wanted me to repot these plants . . . she wiped her hands on a cloth and reached over the dirt heaps for the ringing phone —I think she wants to see you when you come in but, hello . . . ? Yes he is, just a minute . . .

He got in to his own cleared desk, got the phone, —Hello? Jack . . . ? No by the dishrack in the kitchen, I put two tens right there by the dishrack, listen . . . Yes I know you do but listen, Schepperman's off again, that big painting here of his I told you about, he came in here while I was away and . . . No the one I told you about last night, the mural size thing of his they had out here in the lobby, they took it down and . . . I did tell you about it last night but look that's not the point, he came in here and really raised hell when he didn't see it and this place here is like an armed camp, if he shows up here again they . . . No just to find him and keep him out of trouble, I'm going to tour the White Roses as soon as I can get out of here and, just a second, Carol?

—I just brought you some coffee Mister Eigen, you looked like you can use it.

—Thanks just, yes just put it there, Jack? I thought you could look for him in some of those places down . . . no I know it but the first race isn't till one o'clock is it? You can . . . what? What idea you had last night, all you talked about was . . . No all you talked about last night were these two horses look if . . . no but look Jack if you'd had an idea last night that would make a million dollars I'd remember the, just a second, what's all this Florence?

—The pictures and captions for the Annual Report Mister Eigen, Miss Flesch wants to know if . . .

—Yes just a second Florence, Jack . . . ? What do you mean something to do with Baby Jeeter, just a second, Carol?

—Mister Eigen there's this young man waiting to see you Mister Gall, he says Miss Flesch said that you'd . . .

—Just tell him to wait a minute, I . . . what? No what about what suitcase . . . ? No look never mind it whatever it is, I have to get off the . . . Yes by the dishrack, I told you I'd left two tens by the . . . no in the kitchen where the hell else would the . . . the dishrack in the kitchen yes . . . Yes if I remember your idea I'll write it down, yes . . . No I told you there were clean shirts in that suitcase in by the bed look Jack I have to get off, call me later . . . he hung up. —Who's this waiting Carol?

—This Mister Gall Mister Eigen, he's this writer friend of this man that's in with Miss Flesch and he says she said Mister Davidoff said he had some project he . . .

—Yes all right send him in, now what's all this again Florence?

—The pictures for the Annual Report Mister Eigen, Mister Davidoff had some airbrush work done on them and had a set sent out to those schoolchildren but Miss . . .

—Just tell her I'm still working on the captions, Mister Gall? Come in and, Carol where's my other chair.

—Oh I'm sorry Mister Eigen I think Miss Flesch borrowed it to put some plants . . .

—Well see if there's another one out there someplace will you? Sorry . . . he reached across to shake hands, —things seem to be . . .

—No that's all right that's all right I, but are you, you're not the Thomas Eigen? Because I, I mean there was no picture of you on the jacket of your book so I . . .

—I didn't want one I, I'm just surprised that you . . .

—No I always wanted to meet you but I guess I, I mean I'm just surprised to suddenly meet you in an office like this, oh thank you . . . he pulled the chair through the door, bent to brush the dirt off the seat. —I wrote to you the first time I read it, in care of the publisher I guess you never got it but I think it's the most important book I, one of the most important books in American literature and I, since I'm a writer I mean trying to be a writer I . . .

—Well it's nice of you to say that . . . he tipped his own chair back, caught the edge of the file drawer with the sole of his shoe and pulled it out far enough to prop his feet up on it, —a million more like you and I'd be . . .

—But you must have known when you were writing it, you must have known you were writing it for a very small audience, I . . .

—Small audience! his feet dropped, —do you think I would have worked on it for seven years just for, do you know what my last royalty check was Mister . . .

—Gall, I . . .

—Mister Gall? Fifty-three dollars and fifty-two cents, the publisher dropped it cold the day it came out he must think I wrote it for a very small audience too.

—Yes I know I . . .

—I get letters from college kids who have it assigned in their courses, they must be passing one copy around. If he'd let me have the rights back do you think I'd be sitting here now?

—Yes I know, I mean I've been working on a Western I can finish if I can get an advance on this book about cobalt or whatever it is for your company, then with the final payment on the Western I'll be able to get far enough on the cobalt book to collect the second payment and settle things with this Foundation where they're handing out grants to novelists who want to write plays and I . . .

—Yes I've been working on a play myself . . . he tilted back, got his feet up on the file drawer again —I think I . . .

—Yes well to get a grant you have to be a novelist not a playwright but you have to be writing a play not a novel, I've applied for that under the name Jim Blake because that's the name I wrote another Western novel under called Guns of God and if I can change the novel I'm working on now into a play for just long enough to get a grant I . . .

—It's good discipline yes, the play I'm working on now in fact, it started as a novel, sent the first chapter and an outline in to this publisher and got back a fatuous five page . . .

—Yes well before I knew about these fourteen thousand dollar grants I'd already taken a job from another part of the same Foundation to write a book on school television for a lousy five thousand dollars. I worked on that while I was living on the advance I got for this Western and when I took it in half finished I thought I'd use that payment to go back and finish the Western, and then the Foundation just canceled the whole thing. I've been trying to reach the man in charge of it there ever since but it's like trying to reach Klamm in The Castle, he's always busy, always out, never returns a call and now their comptroller's after me for a five hundred dollar expense advance, I told him I'll settle it when they settle with me on the book but he says it's a different kind of money and I . . .

—Like to meet just one of them who'd come right out and say he's really in it for the money, this publisher of mine names himself a six-figure salary I've heard he's written three novels himself, finally hid them in a drawer when his own poor God damn editors read them and had to plead with him not to publish them so Christ awful they were afraid he'd embarrass the whole, yes Carol?

—Mister Eigen Miss Flesch wants to know if you . . .

—Look just tell her I'm talking to Mister Gall about this book project, she . . .

—Yes well this friend of mine who's in there talking to her now is taking over the old publishing house he's been working for, if he gets the contract for this book about cobalt and I can get an advance from him on it and get back to this play I . . .

—Yes just a second, Florence?

—Mister Eigen, Miss Flesch wants to know where the . . .

—Look just, never mind damn it . . . his feet came down, —can't get a damn thing done here . . .

—I've already written the first act, came on behind him toward the door, —but somebody who read it said the trouble with it is my main character . . . pursued him to the dirt heaps, stopped short by the voice from the half opened door ahead.

—It's teachers that make the problems the kids have a ball, all the a v equipment tapes films textbooks slides all that stuff and junk, Carol? Will somebody out there pick up my phone? So when they called I told them what he told me once this product integration followthrough from cable to closed-circuit broadcast with the packaged a v software to go with it Florence did Carol pick up my phone? You have public relations whether you want them or not and I told him PRwise it can't hurt the company imagewise the medium and the message and all that bla bla bla but he said we couldn't get corporate support for all this publishing stuff and junk without support from the company and all they're talking about now is budgets and all that bla bla bla, Carol? Was that the Times calling back Florence?

—It's Mister Beaton's office Miss Flesch, they want . . .

—Omigosh is Mister Eigen out there Florence? Will you see what they want?

—They want copies of any news releases on the educational . . .

—Florence is Mister Eigen out there? ask him where's that news release on all this educational stuff and, Carol? Is Carol out there Florence?

—Mister Eigen Miss Flesch wants to know if you . . .

—Look Florence I'm standing right here, I'll get a copy.

—Hello Miss Bulcke? Yes Carol will bring it right in . . .

—Anyway he said the trouble's my main character coming right on stage and telling all about himself before anybody in the audience is interested in him at all and I . . .

—Thank you Mister Eigen . . . and he straightened from his file drawer to watch her out the door, out of sight up the corridor where the shock of her heels alerted passing glances till blue carpeting stilled them, a door closed behind her and she rounded a corner. —Oh excuse me Governor! Gee sir I'm sorry . . . !

—All right, 'ts all right . . . he listed, gathered way again.

—Gee I'm sorry sir . . . she backed off, backed as far as the sentry desk —Miss Bulcke here's this news release you just . . .

—Yes thank you Carol, good morning Governor we didn't expect the pleasure of seeing you out of the hospital today, is . . .

—Won't be a pleasure for some people, anybody here yet?

—Mrs Selk is right here in Mister Beaton's office sir and . . .

—Blaufinger here yet?

—No sir . . . she got ahead of him for the door, —General Blaufinger called to say he . . .

—When he shows up let him wait in the board room, Stamper gets here bring him right in.

—Yes sir. Excuse me, Mister Beaton . . . ?

—But he didn't hit me ma'am he simply shook me by the lapels and, excuse me . . .

—Excuse me Mister Beaton the news releases you wanted and Governor Cates is here . . .

—I said I wanted him arrested and put in prison.

—Usual gracious self Zona, what poor bastard you putting in prison now.

—What poor bastard, the poor bastard who's been sneaking around selling paintings to ninnies to hang in office lobbies while he lives on my money and Beaton sits here with his thumb in his ass and blubbers about a lawsuit.

—Excuse me sir you can sit right here when I, move this . . . he'd parted his paired shoes and got round his desk to struggle the folds of fur into an armload and start across the room with it.

—Beaton if you can't carry it don't drag it.

—Not a damn carnival worker Zona, expect him to carry a tent like that Beaton just sit down and . . .

—If he wasn't such a little pissant he would have charged this ape with assault and put him in prison where he belongs. You just said he grabbed your lapels and shook you Beaton, isn't that assault?

—Legally yes ma'am with competent witnesses but it seemed more prudent . . . he'd reached his desk again and paused to get breath, —in light of the unpleasant publicity that could result it seems more prudent simply to start an action rising from your original agreement, with private detectives on the lookout for him if he should appear in this vicinity and attempt to . . .

—I'll tell you where he is right now, he's breaking into my Saybrook house and stealing every painting of his he can lay his hands on and I want . . .

—Told you not to store them up there in the first place Zona, dampness ruin all the damn frames now Beaton sit down and be quiet, some things I want you to clear up before this board meeting.

—Just hold your water John, he can clear them up when he's cleared this up, I want . . .

—Zona don't give a damn what you want, Beaton's not your black girl he's secretary and general counsel of this company and he can't drop everything just to . . .

—Yes Beaton what about her, I can't be expected to get along without her this way and I want . . .

—Yes ma'am Deleserea, we've located her and I have a call in to Judge Ude's office to arrange bail but she refuses to cooperate regarding the diamond brooch and it appears we . . .

—What diamond brooch, what are you babbling about now.

—When you reported her missing ma'am, I understood you to connect her disappearance with a diamond brooch you believed she . . .

—Don't be ridiculous Beaton I found that in my steam cabinet weeks ago, if that's all they're holding her for I want her back by lunchtime.

—As a matter of fact ma'am she was originally arrested at a bus stop and charged with soliciting, it's that charge we intend . . .

—Beaton don't be ridiculous who would want to hump Deleserea, you just get the lead out of your ass and have her back by lunchtime.

—Yes ma'am in, incidentally have you notified the insurance company the brooch has been recovered . . .

—That's your job Beaton I don't know what makes you think . . .

—Yes ma'am but of course I was unaware that . . .

—By God Zona that's not his job his job right now's this board meeting and if you want to bring up your black girl you . . .

—You brought her up I didn't, and you brought me all the way in here this morning to do something about Boody's shares didn't you?

—Wasn't for social reasons Zona you can be damn sure of that, talk about this damn fool law lowers the age of minors from twenty-one to eighteen could give Boody and all these young hooligans the right to make contracts and all the rest of it, safe enough in jail right now but if this tender offering for Diamond doesn't go through while you're still her guardian no telling what she . . .

—Excuse me sir I thought you must have seen the pictures in the paper of Miss ah, of Boody's . . .

—If you expect to see those two hundred thousand shares go the way you want them this morning John you can just hold your water. The agreement Beaton drew up for me with this painter has seven years to run and if you think I broke my ass for a corner in his work so he could go out and peddle it on the side while he's living on my money Beaton how much did the company pay for that atrocity.

—Twelve thousand dollars ma'am the actual purchase was . . .

—Would have been a damn fool to turn it down too, seen monkeys do better.

—If he thinks he can get prices like that on his own he can kiss mine, isn't that right here in the agreement Beaton?

—Yes ma'am not ah, yes not precisely in those words of course but . . .

—Both cheeks, if he tries it again while this agreement's in effect I'll dump his work at prices that wouldn't open a pay toilet and he'll stand outside trying to sell one till his back teeth float. Where's that twelve thousand now Beaton, if it's anybody's it's mine and I want . . .

—Yes ma'am of course when you recovered the painting itself we sought to recover the purchase price for the company by locating his bank account and attaching the balance but it appears to amount to less than eight thousand dollars, I understand he bought a ah, an abandoned roller coaster which of course we intend to attach as soon as we can locate it but . . .

—Beaton by God Zona you think I left that hospital to come in here and attach roller coasters? Got Blaufinger coming to sit in on this board meeting'll want to get things cleaned up in Gandia, Stamper out there wants to know what the devil's holding up his pipeline consortium, peace group breaking windows down at the bank and now this damn nonsense in the papers about Typhon grabbing the education market with this Diamond tender hanging fire and you're attaching abandoned roller coasters? See all this Beaton . . . ? Streamers of newspaper were appearing from inside folds, —monopoly, the medium and the message, tell me what the devil it's all about?

—Last night's paper yes sir apparently this news release sent out by Mister Davidoff just before he . . .

—Don't sit there waving it give it to me.

—And stop changing the subject Beaton I want to know how that ape got in here and sold you ninnies that painting in the first place.

—Yes ma'am I believe he was discovered by Mis . . .

—You're telling me who discovered him Beaton? when I found his big one man show with one painting sold and offered half off for the lot they grabbed it because he didn't have a pot to piss in, don't you dare try to tell me he was discovered by miss anybody.

—No ma'am I simply meant the purchase of this particular painting, it was arranged by Mister Davidoff who seems to have been the only person in actual contact with . . .

—I want him arrested too.

—What the devil's all this Beaton don't make head or tail of it, damn nonsense about an iceberg and a two edge sword.

—Yes sir I gather the press had a similar reaction and when they queried our public relations department for particulars . . .

—Department? Thought he was the whole department.

—No sir apparently he'd begun to engage in a little empire building by hiring a woman he described as having a topflight record in curriculum management a few days before he . . .

—What the devil'd he want her for, they got anybody else in that department?

—No sir only a writer, appar . . .

—Well who the devil's this woman.

—According to the personnel file sir she was recommended by Duncan and Company's head of sales a Mister Skinner in connection with this book project, I have the memorandum here on the . . .

—Don't sit there waving it give it to me, told you one business we're not going broke in's the damn book business didn't I? Looked over their operating statement paying ten percent for overhead, ten for their money, ten for warehousing ten for sales and jobbers ten for these damn royalties, bookstore steps in takes fifty off the top sends back what it don't sell leaves you with a wish in one hand and here, what's this their list?

—Those are the titles on their spring trade list yes sir, they . . .

—Who the devil wrote balls in the margin here, crossed out and somebody wrote in, what is it? Round objects . . . ?

—Who do you think wrote balls in the margin, I'd like to know who crossed it out.

—I, I did ma'am I substituted round ob . . .

—Well who the devil's Round and what does he object to.

—Beaton if you cross out something of mine again I'll have you by the round objects if you've got any, these writers Vida collects follow her around with their noses so far up between the cheeks they can't see what they're putting on paper, look at that list.

—Yes ma'am but the, I agree the titles sound somewhat unpromising but the . . .

—See what you can get for a nickel in a used book store why any damn fool wants to add another one to the heap, cut out that ten percent royalty these scoundrels grab they might see a little daylight.

—Yes sir however in this case aside from their reliable textbook area, the majority of titles on the Duncan backlist appear in most college syllabuses and were originally negotiated on most satisfactory terms paying next to no royalties on reprints. I assume this was a determining factor in this Skinner person's decision to set up his own company to buy up the Duncan stock if some arrangement can be made with the bank as corporate trustee following your wish to . . .

—Only damn reason we took it on was a favor, we're not in the book business we're not in the damn public relations business either, we've got Frank Black's office down there handing out canned editorials to every hick paper in the country's all we need and I want anybody who had anything to do with this medium and the message damn foolishness out of here, hear me? Already told them down at the bank any damn fool who shows up wants to go broke in the book business give him a hundred thousand dollar cash option on this Duncan stock, thirty days to raise it and the balance on future earnings if they've got any, can't waste any more damn time on it if Vida don't like those terms she can get a new banker.

—Vida's a silly bitch, raising a million dollars to preserve the spots where our great American works of art were created she just wants her picture in the paper with those red rimmed . . .

—Well by God Zona . . .

—Every writer and halfass American painter and composer she can dig up preserving a lot of filthy garrets so she can get her picture in the paper with those red rimmed eyes staring out like two angry . . .

—By God Zona that any worse than you on television taking every damn fool in the country on that tour of your childhood home? Get it declared a national landmark and you've got a whole corps of army engineers down there in Virginia right now diverting a river to save it, had to move a whole damn town and you talk about Vida's picture in the paper, now what's all the rest of this . . . the newspaper streamers passed in a flourish, —even got that damn Foundation in here.

—Yes I saw that sir, of course the speculation relating your interests in Typhon and Diamond Cable to your connection with City National is hardly a surprise, even though the suggestion that your bank directors who also serve on the Foundation board encouraged expanded Foundation support for closed-circuit school tele . . .

—Damn bunch of sissies what they are, saw something in the papers while I was in the hospital about this little wop up in the legislature tabling your bill on mandatory closed-circuit broadcast for schools and they wet their damn pants, just some cheap construction scandal but they're all so damn scared of being brought up before some damn committee hearing they all ran the other direction, pulled the Foundation right out of school television and put it behind these damn public service community stations, ever see one Beaton? Programs every damn one of them about pollution or strip mining or some damn bunch of Indians nothing but a lot of damn leftwing propaganda and I want this little wop on one side of the fence or the other, sits up there calling the shots on this state banking committee and tables this school television bill to wait us out on the suburban banks see what we'll come up with.

—Yes sir of course I had no reason to feel he might be mistrusted on the mandatory closed-circuit bill at the time he was recommen . . .

—Damn it Beaton don't own them you can't trust them, I told you before I went in the hospital this last time I wanted a full report on that whole situation and now I read about him mixed up with some other wop in a construction scandal just be quiet Zona . . .

—Yes while Beaton sits here with his thumb in his . . .

—No sir I have the report right here in fact Governor and as far as Mister Pecci goes sir, it offers what can only be called an embarrassment of riches. Apparently Mister Pecci's wife recently . . .

—Get to it later if we have time, all I want clear before this meeting's how much his shenanigans and the rest of this nonsense in the paper had to do with a class action against Diamond Crawley said something about. This whole Diamond tender's taken one hell of a lot of putting together and I don't want to see some damn nuisance suit interfering with it.

—A, a what sir? I'm sorry sir I don't . . .

—A class action damn it Beaton, lawyer don't know what a class action is? Crawley said you and he'd discussed it some talk of settling now what the devil was there to it.

—Oh yes sir no, no that happened some time ago but I believe what Mister Crawley was referring to was a threatened stockholder's suit by, another inspiration of Mister Davidoff's sir, to have class six J threaten suit against the company as an exercise in corporate democracy in action I believe he described it, he . . .

—Damn it Beaton what are you talking about, class six J . . .

—Yes sir the class of schoolchildren Mrs Joubert brought in to buy a share of Diamond Cable stock as their share in America you may recall sir, she . . .

—She's a ninny.

—Just be quiet Zona what do you mean threatened a lawsuit.

—Always said Emily was a ninny, had her little pissants running all over the boardroom . . .

—No Mrs Joubert seemed quite unaware of this so-called suit sir, Mister Davidoff seems to have arranged it as a game to give the children a looksee at the system I believe he put it, a few corporate dollars to play with . . .

—What in hell do you mean corporate dollars to play with!

—Yes sir before I learned of any of this sir Mister Davidoff had settled this so-called suit for cash from his public relations budget, he was thoroughly unpleasant when I . . .

—Cash damn it Beaton how much cash!

—Eighteen hundred some odd dollars sir, he . . .

—Some odd dollars by God you can get every one of those some odd dollars right back out of his pay, damned . . .

—Yes sir but I thought you were aware he no longer . . .

—What damned excuse he could have for a stunt like this . . .

—Frankly sir with this and the attentions he gave her class for an Annual Report feature I felt he was trying to make an impression on Mrs Joubert . . .

—Same way that driveling Frenchman got into her pants, what are you doing about that.

—Done it. What's the latest quote on Nobili, Beaton.

—It opened at thirteen and a half sir, I haven't checked the . . .

—Tell Crawley start picking it up again at twelve, probably sold it short himself at about that, hear from Amy tell her we settled her lulu for her shouldn't have any more problems with him.

—Yes sir but she, didn't she get in touch with you sir?

—Been in the hospital damn it Beaton what do you . . .

—Yes sir I gave her that number, she'd apparently met Mister Crawley in the Metropolitan Art Museum and learned of this pressure being brought on Mister Joubert and became quite distraught . . .

—Must have been the Natural History Museum Beaton what the devil would Crawley want in the Metropolitan.

—Wherever it was she was quite frantic sir, alarmed at the way Mister Joubert might react to being pressed to the . . .

—Not a damn thing he can do to her now is there?

—No sir but her concern for Francis was extremely . . .

—Don't see what he can do there either, day she brought her class in here we tied up both those foundations so he couldn't touch either one of them with a ten foot pole, forgot the little lesson I gave you that day Beaton?

—No sir but right now I think her fears concerning Francis are what really. . .

—Better not forget it either, come up with another half-baked proposition like that when she comes in to sign this final set of papers on those two foundations we'll all go to the poorhouse and that fourth dividend, you keep your eye on the date hear me?

—Yes sir it's, excuse me. Hello . . . ?

—That's Stamper I told them to send him right in.

—It's Mister Cutler in Washington sir. Yes, hello? Dick?

—What's he doing down there.

—Yes just a minute. He went down to settle the details of this Endo Appliance divestiture with the Justice Department sir but apparently some question's just come up regarding . . .

—Here give me that . . . Cutler? What the devil's the problem down there . . . Yes I damn well am out of the hospital, spent another day there we'd all be out of business. What the devil's going on, this Endo nonsense should have been cleared up a month ago . . . Took title to the patents didn't we? Without them nothing left but a damn shell, last year's inventory and some lamebrain salesmen I know that, so does the Justice Department whole damn point . . . The what . . . ? Hasn't mentioned it no but . . . Well you tell them this whole damn thing was settled two months ago, they agreed not to give us any problem on this Diamond tender if we tied the can to the Endo outfit and that's . . . what do you mean some question . . . Course I saw the newspapers . . . Well you tell Frank Black I, wait damn it tell him myself. Beaton? Here, get me Frank Black.

—Yes sir . . .

—Put in a call to Monty too, damn nonsense about withdrawing this tender . . .

—Yes sir . . . Miss Bulcke? Yes get Frank Black please and then . . . yes and then put in a call to Mister Moncrieff . . .

—One newspaper headline they're ready to close shop, Beaton what the devil's this about irregularities in the Endo inventory.

—Yes I was going to mention that sir, apparently Mister Davidoff was making gifts from the inventory to . . .

—Just what the devil do you mean making gifts, to who.

—To various schools and institutions apparently sir, he . . .

—What in hell was he doing that for!

—I believe he felt it could be used to bring the attention of the press to the company's . . .

—The press! Bring the attention of the Justice Department the SEC and every damn leftwing politician looking for a headline, nothing left to that Endo outfit but its damn inventory he's giving away with one hand while we're complying with this Justice Department ruling to sell the company with the other, already jeopardized the Diamond tender with this damn fool news story tell me what in hell he thinks he's been doing?

—In his rather inflated notion of improving the corporate image he appears to have . . .

—This keeps up by God there won't be anything left but the damn image, who the devil gave him this kind of authority.

—In Mister Moncrieff's absence sir I believe he had the impression that he, in his own phrase that he was running the store.

—Running the, by God anybody ever run a store by giving away everything in it? Get him in here Beaton, see what else he's given away. And get Crawley, Frank Wiles, whoever's handling this Endo divestiture, find a buyer at any damn price they can get and just write off the rest, get rid of the whole thing and anybody connected with handing out its inventory before this whole deal with the Justice Department blows up in our faces. Get him in here, see what else he's given away damn it Zona just be quiet . . .

—But he's no longer with us sir he . . .

—Gives away the whole damn company and then quits? Where the devil is he.

—I understand he's joined a public relations agency sir but his departure was hardly . . .

—Lucky to get out of here with his hat and his ass and I want him arrested too Beaton. When he interfered with my workmen removing my painting to take to my house he went out of here ass over teakettle John, and Beaton I want him arrested.

—Yes ma'am if there were any possible grounds I'd be . . .

—You're a lawyer think of some grounds, do I have to do all your work for you? He arranged that purchase in direct violation of my contract with that ape of a painter and if that doesn't make him an accessory I don't know what does, Beaton if you can't have them both arrested and tried for conspiracy to defraud and sent to prison you'd better get off the pot because you're not doing anything on it and the next thing I . . .

—Yes ma'am excuse me, hello . . . ? Yes sir just a moment he's right here. It's Mister . . .

—Here give me that. Hello . . . ? Yes it is damn it put him on. Monty? What the devil's going on down there, just had a call from Cutler says Frank Black recommended withdrawing this tender offer for Diamond, had everything settled with Justice on this Endo divestiture and now he says you're afraid they . . . No just heard about it from Beaton, sounds like damn nonsense maybe gave a few stoves away but that don't . . . came down there to see you? What the devil did he think he could . . . No just a damn nuisance, no reason to . . . Broos said what . . . ? Well that's damn foolishness, call more attention to Typhon withdrawing this tender now than just letting things ride and the sooner we . . . threatened to what . . . ? What the devil's that got to do with it, not a damn thing wrong with that smelter contract whole thing was negotiated signed sealed and delivered before you left the company, get some leftwing politician in there threatens to try to lower the cobalt stockpile requirements not a damn thing to do with the government's contractual obligation to Typhon to buy every damn ounce of . . . Well what the devil's Broos doing on the Armed Services Committee, no damned reason he can't step in there and . . . Because management services are management services cost plus contract or any other kind, charge the government or anybody else for management services what's so damn . . . No damn it if Typhon wants to hire management services on this contract from Pythian whose damn business is . . . Monty damn it I know a plant can't be declared surplus and sold until it's built but why in hell we should hold up this Diamond Cable tender until . . . Don't see why that should call anybody's attention to anything, Pythian's interest in Typhon is nobody's damn business, got Blaufinger coming in here this morning and that whole situation in Gandia should be cleared up in a week or two, had Nowunda up there on the platform when Box gave the groundbreaking speech and

Doctor Dé declared the secession of Uaso province same night, Nowunda sending in troops but there's not a damn thing he . . . No, talked to him on the phone, won't see us intervening to support that red regime of Nowunda with all the . . . what . . . ? Yes worked so damn well even got peace groups wearing signs keep out of Gandia and Africa for Africans smashed a window down at the bank this morning, why the devil they always pick the bank about time we . . . No and I don't want to, got Blaufinger coming in here this morning let him get together with Frank Black on it, said something about small arms surplus shipment from Bonn and I don't want to know any more about it . . . What the devil we got Frank Black for highest paid damn lawyer in Washington . . . yes got a call in to him now, one more thing Stamper's going to steam in here any minute want to know whether we're still in this pipeline deal with him or not, still got that bunch of damn Indians camping out right in the middle of the . . . well you know Stamper he don't want easements he wants title free and clear, damn reservation spread out right in the middle of the . . . I told him that but this damn Senate Concurrent Resolution twenty-six disavowing termination's nothing but a damn resolution is it? not a damn law is it? That damn sheep state senator down there making all the . . . well get Broos on to him, I'll get Broos onto him. Beaton? Here, get hold of Broos for me.

—Yes sir excuse me, hello . . . ? Thank you, yes I'll . . .

—Here give me that.

—I'm sorry sir they say Mister Black just left for a meeting at the White . . .

—And Beaton while you're at it I want to know what you found out about that carload of . . .

—Zona damn it will you just let him . . .

—Yes ma'am excuse me a moment Governor regarding that Indian reservation lying directly in the . . .

—Beaton I said I want to know what you've done about that carload of niggers that parks right in front of my door on Beekman Place, I told you to report a stolen car a week ago and they were there yesterday big as life while you sit here with your . . .

—Zona damn it told him to get Broos on the phone Beaton what the devil you waiting for.

—Yes sir excuse me ma'am hello Miss Bulcke? Yes will you try to reach Senator Broos for the Governor please, we did trace the license ma'am but the car appears to belong to the United Nations Trade Commission from Malwi which has only one car it had not reported stolen, and since that is a DPL parking space reserved for cars bearing . . .

—Don't tell me it's a DPL parking space Beaton I paid good money to have it made a DPL parking space so Nick could pull in to the curb and I wouldn't have to wade through an acre of dogshit to get to my own front door, and if you think I believe stories about something called Malwi you . . .

—No but ma'am apparently it is a small emerging country in . . .

—Little country right there east of Gandia Zona about the size of Stamper's place, get all the labor for the mines there so damn poor'll work for peanuts, now Beaton what's this about . . .

—If you think I'm going to keep dancing around piles of dogshit to get to my own front door you'd better . . .

—Damn it Zona try to find some way to accommodate you now just be quiet, Beaton what's . . .

—Yes excuse me sir, hello . . . ? Oh yes he's right here sir just a minute. . .

—Here give me that. Broos? got Stamper steaming in here any minute called to find out what you . . . who? No damn it I'm not holding the phone to my bad ear haven't got a bad ear, what the devil you think I've been in the hospital for this time got two damn inner ear transplants, where . . . Work fine damn it did not think you sounded like Broos, just put a call in to him find out about that gang of Indians squatting in your way up there should have cleared them out twenty years ago, knew the eighty-third Congress couldn't last forever same way they cleaned up the Klamaths and the Menomi, who? Who, Beaton . . . ? No Beaton's sitting right here hasn't said a damn thing to me about it he . . . What in hell you still down there for board meeting thought you wanted to clear up JMI and these Dallas mortgages . . . No, no didn't know that no, what kind of tissue damage . . . In beer? know you do but it sounds like damn foolishness, got Handler putting me back in next week myself wants to implant a damn heart pacer things keep up this way I . . . if Beaton's what . . . ? Hasn't said a damn thing about that either so damn busy running errands for Zona . . . sitting right here yes . . .

—If that's Charley I'll tell his doctors where he got his tissue damage.

—Sends his regards Zona says if you've taken off a hundred pounds since he saw you he'll introduce you to some of his friends.

—Tell him if that showgirl he just married bent over and spread her cheeks his doctors could all . . .

—Into what? What the devil'd you want him looking into that for, sold at around forty back before the war hasn't been traded for years, last I heard deficits running over half a million whole damn thing was . . . Way their tax liens were piling up don't see how they even held onto a few rights of way, ought to pick the whole thing up for a plugged nickel I'll get Beaton going on it . . . Said what? by God anybody knows about these damn mining claims you should not worth the paper they're written on, hasn't said a damn thing to me about any development company either damn busy running errands for . . . No hell get Broos on it do a little logrolling with that old what's his name sheep state senator been in since McKinley came right around last time on that damn waste dumping bill must have something to . . . Write the whole thing off don't be a damn fool think the bank finances a consortium like this expects it to be written off? Just want to hold off on any merger talk till this Diamond tender's straightened out calling Crawley now to withdraw it until . . . want him to call you where . . . ? No what the devil you burning them down for . . . No sitting right here hasn't said a damn thing about any movie film no . . . no be at the bank later call me there, here Beaton and don't take any more calls till you straighten things out here, Stamper says you cleared up his damn Indian tribe why the devil didn't you tell me.

—Yes sir I've been, I believe we'll have no difficulty proving that this particular Indian reservation is not really a reservation as per treaty, appar . . .

—What the devil they all doing camping out there then.

—Yes sir apparently they were removed to this present site around the turn of the century from their original reservation further to the east where substantial deposits of limestone and gypsum had attracted the attention of the cement industry. Our sources say that any claims they might have had through any treaty involving that earlier reservation can be proved without validity regarding these lands they now occupy and that any attempt they might make to obstruct the . . .

—Point is Stamper don't just want easements through there Beaton says he could come in hind tit on the whole deal unless he owns drilling rights and all the rest of it lock stock and barrel and with us banking it can't take any damn chance.

—Of course sir once the treaty matter is determined and the lands recovered by the government their outright purchase can be arranged immediately through the Bureau of . . .

—Get onto it then don't dawdle like you have with this damn Alberta and Western Stamper told you to look into, on their last legs twenty years ago should have had the whole thing signed sealed and delivered for him by now, Zona where the devil you going, don't want that meeting to start till Blaufinger shows up.

—Do I need your permission to go take a . . .

—Sit still Beaton she can get there herself get back to business here.

—Yes sir I've looked into this for Mister Stamper and it appears that just recently this Alberta and Western Power Company was victimized in a scheme of pyramided debenture issues and falsely optimistic earnings forecasts in preparation for merger with this so called Ace Development Company which had of course been set up by the same operators. They had already doubled its ten cent issuing price in a simple buy-back scheme and evidently planned the merger with Alberta . . .

—By God Beaton how many damn millions already tied up in that pipeline deal Stamper sitting on those tar shale deposits up there and you're talking penny stock frauds? Stick them in jail and get on with things.

—Yes sir I understand the SEC has brought mail fraud charges against one of the principals, a Mister Wall, and the man who posed as underwriter is being sought. The problem seems to be in dealing with the interests that bought heavily into both sides of the scheme, the debentures and the development company stock, with the obvious intention of seizing what assets there are when the scheme collapsed, these scattered power company sites and rights of way and the extensive mineral exploration claims that are causing Mister Stamper to . . .

—Well damn it who are they, what the devil's all this . . .

—A report I was putting together from our various sources I thought you might want to review whenever . . .

—Damn it Beaton haven't got time to go through this mess, this the people we're talking about?

—One of them yes sir, this appeared in an upstate newspaper during their takeover of an ailing textile firm called Eagle . . .

—Couple of blacks, are they?

—No I think not sir that, I believe that's simply the poor quality of the photocopy, the one on the left there, a Mister . . .

—Yes Bast damn it I can read Beaton, what the devil'd you get all this trash together for, nickel and dime takeover of a broken down mill only damn thing it's good for's a tax umbrella.

—Yes sir they appear to have made immediate use of its pension fund to acquire a midwestern brewery with very favorable earnings and an attractive undistributed dividends situation, more recently they snapped up a producer of matchbooks whose financial position appears considerably less secure and any long-range plan in their expansion program is somewhat difficult to . . .

—Only damn plan sounds like grab whatever they can get their damn hands on, what else they picked up.

—These are the only completed acquisitions according to our sources sir although a new nursing home issue just rose considerably on rumors of a merger, and we understand they're showing considerable interest in a company called Ray-X which manufactures a variety of battery driven and transistorized . . .

—Management a bunch of damn fools came into the bank last year got themselves tied up hand and foot with government fixed price contracts rising costs didn't know where the devil their operating expenses were coming from should have stayed in toys, started in toys should have stayed in toys. Any damn fool acquires that outfit deserves it, anything else?

—Nothing tangible sir, they do appear to have conducted talks with a privately held chain of funeral homes and I understand are on the lookout for a large cash reservoir like Hartford Fire Insurance or one of the large savings and loan associations, in my most recent information they also appear to have just begun to hedge in commodity futures and . . .

—Keep that up they'll go to jail where they belong, show me any damn corporate charter allows you to . . .

—No sir I meant the principals individually sir, the . . .

—Who this, this what's his name Bast? Looks like he wouldn't know an eight percent debenture from a pork belly damned amateurs don't know the rules come in and ruin the whole damn game for everybody.

—Yes sir apparently they . . .

—Only damn reason they lined up this takeover of these damn mining claims and power company sites to hold up Stamper for anything they can question's where the devil they're getting their information, pipeline's the best kept damn secret since the bomb want all this cleared up damn fast Beaton.

—Yes sir on the other hand it occurred to me they might be acting from some less aggressive motive, according to our sources some timber cutting seems to have begun in the region of these mining claims, with the acquisition of this matchbook producer they may simply have been seeking a dependable source of wood pulp or even cellulose, with the idea of converting their Eagle Mills facilities to the production of synthetic . . .

—Wish I thought they were that damn stupid market's so glutted with imports hardly give the stuff away, damn it ever occur to you to get hold of Frank Wiles see what he knows about them?

—Yes I have sir, in fact he appears to have already handled a few limited transactions for them and apparently Mister Crawley is in sporadic contact with this Mister Bast, who would appear to serve the function of executive officer for operations . . .

—Well by God Beaton everybody in town knows them but you? ever occur to you to pick up the damn telephone get hold of them yourself find what the devil they're up to?

—Yes sir I did approach one of their attorneys on the Alberta and Western matter, a man named Piscator who was hardly cooperative and sounded somewhat ah, unsavory, he said he would speak to his boss but apparently left immediately for Jamaica and . . .

—All you damn lawyers ever do is speak to each other, any damn reason you can't speak to his boss? go straight to this Bast or whoever he's . . .

—Yes sir I've called Mister Bast a number of times at a number given me by Mister Crawley but the secretary who answers sounds, frankly sir she sounds like she'd never got past fourth grade, Mister Bast always seems to have just stepped away from his desk and has never returned a call. Another number given me by this Piscator person for Mister Bast's uptown headquarters office is evidently incorrect, a young lady who answered told me to ah, simply replied with an obscenity and hung up, the only other number I've been given proved to be a pay telephone somewhere on Long Island and . . .

—Say you think this Bast's their executive officer who the devil's running things.

—Yes sir that's the number that proved to be the pay telephone, their organization seems to be so elusive that even the heads of their newly acquired divisions are of no help, in fact the president of X-L Lithography whose name I don't recall sounded like he might have been drinking and the man who appears to be in charge of Eagle Mills seemed grateful to find someone to complain to, apparently some union trouble has risen over the removal of some looms and this brewery acquisition met prominent stockholder opposition, although his main concern seemed to be for a softball team which . . .

—Damn it Beaton stir things up a little up there bring the whole damn umbrella down around their ears.

—Yes sir that occurred to me but I learned that immediately after taking over Eagle they made a substantial management loan which would have to be called if they were deposed, since they represent the management to whom the loan was made, and of course Eagle Mills is in no position to . . .

—Got them by the short hair . . . The white handkerchief came unfurling from the breast pocket and burst as though caught on a sudden gust, —maybe not so damn stupid at that . . . and he blew, hard. —First thing I want cleaned up's these damn mining claims Beaton get Frank Black's office on it find out if they're worth the damn paper they're written on, this outfit's in there on mineral exploration just to cut timber get hold of Monty, Interior serve them with an injunction maybe they'll be ready to do business, when Broos calls get him onto that old sheep state what the devil's his name, whole thing right out there in his neighborhood . . .

—Senator Milliken yes sir, in fact according to our sources they already appear to be in contact with him, it appears that certain sheep membranes play a part in brewery filtration processes which . . .

—Milliken by God that's the one, nose up under the buffalo's tail closer than that damn Indian's smell a nickel a mile away, damn it Beaton trip on this nickel and dime outfit wherever we step I want the whole story on them hear me . . . ? and the handkerchief spread open as though for contemplation of its contents crumpled abruptly, —report like this just a lot of damn newspaper clippings I want facts Beaton, facts.

—Yes sir as soon as we've established their telephones I'd intended asking your authorization to . . .

—Don't ask my authorization damn it Beaton don't tell me what you're doing just do it, here give me that . . . hello? Broos . . . ? Who . . . ? No no wait a minute here Beaton take this, make it short.

—Yes sir. Hello . . . ? Oh, oh yes go ahead . . . yes you mean this just happened? was the boy's . . . Yes but was the boy's mother aware of

. . . No I'd better get in touch with her myself I think she may be quite
upset, thank you for calling immediately . . .

—What the devil's going on up there now.

—They said Mister Joubert simply came up to the school this morning and took Francis out and drove him away, I'm sure Mrs Joubert will
be extremely . . .

—By God of all the damn, get the police on him.

—Yes sir I'll apply for a court order immediately I know Mrs Joubert
was apprehensive about him taking the boy to Switzerland during our
negotiations over Nobili and . . .

—Damn fool thought we'd let him hold us up on Nobili to protect
these U S drug patents . . .

—Yes Beaton where's my Bananx.

—Coming back to join us Zona just pull up a pew and be quiet, what
the devil's she talking about Beaton.

—Yes I have it right here ma'am it's a tranquillizer marketed by our
drug interest sir, one of the . . .

—One they had us up on that patent fraud charge for?

—Tranylcypromine yes sir, one of the monoamine-oxidase inhibitors
included in the . . .

—Beaton just give it to me and don't sit there with your . . .

—Drag in here just to get it free Zona knew you were cheap by God
didn't know you were that cheap, Beaton still have a minute here get
back to that little wop up in the legislature . . .

—Yes that folder right there sir he . . .

—No Beaton I said put it there with my coat and John just hold your
water if you still have a bladder to hold it in, sitting there like a windup
toy with somebody else's eyes and somebody else's ears and try to tell me
what I . . .

—Beaton Zona damn it be quiet Beaton sit down, saw all this trash
in the newspapers one wop throws another one a few highway contracts
gets him a few building variances nickel and dime politics hope you don't
call this information.

—No sir except insofar as these variances have affected mortgages
issued by the local bank which now appears to be in severe difficulties
over these and other unwise extensions of credit, including an unsecured
loan to the contractor in question who our sources inform us has recently
had recourse to a loan shark to satisfy this and the prospect of several
lawsuits which threaten to . . .

—Banker there sounds like a damn fool.

—That would be my impression yes sir, I am also informed he appears to have made a gift of a substantial number of the bank's shares to
the wife of this Mister Pecci possibly in connection with a corporation
formed in both their wives' names to collect fees under contract with the
same contractor under a leasing arrangement involving the local town

dock, though since Mister Pecci's association with the title company set up by his law firm specifically to insure the affected mortgages seems to be sub . . .

—Bank still hold them all?

—No sir they appear to have been bought as an investment by a teachers' union which this current publicity has prompted to bring pressure on . . .

—Not too damn much to go after him with, scandal probably be gone the minute the damn leftwing press finds a new one to take its place, legislature get up and give him a vote of confidence all doing the same damn thing his wife's bank stock may be the only leverage we've got.

—Yes sir of course if that became known, aside from probable grand jury proceedings merely the rather dubious ethics involved could severely injure his campaign for the . . .

—Not talking about any damn ethics Beaton talking about the price of the damn stock, bank going under might see the only damn way to save it's let us bail them out, pass this legislation and the damn fool running the bank will probably take any offer we make him.

—Yes sir though the possibility of his also stipulating a management contract could . . .

—First damn head to fall get him something in Washington if we have to, this bank merger bill ready for the legislature?

—Yes sir I incorporated your changes in the earlier version and sent a copy to your office by messenger this morning before I . . .

—Get Frank Wiles on this bank stock put some pressure on it.

—Yes sir I, excuse me . . . hello? Oh yes thank you. General Blaufinger is in the board room sir, and there was one more urgent item concerning the Senate vote tomorrow affirming support for continued importation of nickel and the native platinum metals from Gandia in the face of yesterday's United Nations resolution supporting the stand of the Nowunda . . .

—Broos calls tell him to call Frank Black settled it with him last night get my arm here Beaton . . .

—Yes sir . . .

—Reminds me Stamper's heart tissue damage doctors tell him some damn government study shows maybe caused by cobalt brewers been using to get a head on beer, great damn beer drinker Stamper want you to get onto that little Jew down in the FDA find out what damn it let go of me . . .

—Yes sir but, excuse me but wouldn't it serve Mister Stamper better to go directly to the National Institutes of Health for the . . .

—Not Stamper's damn heart Beaton point's where the damn cobalt's coming from use it as an additive or find it in the water, find some damn brewery using water where it occurs could mean a deposit around somewhere last thing we need right now some damn fool coming up with that.

Call Crawley about this Diamond tender tell him Stamper's trying to reach him about some damn fool movie they're making, sent Monty a memo on it says they want to shoot hippies in the National Parks probably even the damn Interior Department can't issue permits for that.

—Yes sir I saw a copy of the memo and I believe that was a typographical error sir, I saw the film and their intention appears to be to shoot hippos . . .

—Just tell him call Stamper back in his car, riding around down there burning down all his guest houses been trying to reach Crawley all morning.

—Yes sir in fact I called Mister Crawley myself earlier but was told he was in his bath . . .

—What the devil you call him at home for.

—No sir this was his office he . . .

—Beaton you call Crawley tell him what I told you to about Nobili and this damn Endo divestiture tell him we're holding up this Diamond Cable tender and this time call him at his office and don't tell me he's in his damn bath hear me? While you're at it call Ude's office find out where this damn law stands gives eighteen-year-olds majority rights, safe enough in that Greek jail but as long as this tender's held up I want to be damn sure where her shares stand in case, what . . .

—No excuse me sir just that large folder there I, I thought you must have seen these pictures of her release in the papers sir . . .

—Release by God thought these Greeks gave a damn stiff sentence for drugs.

—Give me that Beaton.

—Yes ma'am it's quite heavy yes sir that was Nepal sir, this time she was charged with transporting incendiary bombs across the border and when our embassy there called Mister Moncrieff to intervene he . . .

—Monty? Comes in throwing bombs you tell me Monty fixed it like a traffic ticket by God Beaton . . .

—No no sir not directly she, the objects she was carrying proved to be ah, items of feminine hygiene whose nature and use the Greek customs examiner was unfamiliar with in his ah, in his limited experience sir, they apparently resembled incendiary cylinders fitted with fuses and . . .

—Perfect pigs look at them, surfacing from a fun stay in the Greek islands with her constant companion on the BP circuit these days, tawny sitar-playing . . .

—Don't have any damn shirt on, who's the nigger with her.

—I understand he's a young musician from India sir, he . . .

—The same one she's stretched out here naked with, how do you like his . . .

—By God Beaton told you to keep a file on Boody don't mean you have to buy every smut sheet in town.

—No sir this appeared in a leading fashion magazine sir she, here I'm sorry ma'am I'll pick them up let me get the door sir . . .

—Anything new on Freddie, Beaton?

—No sir he was out again late last week and apparently eluded his attendants for most of a day but . . .

—Devil's this back here looks like a bus sign.

—A New York City bus sign yes sir, since its meaning is clearly unintelligible I expect to use it in court to support Deleserea's contention that rather than soliciting she was merely asking passersby for dir . . .

—I want her back by lunchtime Beaton and I want that carload of nig . . .

—Whole damn board waiting Zona probably all asleep in there, Beaton get on those phone calls hear me? While you're at it get that damn fool running that bank out there Whitefoot something like that Bulcke's got the number just see if he sounds ready to talk business once we get this little wop straightened out.

—Yes sir . . . and for a moment he appeared to cling to the doorknob for balance once he got it closed behind them before his own black shoes parted to tread by turn a breast, a face, Heiress in Bomb Plot, Andros viewed over tawny buttocks across the carpet to the desk where they drew close again and his hands briefly cradled his face before one dropped to the telephone. —Miss Bulcke I want you to place a call to Mister Crawley and another one to a bank executive with a name like Whitelaw the Governor says you have his number, out on Long . . . yes and Miss Bulcke I want you to try to reach Mrs Joubert it's quite urgent, I suppose the school where she's teaching would be the . . . yes and if I'm on another line when you reach her simply cut in and . . . yes simply say you have a call for me from Senator Broos . . . and his face was gone in his hands again until a button glowed. —Yes hello . . . ?

—Hello, hello . . .

—Paint dropping off the ceiling into my soup and I'm litigating with the landlord, I've brought suits against two publishers and Tuesday I have to go into small claims court for . . .

—Excuse me I have your call from Senator . . .

—Hello . . . ? Shirley what in the hell is . . . no I know it's a crossed line nobody I know'd be in small claims court, if Stamper's trying to get through stay on it and then come in here and fix these electrodes, just hang this up for me there will you Bast? Six thousand shares of phone company stock and I can't reach Billy be damned, well. Brought our magnum opus in, have you? no just put the whole case here in front of me, have to keep my feet in this damn tub, it . . . hand me that letter opener.

—Yes here the, that catch sticks sometimes but . . .

—There . . . wait, probably want to save this piece won't you, might want to get it repaired. Now, let's have a look . . . and he held the page from the top at arm's length.

Alsaka

Alsaka the biggest state of the
U.S. was bought off ob Russia for $
$72,000,000, that was before the
value of it's many natural resources
was known such as precios metals
vergens minerals, coal and oil.
shale, these oil companies paid
$900,000,000 to lease some of
Alsakas north slope interest alone
is $199,320,52 a day, there is
about $70000 a hundred billion barrells
of oil in Alsaka waiting these millions
of years ffor locked in the earth for
the hand of man to release it in
the cause of human betterment also
natural beaties and first 57000 natives
Eskimos and Indians which have no written languge,
which got title
to $40,000,000 acres of land and a
billion dollars cash compesation there
is also much timber and wild life
at Alsaka.

—Oh yes well no that's just . . .

—See how those beggars got off with a billion dollars? Next thing we'll be handing money out to the reindeer up there, sorry . . .

—No I'll get it, it's just something I . . .

—Might just roll up that right trouserleg while you're down there, don't want it copper plated eh? Now, yes this is more like it yes, this the opening bars is it?

—Oh that's I forgot I'd, that's an accordion solo I . . .

—Accordion eh? Sounds interesting Bast but I think we'll want something a little more impressive to open up, looks like a footprint on it too . . .

—Yes the accordionist did that, I just went down there to get paid and he said the dancers were the ones who'd hired me and since they'd both just been fired nobody was responsible for . . .

—Yes come in Shirley tighten up these electrodes will you? Slipping like that no current coming through at all, now what was that Bast?

—Nothing just the first violin was the only nice person there, he said he'd call up somebody he knows at ASCAP and I might get a job listening for their songs on the . . .

—Little tighter there Shirley, ever pick up jungle rot Bast still the best treatment for it there is, did all this by hand did you?

—Well yes but that top part's something I . . .

—Little string of black notes running along here, might be our dik-dik is it?

—Well I'd indicated castanets for the . . .

—Almost see the little fellow running there can't you, glad my slides were a help, yes. Tum tumti, tumti tumti, of course I can't really read it you know that, just a lot of hentracks to me. You know Bast I still find it one of life's great mysteries, people like you who can look at these hentracks and hear those soaring tones that conjure up the vastness of the plains, the purple mountains' majesty, here . . . I'm just looking for one of our big fellows here somewhere, here now this might be one yes . . . his clear nail traced a double mordent, —eland maybe?

—Yes well that just indicates a grace . . .

—That's it Bast grace, did your homework didn't you, and I think you've captured it. Find some game's about as graceful as a hatrack till it moves and then this grace comes in yes, all these notes here looks like you've got a lot of movement in here and I think you've captured it Bast, remarkable, just remarkable. Just tell me something, Bast. When you sit down to compose, do you hear this tumti tumti tum and then get it right down on paper? or . . .

—Yes well that's a little difficult to . . .

—No no don't try to explain it to me probably wouldn't understand it if you did, prodigious Bast, prodigious, that grandeur we talked about

I can almost feel it right here in my hands . . . and the case came up briefly —just the sheer bulk of it, spared nothing have you.

—Yes well I felt you'd want it scored for full orchestra and of course dealing with ninety-five instruments is . . .

—Each playing its part to fill the screen with the breath of life, to make us feel the vastness of the plains, the purple mountains' majesty all down in these little hentracks. Ever happen to read a novel called Trilby, Bast?

—Well no I don't think I . . .

—Probably a little before your time yes but there's a passage in there I never forgot, the man standing there at the piano staring at the music can't read a note and he can't play. All the soaring tones and rapturous sounds that could express his highest dreams and desires right there in front of him and he can't get at them, yes of course that was all back in the days before tapes and records so we won't have that happen here will we. Shirley on your way out there look on my calendar, I think I've got some free time this afternoon in fact Bast and Shirley bring in my check-book, here this may be Stamper now just hand me that will you? I know he'll want to hear the, yes hello . . . ? Who . . . ? Beamish? no don't think I ever . . . oh yes yes heard of your company of course been having your troubles haven't you . . . Yes I don't know why he'd tell you to call me about it though, these people who've taken over X-L Lithograph are still having a little cash flow problem of their own and whether they're in any position yet to settle this old debt to Triangle right now is . . . haven't discussed it with them no just this item in this morning's paper, specula-tion seems to be they went after X-L strictly as an advertising medium, diversifying right and left expanding line of products plan to use these matchbook covers all over the country to put themselves across move in on these markets and saturate the . . . topflight aggressive young manage-ment yes, happen to have one of their principals sitting right here in fact, Mister . . . no no their executive officer, probably clear up the status of this long-term debt right now, Mister Bast . . . ?

—No well if you wouldn't mind speaking to him Mister Craw . . .

—Busy on something else Beamish but . . . what? I didn't . . . oh that's the way it is yes, yes I knew you people were looking around but that asking price what was it? twelve million? probably a little beyond their . . . Go right ahead yes I'm listening, fixed assets seven and a half yes push that pad over here will you Bast . . . ? two million one and eighty percent of the difference back on taxes four million three . . . ninety percent of the inventory two million seven and eighty percent yes . . . four and a half million cash yes sitting right here he'll call you back on it Beamish, probably want to discuss it with . . . whether they'd want to write off your bad debts yes of course I'd advise them to look into the . . . what? Suppose you could call it wallpaper yes it just happens I know a good deal about this Duncan and Company's situation right now and the bank acting as

. . . not receivership nothing like that no, no my point's simply that rather than running around after bad debts Mister Bast's people here might think about just absorbing the whole . . . Which one . . . ? Ritz yes yes I remember them, didn't know you had an interest there too thought the whole thing was . . . good for a tax loss yes let me get all this together and get back to you with it Beamish, Mister Bast will want a chance to discuss it with his . . . Tamarack? play up there myself sometimes think I'll be up there Saturday in fact I'll look around for you, fine . . . hang this up there will you Bast? Lawyer for Triangle Paper Products their real book value must be up toward twenty million sounds like a damn clever fellow, he's got it worked out so you people can pick it up for four and a half cash.

—Four and a half, million?

—Cash yes, wipe out your longterm X-L debt there and pick up a good steady tax loss situation in Ritz Bright Leaf Tobacco didn't know they controlled it . . .

—Yes well of course . . .

—Yes well of course you'll want to discuss it with your associate and when you do you might mention this Duncan and Company too, a fine old firm even though Beamish there calls their list wallpaper and I didn't know they'd let their bills for paper stock pile up that way at Triangle, but I might have an inside track for you people there at the bank acting as corporate trustee if you're interested just give me the go-ahead, might be preferable to running around after bad debts.

—Yes I certainly . . .

—Might make a lot of sense too if you're really thinking of picking up Her.

—Who?

—Your man Piscator's the one who mentioned it to me, take on Duncan and Company too and get all your publications under one roof you might be able to do a lot of cost cutting and bring it around but just let me give you a little advice Bast and I hope you won't mind.

—No no I'd ap . . .

—I like to stay out of corporate affairs and the petty infighting that goes on everywhere but this Piscator of yours, I can't say I take to him.

—Yes I know what you . . .

—Not our sort Bast just not our sort at all, little too fast on his feet if you follow me, even asked me outright to propose him up at Tamarack, no question of prejudice of course but they'd think he came with a traveling dog troupe if he showed up there in that outfit. But that's not my point. You take this Her for instance, fine old women's magazine and all the rest of it but they've been losing advertising revenue up there since the day television came in and they've been trying to sell off their plant for three years. Look at it as a good dependable tax loss proposition fine but I've been around a little longer than you have Bast and it looks to me like you people have about all of that you need, but my point here is since their advertising's handled by these same Pomerance Associates you people have just taken on to do your PR and this Pomerance is Piscator's brother changed his name somewhere along the way and I can't say I blame him, I'd look twice at the whole thing before I held my nose and jumped in.

—Yes well you see Mister Crawley this here whole, I mean this whole thing is . . .

—Nothing wrong with the basics in this rough prospectus for this stock issue you're bringing out once he's got your Jamaica incorporation squared away, can't even say I find anything to criticize in the way he's handling your acquisition of this mom and pop funeral home chain but any first year law student could handle that one, eh?

—Well yes I, I didn't know we . . .

—Didn't know the details no, been busy with your music Bast I know that, why I try to keep as many of these little headaches off your shoulders as I can. Wagner the name of it isn't it? All pretty cut and dried, two brothers built up the chain and the older one just died holding forty percent turns into the same old story, widow and five children controlling the business need cash and the younger brother with his twenty percent wants to plow all the earnings back into expansion but can't buy them out so you people are pledging the widow and children their share of the book value in cash and giving the others a small downpayment plus installments based on future earnings, I don't think you'll miss with it Bast. Younger brother's a real go-getter and it's one business you don't have to worry about dropoff in consumer demand eh? But getting back to your man Piscator here, get into something like this Ray-X situation and you may need more leverage than somebody like him can provide. Looked over that report I sent have you?

—No Mister Crawley and, and listen to tell you the truth about the whole thing I haven't even . . .

—Mind getting that right trouserleg again? Feel it slipping down into the, that's it yes I know you've been busy Bast but I'd better give you a little of the background to pass along to your associate there, he didn't seem very clear about all the ramifications and it's the devil's own time anyhow understanding him on the phone you know. More than half a century there Ray-X was a really prosperous toy company you know but when these peace scares started and you had all these mothers marching around boycotting every toy in sight their inventory backed right up, all the usual kiddie toys machineguns carbines pistols grenade launchers bazookas warehouses full of them and they had to come up with a whole line of new products. Fickle kids cured them of toys but things like these battery-run weapons systems had given them a little expertise so they tried pocket radios but couldn't meet the Japs' competition and went over into these battery-powered prostheses, hearing aids that kind of thing. Other line they went into was thermocouples, grabbed the market overnight but they've been trying to fill twenty-five million in mostly fixed price orders on less than four hundred thousand in working capital, couldn't get public financing and finally had to cut their executives' salaries in half as part of a five million dollar loan deal that dried up their new product planning and R and D overnight. Now they're caught between cost rises and these fixed price contracts and they may run into more trouble on their thermocouples with this pressure to prohibit rhodium imports from places like Gandia as country of origin because of this confrontation shaping up over there, see what I mean about needing a little more leverage than this Piscator can probably give you when the chips are down.

—Yes I, I certainly do but . . .

—Of course I might be some help to you on the rhodium situation if it comes to that, people with substantial interests in the Gandia region there in fact I think this man Beaton's been in touch with you hasn't he? about these mining claims and power company sites your associate there picked up in that Ace and Alberta and Western collapse?

—Mister Beaton yes I think he called but I . . .

—Tell you why Bast this partner of mine in our picture project here sits on their board's got some interests out there he'd like to round off, matter of fact I think he'd be ready to give you people everything you sank into those two ventures and maybe a dollar or two more and I'd recommend you take it. Might help ease this cash flow problem you've been up against since the day you walked in here if I'm not mistaken.

—Yes that's certainly the . . .

—Of course this Ray-X acquisition looks like a good candidate for some of these big government cost-plus contracts your associate there is beginning to press hard for, problem with their R and D in a shambles though whether they can come up with the product and I'd be cautious about overextending too soon. This three million in undistributed dividends you picked up in that brewery deal and recovering most of your purchase price in the pension fund's sale of the stock back to the employees has generated enough cash for things like this move into Nobili Pharmaceuticals I don't mean that of course, talk around the street the only reason you people went after it was its use as a Panama tax haven and transshipping point once this J R Shipping Corp is operative, smart move but right now about all that's carrying Nobili's its far east market isn't it. All this patent litigation in the wings if the VA pulls out on these contracts for ethicals it may just be a question whether they can move into proprietaries fast enough with this crash program in headaches, still having that green problem are they?

—The, the green what? I . . .

—Wasn't clear yes I just meant this trouble their chemists are having with some new aspirin keeps coming out bright green, solve that maybe you can hold things together long enough to tie things in with this insurance scheme for employees your associate here's just come up with if he can get a favorable decision on it may not be easy, SEC can be pretty sticky when they think you're just looking for a cash pool and you know what a stickler he can be for the letter of the law. Expansion program's one thing but when he starts talking in terms of Disney and Kraft and Champion Homebuilders it may be time to stop and regroup, wouldn't you agree? And this hedging he's started recently in commodities futures, it can be a little risky played that close to the margin and this may be a good time to stop and pick up some of your winnings, snap up this offer on these power company sites mining claims and the rest of it may not be there next time you look and I should tell you Bast, this man Stamper's not one who plays to play, he plays to win.

—Yes well that's what my . . .

—And I wouldn't bother to bring Piscator in on it at all just send me the papers and I'll clear up the details, he'd just try to complicate things. In fact Bast as far as your corporate legal work goes if you people follow up on this Triangle deal I'd take this man Beamish right along with the package, that arrangement he just worked out on the phone there sounds like he's got a head on his shoulders and he sounds like the right sort you know, man you can deal with because I'll be frank to tell you Bast I don't like the way this Piscator seems to be trying to nose you out with your associate there.

—Yes but you see I'd really be very relieved if he . . .

—I know what you mean but he's not the type to sit back, take the way he brought this Pomerance outfit in by the back door and brown nosing your associate there on this little nursing homes merger, probably never given you the details on that either has he.

—No but you see Mister Crawley the whole . . .

—Always says he can't get in touch with you or makes some excuse though I must say Bast it's high time you people did something about that midtown office of yours, I called there to ask if there's anything to this rumor about General Haight joining your organization and your secretary Virginia put me on with a Mister Slomin who wanted to take my bet on the Superbowl game.

—Yes well I think she . . .

—And that new uptown number Piscator just gave me girl answered and told me to fuck off give you some idea of the kind of numbers in his little black book eh? You might think some more about that suggestion I made to your associate there some time ago, told me you said you were having a little space problem and I told him to think about taking a decent hotel suite while you're getting this expansion program organized and working out your permanent requirements, use it for meetings that sort of thing.

—Yes well when he called last night he . . .

—Think I suggested the Waldorf didn't I?

—Yes well in fact that's what he suggested last night and I went there this morning, the suite I've taken even has a piano in it not a Steinway or anything like that but a small grand I can use when I . . .

—Glad to hear that Bast yes I know he's as concerned about your music as I am, really thinks a lot of you you know. Why just from this option arrangement he's trying to work out for you so taxes won't catch you on the spread between it and the market price on your new issue see how much he thinks of you as a business colleague, but I think he's just as concerned about you getting time for your music as I am.

—Well yes he's, in fact last night he told me he's setting up this here ah, setting up an arts foundation that could give me a grant to finish the cantata I'm working on as soon as . . .

—Yes as soon as this little project's wrapped up eh? Let's get back to it here yes, everything else cleared up isn't it?

—Yes I just wanted to ask you about my aunts' account, if . . .

—Just reach over and push that will you? black button there . . . ? Shirley? Bring in the Misses' Bast statement and I told you to bring in my checkbook, I'd be careful on this foundation business Bast, tightened up the laws on these individual grants three or four years ago and you could run into some trouble, there just hand me that phone will you . . . ? Hello? No no can't waste the . . . just tell him I've got someone with me yes and bring in my checkbook, hang this up will you? Man who just called there incidentally just walked out of a big spot in corporate PR to join that Pomerance outfit Bast, might get him put on your account in fact so if you run into any problems there you can let me know, thoroughly offensive little man of course just needs to be reminded who's buttering his bread sometimes yes come in Shirley, might take a look over there and make sure these electrodes are plugged in while you're here. Yes here you are Bast, statement up through the twenty-eighth.

—Oh. Is, where it says security position is . . .

—See where we sold their telephone company right here yes, and then this Nobili you people have been buying into, got them a block here at thirty-one, averaged down with another block here when it dropped to twenty-three and got them out at sixteen, gives them a nice little tax loss.

—Oh.

—Yes and here, another nice tax loss in Ampex haven't we, averaged down at twenty yes and again at fourteen, the rate management was handing out false figures to the analysts there was enough to make your hair curl, able to get them out at six though before it hit bottom.

—Oh what was, bottom . . .

—Selling at around five yes and it may be one of the better bargains right now if you think your aunts would . . .

—No but, but what's this one, FAS . . .

—Famous Artists yes, correspondence courses in the arts photography that sort of thing, thought they might find it a bit more congenial than these humdrum industrials.

—Oh. Is it a tax loss too?

—No matter of fact they may enjoy a complete write-off with this one Bast, can't promise anything quite yet of course, went through bankruptcy and we'll have to see how their reorganization program works out, yes now let's get on to the . . .

—Yes but you see Mister Crawley I don't think my aunts really need tax losses and write-offs they . . .

—Cleared up that long-term capital gains situation on their phone stock yes, eleven thousand seven seventy-three now they can think about profits, got them into Natomas here at ninety-seven and it's up just push NOM on that Quotron there let's have a look . . . yes up three-eighths, you see? Of course I think we're both aware your aunts aren't the most sophisticated investors on the street can't expect them to have a completely balanced portfolio overnight can we so let's get back to what brought you here, just push over that checkbook? Now when do we hear it.

—Yes well of course just finding a copyist and going over it with him to prepare the orchestration will probably take . . .

—I think Shirley found some free time for me tomorrow afternoon you think two hours will do it?

—. . . what?

—Yes two hours or shall we make it two and a half, don't want to rush things Bast I want to hear every note from your first violin right down to your accordion here.

—Yes but, but Mister Crawley it, how can . . .

—Don't worry Bast didn't think you had your whole symphony orchestra standing around out in the hall eh? No just tape or records or something, however you people do it.

—No but played by a full orchestra how . . .

—Yes what's this Bast dig a little further down into your score here nothing but a lot of pencil scribbling.

—No but yes that's the rough score the whole thing has to be orchestrated and then the parts for all the instruments . . .

—Don't quite follow all this you don't mean this is all we've got? This?

—Yes but yes that's the score that's the music yes it . . .

—But you just finished talking about ninety-six instruments yes, said something about your accordionist and first violin and now you . . .

—No but but holy shit Mister Crawley I mean what . . .

—What's that?

—No I mean you don't understand I . . .

—I don't understand sir? No it appears we didn't understand each other Mister Bast, when I commissioned you to compose the music for our film here of course I meant music, and to me Mister Bast music is something I hear. Isn't that what music is to you sir?

—Yes of course yes yes but . . .

—Of course yes I think most people would agree that music is something we hear, and in this case I understood our purpose to be to call upon its powers to help evoke the majesty of another kingdom, to summon the breath of life to these fellows as they sweep before our audience on the screen . . . his own arm swept from the teak expanse to summon their vacant stares down from every direction —and I believe . . .

—But . . .

—I believe at that time I told you our primary audience would be a congressional subcommittee Mister Bast, worthy but mortal men cast in a simpler mold perhaps, who can scarcely be expected to share your talents, your ability to glance at these hentracks and hear those soaring tones that evoke the vastness of the plains, the purple . . .

—Yes but I, maybe if I could go through it for you on the piano I could, we could go to that hotel suite and you could . . .

—The piano?

—Yes or maybe I could take a tape recorder up there and play the whole . . .

—Don't think you could do that fellow justice sitting at a piano . . . he hailed hartebeest across the blotter's green, —and even if I were content with such a makeshift expedient I could hardly trifle with the limitations of our audience Mister Bast, to say nothing of my partner in this little venture, and as far as my partner goes I must tell you frankly I had the devil's own time convincing him we wanted music at all. I've heard him sing Don't Fence Me In often enough driving around his holdings there with a can of beer in his hand but I believe that's the extent of his acquaintance with music, and since in effect I commissioned you against his judgment, you may see the spot I'd be in showing him this stack of hentracks.

—Yes but if I . . .

—Or sitting him down to two hours of plunking on a piano, now let me talk to you like a Dutch uncle for a moment Mister Bast because I must be frank to tell you I feel you've been spreading yourself a bit too thin. A look at this, this score as you call it while I listen in vain for the sound of music leaves me little choice but to believe that your recent rise in the world of business and finance has turned your head from your real vocation, and that what you originally regarded as quite a decent fee for this commission has paled before the rewards you now find within your reach. I don't like the word slacker Mister Bast but I must say your intention here appears to have been simply to bring this work to a hasty conclusion and get on with these expanding business ventures you've been sitting here discussing all this time.

—No but no but . . .

—And if I may even go a bit further to say it appears that the more others make an effort to help you, the less effort you seem to make to help yourself. That may sound harsh but perhaps I failed to make myself clear when we were discussing Trilby earlier, Mister Bast. Not all of us have been given your unique gifts, and when I feel you are using them to satisfy what has struck me on more than one occasion as an almost unhealthy preoccupation with money, I am bound to tell you so sir. When you turn these gifts to accomplishing ends any of us are capable of we are all the losers for it Mister Bast, be content to leave these details of leasebacks and writeoffs to us who toil in the vineyards and look to you to lift our eyes up to the stars while standing in the damn trouserleg sliding down again there can you just get it back up for me?

—Yes but I'm no you see I do need the money in fact I still owe my, I still have some things to straighten out with my associate and now I'm getting bills for a rapid reading course and tuition at a business col . . .

—Yes of course all those are deductible, and . . .

—But deductible from what! I . . .

—And of course you realize I can't pay you anything on this little project of ours as it stands, can I. My partner wouldn't hear of it but even if I wished to myself, I feel that such a gesture at this stage could destroy the very incentive I hope to see rekindled. You see I still have confidence in you sir, or should I say in the artist who dwells within you, the artist who disdains such mundane details as selecting a fresh shirt in the morning, who steps forth into the workaday world the rest of us inhabit indifferent to the glances he draws because his shoes fail to match, why? Because his mind has been elsewhere, his inner ear tuned to the sonorous tones of horn and kettledrum, tones it is his sacred duty to let us hear with him. I have the confidence he will and you must too sir, and to show you the measure of mine Mister Bast I'm going to double the ante.

—Yes yes but . . .

—Don't protest Mister Bast I've made up my mind to prove them wrong, those doubters who tell us of the unreliability, the indolence, the ingratitude of the artist but you must help me, four hundred dollars and I think that's a rather handsome offer sir what do you say.

—Yes but you see I . . .

—Let's get on with it then, just push those nitro pills over as you leave that little bottle there yes, and you'll want this whatever it is, stuff it right in your case here . . . and the lid came down on Alsaka the biggest state, —broken clasp yes you'd better carry it up under your arm there, just remember all these fellows looking to you Bast, he came on, arm rising from pushing the case across the teak to sweep the vacant stares down upon them again —to find a home somewhere in our own vast wilds, in our own . . . and he came abruptly upright with the splash of entering —yes Everglades perhaps, ranging its million and a half acres searching its skies for wood stork and heron, sharing its waters with mullet and snook . . . he sloshed unsteadily, gripping the desk's edge like a small boat's gunnels, —looking to you to make this subcommittee hear, to make them see, above all to make them feel the telephone there just hand it over to me will you? And one word of advice, clear your head and get down to one thing. Hello . . . ? Yes, simplify Mister Bast. Simplify. Damn it hello . . . ?

—Hello?

—Other people have help Willie but I've always had to get everything with my own two . . .

—Miss Bulcke? which call is this . . .

—This is the operator may I help you?

—Yes just get off the damn line. Shirley . . . ?

—We have a crossed line again Mister Beaton but both your other calls have finally come through . . .

—When I take them to court I'll have to represent myself . . .

—Damn it Shirley hang up and try Stamper in his car.

—Hello?

—Yes hello I'm calling Mrs Joubert, it's rather urgent . . .

—And come in here and do something about this damn trouserleg.

—Just a moment yes she was right here I think she just passed the, Dan? The door that is to say, Dan can you look out there for Mrs Joubert? Tell her it's urgent yes, hello? Just hold on please yes someone's gone to get her . . .

—Your other phone there Whiteback, probably an award from the Legion of Decency.

—Yes thank you hello? Yes this is the bank ahm, bank phone yes . . . Yes no back not law Whiteback, yes this is Mister . . . who? Mister Beaton? Yes what can I . . . oh. Oh . . . ? Oh . . . Outstanding shares yes well of course this recent unahm, fortunate publicity in terms of the ongoing situation loanwise has ahm . . . Yes well no even if we were receptive the state banking laws would excuse me for a minute, Vern if you can move your foot there so she can . . .

—Mister Whiteback . . . ?

—Yes come in Mrs Joubert this phone here, they say it's urgent . . .

—Thank you . . . hello? Oh Miss Bulcke? what . . . She came to rest along the desk's edge, —no no that's quite all right, I'll just hold on till he's finished . . .

—Yes let me move these papers Dan maybe you could ahm, excuse me I have a call yes, hello? I'm sorry yes go ahead Mister . . . the state banking laws yes even if we were receptive to . . . Pecci Mister Pecci yes and doing a very fine job, he . . . Oh you do . . . ? Oh you, are . . . ? Mrs Pecci yes she ahm, of course we ahm . . . Yes well of course we weren't aware anyone ahm . . . In the nature of ahm, of a gift that is to . . . yes no not something we care to publicize of course we . . . Yes well in that case of course we might be receptive to . . . yes well of course any reasonable ahm offer that is to . . . to stay on in my present capacity of course yes I . . . Oh I see . . . Yes I ahm, I see . . . Yes well in the field of ahm, of education of course I . . . Oh in Washington? Yes well in that case of course I . . . As soon as I can reach him yes, yes yes thank you for calling yes goodbye, Vern maybe you could let Mrs . . .

—No that's quite all right Mister Whiteback I, hello? yes . . . ? And where she drew her hair back it fell again to hide the tremble of her hand, —but how could, how could the school have simply let him drive Francis away without even . . . No no but doesn't anyone know where they . . . No no no I told you he'd mentioned Geneva! by the time you have a court order they . . . No but isn't there anything else you . . . What Uncle John can do! hasn't he already done enough? Haven't all of you already, done enough . . . ! No I, I don't know . . . I don't know . . .

—Mrs Joubert is everything ahm, here let me hang that up for you . . .

—No please I'm all right . . .

—Yes and you've met our District Superintendent, he just dropped in to ahm Mrs Joubert's sixth grade social studies Vern, I'd like you to see the way she motivates these yes in fact right behind you there Mrs Joubert, some pictures just came in I knew you'd want to see right behind you under those clippings somewhere yes in fact you may want to usel, utilize them on the televised portion of your lesson tomor . . .

—No but, but you can't mean, these . . . ?

—Right under there somewhere yes I know our Superintendent here would like to see what really happens on those field trips . . .

—No I'm afraid you don't . . .

—These will show you how she really motivates these youngsters Vern, a really meaningful learning experience yes do you want to just hold them up there Mrs Joubert? show the Superintendent here how you've been getting across to these youngsters what ahm, what America's all about? Just a little modest Vern she ahm . . .

—Mister Whiteback I'm afraid I, I'm afraid I don't feel well I . . .

—Look Whiteback I don't want to know what America's all about, just get her to the nurse.

—No please I'm quite all right I just . . .

—Yes well of course she might Dan you might just walk Mrs Joubert up to Miss Waddams' office where she can ahm, of course she can't lie down there though can she the ambulance hasn't come yet for the ahm, the baby and its ahm, the baby that is to . . .

—I'm all right really Mister diCephalis, thank you . . .

—Yes well thank you for coming in to show us your ahm, coming in Mrs Joubert Dan you might just keep an eye on her down the hall there she did look a little ahm . . .

—Maybe she got in on these pregnancy sweepstakes you're running,

Whiteback. She's certainly a better looking piece than that dried up little blonde who's got your coach here up on assault charges.

—Yes well Vogel of course ahm, of course he was unaware he was really approaching the girl's mother who seems to have been coming to school dressed as her . . .

—Her daughter yes, in other words if he'd shown an eighth grade girl where the horse bit him everything would have been fine. Put that together with these five pregnancies and your newspaper here would name him Father of the Year.

—Yes well the newspaper story on these pregnancies was all simply a mistake since we'd ahm, a mixup in the laboratory that is to say since the samples we'd sent to be tested for drugs got mixed up with some that were there to be tested for . . .

—If you'd sent them there for that in the first place you wouldn't have had this scene in the girls' washroom just now, newspaper called yet?

—No but of course they still seem to be occupied with this ahm, the tragedy of this little retarded . . .

—No problems at all then have we, Glancy and this Vogel story and your stag movie and everything else pushed off the front page when a narcotics agent shoots down a simple-minded boy with a cap pistol and everything's fine.

—Yes well no apparently the boy caught him by surprise and of course the agent's trained reflexes were ahm, yes excuse me hello . . . ? Yes this is the bank's, oh yes this is the bank? Yes . . . his name is Cibo Mister Cibo yes, as of yesterday his signature is required on all of Catania Paving's checks yes he . . . as president of Catania Paving yes he, hold on my other phone is . . . Yes? hello . . . ? Oh Gottlieb yes I was going to call you about . . . yes no we may not have to call your Ace Transportation loan at all no, I just had a call from ahm, a feeler that is to say from ahm, that could save the bank from ahm, wait let me finish this other call yes, hello . . . ? No it's c, c i b o yes you'll find the signature in the Cia Management account . . . Gottlieb? hello? No that was just the bank calling about this man Cibo who's just . . . In labor relations and vending machines yes he's just bought a third interest in Catania Paving from Parentu wait a minute, hello . . . ? Mister Parentucelli yes I was . . . I just spoke to the bank about your Mister Cibo yes he . . . the Coke machines in the cafeteria? Yes Mister Cibo said something to me about . . . yes but you see with so many youngsters buying Coke our entire federal milk subsidy is in danger of . . . Yes I know Mister Cibo's just as interested in the kiddies' welfare as I am but . . . to Mister Pecci's campaign yes I know he is but . . . Yes of course I agree people like a hero but . . . Yes I have another . . . yes but I have another call I . . .

—Come in Major, you and Dan here getting up an act together? Might call it the two white crows . . .

—Look Vern just . . .

——either shit or get off the pot . . .

—Just Parentucelli on the other phone yes, he's . . . No Pecci's political campaign he thinks they should either ahm, either fish or cut bait that is to say, this man Cibo is . . . Yes some sort of publicity stunt to give Pecci a new ahm, make him a hero yes but of course the . . . The smut issue yes but of course . . . Hyde yes in fact the boy's father just walked in, he . . . To transfer the financing right into his name without going through the estate yes I'll . . . no well at this price I don't think he'll mind the ahm, the smell you might say . . .

—Mind if I hang up this phone too Whiteback? Sounds like somebody left a toilet running.

—Yes no go ahead Vern come in Mister ahm Major that was Gottlieb down to the Cadillac agency, he thinks he can put the financing on the car right into your name without repossessing it from Glancy's estate to handle it like ahm, like a used car sale that is to . . .

—What was that about a smell.

—No well of course it was used since Glancy did use it to ahm, I think the Cadillac people prefer to say previously owned yes and he'd only driven it seven miles but of course he'd been in it for a week when they found him down in the woods there and apparently they've been unable to remove the, to restore the smell of a new car interior that is to . . .

—Won't mind a whiff now and then will you Major, be like driving Glancy around in the back seat where you can't see his . . .

—Look Vern I don't have time to . . .

—Yes well I think Vern just means the back seat would have been more ahm, of course we thought he'd taken off to look for his wife until Parentucelli's men found him down there with that hose from the exhaust to the driver's ahm, sitting behind the wheel yes even though he wasn't going, wasn't dressed to go anywhere that is to say, he . . .

—Yes what about his suit, I meant to . . .

—No well down to the bank of course Dan we knew none of his bills had been paid because his wife must have torn up all the checks he'd written against this last loan and then cashed one herself for the total before she disappeared but ahm, yes I don't think anyone was suing Glancy yet they'd hardly . . .

—No no what I meant was my suit I think he . . .

—I think Dan means his wife's suit don't you Dan?

—No I don't think she's not suing anybody no no I just meant a brown tweed suit he got at the . . .

—You mean your wife hasn't mentioned a lawsuit against me Dan?

—Yes well she may not have seen the ahm, of course she knows about the suit against Dan as driver of the other vehicle but she may not have seen the newspaper story about the keys being left in the death ahm, I have the clipping right here somewhere the death vehicle I think they call it suing for a million dollars on grounds of criminal negligence but of course . . .

—Prices like that maybe we all ought to sell out. What do they want for the one with the cap pistol.

—Yes well they're only asking ahm of course they're suing the government too but they're only asking eight hundred thousand in their suit against the school claiming the boy had ahm, might have had a career in music if our testing program hadn't ahm, of course this other boy who just came to the attention of the telephone company when they discovered he was calling Hong Kong and Sydney Australia without going through their ahm, through approved channels had scored near the bottom of Dan's . . .

—Set up a testing program to weed out the bad risks and I end up with . . .

—Yes well he'd been weeded out too that is to say which was why he was home experimenting with the telephone in the first place, of course I've had to write the telephone company that he's only eleven which will probably make them quite ahm, they're already quite put out over our pay telephone booth out here of course being billed nine hundred forty-seven dollars in collect calls which can't be this boy who broke into their long lines because of course he was at home doing a very fine ahm, offered him a very fine salary that is to say but of course I've had to write them that he's only elev . . .

—Then will you tell me how I end up with this other bunch asking a million dollars for a kid with nothing ahead of him but forty years as a gas station attendant at fifty a week? That's a hundred thousand tops if he'd stayed out of jail, I told you this testing program was going to blow up in our faces back when Dan started having trouble with his holes and now you've got every jobless welfare freeloading . . .

—Yes well of course when we found out what Leroy was up to it was too late to stop this ahm, naming Dan in the suit by the family of this boy with the music ahm, with the cap pistol that is to say since his test results had put the boy into that class in the first place and of course Dan agrees that . . .

—Then why the hell wasn't he in it.

—Yes well I think Vern means . . .

—I mean the first thing I told you Whiteback, the only real function you've got here is custodial. If he was put into that class why was he out sticking people up with a cap pistol?

—Yes well I thought you ahm, with the space problem for this expensive equipment our retarded ahm . . .

—Whiteback had to set the little retreads up in business over in east seven Vern, we talked about it the last time you . . .

—No well in fact we had to put them into ahm, out of business that is to say Major we talked about it the last time you were in about that new equipment from your subsiderary for our new ahm, setting up our new home ec center where the kindergartners were ahm, where the kindergarten was . . .

—Where'd you set them up in business, in the halls? their stuff hanging all over the walls out there . . .

—Yes well I think Vern means the ahm, the three dimensional paintings and the ahm . . .

—I mean what looks like a lot of boards with chewing gum stuck on them and painted over.

—Yes well the landscapes that is to say they molded the landscapes in ahm, in gum yes in fact that's all from the adult hobby show isn't it Dan I think Dan's wife worked with the art therapy group for ahm, for arthritics yes even the typewriter portraits received a good deal of ahm, I'm sure if Vern wanted to know more about it Dan your wife . . .

—What I want to know more about Whiteback is the kindergarten. Where is it.

—Yes well of course when all this latest equipment from Major Hyde's subsiderary made it necessary to ahm, made it possible that is to say to set up our new home ec center . . .

—You put the kindergarten out of business too, is that it?

—Yes but of course since kindergarten had been held in ahm, where first grade was scheduled before we ran into problems spacewise with ahm, schedulewise that is to say with the ahm . . .

—Just wait a minute Whiteback, before Vern leads you down the garden path any further I want to know what you're getting at Vern. I've spent a hell of a lot of my company's time trying to let these youngsters in on the benefits of the latest in educational technology in fact I just had an urgent call from my office and I ought to be there now but I stopped in to see Whiteback on another, on a curriculum matter but I'll tell you one thing, when I get up and lay my company's name on the line . . .

—I think he's getting ready to tell us what America's all about Whiteback, all I want to know is whether he's run your first grade out of business too.

—Yes well I think what Mister Hyde meant Vern was ahm, what Vern means Major is of course in terms of the ongoing situation spacewise that is to say we thought Dan might be able to revise some of his testing ahm, testing procedures for the parents of some of our, some of the first graders themselves that is to say whose parents seem to feel quite strongly about the elimination of ahm, finding a place for them among our little second graders that is to . . .

—Wait Whiteback just wait a minute, I just want to say one thing Vern . . .

—That would be a blessed relief, Major.

—I'm getting sick and tired of hearing everything I try to do here twisted around to sound like I'm just doing it for my company as though there's something wrong with company loyalty I just want to make one thing clear Vern, I'm proud of my company loyalty I just want to make that perfectly clear, I'm proud of it. Look around all you see's a bunch of unwashed kids that don't know what loyalty is because they've never had anything to be loyal to they never will, sewing the flag on the seat of their pants the way everything sacred's breaking down the only place left for loyalty if you've got any's the company that's paying your way, when my company says jump I jump! and when I come in here and lay their name on the line by lining up this equipment to set up your new home ec center at no cost to the district it sounds to me like you're just taking Whiteback's little space problems here and twisting them into an attack on the whole situation equipmentwise like this Citizens Union bunch and the rest of these blacks and radicals who try to head me off at the pass every time I see a chance to score for these youngsters and you take Dan here, all this expensive teaching equipment he . . .

—Yes well of course that's what the Citizens Union has been ahm, the taxpayers' reaction to putting equipment like that out in the cold when we've already spent ahm, expended substantial sums on it seemed to be ahm, it seemed to be too late to keep the whole thing from keeping ahm from coming down on Dan's head that is to say. Of course the newspaper speculation that he's been getting rebates on the equipment was hardly yes one look at you Dan and anyone would know if there was any truth in it you wouldn't go around looking like ahm, of course Dan agrees the only practical thing to do is to submit his resignation yes in fact I understand he thinks he may have found an attractive opening in industry and of . . .

—What do you mean leaving us Dan's leaving us? Dan? You're leaving us?

—Yes well Vern felt ahm, Dan that is to say Dan feels it might help clear the air before we submit this austerity budget I had a copy right ahm yes that's what you're looking at there Vern?

—Yes that's what I'm looking at there, books the first thing to go of course?

—Yes well I think books are always ahm, as Vern says the first thing to go in an austerity budget but of course . . .

—But of course thirty-two thousand for blacktopping the parking lot is still in.

—Yes well Mister ahm, I think Parentucelli's appeal to the parents about scraped knees in the old gravel lot was . . .

—And of course he's already gone ahead and blacktopped it anyhow, the way he blacktopped two acres of lawn over at my place.

—Yes well since his equipment was nearby when he finished up Burgoyne ahm, yes Summer Street it's called now isn't it and of course his generous . . .

—I'll talk about that one in court. Still got him in here replacing your front door lintel for another three thousand, you expect your Citizens Union to swallow that?

—Yes well in fact they were the ones who ahm, they seem to have finally discovered that those Greek letters make no sense at all and since there's already been some agitation to ahm, to replace Mister Gibbs of course when they found out it was his idea to make it look like a quotation from Herkahm, yes from the classics that is to say simply by adding curlicues to the letters in that motto his friend Schepperman gave us which sounded ahm, sounded all right at the time of course until we found out it was communist and the whole . . .

—Listen Whiteback I want him out of here, while you're on it I want that, that son of a bitch out of here if you think he's not behind every crazy dangerous subversive Vern do you know him? This, this drunken smartmouth drunk . . .

—Drinks scotch doesn't he? Matter of fact I met him recently in that snug harbor around the corner from the Post Office and he pressed a book on me called The Rise of the Meritocracy, great ideas in it Major I'd pass it along if I thought you could read. Pay these kids salaries instead of giving them grades and they might learn what America's all about.

—Listen Vern this is . . .

—Yes well Mister Gibbs' approach has already ahm, his proscribed openings that is to say have drawn some attention to say nothing of his appearance the last time I saw him about a car loan but of course he was in no financial condition to ahm, no condition to drive that is to say whether he would be as cooperative as Dan here in terms of his ahm, of resigning . . .

—If you think this school board's going to him on our knees Whiteback you . . .

—Yes well no of course but the possibility that firing ahm, firing anyone might reactivate this strike cloud we've been under since that young Mister ahm, Mister his name's on a check right here somewhere apparently our computer issued him one for fifteen thousand dollars which of course was, must have been some more of Leroy's handiwork that is to say they were going to question him about it before he got away but . . .

—Leroy? they just let him skip out?

—No well of course they were getting ready to pick him up when it was in last night's paper I think an elderly lady who complained to police she was here from out of town looking for an office building at number one Marine Memorial Plaza . . .

—Nothing like that around here, just our World War Two memorial up by the firehouse being let run to rack and ruin by these freeloading pacifist . . .

—Yes well it must be a mistake of course the paper said she had a letterhead driving a big ahm, a LaSalle yes you don't see those anymore trying to park it in front of the Post Office when a man answering Leroy's description offered to help her, she got out and stood on the curb to direct him and he simply got in and ahm, and simply drove away which makes it sound like that story of ahm, that book salesman's story who's suing us that Leroy beckoned him right out in front of that asphalt truck might be ahm, might actually be here's this check yes, Bast yes E Bast for the evidently the correct amount a dollar fifty-two but of course since he hasn't returned the other one the insurance company investigators are after him now like everybody else in fact we've tried to reach him ourselves since no one else seems to know anything about this little Ring opera but . . .

—Wait if you mean the one that got up here on the school television with his filthy remarks in front of those Foundation people and lost us that whole support grant Whiteback he's as bad as this Gibbs, that friend of this Gibbs that cut off his . . .

—Yes well right now the whole project seems ahm, of course we'd planned it for our Spring Arts Festival but even this pupil who was playing the part of ahm, with all the bicycle reflectors that is to say up in the nurse's office now may still be absent unless some adoption agency comes through and of course the . . .

—My boy's in that Whiteback plays Call to the Colors, really looking forward to it.

—Yes well of course whether the Spring Arts ahm, whether the new Cultural Center will be finished of course Parentucelli must be ready to blacktop where his men cleared all those woods and trees when they discovered Glancy's ahm, Glancy that is to say but the architects have been waiting for approval on their building plans since that newspaper smear even though the money already approved in the highway bill appropriation plan for the large stabile to stand out in front is ahm, already approved yes . . .

—Thought I'd heard they just found a little readymade cultural center running full blast up there when they cleared away those trees Whiteback, books, music, artistic pictures on the walls, might hold your little festival there it sounds like the Major's boy here could really lead the . . .

—Look Vern what the hell is he talking about Whiteback he . . .

—Yes well I think Vern just means that ahm, an old sort of barn studio beyond the trees there some teenagers had apparently taken over for a dope and ahm, and sex club where the police found a number of these glassine bags among the books and music torn up all over the floor and ahm, obscenities spraypainted on the walls yes but of . . .

—And the pictures Whiteback, I'm sure the Major's boy would be . . .

—Yes well no apparently there were pictures tacked up everywhere of ahm, of women with exposed ahm, exposed I think the newspaper used the word exposing their ahm of course I understand the owners are being cited for maintaining a public nuisance but since condemnation proceedings are already ahm . . .

—I just want to know what Vern thinks he's getting at with these cracks about my boy Vern if you think you . . .

—No offense Major, I just thought after what he'd provided the community here with on the school television he might . . .

—Yes well I think that's what Mister Hyde came in to discuss and of course if . . .

—Yes and I don't know what the hell the uproar's about, I'm pressed for time but I want to clear this up before it goes any further. My boy told me he'd sent away for a film about karate and when he got it and had no way he could see it he did the logical thing didn't he? Came in here and put it on some of the school equipment how did he know it was being broadcast all over the countryside . . .

—Yes well of course we ahm . . .

—He thought it was a film about karate and he said when he held it up to the light all he could see was a couple of tiny figures doing something how was he supposed to know they were . . .

—Yes well since most of our viewers ahm, from most of our calls and mail they apparently thought it was part of our new sex education program and found it quite ahm, the letter from the Senior Citizens found the whole subject handled with it's right here somewhere, seemed to find it quite stimulating here it is yes, handled with refreshing candor . . .

—There, any reason to take it any further? In fact it sounds to me like my boy performed a real community service here after that smutty thing Vogel showed up with about Millie Amp shortcircuiting her shunt and said he'd just followed an outline Dan here discussed with him, if that's . . .

—Yes well Vogel of course . . .

—And how many youngsters here saw it anyhow, just the fifth grade mostly wasn't it?

—Yes well of course that's how it happened to ahm, how they happened to see it over to the parochial school too yes apparently they've been taking Mrs ahm, taping Dan's wife's little enrichment lesson on silkworms and were quite ahm . . .

—Their own fault then isn't it? They've got their own closed-circuit system over there now what do they expect . . .

—Yes well of course I'm sure they didn't expect ahm, rear entry while sitting I believe Father Haight mentioned as something quite ahm, unexpected that is to say apparently that was the only ahm the only sequence he . . .

—A mixed couple though wasn't it Major?

—Yes well I think Vern just means ahm . . .

—I know damn well what Vern means of course it was a mixed

couple, nothing pansy in it at all in fact it sounds to me like my boy helped get these fifth graders off to a good healthy . . .

—Yes but of course some of the parents are ahm, who took an interest in silkworms that is to say are still somewhat . . .

—And if this is all the boy's done Whiteback I don't know why you even called me in, my office is pretty excited about the way I've handled this home ec equipment for them and I've got to . . .

—Yes well no in fact he ahm, yes well he also seems to have been collecting material that ahm, I had it right here yes that was found in his locker and could hardly be confused with ahm, with karate that is to say right under here somewhere they must yes no these are the pictures they sent us out of Mrs Joubert's field trip but ahm, but but wait but wait if these are the pictures of her field ahm what was she Dan right over under those clippings will you see what's under those clippings there . . .

—But, these . . . ?

—Yes hold that up Dan, what you were just discussing isn't it Whiteback? What was that word you were looking for, pudenda? or would you call that a proscribed opening.

—Yes but no I . . .

—Used to call it hair pie back where I came from that is to say, yes hold that one up too Dan. Looks like she's working up a frothy little selection on the old licorice stick nothing pansy about that either is there Major, must be the one Whiteback just finished telling Mrs Joubert to use in her television lesson to show us what America's all . . .

—Yes but she yes that's why she looked so . . .

—Modest I think you said, can't really blame her of course can you, in fact if this is what really happens on those field trips I might like to go along on one myself Whiteback, if you think she'd . . .

—Yes but no I thought I'd put those, that whole pile I thought it was right here, I didn't know I'd left it right out where she could . . .

—Sound like Vogel, he just told me it looked so nice out this morning he thought he'd leave it out all day too.

—Yes no Vogel of course isn't here no he . . .

—He's setting them up in the boys' room right now, just go in and he'll show you where the . . .

—Look Vern will you just damn it Whiteback give me that magazine see where he got it.

—Yes it seems to be ahm, In die Gurgel hineingestossen it says yes it looks like a German ahm, organ . . .

—Look like a German organ to you Major? Looks to me like the biggest black organ I've ever seen, maybe your boy's passing it around to give the other youngsters a really meaningful learning experience in race relations.

—Look Vern just, will you just shut up? It's nothing but, probably just some black GI over there making out with one of the local frauleins how would he know what he was sending for? Stossen die Gurgel I never would have known it myself, now just . . .

—Probably just sent away to get the stamps.

—Well why not he collects stamps doesn't he? Why not.

—Wait what's that one you've got there Dan, looks a little more in the medical line.

—No this just just, it just says the new coitus splint designed for preliminary rigidity it just . . .

—It's all yours Dan, the Major and I are a little old-fashioned I think we'll just stay with the stossen die Gurgel approach, Major? Nothing pansy about . . .

—All right look Vern you've, he's had his fun Whiteback we've wasted enough time clearing this up and I've got to get hold of my office, just push that over here where I can dial Dan? Get a call in to the man who's running the store there before they close up shop watch that cord there Whiteback it's . . .

—Yes wait let me move this ahm, these pictures yes these are the ones I meant this field trip of ahm, Mrs Joubert's field trip yes . . .

—Hello . . . ? Yes give me Mister Davidoff this is . . . No no Davidoff yes this is . . .

—Mrs Joubert's social studies class Vern, her youngsters bought a share of stock in Mister Hyde's Diamond Cable Company to learn what ahm, learn what Am . . .

—Voted to buy it Whiteback get that in, all voted to buy it with their own hello? No no Hyde, my name's Hyde I got an urgent call to . . . In sales yes I got an urgent . . . Davidoff yes Davidoff he's . . . he's what? What do you mean he's no longer with you with us yes what do you . . . No no wait get me Mollenhoff then, Mister Mollenhoff in . . . hello?

—Here let's see that one Whiteback, didn't know you had such a quota of blacks.

—Yes well no I was a little ahm, don't recognize all of them myself that is to say but of course . . .

—Probably see my boy in some of those Whiteback he's usually, yes hello? Ginny? Yes Mollenhoff there? This is Mister Hyde, I got an urgent . . . no no Hyde in sales yes is he there? I got an urgent . . . I'll hold on yes, they took all those for a feature in the company's annual report Vern, youngsters marched right into the broker's and bought a share of Diamond for a good look at the whole, hello? I'm holding on yes . . .

—Looks like a zoo.

—Yes well what I think Vern means is . . .

—Just find one with the whole class then probably see him standing back by the flag he's usually, hello? Mollenhoff . . . ? Yes this is . . . no Hyde, in sales yes I . . . Been trying to reach Mister Davidoff yes I . . . that whole appliance deal yes straight from Davidoff, I . . . he's what? Wait . . . No wait a minute I . . . of course I did straight from Davidoff he . . . Yes but where does that leave me . . . ? You mean this whole Endo subsid . . . yes but where does . . . No but where does that . . . Yes what else can I do, I . . . No but, what else can I do . . .

—Look a little green around the gills Major, something . . .

—I don't believe it.

—This? wouldn't have believed it myself but you just said back by the flag Major, looks like . . .

—No that's not what I, what. What are you talking about.

—Looks like he's about ready to get down on one knee and sing Mammy . . .

—Here what are you talking about, give me that.

—Never met your Mrs that is to say Major but of course every man to his own . . .

—I don't believe it, here give me the rest of those what in, no I don't believe it . . .

—Yes well I think what ahm, what ahm . . .

—What the hell is going on here! Tell by his haircut, blackface in every one of them but you can tell by his haircut what the hell is, who did this. I want to know who did this!

—Looks like you've achieved a nice racial balance here Whiteback, better than busing them out from Queens . . .

—Whiteback did you, what do you know about this did you . . .

—No well yes of course in terms of the ongoing black ahm, nonwhite enrollment that is to say our little family of Koreans out near Jack's Discount Appliance is still ahm . . .

—Damn it Whiteback I'm not talking about Jack's Discount Koreans I'm talking about this boy back here by the flag, this blackface right back here by the . . .

—Yes well of course it might be ahm, yes if there's a sixth grader from that Stye family out near Dunkin' . . .

—That's not Stye's boy damn it it's mine can't you see the haircut? think my boy looks like a . . .

—After all the fine things we've heard about your company Major I think that's where the credit belongs, their annual report going out to millions of stockholders with this little message on corporate democracy, this little group of underprivileged and their share in America probably get one whole vote with it too don't they, a real lesson in what the free ent . . .

—Under what do you mean underprivileged what's that got to do with my boy's . . .

—Just touched up with the airbrush here and there in fact it's probably the most depraved looking bunch of underprivileged I've ever seen, your boy here's right out of Al Fatah and this girl on the end looks like she does it in doorways and look at this one, down front here holding up the stock certificate, ever see so much greed confined in one small face?

Certainly is having a really meaningful learning experience in what America's all ab . . .

—Yes no what Vern ahm sit down Major Dan could you ahm, just a touch of ahm yes a touch of the tarbrush as Vern says Major of course the boy looks ahm . . .

—Looks like maybe somebody in your company's trying to do you a favor Major, give you a fresh image over on your side of town where you're not as popular as you . . .

—My side of what do you mean my side of town these blacks and radicals who are after me aren't from my side of town they . . .

—No I didn't mean them Major no, just your good white taxpaying neighbors, heard they're a little pissed off at the way your great emergency waste disposal system in that shelter of yours has just doubled everybody's new sewer assessment.

—Yes and you watch them, you watch them they'll be the first ones ripping their knickers to get in when the whole thing starts you watch them they . . .

—Never get the feeling history's just passed you by do you Major?

—Passed me what do you mean passed me by you . . .

—Just the gnawing suspicion that this Civil Defense of yours went out with the hula hoop and took the shelter fad with it?

—Look Vern just because CD's turned into some kind of milksop Red Cross rescue mission if you think my shelter's talk about history you haven't seen history you haven't seen anything, Watts Newark you haven't seen anything yet wreck my car, clean out my house, rip off my watch rip it right off me right off my wrist what do you think they're after me for? Because I'm the only one around here with my eyes open the only one who knows what we've got left to protect, that Stye that insurance man Stye remember what I said that day he just sat here without a word taking it all in right over there now with that Buzzie family trying to wipe me out with a million dollar lawsuit and Leroy, that Leroy creeping around punching holes in everything he could get his hands on sabotaging the whole system right under Dan's wait a minute Dan where are you going . . .

—I just, just have to go to the . . .

—Yes well I think the Major means Dan's testing ahm, Leroy of course . . .

—I'm talking about them getting at Dan getting at me through Dan's wife that's what I'm talking about, got my car got my job my boy where's that picture of not the one of him no the one they sent him the blonde squatting over that black look at that sending him a thing like that, that's what I want to know where your wife stands in this look at it that's what I want to know . . .

—But but . . .

—The last time you got into her that's what I want to know Dan, the last time you got into Vern stay out of this I told you to stay out of this, my car my job my house my watch and they set up that accident set up Dan in that accident his wife's suing me too and I want to know the last time he got into her, suing me for loss of his services and you can't tell me they don't look at that picture look at that picture the loss of his Dan come back here, using her to get at me because I'm the only one left who knows what we have to protect the only, look out . . . !

—Major for the last time shut up and listen, all we've got left to protect here is a system that's set up to promote the meanest possibilities in human nature and make them look good. Dan was paid to make Whiteback look good he couldn't do it and he's out. Whiteback's been paid to make me look good he hasn't done it and he's out too Major and that's what America's all about, but if you think I'm going to try to make you look good over there shitting bullets in that emergency waste disposal system of yours when they come over the hill after you . . .

—No no wait Major you're Vern wait you're knocking over the Dan Dan wait . . .

Behind, the door marked Principal bunged in hollow leavetaking of the evasively level stare still cheaply framed high on the wall, still ferreting vacancy for that widely held determination to move courageously toward the prospect of going out and buying a refrigerator or something similarly useful and desirable, still fixing its indifference with benign reproof; before, the face all simple purpose across the corridor suffered a tic, reduced the future and extended the past by twenty seconds; beyond, the cheer of rushing water escaped the sweep of the door marked Boys.

—Why it's Dan, Dan I'm glad I bumped into you.

—Oh yes I, yes hello Coach I didn't know you were still . . .

—Just stopped in to have one for the road, off somewhere?

—Yes well I, I was just going to the . . .

—My treat . . . he led back down the corridor, —join you in a short one for auld lang syne, I hear you're between shows now yourself.

—Yes but I think I have something in, may have something waiting in industry . . .

—And don't forget your friends when you get there Dan, glad enough to be out of the active life myself for awhile you know, looking around for something in research, a place where a man's mind can turn loose and soar. I've been cramped here you know Dan badly cramped. Never notice the smell of sweat in these halls?

—No but I, excuse me I just have to get into the . . .

—He that loves a rosy cheek Dan, just hold out a minute longer? The cheek that doth not fade too much gazed at over there but you see if I stand here alone gazing at it she might be the next one having me up on charges . . .

—Yes but I'm sorry but I . . .

—Spend a minute here helping you with your sling though and who's to say where my glance may fall, around this way yes here we are, resting on one white hand a warm wet cheek there doesn't that smell of sweat get to you now? The air's saturated, comes on like nostalgia for places we've hated doesn't it, knew you hated it the day you walked in and that's the moment you have to tell yourself to never forget, that moment you walked in hating it and knew you were right hating it or you'll be sucked in by the past Dan, look back on it kindly if only because it's your own, finally all you've got and to leave that behind . . .

—Yes but I'm, I really . . .

—That behind God almighty she just turned and look at it, of course she's oblivious standing there looking into her purse, takes a step that bracelet of bright hair about the bone and I hear each one brushing the next, without friction there's nothing but rags and bone you know. Yes yes all right I'll get the door, in fact somebody's just told me it's hide myself not hide my face in thee but after all what never was can have no end now can it. How her pure and eloquent blood spoke in her cheeks and so distinctly wrought I'll tell you between us Dan, I felt their whiteness once. One moment of happiness, the Russian said? One for the road and then blow winds and crack your cheeks why, is that not enough to last the whole of a man's life . . . ?

And the door marked Boys clapped closed on her standing out there tilting her purse to the light, rummaging its depth, alerted in a sudden turn to the rhythmic clank of coins. —Oh J R, I . . .

—Oh hi Mrs Joubert . . . as quickly gone behind the glass panels clattering closed on the first ring. —Hello . . . ? pencil stub, paper scraps surfacing —this is him speaking yes, I'll accept it . . . portfolio jammed up against a knee —hello? Yes hi, boy it's a good thing you called hey I . . . where just now at the hotel? Did you . . . no but wait a second . . . No but see Bast that's what I was just . . . no what kind of full uniform, you mean with a gun and all . . . ? No but . . . no but sure I know we got this here hotel suite so you could partly use it to play the . . . no but see that's the thing hey, I mean for these here business expenses that it's like this company hospitalidy suite for taxes and all see so we . . . No but see you could have just told this here Marine guarding the door you're this company officer and went right in I mean I was going to tell you to anyways because . . . not to play on the piano while he's right in there no I mean just to say hi General glad to have you aboard and does he need anything see because . . . No but . . . no but wait hey that's . . . No but that's what you do! I mean all these here big companies they get some second-handed general or like a used admiral for their board of directors see because . . . Who said I sent away for him, I mean at first I was going to put an ad someplace for like this used four star one see only then they had this big thing over at the parochial school where Father Haight has his brother up there with the flag and all which he's this used two star one which ought to be cheaper anyway see so I just got Piscator to call him up and . . . no well see that's the thing hey, I mean they know all these here other generals and colonels which are still at Washington buying all this stuff for like the Pentagon and everybody where I mean at the government they go out and buy like a million dollars' worth of carbon paper and rubber bands you know? And I mean all these drugs for these veterans' hospitals and all see we can way underbid these here U S companies and . . . sure well that's what I . . . No I know I just forgot to tell you, I mean this here Nobili company it's been selling real low so if we can just move in see they make these here drugs over at Italy someplace without all this crap about patent royalties so if we can way underbid I mean it's like saving the taxpayers' money isn't it what's wrong with . . . He did . . . ? no but . . . sure but I mean how does Crawley know what they . . . that it what . . . ? No well sure I knew about it I mean he's full of . . . no but wait a second I . . . no but look hey I mean all that is it's just this idea I had where why should all these people that work for these here companies we're getting like why should they pay someplace else all this money for insurance where we can like help them out if we can get our own insur . . . No well sure we'd collect it I mean that's . . . no well see I just read in this here little booklet where . . . No but listen hey I, hey . . . ? Bast? Listen I . . . no I know but . . . no I know but I was just coming to that where I was telling you where this here General Haight can help us out see this here Ray-X company it's getting screwed on all these dumb fixed-price contracts see where what we want is these here cost-plus ones where you get to . . . no I know it but . . . no but listen hey . . . No but look just let me tell you how it works okay? See you get this here contract to supply something to the government like and then you . . . how do I know, I mean just something they want to buy off you like that's where this here General can help us out see so what's neat about these cost-plus ones is you get to add this here percent of how much it costs you to fill this here contract so I mean the more you spend the more you get, see? I mean that's the whole . . . no well sure but . . . No I know I was always yelling about low-cost operations see but . . . no but listen a second hey I mean how do you think the telephone company works where they're always yelling how they have to spend all this here money so they need to raise the rates I mean the more money they can think of how to spend it someplace they get to take this here percent where they keep raising the rates till they're like almost bigger than the gover . . . no but wait, see the . . . No I know you don't I mean I'm just coming to that hey . . . no I know I said that but I mean it won't take much longer see we just . . . no well I just mean we like we the company, like not really anybody see so . . . No but see that's the whole thing Bast see it's not money anyway it's just exchanging this here stock around in like this merging it with this here X-L subsiderary which it's worth like twenty times as much as, you know? See we just give these here Ray-X stockholders one share of X-L preferred for their share of Ray-X only this here X-L's common stock capitalization is real low see so we have this here tremendous leverage see and . . . no well I don't exactly either but that's what this Mister Wiles said see he . . . No but . . . no I know but . . . No but see I was just going to ask if you heard anything from the U S Bureau of Mines see because . . . No I was going to ask you about how's old Mister Wonder too see because we . . . No but see I was just going to tell you about this here Indian preservation because like did this here Charley Yellow . . . No I know but wait hey look did . . . No but see that funeral homes thing is just I had this neat idea see you know that big right of way up at Eagle by that there cem . . . No but wait hey wait, I mean how am I supposed to tell you about all this stuff when you don't hardly even come out here I mean what am I suppose to . . . No I know I said that but . . . no I know but see we're just building up these here assets for like getting incorporated with these directors and all for this here stock issue see so we can like exchange it around for these here other assets and get all this here borrowing power to . . . No wait wait I know I said that but . . . No but holy shit Bast I didn't invent it I mean this is what you do! And I mean like I have to do practically everything myself, like I set all this up to try and help you out so you can do your work and all and you don't even . . . No well what about this here stock option on these whole five thousand shares which you get to buy it when it comes out at ten and then you have this whole . . . five thousand shares at ten dollars yes and then you have this . . . No but wait a second wait hey I know you don't have fifty thousand dollars see what you . . . No but wait hey . . . No but . . . what? a job doing what? But what's, ass what . . . ? But like why does this here Ascop want you to sit around listening to the radio for if they . . . what like to make sure if nobody's playing their songs on the radio without paying them these royalties? But like if that's all they're paying you how do you . . . No but wait wait I didn't mean that hey, Bast? I didn't mean you have to save up fifty thousand dollars I mean I didn't even finish hey, see what you . . . No see what you do is you wait till our stock gets up to like fifteen or twenty see, then like if you want to sell some for that you get to exercise this here option for how many at ten which you already sold them for twen . . . no it's not because . . . no because listen I . . . No but I already explained that about if you're getting paid this here salary how you really get screwed by these here income taxes, see but with this option thing you get taxed at this here lower capital gains rate on what you make between this here ten and where it goes up to when you . . . What do you mean if it doesn't go up, I mean that's what I just been trying to explain about acquiring these here assets and all I mean that's what the whole . . . What do you mean wait ten years why should . . . No but . . . no but wait hey I . . . no I know I said that hey but . . . No I was going to tell you I just found that out too but . . . No but getting this here foundation set up tax free is it my fault if they told me this grant from it can't go to some personal individual? I mean . . . No but see so . . . No but see like if we find some group you can get into it which a grant goes to this here group only you get . . . No but like I thought you could think of something, like I don't know maybe like if you played in a band or someplace it would . . . No but wait hey . . . No wait wait hey wait . . . ! Sure no I know hey but . . . No but hey wait a second Bast I mean holy shit what am I supposed to do! Like I mean everything I think of trying to help you out you always find something you get mad at like it was my fault to complain about only you don't hardly do anything and you don't hardly come out here and I have to do everything practically myself, like you don't come out here so I'm trying to get some field trip in there only there's just this one going to this lousy bakery here so what am I suppose to do? I mean now you finally call only you don't hardly listen when I'm trying to tell you about these here Indians and these mergers and all we're doing for this whole stock option thing I set up for you so you complain about that, then I try to fix you up with this here grant thing you get mad at that too I mean you keep only saying what's wrong and I'm trying to do something! You keep only complaining why something doesn't work and I'm always trying to fix it up so it will! I mean like when I said we can use each other so you can do this here work you're always yelling about but this mail comes in which you don't even open it so I get you this here electric machine to open it then you don't hardly read it, I get you this here special telephone put in so you don't have to go down to this cafeteria for these calls which then you don't hardly answer them anyway so I even just got you this here thing you hook onto it for a hundred thirty-nine fifty which this tape answers the call for you while you're doing all this here composing work only everything I do to help you out you don't hardly even seem to try to . . . No well so what I mean you said you'd . . . I did not hey and like even if I did why should everybody . . . Okay so what! I mean that's what you do! I mean like all I . . . No I know I said that but it's like now everybody's trying to use me, I mean like Piscator thinks I'm some dumb . . . No I thought you were him calling just now and he's out on his ass boy trying to screw us on this here getting incorporated in Jamaica thing he must think I . . . No I know I told him to but now he sends in this here expense account he's got airplane fare three hundred eighteen dollars he's even got this here hotel bill two hundred twenty-nine fifty, I mean he expects me to believe that bunch of . . . Plane what do you mean plane you can go there on the subway and like who's going to stay at a hotel in a dump like Jam . . . it's a what? What do you mean it's an island it's this dump where you change trains at going into New . . . No but . . . no but like Piscator never said . . . Okay but how would I suppose to know I mean that's what I need you to . . . no but okay but, I mean like . . . no okay okay maybe I did hey but . . . No well see you won't hardly have to anyways see because that's what this here Pomerance Agency is going to handle all this here kind of stuff only there's this one thing I had this neat idea, see I been getting these requests for like interviews and all see so I got this here little tape recorder which when I talk on it then when you play it you just hold back on the tape like so it goes real slow and the voice goes way down you know? like it sounds like I'm like fifty, you know? See so I can send you these here tapes and . . . no but wait hey . . . no I know but there's just this one more thing which it just takes a second see this here Indian Charley Yellow Brook did he call you hey . . . ? No because see him and his brother they're from this here big preservation where they have all these here mineral and drilling rights see so . . . No but wait wait hey wait who said . . . No but who said anything about drilling hey see it's just this here timber up there like if we leased these here rights off them to help them out like we could . . . No listen it would too hey because some of these here Indians were real broke which wanted to divide up this whole preservation and sell off their . . . what? Oh, okay anyways see if we lease these here rights off the whole tribe these here broke Indians get something and we're like bailing them out, see so I was thinking like if . . . No it's like out by those Alberta and Western sites under them you know? like near all those mineral claims by you know where that big green state that goes along the top of . . . no where they're like all by this here Great Lake under where Minnesota and Idaho both . . . where? No because hey Nebraska's like way out with Kansas and all beside Utah or someplace anyways I was just thinking, see if you took this here Ascop job too you could have this here little transistor radio right in your pocket see and . . . no I know but with this here wire and earplug they have on it see you could be like listening to it anyplace with this one ear like even if you're in some meeting someplace you just tell them it's this . . . Sure and you just tell them it's this hearing aid see? because like I was thinking if this here Ascop wants you to travel somewheres to listen in on some local station like? and they'd pay for your expenses? I mean till we get this here Triangle plane for you to ride around on see because I was thinking when you go out to this here Indian preserva . . . No no wait hey wait I just said like if you go out to this here Ind . . . No sure wait no no I know I did but . . . No but hey . . . No but wait I just wanted to tell you did you get this here golf practice thing I . . . Bast? Hey . . . ? Hey Bast . . . ? The door clattered open slowly. —Oh, oh hi Mrs Joubert I, were you waiting for this here phone?

—Yes and what on earth . . .

—No I didn't know I kept you waiting all this time, I mean I thought everybody went.

—I think everyone has yes, I'm just afraid I don't have the right change for . . .

—Sure wait a second you need a dime? Just a, just a second holy . . . the panels clattered closed again. —Hello . . . ? the portfolio came up

with a tug at its zipper, the handkerchief wad trailing its soiled initial D
to the mouthpiece —David what . . . ? hunched half standing, sweater
parted behind spilling a crumpled shirttail —what that's your last
name . . . ? Yes this is him speaking but look I'm in a hurry what . . . what
at Pomerance? Yes okay but . . . No but like first why don't you talk to
Mister Piscat . . . what Piscator's right there? Put him on will you . . . ?
No I said can't you hear me? I said put on Pis . . . No well look you better
clear that with Mister Bast see he gets Business Week and this here
Forbes both look will you put . . . No well look I can send you some
biographical stuff you mean about me? but . . . No well see look I'm in
a hurry will you just . . . Okay look if you want to discuss this corporate
image and this here company logo thing over lunch why don't you just
take Mister Bast to . . . Look I'm not worried about it, just whatever
Mister Bast says that's what you do, now will you put Pis . . . No well look
if he wants you up to the uptown office he'll tell you see we just took this
here hotel suite up at the Wal . . . No well look see right now there's this
Gen . . . Look I'm not worried about it and this midtown office see we're
closing this midtown office down only . . . Only this here secretary Virginia which we want to hang onto her now look I have to get to this
meeting, will you put on Piscator . . . ? Look I said will you put . . . Hello?
Nonny? Where'd we get him boy he sounds like he . . . No okay look not
now just tell him to write me it in a memorandum look I'm in a hurry
I just want to get . . . No I got it right here wait a second all this, this stuff
on my, desk . . . I said just wait a second . . . ! Portfolio tipped to a perilous
angle, Maine Potato Futures and Hedging Highlights went to the floor
as the tape tore away and lined paper crammed margin to margin came
out with a tug —holy . . . okay hello? Okay then under assets the first thing
is this one dot two million dollar loan we're getting off of . . . No okay so
we can't draw on it it look we're like getting this credit established
paying it off see and it gets in the papers so everybody . . . no this Mister
Wiles he's this bank director too see so anyway we show it over here in
our cash balance and take the interest off these here earnings from
Wonder and all the rest of wait a second look did they do that mineral
essay of that water they're using in this here beer . . . ? No I did see if
. . . No but see if it's got any of these minerals in it we should get to take
this here percentage depletion allowance off the whole . . . What do you
mean we're depleting them aren't we? I mean if we get some tax benefit
off depleting something why shouldn't we de . . . okay so go ahead and
get a ruling on it look, the next thing . . . where? That says mineral assets
twenty million why shouldn't we claim . . . Okay but with all these here
mineral claims we've got how does anybody know there's not these
mineral and gas deposits worth twen . . . Look okay look that's the whole
thing then look, if there's any crap about that we just go ahead and drill
or whatever you . . . What does it matter for what! for whatever they give
out these deductions for these here intangible drilling costs for I mean

what do they expect us to . . . Yes okay I'm in a hurry and look anyway I just discussed these Indians' leases and all with Mister Bast see so you can clear it with him when he goes out there to . . . No see he's going out to this Indian preser, reservation see this Charley Yellow . . . Okay so what if he hasn't called you look Mister Bast is this very busy man why should he always call you, why can't you . . . this girl told you to what . . . ? Okay look is it his fault how the telephone company screws up everything? Like the next time just keep trying see because on this setting up this here foundation grant thing I want you and him to . . . No I told him that he says maybe he can join a band or something because see I want this thing set up fast to make this long-term low-interest loan off it so . . . No see in these here commodity futures if I can get our capital turnover way up further with bank loans on these hedged commodities we . . . what? I don't know what I what . . . ? Okay look now can you hear me? look. We're not working for you. You're working for us, okay? Okay so with these here futures I'm not telling you to do something illegal see I'm telling you what I'm doing and you find how to do it that's all, I mean like if we need to set up some separate commodity futures trading company so set one up, now look I've got this meeting waiting I . . . No look Hopper look I can't always have him calling me like if they're still mad about these here looms we're selling off at South America see I just gave this son of this union leader up there Shorter I just gave him this Wonder beer distributorship for that whole territory and this Bunky I put him in charge of these rebates on all their returns see because if we have to keep them in business to keep this here whole tax loss carry . . . No see I just wanted to know with this big shipment of fiber they got in if we should just like dump it and take the write-off or like ship it to Hong Kong or someplace to make sweaters or something and import them back see if we did that would we still get to keep this whole tax loss carryforward from . . . what? No no wait just wait a second wait . . . The taps on the glass were repeated and the door clattered open a hand's breadth, —gee I'm sorry Mrs Joubert just a second I . . .

—Yes all right but what on . . .

—Okay but just a second I . . . the doors clattered closed, —Look I'm in a hurry but boy Nonny I mean don't you ever say I told you to do something illegal I mean what do you think I got you for! I mean if I want to do something illegal what do I want with a lawyer I mean holy shit where do you think we are over at Russia? where they don't let you do anything? These laws are these laws why should we want to do something illegal if some law lets us do it anyway like selling these looms in this U S aid program at South America that's this U S money coming back here like did we invent this tax break we get with it? I mean if we put a hundred thousand like a million dollars in this here drilling exploration did we invent we get to take off eighty percent for these intangible drilling costs? If we found oil or gas or something we're supposed to just leave it there if they give us this here twenty-two percent depletion allowance to go ahead and deplete it? I mean these are these laws which you're supposed to find out exactly the letter of them and that's what we do exactly the letter! Okay? Okay that's all and look find out about this whole extra twenty percent rapid depreciation if we can use it somewheres on all this here printing equipment from this Her magazine if this other loan comes through and we can generate up some cash selling off their plants and all, did you get me this stuff on Western Union . . . ? Okay I know send it anyway what about this movie company Erebus and this guy Ben Leva, and that whole savings and loan . . . Okay okay and look that letter from the FTC you forwarded me? about these wooden matches from X-L that snap off these complaints they're dangerous? Okay look tell Mooneyham that's how we're advertising them now with this added snapoff safety feature like they tell you when you smoke in the woods and . . . no well sure raise the price, I mean it's this added feature isn't it . . . ? Okay if that happens just forget it then because look I was just going to tell you, we're going all into these paper matchbooks anyway as many as they can print of them as soon as we . . . for these advertisements of all these different products what do you think! I mean why do you think I went after this brokendown matchbook company in the first place for! And look tell them they can start right off with this here new aspirin we . . . I know it that's what I'm telling you! Tell them to go ahead like it is that's how we're advertising it, just it's green that's all we're saying. It's green . . . ! Okay it's true isn't it? Why should it have to mean anything! It's green, explanation point. That's all we need to . . . I said it's green explanation point! That's all we . . . That's what I just said didn't I . . . ! the doors crashed open, —gee Mrs Joubert I . . .

—Well it's all right . . . she turned, eyes risen abruptly into sight over a lavender border of the handkerchief she held there —but what on earth . . .

—No well see it's just, I'm just trying to help out this here friend see and . . .

—And why on earth is that dirty handkerchief stuffed in the . . .

—No well see with this here cold season coming on like maybe that's even where you got yours you know? from these here . . .

—Mine?

—From how your eyes look sure you probably got it from these here germs somebody holy, holy wait a second I'll get it all, holy . . .

—Well why do you try to carry all this around with you? I've never seen such a . . .

—No wait I'll pick it all up see it's just this here portforlio split and all my. . .

—I don't suppose your paper on Alaska's there anywhere is it, but no wonder you never can find anything saving old newspapers and all sorts of . . .

—No but didn't you see this Mrs Joubert? about this here tender for Diamond Cable like taking over education and all? See I thought I'd bring it to class and . . .

—Oh yes I didn't see it, yes do bring it in.

—And this here Alaska paper I'm going to hand it in like even if I have to write the whole thing over, you said you needed a dime before?

—No I really need change enough to call Washington but . . .

—What Washington D C? It's like station to station it's eighty cents the first three minutes then each minute after is twen, you going to talk more than three minutes?

—Well I don't really . . .

—Here fifty, seventy-five . . . the coins came moist, —eighty or if you want to hang around like only twenty more minutes Mrs Joubert see then it goes down to fifty-five cents for . . .

—No no I can't wait really, thank you . . . she sank into the booth, drew her legs away from his sudden breath retrieving Hedging High-lights underfoot and then pulled closed the doors and reached up dialing, sniffed, shook the doors half opened again and reached up, dropping coins. —Yes hello? I'm calling Mister Moncrieff yes will you say it's his daughter please . . . ? His . . . yes his daughter Emily yes . . . Yes I will . . . she waited, and then brought the doors almost closed on him again out there sweeping together papers, brochures, envelopes, —hello Daddy . . . ? Oh . . . oh I'm sorry, I thought . . . Yes I see well, well how long do you think the meeting may last? It's something quite urgent and . . . Oh, no then I'm afraid not . . . No I'm, I'm afraid not no. Thank you . . . and she sat staring at Dialing Instructions where a knifeblade's hasty scars spelled fuck, her handkerchief up and then her eyes caught by movement stopped in the angle of the panel glass fixed patiently intent down the top of her dress, cracked the doors opened and breathed.

—Hi did you get your party okay?

—No but, it's all right but I'm afraid I owe you . . .

—No that's okay but like don't you think it's funny where they always call somebody your party like they're this here party? The arm-load came up and shifted in a turn, —you coming out this way Mrs Joubert?

—No I, yes I might as well, get a train I think there's one . . .

—See because there's these here couple of things I needed to ask you, he came on half a step behind —like are we going to get to futures soon?

—Get to what?

—In class I mean like where you buy these different futures like potatoes and bellies and copper and all see what I wondered is . . .

—Oh, no I don't think there's time to get into anything as com-plicated as . . .

—No but see it's real interesting Mrs Joubert, like now we already learned about the stock market and all with this here our share of America? See so now if we bought some of these futures like if we got in these here bellies and learned the . . .

—Got in what bellies what on earth are you talking about.

—These here frozen pork ones see if we got in these futures of them and learned like about hedging and how you get to help out these here farmers and all, see you just send away for these here free newsletters which wait could you just hold this stuff for me a second . . .

—And we can't really ask the class to bring their own money in again to buy . . .

—No but that's what's neat see you don't hardly put up much cash anyway because like you buy on this fifteen or like even five percent margin so it's the broker who's putting up the wait a second here it is see? Like if we got this newsletter we could learn all these here terms because the thing is sometimes it's like kind of hard to understand like where it says here we are friendly to bellies for the long term and would begin cautious scale-down purchases in the low thirty . . .

—No I really don't think we can start anything as . . .

—Okay but wait then see I got this here little booklet which I just want to ask you, see right here under Bank Financing? where it says there is this opportunity to increase the turnover in a firm's capital with the leverage provided through bank loans on hedged commodities? I mean does that mean you really have these here commodities like all these bellies someplace? or like can you hedge in these futures of them and then get some bank to . . .

—Look please will you take this J R? She held the armload cradled where he'd settled to it like a portable writing desk, even rested an elbow on it —I really don't understand all this that well myself, you'll just have to ask Mister Glan, ask someone who . . .

—What you were going to say Glancy? He got both arms around the load, —I bet nobody's asking him something now boy did you hear about this here brand new Cadillac he . . .

—Yes it was simply terrible, there are so many terrible . . .

—I know like it was this big El Dorado, he came on half a step behind down the corridor —which you know they have this thing where you sit in there and the whole car goes like up and down to stay level the same heighth off the ground even if you're real fat like Glancy? and this thing at night where your bright lights go down by theirself when this other car's coming? I mean there's so much stuff . . . he got the half step ahead, —like did you ever think Mrs Joubert everything you see someplace there's this millionaire for it?

—Is that all you think about!

—Sure I mean look back there . . . he'd blocked the door by way of opening it for her with his back against it, bringing the wind in, —like right now someplace there's this water fountain millionaire and this locker millionaire and this here lightbulb one I mean like even the lightbulb there's this glass millionaire and this one off where you screw the, oh wait wait a second . . . Down that bright empty corridor the telephone rang in the booth, —could you just wait up for me a second Mrs Joubert . . . ? But she reached past him to push the door leaving him off balance there a foot in each direction where the wind brought in a wrapper from a Three Musketeers candy bar —see I just, just, okay wait a second I'm coming . . . and he ran up against her on the steps.

—Just stop for a minute! she caught an arm round his shoulders, —just stop and look . . . !

—What? at what . . .

—At the evening, the sky, the wind, don't you ever just stop some-times and look? and listen?

—Well I, I mean sure, I . . . He stood stiff in her embrace, his armload holding her off between them, —like it's, I mean it's like getting dark real early now . . .

—Yes look up at the sky look at it! Is there a millionaire for that? But her own eyes dropped to her hand on his shoulder as though to confirm a shock at the slightness of what she held there. —Does there have to be a millionaire for everything?

—Sure well, well no I mean like . . .

—And over there look, look. The moon coming up, don't you see it? Doesn't it make . . .

—What over there? He ducked away as though for a better view, —No but that's, Mrs Joubert? that's just, wait . . .

—No never mind, it doesn't matter . . .

—No but Mrs Joubert . . . ? The wind blew her from behind, seemed to blow him after her whirling the leaves up before them toward the station's lights, —like I just wanted to ask you are we going on another field trip soon?

—To a bakery yes, she said over a shoulder, —I'm sure there's a millionaire for that too.

—No but wait I meant like some museum . . . he was up beside her again, —like that one at New York where we . . .

—The Metropolitan, no the home economics class is going in to see their costume collection but you wouldn't . . .

—Like do you think I could go along? I mean it sounds . . .

—You?

—Sure I mean it sounds real interesting, like it's all these olden time clothes and all? I mean that sounds real in . . .

—No don't be silly no you're not in the sewing, is that the train?

—What those lights? No that's over on the highway hey Mrs Joubert? did you ever hear of the Museum of Natural History?

—Of course but . . .

—See well anyways I was thinking like we've been having about Alaska and these here Eskimos and all? he came on near a trot beside her,

—and like you know in our book Our Wilderness Friend? there's this picture of this exhibit they have in there of these stuffed Eskimos? see so I was thinking . . .

—What?

—Of these here, wait you're right in a puddle . . .

—What did you say? exhibit of what?

—Like didn't you see that picture? These here stuffed Eskimos that shows how they live and all these here handicrafts they, what's the matter . . .

—Do you really think that? can you, God can you think that? That they'd take Eskimos and, and . . .

—Sure well no I mean I, I mean like these other pictures they have in there of these exhibits that look real alive like these here stuffed wolves and all I . . . His voice was gone, buried in her breast with his burning cheek where she held him hard for the moment it took him to twist free enough to gasp —holy . . . to drop from reach to one knee wiping his free hand across his face, —what's the matter anyhow I mean why does everybody always . . . and he broke off for the sound of the train above, —but hey? he called after her.

—No goodbye goodnight I can't wait . . .

—No go ahead Mrs Joubert I just got these new shoelaces which keep untying but hey? remember that there field trip that little guy with those glasses? that kept bossing everybody around?

—Yes Mister Davidoff, she called back, tripped against the curb turned to him caught cringing there in a glancing blow of headlights as though about to spring, —that was Mister Davidoff . . . she caught herself at the foot of the concrete steps and then came up them to the top but one, and stopped there dead, caught breath sharply, —oh . . . ! breaking up into the wind, into a run where the train groaned down the platform, —Jack . . . ?

He'd stopped out of reach, newspapers disheveled under one arm wrapped outside with the Turf Guide where wind billowed the jacket so his shoulders appeared to rise turning toward her, —Amy!

—Oh no you're . . . and she stopped. —No . . .

—No no wait Amy listen straighten right up, listen . . . he came on at her wadding his papers tight in a hasty gesture of resolution, —won the double Amy just stopped to celebrate, straighten right up I didn't know you'd be here to meet me listen . . .

—I'm not Jack I'm not here to meet you, I just came for the next train to town and when I heard this one I thought . . .

—Train run both ways told me that yourself remember? Ride you right back in Amy listen . . .

—Back into town? Don't be silly . . . She turned past him after the receding lights already losing distinction in the aimless spread of evening, —you just got out here.

—Quick trip to settle things Amy pick up a few books, tell Backbite shove the job in his proscribed opening get a fresh start listen . . .

—Jack I don't want to listen! She'd reached the billboard, sheltered there from the wind against a breadloaf inscribed Father Haigt eat's it. —Here comes the train now please . . .

—Pope says to get away remember? told me that yourself . . .

—Jack be careful!

The platform shuddered and he flattened up against We kick ass yours too, —to get away . . .

—No please don't get on Jack please . . . !

—To get away . . .

—No no don't don't be careful don't . . . ! Jack you, here, here hold on here . . .

—Got your ticket?

—You can't sit there Jack your foot's Jack your foot!

The bridge abutment passed in a roar. —Tell you about Hardy Suggs sometime wrong God damn foot though listen . . .

—Here can you, can you, help me with the door I can't . . .

—Kick it always helps, here . . . It came back with a crash, —window seat, seat by the window watch the natural beauties rush past the what's the matter.

—What do you think's the, you frightened me! She sat fingertips pressed to her eyes.

—Got beautiful hands Amy listen . . .

—And please . . . she dropped them to open the bag on her lap, find her handkerchief —your knee can you move your knee, Jack can't you just sit . . .

—Trying to pay the fare damn it . . . one foot twisted into the hinge ahead, —reach my pocket . . . the newspapers went to the floor and his hand came up crumpling bills.

—Jack what, where did all that . . .

—Told you won the double Amy get a fresh start, Raindance and Mister paid a hundred twelve forty Mister Fred only six to one, here, here you are my good man.

—Jack stop it you, he can't change a hundred dollars, you . . .

—Not my good man then God damn it find him something bigger, here . . .

—Here stop it here's a five, put the rest away you shouldn't be carrying it all around like that.

—Think you're mad cause I won the double aren't you, thought you'd be . . .

—Don't be silly it's just, it shouldn't be that easy that's all.

—Said that when I found a nickel once Amy not so God damned easy, chance favors the prepared mind sorry . . . he'd plunged after the papers, —Protestant ethic, he said from down there and then, coming upright abruptly —beautiful knees though . . . trying to cross his own and spread the papers up against them, giving that up.

—And what's happened to your throat, you sound like you . . .

—Little bronchitis get some penicillin get a fresh start, newspaper's full of opportunities. Here. Monogrammed doormat sixteen ninety-five how's that, he brandished the page as the train shuddered in to a platform. —Earn your respect making monogrammed doormats how's that.

—Jack honestly if you can't simply . . .

—No no listen look, first time in history so many opportunities to do so God damned many things not worth doing, problem's they start with the sixteen ninety-five have to start with the doormat, went to the woods to live deliberately Thoreau says couldn't escape from the Protestant ethic, be the first ones to redeem it Amy make monogrammed doormats deliberately, sorry . . . Her knees drew away tight. —Beautiful knees I ever saw why, rather watch the natural wonders rush past the windows?

—I think I would yes, she said turning to where laundry strung behind row houses passed the dirty pane, gave way to a store, stores.

—Might open a dry cleaning establishment . . . he slumped, tried to get both knees up against the seat ahead, gave up and got both feet out in the aisle, —get a fresh start . . .

—Even dry cleaning can't give you a fresh start Jack that suit is really the most appall . . .

—I mean be the dry cleaner Amy . . . he was back to turning pages, —watch you teach sometimes problem your kiddies think grownups do what they always wanted to do when they grew up, God damned Protestant ethic can't escape it have to redeem it, have a kid right from the start wants to be a dry cleaner when he grows up how's that . . . They heaved into another platform where the train gasped, failed to a stop. —He grows up gets married has kids want to make monogram . . .

—I have no idea what you're talking about honestly Jack if you can't simply . . .

—Try again then look, Protestant ethic have to justify your own existence be a Chinaman like Lin Yutang and make a million dollars, problem now's to justify the Protestant ethic grow up want to be a dry clean . . .

She cleared her throat without turning from the dirty pane. —What did you want to be when you grew up.

—A little boy.

—I said when you grew up!

—Can't remember Amy, told you once I never really expected to . . . and the pages started again, —find something else here maybe . . . pounding them down in rumpled creases against his leg extended in the aisle where his foot kicked a passing trouserleg black serge all the way up to the round collar, easing into the empty seat ahead. —Well Christ.

—Jack get your feet in, people can't . . .

—New shoes like them?

—Yes but get them out of the aisle people can't . . .

—Can't be alone like a God damned lunchroom, sit down at the empty counter he comes in sits right down beside you, twenty empty God damned stools comes in sits on the stool right beside you . . . A train passed from the other direction with an enveloping shock and was gone, and the door up ahead banged half opened, half closed to the sway of the car past billboards, finished apartments Now Renting, diaper service trucks marshaled against the day to come. —Might start a diaper . . .

—Jack if you say another . . .

—Whole life waiting for this chance favors the prepared mind Pasteur says spend all my God damned time preparing never quite ready when the . . .

—And if you can't simply sit up I think I'd . . .

—Get a black suit and just freeload, problem it's too God damned late now even to be any of the things I never wanted to be. He swayed forward, caught the seat ahead as she stood. —Redeem the Protestant epic have a kid wants to be a dry cleaner instant he's conceived, little conditioning Stella both think dry cleaning next time we climb in concentrate on dry cleaning feel it slip in dry cleaning dry cleaning what . . . She'd already got one knee past him, squeezed the other past his rising knotted up now against the seat ahead where he unfurled the paper full fanning the wisps trailing over the round collar there, folding the pages back and battering them flat without a look across the aisle to where her profile rose beside her in that dirty pane, eyes fixed ahead where slow as though endemic there tears welled, that nearest the glass seized a course down and dropped and she snapped her bag open, pulled dark glasses from the handkerchief tangle and put them on, reflecting the train's shuddering stops and starts as the aisle generated shopping bags, umbrellas, newspapers neatly creased pausing occasionally at the welter gone silent across the way until, beyond it through the dirty pane, buildings aswarm with fire escapes rose from sight as they dropped in a culvert, dropped back as they rose, the tunnel enclosed them like a blow and she waited, joined the end of the line shuffling toward the door, through it, and then a minute later back, pulling the newspapers aside.

—Jack? Wake up . . .

—Wide awake who won.

—Get up, you can't stay on the train.

—Amy?

—You can't stay on the train, get up.

—No came in to take you to dinner . . . the papers went to the floor in a heap, —French restaurant said I'd take you to dinner never showed up . . .

—You're not taking me anywhere Jack but you've got to get off the train. Where are you going.

—Take you to dinner little French . . .

—And you can't wander around like this with all that money, here come this way . . .

—I see crowds of people walking round in a ring thank you? See dear Smyrna merchant Mister Eugenides pockets full of currants how's that.

—Please . . .

—What? He had her arm, a half step behind. —Used to know every word . . .

—Jack I'm, I'm going out this way and I simply can't . . .

—Raining?

—It's drizzling yes what are you going to do!

—We won't worry what to do, won't have to catch any trains and we won't go home when it . . .

—Jack please be quiet, you can't wander around in this with that throat don't you know someone you, do you want to go to a hotel?

—Think they'll let us in without luggage?

—Jack don't you know someone in town? Here's a cab I can drop you wherever you . . .

—Can't Amy. Can't drive and I won't ride.

—Well you can't just stand out here in the rain either.

—Can't drive and I . . .

—You're not going to drive just get in!

—Window side see the natural . . . and they were swept past Girl-O-Rama Live plus Stagette Loops with a jolt that heaped him in the corner.

—Driver? she leaned forward to the glass, —one ten east . . .

—All go to the movies how's that.

—Now, she finished and sat back —you must know someone in town where you can . . .

—Know Mister Eigen probably hates me though.

—Hates you don't be silly where does he live.

—Opened that suitcase make him hate anybody.

—No but you must have friends where you . . .

—No friends Amy just you, sorry that your foot?

And she drew them close, sitting away from him to look out the window until they stopped, released by a doorman in gaping livery. —All right Jack can you, here take my arm and please . . .

—We're here? Thought we're going to a hotel have room service.

—Well we're not and please try to behave.

He had her arm half a step behind into the elevator, half one ahead out and his weight against it pushed the door open at her turn of the key, into the foyer bright at her touch on the switch. —This my room?

—No come along, please . . .

—Nice little room put up print curtains get a hot plate . . .

—Jack! Now please . . . !

—Sorry . . . he came on toward the white expanse of sofa, —looks like Bloomingdale's furniture department nobody live here?

—It's just a, a place . . . She dropped her bag on the sofa and sat on its arm slipping the dark glasses away from her face, her shoes from her feet. —Now will you just sit down and try to think of someone to call who can, Jack stop hopping around and sit down!

—Wet shoe just trying to get off this wet . . .

—Well then sit down and take it off! Jack I just, I'm just terribly nervous I want to take a hot bath and go to bed and you can't just sit here in those awful wet clothes isn't there someplace you, now stop what are you doing Jack you're spilling money all, oh it doesn't matter it doesn't matter!

—Go out find a Chinese restaurant Amy bring in some . . .

—There is no Chinese restaurant! Can't you, I don't care what you do, I'm . . .

—Thought you might want something to . . .

—If you want a delicatessen their number's on a pad under the phone there, I don't care what you do . . . !

He got far enough up to look over the sofa's back, down an empty hallway through an empty door. —Amy . . . ? There was no sound but running water. Movements slowed, stalking the white telephone across white carpet, getting about the place uneven gaited with a kind of deliberate cunning as though outmaneuvering gravity, he finally answered the delivery at the door and came back with it cautiously down to hands and knees, flattening emptied bags under the sofa cushion.

—Jack . . . ? Where, what are you doing what is all this!

—Egg roll pastrami macaroni salad salmon fruit jello . . .

—But it's, you can't spread it out on the carpet it's . . . She sank to the sofa's edge drawing a robe tight at her knees.

—Kind of déjeuner sur l'herbe slip your things off thought we could . . .

—Oh and please look it's something's already spilled on the . . .

—Stuffed that's the what the hell is it something they stuffed, pickles, turkey roll, rice pudding wait this must be the Greek salad have mushrooms in it?

—Why do you do things like this.

—Just thought we'd . . .

—Jack why do you do things like this!

—What. I just thought we'd . . .

—Behave this way! the way you've been behaving since we, behaving like a buffoon Jack I can't stand to see someone I, someone like you Jack a man like you you're too, you almost make me forget what you're really like when you, when you want to be . . .

. He sat there hunched against the arm of the sofa with egg roll. —All right, he said without looking up, and bit into it, —if you want something to eat just . . .

—And don't sit there with your feelings hurt, you don't . . .

—I said all right!

She bent down, dropped the hand holding the robe at her throat to reach out. —What's this one . . .

—Rice pudding . . . he glanced up, from it up the length of her arm into shadow where the weight of her breast hung free, cleared his throat and bit egg roll.

—How's the rice pudding.

—It's quite good really, Jack what about your throat, have you seen anyone for it?

—Got a prescription for penicillin haven't filled it.

—Why not.

—I just got it!

—Yes all right, she said more quietly, —but you must, do you want me to call the drugstore down here delivers, I could . . .

—No I can get it. He came forward between the peaks of his knees for salmon. —Do you want any?

—What is it.

—Smoked salmon.

—No I don't think so really, I'm afraid everything else here looks rather . . .

—Stay away from the Greek salad.

—Yes I wish you'd put it and, and that whatever that is, if you'd put them up here on the coffee table they look terribly oily. Jack do you think we might . . .

—Here . . . he handed them up to her, getting to his feet. —Don't happen to have any scotch? God damn it I forgot cigarettes . . .

—No I'm afraid not, the place is quite . . .

—Mind if I use the phone?

—No of, of course . . .

He stood slumped with the back of that suit to her, dialing, finally dropped it and turned wedging his foot into his shoe. —Friend downtown's wife walked out, he said down working at the shoe, —apartment's twice as empty with him in it probably can't hear the phone.

—You can try him later, Jack if you . . .

—What shall I do with all this stuff? He was down for the fruit jello.

—Just, on the coffee table, Jack if you want to wait and call your friend later you could go in and take a . . .

—Don't have to call him from here call him from anyplace . . . he was down again for a hundred dollar bill stuck to the macaroni salad and up looking, as though looking for a place to wipe it off. —Friend of ours lost in a White Rose bar somewhere and he's probably out looking for him, probably go out and find them both in one, he said backed toward the foyer.

—Jack don't be silly it's raining and your throat's . . .

—Raining and my throat do you think it's the first time I've ever been out in the, do you think I'm eleven years old? One of your class six J eleven-year-old . . .

—You're behaving like one.

—Well what! what do you, you tell me to call tell me not to call, tell me to find someplace for the night tell me not to go out in the rain I don't even know where we are, that sofa must have cost two thousand dollars like camping out in Bloomingdale's window where the hell are we, do you know? Whole place is empty, little room where we came in here with a bed in it do you want me to . . .

—No no please close it it's, it's just a, just a cubby it's . . .

—Well then will you tell me what . . . he pulled the door to it closed, coming back to stand over her there, —what I, what, listen why tears what have I . . .

—No they're, they're nothing to do with you . . . she pulled the robe loose catching it up to her face.

—No but, Amy please what . . .

—They're nothing to do with you I said! and she stood that abruptly, caught the robe's yellow to the full white spill of her breast without a look back —if you want to stay here stay or go out to your White Rose and look for your, for anybody but take off that perfectly ridiculous suit and take a hot shower before you get pneumonia.

—All right he stood there and said, to no one, —all right . . . and came down on the sofa, got one shoe off again and found a plastic spoon down there, up looking for something to dig it into reached the macaroni salad and got down several bites before he turned to look back through the empty door and start for it, his uneven gait silent through it and down the empty hallway past a darkened door ajar toward the one lighted ahead which he pushed closed behind him, half closed, he turned to close it hard but paused, closing it slowly with the douche swinging there from the back of it, before he turned back to stand at the toilet, wrench off the other shoe, jacket, trousers shirt all in a heap and sodden with steam from the shower when he came out to find a lavender towel monogrammed EMJ to wrap around him into the lighted hall, one step silenced in the carpet as the next, as his pause at the darkened door, and his touch on it.

—Jack?

He caught the towel tight at his waist —just, a blanket thought I might need a . . .

—Where are you going.

—Going in to the sofa thought I might need a blanket, shall I get one from . . .

—Don't be silly.

—What? Amy . . . ? he shivered, pushed the door further on darkness, —Amy? Can't see a thing . . .

—Do you have to? And bedsprings strained abruptly as under her weight come up on one elbow, under his coming down.

—God . . .

—Not so, Jack not so tight I can't breathe . . .

—Amy God I, God . . . her head fell back to the pillow his buried in her throat, in her hair lips seeking the details of her ear, moving hands stilled and, stilled, moving again as though life had stopped threatened only to seize it where her breast yielded, to flee that and descend to climb the cradled rise of bone and over perfect smoothness cleave down where creviced fingertips engulfed in taste and smell and raising pinks to purple browns clawed at the confine of their single sense, sudden heat puckered tight against their plunge to depths come opened wide as her knee rose heavy over him, her own hand's rake of nails brushing up from his without hurry, and back, and up to close without surprise where firmness ended, move there in flow all rhythm against the thrust of muscles elsewhere hard with tension and mounted toward her and away as though to force their tension and their strength and very size into her moving hand small as it was and still enveloping all it held, still moving with expectant calm when he went over on his back as though hurled there, hand seizing where hers failed as though to tear himself from his roots and she came up against his chest convulsed with its echo, breast crushed against the hard stiff length of his arm to reach his shoulder whispering —no it's all right . . . holding him, his hand behind her burying a tremble in her hair to press her head down the rise and fall of his chest where her lips, brushing, kissed, but where his hand held firm, chest rising further with each breath until its hardnesses of bone gave way beneath her cheek to muscle drawn tight under hairs bristled at her lips unparted brushed suddenly by a warmth softer than the tongue they curbed and she came up torn away face buried in his neck to cling there, whisper —please . . . half on him as though to swallow up his shudders, —don't please she whispered, —it happens to everyone . . . the weight of her leg warm over his gone rigid for his twist away leaving only his back to her where she kissed his shoulder in the darkness and clung as though for warmth until, as of its own weight, it eased away, and she caught breath at the stealth of springs across the gap, the desolate toss of covers on the bed there and then, for warmth, pulled up her own.

When he waked it was empty, he'd sat up and looked over in shadow spread from the drawn shade and said —Amy . . . ? but it was only a swirl of blankets, and he sank back hands drawn heavily down his face to leave his stare fixed on the ceiling. And then he was up all at once, pulled the closed door open half out in the hall listening, looked both ways before he reached the bathroom with long steps, found only shirt and shorts wilting from the shower rod and tore the seat in the haste of getting them on, coming out that way to find a silent kitchen, open the refrigerator on a jar of honey and opened can of tomato juice rusting at the puncture, a drawer on two lightbulbs, each step slower back up the hall to stop in the doorway and call —Amy . . . ? He cleared his throat, crossed to open a closet door on an empty camera case, another on one patent leather evening pump, back to the closet in the bedroom where he found a soiled raincoat torn pocket to hem pulling it on coming up with a crushed

Gitanes box from one pocket, matches from Sardi's and two weightless five lira pieces from the other, out again down the hall to take the white telephone the length of its cord behind the white sofa where he sat on the floor and dialed. —Mister Eigen please, in . . . Can't remember his extension he's in public re . . . the Gitane he lit blazed up with dryness, —hello? Mister Eigen there . . . ? Still out to what? Wait what do you mean he might be gone for the day for what day . . . But what time is it? Wait never mind listen this is sort of a, not really an emergency but . . . personal call yes it's Butterfield eight, one wait . . . his voice dropped near a whisper, —I'll call him later . . . he put down the phone and hunched there, blew to disperse the signal column of smoke rising over him.

A door closed. —Jack . . . ? He was up from his elbows. —Oh you frightened me! what are you doing there . . .

—I was just, just making a call I . . .

—But why are you making it hiding back there? and what, what on earth are you wearing . . .

—I just woke up didn't know what time it was look I don't even know where I am, how the hell did I know who might walk in the door there and I couldn't find my . . .

—I had to go downtown, Jack I'm sorry it took me so long, she came on to drop all she'd been standing there holding to the sofa. —I was just so afraid you'd be gone . . .

—Gone where! Where could I go like this! Couldn't find my clothes I found this thing in a closet where's my . . .

—Not that suit you had on Jack I took it to be cleaned but it's quite hopeless, and you really don't . . .

—Look I want to get out there and clear things up, tell Whiteback I'm wait where's my money where's my money!

—It's all in a drawer in the dressing table, Jack I called the school this morning and told them not to expect you and it's too late to go out there now, I'm going in to fix some coffee please just sit down, I brought you the paper . . .

—No but I, I can't stay here . . . he turned, —Amy . . . ? stood there for a moment and then sat down to reach for the paper. When she came in with a tray he was holding up the dry cleaner's bag he'd found under it.

—I'm afraid it will be quite tight on you, she said putting the tray down, sitting beside him —but I thought it might do to . . .

—But whose where did it come from, whose . . .

—They've had it since we took it in last summer and when I took yours in to be cleaned they . . .

—But who's, who took it in who's we? Whose is it?

—No one's really now, it . . .

—It can't be no one's how can it be no one's?

—It was just a suit of my husband's, I'm afraid it's just a poplin, for summer . . .

—Fine and he's going to walk in and join us for breakfast?

—Don't be silly he's abroad, Jack you don't have to drink all this juice I just brought it so you could . . .

—He just cleaned the place out and left?

—We're not married anymore if that's what you mean, there was nothing of mine here, I brought this juice so you could take these.

He sank back, pulled the ripped skirt of the raincoat over a knee and muttered —what are they, testosterone?

—Are they what? penicillin, I happened to find that prescription in a pocket of that awful suit you had on Jack I've honestly never, why do you carry so much trash around with you.

—Not trash it's, where is it you throw it out too?

—No it's all right here . . . he watched her back arch bending for the shelf under the coffee table, —honestly look at it, is this anything but trash? and this? and old newspaper clippings this one's so smudged you can hardly read it.

—Yes that's, that's nothing yes, this behaviorist B F Skinner just intrigued the way he's parlayed all his infantile ideas into such a success-ful . . .

She crumpled it, —and this one? about nature's symmetry?

—Yes well that's . . . he came forward, —this report on the decay process of this eta particle's challenged the whole idea of the, you see the . . .

—And you want to keep it?

—This whole question of, have you got a pencil? Never mind, you see it's both a particle and an antiparticle, it has no electric charge nothing to distinguish it as matter or antimatter, for every class of particle there should be its kind of mirror image antiparticle same mass and spin and an equal but opposite charge and this reac-tion they're talking about should produce fragments of equal energy but the positive ones are coming out more energetic than the nega-tive ones, brings up the whole question of a basic lack of symmetry in our part of the univ . . .

—And could you get your foot off the table Jack it hardly . . .

—Only find one shoe yes but you see there might even be galaxies made of antimatter to balance ones like ours that are made of matter I meant to get a copy of this report, published in the Physical Review Letters wasn't it? I meant to . . .

—But Jack the date on this clipping is, it's almost four years old it's no use to you now is it . . . and it joined the crumpled heap with B F Skinner and Clocker Lawton's Selections, —and what's this . . . ?

The unswerving punctuality of chance
A bat as a mouse's idea of an angel
How less like anyone we can be than unlike ourselves
A friendliness, as of dwarfs shaking hands, was in the air
The total depravity of inanimate things (E.M. FORSTER)

Taine's 'Le con d'une femme' as the axis round which everything
    turns
Who uses whom? (LENIN)?)

Of the soul being set before its Maker hatless, disheveled
    and free with its spirit unbroken (K. MANSFIELD)

To see clearly and be able to do nothing (HERACLITUS)

~~As if the roots of the earth were rotten, cold and drenched~~ (KEATS)

Lady Brute: that may be an error in the translation
Growing up as a difficult thing which few survive

                                        (HEMINGWAY?)

Life as what happens to us while we are busy making other plans
The melancholia of things completed
His heart yearning towards the defeated enemy now subject,
    at his free choice, to be spared or killed, and therefore never
    so lovely (T.E. LAWRENCE)

Pascal's being less unlike others than we can be unlike
    ourselves

Beware women who blow on knots

That a work of art has a beginning, middle and end,
    life is all middle

There is a saying, if any stranger enquire of the first met of
    Maun, were it even a child, "Who is here the sheykh?"
    he would answer him, "I am he" (C.M. DOUGHTY, TRAVELS
    IN ARABIA DESERTA)

~~It is true that in the heights of enthusiasm I have been
    cheated into some fine passages, but~~
Gogol's character who in the end became a kind of gaping
    hole in humanity

—More trash, he muttered sinking away from her on the sofa, knee still against hers where he'd crossed his shoeless foot.

—But it's not your hand is it?

—No.

—Well who wrote it it's quite marvelous, whose . . .

—It's trash isn't it? Will you throw it out do we have to go over every God damned . . .

—Oh honestly . . . ! she stood, still looking at it.

—All right it was mine, one of mine when I still . . .

—I like hatless disheveled and gay it's just sweet, and the bat, she said standing over him, —you've got Pascal twice here did you know? And this Taine, surely it can't be the same one? the critic?

Close as though to look, his knee rested against hers where his hand brushed inside, rising. —Why not . . . ? his thumb brushed sudden warmth.

—It's certainly nothing we had in French Civiliza, Jack please don't do that . . . she'd stepped abruptly away, —do you want to keep this then?

—Thought I'd start a little anthology or . . . he sank back, —what are there about a dozen? Write a book with twelve chapters have the epigraphs ready how's that.

—You did tell me once about a book you . . .

—Write twelve books have one ready for . . .

—Jack please! don't, start behaving the way you did on the train it's just, it just isn't . . .

—Isn't what! Told you on the train all I've ever done my whole God damned life spent it preparing, time comes all I've got is seven kinds of fine God damned handwriting only God damned thing they're good for is misquoting other people's . . .

—Jack don't be silly!

—What's so God damned silly about . . .

—It's simply unbecoming Jack I don't like to hear you talk this way as though you could never . . .

—Well what about last night then! What about last night!

—Well what about last night.

—If there ever was a, spend a whole God damned lifetime preparing if there was ever a time I, the one time in my whole God damned life I . . .

—Don't be silly, you'd been drinking and you were tired there's nothing to be . . .

—And the wasted . . .

—Jack stop it! If you'd, Jack if you'll stop holding your head and just try that suit . . . ? she'd picked up the tray, —I thought we might go out for a walk . . . and she turned to the hall with it leaving him there hands drawn down his face, eyes left on the paper heaped crumpled at his knee before he reached for the dry cleaner's bag and came half dragging it on the carpet. —Along the park, the lights should just be coming on, she called from the kitchen, —Jack? Can you see the moon from that window? where the whole corner of it's gone? My mother used to say that's where the fairies were spending it . . .

The only sound was running water, and after the door closed behind them, none, until the doorbell rang, briefly, then long, a brief burst, and darkness accumulated, pierced by the telephone, repeated, repeated, plumbing chortled somewhere beyond the carpeted hall.

—I'm really quite hungry aren't you? Can you get the light? I thought I'd die at the look on Larry's face when he saw you in that suit you wouldn't think doormen noticed those things, do you like lobster Newburg Jack? It's just a frozen kind I got it when you were in the liquor store, I'm afraid there's not much lobster in it and Jack? No I can't really kiss you with these bundles, will you have just one drink? before we eat? I'll try to hurry, no please. There's the paper. I'll hurry . . . He followed her for a glass, back at the sofa undid the waist of the trousers, sitting, did it up at the sight of the tray. —Can you just move those papers, oh and we need a corkscrew don't we . . .

—I'll get it . . .

—No sit down . . . He sank back, turned as the lights went out to a flicker behind him. —It's hardly a candle is it but it's all I could find, she said bending to put it before them. —What is it?

—Nothing. Your throat. I was staring at your throat.

—Jack please, eat . . .

—Hardly see . . . he moved the candle end closer, little more than flame hovering over a pool of wax by the time he leaned for it with a cigarette that flared up as they touched.

—And your throat? those can't help it . . .

—All I've got, I thought you'd bought some in that little bag you came out with.

—Those were cough drops I got for you, where did you find these?

—In that raincoat, must have cultivated cancer to keep down his waistline, he said unfastening it, sitting back, —snappy dresser wasn't he.

—Oh he just wanted so to, he must have had forty pairs of awful socks he'd got in France those really short ones, little designs and elastic at the top and all that dead white skin showing when he crossed his knees but there was no way to tell him, I had to pretend they were getting lost in the laundry and it took me months to get rid of them. It was always a game he had to win, playing against him and helping him win.

—Thought that's what every woman knows.

—No but I was so young, and he did try hard but he had such ideas of himself, of what he thought my family thought he should be and they never quite matched, Jack please don't . . .

—Well what . . . his hand dropped of its own weight, —tell you the story about the lady who has her portrait done by the Italian who scarcely speaks English? When she sees it she says it lacks sympathy, that's a word he doesn't know so he finds the dictionary says it means fellow feeling in bosom and the next time he shows her the port . . .

—I don't like that kind of story.

—Oh.

—Well you needn't be . . .

—What, old Lucien didn't like fellows feeling in bosom?

But she just sat there away from him, her head back and the wavers of light on her throat, twisting a strand of hair until she said —No, no he wasn't jealous really, when he sent back low necks I'd bought it wasn't for what anyone might do if I wore one, it was what they might think, of him, I was his wife and what they might think of him but he'd always point out décolletage to me at parties or a girl in a top her nipples showed through and I never really knew what he, I even bought a cigar once and almost made myself sick smoking it half way down and put it out right there in that ashtray where he'd see it when he came in, and he didn't say a word . . . She drew the twisted strand across her lips in the last flareup of the candle —and it all, it just wasn't fun anymore . . .

—You don't have music here do you.

—No we, we simply never did, we'd go to concerts and things but we never did . . . Her hand closed in his between them, closer until their shoulders touched and he brushed the warmth of her throat, lips lingered at her ear and she turned her face to his in the dark. Suddenly he was bolt upright. —Was that like kissing a man?

—Amy what in, wait . . . ! he was up, after her where lights came on down the hall —damn it Amy . . . ? The bathroom door came closed against him, left him to turn to the bedroom for the light between the beds, shed the jacket in a heap to the floor.

—Look it does, doesn't it! She was there in the doorway yellow robe pulled open where she held up the strand of hair across her lip, —look like a mustache?

His eyes dropped, he cleared his throat, —Yes and stop it or I'll, I'll come tousle the beard . . .

—Jack . . . she pulled the robe closed but paused again, turned to the glass —it does doesn't it!

—Yes and stop it!

—It must be strange, she said turning, coming between the beds holding the robe loosely, sitting across from him, lying back as he fought off those trousers —for a man, kissing a man, wouldn't it be embarrassing?

—I'm sure it would.

—But not as much as a woman with a woman . . . and she caught her breast away from him crowding beside her, brushing the warmth of her throat, lips lingering at her ear and then his tongue abruptly tracing its details, hand gone from breast to breast under the robe until they went crushed under her as he came to one elbow to sweep its yellow from all the whiteness of her back. From his her own hand came, measuring down firmness of bone brushed past its prey to stroke at distances, to climb back still more slowly, fingertips gone in hollows, fingers paused weighing shapes that slipped from their inquiry before they rose confirming where already they could not envelop but simply cling there fleshing end to end, until their reach was gone with him coming up to a knee, to his knees over her back, hands running to the spill of hair over her face in the pillow and down to declivities and down, cleaving where his breath came suddenly close enough to find its warmth reflected, tongue to pierce puckered heat lingering on to depths coming wide to its promise, rising wide to the streak of its touch, gorging its stabs of entrance aswim to its passage rising still further to threats of its loss suddenly real, left high agape to the mere onslaught of his gaze knees locked to knees thrust deep in that full symmetry surged back against him, surges his hands on either side bit deep as though in their possession all her eloquent blood spoke in her cheeks till he came down full weight upon her, face gone over her shoulder seeking hers in the pillow's muffling sounds of wonder until they both went still, until a slow turn to her side she gave him up and ran raised lips on the wet surface of his mouth.

He reached a knee, and scratched. —Think you've got fleas here.

—Don't be silly. You don't really do you?

—They like empty places, nice thick carpet, he said turned from her the moment it took to catch the curl of a single hair from his lips.

—Jack you, no please, she held his hand away, —you didn't see one? I can't imagine how, what could we do?

—Round them up and train them, start a little circus.

—No they don't really have those. Do they?

—Have what, flea circuses? Never heard of a flea circus?

—Of course I've heard of them that's what I mean, it's just a story isn't it. Do you have to scratch so?

He looked down his arm's length where his scratching stopped, pink glistening dark to purple squeezed up between his fingers —make you feel like Lawrence's old warrior Auda . . .

—I think it's dear . . . her head come over on his chest, breast crushed against him as though yearning toward the defeated enemy to trace its withered ridges with a nail, course the quiescent color of a vein all for a moment taken by lips and tongue gone undefined with wetness and as abruptly up pressed back against his shoulder before he could move, until she whispered —can you reach the light?

—Thought I might have a cigarette, he said reaching to turn it off.

—You don't need one, she reached across to hold his shoulder, —Jack? Have you ever seen one? really?

—A cigarette?

—A flea circus, they don't really dress them up in little clothes and train them to pull carts and things? Why would, who would do that?

—Just somebody who . . . he cleared his throat in the dark, —maybe just somebody afraid of failing at something worth doing . . .

—But if they really do it they must think it's worth doing, she turned on her face away from him, —the only bad failure's at something you knew wasn't worth doing in the first place. Isn't it?

And whatever he whispered was gone, turned to her on his side to move his hand down where it rose to rest that night as it might have on a lectern, along the creviced margin between those white slopes opened to the lesson where congregation thronged a dream.

—Jack?

Up on one elbow he brushed sunlight from his face, brought hers in shadow. —How long have you been awake?

—Do you want coffee? Jack no please, let me get up and . . .

—Most elegant throat I've ever seen . . .

—Yes and yours are you taking that penicillin? It sounds . . .

—Not talking about mucosa damn it, Amy . . . ?

—In the living room? where we'll have more sun . . . ? and there, when she came with the tray —who are you calling? And Jack do you know the seat of those shorts is quite gone?

—Hello? Mister Eigen please, in public relations. Like me to put on my dressing gown?

—What that filthy raincoat? She set cups off on the table, —do you want to keep these clippings?

—Thought you'd thrown them all, hello? Mister Eigen yes, in . . . What do you mean no longer there wait, wait let me speak to somebody in . . . What the whole department . . . ? No, no I'll try to get him at home . . .

—What happened? She handed him a cup, —is this the friend who had the. . .

—Friend who apparently just lost his last refuge from reality, sounds like it's too late for him to be the things he never wanted to be either, he's . . .

—Is this the friend who had the accident with the, who hurt his eye?

—Schramm? He reached for a plate. —No. What are these.

—They called them bow ties they're really rather awful, I thought they were pastries with some sort of filling, Jack what happened to him you were awfully concerned.

—He just, nothing . . .

—Is he all right?

—All right yes he's fine . . . ! Pastry crumbs came down on her robe where he leaned back. —Schramm's dead Amy, he just couldn't make it he's dead.

—Oh . . . ! her coffee splashed, she pulled the wet robe away and reached its hem to dry her leg up from the knee, —Jack I'm sorry, I didn't mean . . .

—Nothing for you to, nothing to say he just finally couldn't make it.

—But did he, was it another accident?

—Only God damned thing any of us has done lately that wasn't an accident . . . he came back resting on her leg there drawn up behind him, —all getting to the point there's no time left for accidents . . .

—Jack please don't start . . .

—Well God damn it Amy doing things badly because they're not worth doing, or trying to believe something's worth doing long enough to get it done . . . She'd bent forward over him to put down her cup and he came back against her, robe fallen open where he traced a pastry crumb along a crease of white —it's just, sometimes it's just too God damned long to be able to keep believing something's real . . . he traced back along the crease above, —Schramm standing in that tenement window he'd watch a truckload of smashed car fenders go by and think the poor bastard driving it was doing something real, and the man I just called here, Eigen . . .

—But Jack that was Schramm . . . she brushed a hand at his temple, gone lower, —Mister Schramm, it wasn't you . . .

—This man I just called Eigen, he wrote a novel once some people thought was very important . . . and he paused for his tongue to pursue a crumb along the crease drawn under the settling of her breasts, —finally found everything around him getting so God damned real he couldn't see straight long enough to write a sentence . . .

—But Jack they're not you . . .

—Whole Turschluss generation, kind of paralysis of will sets in and you're . . .

—But they're not you Jack they're not you! She'd pulled back from him against the sofa's arm. —I don't like to hear you talk this way it's, it's ridiculous . . . and she was reaching over him abruptly to stack cups —I, honestly I don't want to hear it anymore, will you help me get these things together so we can go out?

—Out?

—Yes to get you a suit and, and simply to get some air, do you want to keep these clippings and . . .

—Thought you'd thrown them out . . . and his lips blurred on her breast's fall against them as she reached over him.

—No, I . . . her hand came back slowly, empty, —I thought you might want them . . .

—What for, too God damned late to . . .

—Jack don't you see? And her hand, both her hands were up as she sank back against the sofa's arm holding him where his lips drew up the dark circle, tongue traced its pebbled rim, —Jack if you keep talking that way that I'll finally believe it . . . ? her leg falling slowly against the sofa's back with the weight of his hand —and I liked the, about the bat, about the mouse and the angel . . . his hand's weight gone in fingertips brushing down, brushing the soft spread as though by chance —and the rest, about physics and antimatter I didn't understand it but . . .

—That was stupid . . . his free hand down, disentangling for his knee to come up close beside her where her hand ran toward him, nails raking toward him, and he reached up to spread the robe away —all backwards, proving symmetry to call this beautiful God Amy, what immortal hand or eye . . . lips silenced at her knee, run down where all that moved now of his hand were hidden tips of fingers as hers rose and closed tight.

—But it doesn't matter if I understand, it's when I hear you talk about something you care about . . . her hand drew closer, thumb brushed the drop squeezed up and drew it to a thread —that's what I understand . . . where his lips moved she suddenly fell wide, hand drawing closer stripping vein and color as his knee rose over her and jarred the telephone, still holding closed as though against a sudden plunge, or sudden loss, when the telephone rang, her arms came free, came up, her shoulders' struggle against his knee come down and legs drawn tight in a twist away as the telephone box went to the floor and she got the receiver wrong end round. —Hello? knees drawn up tight, she righted it. —Hello . . . ?

—Good, God . . . he recovered the edge of the sofa.

—Yes, Mister Beaton . . . ? No, no nothing I, I just knocked over a vase, what . . . Yes but you told me . . . but when I was in your office yesterday you said, you said you thought . . . But I told you this would happen! I told you it would with your court orders and depending on an old fool like Judge Ude to . . . He's senile and alcoholic and you know how many lawyers have please . . . ! She seized the hand prying past her knee, —what? No I'm upset yes of course I'm upset, if no one else is going to do anything I'll go over there myself if I must and . . . Not what you called about? Well then what . . . Right now? to come down to your office oh honestly . . . ! The phone buried against one breast she rent his face from the other, —now will you please stop it! and she pulled up the tear in the robe. —Yes hello? yes of course I'm all right I . . . yes I told you I'm angry you can tell Uncle John that I . . . That I was made a trustee with what understanding . . . No I certainly don't want to talk to him now tell him I don't care what he arranged, if he didn't have to ask me about selling it all just to destroy this child's father he doesn't have to ask me to come down there and sign things so the Foundation can will you stop it! I'm sorry what . . . ? No tell him that too I don't care what the Foundation does when this tender offer goes through either, if all he and Daddy think about is . . . No he hasn't, when I called him his office said he wouldn't be back in Washington until . . . Well he knows I'm not out there teaching anymore doesn't he? that I'm here just waiting at this number for someone to . . . Well it's my trust fund isn't it? Can't he simply now please . . . ! No I'm sorry but, if he'd just call me, yes . . . and she stood, the robe pulled round her tight. —Honestly Jack, honestly! How can you be so, couldn't you tell this was important? I simply sometimes I simply don't understand you!

—Well what do you . . . he was up with a step toward her and stopped, pulled his shirt together to little purpose —wait where are you . . .

—I'm going in to take a shower, you might use one yourself.

—Oh . . . the shirt parted with his step after her, —fine we'll . . .

—When I'm finished Jack. And I got you a razor, it's there in that bag with the cough drops I wish you'd use it.

—Amy, I'm sorry Amy . . . he dropped his eyes from hers and then, tone dropped to an aside, —love means being able to say you're sorry . . . and he winked.

She looked there, snatched the robe over the dark circled crest peering from the tear in it —honestly! It's not funny Jack you're not funny! and past him she pulled the collar of it suddenly to her eyes.

There was no sound but running water. Back on the sofa he reached down and scratched, brought up the ankle to examine it as though for signs of life, tore open the paper bag from the table and the box in it for a cough drop gone with a heavy crunch of teeth as he reached for that handwriting arabesque and Flaw in Nature's Symmetry? crushed in his hand, opening and closing on the wad of them getting over for the phone, dialing, and the wad went flung to the top of a drapery. —Tom . . . ? Yes it is listen what the hell is going on, I just called your . . . To me? no what do you mean nothing's happened to me, I'm . . . Won the double yes called you that night haven't been able to since, I've been . . . No I know it God damn it I'm sorry Tom listen buy you a shirt, buy you a new suitcase and fifty shirts I won the . . . What Schepperman? you've found him . . . ? no I told you I haven't had a chance to . . . no I know it but God damn it look Schramm now it's Schepperman I . . . For me what do you mean for me what made you think I'd . . . What and the school told you I wasn't there anymore . . . ? God damned right I have yes, found a cleaner greener maiden in a neater sweeter land look has my lawyer called me there? Only number I could . . . She agreed to it? the visiting rights too? Thank, Christ I . . . was worth how much? But . . . Well good God no, broken down old family company I never imagined it was worth . . . Worst God damned best news I ever had though God damn it it's worth it, every two weeks rain or shine writing that God damned money order to the Department of Probation so she can bail out that poor son of a bitch out selling textbooks even brings her his laundry, God damned shirts on the line every time I go out there to . . . What, now? No I'm uptown someplace feels like we're entertaining in Bloomingdale's furni . . . Not Ninety-sixth Street Christ no haven't been there since the . . . What do you mean office equipment no, I . . . Bast? no just trying to write music as far as I . . . No thought I might use the back there though Schramm's place, to . . . No that's not what I mean no, to work in, try to get back to that book I . . . no I will yes but wait, that idea for a game I had have you thought of it . . . ? No down there that night idea for a parlor game Tom God damn it you've got to remember it before we see somebody else come out with it make a million . . . No I almost have it and then it slips away all I come up with is Baby Jeeter and the three God damned . . . To tell me who called . . . ? Didn't know I gave Stella your number·no what did she . . . no good Christ no just what I'm recovering from Tom got a sweeter cleaner . . . Tonight? I, no I don't think so have to call you but I don't think . . . for Schepperman yes but I'll call you . . . he hung up, turned to raise the wad of torn drawers on a toe and came silent down the hall's carpeting, shirt parted brushing behind her where she stood in the bedroom door one hand resting white on a warm cheek wet from the shower, and she held up the towel with the other.

—You can use the shower now, here . . .

—Amy . . .

—Please . . . her shoulder turned from his breath's solicitous warmth, her hand from the solicitation parting his shirt below.

—But Amy . . .

—Jack can't you understand! I'm simply, I simply want to go out for some air if you'll simply get ready, we might look for a suit and that shirt, did you look in these drawers for one?

—Yes all right! He pulled one open, clattered it closed and pulled the next, —good Lord . . . he reached in, —someone you know?

—What? Oh that's, no will you just put it back please.

—Lacks sympathy doesn't she, needs old Lucien in there feeling in . . .

—Put it back! Honestly Jack I've . . .

—Mustache is a nice touch though . . . and he turned to watch the shimmers mounting from her steps through the door where he stepped aside for her a moment later carrying a packaged shirt, to return, wet, unfurling it behind her at the glass where she lined an eye. —Sorry, can I get at that drawer?

—You've got a shirt in your hand, what . . .

—Well look at it damn it size ten, shall I put it on? Size ten for a, now what's the matter . . .

—Nothing, nothing but why you can't simply, laundries make mistakes can't you simply look for another one without . . .

—Well damn it that's why I wanted to open the drawer! He clattered it open again, —one more in here, he said tearing away the gay wrapping, holding it up by the collar, —well Christ.

—Jack I can't . . .

—Well look at it! Clean starched ironed and ripped right down the God damned front, beautiful transparent packaging Your Shirt Sir! Serviced by Professionals God damn it can't you see why I, talk about my negative thinking you tell me how tired you get of my negative thinking about everything but every God damned place I look there's something clean neat packaged serviced by professionals and ripped right down the God damned front . . .

—Will you hand me that scarf . . .

—Some black girl three dollars a day standing there steaming shirts in a window watching the commuting trains up from Grand Central the professional son of a bitch who designed the packaging sold a million on his way home to Larchmont she rips the God damned thing down the front folds it wraps it doesn't even notice . . .

—I'll wait for you in the living room . . . And there, —Jack did you bring that money? It should be in a bank before anything happens to it, wait let me be sure I have my key . . . and the door snapped closed behind them, finally the white telephone rang as though touched off caught by sunlight crossing the room, leaving it behind in shadow, in darkness, —was that the telephone? I thought I'd left a light on . . .

—Didn't know you meant to, I turned it off when we went out. Where shall I put these?

—Just, anywhere. Put them down anywhere.

—Always upsets me to see energy leaking, this place uptown where the hot water . . .

—Everything upsets you, everything seems to you . . .

—Only way to keep something real long enough to . . .

—Is that how you explain that performance you just put on in the elevator at Tripler's? Jack honestly . . .

—Going to get a drink, do you want one?

—Yes. In the bedroom, I've got to get out of these things . . .

But when he came rattling ice on the sides of the glasses she was still sitting on the edge of a bed there, looking at her hands. —You didn't want to talk about it now you want to, Amy?

—Jack whatever made you behave that way? The way that old man was looking at us what possible reason, thank you . . . she took the glass and sipped, —I could see you in the mirror your mouth hanging open rolling your eyes Jack what, no I'm not angry I just have to know, what makes you do these things I just have to know!

—Amy listen just, just listen . . . he came down across from her, drank off half his glass, —sometimes I, let me get off this damned jacket . . . and he was up to pull it off, finished his drink and came down beside her. —I mean sometimes there are situations that just don't seem to have any solution in their own context do you, do you see what I mean? And the only way to, the only thing to do is step in and change the whole context almost like, sometimes it's like a whole little play starting in my head Amy you're so, just so damned elegant wherever we went today everybody so damned deferential, in the bank they would have kissed your feet and that woman in Bergdorf's and I felt like . . .

—Jack all that's just because they know my . . .

—No but finally in Tripler's how God damned helpless you feel in an elevator and standing there this summer suit sleeves halfway to my elbows no tie and that shirt and, and look at the trousers and that prosperous old bastard looking us over, he really looked like he was going to speak to you and I just suddenly thought grab a context before he can, looks like the daughter of wealth and breeding let the old bastard in his ninety dollar shoes think she's taking me shopping, family has an aging halfwit son and she's taking him out to buy a new, Amy? He came down as abruptly as she'd turned away, —I just do things sometimes that, I'm crazy about you and sometimes I just seem to do the wrong things I God damn it I always do I . . .

—Jack don't say things like that! she was up and past him, bare time for him to get in to fill his glass and come back to find her there, sheet drawn up and a gaze fixed on the ceiling that took life brought down to him with —I wished you'd been able to wear that suit out of the store, it makes you look awfully distinguished Jack I can't wait till you have it.

—I can't either, he said unfastening his waist, undoing buttons, down beside her dislodging the sheet.

—At least you got shirts but why you didn't simply get a dozen, didn't you oh! Jack that's not . . . she'd grabbed for the glass rested on the white rise under his hand, —not friendly to bellies . . . ! and the ice cubes rattled with its toss.

—Not what?

—It's just something silly, some sort of newsletter a boy in my class had about commodity futures I just thought of it. We are friendly to bellies in the long term it said, isn't that . . .

—Show you I can be as friendly to bellies as . . .

—No please . . . she caught his forehead as his lips caught its rise, tongue sought water welled there from the glass, —if we can get in these here bellies he said and I asked him what on earth he was talking about, that bleak little Vansant boy and it's not funny, really. He's so earnest so, he thinks there's a millionaire behind everything he sees and that's all he does see, it's just all so sad really.

—Know what you mean, I owe him a dollar.

—Do you I owe him eighty cents, if he were, if only he weren't so eager about all the wrong things, they're not bad things really just, things . . .

—What do you mean not bad things, ever seen him in the Post Office with that kid with the head like a toothbrush? that Hyde kid? See them in there together getting their mail you suddenly know what the industrial military complex is all about.

She drew his head up. —I guess I just don't want to think about it. It was awfully selfish of me to do it in the first place really, taking that job, I simply had to change things for a little, she said against his shoulder where her nails traced down, —and I think at first I really thought I could help but, oh it all seems so long ago that dreadful Mister Whiteback, that poor little Mister diCephalis and his ghastly wife . . . her hand measured ribs, moved on to twine a finger into hair.

—Create a second class profession you fill it with second class people, there's no . . .

—And that poor Mister Glancy and even that poor creature Mister Vogel . . .

—No well Vogel was, tell you the truth I couldn't have held out as long as I did without Vogel. He'd get me aside for discussions on things like the feasibility of sending people by telegraph and . . .

—Jack he was crazy wasn't he? Her hand's inquiry paused, found shapes changing dimension in its warmth, —really quite insane?

—Probably still is . . . he came on his side, closer, —really just a question of technical difficulties though, run into problems of preserving life in the tissue when you lower the organism's degree of activity to keep it stable while part of it's being broken down to be recreated somewhere else but . . .

—No Jack honestly . . . her hand, stilled, moved again, filling.

—Had some interesting theories on the genesis of the steam engine too, he said hand running down her side to descend the slope turned from him, seeking warmth, —great admirer of yours . . .

—Oh I know that's what was so sad but, but it wasn't even that Jack how can children grow up thinking things like, that same boy J R he thought a museum exhibit he'd seen pictures of Jack he thought the Eskimos in it were stuffed oh it's not funny . . . her fingers closed abruptly in their rise, —and when things happened like that poor boy Buzzie and that tragic accident that child who was actually shot I've kept myself even from thinking about it . . .

—Look it would have been an accident if it hadn't happened, point everything's reached Amy it God damned near couldn't not have happened . . .

—No I don't want to talk about it it's all the same thing, that and stuffed Eskimos and sending people by wire and I don't . . .

But he'd come up on one elbow against her, —there's one thing though listen I don't want you to think I'm, in the elevator today that I think being retarded or simple minded is . . .

—Jack I don't want to talk about it . . . her hand resumed its flow, —I'm not brave really . . .

—But if you thought I think it's funny because I, because a boy I knew in boarding school family so God damned wealthy all they exchanged at Christmas were three percent municipals I used to try to help him with his stamp collection, they probably could have bought him the British Guiana two cents rose if they'd ever thought of him as anything but retarded luggage but the Minuet in G you'd look at him and know he was hearing things you didn't, knew things nobody else did my throat still closes when I hear that, sweetest lonely God damned person I ever . . . she pulled him down silenced against her, his face held close as though to free her own for some expression, or for none, fixed on the ceiling as her fingers rose and fell and her free hand came to stroke his temple, —because Amy I wouldn't want you to think I . . . and she pulled him

over lips gone in the curve of her throat, her knees reared till ankle
caught ankle at his back, nails bit his shoulders raking down and her head
slipped from the edge and then her shoulders all rise and fall as they
came off together to the floor between the beds where her feet rose wide,
found purchase to bring her weight up disputing the plunge of his, to still
dispute it when it was destroyed until her nails relented at his neck,
allowed a gasp that almost shaped her name.

—Jack. You're heavy.

He helped her up, got a knee behind her sitting back on the welter
of sheets, reaching his glass. —Always afraid the damned telephone's
going to go off the minute we . . .

—Jack please that's not fair you, I told you at supper there are just
things, some family things I have to straighten out I'm just waiting for
Daddy to call and . . .

—Sounds like somebody I'd hate to meet in a dark alley, he . . .

—No don't be silly he's not like that he's just, remote, I'd talk to him
and he'd always seem to listen so attentively . . . she sank back there
against his knee, —standing there listening and shaping his nose, he'd
broken it in college football and they injected it with something that
softens in hot weather oh I know it sounds awful but it's not, really
. . . She ran a nail along the leg he'd brought up across hers, —so attentive
but I finally realized he was always attentive to something else, it was all
still like coming to tell him something when I was small and he was
watching people play football on television . . . She parted hair still caught
with perspiration to her face, —Mama always said he only watched because he liked to see someone lose . . . and then, as though suddenly
aware how she was sitting, scissored there, —Jack I've never done things
like, like we've done I, I think we need air could you open the . . . but
his leg behind brought her close where he caught away a last strand
clinging to her lips to bring his there, slip them away along her hair, along
a collarbone and off her shoulder coming on his back and staring up as
though such things had never happened anywhere all hair and airless
rutting shrunk myriad crease and fold hid in the simple parting of her
breasts. —Jack . . . ?

—What.

—Jack if I went away for, if I have to go away for a little you won't
go back out there will you? What will you do?

—Thinking about that book I, about trying to get back to work on
that book I . . .

—Would you? I've been afraid to ask, I've been almost afraid it
wasn't true . . . her hand skimmed down, —you told me what it was about
once but . . .

—About a lot of things it's, can't say what a book's about before it's
done that's what any book worth reading's about, problem solving.

—It's a silly question I'm sorry, people always . . .

—No it's about a man who, about the war . . .

—War? but I thought . . .

—And a general who, he's like your father there molding his nose, above the battle, he's a confusion of this man's ideas of his own father and the Lord, the way the Lord sold Faust out in that wager . . .

—I didn't know you were in a war I thought it was about, about art, she said, rested on his knees peaked up behind her, —but it doesn't matter if it's really, if you'll really go back to work on it, Jack? she bent toward him, —who's Stella?

And his rise to his elbows brought his legs tight pressing her breasts close to hide the warmth already rising there between them abruptly stilled. —Stella?

—You mentioned her on the train, I only wondered . . .

—She was, she's just someone who . . .

—The one who came out to the school? in fur? and you introduced me to her as Mrs diCephalis honestly, I couldn't imagine why but, she's quite lovely, isn't she.

—Looking yes, but . . . he eased back up again in view against her where her own hand paused, and fled to measure ribs, —remember that field trip in that Christ awful cafeteria, Edward Bast, she's his cousin she'd just come out there to . . .

—Of course I remember him, someone I know in fact's just given him a commission . . . her hand came back on fingertips, —the last person on earth I'd imagine rescuing an artist but I was delighted someone's helping him along, he's so . . .

—Feeling everybody in sight's helping him along, problem's what the hell he's doing himself.

—But, what do you mean?

—Tell you the truth I don't know, I just heard this place he's working in uptown is filling up with office equipment he . . .

—How really odd . . . she looked down where her fingertips stroked upward, toward her throat, —that card, I never understood what . . .

—Problem seems to be he just can't settle down to one thing.

She whispered —What a shame, that warmth tumescent now gone fierce with color channeled in whiteness as she bent down to reach the distance to his shoulder, slip moist toward color ringed around, —I think he's dear . . . she reached to raise him closer, —Jack!

—What . . .

—Here turn your neck . . . she seized his arm, pulled it across his chest, —how, no did I do that!

—But what . . .

—You're just covered with, Jack there's blood I couldn't have done it there are scratches all down your back deep ones, did I? She pulled him further, —yes and all down your Jack it must have hurt I couldn't have . . . ! she came down on his chest where his arms rose to hold her and then slip slowly down her back, drawing her knees close mounting those slopes abruptly rising in the mirror beyond where her hand came in search and both of his to part them wide, bring them down gorged, all mirrored semblances of curve and line unfaded white and smoothness too much gazed at asunder in his hands for hair and color targeted in her plunges, until they slowed, one leg of hers came straight and then the other, and all the mirror held was bedhead and the lamp where her hand rose, and darkness emptied it. —Jack? don't you want something on those places they must hurt, I feel so badly, Jack? aren't I heavy?

He simply held her closer to say —I . . . and cleared his throat to say, —I love you, and held her there until her weight subsided, turned from him when he raised the sheet in sunlight, cleared his throat gazing under before he dropped it back, slipped out for coffee none the worse for standing overnight, news none the better for a day, or days, he bunched the paper suddenly looking for its date, over the sofa's arm muttering —Christ . . . dialing, —Hello . . . ? Yes yes it is look I . . . No about getting out there to see her today, I've been . . . what? What do you mean yesterday it's . . . Look I'm not trying to change any agreement on anything, I just . . . All right I'm sorry! look can you let me talk to her for a . . . Listen I don't want to get into all that now, if the lawyers say it's settled I don't want to start . . . And with this kind of settlement you can't even buy her one God damned pair of boots? What . . . No I know it you can't pay for her school lunches you even borrow the God damned allowance I send her look can you . . . Look I don't want to hear about your God damned water heater! Can you just put her on the God damned phone for a minute so I can . . . Well then can you tell her next week? Is it too God damned much trouble to tell her I'll take her out to get the kind of boots she wants next week? And can you tell her I'm sorry I . . . and he sat there holding it away, staring at it for a moment before he crashed it down.

—Jack what . . . she came in pulling the robe close, —smashing the phone down that way you know I'm waiting for . . .

—What wait what do you mean? It wasn't for you it was, were you listening?

—Oh, no . . . she sat down slowly, —I just woke up when I heard you on the phone I thought it might be Daddy I'm, I'm sorry I'm just nervous . . .

—Well it wasn't Daddy and it wasn't Mister whatever his name is you don't want me to answer your phone do you?

She looked at him for a moment before she got up. —No . . .

—Wouldn't want anyone thinking you, where are you going.

—Isn't there more coffee? She came back to set it down saucerless. —Do you think you could button that shirt up just a little? and as she bent down to sit, —Jack did you do this?

—What, he muttered concentrating on mismatching button to buttonhole, —get to the point of the English suicide left the note too many buttons to button and unbutton . . .

—Jack?

—Used to have a friend who couldn't stand them even the word called them fifty-threes, what?

—Did you stuff all these paper bags under this seat cushion?

—Oh, forgot all about them yes, he looked up square into nulliparous shadow, swallowed, —that first night we . . .

—But why on earth . . . she brought the robe closed, sitting back.

—I just save paper bags Amy. Anything wrong with saving paper bags?

She just looked at him, brought up her cup. —Is something wrong? and she drank looking over the rim, —Jack? It's not us, it's not me is it?

—No it's just, I don't know look you're not even thirty Amy not even near it I'm old enough to . . .

—But, whatever made you think of that Jack how silly! What difference does it make?

—I don't know just, things you say sometimes I just . . .

—But what, what things . . .

—I don't know just things like, well like Bast this Edward Bast how dear he is and . . .

—But he is dear Jack you can't be, you can't be that unkind Jack you can't be serious he's younger than I. And I scarcely know him but he's so sincere and shy and enthusiastic and that, that kind of touching desperation about him he's so, young is that what you mean?

—I don't know you're not even thirty and I guess I . . .

—But why do you keep saying that do you think I want someone thirty? If I did I'd find someone Jack I don't want someone thirty, nothing's happened to most men thirty there's nothing in their faces yet at all, I've always gone with older men . . .

—I gathered.

—What?

—Nothing . . . he reached for cigarettes, found only cough drops, shook one out.

—No but what did you mean.

—Nothing I, that first night here in bed when I, when you said it happens to everybody when I . . .

—But . . . her cup came down slowly, —but why would you say this to me?

—I don't know Amy just . . .

—No but look at me Jack why.

—Don't know I told you just suddenly . . .

—No but why look at me, because I said that you think I sleep around? with older men is that what you mean?

—Told you I don't know Amy the whole thing the telephone calls the, a douche hanging on the bathroom door I just . . .

—And you thought it was mine?

—Well what . . . he looked up to her finally, —no wait listen . . .

—No please . . .

—Amy listen I didn't mean . . .

—Please!

—No but listen don't, listen . . .

She'd pulled the robe's collar up loose to wipe under an eye, and she let it fall back without gathering it closed. —I'm just so disappointed, she said and let her head back, staring at the ceiling. —No, no please . . .

—No but Amy I . . .

—I said please! She pulled his head up sharply —I don't understand Jack honestly I don't understand you! To say things like that to me one minute and the next minute you expect to make love to me I don't understand you! He pulled his shirt together, joined her search of the ceiling as she broke it off. —If you want to ask me questions ask me questions instead of, I've told you I'm not brave but I've never done anything I thought wasn't right and when you try to make it sound as though . . .

—No all right damn it Amy I didn't mean, I mean what's so damned strange about jealousy I just . . .

—Because it's ridiculous Jack it's ridiculous and unbecoming and to pick on a perfectly harmless young man? Or because I sleep around with older men I don't but what if I had, not if I've loved someone or why I'd love anyone or want them to love me but just who I've slept with or you're afraid I might sleep with isn't that what you're saying? isn't it?

—No but don't you see . . .

—Jack is that why you'd want me to love you? for the one thing any other man can replace? The one thing a woman's afraid of a man loving her for when she thinks that's the only reason he please, Jack no please . . .

—But Amy I . . .

—When you said once you thought you didn't understand women Jack I couldn't bear that don't you understand!

He caught her coming to him on the sofa, caught up an edge of the robe to wipe away under one eye of hers turned full up to him and then the other —I, maybe I do . . . and he let her face go past his, and held her there.

—Jack these must hurt they must, she said at his neck finally, —this one's so deep it must have hurt I feel so badly . . . her hand caught his shirt up and her breath followed a gash down from his shoulder, —Jack no, please . . .

—Why not . . . his lips blurred over the dark margin curled against them.

—Because you're, you're not being . . .

—Friendly to bellies damn it Amy that's not fair . . . his tongue fled up to its depression, —trying to show you I'm the friendliest person to

bellies in the long term you'll ever . . . but her hand drew his head up.
—Trust bellies in the long term they're just friendly by nature, never
know if breasts are going to be friendly or not . . . He brushed beneath,
—much bolder than bellies never know where you stand with them
. . . and his lips came up over color ringed around, —can't define them
too damned simple . . . his tongue sweeping color pebbling to its touch
—can't even devour them, a million squalid tries in paint and words
never touch them . . . his teeth caught at the peak, —sublimely stupid,
always becoming . . . and he came down with a heavy crunch.

   —Jack what . . . !
   —Told you fair warning to breasts.
   —No but . . . her hand there, —what did you . . .
He breathed at her. —Cough drop.
   —Oh! she caught his head away —honestly . . . !
   —No there's no harm look, can't harm them can't harm any of them,
nulliparous, primiparous, multiparous not a trace anywhere look at that
. . . his lips brushed across, —just sheer dumb splendor.
   —Don't Jack don't be . . .
   —Silly? what, nulliparous? Means not having borne a child that's all,
one is primiparous, two is multip, God you're beautiful he said at her
shoulder where the robe came away, coming down with her, beside her,
half behind her drawing her leg over his.
   —Does it mean all that much, really? she said not even turned to
him, her head back off his shoulder.
   —Does if you believe the sculptor . . . his hand brushed up from her
knee to the pleat paused there fashioning it open almost as though by
chance, —the one who called beauty the promise of function . . .
   —No it's all right, she whispered, her free hand caught his raising the
telephone and pressed it back, returned it to the other plying now as
though in search, for entry risen from beneath but still importuning that
bracelet of dark hair along the bone rubbed harder at its crest, faster with
each fall and rise threatening loss restored that quickly gorging the slap
of cheeks abruptly stilled, dead weight at the ring of the phone
and her hand round seizing anywhere to hold him against loss,
before her other rose for the receiver. —Hello? choked near a whisper
then, —hello . . . ? Yes I . . . yes I've been waiting for you to call I . . .
sound like I what? No I, I ran for the phone yes of course I'm all right
. . . No but Daddy I . . . because I just hoped you could do something
quickly to help me find out where . . . No I did tell him that I told him
to tell Uncle John that because this wouldn't have happened if Uncle
John hadn't . . . No I didn't I'm not going to either the only reason he
wanted me to come down there was to sign some . . . Daddy I don't care
if it's important it's important to him it's important to you but it's not
important to me . . . ! her nails bit deeper where they held, her weight
dipped urgently hard on retreat, recoiled with a surge —if any of you

ever thought what's important to me . . . ! Yes right now to go over there myself right now if . . . yes from my trust fund just enough to . . . But . . . Yes but . . . But it's mine isn't it? mine? didn't Mama . . . I'm not then I won't I certainly won't if that's all you . . . There's nothing else no nothing else what else could . . . No no one told me that he had, again . . . ? Daddy I don't care who Mister Wiles thought he saw me with in an elevator I'm simply . . . yes if you'd ever thought what's important to him either . . . ! I . . . I won't no I won't bargain I think it's simply criminal I do goodbye! she held it off, urging her name against the sofa's arm till he reached there to hang it up, her hand clenched in his, ham slipped from its tensing rise and in a sudden turn all of her fallen away beside him up towering in dismay lost in his throat as her hand came to seize him, her arms to pull him down legs flexed against his shoulders' old scars torn across with new till his hands cradling her lunges brought them up cavernous against his breaking upright to his knees as though in anxious wonder to contain it all, postpone one instant to the next claim to the instant just gone by and there the wager taken once for all, until, in surges shuddered like despair, it was too late, their weight came down all weight again. That close, he looked at her as though she were already gone, and she as though there were nowhere to look except away.
—Jack? What time do you suppose it is.

—No idea. His hand came to her shoulder where he held her. —Bet your father's busy right now with that nose of his.

—Oh it's all simply so, simply . . .

—That Uncle John sounds like a charmer too.

—No he's, I suppose he's simply a bully really because he's always been allowed to be that's all, for so long . . .

—Got an idea let's move in with him get his mind off things . . .

—You'd go mad there, that big empty house in Pelham I haven't been in it since after Mama died, he's been getting the same commuting train for fifty years he plays cards on it do you know why?

—Just sounds like a man who likes to win . . .

—Yes dimes to win dimes do you know why? Because all these years he's hated Franklin Roosevelt he still does, he thinks he ruined the country and when that dime came out with Roosevelt's face on it he started to collect them to get them out of circulation honestly he did, he had a pocket in his suits a special one to put them in and the end of the day any he'd got in change or won at cards he'd empty out this pocket into boxes, he still does . . .

—Good God he sounds like he, get the March of Dimes up there march right through his house and . . .

—I haven't been there since after Mama died it was, I was still in school and someone came to dinner he was a man who made fine china and, Mama'd been cremated and he said if, he said right at the dinner table he told Daddy if they'd give him her ashes he'd, he'd make a fine chop plate human ashes make the finest china he said but, but why a chop plate why he said a chop plate . . .

—Amy . . .

—Why a chop plate why he, he'd never met her but why he couldn't think of, couldn't even think of her as something less . . . her hand rose over his closed from one still breast to the other where there seemed neither rise nor fall. —Jack where did you go to school? to boarding school?

—A place up, small school nobody's ever heard of in Connecticut up near Hartford, probably not even there any . . .

—Jack? she was up beside him, brushed the fall of her hair from his face —it's not so late the banks are closed yet is it?

—Banks? I . . .

—Because if I have to, Jack I have to go away for a little to get these things settled and if I need the fare can you lend it to me?

—Why, lend it give it yes what . . . his hand came up as though uncertain whether to steady or to stay the leg gone over him, maw drawn wide in mere promise of the leg to follow, recover the mere function of getting from one place to another, —but to where . . .

—No just to lend it, to Geneva . . .

—To, Geneva? he got his feet to the carpet —you mean now?

—Yes you might phone an airline, she called back to him, —I'm just going to bathe and Jack ask them what time it is . . . ?

—What day it is, he muttered, getting the telephone, scratching as though seeking a place to scratch, dialing, buttoning buttons, getting through in baffled tones and up —forgot to ask what God damned day it is . . .

—Did you find something? she asked to her own image in the glass, bent close lining an eye, —and the fare?

—Got three hours, he said brushed close behind where water beaded white missed by the fallen towel, —four hundred sixty-five one way first class but Amy what . . .

—It's rather more than I thought, she said as the line went on under her eye without a waver, —Jack please . . . eyeliner paused under the other eye for both to rise to meet his in the glass, —it's simply something I must do if I don't go now I'm afraid I, I might never . . . and his eyes fell away, as his hand did, but the eyeliner still paused as though aware his eyes, gone from the glass where he hunched at the bed's edge, had merely dropped to where his hand had been, —there's a shopping bag in the kitchen I think, could you get it? please . . . ?

Back with it, he sat fastening up that waist half following contours now no more than that gone in a half slip, the full fall of her breasts as she bent dropping a skirt rolled into the shopping bag, one shoe and then another in after it and then and with the same dispatch one breast and then the other into the scant suspense of a brassiere. —Amy listen what, how long are you going to be gone this whole thing is . . .

—A few days I don't know really, maybe weeks Jack where will I find you when I'm back?

—Just, I don't know I, getting kind of used to this place feel like I was born here, what's going to happen to it?

—Don't be silly it's, I suppose it will simply stand empty it was leased on some sort of corporate tax arrangement I think . . . she got a shoe on, —some number where I can call you though? Can you just write it down and put it in my bag? There's a pen in it . . .

—Only thing I can, give you Eigen's number only one I can think of . . . he got a shoe on, getting to her bag.

—And your penicillin it's right in the drawer there . . .

—It's gone I took it all, still feel like death warmed over.

—Jack will you see a doctor? if you keep not feeling well will you promise? She turned fastening a last button, —Jack you're not taking that!

—Might rain, I just thought I . . .

—Honestly put it back in the closet! You should have got one at Tripler's you can get one now, I can drop you . . .

—Amy listen Amy . . .

—No Jack please! I, I've told you I'm not brave Jack if I stop now I, it's simply something I must do can you get that shopping bag? I think my mascara's run . . .

—But, God damn it it's not you I don't trust Amy it's life, it's the whole God damned . . .

—Jack please please just, just tell me you'll work on your book while I'm gone that you'll really start today on it that you won't have any more of these silly ideas about, about what's not worth doing and all of your . . .

—But Amy with you gone the whole God damned thing will, get out and see myself in the daylight wonder what in hell you ever saw in me that . . .

—Jack don't talk that way! She leaned close to the glass again, touching at a line under one eye, and then the other. —I love you for reasons you'll never know anything about, she said paused there a moment longer, looking, before she turned away to leave the mirror free to lamp and heads of beds empty across the gap, reached his arm through the door. —What else is this you've got?

—Scotch, hardly drank any of it . . .

—And Jack you won't drink a lot?

—No I, no . . . he cleared his throat, stopped behind her at that expanse of white sofa to sweep up the yellow robe half from the floor there, hold it up with the tear in it —not taking this?

—What? she turned where she had the door opened off the foyer looking up as though he'd interrupted her looking for reason not to go further, and she pulled it closed sharply, —oh that? No . . . She pulled open the front door, —you thought it was mine . . . ? and it snapped closed behind them, a half step before her into the elevator and out of it a half one behind, sealed by a gaping liveried doorman into a cab off with a jolt that left him heaped in the corner staring along the line of her cheekbone, the clarity of her skin and long fingers putting on dark glasses, down the line of her throat. —The bank shouldn't take a minute, Jack you're sure it's all right?

—Yes look why don't I come with you, got enough for two round trips and . . .

—Don't be silly, driver can you wait . . . ?

And out of the bank behind her, —wish at least you'd taken enough for the round trip Amy God damn it suppose you . . .

—Jack don't be silly, driver will you stop at Tripler's please?

—No but, Amy!

—No Jack please . . . she caught his hand and held it there against the seat, turned to the window from him gazing with such concentration he might have been trying to commit to memory each delicate convolution of her ear. —To leave you on a day like this in that poor poplin suit I do hope your new one's ready today, they said it should be . . . they slowed in toward the curb,

—Amy listen . . .

—And it's begun to rain Jack please, please take care of yourself and, not so, Jack please I can't breathe . . .

—When you're back Amy listen instant you're back . . .

—And Jack do get yourself a raincoat too oh I hope your suit's ready . . . her hand gone white holding his —I, I'd so wanted to see you in it . . .

—Amy . . . ! he came a step after the slam of the door, the bottle in the paper bag under his arm threatened by elbows as the light changed, stung there by a horn, abruptly nuzzled by a yellow fender to recover the curb and mount the sheer affront of his reflection against crisp shirtings displayed with discreet worsteds and unworn shoes beyond the glass.

—Mister Gibbs? that's not you is it?

—Me?

—May not remember me my name's Beamish? on the Schramm estate? I, trust I haven't made a mistake . . . ?

—Ay Beamis sí! No es mí no pero que importa, verdad? Porque me acuerdo de ti sí Señor, y la rubia? es tu Señora? Coño . . .

—Good heavens I, excuse me sir we . . .

—Que culo muy rico, mira como tiene el culo el los bolsillos . . . !

—No no please good heavens, Mrs Schramm quickly I think we'd better . . .

—Y el pecho tan bueno también pero falta simpatía, me permites tocar adentro Señora?

—No no good heavens! Excuse us sir yes let's cross right here Mrs Schramm, quickly while we have the light, Mister Duncan you're with us?

—Esperame! esperame . . . !

—He's not coming after us? I can't imagine what, you're still with us Mister Duncan? Mrs Schramm please let me apologize yes let's turn up this way, is he gone? I'm afraid I put you in danger Madame but he did look exactly like Mister Gibbs one of the executors but good heavens! There's a cab Mister Duncan could you hail it, I know Mrs Schramm wants to get home, Madame again please accept my apologies. Since the other executor Mister Eigen failed to drop off those papers, I was a bit hasty when I thought that was Mister Gibbs and hoped he might speed things along but the resemblance was remarkable, and right in front of Tripler's! Goodbye and I'll get another set of those papers right up to you no no Mister Duncan wait, where are you going . . .

—See the lady home . . .

—No I think she'll be quite safe now Mister Duncan let's walk this way, the Waldorf's just a block or so . . .

—I thought you were fixing me up with Mrs Schramm.

—In a manner of speaking Mister Duncan yes but since her position is merely that of a legatee, let's cross here while we have the light, I think your interests will be best served by talking with someone directly concerned with the corporate . . .

—I just want to get fixed up and get back to Zanesville.

—I quite understand yes, there's the Waldorf up ahead, I was going to say in case none of the principals from the parent company is here I'm sure Mister Davidoff will be able to fix you up as you say, but I should prepare you for him, let's go right in this entrance. He's merely their public relations account executive but he seems to have taken a good many prerogatives in the operations area upon himself and if you find him a bit high-handed I would simply counsel patience, the elevators are right over here yes I've the suite number written down somewhere. Apparently they've scheduled some sort of meeting of division heads and even though I've been retained as counsel by the parent company in the course of this Triangle acquisition, I must be frank to say I'm as yet unfamiliar with the entire extent of their holdings which appear quite diverse, this is our floor yes, down this way. In fact the entire situation is moving with a rapidity to which I'm quite unaccustomed but then times change don't they Mister Duncan, that door next after the armed guard I believe. I'm a bit old-fashioned but I put it all down to the decline from status to contract, oh is it locked? Just knock yes, the key to the whole thing I believe, the decline from status to contract . . .

—Come in, is that room service Virginia?

—No sir it's just, oh it's you Mister Beamish did Mister Davidoff expect you?

—I believe I gave you a message for him to that effect when I called yes, we . . .

—That you're bringing up Mister Brisboy that's right I forgot I told him, anyway he's over there on the telephone and the other gentlemen are having something, would you gentlemen like a sandwich or a shot or anything while you wait?

—No I think not Virginia thank you, this is Mister Duncan and I believe he's in rather a hurry let's just wait right over here Mister Duncan . . .

—Maybe you could just fix me up with her.

—Pardon? Virginia? I hardly think so Mister Duncan, I understand she's been with the parent company for some time but she's hardly in a position to resolve your problem, she's only a sort of secretary receptionist after all and hardly the most brilliant one at that, this is Mister Davidoff here and I'm sure he'll be off the phone in a moment or two . . .

—Sir . . . ? Correct General affirmative yes sir an honorary doctor of laws sir they . . . of what sir? of humane letters? I'll ask them immediately sir I'm sure they . . . that they may not have been aware that you painted yes sir they . . . in Life Magazine yes sir but of course that was some years . . . Yes sir the university is fully aware of your help in placing these government research contracts there sir but our new head of R and D at Ray-X is still working out Virginia take Mister Brisboy's coat there excuse me sir, sir . . . ? Yes sir the government contracts with Ray-X are all bought in sir they just have to come up with some products to . . . one called Frigicom yes sir a new method of . . . Cost overruns of course sir Virginia get me that backgrounder on Frigicom to read to the General over the . . . Oh to send your aide for it yes sir we . . . subject to a onceover by our legal eagle here yes sir you know what a stickler the Boss is for . . . When he called this morning yes sir he . . . yes I have trouble understanding him on the phone sometimes too sir but this was in a written memo he . . . his handwriting yes I do too sir but . . . Can do yes sir, Virginia run this last memo from the Boss through the typewriter for General Haight better make eight copies Beamish here will want one too and . . . sir? Yes sir you bet your . . . I said affirmative yes sir goodbye sir, oh and Virginia show me that before you send it out the last time I gave you dictation and you typed dental for oriental where did these scrambled eggs come from, see what it's like trying to run the store camped out in a hotel suite with no exec on board Brisboy oh and Virginia, that black sitting over in the corner if he's here to put in this other phone line tell him to get to it, he's not being paid to sit there looking at what's he looking at, an old Ray-X toy catalog?

—I just gave him it to look at Mister Davidoff, it's got all these pictures and he don't read any English he . . .

—Well who is he what's he doing here and while you're over there Virginia look in the box under that blue chaise longue, the file marked Health Package Mister Brisboy here will want a look at it for the cemetery tie-in that reminds me Brisboy you've got an apology coming, when the press boys called about your Wagner Funeral Homes chain joining up with the J R Corp Family of Companies here I was busy on these

Indians and put Virginia there on the phone with some notes of mine where I'd abbreviated funeral f u n, gave them the idea we'd picked up a string of massage parlors to work into this whole nursing home to cemetery package, really hit the fan if we don't clear it up I thought we could put you onto them later for a statement got somebody working on it now Beamish I know she's been with the Boss since he got started, the only reason I kept her on when he closed down the midtown office and sent her along I thought she had an inside look at operations maybe you can talk Mister Bast into using her at uptown headquarters I couldn't, look at that beam she fills half the room when she stoops over in that print dress takes off her earring every time she answers the phone and then stops to put it back on see what I mean Beamish, I've got to get a gal in here who can see what it's like Mister Brisboy trying to keep score with what is it now Virginia?

—It's this man at the door he . . .

—If it's that soldier boy give him a copy of that feature on Frigicom you'll want to give that a once over before it goes out Beamish oh and Virginia that memo from the Boss I told you to run through the typewriter better give him two copies and give one to Beamish here where is it.

—I just started it Mister Davidoff but this man at the door has this big package for Mister Bast he says it's this golf practice set which . . .

—See what I mean Beamish the piano's one thing but setting up a golf course in the middle of Virginia just give him the headquarters office address uptown let them lay it out up there it's where Mister Bast spends most of his time, the Boss has him all tied up on this foundation music grant project why he wants me here on deck for these brush fires the shape he's in I don't think Mister Bast can handle them, I showed him this big Alsaka Development story and he just drew a blank standing here like that hearing aid was tuned in on outer space looks like he's lost twenty pounds squaring up this music project before he leaves tomorrow for Virginia call Piscator see if he's got the all clear on this company logo, the Boss wants it painted on the tail of the company plane before Mister Bast flies out to that Wonder funeral tomorrow may have told you Beamish, he's stopping off there on the way to this Indian pageant we've worked up to wait if you've got Piscator on the phone I'd better, who?

—It's . . .

—If it's Mister Ten-forty tell him to get up here before we lose Mooneyham, may want to get in on this yourself Brisboy our personnel man's coming in to put the division heads over there through their paces some kind of decision making session the Boss had him work up who is it Virginia?

—It's the hotel manager's office they're calling Mister Bast . . .

—Tell them we expect him any minute he, here give me that, hello . . . ? No this is Mister Davidoff what . . . Not to Mister Bast no you're billing this suite to Pomerance Associates and we're billing the client that's all you . . . what? What do you mean General Haight's suite you're not billing that to us or to J R Corp either no he . . . he's on the board of directors yes but when we took this suite over and moved him up the hall your PR boys took him on as a guest of the hotel for the mileage you could get out of having a retired three star . . . Three no three moved up a grade on retirement he . . . I didn't tell your PR boys he was in charge of commissaries over there because they didn't ask me now what . . . No I don't know how long he's going to stay here no but before you pull that you'd better tie up your . . . yes goodbye somebody at the door there Virginia did you get out that file for Mister Brisboy here?

—Excuse me Mister Davidoff before we go further, this is not Mister Brisboy but Mister Duncan, and I believe he . . .

—Duncan?

—Mister Duncan, yes. In connection with the Triangle Products acquisition I believe Mister Duncan had been led to understand his firm was an object of interest to the parent company in light of its indebtedness to Triangle, however . . .

—Don't worry about it Mister Duncan, Beamish here gets his signals crossed sometimes but everything's under Virginia get Skinner out of the bedroom, show you the dummy he's laying out in there Duncan you'll get a real look at who's at the door . . .

—Some man that says he plays the bass flute with a little mustache he . . .

—One thing we really need right now tell him to try the grand ballroom and tell Skinner to bring out that woman really topflight track record in curriculum management Duncan one look at what she's got spread out in there and you'll see what that big story we got in Monday's Times was all about somebody on the phone?

—Mister Davidoff before we go further, I believe some confusion has occurred between this Mister Duncan's firm, with its reputation as a leading producer of wallpaper . . .

—Wallpaper like his dry humor don't you Duncan oh Virginia if it's those two Indian boys calling tell them to stay right where they are send somebody right out to get them, lose them now and the Boss will really who is it . . .

—It's some magazine they . . .

—Tell them I'm in a meeting and get Skinner out here with wait give it to me, hello . . . ? No he's not who . . . statement he gave you on the phone what statement he . . . Wait you called him where last night he's been out of town since . . . Mister Bast isn't here either no he works out of uptown operations headquarters we're just camped out here handling their corporate PR till the lease is signed on that building at Madison and . . . because right now I'm probably closer to this acquisition picture than Mister Bast is that's why, got the lawyer who set up the Triangle deal sitting right in front of me now what . . . Well who said Mister Bast wasn't still executive officer of the parent company trouble with you press boys listen to each other's rumors instead of . . . what? Because he's been busy on this foundation grant don't even read the releases we send you Virginia get a copy of the press release on this J R Foundation grant to encourage symphonic . . . what? Well what did you call about then . . . Rumor that's what I just said about you boys listening to . . . point eight million this year who wouldn't grab the tax loss but there's no plan to liquidate no, the magazine's being acquired to round out this whole vertical integration picture wood pulp source through paper manufacture with the Triangle deal into this field growing faster than defense getting the publishing end under one roof and any sales of Her magazine's fixed assets are leasebacks or duplication with the Duncan facilities got Duncan himself right here in front of me taking over his whole line, prestige backlist new titles in the trade end pulling together a children's encyclopedia expanding the whole textbook operation and this revamped women's mag laying out the new dummy right now a whole new concept in . . . changing the title to She yes that's all I can tell you a whole new concept in . . . saw that too yes if Time magazine thinks we're going to lose our shirt on it they . . . Because those boys still think à la nineteenth century just ask them how much it costs them to get one subscription one new subscription just one new sub . . . what? Who said anything about paper clothes . . . no we've got the division head from Eagle Mills here I'll check it out call us later Virginia? Get Mister Hopper over there out of that melon long enough to see if he's getting into paper clothes heard anything on that one Beamish?

—No but I believe . . .

—Don't blame you believe anything I hear myself about paper the way they're stripping those power company rights of way and mining claims right down through Virginia I told you to get Skinner out here with those figures the Boss wants on paper consumption rising triple the rate of the GNP for Mister Bast's talk to the security analyst boys, has us bring in a top drawer speech writer on it and then reads them these statements over the phone must be where this Business Week interview came from, Triangle Products acquired for an undisclosed price rumor places substantially below book value refers to him as shrewd downstate interests when it was Beamish here who got the nut down to four million five put Piscator's nose a little out of joint thinks maybe you're trying to crowd him out . . .

—I? Good heavens I hardly . . .

—Probably where the Boss got the idea you were putting something over on him listing this Her magazine's two hundred odd thousand account receivable as a Triangle asset with point eight million in operating losses already this year so he's knocked it off your four million five, three million of that covered by the Eagle pension plan sale back to the employees and X-L selling at twenty-nine with its own paper source handing over fifty thousand shares of X-L common market value over a million four gives you a little margin over this million three balance wants your approval on these figures for the press.

—It is cutting things a bit thin, and I believe we must still review the status of . . .

—This Ritz Bright Leaf outfit don't worry about it, just tell your principals the Boss is sitting tight on it as a tax loss while this USDA experimental program gets off the ground still labeled secret but he wants me to discuss trade names with you as soon as it's checked out with Senator Virginia where's that call we're putting through to Senator him on the phone there?

—No it's the room service did somebody order kippers?

—Probably Mooneyham over there keeping his thirst up, doctor trying to get him off it sends him to five movies a day he's seen so many dirty movies he's gone right back to Virginia tell him you want his glass for a refill and get some coffee into him before Mister Ten-forty shows up, call him that because we got him through some computer management service working on a book on measurement Skinner wants for his spring list Virginia? Tell Skinner to bring that trade list out with him putting through his paper order now reminds me Beamish the Boss said anything to you about recycling that back inventory at Triangle?

—No but I believe . . .

—Must plan to sell it off novelty rolls and all then his last memo he wants that big water tower painted to look like a giant roll of toilet paper even did it himself with orange crayon on an aerial view we'd sent him wanted to make sure there were no legal objections.

—No but I believe the residents in the immediate area of the Triangle plant would hardly welcome the spectacle of a giant roll of . . .

—Don't worry about it then one thing I don't argue with those pieces of lined paper handwritten one end to the other comes in here I just tie up my pantslegs he wants solutions not problems . . .

—Mister Davidoff excuse me sir but that is why Mister Duncan is here. In the haste attending the parent company's eagerness to resolve the status of his firm in the course of acquiring Triangle Products, some confusion appears to have occurred between . . .

—May speed things up to get Skinner out here for a rundown the way these legal boys make twenty words do the work of one get Beamish here going with his whereifs and whereases been here talking for twenty minutes and we're still right over this way Mister Duncan oh and Skinner don't have to introduce you to your old head of sales do I Duncan let him give you a runthrough and I'll fill in the gaps.

—Gosh . . .

—Brought Skinner on board when I left Diamond Beamish, he had a management contract offer from the bank Duncan here set up as trustee tied in with a token hundred thousand dollar option to buy and all Skinner can come up with is joint tenancy in a piece of a three or four million dollar company out here in Long Island City having some reorganization problems got their lawyer coming in later to show you his figures, this woman Skinner just married picked up five percent of it in her divorce settlement putting that up as security for this J R Corp loan to pick up the option and meet the full purchase price out of future earnings probably what's on Duncan's mind here . . .

—I just want to get fixed up and get back to . . .

—Yes Mister Davidoff please, we must interrupt this and get back to . . .

—Don't worry about it, see what it's like running the store with nobody on deck to put out these brush fires Time spread says we'll lose our shirt see why Duncan here's worried about future earnings wants a look at the, where's that trade list comments from your topflight name critics and all, noses a little out of joint when they trip over topflight talent but that's par for the course call this wallpaper Beamish?

I CHOSE ROTTEN GIN The story of a disillusioned Communist, who had not the courage to go against the party.

. . . so ostentatiously aimed at writing a masterpiece that, in a less ambitious work, one would be happy to call promising, for such readers as he may be fortunate enough to have . . .

—Glandvil Hix

O! CHITTERING ONES A serious work which urges us to lay aside our fears and realize our true strength.

. . . the outside world of American life is described so imperfectly and so superficially as to make us feel that the novelist himself has never known it . . . —M Axswill Gummer

THE R I COONS IGNITE Violence in a small southern community, the racial question delicately and faithfully dealt with.

. . . nowhere in this whole disgusting book is there a trace of kindness or sincerity or simple decency . . . —S T Erlingnorf

TEN ECHOES RIOTING A delicately evocative novel.

. . . a delicately evocative novel . . . —B R Endengill
. . . a literary event, of sorts . . . —Newsleak Magazine

THE ONION CREST G I A rousing war novel, adventure with a tough talking sergeant from Wisconsin (the onion state).

. . . does not persuade us that it is based on any but a narrow and jaundiced view, a projection of private discontent . . .

—Milton R Goth

. . . another long and rather dreary saga of modern man in search of a soul . . . —Baltimore Sun

THOSE NIGER CONTI Lusty romance with the Godzzoli family in love and the Italian secret service in Egypt.

. . . a complete lack of discipline . . . —Kricket Reviews

THE TIGER ON SONIC A killer in provincial New England trapped by the brilliant deductions of the author's popular armchair detective, Mr Ethan Frome.

. . . a really yummy read . . . —D O'Lobeer

—I confess the titles are quite catchy ones indeed Mister Davidoff, however we . . .

—Still working one up for this new book on measurement by our Mister Ten-forty went right out and picked up a new suit with his hundred dollar advance and these Haight memoirs, Skinner brought in a topflight name writer to get the General off Virginia try to reach Mister Gall, promised us a new Western himself called The Blood in the Red White and Blue as soon as his play goes into production may have to pull him off the General to give the Boss a hand on this full length bio he wants to bring out, thinks his own success story may rub off on the company and vice versa when he takes the jump into public life sharp eye for a deal but he can use some help on his spelling Virginia? Get hold of Mister Gall? He ought to be in here by now with that Indian pageant script and call the desk, find out if they've seen those two Indian boys better look in the bar tell them to page the Brook brothers oh and Skinner bring out one of your standard author's contracts you know what a stickler the Boss is for the letter of the law Beamish, wants to be sure there's none of your legal doubletalk these writers can horn in on the advertising end . . .

—I doubt there's any reason for concern there Mister Davidoff, I believe these matters are left in the publisher's hands and so long as a book is advertised in good taste and . . .

—Not of the books in the books Skinner get out one of those layouts for . . .

—I beg your pardon you don't mean actually carrying advertising matter inserted in the text of the book itself? There may be no contractual objection however in terms of . . .

—Whose ads don't worry about it, end papers and centerfold go to the J R Family of Companies coming up with the rest from the agency's accounts preference anywhere they tie in with our products and services take Ray-X subcontracting on this line of prosthesises where's Skinner, just told him to get that Health Package layout see how they tie in with this nursing home funeral service cemetery deal . . .

—No no Mister Davidoff excuse me I believe you mistake my point.

Contractual obligations aside sir, surely the arbitrary insertion of pages of advertising bearing no relation to the creative work of an author who . . .

—One step ahead of you there too Beamish already set up a page for Wonder Beer in The Onion Crest G I next printing may even work it right into the . . .

—But the authors Mister Davidoff, the writers . . .

—Best thing ever happened to them ask Duncan here, come in spouting art and literature what they really mean's a big advance on royalties, book finally comes out at fifteen dollars sells two thousand copies they blame him blame the reviewers blame tv blame everything but production costs and your little old lady at the Shady Nook book store spouting art and literature rakes off half wet her pants when the paperbacks came out spread culture grabbed the mass market now you pay hardcover prices for paperbacks, what pays production costs for your tv spectaculars what keeps the Times on the street what keeps Virginia where's that old New Yorker magazine lying around here . . .

—That soldier borrowed it Mister Davidoff he needed some pictures to trace for the General to . . .

—Ran through it yesterday Beamish counted five hundred forty columns two hundred was text the rest of it ads, turns into a catalog and they'd lose their mailing privilege so what you read's as long and lively as the phone book suffocate you if there wasn't a picture of a Cadillac or a bottle of whisky every time you turn a page . . .

—You make your point Mister Davidoff I see it regularly, though I do believe I recall a cartoon some two years ago I found quite amusing, now if we may return to the plight of Mister Duncan . . .

—Don't worry about it, still afraid he won't see his full purchase price out of future earnings why he wants a look at what Skinner's got laid out this way Mister Duncan, gal I brought along from Diamond topflight track record in curriculum management in here spreading out this whole textbook line to take on these ad revenues boys down at the agency bringing them in faster than . . .

—Mister Davidoff you're not suggesting, excuse me for interrupting but you're not also suggesting carrying advertising matter in school textbooks . . . ?

—Not my suggestion Beamish straight from the Boss we just carried it over to the trade list here, whole inspiration came from these matchbooks he picked up Mooneyham's company there for in the first place got the names of every company product plan and service from hearing aids to funerals into the hands of every camper smoker and hophead in the country, need proof just look at the way this new aspirin took off cornered the market overnight with that straight-from-the-shoulder punch line it's green! Whole case of them in there put a few in your pocket when

you leave watch your jacket there Mister Duncan, buttered roll on the
bed better move that coffee Miss somebody on the phone Virginia?

—It's that Mister Hyde Mister Davidoff he . . .

—Just tell him to hold on got our gal here giving Mister Duncan the
fifty cent tour wants a look at her . . .

—Mister Davidoff excuse me but before this whole project proceeds
further I believe certain important legal questions may . . .

—Don't worry about it Beamish just got Piscator back from California on it, get across to these state systems where they buy all their
textbooks in a lump grab a cost conscious ear in the legislature and we're
off and running see these local boards of ed lining up like dominoes when
the word gets out to the taxpayers school taxes up to their wait Virginia
where's that schoolbooks backgrounder you were sending out, have to
call it back I just saw the title you typed scared for sacred want to see
it picked up by the Reader's Digest our gal here trying to reach these
bleeding hearts . . .

—The fear psychology aptitudes reading levels all that stuff and junk,
she came on through bread, the gone bite in the buttered roll smeared
with lipstick like the coffee cup at her knee on the bed and the cigarette
raised quivering now her contact lenses were out she looked at Mister
Duncan with no interest at all, —it's not the kids, if they find a Cheerios
or Reese Peanutbutter Cups spread in the middle of their math lesson
they'll think it's a ball it's not the kids, it's the parents that make the
trouble brought up with tv they ought to be used to love stories docu-
mentaries mysteries all that bla bla bla break off for clogged sinks under-
arms . . .

—But Miss, Mister Davidoff surely you don't intend to accept advertising for such things as deodor . . .

—Don't worry about it Beamish see what she's spreading out for
Duncan right here all pegged to the grade level . . .

—Gum cereals candy bars all that stuff and junk is the primary
grades bikes sports equipment records seventh and eighth on up nothing
till French Three and advanced algebra on deodorants tampons all that
bla bla bla . . .

—Here's a cute one they just came up with for ninth grade algebra
once the USDA opens up and the trademark's registered, smoky letters
rising out of the grass here see them? I'm Mary Jane, fly me. Gets the idea
right across Skinner got that title page? Motto running right along here
under your Duncan and Skinner colophon bringing the world into the
classroom and the classroom into the world gimmick Skinner here came
up with, dug out this name educator Thomas Dewey for the PW an-
nouncement of this children's encyclopedia turned it into a crash project,
team of salesmen out blanketing the city with samples of volume four
pull in enough orders for the set we can go through with the other nine
paying half cent a word all that ad space bypass your little old lady at
Shady Nook hit your educable public right in the supermarket where

they live ought to retail at the price of a package of what's this
Virginia . . .

—This memo I typewrited eight copies of you . . .

—Got your carbons in backwards again the Boss has a Xerox machine
delivered to uptown headquarters place we really need one's right here
oh and Virginia this time you run it through I thought I told you to set
quarter inch margins, something the Boss saw on tv sends out a companywide order to set every margin a quarter inch to save paper whole reason
this publishing end's got top priority in the first place all this paper the
Boss says we might as well print books on it, now he's heard it costs more
to keep presses idle than to run them so he wants them rolling day and
night's why Skinner's got his gal here doubling in brass on this She
dummy give the American gal a whole new image . . .

—Age spots corns ugly veins unwanted hair flabby waistline drooping bust dry skin hemorrhoids all that stuff and . . .

—I hardly see how you expect to sell . . .

—Advertising Beamish sell advertising mail the magazine free to a
guaranteed audience, put out a mag like Her play the numbers game
with your ad accounts spend five dollars to get subscriptions you sell for
four and lose our shirts like the rest of them, She hits the stands and
they'll all line up like dominoes target your ads in on your guaranteed
audience you'll see boat magazines free to boat owners sex mags free to
kids and singles photo mags free to camera buffs just get the lists knock
out this five percent return on direct mail and your ad boys will pay the
difference to know who they're reaching . . .

—Age lines nerves headaches flabby thighs small busts oily skin
cracked nails split ends all that bla bla bla . . .

—Targeting in on every one of them drugstores selling us customer
lists through wholesalers handling the Nobili prescription line gets some
mileage in this feature she's got spread out there let Duncan here get a
look at what Skinner's getting into . . .

—Yes that's . . .

—No here Mister Duncan over here, at last . . . !

—Yes that's . . .

—At last! A Personalized Plan from Nave to Grave, funeral right
through the cemetery with the drug line nursing home tie-in somebody
at the door?

—I thought he was fixing me . . .

—Mister Duncan I quite understand yes, but at this point I believe
you might better join the rest of the gentlemen on the sofa and let me
call you when I find an opening to approach Mister Davidoff in terms of,
of fixing you up as you . . .

—Thought that was somebody at the door Virginia if it's those Indian
boys tell them to sit tight and get that gang over on the sofa off the
firewater . . .

—It wasn't them Mister Davidoff it was just Mister . . .

—Oh and Virginia that call I'm putting through to what happened to that call to Senator . . .

—But that Mister Hyde's still waiting on the telephone for . . .

—Trying to reach me while Hyde holds up the line better close that door behind you Beamish let them get back down to business in there just wanted Duncan here to get an eyeful of what was behind that spread in Monday's where's Duncan . . .

—I suggested he join the group on the sofa until we are able to concentrate more directly on his . . .

—Don't worry about it few things I didn't want to get into in front of him, gave him the three dollar tour to hang on till you or Nonny check out Skinner's option the Boss wants to be sure Duncan's really out of the ballgame dirty looking little man wouldn't have picked him as the publisher of T S . . .

—But Mister Davidoff that is exactly the problem which . . .

—Don't worry about it the only way Skinner and this gal can hold onto it think they'll come up with the purchase price out of some lawsuit you saw his eye and that smile of hers car wreck asking a million each, by the time that's settled the parent company will have called his loan and picked up the option had to take on his management contract to get it he's about as much use as a spare what's this box here Virginia, be lucky to get out with his hat and . . .

—That Indian suit they delivered the one you told me to rent for Mister . . .

—Chief Indian chief, better check it out before he takes it with him can't have him get up there looking like the last of the here just get it off the desk, hello? Hyde? just hold on a minute no sit down Beamish, didn't want to get into this in front of Duncan there the Boss saw that piece in Forbes on this collision course we're running on these mineral interests wants to move fast got this topflight salesman I brought along from Diamond on that Endo divestiture on his way out there with, Hyde . . . ? Haven't shown up here yet no had them paged down at the bar but . . . no if you're driving better leave without them we'll get them loaded on the company plane with Mister . . . what? Six cents a mile companywide yes straight from the Boss not his fault if you drive a Cadillac he . . . time to get rid of what smell in your car . . . Because this whole Endo shipment's on its way out there right now, gets there ahead of you and you'll have them tearing open the crates won't know a toaster from a hair dryer be lifting the tops of the washing machines to climb on them and . . . To hold it off till the last minute with your PR cameras set up when the presentation's ready to . . . No before the pageant starts he makes the presentation they follow up with their ceremony make him an honorary . . . not the Boss no he can't make it been out of the country just called in last night he's . . . Sending his exec out in his place try to smooth their feathers yes . . . Bast yes don't think you've met him he's

. . . what? Young yes but it couldn't be the same one this one's been with the Boss since . . . Don't worry about it I'd handle it myself but the Boss wants me here on deck for brush fires shouldn't be any problems the whole thing's . . . No worked the whole thing up in our shop historical pageant got in a topflight name scriptwriter to help them work up some pride in their history had to do it all himself asked them and they drew a blank, yakked about the Great Spirit warning them the white man would try to take away their language had to get all his background info from the papers and go from there has them sign a treaty for one reservation they're herded off it middle of winter across country barefoot and bottled up in the one they're on out there now, brought in a little famine rapes cholera to jazz up the scenario try to get some togetherness going for them, work up some tribal spirit to get them off their butts and defend this happy hunting ground with these gas and mineral leases they're squatting on find the whole thing in these press releases should be waiting for you when you get out there, want to get them right to the press boys the night before so they can . . . Don't worry about it that's what they're paid for I'd send some of our agency boys out to hold your hand but they're all parceled out on . . . No waiting for final script delivery now don't worry about it just let this Charley Yellow Brook hand out the parts he's been . . . afraid of what? What would . . . no what would they go after you for they . . . No most of them never seen one had to have Abercrombie's send out some top archery types to show them how, even had to throw in some topflight canoeists so they'd know which end of the paddle to put in the . . . No it's Brook Yellow Brook not stream, Charley Yellow Brook and his . . . must have seen a first speech draft joke the Boss came up with about a book called The Yellow Stream by I P Daily thought it might break the ice but . . . get the same feeling myself sometimes I just tie up my . . . your what? Oh your boy want to take your boy along why not, might see something he . . . what America's all about? Show him what we have to protect yes might get him into some pictures want them taken before the action starts hand carried put right on a plane got a couple of photographers from the local papers and a UP stringer doubling as PR for us get them on the wire oh and Hyde before they start shooting Mister Bast ask him to take off his hearing aid, want some good shots of him and the Senator get the Brook brothers in there any local color all those feathers going that hearing aid might look . . . haven't briefed him on it no he's been wrapped up on another project pretty worn down not much of a fireball to start with he may need a little prodding to get into the spirit of . . . don't worry about it goodbye oh and Hyde . . . ? Hung up on me, ties up the phone for twenty minutes and hangs up on me wanted him to check out these appliance invoices at the other end make sure the Boss been at you on that yet Beamish? writing off these appliances at retail?

—No, the entire transaction is one with which I . . .

—Saw that Wall Street Journal crack didn't you about Typhon Inter-national tying the can to Endo in that agreement to divest nothing but backdated inventory whole thing happened before I came on deck here probably one of Crawley's stunts, only reason the Boss could give for taking it on according to Bast was because it was cheap didn't know what to do with it till I thought of this gang of Indians give them the whole kit and kaboodle get them on our side of the fence on these leases and write off the cost but you know how the Boss thinks every loss a profit, wants the tax write-off at retail like those dated drugs in the Nobili . . .

—I would have to review the figures Mister Davidoff but while we have the matter under discussion there are aspects of this enterprise I find frankly disturbing. You may well regard me as old-fashioned but I find posing as benefactors to these Indians simply in order to take advan-tage of their rights to possible mineral or gas deposits on their lands quite as distasteful as advertising chewing gum and . . .

—We don't do it first Beamish somebody else will, got them under the gun now with a move to pull their wigwams right out from under them be lucky to get off the reservation with their hats and their asses, spring this historical pageant to pull them together follow up on the publicity get their claims established and they can sink their teeth in this royalty arrangement with the Alsaka subsidiary put a little wampum under their belts for a rainy day see this Forbes' piece Showdown at Broken Bow? Probably got it all from Crawley on the phone again yester-day about these Alberta and Western sites said he'd talked to you on these mining claims . . .

—He did yes, the other party appears prepared to raise his offer on the power company properties you mention, provided his earlier offer on the mining claims area is accepted in order to avoid what could become a costly and drawn out action threatening the validity of the claims themselves. Mister Crawley was particularly concerned about Mister Bast, he seems to take a great interest in him and stressed his wish to relieve Mister Bast of time-consuming complications, and since Mister Crawley appears to have substantial dealings both with J R Corp princi-pals and the other party a Mister Stamper I believe, and is acting merely as go-between . . .

—Just brought in Stamper for window dressing Beamish, hunting crony of his see the big game film those two put together million zebras running for their lives you'd paint stripes on your ass and run too, rides around his end of Texas in a Cadillac can of beer in his hand answering police calls converted his old slave cabins to fancy guest cottages I just heard he got so mad when he saw his new tax assessment he went out and burned them all down, big overgrown kid never got past fourth grade Bast told me once the Boss never got out of sixth frankly sometimes I believe it, he runs that assay on the water at Wonder Brewery comes across smaltite traces and has Nonny put in for a mineral depletion allowance tipped his hand to the FDA coming down hard on cobalt safety levels now Milliken jumps in to protect home industry only thing they had besides sheep and Indians till he suddenly gets the idea his state is one big cobalt nickel arsenic deposit looks over the stockpile scene and hauls the Undersecretary up before his committee on the contract he negotiated for Typhon to set up this smelting operation in Gandia and buy it back as surplus, supply U S cobalt stockpile requirements from it and sell the nickel and anything else they come up with on the side wherever Pythian Overseas has a market, that's who your other party in this deal is Beamish I've worked with Moncrieff nobody to tangle assholes with . . .

—No I had hardly considered the possib . . .

—Any cobalt in sight Typhon wants to sit on it pressure on them from Pythian has this war going in Gandia to secede Uaso province smelter minerals and all turn the whole thing into a company town, defense minister Doctor Dé steps over declares a republic and you get Broos speaking up in the Senate for self-determination for the people of this gallant little emerging nation, pleads for nonintervention and sponsors a bill prohibiting imports with Gandia as country of origin. Nowunda's government trying to hold things together take help anyplace they can get it so Milliken votes for the Broos bill backs the U N resolution supporting Nowunda's government and wakes up in bed with China Albania and . . .

—Mister Davidoff excuse me again for interrupting but as interesting as all of this is I believe we are straying from . . .

—Just getting to these bellies, Bast been at you about them yet?

—Mister Bast? about, bellies . . . ?

—Pork bellies frozen dried may not know any more about them than I do the Boss has been hedging in them on the side must have Crawley up to his ass on margin some deal going on a trade if Nowunda holds out takes a stiff royalty on mineral exports solve this problem at Ray-X getting rhodium for thermocouples on these government fixed price contracts why the Boss pushed Haight so hard on these Pentagon research contracts had Ray-X borrow on the strength of them, put in later for a cost overrun and come out on top only problem was coming up with the products, got in a topflight R and D man through Mister Ten-forty worked with him for years says he has a topflight track record in the academic field looking for a place where his mind could turn loose and soar, all in that release on Frigicom oh Virginia told you to dig up that Frigicom release, got the City Council biting on the noise pollution end have to check it out with Washington work into this talk for the security analyst boys get me Colonel Moyst on the phone check his new number, Haight got him transferred over to procurement oh and Virginia that black still sitting over there looking at pictures thought we got rid of him doesn't speak English what does he speak . . .

—It sounded maybe like French Mister Davidoff only I don't know what French sounds like so . . .

—Get Skinner's gal out there maybe she can parley vous find out what he's doing here knock before you go in oh and Virginia, something here about a shipment from Hong Kong says plastic flowers must be those sweaters they sent that fiber over from Eagle for, get Hopper out of that whatever he's eating long enough to find out who's this on the phone, Moyst?

—No they said it's for Mister Bast about these musicians that . . .

—Tell them to leave a number have Bast get back to them when he rolls in oh and . . .

—But Mister Bast is . . .

—Here better take it myself can't tell what he, hello . . . ? No he's not what . . . Don't worry about it just give me your figures probably be handling this end anyhow what . . . Taping the whole thing yes told him I thought we should get a topflight name band like the Boston Pops package deal wrap up the whole . . . Mister Bast said what? What's he got against the Boston . . . make any piece of music sound like elephants doing what . . . ? No no go ahead whatever he told you, he's the . . . Wait what about rehearsal time what's the going . . . don't rehearse for record-ing sessions then how do they . . . get ninety dollars for the basic three hour session ought to wrap the whole thing up in one . . . what? Fifteen minutes of usable recording from each session why can't . . . All right suppose they get twenty minutes suppose they get sixty what . . . Fifteen minutes maximum thought you just told me there's no rehearsing what are they doing then playing with their . . . No no go ahead whatever he told you he's the . . . Ninety-five men that brings it to zero, five, eighty-five fifty for each . . . what do you mean eighty-six forty five times nine is . . . Ninety-six thought you said Mister Bast wanted ninety-fi . . . the contractor gets paid double? How many . . . don't know how long it is no he's still . . . Well how long is a symphony give me a . . . just to give me a ballpark figure forty-five minutes that's three of your three hour sessions eighty-six forty each brings us up around twenty-six thousand ought to cover the whole . . . without studio rental just your boys in the band add on . . . orchestra yes add on . . . what? Rental of instruments what do you mean your boys don't even own . . . Look would I take on a job as a writer show up without a pencil? What's the . . . kettledrum no I don't own a kettledrum don't play the kettledrum if I played the kettledrum I'd own a . . . think the Boston Pops has to go out and rent a kettledrum every time they play the Blue Danube? What do you . . . no whatever he told you don't worry about it we'll get back to you see what I mean Beamish, get local eight-o-one in there might as well just get a comb and toilet paper while you're here get to Hopper on squashing that union injunction Shorter brought when the Boss pulled those looms out for South America, gave his boy that whole territory for Wonder Beer making such a mess of it the Boss wants this settled before we have to buy him out might want to bring Bast in on it knows the Eagle picture first hand thought I just heard him in there . . .

—I had thought I heard a piano, however . . .

—Must have come in while we were fixing Duncan up in the bedroom there see what it's like running the store with an exec who . . .

—But do you mean Mister Bast is here? in there? playing the piano?

—In there playing the piano see what it's like running the . . .

—Excellent just let me go in and speak with him it should take only a moment to clear up this . . .

—Wouldn't bother him Beamish gets in there shuts that door wouldn't interrupt him unless the Boss called or the place caught fire, pressure on him to clean up this project get this grant out so there's no legal snag in the Foundation's tax exempt status when he goes into it for a loan to Virginia told you to get Moyst . . .

—Moist?

—Moyst Colonel Moyst told you to get him on the phone don't have to bother Bast on these questions you have about Eagle Beamish probably clear them up myself, the Boss is talking about handing the whole thing over to the town for a park and speedway write these leases off as a gift if you can get him a high enough appraisal on them get some help from Hopper over there on that, any more trouble from this Begg woman with her stockholder suit say he's acting for the stockholders cutting costs move operations south if he has to to hang onto his tax umbrella Shorter's union boys don't like it tell them their jobs are waiting for them in Georgia, set up down there with cheap equipment for fast replacement under deductible maintenance expenses won't have to wait around on this capital goods depreciation allowance think he just wants you to check out that end of it, you know what a stickler he is for the letter of . . .

—The law I do Mister Davidoff I do, however may I say this constant near frenzied emphasis on the letter of the law at the expense of, in fact too frequently in direct defiance of its spirit, is something I frankly find . . .

—What lawyers are for isn't it Beamish wasn't for that you'd be out selling pencils . . .

—Perhaps but however that may be, in this particular instance corporate activities seem so preponderantly inspired by such negative considerations as depreciation and depletion allowances, loss carryforwards tax write-offs and similar . . .

—Way the big boys think Beamish why the Boss is where he is and we're down here pushing pencils, goes right to the gut issue and sends through a directive some of them so blunt almost sound simple minded hardly understand him on the phone half the time either, spend an hour afterward putting the pieces together get the feeling myself sometimes he does the grunting and we do the work but that's Moyst on the phone Virginia? No here just give it to me hello, Colonel . . . ? Oh yes sir . . . No no sir yes sir no sir . . . Yes sir no it won't happen again sir no sir . . . Yes sir I know you haven't been a colonel since nineteen for . . . Yes sir I . . . Saint Fiacre in the Ardennes offensive yes sir I . . . that General Box took all the credit for throwing off the whole German timetable yes I do sir he . . . that Bradley and Ike were completely unprepared yes sir I'm sure the readers of your memoirs will want to see the true light shed on . . . your memoirs yes sir is that what you called about sir? We have a topflight . . . sir? Oh about the university yes sir we . . . all arranged in your name yes sir we . . . in your name yes of course affirmative sir we . . . sir? To name the entire university after you sir . . . ? Yes well no sir we . . . Yes I understand sir yes sir however they . . . through channels yes sir however certain . . . the football team yes sir however certain alumni active in the football team's behalf feel that it might sound . . . No sir that Haight U sir might be misinterpreted as sounding . . . the proper aggressive spirit for the gridiron yes sir however the cheerlead . . . going coeducational yes sir the cheerlead . . . the university's major academic attraction yes sir the cheerlead . . . sir? Yes sir we certainly will sir now if I can take one more minute of your time sir to . . . One minute of your time yes sir to call your attention to an item in this latest memo from . . . sir? The next time I speak with him I certainly will sir now if I can take one more min . . . sir? Magazines . . . ? Yes sir we'll send over any we can find immediately sir and sir? If I can take one . . . sir? Virginia hang this up if he calls again tell him he's, tell him I'm sending over some old magazines anything you can find in there sitting on his royal red white and what's this . . .

—The hotel bill Mister Davidoff this bellboy just brought it up he they want . . .

—Tack it on the agency billing and get that typed up I want Bast's okay on it before he checks out what's wait Beamish . . .

—I do have another appointment Mister Davidoff I'd better be off to it, since telephone appears to be the most efficient means of communicating with you I shall make an attempt to . . .

—Don't worry about it just put out these brush fires and save your dime see the Boss's last memo cutting out of pocket expenses has Bast setting the example, pick up an option on five thousand shares at ten the stock opened this morning at fifteen and an eighth and anybody can turn in an expense account twenty pencils and a string of subway rides and feel no pain who's that Virginia . . .

—I got that Colonel Moyst at Washington you . . .

—Hope you got it right this time walk me into the buzzsaw like you did a minute ago hello? Oh and Virginia, Colonel . . . ? Told you to get

me that Frigicom release hello Moyst? This press release on Frigicom get
your gal on with her pad one of our legal eagles standing by here thought
you could clear it with CINFO direct the Boss wants it on the wires as
soon as . . . what? No this is Davidoff, Davi . . . yes just hold on while she
digs for it running the store here with no CO on deck to . . . What he
called you direct . . . ? Wait how many six thousand brake lining kits at
how much? One forty-nine each he must have gone through Mister Bast
what's the . . . No what storage bill on Long Island I'll have to check it
out with him hasn't said anything to wait here it is under my elbow, she
on . . . ? Dateline New York, Frigicom, comma, a process now being
developed to solve the noise pollution problem comma may one day take
the place of records comma books comma even personal letters in our
daily lives comma, according to a report released jointly today by the
Department of Defense and Ray hyphen X Corporation comma a member of the caps J R Family of Companies period new paragraph. The still
secret Frigicom process is attracting the attention of our major cities as
the latest scientific breakthrough promising noise elimination by the
placement of absorbent screens at what are called quote shard intervals
unquote in noise polluted areas period operating at faster hyphen than hyphen
sound speeds comma a complex process employing liquid nitrogen will be used to convert the noise shards comma as they are known
comma at temperatures so low they may be handled with comparative
ease by trained personnel immediately upon emission before the noise
element is released into the atmosphere period the shards will then be
collected and disposed of in remote areas or at sea comma, where the
disturbance caused by their thawing will make that where no one will
be disturbed by their impact upon thawing period new paragraph. While
development of the Frigicom process is going forward under contract to
the cap Defense cap Department comma the colorful new head of research and development at the recently revitalized Ray hyphen X Corp
Mister make that Doctor Vogel declined to discuss the project exclu-
sively in terms of its military ramifications comma comparing it instead
to a two hyphen edged sword forged by the alliance of free enterprise
and modern technology which promises to sever both military and artistic barriers at one fell swoop in the cause of human betterment period.
Citing as his original inspiration cap p Pater's line describing cap v
Venice as frozen music comma Vogel emphasized the possible importance of Frigicom comma a name he coined from the cap l Latin words
for cold and communicate comma to the fields of music and literature
period with the perfection of the thawing process comma Vogel envi-
sions concerts comma entire operas comma and books read aloud and
preserved by the Frigicom process comma stressing its importance to
longer works of fiction now dismissed as classics and remaining largely
unread due to the effort involved in reading and turning any more than
two hundred pages period new paragraph getting all this? While reserva-

tions have been expressed in some scientific quarters concerning these applications of this promised scientific breakthrough comma Doctor Vogel himself calls it quote merely an extension of an age when a man's mind is turned take out that a when man's mind is turned loose to soar period unquote. Like the tip of the iceberg comma only a fraction of Ray hyphen X activities are visible to the outside observer period other projects unfolding under Doctor Vogel's direction include a method of transport so revolutionary no make that radic wait no better just make that new so new it remains classified top secret hyphen sensitive by the Defense sorry cap d Defense cap Department comma which is backing its development under an undisclosed contract with the company and a major university nearby period quote. It's a basically simple idea that just took a lot of cheek to follow through unquote Doctor Vogel commented when pressed for details comma quote it's going to make your SST caps look like a trolley car period unquote paragraph. Ray hyphen X comma formerly well known as one of cap a America's favorite makers of kiddies apostrophe toys comma recently applied make that has recently devoted its expertise in battery and transistor driven products to the medical field as a major subcontractor in the manufacture of hearing aids comma heart pacers comma and other prosthetic devices in the cause of human bet no just leave that devices comma make that a period devices period. As an important new member of the caps J R Family of Companies comma Ray hyphen X continues to operate as a major producer of thermocouples make that also continues, period want to have your gal just read that back in case she just hold on a minute . . .

—I do have another appointment Mister Davidoff, perhaps . . .

—Right with you Beamish just want to clear up one, Moyst . . . ? While you're on how are you boys fixed for toilet paper . . . No no the Army, the Army, got a backed up inventory in one of our divisions that . . . roll type yes what . . . enough to last till when . . . ? Oh barring a mass defection by the military thought you said a mass defec . . . read what back to me . . . Can't take the time now no just check it out with our legal beagle here waiting for a call from Senator Milliken probably been trying to reach me while you were . . . No what golf game . . . don't think the Boss is too big on golf no probably want to send his second in command here Mister Bast seems really go on it just had a practice set delivered to his uptown . . . his calendar that week's all clear yes set it up any sweat he'll call them at the Senate Office Build . . . don't worry about it, takes care of that Beamish want me to run through this release again so you can . . .

—No no please Mister Davidoff I, I did hear it through and would see no legal difficulties so long as such contracts exist. The details of the actual projects are unfamiliar to me of course but if I heard correctly, I must say the notion of rendering sounds to a solid state by freezing them is simply, is really quite beyond the bounds of even the most childish fan . . .

—Won't argue with you Beamish hard to believe what these science boys come up with people sniffers laser beams cut you in half must know what they're up to, trip to the moon out of Julius Verne one day next day they're walking around up there eating ham sandwiches come back and peddle soft drinks and postage stamps the Boss thinks we might ring one in on promotion when the wraps are off whatever this transport wait there wait, Virginia get Skinner away from that door think he could hear the piano in there hear it playing all the way over here can't you Beamish . . . ?

—Yes in fact I was enjoying it, it sounded a little like Biz . . .

—Where's the here key to the washroom up the hall give him this Virginia thought he knew when Mister Bast's . . .

—But good heavens Mister Davidoff I beg your pardon but, you don't mean the piano is in the lava . . .

—Had to take the legs off to get it in there doesn't bother us at all he . . .

—But good heavens doesn't it bother him? playing in the . . .

—Know what you mean Beamish people trying to help him he doesn't make it any easier sometimes, give him privacy clean well lighted place he complains about the acoustics think this foundation project was the reason we're in business hardly get a yes or no out of him have to make half the decisions around here myself, just thought the next time you're in touch with the Boss might want to put a word in, adding new candidates to his board of directors couple of names I never heard of, company running up toward four hundred million in sales just brought in to do their PR end up running the store thought you might just hold on . . .

—It's that Mister Gall calling Mister Davidoff he . . .

—Who?

—Mister Gall that writer with the hair and his teeth are all . . .

—Just tell him to get that Indian script up here or we'll all be no here give it to me, hello? Yes hold on, oh and Beamish couple of things the Boss wants checked out trademarks I mentioned and this shipping corporation payroll Piscator's set up be right with you, hello? Yes what's holding up that Indian . . . When did he leave ought to be here by wait, oh Virginia see where Skinner's gal's getting with that black probably this messenger been here all the time hand him a picture book and he forgets what he . . . what? What's he bringing up a copy of your play for too nobody . . . Nobody here named Walldecker no I will if he shows up don't worry ab . . . No but what's holding up this profile on the Boss got Skinner in there ready to . . . that's your problem you're the writer all the hard info we've got is in that bio I pulled together from . . . Don't worry about it then leave it hazy, starts off dealing in landfill operations gets into some deals with the government has his eye on Eagle Mills builds up the capital to go after it moves in and . . . Wouldn't say that no just bring in the emphasis on low-cost operations companywide the . . . Wouldn't try the team player image no play with this family of companies angle divisional autonomy just keeps an eye on their tax and prof . . . Don't know that either no tells me the Alabama College of Business but his second in command here lets slip he never made it out of sixth grade probably amounts to about the same . . . Play it up no play it up want to make a big splash in this education market took over Duncan got right to the gut issue how to slash encyclopedia textbook prices help other kids have the opportunities he never . . . Wouldn't put it that way no played against the welfare issue bleeding hearts he's not ashamed of the old-fashioned ideas that made America what it . . . Well go up to the library dig out some of the President's speeches whole Protestant work ethic head of General Motors on free enterprise whole utilitarian pragmatism angle what works, sees how things are not how they ought to be whole approach is what works sort of a two edged sword forged from . . . No getting some sniping from the liberal press want to get across his image sees where the parade's heading before it does gets out in front of it and leads it right over the . . . what? Well why not look at the three we've had in the last ten years oh and this drug donation want to bring in this big drug donation in the southeast Asia market line him up for one of these awards service to humanit . . . have a what? Never heard of one if he has no, might try building one up between him and Virginia here usual warmth trust loyalty she's been on his . . . what one of her? Last thing you'd want them to see no don't have one of him either just use Mister Bast's idea say he's too busy to have his picture taken helps . . . who Bast? Pretty colorless no, went to conservation school dabbles in music on the side here probably inherits it, the Boss says his father's a master tunesmith can't make a living at it has to work as a railroad conductor to support himsel . . . don't worry about it just clean it up and get it in here a s a p got that? Just a profile we're pulling together here Beamish the Boss wants to run a version in She sort of a preview of the full length bio, thinks the aura of his success may rub off on it one thing the gals like it's success, feeling most of his is because he hates to part with a dollar rather find a way to take over the creditor oh Virginia man in the hat there just came in see if his name's Walldecker, getting pressed for time here Beamish can't give you much more something else on your mind we can . . .

—Clear up yes by all means nothing could delight . . .

—Payroll question you just mentioned yes any of your checks drawn on the J R Shipping Corporation?

—No as a matter of fact I have yet to receive . . .

—Subsidiary the Boss had Nonny set up says a check for fifteen percent of his bid on a hull up at auction in Galveston went in wants as many people as possible companywide put on that payroll get in on this six percent government subsidy to U S shipping . . .

—Mister Davidoff again, while the legality of such an approach sounds highly questionable and I would have to look into it . . .

—All the Boss wants you to do Beamish check out the legal . . .

—Setting up a shipping company on the basis of one hull for the purpose of asking the government to contribute six percent of the company's entire . . .

—Know what you mean Beamish small potatoes compared to what these wheat dealers pull down seems to think he may bring something off with these bellies though according to Nonny has him looking into export restrictions on U S commodities going in American bottoms may just end up hanging it on Nobili's Panama branch probably the only reason he bought in there use it as a tax haven transshipping point nothing but a warehouse and oh and Virginia, that letter to Nobili Panama retype it get streptohydrazid right this time and get it off today, one of their drugs the FDA just knocked off the U S market the Boss at you to fight that Beamish?

—No but I believe I read about it in the papers, they think it may cause deafness in children and I would hardly think he would want to continue its . . .

—Same one yes must be dropping it wants Panama to notify its overseas distributors no more coming through when they've exhausted present shelf stocks who is it Virginia . . .

—But good heavens what . . .

—It's the General Mister Davidoff he . . .

—Told you to tell him I here give it to me hello, sir . . . ? Yes sir I see sir we . . . that we sent over Skyscraper Management and Industrial Marketing and there are no pic . . . I'm sorry we'll do our best sir yes sir we . . . That you're leaving tonight yes sir but you do plan to be back by the twenty-first sir? We . . . No sir the date of the field trip by a class of schoolchildren to visit the upt . . . Yes sir I did write the memo sir but the Boss himself came up with the idea a sort of pet proj . . . in connection with our textbook project yes sir the company's expansion in this field growing faster than defense, publi . . . sir? Oh yes sir no sir I didn't mean . . . a figure of speech sir I didn't mean . . . I certainly will in the fut . . . yes schoolchildren to visit the company's uptown headquarters yes sir the Boss is quite proud of it and wanted them to meet some of the company's disting . . . No sir to tell the truth I've never been up there myself either sir but . . . Done this kind of thing before sir yes sir I'll arrange a photog . . . No sir I thought we would just give them box lun . . . He didn't say whether he would be there himself no sir but . . . Yes sir . . . Yes sir I certainly will affirmative yes sir I . . . sir? Hangs up oh Virginia head Duncan off there looks like he's . . .

—I believe his patience has reached an end Mister Davidoff and frankly mine is . . .

—Think he just wait Mister Duncan? Sorry this one's full have to go up the hall second door past the soldier boy by the mop closet Skinner's up there give you the key anything else to clear up Beamish let's skip your legalese get to the point, may have Mister Bast out here any minute few things I have to review with him anybody calls Virginia just tell them who's that . . .

—They want Mister Piscat . . .

—Tell them he's been wait give it to me can't tell what he's been, hello . . . ? Not here right now no he's been . . . Davidoff yes Davi . . . Cohen oh calling on Nepenthe yes ran it up to sixteen today think the Boss is sitting tight on about nineteen percent of the issue just wants control so he can . . . wait no wants to work the nursing homes into this Health Package made to order outlets for Nobili got Hopper here now with his cemetery Brisboy bringing in his funer . . . what? General who? one thing we need right now anoth . . . Oh why didn't you say so without the h yes why didn't you say so, thought you were on your way up brought in one of our own legal boys waiting here now to go over your figures had Piscator run down your Dun and Bradstreet told the Boss you looked a little overextended mentioned controlling interest in another company sounds dead on its . . . Don't worry about it no just took it as security on the loan help this man Skinner out with his option on a publishing deal got him under management contract real topfli . . . don't know no joint tenant said the gal he just married picked it up in her div . . . whose name hers? No didn't see the papers myself the Boss probably has them likes to get hold of those things hims . . . just Piscator's memo yes didn't seem to bother him mentioned your interest in this company dead on its feet a lawsuit you've been running for twenty years and a wrangle with the IRS all par for the course didn't seem to bother . . . what? No what just happened . . . He did? but how . . . Tough yes sorry to hear it Coen wouldn't think anybody would take it that hard see companies going public every day doesn't change the . . . doesn't change the book value though does it what's . . . Didn't mean it to sound like that Coen sounds like a fine man just meant to ask what's General Roll's product line parent company here might be int . . . expanding in paper products yes what about this Nathan Wise you're tied up with they in continuous forms too . . . ? Make what . . . ? What I thought you said yes quite a switch how'd . . . Pill came along and knocked them off their feet did it? how many hundred thousand gross in inventory . . . ? Certainly is yes how'd you people happen to get into . . . what in player pianos? Didn't know they used sheep membranes in the mechanisms no one of our divisions brewery uses them in a yeast filtering process George Wonder out there just died great friend of old Senator Milliken seems to take a lively int . . . who Milliken's family? Big minority stockholders in Nathan Wise pill came in must have wondered what hit them might be able to work something out for you though we . . . waiting for a call from the Senator now yes parent company just retained his old hometown law firm out there keep an eye on some other devel . . . Don't know no have to put you on with our legal eagle here let you two trade legal gobbledy wait where's, Virginia? Where's Beamish sitting right here a minute ago must have gone up the hall Coen have him get back to you oh and

Virginia, call I put through to Senator Milliken what happened to that boy over there unbuttoned down to his what's he doing here . . .

—He's this messenger Mister Davidoff he brought this stuff from Mister Gall he's waiting for you to sign . . .

—Yes where's never find a pencil here give it to him get him out of here looks like he'd cut his mother's man in the hat is that Walldecker said he was coming up here for . . .

—No he said he's this private detective Mister Davidoff he said he wants to ask you some whereabouts of . . .

—Find out what he wants piano just stopped in there Mister Bast probably coming out any minute Skinner's gal make any sense out of that black yet?

—She said he's from this place Malwi he said it's this country someplace he wants . . .

—All want something just tell her to find out what he wants oh and Vir . . .

—He said he's looking for that Mister Schepperman he . . .

—One thing we really need right now help an artist out once he'll never forgive you follow you to the grave, cost me one job to get rid of that lunatic so he follows me here tries to unload two tons of rusty iron calls it a stabile now he's lining up his friends for a handout every black in sight's an artist, can't do anything else suddenly discover they're an artist just tell that one to wait help Mister Bast with that attaché case Virginia lock's broken papers spilling out didn't see you come in Mister Bast in there clearing up this publishing jam not leaving though are you few brush fires to . . .

—There's one thing I'd like to get taken care of Mister Davidoff, I've been waiting for a . . .

—Here sit down put your case just put it here Virginia move this what's this . . .

—It's that Health Package file you told me to get before when you wanted . . .

—Don't think Mister Bast wants to dive into that yet waiting for Brisboy to come up with his funeral figures probably want to get into Hopper's cemetery with him over there first and . . .

—Mister Davidoff there's one thing I want to work out as soon as possible, I'm tired and I still have a good deal of . . .

—Look tired look exhausted hardly have known you though in this new outfit quite a switch, sort of the unisex look isn't it trying to handle most of these brush fires myself so you could put your time in on this Foundation project this all the music here?

—Yes and I've been waiting for a call to arrange to record . . .

—Don't worry about it got them on the phone myself lined up your orchestra just holding up studio rental till we find how long you run how many sessions we'll . . .

—The music lasts two hours and eight minutes.

—Two, hours . . . ?

—And eight minutes yes, it . . .

—Symphony hardly runs forty minutes didn't think you'd want to run over, two hours and, that's four, eight, nine sessions comes to sixty-four, seventy-two and six nines is, should come to about seventy-seven thou . . .

—Yes and while I think of it I told them to start looking for a bass flute player they aren't very common and I said if they could send one up here I'd . . .

—Bass, flute player?

—Yes they're not very easy to find it's a rather new instrument and . . .

—Don't worry about it probably dig one up for you faster than they can oh Virginia want to dig up a bass flute player call the desk might have them take a look in the grand ballroom probably want a kettledrum too don't you?

—Two of them yes and in the percussion we'll want a whip, cymbals, blocks, marimba . . .

—Better just give your list to Virginia here how many you want of what and . . .

—Yes well I think sixteen violins and probably ten cellos and, horns, you see this is the horn part right here and . . .

—Horns?

—French horns eight of them yes and this, this is where the Wagner tuba comes in, it . . .

—Probably able to rent one of those someplace have to go out and rent all their instruments you know trying to get together a ballpark figure on costs want to get another press release out on this grant name the amount this time probably run a little more than the Boss expected but I guess you people want to make a splash here probably could have gotten you a name band like the Boston excuse me Virginia? that Senator Milliken on the phone? Been trying to reach me here all day calls coming in brush fires see what it's like running the store without, who . . . ?

—And you see here I've written a pipe organ in in the background if . . .

—It's that Mister Beamish . . .

—Beamish? what's, excuse me Mister Bast here hello, Beamish? where . . . In the lobby downstairs? what . . . All right yes make it quick Mister Bast and I putting our heads together here on . . . Duncan yes just went up the hall to . . . what do you mean the wrong Duncan he . . . meant to ask him about that Duncan debt to Triangle five years of back paper orders yes Skinner didn't . . . for wallpaper yes Skinner didn't . . . oh he does? All lined up before I came on deck have to run over it with Mister Bast here sounds like . . . Sounds like another of Crawley's stunts can't take time now to hear about Duncan's family complications no go over it with Mister Bast here probably just want to absorb the debt as a down payment come up with the balance out of future earnings if . . . Don't worry about it go for anything in paper oh Virginia, take a look up the hall there for Mister Duncan Mister Bast wants a word with him here little confusion over this Duncan acquisition Mister Bast, Beamish sits here for an hour bends my ear with his legalese never does get to the point has to call back to tell me this publishing house acquisition the Boss meant to pick up this Isador Duncan Company little man gone to the toilet makes wallpaper, wipe out an old debt to Triangle and work out a deal on future earnings . . .

—Yes I think Mister Crawley and I talked about that yes, he was familiar with the company and . . .

—Crawley didn't I tell you? hear me just tell Beamish probably another of Crawley's stunts know him like the back of my hand Mister Bast get him juggling stock and he . . .

—Oh oh yes before I leave that reminds me I meant to, to mention money this money that . . .

—Don't worry about it not pressing for payment but I had Virginia type up Virginia where's that billing you typed up Mister Bast wants to okay it here it is yes just didn't know if you wanted it billed to this new shipping subsidiary or the parent . . .

—What?

—Just didn't know if you, hear me all right? Thought your battery might be running down there think we better bill the parent till these legal beagles get their whereifs and whereases straightened out on the whole . . .

—But what is it?

—Boss wants your okay on any billings over two thousand thought he'd told you, started off at two hundred I told him you'd get writer's cramp billing right here on top for this She project just the preliminary est . . .

—But fourteen thous, it just says title change fourteen thous . . .

—Boss likes his messages brief and to the point yes whole change-over in the magazine's title from Her to She, passive to active image whole new concept came out of in-depth studies on potential readership modern gal's self-image came a long way baby clean break from this old-fashioned passive Her flat on the back missionary position, new concept gets her right up in the saddle putting the boots to here, just the hotel bill next here it's . . .

—This? but it's, you mean all this and then there's fifteen percent added on what's . . .

—Agency fee SOP in the ad game Mister Bast wouldn't want us to starve would you long as the Boss is pushing . . .

—Yes but, but the suite was just billed to the company when I took it I . . .

—Save you the headaches just had them on the phone here trying to give your General the heave ho got him moved up the hall there as

a guest of the hotel long as the Boss is pushing low-cost operations companywide we're willing to take the . . .

—Yes all right but then what's this seven, is this twenty-seven thousand dollars?

—Whole company logo project yes top priority from the Boss going
rate low in fact gave you a break see what Chase Bank Kodak the big boys
ran into for theirs want to get that corporate image across zap! instant
they see it people know they're dealing with a dependable reliable outfit
take your bottle of Wonder beer or an ad for new line of Ray-X products
names don't carry much weight alone but back them up with the parent
company logo audience knows it's dealing with a reliable dependable
outfit builds your stockholder relationships see it someplace and they feel
a nice warmth like somebody in the family just died go out and . . .

—Yes but, twenty-seven thou . . .

—Carried as a tangible asset on your books you're ahead of the game
the Boss came up with that one, agency sent out in-depth interview
teams combed your subsidiaries from blue collar to white find out where
they felt they fit as new members of the J R Family of Companies took
a few guidelines tried to combine their image of the parent with the
profit motif wanted to get away from the trendy block letter IBM ITTs
look like tombstones come up with something alive really get across the
corporate image real pride of belonging stockholders know there are people sweating their asses off all over the place to keep their investments
rolling to go to bed at night know all's right with the world, presentation here the agency got together for you to review been so busy I didn't
bother you with it yes that's, some of the agency teams' sketches they . . .

—These . . . ?

—Some of them a little off target see the deadline pressure the agency boys were under get a real feel for the company what these in-depth interviews turned up little heavy on the corporate tit think they tried working in your woman's lib motive too sense a little resentment here and there of course always happens in these takeovers few sore-heads see their future going out the window liked that one up there too wordy but we picked up the Just Rite use it in institutional promotion right down the line wanted to stress the profit motif without hitting you over the head with it name of the game after all something patriotic about the dollar sign feeling like the flag the Boss wanted that kept right out front said to get your approval . . .

—What on, this . . . ?

—One down here in the corner probably no this corner here yes thought you'd take this one our tastes run pretty close corporate identity there jumps off the page and hits you right between the eyes couldn't get your okay but gave them the go ahead at X-L to print up half a million matchbooks spread them around the country wherever there's a prestige market build up the parent company image bookstores that kind of place where the heavy smokers hang out having a case sent to your uptown headquarters put a pile on the coffee table, Boss sent the word down he wants it painted on the tail of the company plane before you take off tomorrow show the flag to the troops in the field and . . .

—Wait now wait Mister Davidoff where, take off where . . .

—LaGuardia thought you'd want to get out there the night before the funeral do a little fence mending and . . .

—Yes but whose wait no this recording I have to take care of this here whole, of recording this whole . . .

—Don't worry about it music boys I talked to know their business have it all wrapped up for you when you get back the Boss wants me on deck here for brush fires or I'd go along to hold your hand said he'd go himself but he's all tied up, parent company's chief executive officer there to represent him nobody gets their feelings hurt gives this family of companies image a shot in the arm line Milliken up and go from there the Boss said he didn't think you'd met him oh Vir . . .

—Look of course I haven't he knows I've never met Senator Milliken and whose . . .

—Thought this sounded like the best chance you'll get relaxed friendly atmosphere nobody pushing hoist a few to the dear departed and go from there wouldn't push too hard on Wonder's age though Milliken himself must be a hundred takes you right into the Eldercare bill coming up for a vote in the Senate next week need him to do some armtwisting on it goes through and this whole Health Package is off and running might do some logrolling on this free milk program in the schools with the boys from the dairy states trying to get a call through to him offer him a ride out booze it up on the plane a little find out where this USDA project stands government funding to clear out the tobacco and grow pot pull Ritz right out of the red just had Beamish up here gave me the slip before I got to him on this trademark registration can't drag our heels the Boss thought you might have some brand name ideas only one he's come up with so far is Ace, agency boys are trying to talk him around to Mary Ja . . .

—Yes no wait look listen Mister Davidoff he said something to me about this on the phone the whole thing's just absurd, the government helping them even letting them grow marijuana and asking a United States Senator to . . .

—Got hold of the wrong end of the stick Mister Bast if you don't mind my saying so whole point here's just grading and taxing, big market waiting out there all your big interests having a hemorrhage watching kids and amateurs pocket the profits government missing a tax source like letting your moonshiners work in the sunshine, government grading program going all your big boys get in the act sponsor medical studies canned editorials press releases educate the public, get the hopheads behind them pass the laws and put them out of business, caught growing the stuff be like running a still all the big boys' brand names already registered can't drag our heels want to work up some ads for these Duncan lines be all ready to go when . . .

—All right Mister Davidoff all right! I, I'll discuss it with J R and now about, about money I . . .

—Need walking around money for the trip yes a hundred? Oh Virginia get Mister Bast here a hundred dollars out of petty cash better give me fifty too while I think of it taking a couple of the media boys out for drinks later got the Boss pushing this family image might want to work that Just Rite line into this jingle he says you're doing on the side for Wonder Beer oh and Virginia put mine down on the agency's account and Mister Bast's on the parent company's, something on some tuition bills he wanted me to mention too Mister Bast said you'd get no deduction if the parent paid them wants you to take care of them yourself so you can take the deduction really looks after you . . .

—Yes well that's . . .

—Incidentally that check you had from some school for fifteen thousand two fifteen was it? Looking into that stop payment on it local bank out there having some problems asked for their president said he'd quit and gone to Washington going through some kind of reorg . . .

—Yes well that's why that loan you helped me arrange I talked to Mister Crawley about it and . . .

—Call from his gal on it this morning yes just wanted to check out your figures picking up your option on five thousand shares at ten with a loan against some stock he's holding in a family account is it?

—My aunts yes he's taking care of their inv . . .

—Put up your five thousand shares as collateral to borrow against and retire the loan their stock's back in their account and figuring your J R Corp yesterday's opening at fourteen and a quarter that gives you seventy-one two fifty market value margin limit eighty percent so you come up with fifty-seven, fifty paid back on the loan so you come out with about seven thousand less charges sound right? Should be here waiting for you when you pull in from this trip oh Virginia big box that came in where is it Mister Bast wants to take it with him if he's going straight from the uptown office tomorrow want to put a copy of that script in with it where thought you just gave it to me . . .

—That's it there Mister Davidoff what that messenger . . .

—What this oh put his play on top yes any sign of this Walldecker yet? Oh and . . .

—But, but wait Virginia what's in the box.

—It's this Indian suit Mister Bast you . . .

—Chief's outfit box is just big because of the feathers guarantee it's authentic three hundred dollars rental it ought to be, honorary ceremony standing in for the Boss all the rest of them done up in feathers didn't want you to be embarrassed he . . .

—Embarrassed! but what kind of . . .

—Don't worry about it whole thing laid out in the script here might run through it with Milliken on the plane down from Wonder's funeral pep him up about getting in the act want him right up there on the platform with you sending a man out from Endo to handle the appliances topflight sales . . .

—Wait no wait Mister Davidoff I mean this whole trip is something I hardly . . .

—Don't worry about it haven't wanted to bother you with . . .

—I'm not worried about it! Now will you . . .

—But holy, I mean look Mister Bast glad to go to your funeral pow wow with your Indians myself but the Boss wants me on deck here pull your band together set up your taping tramp out these brush fires get as much of this off your back as I can but you don't make it easier Mister Bast try to help you out but you don't make it easier, little communications gap between you and the Boss glad to be the messenger boy but I can't help what's in the message even tried to back you up to him he comes right back with how much he's done for you responsibilities as the parent's chief executive officer option on five thousand shares at ten I might feel a little different but just coming in to carry your PR load see what it's like running the store here brush fires calls gang camped out over there on the sofa feeling I'm the only one that keeps things . . .

—Mister Davidoff listen I know . . .

—Dave just make it Dave time we got on a first name basis Bast look I know the Boss isn't easy to handle never are or they wouldn't be where they are but hire a topflight speechwriter to draft his statements get some mileage out of them hardly reach him myself but some press boy calls him last night he hands out the word on She over the phone, draft of your speech here for the security analyst boys probably call and read them that on the phone too says he'll call here and doesn't when he does sounds like he's in Afghanistan sends through these blunt memos have to fill in the spaces myself wants us to look into Ampex Campbell's Soup Union Underwear Franklin Mint this SSS insurance outfit tie in with his Health Package Champion Plywood Erebus Productions talk him out of Western Union he finds Walt Disney selling for peanuts wants to look into that sounded on the phone like he said he'd just like to get Mickey Mouse by the short hair even asks me how's Russia making out, says he has these Russian Imperial bonds what he's got against Mickey Mouse not saying he's stupid Bast wouldn't be where he is if he was real feeling for the gut issue some of this though I just tie up my . . .

—I know yes but please sit . . .

—Wants a receptacle for these depletion allowances has Nonny set up Alsaka Development Corp all this energy crisis legislation comes along chance to get in on these gas exploration write-offs retains Milliken's hometown law firm out there to represent Alsaka so now Milliken's in touch with the AEC about setting off an underground blast golf game arranged down there for you to discuss it what else can I do carry your golf bag? Even sheep membranes Milliken in on that one too minerals gas timber up to our ass in Indians I mean holy shit Bast what am I supposed to do!

—Yes well, well please just sit down Mister Davidoff I . . .

—Yes didn't mean, just reach the point ask Mooneyham over there for a time cost estimate clean up that pollution mess out at X-L to head off this lawsuit he starts to describe a dream about a hair growing out of his eyeball see what I, what, what's . . .

—Just your, your foot here I'd better just put my case down on the . . .

—Foot? Oh, oh top page there brush right off certainly do meticulous work don't you Bast wrote a novel once myself you know, maybe a little jealous of you boys with a knack for the arts luxury I can't afford never finished it, couldn't just sit on my butt and indulge myself like that why the Boss is impressed the way you keep both balls in the air corporate picture and a hand in the music game had a feeling though since I came on board your corporate hold slipping a little Bast, mind not quite focused may just be the pressure of . . .

—No it's, I'm thinking of leaving it the company I mean, I . . .

—What leaving the, leaving the company? Knew you and the Boss had a little communications gap didn't know things had gone that far though Bast you . . .

—No it's not exactly that it's just, you see I . . .

—Always happens better offer someplace else these headhunters sniffing around first whiff of dissatisfaction they know it before you do the way we got Mister Ten-forty there, have you bought and sold before you know what's happening the Boss know it yet?

—Yes well I'm sure he expects, I mean you see I just came in originally to help him to . . .

—Get things on their feet see why they came after you, not exactly a secret what you two put together overnight here really just starting to take off though can't be planning to pull out tomorrow of course or you wouldn't have picked up this option probably talked to Piscator just so you don't plan to sell . . .

—No I mean I thought that's why the loan was the only way I could . . .

—Don't worry about it just so you're not planning to sell, get it straight with Nonny wouldn't leave you up the creek like the lawyer company I just left little weasel named Beaton father was a law partner of Senator Broos' brother and their Washington lobbyist Frank Black only reason they keep him, left the barn door open when their top man picked up his option day before he quit ten minutes later they're facing a minority suit paid out a fistful . . .

—Yes but all I . . .

—Better ride uptown with you put our heads together with the Boss go over the whole thing Bast heard he started looking at Diamond Cable when it fell to sixteen may be another of Crawley's stunts specialist for Diamond probably sold it short there himself when Typhon pulled back on that tender offer rumor some big blocks in family trusts didn't move when old man Cates cracked the whip but with City National banking Crawley Wiles all the rest of them got the Boss up to his ass in bellies on these five percent margins price drops and . . .

—Yes but listen Mister Davidoff about this stock opt . . .

—Thinking of leaving the company Bast sooner we sit down with the Boss the better see he's expanding the board of directors for instance couple of names I never heard of looked in the Directory of Directors for Urquhart and this other one Teets? Not there either where he recruited them . . .

—No well you see I recruited them all he wanted was I think the law requires a certain number of . . .

—Seen how I've been running the store here Bast might want to put in a word at dinner for what's this Virginia, Angels East what's Angels East . . .

—That bald man Mister Davidoff his name is Mister Wall . . .

—Decker here give him this tell him I'm in conference oh and Virginia gang on the sofa there tell them Mister Bast and I have to get uptown the Boss wants . . .

—No please I'm listen I . . .

—Little embarrassing for me sometimes you know Bast admit I've never met the Boss put this profile together want to get a little feel for him chance to get across his image start grooming him for something big just take this X-L pollution mess, make a front page image as the good corporate citizen but he's so mad at that smartass Boy Scout came up with those color ink samples from the stream there some school science project wants to let them sue get the kid in court have Nonny wipe up the floor with, wait you didn't wear a coat?

—No but listen . . .

—Get mine be right with you put Mooneyham there on the stand they'd end up fining X-L triple damages plus costs shut down production till it's cleaned up, get you or the Boss out there call it accidental spillage study underway get out for five six thousand good corporate citizen image give the little bastard a fifty dollar award engraved certificate banquet at Howard Johnson pull in his scout troop science teacher American Legion Woody Owl get the whole what lose something . . . ?

—No I thought there were some sandwiches here I thought I'd just take . . .

—Must have cleaned them up wait something right behind plate right behind you Virginia what's . . .

—It's that cottage cheese with ketchup Mister Hopper had but he put out his cigar in the . . .

—No no call room service order Mister Bast a ham and like ham and cheese?

—No I'm never mind Virginia listen Mister Davidoff I have to leave and we can't . . .

—Hold out a little longer put our heads together with the Boss over beef Wellington little place up near . . .

—No but listen I'm trying to tell you he's not here he's not at the uptown not in town at all Mister Davidoff he . . .

—Up there last night thought he was still on tap don't worry about it ride up with you anyhow never seen the uptown layout you know, use some of that equipment you're getting in right here if we had it shredder for instance and this Telecopier four hundred reminds me you might want Virginia on staff up there too, good hearted really tries heard you're having some problems gal answering your phone told Crawley to wait Virginia want to call off those media boys tell them to freeload someplace else tonight oh and Vir . . .

—But wait that wait that that woman over there who's . . .

—Skinner's gal thought you'd met her Bast real topflight track record in curr something wrong there Virginia what's . . .

—Listen I have to leave I'm . . .

—She put these contack lenses in this glass of water Mister Davidoff she thinks maybe Mister Mooneyham got it only now she can't see who's . . .

—Yes well look for just tell her to wait where's Mister wait tell Mister Bast to wait be right with him man in the cowboy hat there what's cowboy hat and boots who's . . .

—That's this Mister Brisboy Mister Davidoff he . . .

—Yes well tell him to Skinner's gal there tell her to sit down find who drank that glass of wait get Mister Bast at the door there be right with him if Mister Ten-forty doesn't show up tell Skinner to . . .

—But he's here Mister Davidoff this Mister disomething he's over at the sofa with them he said please don't interrupt them and this Mister Duncan was up the hall he said Mister Skinner got mugged up by the mop closet they . . .

—Ever hear the one about the fellow named Skinner who took the young lady to supper?

—Now if we pay attention this may help us understand our real life roles and aggressive feelings in a merger situation, and help us in the dedecision making process, now Mister . . .

—No no it was Tupper took a young lady to dinner, by quarter of nine . . .

—Mister Mooneyham you sit here and Mister Hopper you sit here now in this little skit I will take the part of the clown and Mister Mooneyham you will be the mouse . . .

—Quarter of nine they sat down to dine by quarter of ten he was up her doesn't rhyme with dinner . . .

—If we pay attention Mister Hopper and you are the cat, remember I'm the clown and I say, let's get a cat, and Mister Mooneyham remember you're being the mouse and you say let's not get a cat, because you're afraid he would eat you . . .

—Tupper that's it took her to supper, by quarter of nine they were ready to dine by quarter of ten it was in her . . .

—And now I go over and open the door so the cat can come in, and I tell him to come in . . .

—Not Skinner, the dinner . . .

—Yes now Mister Mooneyham remember you're being the mouse and you overhear us, and so the mouse comes in where the clown can't see him and closes the door on the cat . . .

—Wait just wait now where's oh Virginia what happened to Mister Bast call the desk get that door there where's Brisboy . . .

—Who . . . ?

—Oh Mister Bast wait, are you Mister Bast? I just saw you slipping out . . .

—I'm, first tell me who you are . . .

—Yes let me help you with your bundle you're going to the elevators? And you are Mister Bast I'm Mister Brisboy from Wagner . . .

—Yes now look Mister Brisboy I'm leaving I'm, I have to get uptown and I can't stop to . . .

—Yes I'll ride up with you here's our elevator, we can have a delicious talk in the cab and you do need help with your things Mother's found me a new analyst up at the corner of Ninety-fifth Street and I simply must . . .

—Mister Brisboy listen I'm just about at the end of my . . .

—Oh I understand Mister Bast that stuffy suite with all those crass people I took one look, we couldn't have heard one another speak and there is so much to discuss do we go out this way? I'd tried to call your office but a girl answered with the most indecent and quite impractical suggestion I'd quite despaired of ever . . .

—Yes well listen I'm in a hurry you don't need to . . .

—Simply abandon you here with this great big box I wouldn't dream of it, what can be in it . . .

—Well it's a, it's just an Indian suit I . . .

—An Indian suit how delish! Oh it does sound like a fun company after all there's a cab oh cabby? Cabby . . . ?

—Mister Bisboy please I'm, Brisboy listen why don't you just get that cab and . . .

—I'd have to hurl myself under his wheels wouldn't I aren't they just obscenely rude with their little Off Duty signs is that the word your mother used too? Oh wait her we are here we are . . . no no get in back we'll put your box up here in front with this savage at the wheel, there. Straight uptown driver, to the very fringe of the jungle oh forgive me was that your knee? What a cute outfit . . .

—Yes well I, I thought you wanted to discuss some, to talk about the company or . . .

—It's all so exciting yes where shall we start, being asked to join your family of companies Mother feels that's what we need and she's never really been one for family if you could see Uncle Arthur, of course I won't go into some of the actual family members I've just met with her except you of course if she found your J R person rather crass on the telephone I can imagine her reaction to your leg and tit person in there from Zanesville but . . .

—To our, who . . . ?

—Your wallpaper person he was discussing the menu with someone who said I'm a ham and eggs man and he said I'm a leg and tit man myself so crass not that unlike Uncle Arthur, he seems to expect your pushy little person with all the cufflinks to fix him up with your blind lady person with purple lipstick on her teeth for fifty cents I can't tell you how relieved I was to see another young face . . .

—Yes well I, I'd expected you to be a good deal older Mister Brisboy I thought Mister Crawley said that your, your business belonged to two brothers and when one died his widow wanted . . .

—Oh he's your stock person isn't he yes he sounds like an absolute bear no it was Daddy who died and Uncle Arthur wants out I can't tell you how relieved Mother and I will be to see him go if your Piscator person can arrange it he sounds quite crass too is he? And you must tell him to stop calling Mother Mrs Wagner every time he calls like Cosima if you please of course that's where we got it if you knew the number of times I've sat through Tristan with her five hours uncut at the Paris Opéra simply relentless, she thought Brisboy sounded a little frivolous I suggested Charon of course but she found that a trifle récherché and felt Wagner might attract a nicer clientèle but of course everyone simply calls it wag-ner even your J R person in our mercifully brief telephone chat kept whining wag-ner wag wag like a doggy's tail can you just lean forward and tap on the glass, oh driver . . . ? Driver? We're not in a mad rush and we don't want to suddenly become statistics Mother told me that's what your J R person wanted me to discuss with you?

—Yes well I hardly . . .

—She said he sounded quite ecstatic to learn that two billion dollars was spent on funerals last year and you simply must tell him the death rate is climbing steadily imagine, only a hundred and eighty million funerals in America since our dear country was born and we count on two hundred million in just the next forty-five years!

—Yes well I'm, I know he'll be delighted yes he . . .

—We get one out of six now in the Fort Lauderdale area and Mother's been constantly after me to bring in that second one to make it two out of six that would be one out of three I think? You know there are over twenty thousand of us across the country but even the largest single chain has less than one percent of the trade were these the statistics you wanted? Because even one percent just think the Social Security persons estimate a twenty percent rise in the death rate between nineteen seventy and nineteen eighty so there should be enough to go round if we can trim some of these frightfully blatant costs we've already tried working something out along the cluster concept so we wouldn't have ten hearses all out roaring down the roads at once and then all of them standing around empty waiting that's why Mother's so entranced with this package approach your J R person wrote her about does he do all his memoranda in lead pencil?

—Yes well you see generally he . . .

—Crabbed age and youth oh I know but what a delicious name to choose for your nursing homes someone's been reading South Wind isn't it the most delicious book ever written! Of course I'd assumed it might be your J R person but when he misspelled Nepenthe among other things and . . .

—Yes well I'm sure he hasn't, never even heard of it no he just bought into this nursing home stock when it first . . .

—Yes how frightfully thoughtful of him all these old dear persons no one wants underfoot to pasture them off in great dank government hospitals at public expense would be quite unthinkable and simply reek of socialism of course free enterprise owes them the dignity of private care after all they've done to make our dear country what it is and Mother tells me you have a Senator person leading the good fight for Eldercare so there won't be those dreary scenes over unpaid bills, and of course the idea of discreet signs placed tastefully about suggesting our services Mother was utterly charmed but I think not in the room itself do you? No near the exits for visitors leaving that delicious old dear person all tucked up in beddy perhaps for the last time just a hint of stained glass and the simplest of messages Uncle Arthur suggested a hearse with the line getting there is half the fun so outré Mother and I thought simply Wagner is ready when you are or do you like they, when they are, of course we thought of when He is but one really must tread on tippy toes it makes Him sound rather like an abductor don't you think? Or don't you think . . .

—Well I really don't think . . .

—No of course not Mother feels understatement is always best and I think she's less than enraptured with your J R person's notion of little booths set up in the nursing home lobbies to sell the entire package, prostheses the nursing care funeral plot and stone it sounds rather like a midway and of course the organized funeral directors are quite gaga over the whole thing rustling up preneed laws and being most unfriendly but if the darkies have been getting away with their little burial societies for ages certainly anyone has the right to plan those delicious last moments at leisure with none of that frantic last minute embarrassment over bills have you worked out the package cost?

—No and I don't . . .

—Know how many packages you'll offer no but there must be a mad variety or it could all turn into the sort of mass burial I suppose they have in Russia Mother says your J R person wants to approach the young married market but projecting costs so far in the future when the average nine hundred seventy-five dollars now doesn't even include vault memorial stone cemetery plot flowers burial clothing even the minister of course having the use of all that money for what might be simply ages before that last surprise party when the package is opened and with people rushing about so even that might happen in some utterly inaccessible place he almost seems to be counting on quite an eventual number of no-shows at your vast cemetery somewhere called Union forgive me was that your foot?

—No it's, it's just my case let me move it I . . .

—Oh I hope I didn't scratch it my new heels are so dreadfully sharp here let me help you, your cabs here are so thrillingly efficient but there's simply no place in them to sit down and my hat is getting careful, your important papers are spilling . . .

—Yes it's, Mister Crawley broke the catch opening it and it's . . .

—He does sound like an absolute bear Mother said he oh! It's all music it's simply filled with music oh I must see! You didn't write it?

—Well yes but it's . . .

—Oh let me see let me see this passage right here how simply delicious what part is it.

—That's the, the harpsichord part it . . .

—Mmmmmmmm! delicious, yes there's a little Rameau there isn't there mmmmmmmmmm . . .

—Well his, his piece The Gnat I just wanted the feeling of . . .

—And you certainly caught it didn't you I feel prickly all over now what's this oh how ominous . . . !

—Yes well that's, that's the string bass but about the cemetery I think you'd better talk to Mister Hop . . .

—Yes Mother said it was simply vast thousands of acres somewhere nearby called Union Falls? that you've taken over an entire right of way for it? Mmmmmm mmm mmmm hmmm . . .

—Well it's no not exactly nearby, this cemetery is in the middle of a right of way up near our . . .

—Mmmmmm hmmmm hmmmm, hmm hmm delicious yes three thousand acres your J R person told Mother and imagine he's concerned about unprofitable plots of course burying the welfare poor has always been a losing proposition simply noblesse oblige the agencies pay such a pittance but his proposal to make it pay by placing them six and eight deep to a plot when he was describing the entire package idea on the telephone as vertical integration Mother was simply aghast she thought he meant darkies and whites stacked in layers like a giant Dubos torta don't you just crave one right now? We could slip over to . . .

—No, no I . . .

—The Hungarians are so clever with pastries but no all he meant was getting into the monument trade he'd just learned it runs over a third of a billion annually but you must tell him those monstrous granite memorials are quite quite passé the maintenance is simply prohibitive, you'll want stones flush with the ground so your lawnmowers can simply whirr past overhead oh how brilliant, mmm mmmmm mmmmm mmmmm mm mm m how simply brilliant and with your handicap Mister Bast oh forgive me, forgive me for mentioning it but I can only think of those cruel people telling Beethoven they heard shepherds' pipes where he heard absolutely nothing and that heartrending will he wrote at the time of his exquisite Second Symphony you mustn't think of taking your life Mister Bast you simply must not . . .

—No well I, I hadn't no I, driver . . . ?

—To think of leaving the world before you've brought out all you have within you no, no you must promise . . .

—Yes well I, excuse me yes I think we're at Ninety-fifth Street, driver . . . ?

—Oh and you must tell your J R person caskets are not worth getting into the profit lag is simply deadly . . .

—Yes driver? Will you stop at this corner?

—Now when am I to hear you play.

—I don't know Mister Brisboy I have to go away for . . .

—Yes we're quite near your headquarters right now aren't we, you don't have a piano hidden there? I know Mother wrote down the address for me I might pop in later and surprise you!

—No that wouldn't no the piano is hidden yes it's not can't be played no, no I'll see you at the hotel Mister Bris . . .

—What fun yes I'm right there in the Towers you know there's none in my suite but I'll have them rush one in instantly goodbye, auf Wiedersehen Mister Bast au voir it's such a joy to be included in the family oh! I'd meant to pay our cabby but Mother sent me off with nothing but fifties . . .

—No that's, that's all right good wait your hat be careful it's, yes goodbye . . . driver? Around on Ninety-sixth Street please, over between Third and Second . . .

—Never saw a real life cowboy where he come from.

—I think he's, he's from Florida yes he . . .

—He from Florida?

—From Florida yes . . . yes down in the middle of that next block, behind that big limousine that last brick front . . .

—Where's all the garbage cans at?

—Yes just pull around and, wait be careful!

—Push that wreck up car right in front of me oweeeee!

—Yes I'd better get out right here, yes and, here thank you, can you push out the box to me, the wind . . .

—Limousine smash right in the trunk oweeeeee!

—Coño!

—Ya mira que haces coño!

—Coño tienes el freno tu, aye madre . . .

—Excuse me . . . he stepped over the glass splintered from framing Z S on the plate, reaching the doorway box and case held high against the wind to pause there for the chauffeur's uniform in full emergency, in to where that bulb seemed to glow with no more purpose than to keep itself warm.

—Say wait could you help me with an address here?

—What . . . ?

—Got this address supposed to be some God damn corporation offices nothing here but Spics and garbage cans, ever hear of a J R Corporation?

—No but, who told you the . . .

—Financial page editor told me supposed to interview a Mister Bast, ever heard of him? Almost looks like some wise guy wrote J R Corp in pencil on this mailbox but . . .

—Oh yes that's, that must be it yes I didn't make the connection that must be Mister Rodriguez up on the fifth floor Julio Rodriguez, that must be what he calls his business he . . .

—Look friend I'm talking about a five hundred million dol, no never mind . . .

—He makes sandals I think yes in fact if you want to talk to him I think he's right outside with his friends, their car out there just had an accident . . .

—Forget it!

—The one with the portable radio . . . and he made the dim reach of the stairs, down the torn linoleum to add case and box to the heap at the door and lift it on its hinges to the splash and fall of waters, down on one knee sweeping footmarked mail from the doormat's monogram in over the sill where it was caught in an abrupt splash of suds.

—Bast? is that you man?

—Yes what in . . .

—I mean look at this, came from the billow rising over the tub where only her face and knees protruded, —like I mean real sudsing power look . . .

—Yes well be careful it's getting on the mail what, where did it come from . . .

—Like all these plastic cups Al found them hanging on the doorknobs but with these sample boxes attached so he had to bring them in too look out man . . . ! A head emerged from the billow between her knees, —like it's splashing out . . .

—But you mean you, he just went around and took them off all the other apartment doors?

—Why not I mean we really need cups but like I dump a box in the tub to throw it away and this happens I mean real sudsing power like the box says man, like I mean do you want to get in?

—Not, not right now . . . he got his box in safe atop 500 Novelty Rolls 1-Ply White, dragged two more packages under the gushing sink and lifted the door closed, in past the tub with his case to find the sofa's length occupied by one the shape of a guitar and, on the floor beyond, —what's this pile of mail back here?

—Like Al just got this postman job for like before the holidays man, I mean he just dumped it there when he came up to sleep off this high.

—Well look it can't stay here and, and this big yellow box where did . . .

—Like that's your golf practice set man, I mean they just delivered it.

—What golf practice I didn't order any golf prac . . .

—Man like how does anybody know who orders what here, I mean these presents you get from these businesses like this lamp made of this old parking meter and these deluxe barbeque tools man I never know what's coming through the door, like right in the middle of I'm getting stoned with this spade cat that comes in to tap your phone and they come to install this Telecopier and like there's the telephone again, I mean all it does is rings . . .

He got back past 36 Boxes 200 2-Ply, —wait Al I'll get it . . . and he
braced a foot, reached up to Round Pkgs QUICK QUAKER to bring the
phone down to his unencumbered ear, —hello . . . ? No this is Mister Bast,
who . . . B S who . . . ? Yes well J R himself isn't here right now no,
who . . .

—Quit splashing man like are you getting in or out.

—Oh B F? Leva? Yes I'm sorry Mister Leva what . . . what? No I'm
sorry I don't recognize your name Mister Leva what . . . Erebus Productions? No, what . . .

—Wait hold still man like I never saw this little wart under here
before, does that hurt?

—Yes well I don't go to the movies very much so . . .

—Like this little vein looks like it's going to pop man.

—Oh, oh yes well . . . yes I heard you yes selling at one sixty-eight
but he hasn't said anything to me ab . . . that you might be interested in
making a deal I'll tell him Mister . . . what? Girl? no where . . .

—Man like how come you never got circumcised?

—Oh you, oh you mean you have a picturephone too . . . ? No no I,
I see you up there now yes well goodbye Mister Leva thank . . .

—Oh wow . . . a splat of suds ran down 24-One Pint Mazola New
Improved.

—Probably yes probably a crossed cable somewhere yes goodbye I'll
tell him to call you goodbye Mis . . . I don't know if they can trace crossed
cables no, good . . . No goodbye Mister Leva I can't hold on another
minute no . . .

—Wait like I need that shirt man what are you hanging it on there
for, I mean like that won't stop it ringing . . .

—Because the man who just, because other people have picturephones too and no wait Al look would you mind just not standing on that
mail to dry yourself?

—Floor's like real dirty man.

—I know it but, well look spread out a newspaper or, here . . . he got
across to lift the door open and drag in the monogrammed doormat,
—there . . .

—Like Al brought up his guitar, man.

—Yes I saw it . . . he got past her for the refrigerator, —wait who put
this in here what, stuffed breasts of Cornish hens à la Kiev . . .

—Like somebody sent it to you man but like it says oven ready your
oven's full of mail so like it says keep refrigerated I mean where do you
expect me to put it.

—Yes but right on these stock certificates it's melting all over them
and this look this is the only place I can keep this manuscript paper
clean . . . He crumpled the top sheet and took some from the stack in to
open his case on Hoppin' With Flavor! pausing to take out the list of titles
and add scribbled notes from an inside pocket before he spread a fresh

manuscript sheet on the top volume of Standard and Poor's Corporation Records, —damn it! crumpling that abruptly —look these are brand new, look there's oil all over it . . .

—Like those little mushrooms man they're packed in all this oil.

—I know it that's what we're using Moody's for that red book now where the, where are all my pencils . . . he came up from the floor with a battered nub —damn it, what . . .

—Like Al was just helping you out trying to sharpen them for you man, came from the doorway where she tugged at a sleeve —I mean that electric coffee grinder somebody sent you like he thought it was this electric pencil sharpener I mean he was just helping you out . . .

—Yes well listen will you tell him to just, I just want to finish this while it's still in my head, just to get this last horn part written out would you hand me that ink? And he turned with it from her reach that gaped the open shirt to find a pen and spread a scribbled sheet of score, settled on Hoppin' With Flavor! licking the pen nib bent over the empty staves where his pen came down pausing, arching, blacking in, pausing as his face drew closer down lips parted, meeting, parting on bleats of sound gone in mere breath and the pen stopped as toes approached the score along the spine of Thomas Register of Manufacturers and clung with a prehensile twinge at plunk . . . plunka plunk . . . —Look Al I'm sorry but I'm trying to . . .

—Man like don't be sorry I mean go ahead . . .

—Yes but your guit . . .

—No like go ahead I mean I'm for like everybody doing what they want to man, plunka plunka plunk . . .

—Look you don't understand I'm . . .

—Like why not man I mean that's how it ought to be like everybody doing what they want to do man, like I mean I'm for everybody doing what they want to do, plunk plunk plunka . . . —like I mean what's that.

—What.

—Like that arrow you just made.

—What this? It's a diminuendo don't you, you read music don't you? Plunk —like why do I want to read music man I mean I play music, like that's what music is isn't it man? I mean I play my own music what do I want to like read it for.

—Oh.

—Man like I play what I feel I mean not what some other cat writes for me to feel . . . plunk plunk plunka —like I mean I'm not one of your cats that has to sit down and play what some other cat hears I mean I make my own sound man . . . plunk.

—Yes well, fine but look I'm trying to . . .

—And like Al says he might bring the Gravestone up here to practice like only they can't get a booking because they don't know anybody like you just have to know somebody, I mean like maybe you could help them out man you know? Like I mean anything you want you always can get it because like you know everybody but like anything they get they have to like get it by theirself you know?

—Yes but, no but even if that were true I don't think any connections I might have in music would . . .

—What because their name's the Gravestone? I mean like you ought to change that anyway man like you can't just keep going around being this Gravestone that doesn't know anybody you know?

—Then like come up with one . . .

—Man like there's four of you I mean you're this whole cemetery like if you can't come up with one how can he get you this booking man, like time is money I mean what about Chairman Meow like I mean did you go to Jersey?

—Like, what day is it.

—Man like how do I know what day is it I mean if you went to Jersey it's like Thursday right? She stooped back to the tub, came up tossing sandals —I mean like hurry man, like tell him I mean don't offices close like?

—Yes well, what time is it they usually . . .

—It's like five of.

—Five of what.

—Man like how do I know five of what, I mean it's like five minutes of something but you hang this big office wall clock from your business over there with like all those boxes stacked up I mean after three o'clock nobody knows what time it is till like nine I mean come on man every day this vietrinary keeps him there it's like four dollars I mean hurry up wait leave me some reds . . . They paused past 24–12 Oz Btls Fragile! —man like what's this, coke? I mean wow . . . she came on, shuddering the door back into place on the flap of sandals down the dark, returning slowly past the rush of waters pulling the shirt closed far enough to thrust the envelope into its pocket and let it fall free again pushing the guitar off on the pile of mail and sitting, feet up toes snubbed on H-O —I mean they give Al this real hard time at Jersey and Connecticut man, like they make him go over there and sign all the time like they won't even mail him his checks you know? Like here at New York they mail him it only then he has to like spend all this New York welfare just to like go get this welfare off Jersey and Connecticut I mean just like you man.

—Like what do you mean me just like me what . . .

—Man like this business job you've got only you're going around with that radio thing stuck in your ear all the time for this other job listening to these songs like you think you have to write down every song they play I mean just make up a list man, like I mean I'll make up a list for you.

—Look I'm just doing it because I'm trying to get something else done here and why you think Al is, I mean if he worked like other people and . . .

—Come off it man like other people I mean like who, like I mean somebody's getting paid to be this weather forecaster someplace telling you fair and warm while you're like up to your ass in this blizzard I mean like who does anything man, I mean somebody gets a job and like the first thing they do they try to figure out how to not do it I mean look at you man, like this business job with all this mail and calls and these presents like only you're up all night trying to make this four hundred dollars writing this music for some band that's getting this money free to play it? Like I mean what's the difference if you get help off that and Al gets it off this welfare, I mean like you're both in music and like you weren't even very nice to him man.

—Yes but, but look can't you . . .

—I mean he brings his guitar all the way up here to talk about music and you won't even talk to him.

—Yes but look can't you see I just want to get this finished and then I can . . .

—Man like finish it who's stopping you I mean everybody's like trying to help you out, I mean like I'm taking in all these packages and like answering the door to these cops and Indians and every . . .

—But what, wait what Indians who . . .

—Like man either he was this Indian or he had this deviated septum like my brother had one I mean like I tell him to get lost and he says he already is lost and like this Treasury Department cop looking for your friend Grynszpan and these telephone calls, I mean just writing down all these telephone calls man . . . legs gaped and the shirt fell wide with her reach to 12–38 Oz Btls Won't Burn, Smoke or Smell for a torn brown paper bag —I mean here . . .

—Yes well, look thank you but if Al hadn't broken that attachment that took them down on tape you wouldn't even have to ans . . .

—I mean that's what I mean like I mean you say maybe it can be adopted to like tape something off your ear radio so Al tries to help you out and when you're like trying to tape this Bach thing it breaks so you blame him when he's only trying to . . .

—Yes all right it doesn't matter look what's, what does this say General who? He held out her pencil markings on the brown paper, —Ball?

—Balls Boll I mean how do I know like that's what I said General who and they said General some company like, and like there's this other general, like council something.

—General counsel? Of, but of what company what . . .

—No man like council general something.

—But, consul general but of where . . .

—Like he couldn't even talk English man, I mean it sounded French so like I say the only French I know and he hangs right up, then like there was this U S chamber of something I mean I didn't even write it down like they said can you come speak at some dinner so I ask like what's on the menu and they don't even know I mean like that must be some dinner.

—Yes well, all right yes what's this one bert, Beaton?

—Like he called twice today man he sounds like this real fag I mean he really wants to talk to you.

—Yes I know yes I'll, I'll call him when I . . .

—And then somebody calls from this office of some Senator someplace I mean they really sound like they think they're hot shit so could they discuss this campaign contribution at your convenience they said they're like counting on twenty so like I say maybe you'll send them twenty bucks sometime so like they say perhaps I misunderstood they mean like thousand so I say they better count again so . . .

—Yes well look maybe, maybe you shouldn't bother to answer the phone anymore if, what does this say Stamper?

—Stamper man like I never heard such a filthy mouth on anybody, I mean like he's in some fucking barnyard . . .

—Yes but what did he, was it about music for a . . .

—He said it's like he wants to talk to you about some rights of something you could like call him back at his car I mean I told him what to do with his car man I never heard such a filthy mouth, I mean you have some business associates man like somebody else calls that says is your boss keeping his long position on bellies man I mean this must be some business you and him are in. And I mean him. Man he sounds like he's calling from under this blanket someplace.

—Did he call? What, what did he . . .

—Man like he can't stop talking I mean he says write all this stuff down so I write this stuff down and, no on the back . . .

—What this? I can't, what's ebus . . .

—Erbus that's Erbus like he said it's some movie company that's losing all this money I mean he sounded real happy, like I wrote it down someplace . . . and her knee fell wide leaning toward the paper gone quivering in his hand, —like down here . . .

—Ebe . . . he cleared his throat, raised his eyes back to the brown paper —Erebus yes that, it must be that man who just called Mis, Mister Leva . . .

—I mean they lost twenty-eight what's that, like million, I mean like he said twenty-eight million dollars making some big movie they're losing like a million dollars a month man I mean like he sounded real happy.

—Yes well there are tax, business tax situations where . . .

—Man like don't explain it to me but I mean like that must be some movie . . . and the knee fell back, —then under there he said like will you read today's Times like about this war someplace you're buying this radium then some other stuff about he's like buying this school will you talk to this lawyer that sent you that dirty mummy joke and then some big bank loan like man let's eat . . . the knees came down —I mean I'm hungry.

—Yes well, go ahead I just want to finish . . .

—Like do you want me to bring in that mail?

—Yes go ahead, I just . . .

—And like shall I open these packages?

—Yes go ahead . . . and the pen moved again, arching, dipping, paused to add a title to the list and his face was back closer to a fresh sheet of empty staves licked lips parting, meeting, parting on puffs of sound against the ripping of paper over the rush of waters beyond, the trickle at his back from under boxes and the massed Musical Couriers

———today. Many were from the finest homes in America. Many were treasured heirlooms . . .

—Like I mean what we really need here, man.

—But what, what is it . . .

—Like it's this electric tie rack I mean can't you see? Like it says you organize them by color on these little wheels and there's this pushbutton selector where they rotate like they must think you're a fucking basket case man, look at this one.

—But what's it for, it looks . . .

—Like it says right on it man Steakwatcher, I mean like it really says solid state computer programmed for broiling steaks and chops to perfection I mean somebody really paid money for these, man.

—Yes well some, there's probably a card from some company in the . . .

—I mean like a lot of fucking money man, like they're scared if they gave you something somebody might like really need you'll think it's this fucking insult . . . An armload of mail cascaded to the sofa, —like I mean things are really screwed up.

—I know it but, look I just want to finish this before . . .

—Before what man. Like I mean the whole fucking scene is coming down . . .

———and any other mouthwash is like the difference between a lovely Beethoven sonata and an ear splitting blast from . . .

—Oh wow.

—What's, no wait wait don't open . . .

—Man I didn't see this box I mean who sent you this!

—Wait no look if you put it on the whole thing will look it's too long, the feathers are dragging on . . .

—But I mean wow like are these real eagle feathers?

—Yes but I don't know but look if it gets dirty I wait, wait you can't wear it carrying all that what . . .

—These cups for grape drink and here here quick get this before it . . .

—Put it on the, here put it on Moody's what is it anyhow.

—It's these enchiladas and like this is remoulade sauce it says on the jar I mean what did you expect.

—I thought maybe this time you look out the grape drink! I thought this time if I gave you that five dollars for food maybe we could eat something that . . .

—Well look man I mean it says niney-nine cents right on the can and this remoulade sauce it says . . .

—No I mean I thought you could buy something, just go in and buy some regular food we could . . .

—Man like what's the difference I mean you're getting like this five dollars' worth, I mean add up the cans and there's like these capers and these fancy snails out there like I mean how am I supposed to save up to get Chairman Meow out of this vietrinary man . . . She shunted mail aside with a ruffle of feathers, —man I don't see how they go around all the time with all these feathers sticking up their . . .

—Well they don't but they do wear, look if you could just button that shirt a little, it's . . .

—Man like my pants got wet with that tub in there I mean I can't wear them wet . . . but she got a button holed, licked sauce from her fingers and tore open an envelope. —Like they're delivering your thousand gross assorted plastic flowers from Hong Kong man.

—Who is what plastic flowers I . . .

—Like it just says owing to backed up warehousing facilities your recent bid on shipment three five nine seven one . . .

—Yes well just, just put it over there wait be careful that looks like a check.

—It's like your Texas Gulf dividend man, fifteen cents, and like here's another one, Pacific Telephone. Thirty cents.

—Yes well those are, I'm putting those in the ice tray in the . . .

—I mean this is what they're always talking about Wall Street? Like I mean I never saw such a . . .

—No but those are just one share people usually own more than, wait don't throw that away it's . . .

—What all this crap that was with them?

—Yes it's the, they send out this literature to their stockholders to keep . . .

—Literature? I mean like you call this literature man?

—No no I don't they do it's all, it's quarterly reports and . . .

—This reduced fully diluted shares outstanding by sixteen percent which had the effect after imputed interest on like you call that literature man I mean I call it bullshit . . . Paper tore, —wow.

—What . . .

—The telephone bill, it's like one thousand eight hundred seventy-six dollars, I mean man you owe them like two thousand dollars and so far you take in like forty-five cents I mean . . .

—No well the telephone bill is, it isn't mine personally it's . . .

—Like here's one you better answer then, personal and confidential I mean it's this executive placement agency that knows of several attractive possibilities if in the near future you should be interested in considering alternatives at the executive vice president level in a major corporate man you told me you're getting out of this crap so you can write all this music . . .

—Yes well I am as soon as I . . .

—Man it's always like as soon as you something I mean here's one will you chair this management symposium on healing the sick corporation I mean that must be some chair. And like who's E Berst, I mean look here's this same piece of mail about buying these free records addressed to E Gast, E Bast, B Best I mean there's seven, eight nine there's like eleven of it the same with all these screwed up names like . . .

—Yes well they think, I think they think it's cheaper just to mail them all than check every name on these lists they buy to see if look be careful, you're getting that sauce on the . . .

—Man like E Berst E Gast I mean how do you expect me to open all this mail I mean . . .

—There's that electric opener right under . . .

—What like you want me to chop off all my fingers? And I mean look what's, I mean look did you know this Eigen is getting all his mail forwarded here too? Like he just sent some more newspapers up here and these books and this box of all these broken toys I mean there won't even be anyplace left to . . .

—No well his mail I've just been putting it on the top oven shelf with here if this is the Grynszpan pile, wait keep it away from that pile Al dumped there he can't just leave it here without what's that one, that foreign one . . .

—Man it's like addressed to J R Corp Famili . . . paper tore, —Dear Madame. I take the liberty to write to you from a strange country, you don, know but don,t be asthonised , because I have heard from your good he. Our famili is quite ruined. My husband is very sick, death sick, without hope of guerishing. I beg you to send for him some cloth and underwear, pijame, all very very used, or second hand which you would wear and would cast away. Do you imagine this awful winter coming and we are allways cold. May I hope that my prayer could reach and touch heart which is always batting for the poor. I beg my God to give you hundred fold. Yours truly and miserable man like I mean how can you pronounce Srskić . . .

—Well I, I don't know but it's . . .

—I mean like why don't you send them those deluxe barbeque tools and this fucking computer for broiling steaks man . . .

—Look, I don't . . .

—I mean her husband's sitting there in no underwear without hope of guerishing man like you could send him that electric heated towel stand that came yesterday to hang his pijame on while his neckties rotate and Mrs Zrk is running around with the deluxe barbeque tools waiting for this solid state computer to boil their steaks and chops to perf . . .

—Look damn it what am I supp . . .

—And I mean then you could like go chair that thing on healing the sick corporation with your heart batting for the poor they'd really be asthonised man like I never saw such sick companies, I mean that must be some fucking chair.

—Yes well look there's nothing I can, I mean damn it will you just let me finish trying to . . .

—No like go ahead man like do you want grape drink? And like what country do they eat enchiladas I mean they're disgusting.

—I think it's a Mexican . . .

—Man like no wonder they're stoned down there all the time . . .

———to join the biggest savings bank family in . . .

—Oh wow. I mean you get some mail.

———selection of gifts for a deposit of only two hun . . .

—Like do you want to know how to say scrotum in Danish?

—Well, well no I . . .

—Bolcheposen. I mean if you just learn all these you can . . .

—Look I don't want to say scrotum in Danish what is that anyhow, who . . .

—Man like it's this letter does your company do business in these foreign countries so you won't name some product you're selling there some dirty word by mistake. I mean you subscribe for like only three hundred dollars a year and they send you all these dirty words in all these different languages so you won't like be going around selling dippeldutters and have . . .

—Look we don't go around selling dippe, we don't sell anything in Denmark we . . .

—No but look man if you subscribe to this you can like make out anyplace, I mean you go up to this Danish chick and say you brought your humørkaep would she like to kusse so she says okay if you use a dråbefanger, so you get this dråbefanger and like go someplace and få et rap. Like do you know what I said?

—No but I, I can imag . . .

—Like, Bast?

—What?

—I mean like did you ever watch us?

—Watch, watch who what . . .

—Like I mean out that back window me and Schramm, I mean like we saw your friend balling that black haired chick back there once.

—Well I, I, once I was, once I happened to look out there and I . . .

—Happened I mean how could you happen to look out, like I mean you have to climb over all those lampshades and papers up on those books to like even see.

—No well I, I mean once I just wanted to see if his light was on I wanted to talk to him about something and, and . . .

—What you saw us screwing? I mean look I'm not mad like I mean I was as good as that black haired chick where are you going.

—I just, I got some of that sauce on my fingers I wanted to . . .

—And like why do you keep that picture up there he had.

—What that, the Baldung? Well it's just up there, it . . .

—I mean do you like those little pointy dippeldutters she's got?

—What her, her breasts? I . . .

—No like that means nipples breast is, wait, brysters look I mean aren't mine better?

—Yes well, well they're larger yes and . . .

—No I mean sit down like she's supposed to be so beautiful to be in this famous painting right? Only she's got these little round brysters and this little round pot and look, no I mean sit here look, under here maybe she's better under here I mean see how heavy this is like? under along here? where she's like skinnier there I mean you are too lift your, all here I mean I got these pants too tight like tomorrow I better go down and get you some bigger ones I mean all up here and, wow like under here in front . . .

—Yes well, well right now they're a little . . .

—Then take them off like, I mean if they're so tight like take them off.

—Well I, I . . .

—No well like then don't. I mean like go set up your practice golf game go ahead, like go turn on your electric fucking tie rack and your . . .

—No no I just, it's just the door if . . .

—If what I mean if that old crap comes knocking my vife my vife Mister? No like go ahead man bring him in and play golf with him if that's what you'd . . .

—No no wait I . . .

—Like be careful man you're going to knock over the look it's that wire will you like take that thing out of your ear? I mean there's no big hurry now . . .

—No but, look all these feath . . .

—I mean here's where I wish I was all nice and firm like you are all under, what like did that hurt?

—No but . . .

—I mean like these must be the bolches in like this is the posen, like

I mean we could both learn everything in all these different languages and . . .

—Yes but look all these feathers can't you, couldn't you just take it . . .

—No but like listen, I mean we had this poem once by this big sea water I mean what was her name, like listen to it in there . . .

—Yes Min, Minnehaha in, in Hia . . .

—No here get your, no like this way I mean it's real narrow get your, there. I mean like aren't mine like do you really like her little pointy dippel oh . . .

—Whose Minne . . .

—No like, hers in the, in the . . .

—No I . . .

—Yes right there, like that like that yes . . .

—Like, there and . . . ?

—Yes oh, oh and here, yes like, yes like that yes and, right there yes wait oh . . .

—But, wait let me, let me move my . . .

—Oh like there yes and, oh . . . you're wait get here and, and . . . not so, not so oh . . . ! like you're, you're built pretty big for not so oh . . . ! yes, yes put . . . yes like not so hurts not so oh, oh . . .

—I, I can't . . .

—Wait don't oh! oh oh oh . . . oh

——highest yield on your savings it's time to join the biggest savings bank family in town . . .

—Oh wow.

—I, I didn't mean to hurt . . .

—Wait like get something it's going all down my, wait move your . . . she reached the brown paper, —I mean my poor fisse, man . . .

—Well I, I didn't . . .

—And I mean wait let me get my, man like that last page you just did those fucking enchilavies went all over it.

—No that's all right I'm, I'll just do it over again . . .

A hand rose to scratch. —Like what do you want to do now.

—Well nothing I, I guess I'd better copy that page over and get back to . . .

—Like I mean you never talk. I mean you're not very interesting you know? I mean like all these other people and like Al I mean they all talk only with us I mean I always have to do all the talking, you know?

—Yes but, I mean when I'm trying to work and not thinking about something to talk about I . . .

—Man like you always think you're trying to work and like you never have something to talk about, I mean like except you're pretty big in the sack there you're like not very interesting.

—Well why should I be interesting! I mean, I mean I want my work to be interesting but why do I have to be interesting! I mean everybody's trying to be interesting let them I'm just, I'm just doing something I have to do so I can try to do what I hope I . . .

—Like then what about Schramm I mean you were always talking to Schramm, like you just said you . . .

—No I didn't really I, he talked and I . . .

—Man like he hardly talked at all I mean you don't know what it was like with him, like with him you never knew what's coming next like this time he couldn't make it and he jumps off the bed and grabs this pencil and throws it down and it, I mean like that's why I hate all these fucking sharp pencils you've got around here you know?

—Yes that was terrible I, I didn't even know you were there when he . . .

—Man I don't want to talk about it! The feathers went off in a heap, a hand came up, scratching a loin.

—No I, I didn't mean . . .

—Then like don't talk about it . . . and the hand came up to dig in the shirt pocket as she stood, —I mean there's the telephone again, like I mean all it does is rings . . .

—Yes I'll get it . . . He passed her paused sniffing by 36 Boxes 200 2-Ply, mounted to QUICK QUAKER, —hello . . . ? Oh Mister Brisboy yes, hello . . . Now . . . ? Oh, no I'm sorry no I don't think it would . . . no no I really don't think . . . Yes well thank you but . . . No not here either no I'm, I still have a lot of work to take care of tonight and . . . I know you do yes thank you but . . . until then yes thank you for calling good . . . yes goodbye thank you for . . . auf Wiedersehen then yes . . .

She followed him back. —Like what are you getting dressed again for I mean are you going someplace?

—No I just feel more, just to work . . .

—Like you're going to be up all night again? She pulled the rumpled blanket.

—No if I can just finish this I, I mean are you all right?

—Like why not man I mean I'm really sailing . . .

—Oh . . . he was back on Hoppin' With Flavor! spreading a fresh sheet of empty staves.

———from the finest homes in America. Many were . . .

—Just that radio man, I mean the water I'm used to like you live by the ocean but that fucking radio, I mean Al put this gum on that mop handle you can like get it in there only to change the station like if you keep wiggling it I mean will you?

When he came down her gaze was gone elsewhere, he stood looking there blowing at the front of his shirt before he sank back to Hoppin' With Flavor! bent over the empty staves where the pen arched, paused, filled, once twice he looked back to find a whole bar missing, crumpled the page staring at the slow rise and fall beyond and pushed the punctured shade aside to bring it into shadow, and licked his lips, parting, meeting, parting on bleats and sudden muted stabs of triumph as he sought fresh pages, drew a hand down his face and stared at the shadowed rise, and fall, and rise, licked his lips, licked the pen nib and dipped it seeking fresh sheets more slowly when the phone rang.

—I can't I can't no! No please I can't . . . !

He was up, caught her head to his trousers bulged against her cheek and held there. —It's all right you, you don't have to . . .

It rang again.

—I can't . . .

—It's all right . . . he held that weight of warmth hard against a tremble of his own, against the next ring, warmth spread suddenly over the back of his hand as he let her down and caught a corner of the blanket up to wipe the blood away, up QUICK QUAKER with the next ring —hello . . . ? Look I can't no I'm busy . . . all right! I'll accept the call operator! hello . . . ? Of course it's me who did you think it . . . who? Al did? No, no Al's just, he's the janitor he's just sort of a janitor who comes in and . . . No I know he shouldn't answer the phone look what are you calling now for what time is it, the candy store can't still be . . . no all right go ahead what is it . . . Well I told you I'd make the trip didn't I? What are you calling about it now for Mister Davidoff gave me . . . expense money too yes a hundred forty-eight cent dollars, thank you look is this the reason you . . . Fine yes did you call just to tell me Mister Davidoff's this real neat guy? I'm trying to . . . from where? I didn't meet anybody there from Malwi no I've never even heard of . . . Of what war, I haven't read the Times no I haven't even . . . what trade deal why did he want to talk to me about a trade deal . . . Well look if you just said they could bring the rhodium out of there through Malwi as the country of origin what's so . . . so who can sell what to China? What bellies, what . . . Look I don't know what you're talking about! I don't think you do either why doesn't your neat guy Davidoff talk to this Senator Milliken about trade with China and this export license, why didn't he talk to the man from the Malwi Trade Commission and get the whole thing straightened . . . Well why doesn't he know about it, he seems to know ev . . . No I know he's not an officer of the company like I am look make him one, there's nothing he'd rath . . . well of course you'd have to pay him more what do you . . . Yes I know it but that second hand General's never met you either neither has poor old Urquhart and that, that terrible Teets so . . . Yes I know I did look you said you just wanted a distinguished looking old man and somebody who looked like he'd run over his own grandmother for . . . Yes all right but for ten dollars each where did you expect me to look, in the Directory of Dir . . . I'm not getting mad, I just have to get back to . . . I did see Mister Hopper yes but he didn't wait is that where these plastic flowers are supposed to be going . . . ? Just a shipping order yes it sounds like millions of them look I just don't want them delivered here, tell somebody to . . . Well you can't have them delivered to Mister Brisboy's hotel no I met him he's a real, really enthusiastic but . . . yes he wanted me to tell you the death rate should rise twenty percent in the next ten years I said I knew you'd be delighted now look . . .

—Hello Mister . . . ?

—Wait somebody's at the . . . yes she wrote them all down wait somebody's at the door . . . and he was down past 200 2-Ply, reaching under the sullen heave on the couch.

—Hello? Mister . . . ?

—Go away! He got back up smoothing the brown paper out on 24-One Pint Mazola under the bulb —it was nobody, nothing, now what . . . Your call yes I just told you she wrote it all down and then this Leva called B F Leva, he said he might want to make a deal I told him you'd . . . yes well fine then tell him that, don't shout at me who does he think he is he might want to make a deal shout at him shout at Piscat . . . Well if you've already told Piscator to figure something out what do you want me to . . . Yes it's right here, the stock's book value is six wait, one sixty-eight and . . . I told you she'd written it all . . . because it's a little smudged that's why look what makes you think that, of course she's dependable she . . . Well what do you mean company loyalty! she's not even . . . No no listen that's very kind of Mister Davidoff but I don't need Virginia up here no, everything's . . . Yes I know she is but I don't need her here and look what do you want to go over these figures in the middle of the night for anyhow, I'm . . . from the Times? When today . . . ? No I haven't just given an interview to anybody no and listen . . . Well listen what did you do that for look Mister Davidoff's your public relations that's what you're paying him for let him call them, he's already upset the way you tape these statements and play them over the phone to every . . . No of course he doesn't know you do it so you can hold the tape back to make your voice sound deeper he doesn't even know you tape them, he just doesn't like being taken by surprise every time you . . . No I didn't see our neat write-up in U S News and . . . I didn't see that one either no but . . . Yes the new company logo's real neat you're welcome now is this all you . . . Yes she did but you know more about them than I do anyhow, Mister Beaton called and this man Stamper but I thought you said this neat lawyer you got from Triangle this Mister Beamish was supposed to be handling that whole . . . well look he's a lawyer isn't he? And this law firm you got out there Milliken Mudge whatever it is that represents this gas business let him talk to Senator Milliken about gas exploration and all the rest of this Alsaka Devel . . . what? What do you mean who changed it nobody did, you . . . because you spelled it that way in these memos you send out that nobody dares . . . Look I know how to spell Alaska but you spelled it a l s a . . . Because I know you did!

Piscator sent me your memo when he registered the . . . Yes you did
. . . you did so . . . you look goodbye I'm not going to spend the rest of
the . . . what? What one more little thing . . . Listen we just talked about
that, I said I was going didn't I? to . . . No now wait wait what do you mean
take the bus what . . . The General took it? he just took it . . . ? Yes but
who said he could just take the company plane any time he . . . These
neat research contracts at Ray-X yes but does that mean he can just take
it to go get some honorary degree from this broken down Tex . . . look
I don't want to hear about this neat real estate deal with them no why
didn't you just send away and get him one from Alabama like the rest
of us, he . . . Yes all right! but that's no reason to take a bus I can get a
regular . . . No now wait . . . No no wait wait how many Indians . . . No
wait look is this why you really called me tonight? to tell me Charley
Yellow Brook and his brother are waiting for me at some bus station and
you . . . you said I'd meet them when . . . ? Yes I know I said I'd be out
there in time for the funeral but . . . No but you mean twen, twenty-four
hours on the bus with the Brook bro . . . What do you mean this neat
chance to get acquainted by the time we get there we'll all be . . . No
now wait look it's always just this one last time! will I just do this one last
. . . Yes I know it but . . . Well why shouldn't Crawley tell you I'd exercised
my stock option what did you expect me to . . . no who said I was going
to sell it I just . . . All right yes I know it but . . . Yes my work is, it's fine
yes I know you do I didn't say I don't appreciate this music grant but
that's what I mean, you say just this one last time and now you're talking
about two hundred thousand shares of something and meeting Boody
somebody when I get back and some golf game look did it ever occur to
you I might not want to learn to play golf . . . ? All right yes all right! just
don't start to talk to me about company loyalty again and look I can't
listen to all the news about school now I can't listen to your plan for a
field trip just tell Davidoff to . . . yes and tell him I'm dropping all the
music off at the hotel desk he said he'd arrange the whole . . . Well then
why don't you just not call here at all till I get back just let him . . . what?
I just told you, a hundred dollars . . . No but wait if the round trip is
eighty-eight fifty-five that only leaves me with . . . Look I'm, I'm just too
damned tired to argue about it if we're taking the bus just because
they've already got bus tickets tell me what bus station they're at and
. . . at what? Look don't try to explain it just tell me where the police
station is and I'll . . . Well I said I would! just don't tell me to have a neat
time at a funeral and twenty-four hours on a bus with two . . . Yes well
I wish you could too goodbye . . . you're welcome yes goodbye goodbye!
 —Bast . . . ?
 —Yes I'm coming . . . he paused to wet a shirttail at the sink.
 —Man like is that you?
 —Yes are you all right? you, you had a nosebleed . . . and he reached
the wet cloth down as white spilled full with her sudden turn toward him
blotting pinks against his knee there.

—Oh man . . .

—I think you had a bad dream . . . he licked his lips come down a breath away to draw the blanket up, yanked to her in her sharp turn from him leaving white massed now in featureless descents to the dark fissure where first his eyes and then a hand came down to hesitate, draw back abruptly at her voice in the sofa's crevice.

—Like are you coming in?

—No I, I can't . . . he cleared his throat and took both hands to pull the blanket down, turned back to spread fresh staves on Standard & Poor's, scarcely looked up from one page to the next till light came separating the blind askew behind the punctured lampshade, reaching beyond to 36 Boxes 200 2-Ply by the time he capped the ink bottle, preceding him past 24-One Pint Mazola to the torrent at the sink where he'd pulled off his shirt, propped up the cookie tin top and got a razor from its plastic display when the door sounded with a knock.

—Hello . . . ? It shuddered in with a familiar care for its infirmity, —Bast? Anybody here . . . ?

—No who, oh oh Mister Gibbs . . .

—Little early, I'm not disturbing you?

—Oh no it's, it's all right yes come in . . .

—My God I forgot your waterworks here, like living under Victoria Falls. Is everything all right?

—Yes it's, everything's fine yes it's . . .

—Can't say you look, tell you the truth Bast you look like hell.

—Yes well I'm just, I haven't had much sleep I've been working and I have to go somewhere I . . .

—No go ahead and shave don't let me interrupt you . . . he got the door into place with his back against it. —Came up to find some papers I thought I might do some work up here, won't bother you will I?

—No, no fine but wait before you . . .

—Place seems crowded you've moved things around a little, hardly get past these God damned . . .

—Yes well some more things some boxes and papers of Mister Eigen's came, I just put them . . .

—Probably get some more up here today I spent the night down there helping him pack up his, this isn't his is it? What the hell is it.

—Oh no well that's just a, it's just an electric towel stand and oh and those, yes those are just barbeque tools I . . .

—But where the hell did they, what are all these where did these come from, what is it soap powder?

—Yes well it's detergent yes those are just those are samples they were, they were just left here wait before you . . .

—Blue folder around here someplace have you seen it? Getting a fresh start on a book I was working on Bast, getting a fresh God damned start on everything really going to get down to work again, you might want to hear some of it sometime like to get your, what, what's that is that a telephone?

—Oh that yes well that's a, it's sort of a picturephone I think they call it yes it's . . .

—But what the hell is it doing up there? and what, this thing under it what . . .

—Yes well that's just something we use for, I mean we don't really use it it's for sending pictures by telephone it's just look Mister Gibbs wait before you go . . .

—Thought you were writing music up here all this time Bast let's see what you've got set up in the good God I beg your pardon . . . !

—Yes well I was just going to tell you she . . .

—Man like what are you staring at . . . knees came up with the welter of blanket —I mean like you never saw one before?

—Why, why yes quite recently in fact Miss . . .

—Yes well Rhoda this is Mister Gibbs you remember Rhoda she was . . .

—Never had the pleasure Bast good Lord relax, didn't mean to interrupt you I can come back up later and . . .

—No don't go no I'm, I just have to hurry I . . .

—Pleasure my ass man I mean that night you're over there with like one shoe giving these cops all this grief? And Bast like while you're in there dump one of those little red boxes in the tub? and then I mean like get out of the way . . .

—Rhoda of course, yes go ahead and shave Bast . . . he came down cautiously on Hoppin' With Flavor! —I'll just sit down and chew the fat with Rhoda.

—Man like try that and you'll get a fat lip, and like watch that can by your foot I mean do you want grape drink?

—Good God no I . . .

—Well I mean will you just hand me the can then? and like that red cup off the, man not this can I mean look at it like does that look like grape drink?

—Frankly I didn't want to say, but since you . . .

—It's enchilavies I mean what's the matter with enchilavies, like I mean what do you have to put everything down for man.

—I? Wouldn't have you think that for the world, I've been marveling at the woman's touch everywhere since I came in in fact really cozy, pants hanging on the dishcloth rack in there, dirty cups on the sill and Mister Bast's greasy diploma up here on the wall like an earnest young dentist, milady's lemonfresh bath scenting the air and, yes what's that behind you on the floor . . .

—Man like what are you trying to, I mean what do you mean what is it it's this Indian hat what does it look like.

—Mister Gibbs? Is it all right if I, I've been wearing these shirts you left here once and . . .

—No by all means, neck size makes you look a little cadaverous and those trousers are, where in God's name did you get that outfit anyhow.

—Man like what's the matter with his outfit I mean look at yours, like you're wearing this old summer suit of somebody's man.

—Yes well it's all right Mister Gibbs I can't stop to, you don't know what time it is do you?

—It's like ten after man I mean don't ask me ten after what, and I mean before you go like can you leave me some coin? Like I have to go to this vietrinary before they stuff him.

—But I thought you, when I gave you that five dol . . .

—Five dollars I mean like that new razor I got you was like three ninety-eight and those pants were like eighteen dollars and that jacket man, I mean you've got all these checks in there like just tell your friend to like cash them.

—Yes well if he, if you could Mister Gibbs they're just some dividend checks and, oh and wait this check here I meant to give you this check for the rent sixty-one forty, I think Mister Eigen said . . .

—Didn't expect you to pay it all though Bast after all we . . .

—No no that's all right it's all made out and, I mean it's really not exactly me anyway it's . . .

—But who's, who the hell is the J R Shipping Corp.

—Yes well it's just a, just I don't have time to explain Mister Gibbs it's all too, if you could move your knee I just have to get that music there and . . .

—What this whole pile? Good Lord what's, is this your what was it? your oratorio? No wonder you look, Bast that's great you've finished your oratorio?

—No well the, the oratorio, it's not exactly an oratorio now it's, it's just going to be a suite for small orchestra but it's not exactly finished I, I'm . . .

—Small orchestra good God, must be enough parts here for a whole Berlioz . . .

—Yes but, but this isn't it this is, this is just something else I've been working on so I could . . .

—Man like don't let him get started I mean when he starts explaining like why he can't do this one thing until he does this other thing he's not doing either because there's like something else he has to do as soon as he finishes this other thing I mean can you move your foot . . .

—Yes if can you just hand me that Indian . . .

—Better help your squaw with her blanket in back there too Bast wouldn't want people in the street to . . .

—Look man I'm just going in the tub I mean where do you think I'm going.

—Oh and Mister Gibbs I meant to say if you're going to be here if any phone calls come they may sound like business I mean they are business and . . .

—You mean that phone in there works?

—Yes oh and that's something else if you can keep something hung over it, I mean it's a picturephone and if somebody's in the tub or anything I wrote a number down there you can just tell them to call Mister Piscator he's a lawyer, I wrote his number down there too if he calls about a movie company called Erebus somebody called Mister Leva if you could just help me with this box here I . . .

—Look Bast I'll do anything I can for you but God damn it can you take two minutes to sit down and tell me what this is all about? This business these dividend checks what's . . .

—They're in the icetray yes if you could just cash them for her I'll try to explain it all when I get back oh and don't let Al answer the phone anymore he . . .

—Al who wait look how long are you going to be gone where the hell are you going?

—It's just, it's something I said I'd do Mister Gibbs so I, I have to do it if you could hold the door for me . . .

—Yes here but listen Bast there are some other things I wanted to talk to good God no is that a hearing aid?

—Yes no Rhoda can tell you goodbye thank you Mister Gibbs goodbye . . .

—Good, good luck . . . his weight and the door's supported one another till it shuddered back in place, —good . . . God.

—Man like could you hand me one of those red cups by the sink?

—With grape drink? Look will you tell me . . .

—Like I just want it to dip over me man I mean all this real sudsing power, like do you want to get in?

—In, the tub?

—Well like what do you think I . . .

—No look Rhoda I just came up here to get some work done, I thought Bast was shut up here alone writing music find all this going on and him never seen him looking worse, never saw anybody look worse what the hell was that hearing aid he's wearing.

—Like that's this little ear radio man I mean it's this job he has on the side, like he writes down every record this station plays so these musicians don't get screwed on like royalties and . . .

—But of what, this job on the side of what you mean he composes with that thing playing in his ear all the time?

—Like that's all this music he's getting this four hundred dollars for so he can write this other music I mean that's why he doesn't even know what it sounds like till he goes to this hotel someplace to like play it on the piano there, I mean like he was trying it here only he couldn't find these octaves on the piano, like I mean he'd just find them and some more stuff would like come and get piled on them and I mean now you can't even find the fucking piano anymore.

—All right but what's all this got to do with his, with this business this J R Shipping Corp and all these . . .

—Like that's what it's on the side of on the side of, I mean wait till you see the mail like there must be these fifty sick corporations man, I mean when the telephone rings you never know what it is like can you lend me your hand so I don't slip getting out?

—Yes here but . . . he cleared his throat —be careful, this lawyer he mentioned this Piscator . . .

—He's this lawyer they've got that like could you give me that shirt to dry off? And his boss, I mean when he calls you never heard such a creep like could you throw me those moccasins?

—Yes listen on second thought I'd better just forget the . . .

—I mean like whenever he calls man he's got like this whole list of stuff and you can't hardly . . .

—Never mind listen I shouldn't have asked, came up here to do some work and . . .

—Man like do it then I mean who's stopping you, like I mean what are you climbing up there for . . .

—I'm looking for a God damned looking for a blue folder and some boxes of notes Tootsie Roll boxes, they say Tootsie Roll on them have you seen . . .

—Like this blue folder's someplace I mean I saw it once but these Tootsie Rolls man, I mean you could dig for look out! Like that whole pile's going . . .

—God damned . . .

—Like before you get buried I mean could you come down and cash these checks like you said?

—Look I didn't say . . .

—Man like it's not this million dollars and I mean by your foot like throw me that raincoat?

—All right just, wait hold those film cans before they, there . . .

—They're like right in the refrigerator I mean that's where he keeps . . .

—Yes but wait what, good God what is this in here . . .

—That's all this literature for these investments man, like . . .

—No this, this Cornish hens à la Kiev, classic dish of the Imperial Court of Old dripping all over these . . .

—It's some present he got like it says keep refrigerated I mean just look in the icetray.

—But, all these? you expect me to cash all these U S Steel what the, forty cents? International Paper forty-three cents what are all these on one share? General Telephone forty cents, Typhon International . . .

—Man like don't ask me I mean just add them up okay?

—Columbia Gas forty-seven, El Paso Natural Gas really God damned diversified portfolio, Walt Disney . . .

—And there's like this forty-five more cents of them under the couch with the . . .

—Western Union look they're not even endorsed, I mean what do you . . .

—What like signed on the back? I mean endorse them then like just sign a fucking x on the back what do they want for thirty cents, Abraham Lincoln's autograph?

—One eighty, two ten, two thirty look I'll give you five dollars for the lot, here . . .

—Five dollars? Man like I need cab fare I'm going shopping.

—Now? like that?

—Like what, I mean can you see through it?

—No but it's, you'll freeze your pants are hanging in there on . . .

—Like what do you want me to do leave them at Macy's? And I mean I could get you something man, like that suit you've got it looks like out of some old movie and I mean it's this big sale down there today I could get you a . . .

—Look what difference does a sale make if you're just going down there to . . .

—The crowds man the crowds, I mean they're so cheap like for a hundred people they've got this one spaced out sales person that's like trained not to see you, I mean look is that this blue folder you're looking for up there? No like over the refrigerator on that Flakes box . . .

—How'd it get up there yes lost this and I'd really be, what in, what the hell . . .

—Oh wow, I mean like there was this frozen pizza up there . . .

—Frozen what do you mean frozen cheese and tomato all over the whole God damned throw me that shirt God damn it, I mean God damn it if you and Bast are staying here at least you could . . .

—What man at least we could what, I mean he just gave you some rent didn't he? And I mean like you weren't even very nice to him, man I mean this one time I ever saw you before you're up here that night waving this bottle around with like one shoe and I mean now you come on like you're this really different person, man like I mean really up tight you know?

—Yes well listen . . .

—I mean you just come in here all at once from like nowhere and everybody should drop dead while you look for your Tootsie Rolls and this great folder with cheese and tomatoes like it's War and Peace I mean what . . .

—Listen it is it's, look . . . he wiped a hand, sank back on 24–12 Oz Btls Fragile! —chance I've been waiting for to work on this book again I've finally got it, worked on it before never any reason for me to finish it anything to make me really want to do it now there is that's why it's, why I've got to really damn it . . . he got to a knee, reached up, —hello yes who . . . ? Wait who is it what do you . . . Monsieur Bast oh, no il n'est pas là . . .

—Man like just say j'ai mon foo and they hang right up . . . the door shuddered, hung, —I mean I'll see you man . . .

—Comment . . . ? Le commissionnaire du, du mal oui? comment? C'est un pays . . . ? Yes all right bon no offense damn it qu'est ce que vous . . . qui moi? Moi je suis ahm, je suis son aide oui, Monsieur Bast est parti mais je . . . Urgent oui mais je . . . de quel catalogue . . . ? Rouge et vert, de quoi? Ray X? Don't see one here no je ne . . . Que vous êtes pressé bon je le dirai au Monsieur quand il re . . . yes well look écoutez God damn it what do you want me to qu'est ce que vous . . . comment? De bonne vente oui mais you mean acheter tout . . . ? Oui fine prix convenu mais l'inventaire tout entier . . . ? Tout à l'instant même fine see what I can . . . qui moi? Je m'appelle ahm, oui je m'appelle Grynszpan oui, Monsieur Grynszpan . . . bon, si vous . . . plus tard bon pas de quoi good God . . .

He came down wiping a hand, caught the door tipped on its hinge and set it firm before he wet the shirt's tail at the sink torrent and came in to the couch wiping the blue folder —try to get anything done here . . . sitting to open its pages and wipe at margins, pausing with —I hope every weeder . . . to clear his throat, —I hope every reader will, from this history, take warning, and stamp improvement on the wings of time . . . and his feet came up to rest on Thomas Register. —Pursued by the crippled ghost of exquisite and delicate sensibility, Frank Woolworth fled to wait . . . he reached, dug, came up with the nub of a pencil. —Fleeing that crippled ghost of exquisite and delicate sensibility to Lancaster Pa where his best would be good enough, Frank Woolworth secured success with a line of ten cent items to stamp his nickel's worth of improvement on democracy even then being flushed from elsewhere in Aristotle's lecture notes as forlorn delusion rising out of the notion that those who are equal in any respect are equal in all sounds fine doesn't it, nothing hard about that. Roused by the steam whistle, democracy's claims devoured technology's no wait. Roused by the steam whistle, democracy claimed technology's promise to banish failure to inherent vice, where in painting it survives today, and America sprang full in the face of that dead philosopher's reproach to be always seeking after the useful does not become free and exalted souls. By the nineties the arts were already seeking refuge at Hull House dressed as, by the nineties the arts showed up disguised as therapy at Hull House seeking refuge from streets ringing with Jack London's howling discovery of Spencer's immutable law, Give me the fact, man! The irrefragable fact! and elsewhere their torrent catalogued as literature to trample Maggie the Girl of the Streets where John Dewey came groping for the close and intimate acquaintance got with nature at first wait. And elsewhere their torrent no. Catalogued elsewhere as literature, these . . . the pencil nub drew lines, an arrow detouring a tomato blot —published this ten years ago it would have been damn it have to type it over anyhow where I put those cigarettes . . . he rummaged. —Give me the fact man sound like I mean that's Spencer's law? howling discovery of Spencer's immutable Christ anybody thinks Spencer would say give me the fact man no business reading this in the first place. Now . . . smoke rose. —Catalogued elsewhere as literature, these no. These, catalogued elsewhere as literature, catalogued as literature to trample made it an active verb, conspired no . . . smoke rose, the cigarette finally dropped into the enchiladas, his head rested back. —These . . .

The smoke drifted through planes of light from the askew blind mounting 24/One Pound H-O and Won't Burn, Smoke or Smell, crossed the plateau of bound volumes of the Musical Courier to climb NO DEPOSIT NO RETURN and fail against the arc of the clock where the long hand pursued the small, passed it, descended and was gone. He sat up abruptly —damn it get anything done in this place . . . and he was in past 36 Boxes 200 2-Ply —hello . . . ? Not here no Mister Bast left this morning, who . . . Mister Grynszpan? not here either no, who's . . . oh. Oh they did . . . ? and they said they'd just talked to a Mister Gryn . . . can't understand them at all no matter of fact Mister Piscator they ahm . . . No, no it's French yes talked to them myself, I . . . me? Grynszpan yes I just said that because I'm up here getting some work done didn't want to be dist . . . just helping Mister Bast out yes took this call from . . . radium? No they . . . oh, didn't mention rhodium no sounded like they had a catalogue of x-ray machines red and green catalogue want to buy the whole . . . Ray X that was it yes red and . . . all outdated inventory? Didn't even ask didn't seem to care no I don't think they could read the specifications either, sounded like all they could read was the prices they want immediate . . . discount no didn't ask for one they just want im . . . in the catalogue yes everything in it I sold them everything in the catalogue complete inventory if they can get hold of it immediately, just want to know where they can . . . got it all warehoused where . . . ? Fine yes I'll tell them that, goodbye . . . you're welcome yes, good . . . what? No, no Mister Bast mentioned it said this Leva might call but he didn't give me any details just left here this morning in a hell of a hurry and . . . Yes well look I'm busy I can't . . . sorry yes but look I can't get into . . . who B F Leva? worst God damned moviemaker in . . . losing how much . . . ? You mean your company's looking for tax credits up in the range of . . . who Bast? No didn't say anything to me about a threat to the tax loss status of your textile wait look Mister Piscator don't go into it please, I'm working on something up here and . . . yes I . . . All right look all five studios what's the book val . . . what just in carrying charges . . . ? All right look take on the whole thing get rid of that two and a half million cash outlay in carrying charges by dumping these four smaller studios well under book value, say you sell them off at two million one bring your tax credits up around forty million just hang onto the big studio rate this Leva's going you'll be . . . problem getting hold of their stockholders list quote the book value at a hundred and sixty-eight a share real God damned point's how active it is, stockholders probably watching these losses sitting on their look I don't know the whole story shouldn't be trying to . . . can't no I told you I'm working on something I . . . help Mister Bast out yes but he didn't say anything about a . . . Didn't mention that either no he . . . no look I . . . didn't tell me about that either damn it look Mister Piscator trying to help out but I've got something here I'm working on that's . . . I don't know when I'll finish it no! Now will you . . . you're welcome yes good . . . I will yes goodbye.

He was back in muttering, dug out a cigarette and lit it before he came down to the sofa —forty million tax credits Christ thought he was up here writing music what the hell he's been, where was I . . . he picked up the folder, set the enchilada can on Moody's —get anything done here ought to just let the God damned thing ring, consoled only by the fact that Madame Bernhardt had allowed herself to be photographed in a yellow mackintosh as ungainly as his for the jaunt, Wilde still knew no country in the world where machinery is so lovely as in America. I have always wished to believe that the line of strength and the line of beauty are one. That wish was realized when I contemplated American machinery. It was not until I had seen the waterworks at Chicago that I realized the wonders of machinery. The rise and fall of the steel rods, the symmetrical motion of great wheels is the most beautifully rhythmic thing I have ever seen. Spread broadcast, this particular aesthetic experience of Wilde's was now leveling men's claims to being absolutely equal since they were absolutely free, the symmetrical motions of those great wheels homogenizing their no, no wait spread broadcast, this wait. On less aesthetic levels, Wilde's experience spread broadcast leveling no damn it leveling levels wait. In less aesthetic versions, the symmetrical motions were, motions were, no, no elsewhere. Elsewhere the symmetrical motion . . . he tapped ashes into the enchiladas, tapped one foot against the other on Thomas Register. —Leveling men's claims to being absolutely equal since they were absolutely free, the symmetrical motion of, symmetrical motion of God damn it, the symmetrical motion . . . he sat there tapping, —where the hell did that come from . . . and he had the guitar by the throat, plucked it, cradled it and strummed a chord —can't be his no whole God damned thing's out of tune . . . he hunched over it trying strings, tightening keys —owner must be a deaf mute . . . he plucked, tried chords, loosened a key, tightened one, tried a string, a chord, a bar —thing of Granados how the hell does it go . . . he made a fresh start. Another. The long hand crept from NO DEPOSIT, passed the short, the second hand swept past them both to NO RETURN, reappeared and was gone —almost had it that time God damn it just try to get anything done here . . .

He got in past 200 2-Ply, braced a foot and reached, —hello . . . ? No wait this is . . . wait this isn't . . . Look this isn't Mister Bast he's not here, he . . . Lunch? but it's . . . too bad yes but . . . Well look it's not his fault if you brought in Pouilly Fuissé and this salmon mousse before you called, he's not even . . . that you've got a grand piano in your suite now fine I'll tell him, good . . . what? Me? No that's . . . yes that's very kind of you but . . . no I have a lunch appointment just leaving for it, good . . . I will yes, au voir . . . he came down cautiously, —seems to lead quite a life up here . . . and he picked up a red cup to rinse it under the torrent in the tub, fill it at the one in the sink and drop in a teabag, back to set it on Moody's and find a cigarette —get through one simple sentence here before something else where the hell was I, published this ten years ago it really would have been here, disappointed with Ni, spread broadcast yes. Spread broadcast, this aesthetic no wait what did I, elsewhere yes. Elsewhere, close and intimate acquaintance got with the wonders of machinery at first hand were lev, was leveling men's claims to being absolutely equal since they were absolutely free, the symmetrical motion of those great wheels homogenizing their differences till Christ damn it now. At less exalted. At the less exalted levels where close and intimate acquaintance was, with the wonders of damn it God damn it . . . ! He reached for the cup, spilled it back on Moody's —get something to eat just no God damned energy, where I put those cigarettes. Now. At less exalted levels the synep, symmet, the symmetrical motion . . . his head came back, his eyes climbed 2-Ply Facial Tissue Yellow through planes of sunlight from the askew blind to rest on the Baldung propped up there, —that symmetrical motion . . . and the cigarette, dangling unlit, finally fell.

———mouthwash with the distinctive continen . . .

—Wha . . . he sat up abruptly, brought a hand up against the sun come round full on his face.

———to perk up your personality. Do something nice for . . .

—Perk up your personality you bastard, thought that God damned thing was dead . . . He was up, —thought I, somebody at the door . . . ? he got through past the torrent at the tub —one minute's peace get anything done here, yes?

—Mister Bass . . . ?

—Just a . . . he got it opened —good heavens! He stared down into décolletage —he's, he's not here, what . . .

—Erebus Production buy im a fuck an ere I am.

—Oh, oh I see, well . . .

—E's not ere Mister Bass?

—Not, not right now but it's hardly . . .

—I ave a eavy schedule you know? Wen e's ere.

—Don't know but wait, wait I've seen you somewhere yes in a drawer once, saw you in a man's shirt drawer . . .

—Don be crazy I don go in man's drawers no, goodbye . . .

—Bet you don't, had a mustache too yes last time I saw you you had a mustache . . .

—You very crazy goodbye . . .

He dug a cigarette out and lit it before he got the door closed —couldn't have been, Christ imagine that . . . barely past the tub —now what, God damn it . . . he braced a foot —hello . . . ? Wait who's . . . ah oui. Oui c'est fait, tout . . . l'inventaire complet oui, même que dans le catalogue c'est warehoused hell's the word for warehouse. Déposée oui déposée au port de Houston . . . non non comme owston, en Texas . . . comment? No, non c'est un état, Texas . . . Oui tout reste ahm, préparé . . . Argent oui on peut payer là . . . là oui en Texas même si vous . . . look écoutez damn it just pay for it and get it out of there packed ready to go tout préparé oui . . . you're welcome yes pas de quoi monsieur what the hell that's all about never heard anybody so excited . . .

———to join the biggest savings bank family in town . . .

—Problem's I'm the God damned aerial, get in under their signal here . . . he crouched, dragged 24/One Pound H-O from the heap, dislodged a cache that clattered to the floor like broken glass —God's name was that . . . he was down picking them up, held one to the light, another —who the hell's been taking pictures of zebras, damn it got to get through this thing . . . He reached the folder, sat hunched on H-O —get through one simple sentence here, just one. Spread broadcast no, what was, at the less, at less exalted levels the symmetrical motion leveling God damn it, well God damn it what's wrong with it like it was. Spread broadcast, this aesthetic experience of Wilde's was leveling men's claims to being fine what the hell's wrong with that, homogenizing their fid, their differences didn't write it to be read out loud anyhow, homogenizing their differences till by the time Horatio Alger died the hand at the machine had a distinctly childish cast and Ragged Dicks were everywhere, one and, one and? Supposed to be in, one in seven children between ten and fifteen out working for wages, a body thirty times the size of the U S Army for whom refinements on Cartwright's loom and advances in the canning, in canning machinery and the glass problem's that God damned till. Homogenizing their differences till by the time wait, shrinking, just use shrinking. Shrinking their differences till the hand at the machine had a distinctly childish yes Cartwright's loom advances in the canning, in canning machinery and the glass industry swelled the coercion of equal opportunity to the turgid proportions of Alger's own achievement in a hundred and nineteen works, a generation indoctrinated in the comforting assurance that virtue is always rewarded by wealth and honor nothing wrong with that is there, and a century labeled one of the most fascinating chapters in the history of man's upward progress by one of its survivors, Reverend Newell Dwight Millis. Where the hell did I find Reverend Newell Dwight Millis Christ start checking all my sources I'll be, have to look for those notes. For the first time government, invention, art, industry, and religion have served all the people rather than the patrician classes. The millions join in the upward march now what the hell's wrong with all that, nothing so God damned difficult why everybody says it's difficult, now. And while those millions saw where they were marching much as no, much the way, much the way Mark Twain saw them through a glass eye, darkly, the one eyed man, these one eyed men no. And while those millions, while those millions . . . he came forward to pick up a slide —never saw so God damned many zebras . . . he picked up another, another, finally swept the entire pile toward him and settled back against Won't Burn, Smoke or Smell to hold them one by one up to the failing light, —antelope looks like eland where the hell did all these come from . . .

The long hand drove the short before it into NO RETURN. —Christ! he came forward —where was I. And while those millions yes, and while those millions saw where they were marching up to the one eyed man, these one eyed men no. And while those millions where's that pencil, must expect to clear thirty or forty million next three or four years . . . Figures appeared in the margin —how the hell many shares outstanding though can't figure the . . . he sat there tapping, finally came up all at once and in to find a number penciled under KER and dial. —Hello? I'm calling Mister Pis . . . yes this is Gryn, Piscator? Listen yes just had an idea on your Ereb . . . is who here? Whose boss your boss? here? No I don't even . . . been reading what statements to the press no I don't even . . . No told you this morning Mister Bast didn't mention any leases on . . . Look I don't know anything about this subcommittee either just this Ray-X inventory whatever the hell it is they're picking it up tonight down there paying cash on the . . . don't know anything about that either look I just called on this Ereb . . . class suit no he didn't mention that either I just called with an idea on Erebus if you'll listen for a min . . . Leva no Leva hasn't called sent up a Mother's Day greeting a little while ago but . . . Never mind no, no let's forget the whole thing sorry I bothered you I . . . All right can you just listen for a minute then? Know how many shares of common Erebus has outstanding . . . ? No but . . . book value of the stock's one sixty-eight yes but . . . Look why waste the time chasing down their stockholders' list just publish a flat offer eighty-five ninety dollars a share knock the bottom right out of it, talk that's going around on these losses small stockholders must be so God damned scared they'll trample each other to death dumping it in your laps probably be picking it up at fifty or sixty before the . . . who Leva? Why should he be, he'll still have the big studio won't he? Go right on making his Christ awful pictures build up your tax loss pos . . . you're welcome yes good . . . Crawley no nobody named Crawley's called goodbye, I . . . Look I'd like to help out on it but . . . No, I . . . no . . . I don't know no, now . . . No listen I . . . listen I just told you I don't know a God damned thing about these loans voting trust rumor or anything else Mister Piscator, something God damned important here I'm working on and . . . what? All right yes I'll take a message for Mister Bast if it's brief, what . . . yes a shipment of sweaters ready to be flown back from Hong Kong, what . . . What, it's overloaded . . . ? If the pilot's ready to fly it anyhow what's the difference if the plane is over . . . oh. The price the insurance company's named for the premium would wipe out your profit I'll tell him when I . . . no I . . . no I told you I . . . and the what . . . ? No I don't know when he . . . No now wait listen, listen. Save us a lot of trouble here look, there must be a girl around the Hong Kong factory there who'd like a free ride to New York, give her a handful of quarters how much are the sweaters worth at retail . . . Fine just insure her for a quarter of a million write in the company as beneficiary if it goes down you're . . . fine yes you're . . . you're welcome yes good . . . yes goodbye! Christ, give him an inch he wants what the hell did I come in here looking for, dictionary . . .

Film cans crashed as he got a foot against 24-One Pint Mazola in ascent —probably have to go through every God damned box in the place . . . but he got no further than Stack Top Side Up and the first book he took from it, slowly settling back up there turning unhurried pages motionless till he reached for the bulb strung overhead, rummaging occasionally for a cigarette and reaching the top of a film can up for an ashtray, turning page after unhurried page till he started up abruptly snapping the black covers closed with an emptied cigarette pack thrust in at page 149 —never should have called him back Christ, tell him Grynszpan's taken cyanide . . . he stretched across QUICK QUAKER, —hello . . . ? the what . . . ? It was John Adams yes what the . . . what . . . ? Look I don't . . . look God damn it I don't want a free dance lesson no, goodbye!

The second hand rose from NO DEPOSIT and swept the vacant arc to descend to NO RETURN —whole God damned day gone . . . he sank down on H-O, reached the blue folder, —out of cigarettes can't be . . . he was up again rummaging pockets, —out for something to eat probably work better at night anyhow all these God damned interruptions, she can't be back before Christ! He was back at QUICK QUAKER, reached up to dial, —Tom? Yes listen I . . . Ninety-sixth Street yes listen just realized there's a phone up here, told you I gave her your number there when she calls you can . . . No I know she can't be back yet but . . . what you knew Bast had a phone put in here . . . ? No wait look if you're doing that just have all your calls transferred to this number, anything went wrong now I'd . . . Haven't even been out to eat up here all day working yes, hardly get through one God damned sentence people at the door phone ringing gets calls from every . . . no just trying to help him out sounds like he has about twenty part time jobs left here this morning with an armload of music Indian headdress God knows just trying not to think about it, I

. . . Fine yes read you some of it right now if you . . . what? Oh, no well not, not yet not exactly I didn't mean actually writing no can't find the God damned typewriter, thought we'd brought Schramm's in but . . . going over this first part again yes read you some of it right now if you . . . yes I know it Tom but . . . know how many times you have yes but I've made some changes thought you might . . . know I said that too but . . . look I know it but God damn it I can't without my notes, spend half the God damned day up here looking for my notes so much stuff piled up by now the place is like Kafka's . . . what this last load of yours? Hasn't come yet no thought it was going back into Schramm's no place left here to put a . . . no just out for something to eat haven't felt too God damned well either I . . . really? Which tooth is it . . . Sounds more like a nerve dying not a God damned thing you can . . . know it yes hard as hell to concentrate on any . . . know it yes not a God damned thing you can . . . know it yes look I've got to get off go out and get something to . . . Who said that your lawyer or hers . . . ? that you have to pay her lawyer's fee too just part of the God damned system nothing you can . . . no I know she's the one who pulled out look Tom . . . I know he's your son yes but . . . look from now on you've got responsibility without authority, whole thing's like driving the back end of a God damned hook-and-ladder downhill at night I've got to get off Tom I . . . who? Well what the hell did you think he'd . . . know what a fatuous bastard this German publisher is what the hell did you expect, look I've got to get something to eat working up here all day haven't had anything think I can work better at night anyhow and wait listen, this phone call . . . Well she might, anything went wrong now I'd cut my . . . know it yes look I've got a good root canal man if you need one just . . . two or three hundred depends on the tooth, let me know if you . . . know it yes won't keep you on, goodbye . . .

The door brought in a cascade of mail swept through with a foot, the last pieces kicked in from the hall as he got it closed against the lull of falling waters broken only by occasional peals of the phone until it shuddered in again, hung open behind the flap of sandals past the tub and 200 2-Ply, dump of mail and the bag shaken over it at the sofa where motion came down stilled against

————prompt temporary relief by reducing painful swelling of . . .

The peal of the phone convoked 24-One Pint Mazola and NO DEPOSIT NO RETURN, Moody's, H-O, Musical Couriers and lampshades, paper bags, Appletons', 500 Novelty Rolls 1-Ply White and the collapse on the sofa alike, abandoned them to

————Alsaka Development working day and night to bring the American family its full share of the world's energy. Alsaka. A proud member of the J R Family of Companies. When you see a product. A service. A promise of human betterment for all. If it's J R. It's just right. J R. An American family of American com . . .

And the flap of sandals took up from the dark, the mail bag dragged empty past 200 2-Ply out the door left hung open on the tub's three gallon a minute torrent to the sink's two.

—Thought I closed the God damned door, Bast? Anybody here? What's her, Rhoda . . . ? He got it closed, in over mail to the sofa where he dropped a paper bag —get right back to this before I, get it done Christ published it ten years ago it would have where the hell is that light . . . he got the punctured lampshade, yanked, dug in the paper bag for cigarettes, —now. Where the, where was I tripods of Hephaestus no back at, millions here those God damned millions here. And while those millions saw where they were marching much as Mark Twain saw them through a glass eye, darkly, the, what, what the God damn it . . . He reached to shake the lamp, the light came on again, —much as Mark Twain saw them through a glass eye, darkly, the one, the good that's it yes the good the good eye could now peer into hell's that pencil, the good what damn it God damn it! Must have loosened the God damned plug when I, well Christ! Just look at the God damned thing and it comes on again what was I, get through one sentence get through one God damned word this way . . . The longer hand lapped the shorter, the arc went dark —could have cleared up the whole God damned thing tonight first God damned peaceful no, can't be no middle of the . . . he was up, —might be no she might be back . . .

He was through to QUICK QUAKER —yes hello? to who . . . ? Bast look God damn it Mister Bast isn't here what do you . . . what? from Mister Bast? I'll accept it yes operator \ here . . . Bast? Where the . . . look no Akron's in Ohio not Indiana middle of the night what the hell are you doing in . . . No no it's all right damned good thing you called I've been . . . what? Yes I'm listening what . . . nobody named Crawley no but I've had . . . wait you forgot to tell who what . . . ? Want the tape sent right down to him when it's finished fine, what tape . . . All right I will yes be sure to, listen I've had this Pis . . . no no this Piscator of yours had him on and off the phone here all day says your company's stock's being hurt by pressure on some big loans they've got out against some government R and D contracts with this Ray-X division rumor there's a . . . Whole point look I don't know somebody called this morning sold them the whole inven . . . No I, Grynszpan yes Grynszpan stopped by just helping out said he'd sold their whole outdated inventory to . . . what I'm trying to tell you no idea what it is just said inventory, Piscator says may take some pressure off this Ray-X some Senate subcommittee starting a feasibility study looking into cost overruns on these contracts has your boss trying to head off rumors these lenders may force his stock into a voting trust protect their old loans and these new ones he just . . . Well damn it Bast I don't know that's what I'm asking, maybe trying to get in under the wire with this Erebus deal pick up their tax loss offset rumors some textile mill losing its loss carryover if it goes out of production town takes

over for a park and speed . . . Eagle yes said there was some class suit
shaping up over the way your boss converted his preferred to common
to get control look Bast if you can just tell me . . . hasn't called here at
all no Piscator says he's been calling the press reading them statements
on these oil and gas leases you're securing on some Indian res . . . Well
damn it Bast I wouldn't have either thought you were just sitting up here
writing music can you tell me what the hell is . . . explain it all someday
fine meanwhile how the hell shall I . . . Bast damn it look how the hell
can I use my own judgment if I don't even know the . . . I'm not angry
at you no damn it look you're welcome but can you . . . my work? Been
on it up here all day yes going fine going pretty well I . . . of plastic what?
Hardly hear you . . . wait get to whose funeral at noon, Bast . . . ? She's
not here no wait get to whose . . . I will yes but damn it wait she . . . what?
Wait wait what bus is leaving, Bast? Bast . . . ? Good, Christ! He came
down, a film can followed to crack open on the floor and send the roll
merrily unfurling before him, came to grief at H-O where he sank for a
moment—get it done Christ could have cleared up that whole first part
tonight . . . and he reached under the dark of the punctured shade, made
the sofa and pulled the blanket up, crooked an arm over his head against
the torrents beyond and, nearer, the trickle of

————treasured heirlooms, many were from the finest . . .

Light came finally separating the blind as though cautious what it
might disturb, broadened as though emboldened where nothing moved
but the second hand spanning the arc alone till the long hand rose from
NO DEPOSIT and, after repeated tries, came up dragging the short behind.

————to let earnings on your idle cash go down the drain when you can convert it
to . . .

He came up on one elbow —who the, who is it!
—Got a delivery . . .
—Just wait a minute . . . he came fighting the blanket, got the door
opened —stuff from downtown? Just bring it in and, here close the tub
cover just pile it here.
—What you talking about pile it there.
—What the hell's the problem just bring it in and pile it here . . . he
clattered the tub cover down passing, —busy with some work I can't stop
to . . .
—Take a look out your window there.
—What that truck? Biggest damned truck I ever, look who's this for.
—Mister Bast J R Corp whole fucking truckload here's your invoice,
shipment three five nine seven . . .
—That's absurd here let me, look you can't bring a hundred thou-
sand plastic flowers up here good God, what . . .

—What I'm telling you, so where do you want them.

—I don't want them look take them back where they came from or, wait drive around the block while I call . . .

—Came from Hong Kong take me an hour to get that fucking rig around the fucking block what do you . . .

—Good great take two hours ride around the block go back to Hong Kong look God damn it don't give me . . . he caught the door, left it hanging till he was back from the dim recess of plumbing in the hall examining a square of tissue in the light —business is very good where the hell this came from, can't be Bast must be Bast . . . it dropped crumpled, —God damned morning half gone not even a chance to get started here . . .

He came in with a red cup floating a teabag, set it beside the red cup submersing a teabag on Moody's —run right through it today Christ got to get it done, another day like yesterday and I, where those matches . . . he drew the enchilada can in reach —where was I, where John Dewey came groping wait, damn it, well God damn it missed a whole page . . . He picked them apart —groping for the pages stuck together with this God damned cheese, close and intimate acquaintance got with nature broke off in the middle of this Dewey quote didn't even notice it, intimate acquaintance got with nature at first hand, with real things and materials, with the actual processes of their manipulation, and the knowledge of their social necessities and uses most awkward writer in the God damned language, break off in the middle of one of his clumsy God damned sentences don't even notice it. Now. In a Cambridge house where William James was busy pasting up a collage of what worked into a philosophy, E L Thorndike emerged from actual processes of manipulation in the cellar with his book Animal Intelligence to lay foundations for modern public school testing in terms got from nature at first hand in the intelligent behavior of chickens, terms irrefragable enough to be measured and compared as time and motion were currently being straitjacketed by F W Taylor in a Bethlehem steel plant, to be sorted and evaluated as readily as the nickel and dime items on Frank Woolworth's expanding counters, ingredients of the tangible world Mary Baker Eddy was profitably demonstrating could be classified and organized in unruffled confidence that it did not exist while, as profitably confident it did, the shoe machinery trust was showing such organization to be as vital to the prospects of the shoe machinery industry as shoe machinery itself. Disappointed with Niagara there, follows beautifully reads God damned well out loud too . . .

Foot tapped foot on Thomas Register as he dug for matches, —follows so God damned well though how can I leave out a whole page never miss it, skipped a whole God damned page never even missed it probably ought to take it right out speed up the Christ . . . his feet came down —start thinking that way be nothing left of it but the God damned title right back where I started . . . He came forward, picked up the roll of film —end up reduce the title to a God damned period give an intelligent reader the essence of the whole God damned thing . . . he stretched an arm's length of film up to the light —incredible, look at this German footage think they staged the whole God damned war for their combat photographers . . . and another arm's length of film came up, another, it rose in coils at his feet —Huertgen Forest must be Schramm's didn't know he, damn it just let the God damned thing ring try to get anything done here no . . . he was up, —might be . . .

Film trailed him through in a tangle caught on his foot mounting 24–12 Oz Btls Fragile! —hello . . . ? Mister Bast no he's . . . who? Leva? Not the B F Leva . . . ? he settled back. —Quite an honor Mister Lev . . . right number yes Mister Leva Mister Bast said you might . . . this morning's paper haven't seen it no, anything interesting . . . ? Erebus yes of course Mister Leva, all America knows your . . . Ad offering sixty dollars a share? Why no, thought I'd suggested eighty-five or ninety Mister Leva they must have . . . my idea yes just helping out here I . . . pardon? Why of course I do, all America knows the name B F Leva Mister Leva, whole world . . . joke no certainly not Mister Leva, whole thing's on the . . . Sorry you're taking it this way Mister Leva we thought you'd be delighted, all America knows your reputation for cheap . . . no no I meant cheap ideas Mister Leva, wouldn't think of implying . . . pardon? the tub . . . ? Oh you have a picturephone too . . . ? No, no you just happened to catch me on location here Mister Leva, making a little film ourselves story about an Estonian refugee family, father's a blind diamond cutter daughter's just lost her . . . oh you did? Yes, yes I see your fat face up there now always wondered Mister Leva, are you German? Hungarian . . . ? No no didn't mean that no just the general level of vulgar stupidity you . . . Don't know why you'd say that Mister Leva really thought we were helping you out, got a lot of confidence in your . . . Sixty dollars a share yes look Mister Leva afraid you're putting the wrong interpretation on the whole . . . confidence yes real God damned vote of confidence Mister Leva, company's looking for a good solid dependable long-term tax loss proposition really confident you'll always find the sleaziest best seller pay the highest price for it and keep on turning out big budget money losing flops consistent tasteless stupidity God damned valuable asset B F all very complimentary, don't find too many real professionals like you around any . . . pardon? Didn't think you'd take it this way B F, after all it isn't if you win or lose it's how you played the game isn't it, thought you'd . . . What I mean yes B F yes we're playing dirty, don't mind if I call you B F? Always thought of you that way connotation in England you probably . . . no bloody fucker, thought you'd . . . pardon? Oh, it's Grynszpan yes, g r y . . . that nobody ever talked to you like this? Well now you . . . come out there to work for you? God damned kind of you B F but . . . working on something here I have to finish up yes . . . yes any time

B F any time . . . He came down kicking free of the coils of film —day's really getting off to a good, what was that somebody out there? Who's out there . . . he got the door on the sound of footsteps down the dark stairs, the mail still settling at his feet —God damned coward come back here . . . !

The door banged below and he stooped to sweep it in with the rest —rain nor heat nor gloom of night can't stop them get a God damned bear trap . . . he scooped it up, —sort it out while there's still room here to move . . . and he came leaving a trail to the sofa where he let it go over the armless end —whole pile already here where the hell did all this come from. Ace Hand Laundry, two twenty West Eighty what the hell they're delivering this here for, Miss Olga Krupskaya four thirteen West start a pile here for the West Side. G Berst this address who the hell, Grynszpan pile for Grynszpan, Thomas Eigen Author of God still girls around who dot their i's with circles, send him her picture naked he'd be there return mail. Bodega de West Side pile, Grynszpan Connecticut State Highway Department sounds good, Edwerd Bast Esquire from Beaton, Broos and Black sounds like the God damned Spanish Main, telephone company, Grynszpan Britannica still after him, Bast return envelope Henry Street Settlement, somebody so God damned cheap they cross that out address it to him in pencil, phone company, E Gerst new pile . . .

The long hand drove the short higher, dropped toward NO RETURN. —Señora West Side pile, Thomas Eigen Family Court better call him, there. Now. Try to get anything done here where was I, millions yes. And while those millions so God damned many piles no place left to sit down, millions, those one eyed, that one eyed wait God damn it had it last night when that God damned lamp went one eyed no, that, that, well God damn it! He whispered into hands pressed against his face —why the hell I'm trying to do it this way anyhow should have gone right into those God damned notes, get going on it Christ have to get going on it find those God damned notes . . . He got a foot on 24/One Pound H-O —Tootsie Roll, remember the box it said Tootsie Roll Twelve Count . . . he pulled himself up to Won't Burn Smoke or Smell —hell's all this . . .

Letters, string, shoe polishing cloth, glue, a Liberty head quarter —Christ might be worth something . . . cigarette lighters, view of the Ghiralda, snapshots —think she was ever that small . . . undeveloped film rolls, clippings, typed pages held together with a rusty clip —How Rose Is Read, God forgot I ever started this published it five years ago it would have been . . . he stretched back up there head resting against NO DEPOSIT. —Rose, young but no girl, beautiful out of context and aware of that, stayed out entirely or until her late presence merely confirmed one she'd established of her own where she'd sit quietly and watch as though she'd never been elsewhere, and though it must have been one young man's persistence after another that drew her to say she always understood people's motives but sometimes not their words, she'd go on appearing to take each at his own evaluation and let that build without her interference out of all proportion till when she sidestepped, and it fell, it came from such a height there were a good many pieces and time, too much of it, to pick them up in and examine for their delicate contrivance. And there were pieces everywhere. Mention her name and you'd see them, or their sharp edges, surface briefly in the young men's eyes dropped quickly elsewhere once they'd learned how many times she'd read Go lovely Rose, in how many different hands, forcing her door with flowers, fleeing it home to books to flee her there. Elena in Turgenev's On the Eve flung down at two am as elsewhere pages feverishly turned to find her serving tea to friends by one gone back to bed to toss alone till dawn came in another part of town where someone else gave up importuning her shade through Gluck's underworld with a twist of the dial to study in his own unsteady hand of the night before beware women who blow on knots and then take all of an hour to find perhaps it was right to dissemble your love, but why did you kick me downstairs? No book heroine as they wanted, this crowd who would not understand how much more human she was, like old Auda after battle and murder, heart yearning God damn it just get through one sentence in this, just one simple God damned sentence . . .

He was down brushing himself —filthiest place in the, hello . . . ? No, who's . . . called last night from Ohio yes said you might call about a tape he . . . no Ohio Akron Ohio, something about a tape you . . . No I don't no look Mister Crawley I don't know what anybody's doing in Ohio, said something about a funeral guess they all just go there to . . . Didn't mention any margin money no he just said there was a tape he wants to be sure you . . . just helping out up here yes got some work I have to get right back to, now . . . Who this Leva? called this morning yes sounded damned excited about the whole thing, got on a first name basis reassured him about the company's confidence in his . . . Piscator said what . . . ? No wait my idea but not my decision look . . . no what president, president of oh you mean the company Bast's company hasn't been in no just . . . hasn't called no, just . . . bring what lenders down on him look Crawley I don't know the company's cash position don't even know the . . . didn't know the stock opened off two points this morning no, look I . . . wait listen, I . . . Listen I don't know where the hell he is no, don't know a God damned thing about these statements he's calling in to the press gas exploration pollution suit mining claims voting trust margin money or anything else no, I told you I'm working on something important up here and . . . Look if he calls I'll tell him to call you tell him you're being pressed hard by these commodity exchanges for margin on . . . should have seen it coming laid out your supply and demand curves bigger the gaps get just watch the whole God damned cobweb develop pick a point anyplace on it you know where the . . . watch your corn sales, price of hogs a hundred pounds goes over eleven times corn a bushel they'll feed the corn to the hogs, goes under eleven hell with the hogs sell the corn should have kept an eye on the . . . Can't no look I told you working on something here that's . . . no just this tape Mister Bast wanted to be sure you . . . oh you did? Fine I'll tell him you got it goodbye, I . . . what? No just give me the message sure I can remem . . . captures those soaring tones that evoke the vastness of the plains, the purple mountains' majesty certainly won't forget no, good . . . sonorous tones of horn and kettledrum evoking the majesty of another kingdom won't forget that in a hurry no, good . . . what? Tell him you've had disappointing news on the film but you're a man of your word sending him his fee anyhow sure he'll be God damned glad to hear that yes, good . . . Thanks yes very flattering Mister Crawley just not looking for a job right now really not my field anyhow, good . . . no just, put it this way just happen to be friendly to bellies in the long term, now goodbye . . .

He was back at the sofa spearing a sharp pencil into an open jar —choice of fancy snails or a rotting classic of Imperial Old Christ where was I when that idiot . . . he got the folder, came down on Hoppin' With Flavor! —clear line of thought going bastard comes in with his sonorous tones of horn and millions here, through a glass eye, darkly the one eyed, had that God damn it had it last wait the good eye yes, the good eye . . . he licked the pencil's point, —the good eye could now peer into Aristotle's kingdom where if every instrument could accomplish its own work, obeying or anticipating the will of others, like the statues of Daedalus, or the tripods of Hephaestus, which, says the poet God damned cheese and tomato right down the which, says the poet, of their own accord have to type the whole God damned thing over anyhow . . . he reached for the punctured can —Jesus . . . ! purple dripped from his chin —Christ what did I think I, go anywhere like this . . . he was up brushing at his trouserfront, each stroke slower until he was simply standing there staring through the blind below —poor bastards got all five of them fixing a tire so they can push their God damned clubhouse across the street almost envy them, all that senseless God damned energy look at them . . . He came down more slowly on Hoppin' With Flavor! —problem just no God damned energy . . . and where his gaze fell short to the sill, a clothespin dropped. The long hand peaked to lap the short between NO DEPOSIT and NO RETURN —half the God damned day gone . . . and his head came slowly back to rest against 24–7 Oz Pkgs Flavored Loops, where the sun more slowly left it.

——What have you done for your mouth lately?

—Wha . . . he sat up abruptly, brought a hand up.

——continental mouthwash with the distinc . . .

—Get that God damned thing . . . and he was up, crested the plateau of Musical Couriers and seized the mop handle, put his ear to the crevice and pounded the mop handle up and down.

———really time to do something nice for your mouth . . .

—Do something nice for your mouth God damn you, you . . .

———like sending your mouth on a vacation . . .

—Send your mouth on a vacation you son of a bitch there!

——**actually helps shrink painful hemorrhoidal** . . .

—Bastard!

——**prompt temporary relief by reducing painful swelling** . . .

—Oh you bastard you bastard! he plunged the mop handle, pounded it up and down.

———what America is today, so look for volume one of this exciting new children's encyclopedia at your neighborhood supermar . . .

—God damn you Christ! how do people . . . he was on all fours up there back against the ceiling —have one thought one God damned thought one God damned civilized thought in this whole God damned get that God damned thing once for all God damn it . . .! he flung the mop handle pulled aside 1899's bound Musical Couriers, Trade Extra 1902, 1911, 1909 —no place to put the God damned things . . . 1903, 1908 —must weigh twenty pounds . . .

———product. A service. A promise of human bet . . .

—Little bastard you . . . he heaved at the volumes, dragged up 24–10 Pad Pkgs, 2 Dozen 57 The World's Largest Selling Ketchup, Tonic Water Twist Cap —hell that ironing board get down there . . . he yanked at 48 No 1 Cans Beef Gravy and books slithered across the heap —can't do it God damn it no place to put them . . .

———join the biggest savings bank fam . . .

—God damned ironing board . . . he pulled, yanked, finally ripped at the next one sending papers streaming down —good, Christ . . . and he followed, holding together the torn sides of Tootsie Roll 12 Count, moving more slowly with each sheet after pasted sheet of paper he picked up —God hundreds of them . . . finally coming to rest on H-O with the torn carton drawn close —started with eighteen seventy-six have to get them all back in, Christ how did I, look at that what did I think I was doing!

The long hand pressed the short ahead till only the sweep of the second hand crossed the arc up behind him, hunched there on H-O turning up page after page —ANI, LEM abbreviated all these God damned references can't remember what they, go through every book in the place again Christ, how I worked on this . . .

1920

cv. PPC 32, 34, 83, 87ff, 137e9, 143e4

1920

1920

the Sackbut London vln2 The Pianola as a Means of Personal
                          Expression / Alvin Langdon Coburn
He holds that it is an instrument for the artist, 2hrs practice a
day for a year to master it. Its deadliets enemy the mediowre pianist
Diff frm gramophone whose records are invariable perfs (pianola's
fingers drop 1/2") "the arts must accept the new conditions and make
the most of them"

23rd US depression 8mce 1790 (6/1/23)   0 Little Town of B'hem
HFord's antiSemitic campaign wcr65ff/KS   That old Irish Mother of Mine
Mah-jongg pop (depression)   Holst's The Planets
RUR (Eng trans 1923)   Caruso last appirnce Elgar 'Enigma Variations'

1920 Lasky had got to Hollywood to combat hostility of dramatic critics
£ littérateurs toward movies Maeterlinck Maugham Grtrude Atherton EGlyn
arrived there in 1920 'It did not take the authors long to discover
their presence in Hwood was only windowdressing' they left angry sorry
"Maeterlinck's first scenario was 'a charming little tale about a small
boy who discovered some fairies. I'm afraid (wrote Mr Samuel Goldwyn)
my reactions to it were hardly fairy-like.'" (R 1921? v VMC)
EGlyn of Valentino: Do you know he had never even though t of kissing
the palm, rather than the back, of a woman's hand until I made him do it!

downgrading music ed. standards (democratising) LEM58 - musician as menace,
                                                         one-sided ec. LEM63
1,060,858 children between 10-15 in US gainfully   high ideals 735
    employed :mfrng & mech industries 185,337; textiles 54,649
        8. Gigli debut in Boito's Mefistofele   College Boards too tough,
KDKA Pittsburgh first regular radio broadcasting srvice dropped - LEM163
                                                    #1 Masters degrees "167
Dame Nellie Melba sang over radio at Chelmsford Eng. hrd in Persia '167
    5000 radios in US   art for art's sake obsolete - 192
NY Wall st bomb exp WA141 committed OY59   #9 music teachers 130,265 "198
Sacco-Vanzetti accused in murder WA141 also 1921, 27
Ponzi - 144AF arrest 149 edemonstrations ebroad OY60 Sec. of Fine Arts LEM60
Gaston B. Means joins Justice Dept. AF181   1920s - 1950 perfectionism
employees militantly antiunion, see Cabot & Boston   passe - 61
                             promoted Symph.   " music ed 186
         'American Plan' (est open shop,   " music conditioning
total 3411 strikes   destroy unionism   cf. Pavlov 203

NYrs day A Mitchell Palmer arrests cmmnsts FLA40 & union tieins
    Reed as a cmmnst leadr was indicted in absehtia, in Russia in
    fact where though he tried to get home died age 33 typhus lay in
    state fr a week in Moscow's trade union center   hurt musicians
top b.s. The Man of the Forest Zane Grey (the Star of Paradise Mann   (amendment
                                          (the age of innocence street)
P voted for first time in 1920 election- helped put across prohibition
Al Capone signs up with Torrio in Chicago (MM I)   as foundation for
                                                     organized crime
AT&T patent agreements US PS 73 dial phone introduced   OY174-79 e183
Eastman film monopoly US PS275   O'N's Emperor Jones
5KW essay on Fed Seddion Law (p67)   Man o' War 2min 14 1/5 sec
Ford 1 a minute KS42 Ford income KS284   1 3/8 mi stretch - Belmont
Divorce rate 13.4 per hundred marriages OY81   Chicago White Sox
Mayakorsky- anotha poem to himself Bd 137   indictment
      prize fighting legalized in NY (Walker)(in senate) Chicago theatre strike

He turned the pages more slowly, finally hunched toward the sill for the failing light —must have thought I could, like Diderot good God how I ever thought I could do it . . .

On the sill where the clothespin lay, a string had appeared lowered from above bobbing a wad of gum. He stared at it, picked up another page and stared at that —done it then Christ gone ahead and done it then, written it ten years ago with no pressure on me but now . . . ?

He was watching the gum wad bounce off the clothespin when the phone rang —God suppose she . . . He got up slowly, in past 200 2-Ply, hesitated before he reached up —yes hello . . . ? He cleared his throat —not here no, oh it's you Mister Bris . . . not disturbing me no that's all right, Mister Bast's still off on some sort of business . . . oh you are? Didn't realize you and he were business associates Mister Brisboy thought it was more ah . . . no no didn't mean you didn't regard him as a dear friend, I . . . just wouldn't get this upset Mister Brisboy I'm sure he wouldn't let that happen, now . . . No I'm sure he wouldn't mind if you talked to the president of the company, best thing to . . . here? Sorry I can't no, I . . . wait no you don't under . . . Look Mister Brisboy I'd be glad to switch you over if I could but . . . because I don't know where the hell he is no look I'm just not that familiar with the company's activit . . . Haven't seen his statement in the paper about franchising out the entire health plan but you can't believe everything you read in the . . . Rumors of what . . . ? No I heard the stock was sagging a little but . . . well I'm sure it really is a fun company Mister Brisboy what I've seen so far it certainly . . . to tell your mother what . . . ? Good God wouldn't want that to happen no, look I'd just . . . listen I'd just wait till Mister Bast gets back and . . . I'm sure he will yes no reason some story about these Indians having a clouded title to this reservation means he'd be . . . I'm sure he'll bring his Indian costume back yes never mentioned playing dress up but of course Mister Bast seems to have a number of talents I nev . . . he certainly is yes, now . . . No no I wouldn't do that no, no don't bother to come up here to wait for him no telling when he . . . No no very kind of you but I . . . yes good, auf Wiedersehen that is yes . . .

The gum wad bounded off the clothespin, drew up, dropped and missed in the near dark, drew up again as he came back to stand at the sill knuckles gone white one hand grinding the other, the gum wad bounded, drew up —like Robert the Bruce, Christ! he pried up the window and his fist shot out, pounded the gum on the clothespin snapped up from sight past the blind and he banged down the window —got to get out of here . . . tripped against Tootsie Rolls 12 Count, suddenly had it papers jammed in held together and up behind Won't Burn, Smoke or Smell and he was through to the door left tipped on its hinge against a shuffle in the dark hall, a tap.

—Hello, Mister . . . ? and then no sound but the falling waters until the door shuddered in again with his weight in the darkness threading

past 200 2-Ply, coming down among the stacks of mail on the armless sofa
where a hand hung off extended open toward the sill as though to seize
the day, or hold it off, when it appeared.

There, a pink hair curler dropped, rolled toward the edge and
stopped. He came up on one elbow and waited, finally came up all
together and drew a hand over the roughage of his chin. The long hand
rose from NO DEPOSIT driving the short before it —Christ got to get
started got to, to get started . . . he bumped against Won't Burn, Smoke
or Smell, picked up both cups floating teabags on Thomas Register
—brought that in last night somewhere just have one to get started
. . . and he was back to set a cup of water on Moody's, tip a bottle over
the other. On the sill where the curler lay, string appeared lowered from
above bobbing a wad of gum. He stared at it, drank off one cup and then
the other, picked up the blue folder and stared at that, patted pockets,
rummaged —out and get cigarettes get something to eat come back and
get started . . . and he was through to the door left tipped on its hinge
against a tap, a pounding, an expletive, finally the thud of bundles against
it.

—Man like what's all this I mean you can't get in the door.

—Like climb over it man and I mean help him, like get his foot wait,
like help me get the box through . . . and the shuffle of moccasins, the
flap of sandals repeated passing tub and 200 2-Ply —like you bring him
up here this morning to practice I mean he doesn't even bring his inster-
ment . . .

—Like he'll hum along then man . . . the mailbag shook over the
sofa's end, the guitar came up.

—Man like he's still so spaced out he can't hum shit . . . she swept
the mail from the sofa to join the heap on the floor, dropped a battered
paper shopping bag there and opened the box beside it —come on kitty
kitty, man like they really shaved his ass I mean where they sewed him
up it looks like this fucking football come on kitty kitty kitty . . .

Plunk. —Like come on man, hum . . . plunka plunka . . .

—Man look out for your, oh wow did you see him go up those boxes?
Move his, I mean that telephone it's like this burgular alarm move
his feet man, like I just come in the door and I mean move him!
Hello . . . ? He's not here man, who . . . Like what do I sound like his cat?
I mean if you want to leave Mister Bast this message I mean leave it, like
I mean who is this . . . Man like don't give me this family history I mean
you're just some bank, right? So like what do you mean you want more
collateral spell it man . . . So? His stock drops to twelve and an eighth like
that's no skin off your ass, what . . . Like what do you mean the bank's
ass I mean why should he bail you out man, like I mean if you need
money so you expect him to bring in like five thousand two hundred and
eighty dollars? I mean Bast . . . ? Man like wait I mean nobody gives
money to banks like I mean you get money from banks because like that's

where all the fucking money is . . . No man look I mean don't put me on with this eighty percents margin of some falling collateral, like you just said you're selling his stock if he doesn't bring you in this five thousand two hundred and eighty dollars man I mean when you open this ice tray you've got this real surprise coming . . . No look man I mean look, like you're this fucking bank, right? So I mean if you're so hard up for this fucking money go look in your fucking bank vault that's where . . . oh wow.

Plunk. —Man like hum . . . plunka plunka . . .

—Listen man I have to call about this job will you, I mean I don't believe it. Hello . . . ? He's not here what do you want . . . Look when some chick calls him I . . . so like what's the matter with this Mister Wiles can't he dial the . . . hello? Man like I just told your secretary Mister Bast isn't here what . . . who? What president man, I mean don't put me . . . what of his company? You mean here in this . . . man like how do I know his position on bellies I mean look Mister Wiles you and him must really be . . . Look man I don't know about some voting trust taking over like I mean if this commodity exchange has you against the wall and you expect to get this margin money here man? I mean look I just talked to this . . . no I mean just go to the bank like everybody else does man, like I mean they just tried to put me on the same way you are I mean like go look in their fucking bank vault man that's what banks . . . oh wow. I mean are these people rude, man.

—Man like hum . . . plunka plunka —hum, man . . .

—Like where's that telephone number I have to call man . . . she braced a foot coming down —like I knew I got these pants too tight . . . she reached the sagging denims down from the dishcloth rack, sank to 24-12 Oz Btls Fragile! to tug at a clasp —I mean look at that, like I hardly get them and it rips right out I mean they make everything now like they don't give a . . . she freed a foot from plaid, —man like I don't believe this fucking telephone . . . and she was up on a bared knee —hello . . . ? Look man who are you calling . . . no like this is his number but he's not here, what . . . who? What company spokesman look man if . . . no look I mean you said you're this newspaper what are you asking me for, go look in . . . So they're setting off these four twenty kilotons to release this natural gas I mean what am I supposed to . . . Man I mean you're the one who just said they rushed this AEC approval through to beat these envirementalists' injunction I mean what are you ask . . . No man I mean look, I mean you don't give news to newspapers you get news out of newspapers like I mean that's what newspapers are man, like I mean if you're this newspaper and you want to know if some under- ground explosion is dangerous I mean go read your fucking news- pap . . .

—What in, what Tom? are you . . .

—Man like are you kidding? I mean like what's the difference if the whole fucking state blows up who would even miss it . . .

—What the hell is this . . . he brought a newspaper bundle to the floor with him getting through, faced the expanse bared of plaid where she'd turned reaching up with the telephone. —God damn it what's all this doing here.

—Man like it was there when we came in, I mean . . .

He got two cartons up balancing a shoebox, —never occurred to you to, wait what do you mean we.

Plunk.

—Like just Al and his group man they came up to rehearse . . .

Plunka plunka plunka plunka

—Mmmmmmmmmmm . . .

—Good Christ no . . . he came bumping the cartons past tub and 200 2-Ply —what the hell is . . .

—Man I just told you like when the rest of the group comes . . .

—Mmm mmm mmm mmm . . .

Plunkaplunkaplunkaplunka . . .

—Jesus Christ listen this can't, well God damn it! he was down picking up a red mitten, paperclips, marionette in a tangle of strings —when the rest of who comes look God damn it . . .

—There's only like two more of them man, they . . .

He got the broken music box, car without wheels, a three legged sheep —look Al I'm working up here . . . a purple crayon, the Virgin one arm spread in mild surprise at the loss of the other, an arm cocking a bugle —now God damn it can you understand that Al?

Plunk. —Man like go ahead I mean I'm for everybody doing what they want to do man . . . plunka plunka —I mean that's how it ought to be everybody doing their own . . .

—Tell you something Al, if I did what I want to do right now you'd go out of here in a God damned sack. Now get this one up off the . . .

—Man look I mean he's having this identity crisis man don't hassle him . . .

—Great, all for him doing what he wants to too just tell him to go have it someplace wait, here God damn it give me that . . .

—Man like let him keep it what is it, I mean . . .

—It's a Wide Man what the hell does it look damn it let go of it! he twisted a turbaned figure clutching a casket from the desperate grasp —bring them up Christmas Eve I'll tell them the story of Baby Jeeter and the Three Wide Men right now just get them both the hell out of here . . . he followed her hitching gait as far as the tub where she stopped to finally free the other leg, followed the flap of sandals to the door where he dragged in a bundle of newspapers.

—Man like how did we know you'll still be here this morning . . . She balled the denim under an arm, shook the plaid legs out their full length —I mean like Bast he didn't come back yet?

The newspaper bundle cleared QUICK QUAKER to slide off and settle among lampshades and he turned to drag in a carton, —last I heard he was in Ohio . . .

—Oh wow. I mean like where's that. She held up the plaids —like I got him these bigger pants but I mean you really need them man. I mean like what happened.

He heaved the carton up past Stack Top Side Up , dragged two more in past the sink —what do you mean what happened.

—I mean you ought to see yourself man, like I mean once they gave Al this kidney test where he pissed purple right down the front of your pants and this black all over your face I mean you look like you didn't even shave since I saw you . . .

—Wash and shave as soon as I get these God damned boxes in been moving boxes around this God damned place since I . . .

—Man look out you busted the, don't throw it!

—Where in, what the hell . . .

—What does it look like I mean it's about a million book matches, I mean I just told you it's busted don't try and throw it didn't I? Now look what you did you got them dumped all over the . . .

—All right! look just get the corner there and push it in will you? Who the hell's sending a case of matchbooks . . .

—Man like who the hell's sending anything and I mean what are you pushing all these boxes in there around for anyway, you found your Tootsie Rolls?

—What my, no my notes no looking for a typewriter have to type this whole God damned thing over again cheese and tomato all over it where you and Bast . . .

—Me and Bast what man I mean like Schramm's typewriter it's right in by those brown books, I mean all this work you said you came here to do and you . . .

—Yes well God damn it look! get anything done here, get through one simple sentence without somebody banging on the door troop of idiots comes in to rehearse phone ringing . . .

—Man like so let it ring . . . she was unwadding a tattered scrap of newspaper —I mean like why answer it then.

—Because I've been waiting for a call . . . he scaled a bundle over Appletons' —waiting for an important call, now what . . .

—Look man I mean I just need to make like this one call okay?

She turned away to reach up and dial, drew his eyes up —whole God damned reason I'm trying to get this work done . . .

—Hello? Like did you have this ad in the paper about . . . hello? I mean look my friend showed me this ad in the paper where you want this girl to . . . No but like for how much, I mean . . . no but I mean like what do you want me to do screw a horse in . . . what like right now? I mean I can come now if . . . ask for Mister what? Like c h . . . i? c i . . . ? No man I mean I know where the hotel is I'm coming right down

. . . She sank to 24–12 Oz Btls Fragile! to tie a moccasin —man like these pants I just brought you, I mean like can you give me five dollars?

—Five what do you, you didn't bring them to me I didn't ask you for them look I've got a suit to pick up at Tripler's why the hell would I want . . .

—Man like walk into Triplets like that I mean they'd call the police, I mean look man these cost eleven ninety-seven look at the tag and I mean I need cab fare they said come right down for this inter . . .

—Christ here take the five dollars . . . he straightened up from the last bundle of newspapers —well now wait what, you just sold them to me what the hell are you putting them back on for.

—Man like I'm borrowing them I just said I have to go to this interview, it's like some publicity thing I mean how do I know what they want me to do . . . her leg gaped fighting a foot back into the plaid from 24–12 Oz Btls Fragile! —screw a horse in Macy's window?

—God damndest customer loyalty to Macy's . . . he heaved the last bundle toward Appletons', lifted the door closed —how they ever earned it from such a discriminating . . .

—Man like once I bought this rug there you know . . .? She got the other foot in, got up pulling them high —and I mean when it came the color really stank so like I returned it and then they keep sending me these fucking bills for it, like I mean I write to them and I go in there and I mean they won't stop man . . . she was down rolling a cuff up inside —so like it's a year later I'm trying to get this real job someplace working I mean I even buy these clothes and everything for it, so when I come in they say they're informed I have this lousy credit reference for this fucking rug I never paid for and like I don't get the job I mean that was the last time man, I mean the last time . . . she fought the clasp —I mean this way I save them all this grief of some spaced out old bag writes these sales slips and sending you these bills and lawyer letters it's like simpler for everybody I mean what's wrong with that . . .

—Can't argue with you no . . . he pulled off his shirt, —Grynszpan has a similar arrangement here with the Edison Company . . . he leaned close over the torrent at the sink looking into the cookie tin top —Christ . . .

—Oh wow, man I mean turn around a little . . . she paused closer pulling on the raincoat, —like I mean that must have been some screwing man . . .

—What are, what do you think you . . .

—Man like what do you think I think, you were out picking blackberries? Like all these old fingernail scars right down your back man I mean she was really hanging in, like who was it that black haired chick?

He shuddered at her blunt finger run down from his shoulder, turned abruptly backed against the sink there —but what do you, how did you . . .

—Man like what's wrong I mean I just asked was it that black haired chick you were balling that time . . . she got the door, —I mean I bet she really stayed screwed . . .

He turned back slowly to the sink gripping its edge —Christ, what . . . reached suddenly up to seize his shoulder and try to bring it under his twisted gaze, then as abruptly thrust his head under the torrent, banged it on the tap coming up —God damn it . . . wiping his face, trampling film cans, reaching up a wet hand —hello . . . ? No he's . . . said he was having calls transferred to this number yes but he's not here, who . . . who? Can't accept a collect call from Mrs Eigen no, I . . . look operator I'll tell Mister Eigen she's trying to reach him but . . . said I can't no! goodbye . . .

The gum wad bounded off the sill, rose, dropped again. He tipped the bottle over the empty cup —all I need right now little encouragement from Marian . . . he came down on H-O with the blue folder, set the cup aside emptied again —just need to loosen up a little, run through the rest of this before I type it where the, one eyed, good eye yes the good eye could now peer into Aris tripods here, tripods of Hephaestus which, says the poet, of their own accord entered the assembly of the gods, if, in like manner, the shuttle would weave and the plectrum touch the lyre without a hand to guide them, chief workmen would not want servants, nor masters slaves. For though the tale how for art's sake Wilde had faced Leadville's bullies to a standoff continued to amuse long after he'd withdrawn to join the compost smoldering in Europe with Pater's recipe for, fueled by Pater's no. The tale no. For though, and though the, for now the tale . . .

Long hand drove short toward the summit, descended into NO RE-TURN. Gum wad bounded, withdrew, dropped again —still smoldering in, no the compost ignited by, lit no, hell's that God damned dictionary . . . He tipped the bottle over the cup, edged closer to the sill as he raised it, put it down empty on Moody's watching the gum wad bound, rise again, gradually reached to raise the window, chin on the sill blowing gently. The curler wavered. The gum wad hesitated, dropped rose and bounded off. The curler wavered to the edge, rolled back, the gum wad rose. The long hand climbed from NO DEPOSIT. At the sill's edge the curler trembled and was gone, the gum wad swung aimless and slowly rose from sight.

—Get anything done here God damn it . . . he grabbed up the shirt coming through —catch pneumonia this way, hello . . . ? No now wait who do you . . . no company spokesman here right now no, goodb . . . never heard of Teletravel no, now . . . Frigi what? Look . . . no listen . . . look I don't know a God damned thing about filing an environmental impact statement on the . . . effect on marine life of disposing of what sound shards at sea look I don't know what you're talking ab . . . Yes well look if that's what their head of R and D testified before the Armed

Services Committee what else do you want, if I was a tuna fish I'd . . . because I'm not a God damned tuna fish! now . . . President of who you mean the president of the company? here? are you out of your . . . Well look if he called you and . . . look if he gave you all that in a phone statement what are you calling . . . Look I'd like to be in Honduras myself, now . . . because I don't know God damn it, good . . . no comment yes goodbye . . . !

He ducked to Hoppin' With Flavor! to tip the bottle over the cup —just stop answering the God damned thing call Tom work out some kind of Christ, try to call him there they'll tell me to call him here . . . he set the cup down emptied —now. For though, for now the tale how God damned tomato and cheese right down the, wonder how old that pizza is . . . he got a cheese clot off Wilde with a thumbnail, bit, blew it out —should have brought something in damn it, shoot the pianist just get to the end of this God damned sentence shoot the pianist. For thow, damn it God damn it! His hands went white against his face, drawn down for fingertips to press his eyes, dig at them, fall away to leave them staring —find the God damned typewriter should have done this in the first place . . . he dragged the case from behind Thomas Register of Manufacturers, squared it on top and snapped it open —retype the whole thing right from, be God damned . . . he caught the stained manila folder sliding off the keyboard —wondered what the hell happened to this . . . he opened it and turned a page, sank down on H-O with it and turned another, found a cigarette and brought the enchilada can closer tapping ashes, settling back against Won't Burn, Smoke or Smell tapping ashes, leaning forward to tip the bottle, back to where the sun streaked down one margin crossing closer to the other with each turning page till it had left them altogether when the peal of the phone brought him up steadied against Hoppin' With Flavor! —coming God damn it . . . against 200 2-Ply as he passed it on the fourth ring.

—Yes hello . . . ? Not back yet no goodb . . : oh it is? Put him on yes thought I forgot his, hello? Thought I forgot your message didn't you, sonorous torns of hone and kettle . . . the who . . . ? No no nope boss company president whatever the hell he is not here either hasn't called no, not a . . . you what . . . ? Wouldn't say that Mister Crawley, he prob . . . no no wouldn't think he'd do a thing like that good Christ see a fine man like you go under just for a little margin money, company like this one he must hold enough stock to cover any . . . closed down four points? God damned shame, what's . . . They what . . . ? Who filed it Piscat . . . God damned shame atmosphere of mistrust these days isn't it, old Piscator files an affidavit accepting service of the summons these lenders go ahead and attach his stock anyhow tell you what it is Crawley whole God damned decline from status to contract what's wrong with the whole God damned modern . . . Sounds like to me see them attach his stock to guarantee his court appearance sounds like they're trying to grab

off his company what it sounds like, what's wrong with the whole God
damned country atmosphere of mistrust say incidentally Crawley, don't
happen to be planning a trip to Honduras . . . ? Honduras yes, just
happened to think you might bump into him down there, newspaper
called says there's a rumor wait, listen . . . no no listen . . . hear a funny
nose in this phone? noise . . . ? He held it up and shook it, started
unscrewing the mouthpiece —what? Why not sounds like a God damned
exciting place Honduras might be thinking of buying it, vastness of the
plains the purple hello . . . ? hear me . . . ? Can't hear me . . . he had the
cover off holding it closer, forcing a nail under a wire, twisting —God
damned bug in it . . . he pulled it out, —hello? screwing the cover back
on, —hello Crawley? Bastard hung up . . .

He tossed the thing ahead of him coming down, steadied against 200
2-Ply to crush it under a heel —whole God damned place probably
bugged . . . the bottle tipped horizontal and he held it up to what light
there was —Christ . . . he raised the cup —what, something move God
damn it saw something move up there looked like a . . . he reached to
Won't Burn, Smoke or Smell to pull himself up —well God damn it! and
he was down picking up cigarette lighters, view of the Ghiralda, glue,
—God, suppose she . . . and he steadied against H-O, came down on it
—what was I, typed yes get it typed Christ, get something typed . . . he
dragged Thomas Register closer, reached the bottle over, rummaged in
Won't Burn, Smoke or Smell beside him, —now . . . He hit R.

—— your loved ones, open a trust savings ac . . .

—Get under their God damned signal, here . . . he emptied the cup,
hunched closer, typing —God damned apostrophe hardly see in here
. . . the roller turned, turned again, each time more slowly till he was up
abruptly shaking the punctured lampshade, rattling open the battered
shopping bag from the sofa as the lamp lighted —knew they eat snails
Christ but, catfood . . . ? The lamp went off, came on —chicken parts
necks and backs, palmitate, d-activated plant sterol choline chloride pyri-
doxine better not no where the, where those cigarettes . . . the lamp went
off.

When it came on he was sitting on Hoppin' With Flavor! staring at
the vacant sill outside. He reached the bottle. The second hand sprang
from NO DEPOSIT, plunged to NO RETURN and suddenly he was up digging in Won't Burn, Smoke or Smell, had the glue squeezing it on the
Liberty head quarter as the lamp flickered off and on for him pressing
the quarter on the sill, banging the window up steadying an arm on
2-Ply Facial Tissue Yellow —couldn't, couldn't be God suppose she
. . . It rang again. He looked down his front, brushed at it, tripped against
H-O getting through to steady against the tub, let it ring again. —Hel,
hello . . . ? Christ that you Tom? did, she didn't call did she . . . ? no no
just, that's right just thought . . . no couldn't have missed her no been here
the whole God damned day been here got Schramm's typewriter, found

Schramm's typewriter been . . . what? Notes? find my notes told you I can't find my notes whole place is . . . Schramm's notes? in what typewriter . . . old manila folder got what spilled on it . . . ? Keep an eye out for it Tom I'll keep an eye out typewriter manuscript old manila spilled on God damn it . . . Nothing no foot just slipped on this God damned what . . . ? Drink two drinks yes had three drinks been up here all . . . well God damn it listen I . . . know I said that yes but God damn it look Tom she . . . listen say something like that listen Tom told you I haven't felt too God damned well I . . . no what . . . Didn't tell me that no, what . . . no which eye . . . No but look if it was your . . . heard of that happening listen Tom had a detached retina you'd really be . . . Wouldn't try that Christ no find a good eye man a good, eye man, not a good eye, the good eye could . . . the what? Called who, here? Oh called here yes she called this morning collect didn't even . . . visitation rights make the kid sound like John the Bap wait listen ever think of that game idea we . . . no just reminded me jumping for joy in the womb Mary visiting Elisa wait Christ listen what day is it . . . ! no no now today what . . . Not the God damned date the day the day! got a God damned name like Monday Tues . . . Christ.

———court begging for permission to see my own son? Jack . . . ?

The phone swung free. His foot slipped again, recovered 24–12 Oz Btls Fragile! and he stared down at his front, brushed at it, caught his balance and grabbed for the phone, clung to QUICK QUAKER and tried again, caught it and reached his free hand up to dial. —Hello? Yes listen I . . . know it yes but listen I . . . know it yes I know what day it is that's what I'm . . . Because I couldn't God damn it because I couldn't! will you lis . . . Don't no I don't want to tell her myself no I, look can you tell her next week tell her get the new boots for her next week can't you just . . . Look I know it's getting cold that's not what's God damn it couldn't you . . . Because I can't talk to her right now that's why! Look at me! I, can't you just once can't you, just once couldn't you, once just not have to win . . . ?

String came lowering a gum wad into the cast of light at the sill abruptly gone with his lurch against the punctured shade coming down on Hoppin' With Flavor! —Christ what I'm, Christ . . .

———merican family its full share of the world's health. Remember. It's green! Another fine product of Nobili Laboratories, a proud mem . . .

—Man like you didn't even bring in the mail . . . the door shuddered in on her wading through envelopes, kicking ahead the Journal of Business, Modern Packaging, Financial World —and like there's this big fucking box out there I can't even move it. Are you in here . . . ?

—In the library quick just been attacked by Cruden's Concordance . . .

—Man like what are you sitting in there in the dark and I mean what's with the telephone, it's just hanging here . . . she freed an arm, passing, to reach and hang it up.

—Got my call took it off the hook . . . the lamp flickered on, the gum wad took up again, bounded merrily off the quarter, drew up, —got my call won a free dance lesson . . .

—I mean look I'm expecting this very important call . . . she came in trailing mail, dumped the raincoat's pockets of cans, jars, a clothing wad as she pulled it off —like I mean this job they said they'll call me on this very short notice . . . she yanked at a zipper.

—Charming little frock never pictured you in a charming little frock . . . he stared up from the cup's emptiness, edged over to H-O in reach of the bottle —why you taking off charming little . . .

—Man like this place is so filthy I can't even sit down in it, I mean they gave me this twenty dollars for it to look nice for this job like can you hold it a minute?

—Sound like a God damned fastidious horse what's the . . .

—No I mean hold it up off the floor man . . . she shook herself into a shirt —like I'm supposed to be this secretary that's got these personal problems like am I pregnant or something I said how do I know . . . she got through over his feet to hang the dress on the dishcloth rack, —I mean for when this public figure grabs me in the window like you should see this place man, I mean they must all shit American flags up there it's so patriotic.

—God damned disappointment public figure thought you said a horse . . . the bottle tipped, wavered —like the flags though, Macy's draw a nice genteel crowd nothing vulgar . . .

—Man like what do you keep saying this horse I mean I just told you it's politics, I mean this Mister Cibo that hired me he's like right out of the Mafia . . . she paused mismatching button to buttonhole, —I mean I'm jumping out this window with these personal problems and this politician saves me to make him this big hero, like I say how his coura-geous act shows he cares for people and gives me this courage to face life's battles once more and they pay me this hundred bucks and I mean what's with this lamp . . . she shook it, got around tugging at 24–7 Oz Pkgs Flavored Loops —like there's this other lamp back here they sent him I mean have you got a quarter?

—Gave you five dollars this morn . . .

—Like I'm not selling it to you man . . . she dragged it out, set it up on Moody's —I mean it's made of this parking meter you need a quarter to make it go for an hour.

—Take twelve minutes here's a nickel, careful that bottle . . .

—No look man I mean a nickel's too fat to go in the slot what do you wow, like you drank this whole bottle just today?

—Grynszpan dropped in heavy drinker he, look! See it? damn . . .

—Man what's, see what . . .

—Football up there box in front of the clock wait till the light comes back on, old football climbing out of No Dep there! See it?

—Man like that's here kitty kitty I mean that's Chairman Meow man, here kitty . . .

—Hell's he doing here looks like a . . .

—Man like where was I supposed to take him and I mean where's that opener, like I had it in here for those enchilavies . . . and her sharp bend away looking under the sofa snapped the shirttail up where he swallowed abruptly on nothing, licked his lips and spilled the cup over the back of his hand getting it to them. —Here it is it's still on the can I mean what a disgusting mess, like I mean these cigarette butts and enchilavies man couldn't you even put garbage out in the hall like you're supposed to?

—Little old lady comes down cleans out the tunafish cans . . .

—Man like we don't even have tunafish and I mean the last time she tried that they almost put her in this little green panel truck and took her with it here kitty kitty . . .

—This keeps up put us all in a little green panel . . .

—No I mean this one that comes for the trash every night man like Bast says it's some service his company must have fixed up kitty kitty kitty . . . she tapped the opened can on the floor.

—Company his service fixed up just found a bug on the phone that's who . . .

—Man like that's what I'm telling you, I mean this place is so filthy I expect to wake up with bites come here kitty . . .

—Bite bug not a bedbug no a tap phone tap, on the floor in there just ripped it out of the phone I . . .

—What that you ripped it out? Man like why'd you do that I mean he'll just have to come back and fix it kitty kitty . . . ?

—He who, what . . .

—This spade cat that works for the phone company man, I mean like he installs these telephones and these taps he does on the side so I mean like when they don't hear anything they'll just tell him to come put on another one I mean are you hungry?

—Not that hungry . . . he moved a foot from the stealthy approach to the can opened on the floor, —ever see a football eating don't disturb . . .

—What do you have to say it with him standing right there man . . . she'd gone round on one knee on the sofa's edge thrusting among mail for a jar, a can, inching the shirttail up —I mean can't you look at somebody's face instead of their ass? And like didn't you find a quarter I mean this fucking lamp going on and off I can't hardly see what . . . she was down biting open a transparent packet —like do you want some?

—What, some what . . . he tipped the bottle over the cup, shook it.

—Some what man how do I know some what I mean it says cheese type processed food product do you . . .

—Wait! Christ . . .

—Like what's the matter that's grape drink I mean I just poured you grape drink what's . . .

—Last of the whisky poured it right in the last of the God damned whisky . . .

—So now you've got like grape whisky I mean you're so stoned you won't know the difference man what are these . . . she held it up, pried off the lid —raviolis you want some raviolis . . . ? The lamp flickered, beyond her the gum wad bounded and slowly rose from sight as she licked fingers, tore an envelope —Dear Mister Eigen, it is my pleasure to inform you that the Admissions Committee of the PEN voted at its last meeting to ask you to become a . . .

—Wait what's . . . he coughed into the cup —what are you . . .

—What man I mean I'm reading the mail, like I mean when Bast and I eat that's what we do man . . . she paused parting the shirttail on a flank to scratch there, —I mean like what else is there to do.

—No look problem's just problem Mister Eigen God damned touchy sometimes might want to open his mail himself look . . .

—Man like what's the difference I mean it's all mail . . . paper tore, she licked fingers and set the jar down. —This is a periodic report which the trustee under the indenture mentioned below is required to make by reason of all this bullshit Bast gets I mean who wants to read all this Kissinger Tax Letter, U S Bureau of Mines Taxwise Methods for the Executive, Bureau of Indian Affairs U S Department of bullshit . . . she was digging in the heap beside her —I mean I thought I had this herrings someplace . . .

—Try Grynszpan had it all sorted out, what the hell happened just sorted it out . . .

—Like can you open this can? I mean they don't even give you this key thing anymore here's one, dear Mister Grynszpan. Since we believe you are a deeply concerned citizen whose opinions on the vital issues of the day are formed after careful and intelligent consideration, and since the continued survival of our republic as we know it depends so heavily upon the free expression of such independent views as yours at the highest levels, a letter is enclosed for your convenience which you may rewrite in your own words and mail to your Senator and Congressman immediately dear sir, as a concerned citizen I wish my voice to be heard expressing strong support for HR three five nine seven and the companion Senate resolution sponsored by Senator Broos firmly backing nonintervention in the civil conflict in Gandia, and the earliest possible recognition for Uaso province as a sovereign and independent look out! man you're spilling . . .

—God damned cat what . . .

—What I mean he just jumped on the windowsill man like why shouldn't he look out the, what's he, what's that, I mean look there's something out there dancing up and down on this string man look . . .

He righted his cup, recovered his seating on H-O —went back up and reloaded looks like double bubble . . .

—Man look there's this quarter out there . . . ! the shirttail tugged up with her turn to shake the sash, raise it, a paw shot out past her at the glistening pink wad —man like hold him! She bent further —it's stuck here, I mean it's stuck here man I can't get it off . . . the gum wad danced above, plunged, the paw shot out —man will you get this fucking cat off my in my hair what's, oww . . . ! the string tautened, yanked again, she was in, banged the window down —man who's with that fucking gum up there and I mean if that's that my vife Mrs at the door I'm really going to hand him his . . . she was through past 200 2-Ply, —like who is it!

—Good evening madam . . . it shuddered open, —I trust I am not interrupting the dinner repast, am I addressing the lady of the house?

—Look man what do I look like the . . .

—I see immediately that I am speaking with someone who has enjoyed the benefits of a fine education, surely madam you would not wish to deprive your youngsters of similar advan . . .

—What youngsters man look . . .

—Madame unless my eyes deceive me . . . he raised them, —if your husband has indeed let you go childless he should be prosecuted for criminal negligence ha ha, of course I am sure he is a person of breeding and culture like yourself one glimpse of your lovely home and these are clearly the surroundings the publishers of our fine new children's encyclopedia would like to see it displayed in to be seen and admired by your many friends and neighbors of similar cultural . . .

—Look I mean get your foot out of the . . .

—Ex, excuse me madam if you interrupt me I'll have to start all over again of similar cultural pursuits, this is why we take pleasure in inviting you to accept a complete set of our fine new children's encyclopedia at the special introductory prepublication price and in order to help you make this rewarding decision this advance copy of volume four has been reserved in your name for your perusal over a ten day period during which you may examine it here in the comfort of your own lovely home at absolutely no obligation, hold this fine volume in your own hands sir or madam as the case may be show it to family and friends, study its physical format if you'll let the door it's hurting my foot note the fine grain binding a new substance designed to outlast ordinary leather and outshine its beauty for untold years to come, each volume in the set is richly gold tooled and the perfectionist binding gives them the elegance of fine volumes costing far more than our special introductory price take this fine volume into your own hands sir or mad . . .

—Man come help me here!

—Note the fine binding and paper stock, the quality printing, the intensity of the many color illustrations in addition to these each volume contains detailed charts, diagrams and graphs to enhance your exciting journeys through these pages of the world's history, culture, civilization, government, history, art and literature and and, and science yes for though written and designed to inspire and reward the child's thirst for knowledge this is in fact no mere children's encyclopedia but the ideal reference work for the casual browser, the armchair traveler, the dedicated scholar alike, the crowning result of many untold thousands of hours of painstaking research by world renowned schol, is, is this the, the gentleman of the house . . . ?

—It's the fucking armchair traveler what does it look like now get your foot out of . . .

—Madam madam I see I am speaking to a lady of liberated opinion as a special inducement our publishers have also set aside in your name a charter subscription to a new publication designed especially for you the exciting new magazine She at absolutely no obligation be the first of your friends and neighbors to thrill to . . .

—Got his God damned foot caught under the . . .

—Thank you if you will just give me your name and sign here sir or mad . . .

—Like get it down by the hinge and push, man . . .

—Thank you perhaps your neighbors will be more receptive to our generous offer if you will, sir if you will kindly just return the fine vol oww . . .

—Harder man harder till it's all the way, wow . . . she led back in past the tub, —like I mean why'd you take it I mean that's all we need here another fucking book . . . and she brought the punctured shade to light with a punch —I mean if we had that quarter like where's the raviolis, you ate them?

—No no grape whisky just fine thanks . . . he steadied against Won't Burn, Smoke or Smell coming down, —peruse this fine volume . . .

She got the jar from the floor —I mean what's the matter with the raviolis . . . licked fingers, paper tore —like I mean why don't you just go out to dinner then dear friend, complimentary tickets are being reserved in your name for the Second Anniversary Dinner of Rancho Hacienda Estates, a full course dinner will be served and you will view a fascinating motion picture, informal dress banquet room man I mean you could really go . . .

—Lost your pants both go, they all clap when we arose for your sweet . . .

—Informal dress like you could really go man I mean you should look at yourself, I mean you're like already shaving when I went and I come back you're sitting here stoned like I mean you didn't even shave.

—No been, been typing found the typewriter been typing . . .

—Typing what. Man I mean you're like waiting this hundred years for this big chance so everybody should drop dead when you come in and find this dirty folder and these Tootsie Roll notes and then I mean I come back and you're like sitting here stoned watching this wad of gum out the . . .

—Tootsie notes can't find them no typing, found the typewriter been typing . . .

—Can't find them man they're like right behind you and I mean typing what. I mean the typewriter there's no paper in it man, look . . . her leg fell wide leaning forward to turn the roller, —sit down I mean look there's no fucking paper in it man there's nothing look out! you're tipping that whole thing over . . .

—What I just, tipping not tipping typing said typing whole God damned thing over I, God damn it . . .

—There didn't I tell you you're tipping it over? And I mean the box says Tootsie Rolls all over it like I mean you can't find your notes man they just found you . . .

—Christ . . . he came back down slowly, got a foot out dredging the papers together —God damned Pandora box follow me around how many God damned thousand hours in it sixteen years, live with it sixteen years begin to look for it in bookstores come back waiting like you left it publish ten years ago it . . .

—Man be careful you're tearing . . .

—Sixteen years like living with a God damned invalid sixteen years every time you come in sitting there waiting just like you left him wave his stick at you, plump up his pillow cut a paragraph add a sentence hold his God damned hand little warm milk add a comma slip out for some air pack of cigarettes come back in right where you left him, eyes follow you around the room wave his God damned stick figure out what the hell he wants, plump the God damned pillow change bandage read aloud move a clause around wipe his chin new paragraph God damned eyes follow you out stay a week, stay a month whole God damned year think about something else, God damned friends asking how's he coming along all expect him out any day don't want bad news no news rather hear lies, big smile out any day now, walk down the street God damned sunshine begin to think maybe you'll meet him maybe cleared things up got out by himself come back open the God damned door right there where you left him . . .

—Man that quarter out there . . . she'd sunk back, a hand dropped scratching where her leg lay fallen wide —did you stick it there man?

—Told you come in look out one eye yellow other eye seeing green try to put two God damned thoughts together make an idea . . . he caught his balance on H-O, reached the blue folder —God damned friends getting indignant tell you bring him out, tell you bring him out like he is little crippled maybe don't give a God damn, quick and dirty just dress him up a little bring him out anyhow go back waiting, plump the God damned pillow move a clause around . . .

—Did you man? glue that quarter there?

—Told you tale, tale . . . pages flapped under his hand —for though the tale left right here for though the God damned eyes wipe his chin wave his stick figure out what the hell he, for though, for now the pencil where's a pencil God damned clauses look just turned around pencil quick . . .

—You did didn't you man, you glued it didn't you . . .

—Clauses turn right around look. For now long after Wilde had withdrawn to join the compost smoldering in Europe with Pater's recipe for success in life, the tale how for art's sake he'd faced Leadville's bullies to a standoff continued to amuse here where invention was eliminating the very possibility of failure as a condition for success precisely in the arts where one's best is never good enough and who, now the song would play on without losing a note, could resist the temptation to shoot the pianist? How's that.

—How's what. Look man I mean . . .

—What don't like it?

—No I mean I don't get it, like I mean I don't even understand it.

—God damned problem not read to be written aloud you read it then start here read it, here.

—What like here? The only rat, rational method of art criticism I have ever come across Wilde had observed, now elsewhere and dead, a mildewed chimp, and Ste . . .

—Chump God damn it says chump not chimp, here . . .

—It says chimp man look chimp, c h i . . .

—Chump mildewed chump think Crane call Wilde a God damned chimp?

—Man how do I look out, I mean that's my ankle . . .

—Chimp make it sound stupid don't you, hate it try to make it sound stupid . . .

—Hate it man like how can I hate it I mean I don't even know what it's about . . .

—Shoot the God damned pianist what it's about just told you, player piano play by itself get to shoot the pianist just read it God damn it says it right here, here where invention was eliminating the very possibility of failure as a condition for success precisely in the God damned arts there, says it right there.

—It says what, I mean this player piano where does it say that.

—Invention says right there invention God damn it means player piano . . .

—Man I mean that's what I mean, like I mean if it says it why doesn't it say it? And I mean this is the name of the book agape agape? that's the name of it?

—Can't, look pē mark right over the God damned e pi eta pē agapē can't see God damn it? pi eta pē?

—Man like who's supposed to know piéta I mean . . .

—Didn't Christ! didn't say pietà whole God damned different Christ any God damned use look, book don't bring a God damned thing to it can't take a God damned thing from it don't know something look it up no God damned obligation encyclopedia right here look it up ag, ag, glass golf wrong God damned volume . . .

—Look man I mean it doesn't mat . . .

—Whole God damned point doesn't matter why agapē's agape, whole God damned point just look up something else Gordian Knot the, casual bowser look up Gordian Knot the. Known as Chinese Gordon for his brilliant military exploits in that country, Charles George Gordon later undertook the heroic defense of Khartoum where the knot that bears his name of Christ!

—Look out! you could have broke the window man I mean Chairman Meow you scared the shit out of him here kitty, I mean like why'd you throw it at him man here kitty kitty . . .

—Whole God, damned, try to tell you tell them too God damned late love feast all over shoot the God damned pianist doesn't matter laughing string whereon mad fingers place of stone Christ, feel like I was born here . . .

—Man look out that's my leg . . .

—God damned many years worth doing God damned eyes follow you start to hate him still waiting shake his God damned stick nothing happen, bandage dry up falls off milk sour world go by out in the God damned sunshine friends finally too God damned embarrassed to ask, come back open the God damned door right where you hate him God damned eyes staring out see where he was going thought you were taking him see what you don't . . .

—Look out man sit up I mean you're hurting my, here kitty . . .

—Move a clause plump the God damned pillow doesn't matter wave his stick doesn't matter cut a paragraph hands on his God damned throat squeeze the whole God damned thing down to a period hate it!

—Wait don't man I mean you're tearing . . .

—Ten years late staggers out God damned pianist already shot God damned sunshine everybody step right over him God damned hurry go noplace nobody give a God damn book everything's happened book about everybody knows hate it!

—Man like that's what people want's books that tell them what they already know, I mean that's why they're all such bullshit get my foot out of under your, ow . . . she drew its moccasined heel up hung on the sofa's edge her fallen leg's length from his perch there on H-O —like I mean look at all the fucking books in this place who asked you to write another one anyhow.

—Said I would.

—Like said to who, I mean that's this big important call you're waiting for?

—Said don't answer it, only God damned thing I ever . . .

—Man those must have been some dance lessons, like I mean if you hate it man how can you do it.

—Can't! told you only God damned thing I ever . . .

—What man ever what . . . her hand came down from the flexed knee scratching —I mean that's like I always said I'll be this model you know? Like I used to read all these dumb comic books like Millie the Model when I'm like ten and I mean I already have these little dippeldut-ters like her up in that picture so I'm going to grow up and be this big model you know? Like if I can't be it I'm nothing, I mean I break my ass so like finally I'm out looking and they tell me my nose shadows wrong and my tits are too big and I mean I really came down man, I mean I'm really nothing, only like there's always like somebody crowding me up trying to slip it in you know? I mean I even meet this big model that's like going to help me out and I mean she's climbing on too and I'm finally thinking like wow, like I mean which one is real, I mean like I changed and this big idea from when I'm like ten didn't change and it's still hanging me up, you know . . . ? her hand dropped to scratch the dry mound, —like I mean I'm the one that ought to write this book, you know?

—Ought to teach too . . . he caught his struggle for the cup, reared back with it on line with her fallen knee —lecture like wow which one is real get to give neoplatonism whole God damned rebirth start a little school . . .

—Man like you think you're kidding I mean I wouldn't hand them any bullshit, I mean you can ask my friends man.

—Little book you and your friends call it Old Foes With New Faeces sell a million . . .

—No look man cut the bullshit I mean this book I could write like if it sells a million of it I mean that means it's good, right? Like I mean I could write this book people would read, man . . . the scratching slowed from palliative to ruminative —like without all these phony big words you use I mean like, I'd communicate . . .

—Try that God damned Christians strip you naked tear you up with oyster shells take your Christ! he blew back into the cup, dropped it empty into Won't Burn, Smoke or Smell dredging pages up with his foot —give you a title small words mint condition how's that, Agapē Agape never used how's that.

—Man like I mean I just said who wants your fucking title if nobody even knows what it means . . . the flexed knee sagged, —I mean look man do you want to ball?

—Drop that knee little further everybody know what it means, picture on the jacket Taine write your jacket blurb sell a million . . .

—Look, I mean do you?

—Told you I'm, why . . .

—Why, I mean like what else is there to do . . . her scratching fingers stilled, —I mean there's nothing else to eat there's nothing to even smoke so like you're going to sit here reading this dirty book you wrote in the moonlight?

—Told you too late no, fairies spent it.

—What fairies man! she came forward to punch the punctured shade into light —I mean look, do you want to make it with me or not.

—Told you too God damned late didn't I! Why agapē's agape little bastards up there spent it didn't I?

—Man like forget it . . . she'd undone the shirt's button sinking back, dug in its pocket —I mean those must be some fairies.

—Didn't mean just meant . . .

—I mean forget it!

—Just meant something just, just trying to hold onto something just . . .

—Like go hold onto it then! She sifted out a fold of white paper, stretching back —I mean go hold onto your Tootsie Roll man like I mean you're going to end up . . .

—Didn't, end up . . . he braced an elbow, got his feet closer —sniff what I think you're sniffing wake up with a bloody nose . . .

—Man like doesn't everybody? I mean gluing that quarter out there typing this great book with no paper in the fucking typewriter I mean you're, you're going to wake up like Schramm coming up the . . .

—What . . . he steadied against Thomas Register coming up —what, coming up what . . .

—Like you don't want to know, man.

—What coming up what . . .

—Man you don't want to know! watch your, I mean if you make me spill this . . .

—Wait wait listen . . . he tripped against Hoppin' With Flavor! —don't move listen . . .

—I hear it man it's the fucking telephone I mean go answer it.

—Told you wrong number listen!

—Look man the phone's not up there it's in the other . . .

—Quick toward the window move you're the aerial listen . . . ! Tonic Water Twist Cap capsized into Won't Burn, Smoke or Smell as he gained the plateau of Musical Couriers —little further listen!

—Man I have to answer it maybe it's . . .

—Don't move . . . ! he was gone between 24–10 Pad Pkgs and 48 No 1 Cans Beef Gravy —there!

—Look I'm answering it man maybe it's my . . .

—Bastards!

——selection from Bruckner's eighth symphony brought to you by . . .

—Bastards you ow . . . ! he caught his head, came down pounding Trade Extra 1909 slipped against 2 Dozen 57 The World's Largest Selling Ketchup and kicked, got the mop handle —bastards!

——wedding of the grand alliance of education and technology forging the two edge . . .

The mop handle flailed, he plunged it down, pounded —can't play the whole symphony can't even play the whole God damned scherzo bastards . . . ! Musical Courier 1911 skidded offside, he twisted, pounded, kicked against 24–10 Pad Pkgs forced a knee against it, forced the other against 48 No 1 Cans Beef Gravy and sank further, tried a shoulder against the abrupt decline of 2 Dozen 57 The World's Largest Selling Ketchup, fought a hand out —ooph! Trade Extra broke against a rib —bastards . . . !

——pedia, bringing the American family its full share of the world's knowledge. Look for it in your local supermar . . .

—Man like what's happening in here are you up there? I mean it sounds like the whole fucking place is going through to the cellar what happened.

—Shot the pianist.

—Like it's his boss on the phone I mean Bast's, like I mean he's really strung out man you coming down?

—Can't.

—Look he said he heard this Mister Grynszpan's here he wants to talk to him man I mean he wants to talk to anybody . . . she got over the collision of Tonic Water Twist Cap, brought moccasins up on it settling back —like go talk to him man I mean you know what's with Grynszpan . . . she tapped the paper crease, held it up —I mean he's really strung out in there like he's yelling like you don't know if he's laughing or crying kitty kitty kitty? I mean he must be some creep, kitty kitty? Is he up there man? Chairman Meow is he up there . . . ? her free hand scratched where it fell —like he's probably so scared we won't see him for a month, man? I mean what are you doing up there.

—Peruse this fine volume . . . Trade Extra's cracked leather spine sailed over NO DEPOSIT to hit the clock, the second hand fled into NO RETURN —armchair traveler God damned exciting journey no obligation

. . . paper tore. —The music of the world is free to all. How's that.

—Like I mean I could really tell them man, you know? I mean like why should I have to be this fucking model just because this spaced out ten year old said I will, I mean I'm the one that ought to write this book you know?

—For those whom classic pieces interest, Scarlatti, Bach, Haydn and old Handel have written oratorios and fugues how's that.

—Like I tell all my friends and I really break my ass when I get out of school like I take this charm course and how to do makeup and all and I mean then they're all getting pissed off buying Vogue when I'm like never in it and I'm like nothing you know?

—Unhappy Schubert speaks to them in the sweet tones of Rosamunde. Beethoven, master of masters, thrills alike the listeners and the performer of his Appassionata or beautiful Fifth Symphony . . .

—And then I mean I finally figure out like all this time I'm trying to be it I really hate this fucking model I always said I'll be, you know?

—Chopin bemoans the fate of Poland in his nocturnes or breathes the fiery valor of his countrymen in Polonaise . . .

—Like I mean you forget how you know? I mean like hating all these wise-ass generals and fucked up presidents we get and like these banks and faceless reverend garbage peels and asshole politicians I mean it's just this big drag and like you forget, you know? I mean like really how to hate?

—For other tastes great Wagner comes and, lifting them aloft above the clouds, transports them to the mighty Halls of old Walhalla, in Ride of Walküres, or takes them to the cool, green depths of classic Rhine in Nibelungen Ring . . .

—I mean like when I finally find out I'm fine like just who I am, and I mean this model I always said I'll be like I find out all this time I really hate her you know? I mean I'm breaking my ass and she's like making me hate who I really am, you know?

—The Pianola is the universal means of playing the piano.

—I mean I could write this book people would read, you know?

—Universal, because there is no one in all the world, having the use of hands and feet, who could not learn to use it with but little effort.

—Like I mean I'd communicate, you know?

—The striking of the notes of the selection, in proper time and place, is no concern of the player. This is correctly done by perforated rolls of paper . . .

—Man you glued that quarter out there, I mean didn't you . . . ? She creased the paper closed coming forward —I mean this fucking lamp . . . she yanked it, hand fallen fumbling arm's length in the dark where she stretched back. —Like listen to the water in there I mean I'm like I'm floating, man? you're still up there . . . ?

————homes in America, many were treas . . .

—I mean listen it's getting closer listen. Man? Like I mean we could all drownd and nobody would even know it listen! I mean it's getting closer man I can't see are you up there? Man like my feet are caught in, help! Man like we're tipping over help! Where's, here kitty kitty it's this big fucking storm Bast are you up there help! my feet are caught help! I can't, man I mean it's so deep I can't, man it's so warm I mean it's running all down, oh wow, oh wow . . . and the torrents at sink and tub seemed to rise in the dark swollen by the sound of rain driven against the glass, where light came finally graying a sunless day. —Man like I'm having this nosebleed can you bring me something . . . ? she waited up on an elbow, hand to her face —I mean are you still up there . . . ? and she kicked free the knotted blanket, each step a bright splash on the fall of envelopes and pasted notes and letterheads, Modern Packaging, Financial World, over the collision of Tonic Water Twist Cap past 200 2-Ply where she caught up a damp wad of shirt to her nose —wow who dumped all the, man are you under there . . . ? her free hand swiped through the billow of suds, rose pulling off her shirt and dropped to scratch her leg spread poised at the tub's edge to kick off a moccasin —who's, man is that you . . . ?

The door shuddered. —Got a delivery . . .

—Like who's stopping you . . .

It sagged in —look I been here before I'm trying to deliver a truckload of where are you anyways . . .

—Where does it look like . . . she batted the rise of suds from a shoulder, —I mean what are you staring at, deliver your delivery . . .

—Thousand gross plastic flowers down there look, how you expect me to get a thousand gross plastic flowers in here you . . .

—Man like who said I expect you to do anything? Like I mean that's your problem, I mean you're supposed to be this big delivering man do it how they told you in delivering man school, okay . . . ? The shirt wad came up wet abruptly jostling pebbled pinks from the suds —I mean look man at least can you quit standing there pulling your pork and like answer the telephone? No I mean look it's like right up there behind you . . .

—The, oh . . . hello . . . ? want the, who . . . ?

—Like who is it I mean if it's for me I'm expecting this imp . . .

—Somebody says where's the boss at says he supposed to be in court . . .

—Like tell them to fuck off I mean I'm expecting this very important wow, like I mean what's this Macy's window?

—What in, look who the hell are you what are you doing here where's . . .

—Man he's answering the telephone I mean what does it look like he's doing here, I mean . . .

—But what, where's Jack what's . . .

—Like how do I know where's Jack and I mean who's that, like I mean what am I supposed to be some fucking sideshow?

—Who's what wait, wait who are you . . .

—Yes you're Mister Grynszpan? I have a summons here for . . .

—Look damn it I'm not Mister Grynszpan my name's Eigen, now what the hell's . . .

—Oh, this Mister Grynszpan on the phone then? Here you are sir, U S District Court Southern District BMT take you right there, now Mister Bast? One here for you from the United States . . .

—Man look at these I mean do I look like Mister anybody? I mean get out everybody get out of here!

—Sure you're not Mister Bast either sir? I have a subpoen . . .

—I'm damn sure yes now get out of here you too, get down from that phone and get the hell watch that door! Look where's, what are you doing here where's wait you're the, your name was Rhoda wasn't it you· . . .

—Like what do you mean was and I mean what are you staring at, what does it look like I'm doing man I mean look hang that telephone back up I'm expecting this important call and I mean that door, like push something against it before he gets that stuff in here . . .

—What stuff who . . .

—This delivering man I mean he's like delivering this thousand plastic flowers, like I mean can't you hear he's knocking the fucking stairs down out there . . .

—Oh that's no, no that's all right that's somebody else, friend of Jack's and mine he's just bringing a big easel up to . . .

—Like you and him have some friends man I mean hand me that shirt . . .

—It's all right he's not coming in here with it he won't bother us, he's a painter been looking for a place to work he's just putting his things back in the empty, here let me . . .

—Look I mean I said just hand me the shirt. I mean like I can get out by myself okay?

—Yes I just, here . . .

—And I mean look man I mean I can dry myself too, okay?

—What's the matter I just . . .

—Like nothing's the matter I mean I just don't need your hand there okay?

—No but what's . . .

—I said I can dry there myself!

—What's the matter what's so . . .

—I said nothing's the matter just get your look man I mean the telephone's man I'm not kidding, I mean let me answer the fucking telephone get your . . .

—Just, wait damn it I'll answer it just . . .

—I mean I'm expecting this very important . . .

—Hello . . . ? He's not here no, who . . . Oh it's you yes Jack's been waiting for you to call he's . . . just went out a little while ago yes but where can he reach you, I know he can't wait to . . . Yes he's told me about you it all sounds . . . pardon? No, no it's e i g, I thought . . . Thomas yes Tom I, I thought Jack had probably . . . No he was but I'm giving the place up you see my wife just pardon . . . ? No it's a, it's sort of a studio uptown he's been working here since you left I'm just having my calls transferred here, I thought if my wife wanted . . . No not recently no something I wrote a few years ago's out in paperback picked up some kind of an award but pardon . . . ? Oh, oh you mean his book yes, yes he's been working on it driving himself pretty hard since you left been having a few problems with the . . . I don't think it's really that though someone who's not used to the kind of self-discipline that . . . No but every writer has dry periods I'm just coming out of one myself, quit my job I feel like I just got over a long illness but I've been having a little pardon . . . ? Oh you're still at the airport you just got in? I didn't . . . just said Geneva yes he thought it was some family problem I know he'll be glad to hear you've straightened it out, once these things get started I know my own lawyer's said he thinks I should . . .

—Look man hang up I mean I'm expecting this very . . .

—Pardon . . . ? Oh you're, you're welcome yes I . . . yes I'll tell him that I know he's . . . I will yes I'm looking forward to meet . . . hello?

—Look I mean I'm expecting . . .

—Yes I heard you, listen that's a call Jack's been waiting for, someone he's . . .

—Somebody he really doesn't want to see man I mean I heard all about it.

—Heard what don't be silly, it's the only thing holding him together he's . . .

—Man like nothing's holding him together I mean if there's really somebody he doesn't want to see it's her, like I mean who took my pants . . .

—Well damn it where is he, keeps saying he thinks he's sick I've been telling him to see a doctor listen was he drinking last night? Where the hell is he.

—Like I said how do I know where is he, I mean these plaid pants I can't find them maybe he wore them to go to the doctor place man I mean maybe he's still up in that pile of boxes in there from last night.

—Whole place is such a mess hardly get through the, what are all these matchbooks dumped my God what happened in here anyhow, books and mail dumped all over the look how did this happen, these toys I sent up here how did they get . . .

—Look man I mean they're all broken anyway what do you . . .

—No but look film papers cans all over the Christ is that a cat up there?

—Oh wow, like I was scared he got drownded . . .

—Got what?

—Like this shipwreck man, I mean this big storm last night there was this shipwreck here kitty kitty . . .

—Listen what are you talking about, this . . .

—Man I mean I was in it!

—All right never mind look, I just . . .

—Like what do you mean never mind I mean what does it look like happened here man.

—God knows, I thought Jack was . . .

—Knows what I mean I'll tell you one thing he's no fucking good in a shipwreck. Kitty kitty . . . ?

—All right listen I may have some important mail here and I'm looking for a, damn it look there are a lot of valuable papers stored here whole manuscript of my book splitting right down the side that box that says Hoppin' With . . .

—Man like that's where the armchair traveler . . .

—And this folder I'm looking for something I, some work I started it's an old manila folder with tea stains all over it think I mislaid it someplace have you . . .

—Man like the only old wait look out look out, I mean right by your foot that piece of folded paper . . .

—What this? but what . . .

—Man don't spill it I mean wow I didn't know I still have some left move your, look I mean there's hardly room to . . .

—Get your feet up then I'm just trying to see what these, Christ look how did this happen! all the notes for his book how could . . .

—How could I what I mean he's sitting here scraping it up with his feet like what am I supposed to do, I mean he hates it man.

—Hates it don't be, it's the only thing holding him together reason he's working on it again I told you this call he just got, she's . . .

—What man she's what, I mean I'm telling you nothing's holding him together man she's why he hates it! I mean the telephone rings he says it's the wrong number, like this big important call he says he already got it he won this free dance lesson man I mean you're in there talking to her like she's this big fucking inspiration I mean this load she put on him she's really wiped him out man he doesn't want to see her!

—Sounds to me like you're . . .

—I mean you're supposed to be this big important novelist and you don't even get that? I mean he's got this book so screwed up with this free dance lesson he comes out feeling like I said I don't need your hand right there man if you . . .

—No relax I just meant, I just meant she sounds like an elegant woman hear him talk about a neater sweeter maiden it all sounds romantic enough but she sounds a little chilly, a little bit . . .

—Chilly? I mean it's this black haired chick he's been balling right?

—Has he told you ab . . .

—Like what does he need to tell me I mean he was right through that window over in Schramm's balling her wasn't he? And I mean if you think she was look I mean I'm not kidding get your . . .

—No relax look I just meant, I mean meeting somebody like you who doesn't lay down all kinds of old-fashioned conditions like commitment and intimacy on something that's as healthy and natural as . . .

—Look man if this spills I mean get your . . .

—What is it, is it . . .

—What does it look like snow? I mean look I don't need your . . .

—I've heard it's kind of an aphro . . .

—Afro nothing man look I said I don't need your fing . . .

—Just, look relax don't be, don't get excited just . . .

—Don't get excited I mean then what's your finger trying to look man I'm not kidding I . . .

—What's the matter just . . .

—I said nothing's the fucking matter I mean I just don't need your finger . . .

—Then how, how about this . . .

—Oh wow, wow I mean come on . . .

—What's the matter what's so . . .

—Look I, I mean come on get your, I mean the telephone's man you're hurting my mean I'm not kidding I'm expecting this very . . .

—You damn it, you . . .

—I mean I said I'm not kidding!

—Go ahead damn it! go . . .

—I mean let me past . . . !

—Spread it for Schramm for Jack why can't you . . .

—Hello . . . ? this is her yes, I mean . . . Like whenever you want Mister Cibo, I mean now . . . ? No I mean I'll come down there now if you want like all I have to do is . . . this dress with these little checks on I already got it yes I'm coming right . . . At suite what . . . ? Yes I'm coming right down . . .

—Spread it for Schramm for Jack for any, Bast probably for Bast too why can't you . . .

—Look I mean go back in there man leave me alone, I mean I need to get on this dress . . .

—What's the difference just tell me what's the difference you spread for . . .

—I mean look man are you going to stand there like that . . .

—Just tell me what's the difference you're the, you're what the young man from Racine invented aren't you no intimacy no, no commitment nothing, concave or convex to fit either sex aren't you . . .

—Man you're, I mean you're this real bastard aren't you . . .

—Beefy face and grubby hand didn't Jack ever quote the rest of it to you? Ever quote anything to you ever talk to you at all? So jealous of this woman who just called you can't see straight can you so stupid it's the only intimacy you can offer anybody isn't it, easier to get laid than try to talk about something isn't it just a, a mechanical lay aren't you you . . .

—I mean this, this real bastard aren't you . . .

—Aren't you no ideas no passion the world's no bigger than your, than your dumb appetites why you have to sniff that stuff the only way left you can feel anything isn't it, getting laid's about as interesting as a, as washing your face no more feeling than a, than a milking machine just a . . .

—Like go get one then! Man I mean standing there like that go get one of those plastic things with hair on you put warm water in it that's all you been grabbing for that's all you . . .

—Joke was on Schramm wasn't it all he . . .

—Man like get away from me I mean what Schramm . . .

—What Schramm wanted that's how much you know listen what Schramm wanted was a woman he could trust with everything he had, wanted it so much he knew if he thought he had it and lost it he'd cut his throat so he found you instead didn't he, took the safe way no commitment no intimacy no passion no conversation but fucking this and fucking that nothing to hold back but your slit just to prove you can offer it to anybody who goes by and he finds he's even jealous of you you, you couldn't even give him that could you came back here that night you couldn't even . . .

—Look man I mean, I mean how do I know what he's going to do like he's down in your apartment you're the one, I mean you're the one man you're who knows what he's . . .

—No no I'd talked him out of it he thought you'd be here, only way I could talk him out of it he thought you'd be here waiting and you couldn't even . . .

—Talked him out of bullshit man I mean you're leaving out this whole fucking step, I mean you talk him out of it so he jumps out your fucking window he comes up those stairs blood all down him his bandage all . . .

—How do, wait you were here . . .

—Leave me alone get your . . .

—You were here when he came back weren't you!

—Man you're tearing my, look I have to go to this job if you screw up this dress man you're hurting my . . .

—You were weren't you!

—Like what if I was!

—You you what did you . . .

—Man get your ow, I I hear him dragging up the stairs I see him through the rails all this blood this hole where his bandage was these, these noises he's, he's making these noises what am I supposed to man you're tearing my . . .

—Why couldn't you couldn't even . . .

—Get your ow! I'm, I'm in these dark shadows he gets up the stairs and I, I get back in this dark landing till he's inside I'm scared I mean I'm scared I creep past his door for the stairs how am I supposed to know what he's you're, you're hurting my . . .

—You couldn't even . . .

—How am I supposed to know what he's doing in there! No get, get away from me you're . . .

—Pretend you're, try to pretend you're crying you're just . . .

—No get away you're you're, man you're like some, you're like some fucking graverobber aren't you you're . . .

—What do you, listen you . . .

—No I mean you're like this fucking graverobber aren't you man I mean like all you want me for is I was Schramm's isn't it . . .

—Don't you, you don't know a damn . . .

—No I mean you're telling me I'm so stupid like man like, like when you know as much as I do there's no place to go I mean what about his get away! I mean what about his stepmother that's the ass he really wanted go dangle it for her you come in here with your . . .

—Shut up listen you don't even, you're so high on this stuff you've been sniffing you don't know what you're . . .

—High man I mean I'm flying like I mean I'm really flying, I mean you come in here where's my tea stain folder get away from me! my tea stain folder I may have mislaid it like you think I don't even know whose fucking tea stain folder with everything he ever wrote's in it that's all you . . .

—Just, just shut up relax look . . .

—I mean that's all that's left for you isn't it my ass and this tea stain folder isn't it, I mean you're telling this chick on the phone how you're this big important writer how Jack's this big friend of yours all the time you're putting him down like he's some schmuck like you're telling me she's this cold stiff I mean I saw those scars down him man, like I mean all this passion and intimacy you're telling me I don't know what it is man I mean that was some free fucking dance lesson you don't trust him none of you trust anybody you're all scared shitless of it aren't you, I mean he's so hung up on this book he's scared to lose this lousy opinion of himself that's why none of you can . . .

—Look Rhoda just, look just relax wash your face and . . .

—I mean like what are you calling me my name all of a sudden for get away, I mean you don't think I wanted somebody that will talk to me that will, that will still like me anyway after we screw?

—Look you can't leave this way come back in and, you can't go to a job this way you're . . .

—Man I'm not kidding let me get my raincoat I mean get out of my I'm not kidding man get out of my way . . .

—Just, get out . . .

—I mean answer the phone man maybe that's her calling back, I mean maybe she'll give you a free dance . . .

—Get out! and, and don't come back either you don't need to come back either . . . ! he stood between the torrents there getting breath before he turned, tripped on a film can reaching —hello . . . ? No what do you . . . what Indian uprising no you've got the wrong . . . I said you've got the wrong number! and he got as far as 36 Boxes 200 2-Ply —now what . . . ripped his foot from a tangle of film, —hello . . . ? He's not here no, who . . . lawyer for who . . . ? Wait no you've got the wrong one, this Mister Gibbs never worked for a general . . . oh, oh a company yes, yes he worked once for some small family comp . . . Eigen yes, I've known him for . . . Mrs Angel? No I don't think I, wait yes that's Stella? Yes he's . . . I usually do yes but . . . yes I'll tell him it's urgent don't know when he'll be back though, he's been . . . No he's mentioned it to me but I don't know the . . . no, no I think he just signed the stock certificate over to his ex-wife in a lump settlement, I'm having a similar kind of what . . . ? No I doubt it no their relations are hardly cordial, she's got custody of his daughter makes things pretty difficult for him the way my wife just walked out took my son with her and she thinks she's granting me a privilege letting me see him can you imagine that? I went out to see them yesterday a house I'd rented myself when I still thought we could what . . . ? Oh, oh yes yes I just . . . yes what kind of a misadventure . . . yes I'll . . . minute he gets in yes I'll tell him to call you Mis . . . ven one four seven I've got it yes c, o . . . oh without the h? Yes I'll tell him, goodbye . . . And he got no further than 24-12 Oz Btls Fragile! —Yes hello . . . ? Wait no wait who do you . . . if who? To defend what paternity suit look who do you . . . No look you've got the wrong . . . look damn it you've got the wrong number!

And rain took up again against the pane where he came sweeping Dun's Review and the Journal of Taxation before him with the crunch of slides underfoot, emptying Tonic Water Twist Cap into Won't Burn, Smoke or Smell raised to the heap and squared, lifting, stacking, sorting —Grynszpan, Eigen, Bast, Bast, Gerst . . . ? The long hand rose to drive the short behind the silence of the cat posed there unblinking as it dipped to NO RETURN, emerged from NO DEPOSIT —E Berst? Grynszpan, Miss Bertha Klupp where the, God what a mess . . . Light filled the punctured shade, was gone, came on again as though enlivened by some demented electric eye scanning the gloom beyond the glass where the gum wad leaped and splashed on the sill. The typewriter clattered, failed, clattered and was still. The long hand dipped to NO RETURN. He edged closer, abruptly pulled up the sash grabbed the dancing string and yanked hard.

——provide a meaningful way of life for older persons so they may continue to contribute to their community in a dignified and productive manner. This is Senior Citizens' Month . . .

He freed the second head string, held the controller up and turned it to the side, the marionette's head nosed the tangle of hand strings and he followed one to its source in the back string's tangle, held the thing up and bit a shoulder string free, shook the controller and held it up tipped forward, pulled the back string and the marionette sank slowly seated on Hoppin' With Flavor! arm hanging numbed, leg drawn indifferent in the tangle that remained to spring up clearing Moody's in a single vault and tread the Journal of Taxation laocoön in the small.

—Just wait out here a minute Freddie not sure what's, Rhoda? Anybody here . . . ?

—Jack? The marionette dropped back in a tangle with the broken music box and red mitten, maimed Virgin and sheep, —is that you?

—Tom that you? Any calls? Look Freddie wait out here a minute let me get this box in help me get this box in Tom?

—Yes but what's, who's that . . .

—Tell you inside just get this box in careful don't break it, looks like another case of matchbooks, just get that corner in past the sink listen Tom be nice to him, knew him in boarding school a little bit simple but he's one of the sweetest . . .

—But what's he, why'd you bring him up here he's . . .

—Bumped into him outside Grand Central soaking wet look at him, knew me the minute he saw me he hasn't changed since he was ten look at him, what the hell could I do leave him there? Bronze plaque outside the station standing there in the rain reading his family names all over it probably still own the whole God damned block looks like they keep him put away somewhere, Freddie? No come in come in doesn't matter if you're wet look at me Christ get that wet jacket off, where the hell he got it says Bob Jones U across the back wait watch that bag, brought in some groceries whole bottom of it's falling out here put the, wait look who left the God damned phone off the hook . . .

—I did Jack I took it off, ringing every time I turned around people calling about an Indian uprising somebody's supposed to be in court to defend a paternity suit what the hell's going on here anyhow, I came in this morn . . .

—No but God damn it suppose she called how long has it been hanging here suppose she tried to . . .

—She did just listen for a minute, she called this morning she was still . . .

—Amy? she called? Christ why didn't you tell me! where is she what did she . . .

—She was still at the airport she said she'd call back where the hell have you been, I . . .

—What I've got to tell you I've wait God damn it how could she call back if the phone was look where can I reach her, did she . . .

—She couldn't say Jack she'd just got in, she said she had some things to settle she wants out of the way before she sees you may take a day or so, she just wanted you to know she's back and everything's . . .

—Day or two! Christ a day or two listen I, something I have to talk to you about Tom wait wait Freddie here, give me the newspaper get the tub closed put that bag down before the whole God damned bottom falls out get those cigarettes Tom, must have carried it three miles in the God damned rain we got in a cab downtown radio playing Gluck's Orfeo drove all over hell so Freddie could listen to it, just getting into Che faro senza Euridice counted my money and we had to get out at the God damned Museum of Natural History driver so God damned obnoxious about his eight cent tip I left his back door open pouring rain he roars away rips it right off against the back of a bus Christ look at this suit, two hundred dollars two hours ago already looks like the Salvation Army listen something I've got to talk to you about Tom, I just spent the whole morning down at . . .

—Wait look out for his, God you're both soaked look Jack he can't just, where is he going to . . .

—He's all right aren't you Freddie here just come in here watch out for, over here that's it sit on this box here get that wet sneaker off I thought we could just put him up back in Schramm's there till I find out what's . . .

—He can't no Schepperman's back there, I was just . . .

—Schepperman where the hell did he come from.

—Standing on line in the unemployment office he's desperate, detectives after him and everything else what the hell else could I do leave him there?

—No but Christ if he's . . .

—I mean I feel partly responsible Jack, that big canvas of his the company bought that old Selk bitch claims everything he paints is hers why he's barricaded himself in back there, a painting he put aside years ago when he was still doing figures now he's frantic to finish it says its time has come he just moved in with all his junk and two bushels of potatoes, the old bitch even froze his bank account he'd just done a monstrous stabile big David Smith kind of atrocity palmed it off on some corporation and I had to give him ten dollars for potatoes, he . . .

—Christ glad you mentioned that listen I've got to have ten Tom or twenty, twenty, same God damned thing I stopped in the bank where Amy had me put what I won on that double keep it safe the God damned Internal Revenue found it there attached every God damned penny, brown nosing banker said they've got a lien against me for twenty-eight thousand dollars where the hell they came up with that figure hate to miss the pleasure seeing those bastards sue my estate look I've got to have twenty, got to get out and meet her the minute she calls back tell her what I've got to tell you about this Tom spent the whole God damned morning down at what's the matter . . .

—Just his foot here damn it Jack look, it took me two hours just to sort all this mail that whole pile from the West Side where the hell did it come from. I even found a mailbag back there tried to clean things up Jack the place looked like a, it looked like a shipwreck what the hell have you been doing up here I thought you were up here working, I found your notes for your . . .

—Tom it's not that important now that's what I'm . . .

—What your book's not? is that what she . . .

—Yes if you'll listen I . . .

—Damn it you listen can't you see what she's, she told me you hate it you can't finish it you're afraid of losing your rotten opinion of yourself she said all of us were . . .

—No but how could, when she called? Christ what did she say you just told me all she said was . . .

—Not her God no I mean Rhoda this Rhoda you've been, what the hell has she done just moved in here? I came in here this morning door standing open a process server right behind me some slob in overalls on the phone she was in the tub bouncing her . . .

—Look Tom she's just a, little outspoken but there's not a mean bone in her body really just a sweet kid who . . .

—Sweet kid? Rhoda a sweet kid? She's a, my God she's a pig Jack sitting here scratching nothing but an old shirt she sat here spreading her legs nothing but an old shirt around her sitting here pushing it at me what do you think I . . .

—Glad things worked out Tom listen, something ser . . .

—What with her? Be like, my God it would be like one of those plastic things you fill with warm water will you tell me what the hell you think you're doing with her Jack? She said the last person you want to see's this black haired chick she calls her says you wouldn't even answer the phone . . .

—No listen . . .

—Can't you see what she's trying to do? So damn jealous there's a woman you have halfway intelligent intercourse with she only knows one meaning because it's all she's got to offer sitting here spread out sniffing what is it cocaine? She went out of here this morning for a job so high she could hardly . . .

—Tom what the hell do you expect, kid like that she lives in a scene where hallucination is confused with vision all she . . .

—What like seeing you and your neater sweeter maiden making, balling was that a hallucination?

—Couldn't have said that it's ridiculous, she . . .

—That's what I'm telling you believe a damn word she says, she said she watched you balling this black haired chick through that back window in Schramm's said it was some . . .

—She couldn't have we never, wait that blonde look it was just that blonde from the subway I found in Penn Station she showed up here once in a black wig Christ the whole thing's irrelevant anyhow if you'll just lis . . .

—Jack she's out to destroy you is that irrelevant? The way she destroyed Schramm she's out to destroy all of us is that irrelevant!

—No now listen you know God damned well she didn't destroy Schramm, you know God damned well what destroyed Schramm sitting on the floor back there babbling Hart Crane there is a world dimensional for those untwisted by the love of . . .

—She could have stopped him what's the difference and it's not a world anyhow, it's the world. There is the world dimen . . .

—Tom Christ! time for such God damned quibbles listen something I . . .

—No you listen she was here that night, did you know that? Here waiting for him when he came back right out in the hall there waiting she finally admitted it, broke down here this morning admitted she'd been . . .

—Wait she couldn't have been there when he . . .

—Hid she hid, she watched him come in hid in the stairwell in the dark there sneaked out when he got inside I told you that night didn't I! that she could have stopped him? that she was . . .

—Tom?

—What?

—Nobody's blaming you for Schramm.

—What do you, what the hell do you mean nobody's blaming me who's blaming me!

—I just said Tom, nobody.

—But why did you say it what the hell made you say a thing like that you, you know damn well she's the only reason I let him leave that night, last shred of confidence as a man he was down there with those lines of Tolstoy there was something terribly lacking between what I felt and what I could do and she, she might as well have strangled him herself that knot between her legs she . . .

—Christ look can't you see it wasn't any of that! it was, it was worse than that? It was whether what he was trying to do was worth doing even if he couldn't do it? whether anything was worth writing even if he couldn't write it? Hopping around with that God damned limp trying to turn it all into something more than one more stupid tank battle one more stupid God damned general, trying to redeem the whole God damned thing by . . .

—Yes that folder of his, have you seen it? Old manila folder you were waving it around at Beamish that night? Jack?

—What.

—Meant to tell you I found a letter from Beamish in this mess we each owe Schramm's estate sixty-eight dollars for estate taxes, has to be paid before these bequests can be handed out reminds me these papers I told him I'd give Mrs Schramm, I found them in the pocket of this jacket this morning completely forgot to, what's the matter.

—Never mind. Look, do you want something to eat?

—Eat? I thought there was something you wanted to talk about.

—Just going to tell you I spent the morning down at the hospital being tested, they . . .

—What are you upset about then aren't I the one who's been telling you to see a doctor? Where did you go, I . . .

—Went down to . . .

—Should have gone in myself while I still had that company insurance plan, this pain I've been getting right under here it's . . .

—Wait tell me about your eye Tom, first tell me all about your eye.

—My eye?

—Detached retina, told me you had a detached retina . . .

—Oh, oh you know what happened I think it healed itself, the doctor I called said that was practically unknown in medical . . .

—And your tooth yes I meant to ask about your tooth, reminded me of that great line of Pascal's about toothache how the hell's your tooth.

—My too . . .

—Angry looking vein in your forehead there too, hope it's not . . .

—Look Jack what the hell are you trying to . . .

—Trying to tell you I'm going to die.

—To, what do you . . .

—Told me I've got leukemia haven't long to live that's all.

—But you, who told you who . . .

—Blood tests laboratory doctors the whole God damned crew down there, got a white count up in the bil . . .

—No but look that's absurd you couldn't just . . .

—Why what's wrong with being absurd, people all over the place being broiled like chops on the highway getting heart attacks cancer dandruff I just drew one that's . . .

—And look Jack don't try to pretend to me you don't think it's serious, you . . .

—Well God damn it I know it's serious! what do you think I, told me to come back in the morning to check it but good Christ . . .

—Why didn't they just keep you there if they really thought you no look Freddie, Jack ask him not to fool with that marionette will you, I've been . . .

—Not hurting it Tom the God damned thing's already . . .

—No but I've been trying to fix it I thought I'd take it up to him next time, familiar old toys they might give him back a little sense of security

Jack we, we told him about it yesterday the worst thing I've ever been through. She wanted me to tell him I said look damn it you're the one who's done it who's moved out you tell him he just stood there he, he turned and walked out he hardly made it Jack I went out and found him just standing there carried him back in crying all he could say was, was wouldn't I, wouldn't I be lonely can't even talk about it . . .

—Tom there's noth . . .

—Marian up there acting like a, I rented a car drove up there to see them acting like a brave war widow she's already papered his bedroom herself, four years she couldn't even clean his room downtown now she papers one overnight wants to know if I'll pay for a bed he's, Jack he's got four pictures of me lined up by his, by this little cot he sleeps on so used to him being right where I God I, I stopped in a bar last night two or three drinks a man standing there with his shoe untied I almost grabbed him told him to tie his shoe I've got to get out of that place downtown Jack, came in last night I had a few more drinks woke up at three sitting on the couch I jumped up ran to his room to make sure he was all right just the, nothing there just the bed I, look I think I'll have a drink where's the, what is it what's out there.

—Where.

—Out the window, I thought you saw something out the window.

—Just looking out the window Tom. I'm just looking out the God damned window.

—Oh. Did I tell you she's already complaining about the house up there? Says the refrigerator's too big things get lost in it the one we had downtown she complained was too small she couldn't shop ahead but one night I remember when I found some veal gravy she'd put behind the, where are you going . . .

—Fix something to eat, fix some veal Marengo how does that sound Freddie? Haven't eaten all day God knows the last time Freddie had any God damned string tangled up here what's, gum stuck all over his here wait get your sock off how the hell did this get here?

—Somebody jiggling it outside the window there I finally reached out and . . .

—Tom why the hell did you do that.

—Why did I do it because it was driving me crazy! trying to, to get some work done here I finally . . .

—No but why did you have to do it Tom, somebody up there only God damned thing keeps them going's maybe they'll get that quarter out there why couldn't you just let them . . .

—What quarter what are you talking about Jack how can you, fixing chicken Marengo look you're not even . . .

—Veal Marengo Tom, veal Marengo.

—All right veal Marengo! You can't even, how the hell can you fix it the oven's full of mail there's no gas anyhow what do you . . .

—Freeze dried Tom don't need the stove at all do we Freddie, add hot water got plenty of God damned hot water here just drop this dried up thing in it unfolds into veal Marengos like those God damned Japanese paper flowers got some grape drink too, we can . . .

—Damn it Jack listen what are you trying to do I mean how real is all this anyhow, they gave you some tests told you to come back tomorrow what . . .

—Anemia swollen lymph nodes astronomical white count how God damned real do you want it to be! Kills thirty thousand a year chronic and acute models, chronic lets you hang around a year or two tell all your friends goodbye twenty times, mine looks like the God damned sports model get there faster now do you . . .

—So you're going to sit here in wet clothes and . . .

—Going to sit here with Freddie drink this God damned grape drink and eat this God damned veal Marengo aren't we Freddie, read aloud from Skyscraper Management have a few choruses on the guitar and wait for the God damned telephone to look out there she is . . . !

—Watch that mail! damn it . . .

—Yes hello? hello . . . ? No who's . . . looking for what . . . ? Look call the company's public relations agency they can . . . no what here? No listen . . . wouldn't advise it right now no we . . . No no just a, a bomb scare yes we just had a bomb scare they're . . . yes clearing the building right now goodb . . . sorry can't wait yes goodbye . . .

—What was that, see why I took the phone off?

—Christ knows something of Bast's, school field trip wants to tour company headquarters can't find it listen Tom how long was this God damned thing off the hook she might have called back and . . .

—She didn't call back I just told you that Jack, the only call you had was some lawyer named Coen he said Mrs Angel told him I might know where you were, look while I think of it . . .

—No but wait did he say what it was about?

—Something about what you did with that stock you had in her father's company and her husband, he said her husband had had a misadventure look while I . . .

—What Norman? What happened what did he . . .

—Just said he's had a misadventure look while I . . .

—No but Stella did he say she'd call or anything, or . . .

—Didn't ask him I thought she was the last person you wanted to hear from, things you've said about her God compared to Marian with the knives out demanding a winner you just ask for it sometimes Jack, you . . .

—Whole God damned point no you don't know what Stella's asking of you, finally realize she's not asking a God damned thing never expected a God damned thing you end up not asking a God damned thing of yourself that's what I, this book why it's going to be so God damned hard to tell . . .

—I know look while I think of it, has somebody named Gall ever called me here?

—I just, no.

—Young writer I gave him my play to read strange I've never heard from him, he really pressed me for a look at it I thought he could read it with a fresh eye sort of this generation point of view he showed up there one day in my office just before I quit, said he was a great admirer of my novel did I ever tell you what that secretary asked me Jack? Girl named Carol she'd just heard I'd written a book she was really wide eyed, first the standard what's it about how long is it how long did it take you and then do you know what she said? Where are you going . . .

—Get some grape drink. Like some grape drink Freddie?

—Jack what the hell is this about grape drink haven't you got some scotch?

—Just grape drink Tom, acquired taste have to get used . . .

—No look something like this happening and you're drinking grape drink Jack what do you . . .

—Like what Tom. Something like what.

—I mean your, what you just said they told you at the hospital what do you think I . . .

—Just didn't think you'd heard me.

—What do you mean of course I heard you, why I can't see you sitting here waiting for the phone drinking grape drink with this hanging over your . . .

—Because I don't want to show up full of scotch when she calls can't you see that! because it's going to be hard enough to, to tell her this, about this book tell her I'll never finish it never write it Christ one thing the one God damned thing she ever really thought I . . .

—Wait what's that, listen . . .

—What . . .

—No I thought I heard something, somebody out there at the door did I bring in those cigarettes?

—Right there under your . . .

—Yes and Carol I was telling you did I tell you? what she said? She asked me if it was interesting, if my novel was interesting imagine asking a novelist that? if his novel's interesting?

—Really can't, Tom. Imagine that Freddie? Asking a nov . . .

—No it's strange you know that sense of order you get in an office I almost miss it? that sense of intimacy this girl Carol she'd sit on the edge of my desk God I really was stupid you know? short yellow dress probably why she sat that way look right up wherever I look I, Jack I took David for a walk in the woods yesterday even looking up at a tree that open scar where a branch is gone that long oval shaggy edge like the lips pulled open God even coffee this morning, pouring milk from the carton how it comes out in spurts Jack I've got to tell you this I, last night coming back

I stopped for a light down on Third a girl came over and, she came up to the car ten dollars a french right there in the car all I had was a twenty she said she, she said I live right in here my sister can change it Jack I gave her the twenty I just gave it to her, sat there waiting I sat there watching the building waiting for her to come out I must have sat there for ten minutes before I, till I finally . . .

—Really can't give me this can you Tom.

—What give you what . . .

—Never mind look, do you want something to eat?

—No now wait give you what I, Jack I just told you something I'd never tell anybody all you can say is . . .

—I said never mind God damn it do you want . . .

—No now wait damn it this book is that what you mean this book? this excuse you've got now for not writing this book you've been . . .

—Excuse Tom Jesus!

—I just meant look I mean being objective Jack facing it honestly instead of this turning it into this Tolstoy play this, to make the whole world know what it lost that's all I'm saying, this I shall write nothing the world will have to understand all by itself . . .

—Even take this away wouldn't you Tom, even try to take this away wouldn't you.

—All right listen do you know what I found on the floor here cleaning up? Your notes all your notes for this book I put them up here look, footmarks pages torn look at them Jack it was all over before you found this out wasn't it, before you even went down to the hosp . . .

—Like that string there, God damned wad of gum on that string out there rain or shine hope they'd get that God damned quarter you couldn't even let them have that, could you Tom.

—No now wait . . .

—You hungry Freddie?

—No wait listen can't you see what I, Jack I stopped at a diner last night on the way down sitting alone at that counter I could feel a, grilled cheese sandwich I could almost feel a head inside mine chewing I could hear it like a hollow, like an old head like an old head inside mine chewing I even looked around to see if anybody else heard it or, or saw it God can't you see what . . .

—Look just tell me one . . .

—Cigarette look at the end of it's wet teeth separating I mean can't you see what I . . .

—Look Tom, do you want any of this God damned veal Marengo or not.

—No I, no . . .

—You Freddie? What do you, wait what the hell's going on out there . . .

—Is that, sounds like somebody at the door . . .

—First class funeral out front three, four black Cadillacs bastards came a little early didn't they move your, here get Moody's out of the way sit right here Freddie vea pasar los cadáveres de sus enemigos how's that.

—Jack? Man at the door here you'd better talk to him he . . .

—Sit in the front door watch the bodies of . . .

—Says he's a deputy U S marshal Jack he's got some kind of subpoena for . . .

—Bring him in, come in Mister Marshal pick up that cup by your foot there pour you some grape drink, want to bring in the can Tom?

—Wait now who's Mister, sorry somebody taking a bath here?

—No no tub's free now go right ahead, don't stand on ceremony here do we Tom hand Mister Marshal one of those little red boxes . . .

—Jack stop it look this man's a federal marshal, he's . . .

—Drovie my name's Drovie now which one of you's Mister, papers right here wait a minute, Urquhart? Mister Teets? Mister Bast? Mister . . .

—Look Marshal my name is Eigen Thomas Eigen I'm a writer this is Mister Gibbs, whatever this is all about we're not even . . .

—Don't get all hot and bothered friend, SEC just wants your company's officers and directors downtown to answer a few questions bring along your records . . .

—Got the Boswell Sisters doing Down on the Delta think they'd like that one Tom? Muddy water used to be my playground, dudu . . .

—Be quiet Jack look Marshal, whatever this company you're talking about we don't even . . .

—J R Corp isn't that the name of it? Papers right here yes, see here? J R Corp, now what about that rear apartment is that part of . . .

—Wouldn't go back there Marshal got the abominable snowman back there he'd . . .

—Jack be quiet . . .

—Be quick, jump over the God damned somebody else at the door . . .

—Don't pay any attention to him Marshal he's just had some news that upset him acting a little difficult but . . .

—See all kinds in my business friend, like to use your telephone though if you . . .

—Can't use it, Tom? Tell him no outgoing calls God damned door here's ready to, just a minute, Tom? Only take incoming calls show him the phone bill I said just a minute!

—Mister Gibbs? is that . . .

—Yes just a, Bast . . . !

—I'm sorry to bother you Mister Gibbs I've just . . .

—No no here wait get the door . . .

—What are you whispering for what's . . .

—Before you go in look there's a U S marshal in there he's, wait turn around Christ what's happened to you!

—No I'm all right what does he want, is it the bomb?

—What bomb he's got a fistful of subpoenas for this company you're mixed up with will you tell me what the . . .

—But I have to get my mail is there any mail for me?

—Roughly sixty pounds now look . . .

—But Mister Crawley do you know if he got that tape? did he send my . . .

—He's delighted yes told me to tell you the sonorous torns of ho, toes of damn it listen . . .

—But the check he was going to pay me, did he say . . .

—Said he'd sent it yes some project didn't work out but he's a man of his word now look can you tell me what the hell's . . .

—Jack? Who's out there . . .

—Nobody just the, just the mail Tom be right in look Bast, go across the street watch the front window soon as this marshal leaves I'll . . .

—I can't no I ran into somebody some people they're waiting for me out there Mister Gibbs if you could . . .

—Not that funeral now listen . . .

—No well sort of yes if I can get a ride home to get some clothes, if you could sort of entertain the marshal till they're gone the cars I mean, if you could look in the mail for me Mister Gibbs that check before anything happens to it . . .

—I'll try yes but God damn it some things I have to talk to you about Bast something I, look out wait what the hell is all this?

—You the place order the box lunches?

—Christ bring them in why not, Bast? you all right?

—Not really but if you could look in the mail Mister Gibbs could I take a box lunch?

—Here take two good God don't look like you can get as far as watch your case, whole God damned thing's coming apart there watch the stairs . . . !

—Jack? Who's this what's all this . . .

—Box lunches Tom ordered in some box lunches, not enough veal Marengo to go round if this keeps up here just put them look put them on the God damned floor, want to sign for them Tom? Got another customer here . . .

—How do you do my name is Bailey, I have a sub . . .

—Come right in Bailey just step over that's it, pick up a box lunch go right in join the . . .

—Whole damn door just came off Jack.

—No place to put it just lean it against, yes? help you?

—Come to do the phone, man.

—What do you mean do the phone.

—Like the tap man I mean do the tap, like my people tell me the tap's out I come up to replace it, like I mean where's the chick.

—No more chicks look just do your tap and do it God damned fast waiting for an important call here and I'm wait Bailey this way, go that way the lampshades will get you come in and meet Marshal Drovie, bring in another lunch for the marshal there Tom?

—Hey there Bill how they hanging.

—Hey Bill, you on this one too?

—Civil action thought I'd never find it, sorted out the players yet?

—Looks like Teets and Urquhart here where's my scorecard, might be Bast there by the . . .

—Got his picture here from yesterday's paper, hard to tell what he looks like all these feathers but . . .

—Look Marshal I just told you my name's Eigen and this is . . .

—Who's that by the window Bill, description of the company president they gave me from some magazine here says steel blue eyes bulldog jaw . . .

—God damn it wait a minute, him? I mean look at that face Marshal not a God damned thing's happened there for thirty years, completely uncontaminated by getting on in the world think you'd ever see that face in a God damned board room? Find a trace of one mean small God damned thought there other little bastards trying to take advantage of him Marshal, get his National Park set imperforates for those God damned Duetsches Reich surcharges . . .

—Look Jack will you stop . . .

—Never see faces like that do you Marshal, hope without expectation never see that do you, acceptance without resignation . . .

—Subpoena here for the company records too, books correspondence memos any phone tapes . . .

—Got a spade cat in there doing a tap for you right now all got rhythm haven't they Bailey, try to dig up some records for you just promised the Boswell Sisters to the marshal here but . . .

—Jack listen . . .

—In the bottoms how I used to play round, Lordy what a spankin I got . . .

—Damn it Jack stop singing these men are serious they . . .

—Just trying to entertain them Tom looking for books too, anything special Marshal? Twenty years of the Musical Courier right over here how about novels, got some God damned fine novels just have to dig for them, like Broch Bailey? Came across his Schlafwandler the other day spent the whole God damned afternoon with it . . .

—May better just get a fire inspector in here and then get an order seal the whole place up Bill, any other agencies in this?

—Probably get Tippy up here from Internal Revenue better get a postal inspector in here too, take a look back here Bill . . .

—Now just a minute Marshal I have some personal mail that . . .

—What's these piles E Gerst, B Best, R Gast all sound like AKAs don't they Bill, haven't seen a mess like this since the Scungilli brothers.

—Infinite riches in a little room, Merchant of Venice isn't it Bailey? Want to read us the whole passage there's probably a copy in that H-O box there, don't mind if I run through these piles while we're waiting do you Marshal? Sent away for some dance lessons I can't wait to . . .

—Seriously Marshal you can't simply come in here and subpoena everything in sight I have some personal effects that . . .

—Box he's pawing through there Tom ask him if he's got a subpoena for the Three Wide Men listen ever think of that God damned game we made up that night? Remember it we could sweep the country make a million dollars tell you what I'll do, leave you my royalties if you can ever remem . . .

—No now seriously Marshal I have some papers here that may be worth a good deal, manuscripts that sort of thing they've got nothing to do with whatever you're after here that box right behind you, it's got the manuscript of a book I wrote in it and there's another one, a folder I've been looking for notes and manuscript it belongs to an estate . . .

—Don't get hot and bothered friend everything gets inventoried, wait listen there Bill hear that?

——ther report brought to you every day at this time by She, the magazine today's wom . . .

—Sound like it's coming from over there Bill somebody under the . . .

—Meant to tell you Marshal shipwreck here last night may have caught the cabin boy when the cargo shifted, they still in business out front there Freddie? Kids all over the place truck a block long's got the funeral hemmed in can't leave now Marshal, haven't even opened your box lunch let's see what they gave you, ham and cheese banana cupcake pickle wedge not leaving now are you Tom?

—These papers I found in my pocket yes, I ought to . . .

—Golf game in the corner there thought we might spread it out get up a foursome water hazards and all, like golf Bailey?

—No seriously these papers I ought to take them down to Mrs Schramm and Marshal? That folder I mentioned if you come across it, I'm an executor of the estate it belongs to it's a plain manila folder with stains all over it just be sure I, I just want to be sure nothing happens to it you know she might have some interest in it Jack I, Marshal there's no reason I can't leave? Those names you read I'm not even . . .

—Parties answer their subpoenas in court or we're out with an arrest warrant that's all friend, hear that Bill it's coming from way under there . . .

—————Family of Companies. And now the weather. Forty-eight degrees in sunny mid-town. Listen every day at this time for the weather report brought to you by She, the magazine designed for today's wom . . .

—Wait one thing before you . . .

—That ten you wanted I forgot it yes, wait . . .

—So had I, that's not what I . . .

—Five, ten here and, these papers may not be any good to her I've been carrying them around so long I just thought I ought to take them down and . . .

—Meet her yes, probably be God damned grateful, shame you can't take that folder along too show her he was on the threshold of great things, might have kicked the world to pieces . . .

—I don't know what you're, why you can't give me this either can you any credit for, credit for any loyalty to his memory my God see him in that canvas sack it's like being loyal to a nightmare . . .

—Had your choice of nightmares go ahead I mean you've got custody of his memory Christ, all you've done for it certainly got the right to sweep it up with the trash why not take along that picture he had of her too, see you waiting there in the lofty drawing room her pale face floating toward you in the dusk takes both your hands in hers no chick but good Christ she's survived hasn't she, probably tell you she knew him better than you did want to hear his last words give her something to live with, dream the nightmare right through to the God damned end when you come out with it . . .

—What with, what do you mean I . . .

—Mean you'd better fix your trousers in front there first that's all.

—What I, damn it why didn't you . . . he paused half backed between the torrents on either side —Jack damn it you, why the hell you're acting this way . . . he reached his free hand for the doorframe, backed from the light of the doorway —I, I don't understand you . . .

—I know Tom . . . came after him in the dark of the hall where he turned, hand running on the rail feeling for the stairhead and suddenly down two steps at a time from the voice up there in the darkness, —I know . . . he made the door with a final tug at his waist and, hand plunged in an inside pocket as though to clutch the desperate consequence of the papers he'd found there, came out with the lunge of a man abruptly threatened by the weight of the overcast sky.

—Say excuse me, could you tell me where the . . .

—One flight up end of the hall, the door's open . . .

—Want to move that truck buddy? You're blocking the whole . . .

—What's this kid in my car!

—Excuse me just let me get past here . . .

—Out of this God forsaken place, taxi? Taxi . . . !

—Watch where you're pushing that junk heap you crazy bunch of, look out!

—Coño . . . !

—So who finally died?

—This green panel truck where's the driver, tell him to get it the hell out of there.

—Excuse me I'm a reporter from . . .

—Hey Mister Bast we going to the movies?

—You're not going anywhere no now get back in the cars, now where's . . .

—Excuse me I'm a rep . . .

—You kids get away from that car I'll bust your . . .

—Wait I thought these cars were hired for this school group . . .

—This here's a private limousine now get that kid out . . . and the door swung open on the figure cringed in the back, battered portfolio spilling from knees quivering at anchor where a sneaker worked wedged in a gleaming hinge of the jump seat, —out!

—Private limousine what's it doing here, they told me these . . .

—Come up to see my mother that's what it's doing here now get him and his pile of crap out of there before I . . .

—Okay okay holy . . .

—We going to the movies Mister Bast hey wait what happened to your . . .

—I told you to get back in those cars, come on J R hurry up . . .

—Okay how was I supposed to, wait could you hold this stuff a second while I . . .

—I can't no I'm holding enough stuff now get in that first car up there, the rest of you get in the other two hurry up!

—Look at the cowboy coming hey!

—Be quiet just do what I no, it can't be no . . .

—You getting in with me hey Bast? because boy I got this whole bunch of stuff to ask you like . . .

—Yes well I've got a whole bunch to ask you too just get in quick here, get these boxes before they slide off my . . .

—Wait look out for my . . .

—Well get the door closed!

—No but holy, I mean what happened to you anyways you . . .

—I've been on a bus for twenty-six hours I've got a cold I haven't eaten since here look over my shoulder, is he out there? the man in the cowboy . . .

—He's like standing there by these garbage cans looking up at this dump we're parked at who's he suppose to be, I mean what are we doing here anyways we . . .

—That's what I'd like to know! that Mrs diCephalis when I saw her I thought I was having a . . .

—No but where are we, like we fix up this here whole field trip which Mister Davidoff gets these here limousines so we go to this Waldorf place where this general's suppose to excort us which he's not even there and Mister Davidoff they say he already went someplace and will we please leave so . . .

—Driver let's, where is he where's the driver . . .

—So like Mrs diCephalis is suppose to have this here headquarters address to meet you so then we ride around awhile and stop at this dump where she can go in that lousy looking place where its says bodeega to call and they tell her it's this bomb scare then you come down the street in these here funny looking clothes with your . . .

—Just be quiet a minute where's the driver where's that woman look, go find . . .

—What Mrs diCephalis she already went in this taxicab she . . .

—What do you mean went, where . . .

—Well see she has to go to India to show them how to do birth control and all see she's got social studies since Mrs Joubert went so she's always telling us how everybody's real poor down at India so mainly all they do is . . .

—Stop no stop, you mean she brought you all in here and dumped you and went to Ind . . .

—No see she has like this interview at this government thing someplace so she brings us in where it's all fixed up with this here new principal this Mister Stye we got where Mister Davidoff thought it's this neat publicity idea for where we're like buying the school you know? So there's suppose to be this photographer and these here box lunches and you're suppose to excort us and take us around like, so now you come down this street with these wrecked up cars and garbage cans all over in this here funny looking suit with these ripped pants and your eye and all I mean didn't Mister Davidoff even say to . . .

—How could look can't you understand I just got off the never mind let's just get out of here before here, get out your side get the driver and tell the other cars to follow hurry up . . .

—This truck here I can't hardly, wait open your side hey he's coming over this man in this cowboy . . .

—Will you do what I tell you!

—He's knocking on the window wait how does it open there's no turner thing how do you, look hey this button you just push . . .

—Damn it leave it . . . !

—Mister Bast thank heavens I've mercy! what's happened . . .

—Hey who's . . .

—I said get the driver!

—But what's happened are you all right?

—I'm yes I'm fine yes Mister Brisboy I'm sorry we're in a little hurry we . . .

—But what is it who are all these dreadful urchins Mister Bast I simply must talk to you Mother called she says she's been fired! She's simply livid of course that letter from your Piscator person about franchising out the entire health plan already had her in a perfect tizzy I know it's all some sort of ghastly mistake, I told her I knew you wouldn't stand for it of course you're in rather deep yourself aren't you and she's seen all these frightful things in the papers I've had reporters battering at the door of my suite all morning, of course I've told them I won't hear a word against you I know you'd never dream of knowingly doing such a thing but . . .

—Yes well I'm sorry Mister Brisboy I really don't know all the details yet but . . .

—Oh I know I know they're so fearfully rude aren't they, whoever dreamt up that soubriquet gentlemen of the press must have been demented it might have been Kipling mightn't it if there's anything in the language more excruciating than his little ditty If thank heaven I've been spared it I simply don't share the talents for dealing with them your crass little person with all the cufflinks . . .

—Mister Davidoff yes do you know where . . .

—Oh isn't he yes I do think he rather revels in it, if you could have seen him this morning in the company suite making tales up faster than Scheherazade before they pranced off to court all baying after him like jackals about your J R person's court appearance today in this business squabble, of course they're merely whetting their carrion appetites for his squalid paternity suit I'm not one to point a finger you know, but I must say the vision of that Virginia person's bulk wallowing unsheathed on a desktop does add a rather unsavory dimension to our little family of comp . . .

—Yes well I'm sorry Mister Brisboy I can't really . . .

—But there's no earthly reason you should Mister Bast your cold sounds perfectly ghastly and they are such bullies, whining about rude responses to their prying phone calls why I've talked with your Grynszpan person he sounds terribly gracious and I've had no difficulty at all finding the place we're right in this quaint doorway aren't we? I'd just rushed up to my analyst after this excruciating call from Mother so near your amusing neighborhood here I thought I'd run up for a chat . . .

—No what I meant was I've been away I don't really know all the de . . .

—Oh your trip yes of course I simply can't wait to hear every chilling detail, that hilarious story in the paper about the drunken brewer chasing you among the vats with a gun how fortunate the eye came through quite unscathed didn't it, simply all that rather bilious discoloration thank heaven they got your good profile in that splendid picture in Indian attire I do so love pageantry, of course I sent it right off to Mother to reassure her after all these gloomy items in the paper when your stock stopped trading at four your Crawley person's simply gaga over the whole thing isn't he of course they say the poor man's going under what a cutting wind! It does look so cozy in there I wonder if . . .

—No well I think we, I just sent someone to look for the driver I think he . . .

—That urchin yes he's coming with him now of course you know I don't approve your going at all you must be running a frightful fever but I know the courts cannot abide tardiness Mister Bast you must promise me one thing, you must not simply not permit yourself to fall victim to misguided loyalties you know I wouldn't dream of sowing dissension but I simply must say your J R person does begin to sound rather un . . .

—Yes well we, driver? I think we'd bet . . .

—Just a second hey let me get my . . .

—of the confidence Mother and I have in you to mercy one just crept in beside you . . .

—Yes well it's all driver we'd better leave goodbye . . .

—your own work I know you've had so little time but . . . waiting breathlessly to hear . . . only living soul I know with something worth doing . . .

—Hey holy . . .

—about the concert grand . . . ? of a charming Chambolle-Musigny you'll adore . . . care of yourself . . .

—Hey look he's going to get run over if he runs along by us like that holy . . .

—found this delicious new Czech recording of the Kindertotenlieder . . .

—Yes goodbye, goodbye . . .

—to know you're all we have left au voir au voir . . .

—No but who was that suppose to be hey.

—Just be quiet for a minute.

—Sure okay but I mean who was . . .

—Nobody! it, wasn't supposed to be anybody . . .

—Okay I mean you don't need to get mad hey you know what took me so long back there? This here tremendous truck that had us blocked in you know what it was hey what's the matter your eye still hurts?

—Yes.

—Anyways what it was it was this whole shipment of these here ten thousand gross plastic flowers we got at this dock auction from Hong Kong so cheap because the colors were all screwed up you know?

—No.

—Like all these here red daffodils and blue roses and all see these here Chinamen which made them like they had pictures of the shape and all only they don't have them real down at China like here so they just made up all these here dumb colors, I mean I heard this dopey truckdriver he's yelling about all this plastic crap in his truck from Hong Kong I thought it's these here sweaters we sent over there to make them for Eagle I mean didn't they even come yet? And I mean it's both suppose to go up to Union Falls anyways like what's he doing yelling around that dump about J R Corp this address, this here big delivery at J R Corp this address what's he . . .

—You wanted a low-cost operation didn't you!

—Sure but holy, I mean, I mean holy . . .

—Sixty-one forty a month what did you expect for sixty-one forty! what do you think I've been . . .

—No but, no but I mean holy, I mean that was it this here whole world headquarters? that, that dump . . . ?

—Well how do you think we . . .

—No but, no . . .

—Down Park sir?

—Down Park down anything driver it doesn't . . .

—No but wait hey Bast we're not going back now are we how come you . . .

—Because it's the only way I can get a ride home that's why, because I've . . .

—No but we only . . .

—Because I've got exactly thirty-seven cents that's why! because I've got to get rid of these clothes because I've got a cold and a fever and my head's splitting that's why! Because I haven't slept I haven't eaten since that box give it to me, that white box . . .

—No but . . .

—Take the other one eat it go ahead open it eat it it's your, one of your forty-eight cent tax dollar box lunches your neat guy Davidoff got for this so-called what made you do this anyhow, now today what made you do it!

—It just, it seemed like a good idea . . .

—Well it wasn't it wasn't a good idea, of all the . . .

—I wanted to see it! I, I just, wanted . . .

—All right don't, here get your foot down have you got a handker-chief?

—Sure just, just a second . . .

—No you, use it. Stop sniffling and use it.

—I just, always, I mean I always thought this is what it will be like you and, and me riding in this here big limousine down, down this, this here big street . . .

—Well we, we are, here . . .

—No I, I mean like we . . .

—I know what you mean here, eat your sandwich.

—But, okay . . . hey?

—What.

—Right there that big white place, what is it . . .

—A club an embassy I don't know, why.

—I just always thought we'd, we'd, nothing. You want your pickle?

—No.

—Like I'll trade it for half my . . .

—Just take it!

—Okay I mean you don't have to get mad about it, I just . . .

—I'm not mad about it about a damn pickle haven't you heard anything I've said? Don't you know where I've been what's going on out there haven't you seen the . . .

—Like that's what I'm trying to find out only you keep interrupting, I mean this here whole big thing where you're dressed up in this neat Indian wait a second it's under here . . .

—Look that's yesterday's paper I mean what just hap . . .

—No but I mean all this expense we went to and all and this old chief giving you this here pipe he looks like he's wearing this cheap kid's Indian suit with these crumby chicken feathers sticking up and like who's this old fart standing back here looks like a . . .

—That's Senator Milliken and those are crumby chicken feathers, when I got up in this fancy dress Davidoff rented for three hundred dollars Charley Yellow Brook's father showed up for the picture in smelly jeans and that idiot with the appliances said he didn't look like a real Indian, he sent that stupid kid of his to the dime store and that's what he brought back size eight that's what started things off . . .

—I know it tells about it in this here neat story, echoing to the dip of paddles the hum of arrows and the legendary cry Howee! the dramatic reenactment of history unfolding here today promises to rekindle tribal hopes and loyalties smoldering from bygone times like the coals of some forgotten campf . . .

—Look this here neat story was written before anything happened like that picture, it was taken before they'd been pushed too far and exploded can't you understand that? It's a press release your neat guy Davidoff wrote from the script what he wanted to happen not what really happened, it was handed out the night before to get it in the papers the same day the . . .

—No but what do you mean exploded like they couldn't even do it? I mean we have to go spend all this here money learning them how to row these canoes and shoot off these here bow and arrows like they can't hardly do anything for theirself? Like we're trying to help them out to like rekindle this here tribal spirit and defend their hunting grounds and all only they're so dumb they don't even know their own history so then we have to go pay this here topflight writer to fix them up with one so they can have this here dram . . .

—He did that all right he rekindled their tribal spirit that's what I'm telling you, when they read it when they read about the rapes and famines their forefathers forced off their treaty reservation marching a thousand miles barefoot in the middle of winter to the one they're on now the hum of arrows I wished Davidoff was there to hear them, these stoves and washing machines and the rest of that junk pieces of it spread all over the . . .

—No but wait hey wait hey wait a second holy, I mean like that

inventory was worth like holy shit I mean one washing machine retails
at a hundred nine, ninety-sev, they couldn't of I mean they, they couldn't
of . . .

—Well they did nobody ever thought of finding out if . . .

—No but wait a second I mean, I mean just because they get mad
about these here forefeathers marching around in the snow in these here
bygone times so they go wreck up this whole tremendous gift which
v e're trying to help them out like what did we ever do to them! I mean
no wait a second like it says down here look, forging this here human
betterment wait a second here, cause of human betterment to forge a
two edge sword severing past from future at one fell swoop in the un un,
unprecedented gift of a full range of modern electrical appliances from
the Endo subsider, sidiary of the worldwide J R Cor . . .

—That's the point they don't have electricity! Nobody ev . . .

—What?

—Electricity they don't have electricity! these Indians the reservation there's no electricity nobody ever thought of finding out if . . .

—How can't they have electricity I mean everybody's got electricity, I mean you just turn on the . . .

—That's what that Hyde idiot that Mister Hyde you sent out with
your appliances that's what he thought, the little talk he wrote bringing
them civilization he even sent you a copy in this mess somewhere do you
want to read it? Markets production lines what America's all about till
they came after him with . . .

—No but, no but wait a second was he . . .

—He was out there waving a hair dryer at them shouting come and
get me they did too when that awful kid of his started . . .

—No but wait Bast wait wait was that wasn't this same Mister Hyde
that's holy, this kid was he . . .

—Up there with his knives and coils of rope blowing the Call to the
Colors on his bugle he would have been scalped if he'd had enough hair
to . . .

—No but I, not this same kid I, this same Mister Hyde at the school?
How could . . .

—Well you hired him didn't you?

—No I mean, like I mean how did I know that's where he works I
thought . . .

—This kid of his you knew he was going didn't you? he's a friend of
yours isn't he?

—No but, no I mean he just said he's getting this special permission
to go on this here very important trip with his father so he'll write this
here essay what America has to protect and all where, but what happened where . . .

—Somebody finally got him with a shovel they're holding his father
till you give them this thirty million dol . . .

—Dollars? thirty million dollars for him? I mean what do they think we . . .

—The thirty million you already agreed on for this twenty year lease they want it now in cash, Charley Yellow Brook drove me to the bus in that smashed up Cadillac they . . .

—No but wait a second I mean we already agreed we'll give them it in these royalties out of earnings I mean why should they get it off us now before we even get to . . .

—Because this here neat history you fixed them up with, it got them so upset about that thousand mile winter hike they're afraid the government will send them back to that original treaty reservation and put this one up for sale they want the money to buy it that's all, just give them the money and . . .

—What do you mean just give them the money! this old man Hyde you think he's worth like thirty mil . . .

—I don't think he's worth a nickel no! but if they have to buy something that's already theirs you've got what you wanted haven't you? these leases? You've already agreed to thirty mil . . .

—No but that's different than like getting it all at once . . .

—Where do you ever get it borrow it, that's all you ever talk about building these here assets so you can borrow another three five ten what's the difference it's just numbers isn't it? Just numbers on paper half the time you don't even know where the dot goes you don't even . . .

—No but you didn't already tell them we'll do it did you? I mean like give them this here whole lump thirty mil . . .

—Of course I did, Charley Yellow Brook yes I gave him my word we'd . . .

—No but look hey . . .

—Look hey nothing all you've done from the start is whine about what I don't do I don't take an interest don't take responsibility well this time I have, I gave him my word I expect to live up to . . .

—No but anyways that's okay you don't have to live up to anything see because you didn't have this here arthurization to . . .

—Why didn't I have it I'm supposed to be executive officer of this whole, this whole mess nobody has to give me authority to . . .

—No but see that's the thing you're not.

—What do you mean I'm not that's all you've been . . .

—Because you got fired that's what I been waiting to tell you, I mean after how you loused up everything like I mean I try to fix everything up for you and I mean if it's just you you're lousing up but like you go lousing up everything for everybody what do you . . .

—Stop no stop of all the, get your foot down what do you mean, you've been waiting to tell me you fired me while I was gone? Waiting to see if your Indian deal worked out now you think I loused everything up so you decide I was fired before I ever went out there so you won't have to part with this thirty mil look don't start getting out these torn up newspapers I don't want to see them just tell me, is that it?

—No wait a second see it's not even . . .

—I mean don't misunderstand me being fired nothing could be better nothing could make me happier, this helping you out again just this once if I'd never . . .

—No but it wasn't me Bast I didn't fire you they did, you . . .

—It's never you it's always they who's they, if you'd . . .

—These here lenders that got pissed off when you sold your stock and screwed up everything that's what I'm trying to tell you, these here banks and . . .

—What do you mean when I sold my stock, all I . . .

—I mean boy you can even ask Nonny if there's this one thing I always said it's to keep this here whole thing exactly legal and I mean with all these here option terms and bylaws and all if there's this here one thing I thought you wouldn't do it's that, I mean after I go fix everything up so you don't get screwed by these income taxes and you go sell it off so it's taxed like this here straight salary I was saving you from? Like this here suit says you sold at eleven and a half that's like fifty-seven thousand five hundred I mean that's over fifty-four thousand dollars, that's this fifty-three percent rate that's like they're taking like twenty-seven thousand just the government that's not even the state which they're these real shits boy and I mean that's not even . . .

—Wait the only thing you've said I ever heard of is this salary you've been saving me from that's the whole . . .

—No but that's not even counting all this legal stuff too, I mean like they're always saying this here friend in need is this friend indeed boy I must be this real big friend then I . . .

—It doesn't mean that it doesn't mean the one who's in need, it means the friend who comes to help the one who's in . . .

—I know boy I mean you've like got this whole fifty-seven thousand dollars and boy am I in nee . . .

—No now stop look, listen what makes you think I just told you didn't I? I've got thirty-seven cents? What makes you think I sold my stock I just used it to borrow some money, this salary you've been saving me from what did you expect me to do I had about four dollars it's the one thing your neat guy Davidoff's ever done that made sense, he worked out something with Mister Crawley so I could . . .

—No but okay what's the difference, I mean you go sell off your stock for like fifty-seven thousand dollars or you give it to this bank someplace for collateral and loan this here fifty-seven thousand dollars off them then they go sell it for fifty-seven thousand dollars, I mean you still got this here fifty-seven thou . . .

—I don't have it! I never had it listen . . .

—And I mean this whole option thing like when I fixed it up to help you out so instead you're yelling at me on the phone where were you suppose to get this fifty thousand dollars so you could like exercise it so now you . . .

—I borrowed it and paid it right back how do you think I . . .

—No but I mean how could you pay it right back if you didn't go sell off this here stock that's what I mean! And I mean anyway there's this whole law which you can't loan money off banks to go buy stock with it on top of you even told me that time on the phone you're not selling it, I mean that's what's this here tremendous like disappointment you know Bast? I mean like you didn't have any confidence in this here whole enterprise and like all this here corporate loyalty where we used each other and all like you didn't even hardly be . . .

—Listen first I didn't sell the stock I didn't tell the bank to sell it either, second I didn't borrow money from a bank to buy it I borrowed it from my aunts. I used their stock to borrow enough to buy this stock on this option and then I used this stock to borrow seven thousand dollars Mister Davidoff said would be waiting and the rest of it to pay back the loan on my aunts' stock and put it back in their account with Mister Crawley, now that's all I . . .

—What he keeps it all in this street name down there?

—Here we are, sir.

—Because if he does these here aunts better watch out hey . . .

—Wait a minute, what driver? Where, we're where . . .

—Pennsylvania Station.

—What are we doing here, we want . . .

—Our instructions sir, bring your group back to the Penn . . .

—I thought you were taking us back out to Long Island, we . . .

—See because if Crawley and Wiles and these here brokers need all this collateral for these here big loans they're . . .

—Be quiet, driver? Listen take us out there anyhow you can just put it on the same bill, this company that . . .

—Can't do that sir I don't have the authoriza . . .

—Well I'll give it to you I'm giving you the authorization!

—Can't do that sir I don't have the authorization to accept your authori . . .

—See they're getting this real hard time from these commodity exchanges for all this margin money since these here bellies dropped so . . .

—Be quiet! look do you know who, wait have you got any cash?

—Well, well sure but . . .

—All right, driver? We'll just pay cash then how much will . . .

—Can't do that sir our franchise don't permit . . .

—Why can't, why didn't you just say so! Here come on, let's . . .

—You want this rest of this here cupcake?

—Bring it bring everything yes you can't leave . . .

—Okay could you hold this a second while I . . .

—I can't hold anything a second here give me that box and get what's that on the floor there . . .

—Boy if I lost that it's this tape player thing, have you got these here tapes off the phone hey? Because . . .

—Get that banana on the armrest please sir?

—See because Piscator said they're like subpoening all these here phone tapes which we want to hear them before . . .

—Will you get that damn banana! Here the rest of you, this way, this way . . .

—We going to the movies Mister Bast?

—That guy with all the heads could we go see him hey?

—These women wrestling these eels . . .

—We're not going anywhere we're going home! now here stay together . . . !

—Because this whole trade deal was loused up too you were suppose to fix up where Ray-X can't get this rhodium from this place Gandia where they're having this here war so there's this dumb law you can't buy exports off them so there's this trade delegate guy from this broken down country Malwi right by this place Gandia you were suppose to see him at the Waldorf before you . . .

—Down this way stay together . . .

—Where you couldn't get this export license to like export these bellies down to China so like if we exported them to this place Malwi where they export them down to China we could like one percent this money from them into this Gandia and one percent this here rhodium back out and then like just import it here with this Malwi as country of origin do you have to walk so fast hey? I'm dropping . . .

—Here this way all of you hurry up . . . !

—So then this here Malwi place goes and gets sucked in this same dumb war . . .

—I said stay together!

—And these talks they're having at the Senate about trading with China and Russia and all, this Senator Broos breaks them off and all these bellies drop so Crawley and Wiles and these brokers get pissed off at me because they're getting this hard time from these commodity exchanges over all this here margin money which I haven't got it so they have to hey wait a second . . .

—There's our track hurry up the train's in four min, where's where did he . . .

—He's over there getting a newspaper could we get some candy?

—No! get the train I'll get him, of all the sorry excuse me, of all the, sorry . . .

—Oh hey Bast? Have you got some change I can't reach my . . .

—Just leave it! the train's . . .

—But I already took the paper you said you have thirty-sev . . .

—Just, damn it here! Now hurry up . . .

—Boy you almost knocked that old wom . . .

—I don't care hurry up!

—Hey wait up hey my shoelace holy . . .

—Stop that pushing up there! stay togeth . . .

—Boy I barely made it if you would have . . .

—Just sit down will you? The rest of you up there sit down . . .

—Do you want by the window or . . .

—I don't care just sit down!

—Okay just let me get my foot over these new laces boy I almost lost my sneaker back there, could you move your . . .

—I can't move anything no get your foot down, can't you just . . .

—Where am I suppose to put it!

—Try the floor! and get your knee out of my . . .

—No but I have to set this thing up to play these here telephone tapes so we can hear what . . .

—Listen if you want to play tapes go find another seat, I'm . . .

—No but we have to hear them before they get subpoened I mean how do we even know what's on them. I mean like you sent me one once where right in the middle of I'm telling you where we're getting this hard time on these Ace mining claims from this here Interior Department suddenly there's this singing and you hear this guy say you have just heard somebody Fisher dishcloth singing this here foreign . . .

—I thought the tape was blank! I, I tried to get some things off that junk pocket radio that's all, what difference does . . .

—Because if they subpoen them that's why! Because this here old lady Begg she's suing me too she's subpoening everything for where we took over at Eagle so if there's this tape where I'm saying how we're protecting these here stockholders like where Eagle's losing all this money so we move everything down at Georgia so we can . . .

—Look you're spilling papers all . . .

—Wait it's under here, I mean we even try to help out this dump Union Falls with this whole big cemetery thing and like giving them these Eagle properties for this here park and speedway so how this old lady Begg thanks us she goes around telling these here other old stockholders how I screwed them converting my preferred stock into common to like get control so I could wait here it is look, the Begg Action is a consolidated class action brought by former stockholders of Eagle wait no this one's yours, where's . . .

—My what, what's . . .

—Where she's pissed off at you too here, the Action arises out of alleged violations of Section ten b of the Securities Exchange Act of nineteen thirty-four and rule ten b five progul, mul, progulma . . .

—Promulgated give me that! what's, she's suing me too?

—You didn't need to grab it, I mean you didn't get one? Piscator sent me this here cop . . .

—Wait now just because she's suing you I didn't even know what the, I just went up there and ate that disgusting candle salad with . . .

—No but see she's suing you for this whole other thing hey, like where I took over this control to protect these here stockholders where their J R Corp equity went way up if they would have sold see? Only when it went down and they sell at like five and an eighth like this old lady Begg so they're all pissed off at you for getting this eleven and a half where you knew what's going on inside ahead of time . . .

—Inside what, I . . .

—Like inside the company and all that's why they call it this insider suit see where you're this here . . .

—Inside? that's, how could I be inside there isn't any inside! How could anybody believe the, the only inside's the one inside your head like these statements you make, these tapes you play over the phone to these newspapers virgin minerals gas discoveries the health plan of tomorrow travel of the future some reporter even found me out there he said he understood we were freezing sound now what kind of a . . .

—No but wait that was right in the paper hey, just . . .

—Look don't start digging through that trash again can't you see it's all just . . .

—No but that's what I been telling you about protecting these here stockholders trying to keep the price up of their stock, I mean where these like security analysts are making this big deal out of like where Ray-X is getting screwed with these big penalties on these old fixed price contracts where they can't get this here rhodium and like recalling these products, like these old cruds with these heart pacer things quit working so they have to go get these new ones replanted in them where we even have to pay the hospital and all, and I mean right when we get these here big cost-plus look, here it is look. Frigicom, a process now being de wait, operating at faster than sound speeds, a complex process employing liquid nitrogen will be used to convert the noise shards . . .

—Listen can't you understand? it's just like that story about the Indian res . . .

—What where they wrecked up everything? No but see why these here students threw rocks at General Haight see this university down there by Ray-X where we did them this big real estate favor right when he comes down there to get this here honorable degree these students get pissed off at these big military contracts we got them for research development to like help them out you know? Where this same shithead this Senator Broos he starts these secret hearings where they're like reviewing this defense budget, I mean it's like this here hundred billion dollars so his crumby Armed Service Committee they're making this big deal out of this lousy thirty-eight million about cost overruns where they

been having these technical problems with these here shards and all hey?
hey Bast?

—What.

—You looked like you weren't listening, I mean did you ever know
we hired Mister diCephalis hey?

—No and I don't really . . .

—I mean I didn't even know it either, see they got him from this
computer executive employment place where everybody's this here
number so we're looking for this skilled psychological personnel guy
which it exactly matched his number isn't that funny hey?

—Funniest thing I can . . .

—I know I mean I didn't even know it till we just sent him down to
see this big scientist he hired us down there at Texas this here Doctor
Vogel you know? Like I even saw in the paper we told him don't come
back if they can't fix up these technical problems with these here noise
shards and this big thing I been waiting to tell you hey look. See where
it says here a method of transport so new it remains classified top secret-
sensitive by the Defense Department I mean I couldn't even tell you it
over the phone you know? I mean we already set up this here whole
subsiderary for it what it is it's called Teletravel, see what it is is this hey?
Hey Bast?

—What what . . .

—I thought you went to sleep, I mean I'm telling you this here
tremendous . . .

—Look the conductor's waiting will you pay him for my . . .

—We all got return tickets this time see so I don't . . .

—Well I didn't! Pay him.

—Okay don't get mad, I mean could you just hold this stuff a
second . . . ? Paper scraps, handkerchief wad, the wadded bills came out,
coins —hey? Could you give me . . .

—Look I just bought your newspaper I don't even have the thirty-
sev . . .

—No I mean if you give me seventeen cents I won't have to break
this here quarter see then you can . . .

—Pay him!

—I am! but, wait give me two cents then I won't have to break this
nick okay okay! You don't need to get so mad and I mean this here
newspaper you can put it on your expen wait, wait where is it . . .

—You . . .

—No but where is it! holy, it must have dropped is it by your feet
hey?

—You probably dropped it in the station get another one, what
difference . . .

—No but all this stuff's happening today I have to see what happened, I mean this here whole court thing and this explosion they're like

setting off underground out there for this here big gas deposit where these like radicals they've been going around telling the newspapers and everybody it's so dangerous and getting this here injunction to what's the matter hey, how come you're shivering.

—Be, cause I'm cold . . .

—How could you be cold you're like sweating all down your . . .

—Look just, just get this stuff of yours off my lap I'm going to take a nap.

—What like go to sleep? No but wait a second we got all this stuff to go over and these tapes and all I mean . . .

—I told you get another seat, you can lis . . .

—No but you need to help me out listening I mean how do I even know whose voice they are talking, I mean like I'm always reading this stuff in the paper where this company spokesman makes this statement which I don't even know who it is like this here whole explosion thing, it says this company spokesman which prefers to remain anonymous says what's the difference if the whole state blows up who would even miss it so Senator Milliken gets real pissed off and we have to go . . .

—Look I haven't even been here how can I . . .

—No but that's what I mean Bast, like who just said it's this bomb threat and these here company spokesmen I don't hardly know who anybody is anymore like this here Mister Greenspan, I mean Piscator said he's up there helping you out when you went which you didn't even tell me so he goes and sells off this whole old Ray-X inventory right when we're writing it off did you even know that?

—No I don't even know where he . . .

—Me neither I mean I ask Piscator so all he knows he says they talked French so it must be somebody down at France, see they bought it all at retail and paid cash so at first Piscator's taking all this credit like he tried that time with that neat Triangle deal it was really Beamish that figured up, see so if we hear these here tapes we can . . .

—Can't you understand I haven't been here? Any tapes I've got were made before I left I've just been carrying them around to give you with the rest of this trash. I don't know what's on them I don't even know if that tape thing's still on the phone, I come back and the place is full of marshals waving subpoenas somebody sticks his head in the car window and says you're firing everybody franchising your health plan on your way to court Crawley's going under how am I sup . . .

—But that's what I been trying to tell you! I mean where Crawley and these here brokers get pissed off at me where they have to go borrow all this here margin money off these same banks they helped get us these big loans off of so then these big lenders start yelling how they have to protect theirself, so I mean I have to go put all this stock in this here voting trust which they control it so they won't call these here old loans on us and they'll go through with these here new ones so then you go sell off your stock and they're really pissed off, I mean then they get to dump our directors and hire this bunch of new ones which get to fire the whole J R Corp management and sue me for this here erotic . . .

—So it's my fault is that what you mean?

—No well sort of see bec . . .

—Because a bank sells my stock and gets me fired for selling it and then somebody sues me while you're running around getting loans for this here asset to borrow against for this here new asset to look haven't I told you to stop? when the whole thing started? just stop and let somebody help you pull things together instead of this more! more! The more you get the hungrier you get by this time you don't even know how much you, I mean who would believe it who would be, any of it who would believe it.

—No but that's what you do! I mean where they said if you're playing anyway so you might as well play to win but I mean even when you win you have to keep playing! Like these brokers these underwriters these banks everything you do somebody's getting this percent for theirself this commission this here interest where they all know each other so they're fixing up these deals giving you all this here advice which they're these big experts how am I supposed to stop everything!

—If you hadn't been so cheap if you'd just hired somebody who knew what. . .

—Okay so I even write out this whole bunch of rules where one says hire smart people but run things yourself if they're so smart how can you run anything! I mean this Mister Greenspan he's so smart everybody else is hiring him like Crawley says he has this surefooted grasp of market trends he tries to hire him he even said this Leva tried to hire him so I mean I try to call him up they just leave the phone hang there I don't even know . . .

—Look will you just get this pile of stuff off my . . .

—Okay wait let me find this one financial column it says he's like maybe this like greasy eminence behind the whole meteoric rise of J R Corp I mean I don't even know who he is! I mean it even says there's this rumor where these new directors even want to hire him for how he figured up this Erebus deal where they're suing me for this here erotic management for the same thing hey, hey? Can't you even . . .

—I can't even move my knees no now will you get this stuff . . .

—No but you're not hardly even listening Bast I mean . . .

—Well what do you mean! How could you be sued for . . .

—I just told you erotic management how do I know, I mean that's what Piscator said wait where's, I wrote all this stuff down like they just stuck in everything they can think of see look hey, our next quarter earnings that they're grossly overstated like where we put in this here forecast for J R Shipping Corp where there's all these rules about shipping U S exports in American bottoms, see so we were like building it up to ship all these bellies in these here American bottoms I mean what's so erotic about that.

—I don't know I don't know what you're talking about, look Piscator's the only one who can do anything why don't you just . . .

—No but he already did it boy, I mean he goes and files this here affidavit which he said it means I allowed myself to be served I mean how did I know what that means it sounds like some crumby lunchroom, so like then some dumb newspaper says this here company spokesman confirms I maybe went to Honduras which I never even heard of it so these here new directors get this court to attach all this stock in this here voting trust to like make sure I'll be there today to defend everything, like this here Judge Ude I mean he wouldn't even give this postponement while we figure up some laws I mean holy shit how can I go to court!

—To court! but you, look this might be serious look . . .

—That's what I been trying . . .

—No but what can, what did Piscator say they wouldn't just come and arrest us I don't even . . .

—No wait see it's these whole different things, see where these here stockholders say you screwed them it's like this thing you did just for yourself see only this thing today I wouldn't get arrested because everything I did I'm like acting for the corporation, I mean that's the thing of this here limited reliability you know? See where these new directors get pissed off at me for this here erotic management only I'm like acting for the corporation doing all this stuff for these here stockholders with this limited reliability it's like the corporation did it itself which you can't go put a corporation in jail, I mean it would be like sticking this bunch of papers in jail see so . . .

—So I can go to jail and you've got nothing to worry about you don't even go to court you just . . .

—No no that's what I'm telling you hey! I mean if I don't show up and they get this here judgment and take all this stock off me where I lose control then I can't even . . .

—Yes but that's, then it's over! It's all over!

—No but wait a sec . . .

—Today right now you're supposed to be there aren't you? and you're not? So you lose it you lose your stock you lose the whole thing the whole mess you're out of it why didn't you tell me!

—Okay but wait a . . .

—Okay what do you mean okay it's the best thing that ever happened why didn't you just tell me instead of, look what's going on anyhow! You knew about it about the court the whole thing but you show up today with this field trip you pretend everything's . . .

—No but how did I know this court thing's going to happen today! I mean boy is Mister Stye going to be pissed off, like I mean him and Davidoff fixed up this trip ahead of time for this whole publicity thing for where we like bought the school off that Superintendent that Mister Teakel before he just got killed in this car wreck see it's going to be like this here showcase . . .

—Stop it! you can't buy schools you can't even buy . . .

—No well see the deal is where these taxpayers have this here referendum wait I got this thing out of the paper, see they're pissed off about all these school taxes so there's this referendum where J R Foundation like takes over the school and J R Corp like buys the plant off it on this ninety-nine year leaseback deal where we pay these here operating expenses which they're all deductible anyway see, so then we have like this here whole showcase of these new D and S subsiderary's textbooks and these here other education enervations you know? What's the matter . . .

—Just let me get my foot . . .

—I mean where school's always this bunch of crap which it never has anything to do with anything real you know? So like when Whiteback quit we got this here Mister Stye which he's like this branch manager, I mean he used to be this insurance man so he knows what everything's worth, you know? Like there's this neat idea where instead of getting these dumb marks you get paid see like a dollar is A, fifty cents is B C is a quarter D is like nothing see then instead of E you have to pay a nick wait what are you doing hey . . .

—Just move your knees I'm getting another seat, I just can't listen to . . .

—No but wait a second! I mean what . . .

—You just told me it's over didn't you! The whole thing it's all over can't you stop . . .

—No but you didn't let me finish where we get to countersue hey! I mean like they sue us so we sue them right back I mean that's what you do! I mean for like antitrust and conspiracy and all where they fixed up this here whole voting trust thing just to screw me out of ev, hey? hey what's the matter . . .

—I don't, don't feel very . . .

—You got all white hey wait get your knees wait let me get my, just hold this stuff a second sit back I mean just to get me by the short hair you know? Where they use these old loans to make us get these here new ones which we're building these here assets where you're like dribbling on your chin hey, I mean then they start yelling we're overextended and fix up this here voting trust where I'm like this captive borrower which stop jiggling your knees I'm trying to find this here article, look . . .

—I, no . . .

—Okay wait I'll read it listen. The small closely held company which rose almost overnight from the ruins of a failing upstate textile mill to become the multimillion dollar multiface, facet, faceted J R Corp appears threatened by a credit squeeze whose dramatic repercussions could be felt throughout the corporate and financial world it was reported here today, I mean that was like Tuesday. Attracted by the smell of here it is listen hey, smell of profits and the corporate daring which have characterized the company's abrupt entry into such diverse areas as pap wait where does it tell about me down here someplace I thought I marked it, reputation both as a ruthless corporate manipulator with a shrewd see this is me hey, a shrewd eye for tax situations, and a man of vision whose almost clair, clair something see this is still me, clairsomething ability to cut through to the heart of a problem and post an answer in profits before the competition has understood the quest continued on where's the rest of it wait, I even marked it where I have this here bulldog jaw and all might prove there's more truth than why'd I mark that for it's, wait no wait this is you hey listen. You listening?

—Just get this stuff off my . . .

—Okay just a second listen hey. Might prove there's more truth than poetry in the bard's words music hath charms to soothe the savage dot dot dot when intimates report funloving millionheiress Boody Selk shedding her swarthy zitar strumming playmate to slip on an eyecatching topless by daring new designer Harry Bosch for her latest teetateet with suave young business exec Edward Bast, seems Ed dabbles at the ivories between corporate mergers we hear his dad's a prominent conductor on the Long Island Railroad who does a little tunesmithing on the side but with Ed's head for figures these days he may be planning a merger of a diff . . . hey wait what do you . . .

—Think I, feel like I'm . . .

—No wait sit up I got this here picture too Davidoff sent me to show you from some magazine it's right under here she is look hey, surfacing from a fun stay in the Greek islands boy that's some pair of look out! you're coughing right on . . .

—Feel like I'm going to . . .

—I mean you got spit on these holy, hey wait swallow real hard quick let me get this stuff away try to swallow real hard hey, let me get this handkerchief . . . and he huddled away, dabbing the wad down a rise of tawny buttocks against the sparkling Aegean, licked his lips —you okay now hey? hey Bast . . . ?

The train shook abruptly to a halt and he held the heap close, wedged a toe deeper into the hinge of the seat ahead to bring his knees up under it —I mean you don't need to get so mad at everything, I mean you even got spit on where it says about a man of vision and all . . . and the handkerchief wad wiped that, came up clutched tight for the back of his hand to wipe across his nose and he hunched deeper under the pile peeling up ragged ribbons of newspaper, magazine pages torn jagged —with his sure instinct for the pulse of the market in a companywide search for ways to serve the customer better see this is me too hey, but it is his outstanding talent as a manager's manager which is held most in awe by his corporate peers see then it tells about this whole paper empire see that's what it's called here Paper Empire, I mean it starts off with this here surprise coop where we took over Eagle see then it tells where I thought up buying X-L for this here advertising on all these matchbooks to like fermiliarize everybody with this here rapidly expanding line of products where we went after these timber reserves when we went after Triangle and this here Duncan and hey? did I tell you hey? I mean where this here D and S subsiderary now they want me to write this whole book to publish? Like they said they want to name it How To Make a Million see only I think earn, like How To Earn a Million I mean it sounds more dignified you know? Like this biographical stuff which they fixed it up a little like where they stick in my golf game is in the eighties and all see they'd help me out with this book, I mean this Mister Davidoff said they'd like write it for me you know . . . ? And his elbow, come to rest high on the seat's back, left a hand dangling by his nose where the thumb promptly sought employment —like this here thing Virginia just wrote all about me in She where Mister Davidoff said it's to like create this masculine image for this here feminine reader appeal which they wrote it for her see, I mean it's like this intimate picture of her boss which she's like been with me since the start up to this rise of success and all like I thought it would give the magazine this real success feeling about it if it was like tied onto my own success you know? I mean like where it said in the paper about leading this parade wait a second . . .

The train jolted, glided ahead, stopped, his free hand caught the heap against lock steps past his elbow, came up with a tattered streamer —listen hey. Men who have worked with him I mean that means me that him, with him for years say his chief characteristics are enormous powers of concentration and a dogged persistence in attacking a problem until he comes up with a completely satisfactory answer . . . the thumb dug deeper, emerged for brief examination —which gives the clear impression here it is hey, impression of a man who sees where the parade is heading long before the paraders themselves do, and calmly steps in and leads isn't that neat? Qualities which u, uniquely fit him for the career in public life which has already created a groundswell I mean what's a groundswell, which faces only one major ob wait, obstacle, see like some of these words I didn't have them yet only I keep reading this stuff over again obstacle, an innate modesty that is evident in his words crediting his own success to a mysterious thing which is hard to identify, the vital creative force of the whole J R Family of Companies I mean see I never quite exactly said that you know? See but then it says when discussing the profit picture which has made his company's stock a leading glamour issue overnight however, a gleam of quite pardonable pride appears in his hey? Bast . . . ?

He'd come forward freeing his hand to drop between them and scratch, to rise and wipe the frayed edge of the sweater's sleeve across his nose and leave the lip trembling there turned toward the inert profile jolting between him and the dirty pane where the trembling lip tightened at the abrupt encounter, where the eyes hesitated as though caught by a passing gleam in the near darkness beyond —okay don't even listen then . . . ! he hunched back, thumb snagged back at a nostril —if you don't want to even hear this letter where you get to go to this here banquet for helping out the arts and all, I mean where I went and fixed up this big grant to play this here music you're always yelling about after all I did for you boy, what did I do with it . . . and the portfolio pocket tore a little further. —It gives us great pleasure to like there's this here other one too for where we gave out all those old Nobili drugs down at Asia so Davidoff writes right across it be glad to stand in for you on this one if Mister B is otherwise occupied, I mean how does he know maybe I want to go to this here where does it say it, this Brothers Keepers banquet and accept this award it's mine isn't it . . . ? The thumb dug savagely —like everybody's always going to all these banquets I never even got to go once . . .

The train shuddered to a halt, moaned at the platform, jolted the silence beside him moving on with —you want this rest of this here cupcake hey . . . ? and he crammed it away, dug the sneaker toes tighter to come up cantilevered and scratch —his dedication to the traditional ideas and values that have made America what it is today . . . he came down brushing crumbs from the tattered magazine page. —A quiet, soft voiced rather modest man who looks out from a calm impassive face and beetling brows, with deep set eyes that have such a startling clarity which makes them seem almost hit, hypnotic. They have a blue steel chill about them that suggests an austere, indrawn indwellingness. But they can sparkle with an engaging warmth and the bulldog set of his jaw breaks in a boyish grin when asked about his youth . . . he hunched closer to blow at an icinged crumb, —ful, youthful surroundings and the influences that shaped his formula for successful marketing bluntly expressed in a recent interview as, simply, what works. As the moving force behind his publishing subsiderary's slash in textbook prices and the, the ubisomething new children's encyclopedia as well as a sweeping breakthrough in education about to be announced by the parent . . . his thumb rose to burrow, his free hand traced back up the lines to —a calm impassive face and beetling brows . . . he sniffled and looked up, edged forward to peer past the form rocking beside him to the window mirrored with dirt and the darkness beyond lips shaping —beetling brows . . . and the eyebrows gathered in a wince, widened with —a blue steel chill . . . as the train gasped to halts, moved on, —but they sparkle with what did it say . . . ? and the eyebrows went up and down desperately projecting —engaging warmth that was it, and the bulldog set of his jaw . . . the narrow chin thrust forward, came up, protruded like an exhibit of orthodontic despair, all of it giving way suddenly to a face beyond the glass thumbing its nose from the platform. —Holy, we're here holy shit wake up hey Bast wake up!

—What what . . .

—Quick wake up we're here they all got off boy that wiseass, hey wait we have to get off! Quick get your stuff . . .

—Leave it there I don't . . .

—You can't leave that hey! wait hold the case together . . .

—Here let me get your shoulder I don't feel very . . .

—Hey wait we're getting off! you okay hey? Boy it's cold wait a second . . . he squared his armload sheltered behind We kick ass yours too as the train receded into the desolation of the evening, paused again at the breadloaf inscribed Father Haigt eat's it to mash streamers of paper into the portfolio and tug at its zipper —boy if there's one thing I really hate it's the wind you know . . . ? They reached the concrete steps, came down them. —You okay hey? I mean can't you carry some of this stuff I have to stop at the, holy shit it's closed look the candy store, it's closed!

—Don't want any candy where's a cab.

—No I mean the paper I can't get the paper, I mean now how are we suppose to we know what happened at that court thing and that underground . . .

—I don't care what happened where's a cab!

—There's not any there's not even buses hey wait up, I mean didn't you hear what happened? where this same new bank from the city which took over they called Gottlieb's loan which he couldn't pay it off so they seize his Ace Transportation assets which that's both his cabs and all these school buses I mean it's this same bank that wait where you going . . .

—Where do you think I'm going I'm . . .

—No but wait up . . . leaves swirled behind him, rushed past in the street where the sweeping lights of a car hurled his shadow over the figure mounting the curb ahead —hey Bast? I mean it's this here same new bank from the city can't you even listen a minute! It's this here new branch of one of these same banks that's screwing us too I mean they never lose these banks don't, I mean where we're getting screwed Crawley's getting screwed everybody's getting screwed except these here banks they never get screwed, they're always in there getting this per-cent of everything I mean I should have thought of it my . . . he stumbled, —I mean I got all this stuff I can't hardly see where, hey . . . ?

A car passed joining their shadows in a leap, flinging them aside to raise the shell of the Marine Memorial ahead in crumbling detail —I mean some bank getting some bank I should of thought of that by myself hey? Like where this newspaper just said the parent company I mean that's me, how the parent is going after this SSS Savings and Loan with these big cash reserves that's how I thought of it I just saw it in the paper, like where the paper's always saying the parent this the parent that I mean that's me the parent! See I hardly got started hey once we get things fixed up I had all these plans . . . his teeth were chattering —I mean like banks we could have these different kind of banks like this regular bank and these blood banks these eye banks these bone what, where you going . . .

—Have to sit down I, I feel like I . . .

—Wait get back up here where there's no wind hey . . . he stumbled against the crumbling edge of the Memorial's shell —let me put this stuff down where we can wait you going to sit here a second?

—Yes I, I feel diz . . .

—Okay because these here tapes you got I just remembered, I mean we can play them and boy this here nice attaché case I got you you really let it get busted up where's my, I can't hardly see what's wait a second I left one in here . . .

———ca's all about and holds everything together because nothing works unless there's something in it for somebody, so the . . .

—Hey this is a tape I made there's this eighth grade at some orange place at New Jersey buying this here share of America where they wanted this here speech I thought you could, hey? you want to hear it?

—No!

—Okay we better do these others first anyway these batteries are real weak where's your, when this car comes I can see what I'm doing they think they can screw me out of everything boy I hardly even got started what's the, this thing's suppose to fit right into wait I got it in backwards once we get things fixed up boy this whole health plan thing we franchise it out and that whole Endo deal when we find out how much all that goodwill is worth and like Wiles said we have this here friend at Chase Man there, listen . . .

———medicine capsules only cost Nobili a nickel each to make which their dates are like expiring we'd have to dump anyway for this lousy nickel deduction see but like they sell for a quarter so every one we donate we get this whole quarter charity deduction for a nick . . .

—Sit down hey these batteries are real weak you have to listen real . . .

———this here fifty percent tax bracket, see so every nickel capsule we give out we make this here ten cents net profowwwrr ja ach ja ich bin verlor . . .

—Hey what's, it's doing it again!

—Wait listen . . . !

———nein du bist erkoren . . .

—This singing you did this one too! Right in the I mean holy shit right in the middle of I'm talking about ouch! What's let go my shoulder what's ouch!

—Just listen! shut up for a minute sit still and listen!

——nein du hassest mich . . . !

—No but holy shit Bast! this here tape was . . .

—I don't care what it was! I didn't know I had it I forgot I'd even sit still! Now listen. Once, just once you're going to listen to something that . . .

—No but ho . . .

—And stop saying holy shit! it's all you, you want to hear holy you're going to hear it wind the tape back, just once you're going to keep quiet and listen to a piece of music by one of . . .

—No but look hey I'm cold I mean how can we sit out here in the dark and lis . . .

—I'm cold too! I'm cold dizzy sick at my stomach if I can sit here and listen to you talk about how much this goodwill is worth and this here friend at what makes you think we've got any friends anywhere! How much goodwill do you think we . . .

—No wait hey I mean holy shit I don't mean where everybody's crazy about us and all, see goodwill that means the excess of the purchase price over the value of these net tangible assets where they really screwed us on that Endo deal see so ouch!

—That's not what it means! That's what I'm trying to, listen all I want you to do take your mind off these nickel deductions these net tangible assets for a minute and listen to a piece of great music, it's a cantata by Bach cantata number twenty-one by Johann Sebastian Bach damn it J R can't you understand what I'm trying to, to show you there's such a thing as as, as intangible assets? what I was trying to tell you that night the sky do you remember it? walking back from that rehearsal that whole sense of, of sheer wonder in the Rhinegold you remember it?

—Well I, sure I mean we're still having it Mrs di . . .

—How it can lift you right out of yourself make you feel things that, do you know what I'm talking about at all?

—Well sure I, I mean like where there's this storm so Mrs diCephalis gets the art class to cut out these here big clouds which they pull them over you on this closeline and like somebody's rolling these marbles around in this piepan you get this here real feeling . . .

—It doesn't have to be like that's what I mean! Music's a, it's not just sound effects there are things only music can say, things that can't be written down or hung on a clothesline things that . . .

—Okay! could you, I mean could you let go my shoulder this thing's wound back what am I sup . . .

—Listen to it then! look hold it up you'll hear two voices a soprano and a bass, it's sort of a dialogue between the soul and Jes . . .

—Okay okay! I mean how can I hear anything if you keep . . .

—All right listen to it! and his hand dropped from the torn shoulder, his other rose to join it covering his face against a sweep of lights from the road.

—Okay I heard them, I mean it's like starting to rain can we . . .

—All of it! he came forward and coughed, caught one shaking hand back in the other to draw his knees close where his head came down from the wind hollowing the empty shell around them, raising dead leaves in a rush and falling away, driving them back.

—Hey? Okay I heard it I mean that's the end of the . . .

—Is that all?

—Sure I mean that's the end of the . . .

—That's all you can say? okay I heard it?

—Well I, sure I mean what . . .

—Look tell me what you heard then, just tell me what you heard.

—Well I, I mean you know . . .

—Why can't you just tell me what you heard!

—Well just, because.

—Because what! what's . . .

—Because you'll get mad I mean you're already mad! I mean I, everything I say you get mad somebody gets mad I mean how come everybody's always getting mad at me! What am I sup, hey wait I thought you're going to sit here a minute I mean just because I . . .

—It doesn't matter!

—No but wait up hey! I mean all this stuff, I . . .

—Leave it there what good is it!

—No but if they subpoen it I mean I have to get it back in my locker at school for this here whole . . .

—Can't you damn it! can't you see it's trash it's just trash it's always been trash all of it! The net assets the nickel deductions the man of vision all of it, can't you see that now?

—No but, hey? hey Bast? Wait up I can't hardly see where I'm, hey . . . ? he came on kicking through leaves for a remnant of sidewalk, —I mean what did you say this, this here man of vision I mean what's so trash about that!

—Because you know it is all of it! You know it's been right from the start your surprise coup taking over Eagle you were more surprised than anybody, you didn't even know what X-L made when you had to buy it you asked me what's a lithograph you never thought of flooding the country with those damn matchbooks till you read someplace you'd already done it like you read the reason you tried to grab that insurance company was its cash reserves, all you wanted it for was you hated to see all those employees paying premiums someplace else you just wanted to pay them with one hand and take it back with the other you know what really happened! That timber you didn't go after it at all you got stuck with some mining claims and land you didn't even know where it was in a penny stock swindle like your shrewd downstate interests in that hopeless Union Falls paper right at the start, you knew it wasn't shrewd downstate interests any more than this man of vision this, these intimate glimpses of you by that cow Virginia you know they're not real!

—No okay but hey listen . . .

—It's not okay! that, dabbles at the ivories my father's a prominent
conductor on the look how could anybody be a prominent conductor on
the Long Island Rail . . .

—No but that's what you told me once hey and besides . . .

—Besides what! I never told you such a grotesque thing in . . .

—No but besides you never let me finish about that hey wait up holy,
my whole sneaker got wet hey wait up!

—For what wait up for what! finish about what! Your suave young
exec's teetateet with look you know it's not real any of it!

—No but wait I know it's not real hey! I mean it's just this neat idea
I had where this here naked girl picture I read you it on the train where
they got this gossip calumnist to like fix you up with her hey Bast? I mean
just this once see where this whole Teletravel thing see once it gets like
operational I mean she's this here whole heiress of these two hundred
thousand shares of Diamond Cable hey Bast? where she gets these rights
to them once you marry her to vote them when we make this here
tender offer hey? then you get this divorce just like everybody hey Bast?
Look out . . . ! Headlights swept down the highway's unkempt shoulder
where it parted on the ruts of a dirt road —that shit boy! he splashed all
over my, hey wait up I can't even see where you, did you hear me? Just
this once hey? Then we go after Western Union we get this whole complex of this cable travel going they think they can screw me out of
everything boy I hardly even got started, I mean we get these here banks
going we get this energy complex going with this here big gas deposit
and this mineral one where you just fixed up this here neat deal with
these Indians we get this here whole education market by the ow! Ow
ow ow . . . ! The wind held his hair on end hunched down on one knee
there, lights loomed a shadow back over him, dropped it as they passed
—oww . . .

—Well what happened.

—This busted sidewalk sticking up I hit my ankle I mean everything's getting wet holy, I mean couldn't you even carry this here tape
thing it keeps bumping my . . .

—All right but where! what do you . . .

—I mean I couldn't even see you ahead of me just then did you hear
what I said? I mean just this once no wait! or I mean what's, like what
was it all for!

—That's what I've been trying to tell . . .

—What tell me what! I mean you're telling me how neat the sky
looks you're telling me listen to this here music you even get pissed off
when I . . .

—I asked you what you heard! that's all, I . . .

—What like it lifted me out of mysel . . .

—Not what I said no you! what you heard!

—What was I suppose to hear!

—You weren't! you weren't supposed to hear anything that's what I'm . . .

—Then how come you made me lis . . .

—To make you hear! to make you, to make you feel to try to . . .

—Okay okay! I mean what I heard first there's all this high music right? So then this here lady starts singing up yours up yours so then this man starts singing up mine, then there's some words so she starts singing up mine up mine so he starts singing up yours so then they go back and forth like that up mine up yours up mine up yours that's what I heard! I mean you want me to hear it again?

—No!

—See I knew you'd . . .

—Never want you to hear it again I never want to hear it again myself! you, everything you ruin everything you touch!

—Wait wait hey quit . . . !

—Think I could ever hear it again without hearing your, everything everybody! you destroy whatever you . . .

—Quit kicking it! you, it's smashed what did you . . .

—Why not why not smash everything! Charley Yellow Brook in that smashed Cadillac waving a pint bottle telling me the earth is his mother telling me corn is a god talking about water water thanking me for trying to, Mooneyham weeping in his omelette before his heart attack George Wonder hanging onto me when the police took the gun away from him I can trust you Bast you're the only friend I've got if there's one thing I know it's brewing they're pushing me out, it's all I've got Bast you're the only friend I've got and that, that poor Brisboy you're all we have left smash all of them! Union Falls wipe it all out but your cemetery that simple minded Bunky there selling your purple plastic daffodils to help him out help everybody out everything everyplace there's nothing you can't destroy even, even music a glorious piece of music I thought it could rise above anything even your, even you I thought maybe you'd hear something there some speck just a speck in you somewhere might wake up might be exalted for an instant you hear me? Even an instant!

—Boy after all I did for you . . .

—All you did there's nothing you haven't done for me nothing wherever I go I, that junk pocket radio there was one station with decent music the only station left on the radio anywhere it came on one night noises screaming pounding noise brought to you in this new popular format by the J R Family of Companies bringing America its full share of of holy shit!

—No but . . .

—No but nothing! that was you too wasn't it? even that it was your idea wasn't it?

—Okay what's so . . .

—Okay nothing it's the whole thing! the whole rotten thing it's a perfect example even you can understand it! the one station that played music great music left in the whole loud cheap pounding stupidity of radio you find it and make it cheap and stupid like all the rest if you could, if there was one flower out here in this mud and weeds and broken toilet seats you'd find it and step on it, the minute you . . .

—Okay wait look is it my fault if . . .

—The minute you get your hands on something the power to keep something like that going you couldn't do it you couldn't even leave it alone for a few people still looking for something beautiful, people who'd rather hear a symphony than eat who can still, who hear a magnificent soprano voice singing ach nein when you hear this here lady singing up mine you can't get up to their level so you drag them down to yours if there's any way to ruin something, to degrade it to cheapen it . . .

—Look is it my fault if this here symphony takes like half an hour to play it! And I mean you say cheapen boy this whole deal it's like two million dollars in it and I mean like who wanted to buy their lousy station anyway! I mean this here Pomerance's agency they go around there for us where all we want is like this one hour a night to get our message acrost so they tell us how much and then they get real snotty and say they still control the program content which that's these here symphonies and all so I mean how many messages are you suppose to get acrost in this here hour where it takes this band half of it to play this one symphony for these here people which aren't hungry where this other crap takes like three minutes each, I mean what do I care what they play there! Like we're paying them for this here whole hour aren't we? I mean if they could get through these here symphonies in like five minutes where we're getting this bunch of messages in we're paying for I mean what do I care what they play! I mean who's paying them to play all this here great music these people which aren't hungry like at Russia? where the goverment makes everybody listen to it? Like I mean this here station it's losing so much money it can't hardly last anyway so I mean we have to buy it to help them out I mean what am I suppose to do! That's what you do!

—All right all right! Listen I can't . . .

—No but holy shit Bast I mean that's what you do! Like I mean these here Indians is it my fault they think corn is this here god they don't even have electricity? is it my fault if I didn't get these here leases off them and leave them stay there somebody else is going to screw them out of the whole thing? Is it my fault if I do something first which if I don't do it somebody else is going to do it anyway? I mean how come everybody's always getting mad at me! Like we get Milliken to help fix up these here laws to start selling this marijuana to help out these here Ritz stockholders so Beamish gets pissed off and goes and quits just because I did it first like these ads in these here textbooks and all, I mean he gets pissed off at that just because I do if first so then he gets pissed off where I do just like everybody like where we're franchising out this here health plan, I mean where these nursing homes and funerals and all they have to buy everything off us where we get to charge them what we want and squeeze them out anytime we want is it my fault that's what franchising is! I mean Beamish even gets pissed off where we paint this Triangle water tower like this here giant roll of toilet paper then he respectfully submits why don't we recycle this here whole encyclopedia I mean is it my fault if we've got this like third of a million dollars sunk in it when some wiseass finds out these writers they've just been making up entries only nobody knows which ones? I mean then where one of them even says what do you expect for this half cent a word what am I suppose to do, recycle it and throw all these here printers and binders and salesmen out of work so they all get pissed off like at Eagle? I mean like we close the mills so they're all pissed off about this here vacation time they been saving up like it's my fault they didn't take their dumb vacations so they're going to strike and sue us and all so this here Billy Shorter, I mean just to shut up his union we go and give his stupid kid this Wonder beer distributorship which he screws it up so bad we have to buy it back off him for like fifty thousand dollars I mean what do you expect me to do! Hey. . .? My ankle I can't hardly, hey? Bast . . . ? he pushed shoulder deep from weeds to gather his armload close stepping high over the rutted mud, —I couldn't see you hey wait a second . . . he paused against a pole of rust signaling the opening with an indecipherable sign —I mean did you even hear what I was just telling you?

—No I just want to get . . .

—I mean you're telling me how I wreck up everything and you don't even listen! Like this here Bunky, you even said I screwed him sticking him out selling these plastic flowers at this cemetery boy do you know what that shit did? I mean you think he's so simple minded when we took over Eagle I do his father this big favor, I give him this job handling all these rebates on this cloth where there's something wrong with it? So this one place they're getting like twice as many rebates which they're always way bigger than these other ones too so I'm trying to find out how come they wait up . . . ! the weeds closed behind him —how come this one place is always getting so much lousy cloth so I find out there's no such of a company! I mean we never even would of found out he went and set up this here fake company to give all these big rebates to if he would of just gave them like the same as these real ones only he has to try to grab all the listen! I mean I'm telling . . .

—I heard you! can't you damn it didn't you learn anything from that? grabbing ev . . .

—I mean that's what I'm telling you! I mean why should somebody go steal and break the law to get all they can when there's always some law where you can be legal and get it all anyway! So I mean I do what you're suppose to and everybody gets . . .

—But why why are you supposed to! that's what I've . . .

—No sir boy you, I mean like you're telling me listen to this here singing just tell me what you hear so when I tell you you get so pissed off you smash it because I didn't hear what I'm suppose to like you're telling me how great the sky is and all like, I mean like this here night Mrs Joubert grabs me to make me look at the sky where she's pointing see back there? that top of that like round white thing lit up back of those trees back there she's holding me against her tit pointing at it so I can't hardly breathe telling me see the moon over there coming up? is there this millionaire for that? and I, I duck away and she's pissed off at me too it doesn't matter she says why couldn't, I mean why can't anybody just . . .

—But she's can't you see what she, why did you duck away! can't you see what she was trying to tell you she . . .

—What tell her it's this top of this here Carvel icecream cone stand? tell her does she want to bet her ass if there's this millionaire for that? I mean you and her boy you're telling me it doesn't matter I mean you got what you wanted to didn't you! I mean you're blaming me for wrecking up everything and everybody like this here Bunky you know why he did it? I mean this dumb shit he goes and signs up for these like nineteen thousand four hundred dollars of dancing lessons he should have went to jail only I try to help him out, I give him this here franchise of all these plastic flowers where I even tell them to put up these signs you can't bring any fresh ones in the cemetery on account of cleaning up and helping out pollution and all to pay off these dancing lessons I mean just almost like you can't you even . . .

—Like me what what do you . . .

—This here music I mean what do you think! I mean okay I don't mean you stole something like him or you walk around like this here funny looking windmill like you said he does only these dumb dancing lessons he has to have I mean this here whole big opera music thing you got to do it didn't you!

—But I, why do you think . . .

—These a hundred musical insterments all playing at once where they like taped it for you and all I mean didn't you? where you said it's something you have to do like it's your only reason to be anybody so I mean what's the difference if maybe I couldn't even understand it! I mean just because you know what you have to do without somebody's always telling you what's the difference if I look over there and see this icecream cone thing where Mrs Joubert sees this here moon coming up where I'm trying to find out what I'm suppose to do so you say it's trash? where this here paper says I'm this man of vision so you say it's trash? where I'm leading this parade where there's this groundswill of I'm like fit for this big career in public life I mean this here eighth grade at this orange place where I'm telling them play to win only it's not this game anyway even if you do what you're suppose to I mean even if it's trash boy, I mean you got to do what you have to do out of it didn't you?

—But I've, this music listen that's what I . . .

—No that's okay I just mean didn't you, that's all. I mean you don't need to go around thanking everybody Bast but like where we said we'll like use each other and I mean where even Crawley he's telling me how this music's so important where you're working so hard on it and all so I mean even where you didn't hardly open the mail or like even answer the telephone hardly and I didn't get pissed off because all the time I had these here big plans you know hey? I mean not just for me for the both of us . . .

—Listen that's what I'm talking about! I, this chance, I had the chance and I didn't do what I . . .

—No but that's what I'm telling you either did I! I mean from right at the start where I think it's this big deal loaning money off some bank where I find out you can't hardly not loan it off them till by now they've like got everybody by the short hair I mean I should have just went after some bank myself right at the start! I mean I get all screwed up with these low-cost operations all over the place like that dump I made you have your office at and these bus rides and these forty-eight-cent dollars how did I know the more you can spend the more you get, I mean I should have only went after all this here cost-plus stuff right at the start! Like I mean these here little booklets they never tell you how you get to take this percent of the more you can waste where all these here regulartary agencies like this FCC and PSC and all they're like right in there helping you out to get all you can? I mean like where you just said I should have went after this here insurance company for this big cash reserve at the start instead of just to insure all these dumb employees which it's not even them that's insured anyway hey? where this guy which he's like getting his insides taken out it's not even him it's this here doctor which the more he takes out the more he gets I mean it's him and these hospitals and everybody, they're insured they'll get paid whatever they want because they've got these big lobbies and all I mean I didn't even know what's a lobby hey! I thought it's just this place in some hotel where you get to sit down, I mean I'm just finding out everything's like just the opposite of how I thought is that what you mean hey? Bast . . . ?

—No it's, look it's useless no I give up, I can't . . .

—No but you can't give up now hey wait up! I mean just when we find out how everything works hey? Where I mean just because I screwed up this once where we didn't do all this here PR stuff right hey? I mean like Davidoff and those guys if they wouldn't have screwed up on all this PR stuff where now everybody's blaming me for how the whole market's like diving and all I mean once we do all this PR stuff right hey Bast? where you're in the paper going to these important functions with this here tuxedo like all these big politicians go around in all the time to these banquets and all hey? where you get to play golf with like Billy Grahey? Wait up I mean this rain it feels like it's turning into snow hey Bast? I mean listen wait up, like do you need any money before you come to school tomorrow to like pick up your check hey?

—No . . . !

—Because I can't hardly see you I mean what are you going to do then hey, hey? Because like I was thinking hey Bast? I mean where you could go on this here lecture tour just like everybody hey? where you screw everything up so then you get to go on this lecture tour at these neat colleges and all and you write this here book and get to go on tv where you make all this money while you're figuring up what to do next at these banquets and all hey? Like even that Finders Keepers one I read you on the train if you could just have went to that, I mean I never even got to go once! he stumbled, kicked in the wet weeds and a can tumbled out to the highway's broken shoulder —like that Union Falls one you told me about right at the start hey? with this banana sticking up out of this pineapple with this peanut butter and marshmallow and all? I mean I always remembered that . . . he got an arm up to pull the wet sleeve across his nose —hey? Because with this here Begg lawsuit and all if we can't fix something up I mean maybe you could just go bankrup awhile you know hey? Like I got this thing someplace how you get to be declared this here bankrup for like seventy-five dollars then you get to start over hey? I mean it says did you just turn twenty-one been reprosessed bad credit we finance anybody walk in drive out? Then I mean we could just hook that onto that ten dollars that time from those train tickets with interest where you can just pay me it all back on time when you get to start all over hey? I mean I'll bring it to school tomorrow when you come for this here check and hey listen . . . came blown over the wet weeds, —I even got this here old booklet off the goverment where you still get to homestead like we had at school in the olden times hey? Where you get like this whole hundred sixty acres free which you just improve it by like chopping everything down I mean I'll bring it tomorrow too okay? And hey Bast? I mean sometime . . . the wind flung the voice into the weeds, raised it abruptly with —hear this here tape they made you sometime hey . . . ? bill for all these horns and kettledrums and all I mean . . . hear it I mean I bet it's as good as this thing you just made me . . . hey? even if I don't hear exactly what I'm suppose to . . . ? the wind came down, lost any voice but its own till it seized the clash of branches tossed bare over ruts leading into more ruts and the remnants of pavement, the rusted length of a car's muffler and the sodden heap of a mattress, torn pennants of paper swirled in the leaves and then the sudden iron nakedness of a piano frame still strung pounced shaping in the mud as though to fossilize a bedspring fused at this lonely height of passionate deformity caught now in a glance of lights where the ruts broke off on darkness spread glistening beyond, lights sweeping in with maritime disdain to stop and add a burst of flashlight reduced to the jarring cadence of a man on foot.

—Hello? this man's looking for the Bast house, do you . . .

—So am I where is it!

—Just a minute officer, who's . . .

—Wait who are you buddy what's the . . .

—But I'm that's who I am Bast I'm Edward Bast I'm . . .

—Mister Bast good heavens! you, I'm Mister Coen the attorney for your . . .

—But where's the house where's my, where's where's anything where's the . . .

—I'm equally confused Mister Bast yes, I recalled it being just off this corner behind a long hedge but the officer here says all he knows is that this is the new Cultural Plaza, I'm afraid we're both mis . . .

—Hedge the hedge yes where's the hedge where the trees where's my, wait he's the you, you you're one of them one of the police you were here that night the barn, the studio, right here a big room right here you were standing in it a big stone fireplace there was a piano right here right where this car is, a grand piano you told me to get it boarded up you, books there were books torn up all over the floor you said some kids had broken in can't you . . .

—Get calls like that every night buddy, want to stop in the precinct check the records if anybody turned in a complaint . . .

—I want to know where my house is!

—Told you all I ooph! All right you're coming in . . .

—Ow!

—No wait officer please! he's, I'm sure he just slipped he's obviously quite distraught if you'll just let him come with me I'm an attorney, he's needed on an urgent matter I fine thank you around this way Mister Bast thank you officer . . .

—Just get him out of here.

—Fine yes thank you no this door Mister Bast, be caref . . .

—Who are you.

—I'm the, my name is Coen Mister Bast please get in, I tried to reach you some time ago your aunts must have mentioned my . . .

—Where are they!

—I don't know Mister Bast I have no idea, I've tried to reach them or you all day I was told the phone had been taken out that's why I finally drove out here to please Mister Bast get in, you're soaking wet we can't stand here it's beginning to that's it yes, just get your hand in so I can close the . . .

—Where the trees.

—My coat's on the back seat there put it around you before we, yes could you move your feet I can't drive if you . . .

—What's that thing! that, thing . . . !

—That yes it's some sort of a huge metal sculpture that's what brought the police here, there's a child caught in it they're waiting for the insur . . .

—Look!

—Where oh, the shopping center yes I confess I don't recall it across from your Mister Bast close it! Close the door you can't, you could have been badly injured please, you must . . .

—The hedge where's the, flowers that was a field dahlias chrysanthemums and dahlias where, where . . .

—If you can just sit back Mister Bast yes I think we turn up this way, I'm afraid I have some extremely unfortunate news to . . .

—Stop the car stop the car . . . !

—Mister Bast it's sleeting quite heavily, I don't think we . . .

—I'm going to be sick stop the car!

—Wait wait yes, yes I'm stopping no push that down, yes down that's, yes can you lean a little further out over the, that's it yes just get this coat sleeve out of your, there, there yes that ought to, let's hurry yes we're right in front of a church they might misinterpret the, you're sure that's all now? Yes just just before you wait wait here's a don't have a handkerchief wait just, wait here it's just a polishing cloth if you can wipe off your, you're sure that's all? If you can get your here let me slam this door a little harder there, feeling better now? Get that coat around you yes if you can just settle back, it's quite difficult to see the road . . .

—There it is! stop there it is! there it is!

—What there's what what . . .

—The house stop we just passed it!

—Mister Bast please we can't keep, I can't drive if you . . .

—I saw it we just passed it I saw it!

—Just push this down make sure your door's locked Mister Bast I may have been mistaken in recalling your house being right off that corner back there but I'm absolutely certain it was not practically next door to a Catholic church, in fact the vehemence with which your aunts expressed their aversion to . . .

—You a lawyer Mister Coen?

—Why I yes that's precisely why I . . .

—Ever handle a bankrup?

—Why why yes it's quite a routine procedure Mister Bast but I've come out here on an extremely urgent matter concerning your cousin's husband Mister Angel, I take it you haven't heard . . .

—Get to start over right?

—Pardon? oh, oh in a bankruptcy yes in a manner of speaking Mister Bast but your cousin's husband Mister Angel is in the hospital I, I take it you don't know what's happened . . .

—What's happened wait. Sixteen die in Chicago plane crash?

—No, no he wasn't in a . . .

—Sixteen die in Chicago plane crash I saw it in the paper, don't you believe me?

—Why why, why yes but that's not the, you see Mister Angel is in a coma as the result of a gunshot wound and Mrs Angel your cousin, your cousin Stella, the police have . . .

—Get to start over, right?

—Mister Bast perhaps I, I mean you are Mister Bast aren't you? Edward Bast?

—With an e Edwerd with an e, Ed . . .

—An, an E of course yes you understand meeting you for the first time under these somewhat extraordinary circumstances it just occurred to me I might have picked up some wandering please your foot! I can't drive with your foot under my, that's better yes of course if I'd left you to that policeman and you really are the Edward Bast I've no no be careful! we almost went off the, a terrible cough yes you're really not well you, you're not going to be sick again are you? Try to, here pull the coat around you you're shivering let me turn up the heat, now. Your cousin Mister Bast, your cousin Stella, Mrs Angel? The shock has shaken her severely as I'm sure you can understand, the initial shock of the, the discovery itself of course and then the ordeal of the police investigation questioning, taking descriptions photographing the crime search scene as they re . . .

—Get the whole place boarded up.

—Pardon?

—Dry place to screw where they won't freeze their nuts board the whole place up.

—Mister Bast I'm trying to, I'm talking about Mrs Angel your cousin Stella, when I left she'd gone in for a paraffin test whose results I have no doubt will prove negative, howev . . .

—Weather like this find a dry place to . . .

—However since her husband's chance of survival appears extremely slim, and as a matter of course such situations become the province of homicide investigation and are approached as assault with intent to commit murder until any such possib . . .

—You a lawyer Mister Coen?

—Yes I am a lawyer Mister Bast! and I, this is an extremely grave situation in which I am trying to be of assistance. When I left her, Mrs Angel appeared unable to distinguish between the likelihood of being called as a material witness and the idea of being held on suspicion and I thought, I had hoped that if you would talk to her it might . . .

—Don't need to go around thanking everybody?

—No I hardly think that would, Mister Bast I meant only that if you were willing to talk sensibly with Mrs Angel I believe we should be able to secure her release. Otherwise even in the absence of sufficient evidence to detain her on suspicion, the probability of her commitment to Bellevue for the standard ten day observation period would be . . .

—Get to start over right?

—Mister Bast I'm afraid you no sit up! You've, there's simply not room for you to lie down in the front seat here while I'm . . .

—Not pissed off at me are you Mister Coen?

—Why why, why no but . . .

—I mean why is everybody always getting mad at me!

—I, I'm sure they're not Mister Bast but I do find it difficult to drive in this wind and sleet, if you could . . .

—Rain or hail fire or snow rift the hills and roll the, get to roll these here marbles around in this piepan board the place up she tell you that?

—No I, I'm afraid not Mister Bast she, the last time I spoke with your aunts on the telephone I got the impression you were away on a business trip and I have a number of matters I had hoped we . . .

—Shoe business she tell you that? Place called Trib, Trib, place where the muck runs down to the sea . . .

—Mister Bast I think, I think under the circumstances . . .

—Import export place called Burmesquik where they make the crooked. . .

—I think it might be wise to postpone your seeing Mrs Angel, considering her present condition and of course having met your please! be careful of your foot, had the pleasure of dealing with your aunts of course I should have been aware that stability is perhaps not your family's most promin . . .

—All got pissed off because their bellies dropped I mean what's so erotic about that.

—I, I'm sure I don't know Mister Bast why don't you just rest for a few minutes, perhaps we can find some music to . . .

—Soothe the savage dot dot dot, get to wed some savage woman she will . . .

—Rest your head back yes I believe we share an interest in your knee Mister Bast if you can move your knee, in fine music . . .

—She shall rear my dusty race want to say scrotum in Danish Mister Coen?

—Not, not particularly if I can, if I can just find some music yes if there's one thing I dislike Mister Bast it's disorder I don't like surprises, the caterwauling on most of radio that's why I felt the expense of having this FM here here listen! it's, I think we have Handel that's better isn't it yes Jephtha? Handel's Jephtha I remember this part yes when I was a child, I thought the soprano here was singing get away! get no no stop! stop! we almost what made you do that! We we could have been killed no get your foot down!

—Up yours Mister Coen.

—But you, you put your foot right through the . . .

—Up mine up mine du haaaassest mich!

—No no listen Mister Bast stop it stop singing! I can't no, no you'll have to sit still I can't drive if you . . .

—Help each other out Mister Coen make seventy-five dollars?

—Why why what . . .

—Ever handle a bankrup?

—Mister Bast I . . .

—Believing and shitting are two very different things Mister Coen.

—I see yes I, I'm sure they are Mis . . .

—Two very different things.

—I'm sure yes I, I'd never really thought in precisely those terms now please . . .

—Better think in precisely those terms Mister Coen drive in walk out, two very different things.

—I will yes Mister Bast now sit back or we'll have to . . .

—What's that what's that! that, that white thing that round white thing . . .

—It's simply the knob to control the ventilator, now please . . .

—Bet her ass if there's this here millionaire for that like to win that bet wouldn't you Mister Coen? Once just get a good look at it winked at you just this once get a divorce just like everybody wouldn't you?

—I'm sure I would Mister Bast that's better yes, settle back . . .

—Win the Finders Keepers award get to go to that banquet, where you shipping them all there in American bottoms?

—I think we'll go directly to the hospital where they've taken Mister Angel, I'm sure his physician will have you admitted you're here get the coat over you you're shivering where's the, that cloth you're perspiring heavily yes, yes I had thought if Mrs Angel should go to Bellevue I could certainly have you admitted there too but getting you out again might prove somewhat more diff . . .

—Open a bank there wouldn't you? Shrewd downstate interest lead the parade open the bank there first national bank of Burmesquik no deposit no return, wouldn't you?

—I'm sure I would Mister Bast yes, yes we won't be long now . . . and his hand dropped from wiping the inside of the glass before him to lift away the foot renewing its errant threat to join his on the accelerator, rose to wipe again where the bursts of passing lights became more frequent, gave way finally to the sheltered glare of the tunnel, the open glows of green's consent and red alerts in BAR, DRY CLEANING, EAT, EMERGENCY —yes here we oh . . . ! where the glass doors hung still behind his haste through them as though content to reflect the novelty of the fender crumpled in his fervor of arrival until they were swept wide on the pursuit of a wheelchair —wait yes I think he's still asleep, here let me . . .

—No I can lift him he don't weigh nothing, just get the blanket . . . and the doors outside returned to their diversion, inside deflected —he go to admissions?

—Where the trees . . .

—He wha'd he say?

—He, no no I think that won't be necessary I just arranged his admission with Miss, Miss . . . ?

—Is this the new boy? He'll have to tell me all about it . . .

—I don't think he can he's quite feverish, he became incoherent on the way in he's been using language I'm sure he never . . .

—Don't worry he can't shock me I just came here from working at a public school, oh this man in intensive care you just asked about, this Mister Angel? They said his condition's unchanged, this bullet entered beside the eye it's lodged in the brain if you want to stay awhile maybe they . . .

—No I can't no I have to get over to the nineteenth precinct if he should, if his condition should change they should be notified immediately and, Mister Bast? Goodnight I have to leave, I'll look in tomorrow perhaps we'll have a clearer picture of things . . .

—Off we go, Mister Bast is it? We're going for a little ride . . .

—Walk out drive in.

—Yes we'll get those wet things off and something to help us sleep won't we, Joe? Tell the doctor room three nineteen you better see about an oxygen tent too just in case . . . and the wheels spun through bull's eye doors for the lull of an elevator, down corridors of greens unknown in nature. —Here we are . . .

—Where the trees.

—Silly there aren't any trees . . . only the flurry of hands and sheets, the rattle of carts and trays and finally of a shade coming down on the glow at a wall socket indifferently exchanging day for night, night for day.

—I'm telling you this place is a dream after where I was at, did I ever tell you what was . . .

—Wait, hello . . . ? He's in three nineteen yes wait here's Miss Waddams she can . . .

—Hello . . . ? Oh hi . . . last night yeah but I just went on days this morning, he's coming along fine he didn't even wake up since you . . . now? with him? No we got him in a tent he's not even . . . no an oxygen tent Mister Coen he's got enough trouble breathing already without trying to talk on the tele . . . I know yeah he really hit the jackpot double pneumonia nervous exhaus . . . what? Malnutrition yeah I don't know a couple of days maybe, they always worry about complications with this you know? So how's your other patient . . . No I mean your friend they got here in the intensive care . . . You really got your hands full haven't you Mister Coen . . . I sure will Mis . . . you bet Mister Coen goodbye, anyway this place is a dream after where I was at . . .

—No lunch for three nineteen either?

—No he's on iv maybe I better go check him now, don't go away wait till I tell you what they found stopping up the junior high plumbing

. . . and she came hedged by that despair of color down the corridor to weigh in green's arrest OXYGEN NO SMOKING with a shoulder and search a pulse among whites left sallow with her steps away in the wall socket glow's indifference day to night, night to day.

—Anyway like what I was telling you yesterday can you imagine that back when you were in junior high? I'm telling you this place is wait, hello . . . ? Oh hi Mister Coen? It's me yeah he's coming along fine he still didn't really wake up since you . . . no I mean just for tests and all but he's still on the . . . no but even if you have these important matters to discuss with him he couldn't even . . . I sure will Mister Coen so how's your other patients you really got your hands full haven't you you must be . . . you bet Mister Coen goodbye. I better go check him don't go away I didn't even tell you where we had this kid that was always sticking people up with a cap pistol . . . and she was down the corridor shouldering in OXYGEN NO SMOKING, —how we feeling today Mister Bast . . . ? flashing a light, searching a pulse —just take one day at a time . . . and leaving that one behind, undistinguished by the steady glow from the one that followed.

—I'm telling you after where I was at only don't you get bored here? Hello . . . ? for Mister who . . . ? No it can't be three twelve three twelve's a hysterectomy . . . seven till eight yes goodbye, anyway did I tell you where we had these junior high girls leaving their samples for wait, hello . . . ? Oh hi there Mis . . . much better yeah he's out of the tent I bet he'd like to see you Mister Coen, he seems sort of lone . . . no he's talking sure but . . . sure but he's saying things like a dollar is e, fifty cents is d, a quarter is . . . yeah then he tells me if corn is this god we don't even have electricity and he's only fit for public life then he tells me some poetry about some ancient founts, what he said about this place where he said he's been what they do there I wouldn't even . . . I sure will Mister Coen so how's your other pa . . . you really got your hands full I'll . . . you bet Mister Coen, goodbye. What's this . . .

—A postoperative for three nineteen.

—Good he'll be glad for some company in there.

—Yeah . . . ? they swung the bed down the corridor, —wait till he sees it.

—Mister Bast? you awake? We brought you a roommate see . . . ? but all that emerged from the heap on the rolling bed once in place was a rude sound which set its pattern of response for the night.

The shade clattered up on a gray that seemed to draw light from the room itself. —And how are my boys this morning? Mister Bast? are you awake?

—He went back to sleep, what's your name.

—I'm Miss Waddams, did you boys both wash?

—Get me some newspapers I haven't seen one for a week, what are you doing there.

—I have to take your pulse, would you get your arm out of the covers?

—You try to find it.

—Now now let's act our age, did you and Mister Bast get acquainted last night?

—Thinks I'm his father, he says let's improve this orange place by chopping everything down like the olden times.

—He doesn't mean anything by it, he tells me somebody broke in his house and I say who and he says you did! Then he tells me some creepy poetry about the dreary moorland and wants to see the scar around my neck he said he heard I'm a witch, he heard I screw my head off at night.

—I'll bet you do too Waddles, come around tonight and we'll . . .

—Now now let's act our age . . .

—Just want to get fixed up and . . .

—We'll fix you up don't worry, I'll get your newspapers . . .

—Bast? you awake . . . ? and he subsided till the rustle of sheets gave way to the ruffle of newspaper, the clatter of trays —don't think he even wants to wake up for lunch. What's this, fisheye?

—It's tapioca.

—It's fisheye . . . a clatter that gave way finally to a variety of solitary expressions of relief, and a silence broken eventually by the ruffle of newspapers. —Bast? you awake? Read you the paper and cheer you up, so full of other people's misery it's enough to cheer anybody up listen to this one. She told investigators she had not seen her husband since one evening last week, when she hid herself in a closet and watched him carefully make up his face and dress in an elaborate array of woman's clothing before slipping out. Answering a knock minutes later, she said he confronted her at the door insisting he was his own sister on a trip through town and just wanted to say hello. Unmoved by her demand that he come in and stop the nonsense, she said he suddenly turned and left and she has heard nothing from him since. In recounting her discovery, Mrs Teets appeared most annoyed by the variety of silk underthings she found hidden in his shirt drawer, since she had been restricted to cotton and synthetics throughout their marriage to save money. Mister Teets is being sought in connection with a subpoena for . . .

—Have we used the bedpan today?

—Think it'll hold us both? Let's wait, don't go away Waddles I've got a stiff proposition here for you . . .

—Now now . . .

—Real spoilsport isn't she, listen to this one. For a fifth straight day, the brave little fourth grader trapped in the soaring steel sculpture Cyclone Seven patiently awaits court settlement in a case that promises to set precedents in art and insurance circles alike. As tightlipped members of the local fire department stand their lonely vigil with acetylene torches ready, prepared to free the boy from what has been called one of the most outstanding contemporary sculptural comments on mass space, insurance company attorneys continue to work around the clock assembling briefs covering interpretations of the health, accident, life and property provisions contained in the numerous subclauses of the policies directly and indirectly involved in the controversy. Prospects for the out of court settlement rumored yesterday were suddenly dimmed by the intervention of a group calling itself the Modern Allies of Mandible Art. Through its attorneys, MAMA is seeking an injunction against what it terms willful destruction of a unique metaphor of man's relation to the universe, stating its contention that altering the massive work in the smallest detail would permanently destroy the arbitrary arrangement of force and line that pushes Cyclone Seven beyond conventional limits of beauty to celebrate in the virile and aggressive terms of raw freedom the triumphant dignity of man. Braving the sleet and freezing rain that continue to sweep the bare expanse of the Cultural Plaza where Cyclone Seven stands, protesters picketing within a stone's throw of the makeshift tent hastily suspended by friends and neighbors of the boy's parents to give him some protection from Bast? Look at that picture looks like he's being eaten alive, what's this Waddles. Fish?

—It's your supper.

—It's fish.

—Mister Bast? Suppertime, let's wake up and eat.

—Cheer up Bast the worst is yet to come. Wait till you try this fish, remember anything you told me last night? not to bring fresh flowers into the cemetery? You don't even know what failure is at your age how can you call yourself one when you've never done anything, talking about your father picking the wrong boy what you're worried about inheriting from him I've been trying to get out of the wallpaper business for fourteen years how do you like that, these great plans he had for you to be somebody? get your picture in the paper wearing a tuxedo? I never tasted anything like this before I don't see how you can get it down, I'll tell you a story about my boy. Tell me about this limited reliability you found in the trash I'll tell you a story about him. That war those same son of a bitches were running when they ran the whole country into the ground ten years ago he met a girl overseas and brought her back she was pregnant all right, I think this fish is going to make me vomit. He finally told me he couldn't swear it was his I could have told him that with one look at her he told me it didn't matter, he just wanted to save somebody love somebody help make up for some of the hands and feet we blew off over there it wouldn't matter, there didn't anybody ever need to know if it was his he married her and she had the baby it was black as your hat, how do you like that. A little boy now he's in second grade as black as your hat see what I mean? It's taken me fourteen years to get out of the wallpaper business people think winning's what it's all about just ask those son of a bitches who ran that war, ran the whole country into the ground while they were at it where's that woman, Waddles? Come in and get this tray it's the worst meal I ever ate.

—Did we take our medication?

—What medication just get this tray out of here.

—This little white cup yes you took it didn't you, if milk of magnesia doesn't help we may need an enema.

—Just crank me down a little I thought it was the sauce for the fish, here give me those papers read about other people's troubles see what I mean Bast? Can't get her mind off enemas here's one, remember the shelter fad? Here's one somebody built on Long Island it's got such a fancy big waste disposal system the whole district's sewer assessment's in trouble look at that, afraid of losing federal funding so they're condemning the whole thing turning it into a public convenience look at it, make a nice fifty holer won't it Waddles, ever been to Long Island? It says here the water table's so high the whole island's turning into a leaching field it may have to be declared a disaster area, one look at it I could have told them that . . .

—Are you finished too Mister Bast?

—If that fish didn't finish him nothing will you better take his pulse see if he still has one, here's a Senate subcommittee that still thinks winning's what it's all about holding hearings on a project part of a company the same son of a bitches that got me out of the wallpaper business listen to this. Testifying before the Broos committee on operational difficulties, Doctor Vogel stated that the only remaining problems appear to be those encountered in handling the noise or sound shards as they are called, and in perfecting the timing element in the thawing process. In what Doctor Vogel described as perhaps too ambitious a trial in this early state of the art, the shards comprising Beethoven's Fifth Symphony proved more difficult to handle than had been anticipated, and the sequential thaw technique was not entirely reliable. Appearing before the committee with his left arm in a cast and his face partially hidden by bandages, the colorful research director stated that the injuries sustained by himself and three of his technicians occurred when the entire first movement thawed in an unscheduled four seconds, ascribing the damage mainly to the strident quality of the musical work's opening bars . . .

—Move your feet let me tuck this in here, I don't think Mister Bast hears a word you're saying I think he's gone back to sleep.

—He knows how to get along with people he's a good listener aren't you Bast, pass me his orange drink he never touches it. The next test series will be conducted with a selection from The Red Mill by Victor Herbert, which Doctor Vogel chose as being less hazardous to personnel in the event of a repeated malfunction in the thawing process. Initiated by the Defense Department for reasons that remain unclear, the Frigicom project is being carried on in conjunction with noise environment studies in several cities and has attracted the interest of the recording industry due to the complete absence of friction associated with conventional transcription. Concluding his testimony with a jocular reference to turning the other cheek, Doctor Vogel was believed to be referring to cost overrun and feasibility studies in connection with a highly secret project said to involve a revolutionary method of transportation which is the focus of acute military interest. Informed sources stated that his abrupt departure for Texas this evening signaled the probability of a trial run of the new what are you looking for under there Waddles.

—Nothing silly I'm just checking your dressing.

—Check a little further you may get a surprise.

—No now Mister Duncan let's act our age . . .

—Just want to get fixed up and get back to Zanesville, crank me down a little will you . . . ? came from the tumult of newspaper, and she drew the door behind her on —here's a nice one, Bast? you awake? Here's a politician who pushed a girl out an office window he says she told him she could fly . . .

And down the corridor, —there's a call for you on two I think it's that same lawyer . . .

—Hello Mister Coen . . . ? Sure he's much better this eve . . . no he sleeps a lot but he seems much more . . . no, no he didn't have any visitors yet but he's got this real character in there with him now, they really . . . tomorrow? Sure, you . . . you bet Mister Coen yes see you tomorrow then . . .

Through bull's eye doors from the lull of an elevator, down those greens lost to the morning sun already failed elsewhere for the decline of afternoon's —excuse me nurse, I'm looking for . . .

—You the man to fix the diathermy? It's right in . . .

—No no I, I've come to see a patient is Miss Wad . . .

—It's not visiting time, Miss Waddams . . . ?

—Oh hi Mister Coen you finally made it, he's down this way. So how's your other patients.

—I just stopped at intensive care yes they, his condition's unchanged of course they don't dare operate but . . .

—I know they really hang on sometimes don't they there's no . . .

—Yes well how is Mister Bast, has he . . .

—Oh he's fine he ought to be out in a couple of days, he woke up this morning he wanted fifty sharp pencils he's been in here drawing pictures all day no right in here, wait till you meet his friend . . .

—across supermarket counters today following what was explained as an unfortunate lapse in inventory control by a spokesman for the Triangle Paper same son of a bitches who got me out of the wallpaper business how do you like that . . .

—Mister Bast . . . ?

—Intended for eventual distribution to novelty and mail order houses, sixteen thousand cases of toilet tissue appearing on supermarket shelves in many parts of the nation are the novelty roll variety, so called because alternate sheets bearing ribald messages . . .

—Mister Bast look you have a visitor!

—We've got a case of that they sent us in Zanesville you know what the message is?

—Mister Bast? I'm glad to see you recovered, you look . . .

—Who are you.

—It's your friend Mister Coen.

—It's your friend Mister Cohen Bast maybe he brought your pencils, you know what the message is on these . . .

—Yes you probably don't remember our drive in together Mister Bast, I must say I'm greatly relieved to see you up and, what is this you're doing . . .

—He's writing a piece for the unaccompanied cello because all they'll give him is a crayon, he said he has to finish something before he dies.

—Silly he's not going to die, now let Mis . . .

—Well then give him his fifty pencils, how do you know who's going to die Waddles you give him this drawing paper and one purple crayon all he can write is something for one instrument, give him his fifty sharp pencils he can probably write us a whole concert and bring me some more newspapers . . . !

—Mister Bast? You may not recall my telling you about Mrs Angel, your cousin Stella? She's still, still somewhat uncommunicative I saw her downtown last evening where I believe I mentioned she might go for observa . . .

—Before you sit down Cohen reach across him in that night table and just hand me that urinal?

—Why why, yes excuse me Mister Bast no go ahead with what you're doing just let me, there. Now. About your aunts Mister Bast I've been making every effort to learn what became of them, it occurred to me they might even have returned to Indiana? Recalling their devotion to their local newspaper out there fortunately I remembered the name of it and placed an ad urging them to get in touch with us, I've also renewed my efforts to reach their attorney out there a Mister Lemp? Their position seems to have assumed particular urgency since . . .

—Mind putting this back Cohen? careful . . . ! just got the cuff you won't even notice it when it dries, listen to this one . . .

—Excuse me Mister Bast if I might borrow that washcloth yes now, yes in looking into the complications implicit in Mister Angel's present condition and possibly also that of his wife as affecting your aunts' position with regard to settlement of the estate and attempting to verify their original holding in the family company, I learned that they appear to have had the bulk of their securities in a discretionary account where they have already suffered substantial losses through unsound investment decisions on their part, and since what stock remained was being held by this broker in a street name, in all likelihood it was included in the collateral he put up for very substantial loans he now appears unable to . . .

—Listen to this here's a couple of wetbacks one of them got a new Cadillac for five dollars, the other one's got an eighty foot yacht for ten how do you like that.

—To, I assume you've, Mister Bast? I assume you've had no word from the, from your father?

—I can help you out on that one Cohen.

—Pardon?

—Is that it? Cohen? with an h? You a lawyer Cohen?

—Why why yes, yes that's . . .

—Try this one on tell me if I can sue the city, walking down the street here a chippy came up she said she'd fix me up right there in the doorway for five dollars all I had was a ten, you know what she said? She said she'd go upstairs and get her sister to change it for me I'm not that dumb, I said I'd go up with her, hallway up there black as your hat and wham! That's what I'm doing here, ruptured spleen three broken ribs a torn . . .

—Frankly I doubt if you would have any success in attempting to sue the city Mis . . .

—Duncan Isadore Duncan, maybe you heard of my . . .

—The name sounds familiar yes but I'm afraid I . . .

—Just want to get fixed up and get back to Zanesville.

—I see yes I, I can hardly blame you and now, Mister Bast? Yes what was I, Mrs Angel yes, as I assumed the results of the paraffin test proved negative as of course so did the prints when they dusted the weapon an old octagonal barrel twenty-two, a sort of relic of Mister Angel's boyhood I believe. Of course I had had no doubt that the wound was self inflicted, I don't know whether you were aware of the growing despondency that had overtaken him lately but for a man of his fiercely independent nature seeing the comp. . .

—A man in the paper shot himself performed a perfect lobotomy, you read about that one Cohen? Held the gun up to his temple and fired put it down and walked away, the bullet went right through his head performed a perfect lo . . .

—That's very interesting Mister Duncan yes but I, I wonder if you would excuse us we have some rather important . . .

—Just put the gun down and walked away he didn't even know what he'd done, left him a little simple minded but I guess but that's better than being . . .

—No go on with what you're doing Mister Bast I'll simply try to keep my voice down, for a man of his background and temperament of course seeing the family company he'd worked so hard to build forced to go public in order to satisfy these estate taxes he took it all quite personally, especially these recent developments you may be unaware of? You, you do hear me Mister Bast? Yes, at any rate in what now proves to have been a futile attempt to forestall the halt in production and layoff that followed the, following the accident, I had undertaken negotiations for the sale of a roughly twenty percent interest in the company in order to satisfy these tax claims as a way of sidestepping going public in the full sense which Mister Angel found so disturbing. Unfortunately as these negotiations progressed he became even more alarmed at what he saw as the threat of a takeover through the direct sale of this minority interest to the large diversified corporation which had already in effect . . .

—Can't quite hear you over there Cohen.

—No well I, don't let us disturb you please we . . .

—Sound like the same son of a bitches that got me out of the wallpaper business.

—I see yes, what was I, in effect yes since they had in effect already gained what might be called a toehold with a five percent interest which had come into their hands as security for a loan to a person named Skinner setting him up in a publishing enterprise which he lost when he failed to meet his option . . .

—This the same Skinner that took out the girl to supper Cohen?

—Please I haven't the slightest . . .

—Took her out to dinner at quarter of ten it was up her something like that, purple lipstick on her teeth is that the one?

—I have no idea I, the man I mentioned I understand received a modest settlement on his management contract and has embarked on a new enterprise in fact, Mister Bast, since the personnel layoffs which occurred would naturally arouse your concern, you may be pleased to learn that some chance remark I made during the negotiations regarding the availability of two rather personable young ladies from Mister Angel's office appears to have led him to employ them in this new enterprise where their natural talents are apparently being given full . . .

—Quarter of nine it was in her the supper, something like that Cohen I can't remember . . .

—I see yes that, that may be just as well now as I, this five percent Mister Bast yes apparently it came into this Skinner person's hands through the former wife of a former employee who turned it over to her in a divorce settlement all of which may be somewhat beside the point, while its value at the time of transfer in the region of a hundred twenty thousand dollars clearly reflects the company's remarkable growth in the comparatively brief interim since he received the original stock when it was probably worth a mere seven or eight thousand, any long-term tax obligation perhaps twenty-five or thirty thousand dollars he may have incurred on the increment has nothing to do with the company itself of course. In fact the issue is not even the stock's current value which under present circumstances is probably severely open to question, but rather that of controlling interests in the light of recent, pardon? Mister Bast? No I, I thought you spoke, you can hear me? Since I am still unclear on whether you intend to exert any claim yourself? Because you see if the law . . .

—Why break the law to get all we can if we can get it all legally.

—Please not so loudly no, no I have no inten . . .

—Got you there hasn't he Cohen.

—Mister Duncan please, we . . .

—Change the law after he breaks it and where does that leave him, listen to this. National Commission will propose legal private use of marijuana, how do you like that. There is increasing evidence that we are approaching a situation similar to that at the time the Volstead Act was repealed wrote Doctor James Carey, a professor of criminology at the University of Cal . . .

—Please Mister Duncan please, this has nothing to do with . . .

—That's all right Cohen you didn't let me finish, the recommendation does not amount to full decriminalization because persons who use marijuana could still go to jail for such actions as growing it, giving it to friends, transporting it or smoking it in public how do you like that. Studies have shown . . .

—Mister Duncan please! What I am attempting to discuss with Mister Bast has nothing whatever to do with mari . . .

—Just depends whose ox is gored is that it Cohen? The conservative majority has insisted that criminal penalties be retained for the simple sale of the drug, that is sales between friends and others not in the business of trafficking drugs keep the world safe for Seagram Distillers National Tobacco Company and those son of a bitches that got me out of the wallpaper business is that it Cohen? How do you like this, in Houston a young civil rights activist is serving a thirty-year sentence for giving marijuana cigarettes to an undercov . . .

—Mister Duncan! I hold no brief whatever for the special interests you mention, I am here simply to discuss a rather grave and complex family matter with Mister Bast and I must ask you to find some other source of entertain . . .

—Want to discuss a family matter Cohen I'll tell you what my wife did, I put part of the business in her name just for the tax angle when I wanted to get out she wouldn't let me how do you like that. Nothing she wants nothing she hasn't got, fourteen years of it I built her a house so big she still carries her handbag from one room to the next one she won't even give me a divorce, she turned me in to the IRS for ten percent had me followed by detectives got herself a Jew lawyer how would you like to handle it for me.

—No no thank you no, no I'm certain there's nothing I . . .

—Always heard the only way to fight a Jew lawyer's to get another Jew lawyer I've been trying to get out of the wallpaper business for fourteen years, you know what I finally did? Ran up the biggest bill we could with our paper supplier and just left it lie there till a company took them over and offered to write it off as a downpayment, said they'd take the rest out of profits son of a bitches finally got me out of the wallpaper business, how do you like that.

—It's very interesting yes clearly you have no need for a Jewish attorney, now . . .

—Tell you what I just read about here this wetback who bought a new Cadillac for five dollars, one of these Texas millionaires died he left the proceeds of the sale of his Cadillac and the yacht to some chip, what do you want now Waddles.

—We're going for a ride Mister Duncan, they want to take your picture up at x-ray, let me get the chair closer here let's get our feet out and . . .

—I'll try to make it quick Cohen, don't . . .

—No no please don't hurry back on my account Mis . . .

—Mister Duncan!

—Told you I had a surprise for you didn't I Waddles? Don't go away Cohen, something else I wanted to ask you . . .

—Yes thank, heavens. Now Mister Bast perhaps we can concen, what is it you need more paper it's right down here let me, there, yes I'm sure you can follow what I'm saying while you continue with that you see Mister Bast under the circumstances, you appear to be the only family member available and, and competent to discuss this matter and in light of your own real or possible interest in its outcome I'm sure you can help me to clarify some of its aspects, I'll try to be brief. As you may or may not have been aware, an element of mistrust appeared to have developed before Mister Angel's accident between him and his wife your cousin Stella concerning the controlling interest in General Roll. What gave rise to this growing mistrust on both hands of course I have no way of knowing, though I may say that from my frequently close contact with Mister Angel and certainly in light of this recent unhappy event, assuming my interpretation to be the correct one, his was motivated immeasurably less by anything resembling what might perhaps in another instance be construed simply as greed, considering the rather substantial sums of money involved, than by the very understandable fear in a man of his, his ah . . .

—background and temper . . .

—Background and yes, yes you are following me then . . .

—No I'm just listening.

—Yes that's what I, I see yes at any rate having drawn up Mister Angel's will in which I am named executor while of course I am not at liberty under the circumstances to divulge its contents whatever its provisions, even were his wife your cousin Stella to be excluded, we are all aware of her incontestable claim as his wife to a portion of his estate which after taxes should amount to approximately eighteen percent of the company, her share of which combined with the half of her father's estate to which she is clearly entitled giving her altogether about eighteen and one half percent as opposed to the twenty-five percent now controlled by this conglomerate and the twenty-seven controlled by your aunts and their brother James, your father I mean to say if such indeed proves to be the case, in which event of course her claim your cousin Stella's to her father's estate in its entirety combined with her minimum portion of that of her husband assuming his failure to survive would secure her . . .

—Who's Mister Duncan here.

—What? pardon? Oh, oh he's not here Miss no I believe he went to be x-rayed he . . .

—Tell him to call the office about his insurance will he be right back?

—I sincerely trust not but of course I'm in no position to . . .

—Just tell him to call the office about this health plan he's got before supper all right? He'll be back by then?

—I would have no doubt yes now the, Mister Bast? Yes, now this question of the, of Mister Angel yes where, what was I . . .

—of his amusing failure to survive you said . . .

—His yes which would of course secure her control with roughly thirty-one percent barring a surprise from other quarters, by which I refer of course to your own status in the matter regarding which I have been making every conceivable effort to reach you for what seems an eternity and which would, of course, assume substantially more complex proportions should it prove in turn related to the intentions of the conglomerate I have just spoken of as these become clarified by the parties to its reorganization with the wealth of possibilities for protracted litigation its rather spectacular dissolution will undoubtedly present, to say nothing of the effect already apparent on the market insofar as this unprecedented downturn which shows no indication of reversing itself, most especially in terms of the overwhelming loss of confidence that has led to the headlong flight of the small investor, is ascribed by growing numbers of market analysts to the events stemming from this particular corporate situation which has filled the papers this past week as I take it under the circumstances you may well have been unaware? Mister Bast? I, I thought you spoke . . . ?

—Have you got a pencil?

—Why why, yes, yes I should have thought of it of course here, yes I mention this simply in passing Mister Bast because the remote possibility that the right hand might be ignorant of the left hand's activities suggested itself to me in these news stories to which I refer, where I came upon an elusive company officer bearing the same name whose activities appear to have provoked at least one lawsuit and I even saw pictured in the midst of a disorderly episode where unfortunately his features were obscured by a feathered headdress in somewhat . . .

—This the room that asked for the newspapers?

—Par . . . ? oh, oh that bed there I think yes, thank you. Yes it even occurred to me Mister Bast during the negotiations I . . .

—That's a dollar ten.

—The, oh? oh I see all right yes, yes here, in these corporate negotiations I just discussed it had even occurred to me that this coincidence might have inspired their part in General Roll's divestiture of its long-standing major interest in the Nathan Wise Company through a bill sponsored by a Senator whose family happens to be among the original stockholders, providing family planning assistance to our prolific neighbors on the Asian subcontinent, and in turn enabling Nathan Wise to write off at retail its vast inventory accumulated since pharmaceutical measures to deal effectively with this historic dilemma have gained such popularity here among our own popula . . .

—Still here Cohen? good . . .

—Heavens I, that was quick . . .

—Technician broke his glasses how do you like that, careful there Waddles . . .

—I see yes well, yes some newspapers just arrived for you there Mister Duncan I'm sure you'll find plenty to interest you while Mister Bast and I finish up here in terms of fixed assets you see Mister Bast, the Nathan Wise divestiture leaves the company with only the Astoria plant and its appurtenances, however you may be unaware of the enormous ramifications in terms of extensive damage suits throughout the data processing and punched card industries that may be expected to follow upon final resolution of a lawsuit originating well before my own connection with the company against a firm called JMI Industries then known as the Jubilee Musical Instrument Company, relating to applications of the Jacquard loom approach to information storage and retrieval in the form of punched holes as in the player pi . . .

—On the hole business is very good, is that the one Cohen? That's the message you asked me what was on those novelty rolls?

—I see yes I, thank you Mister Duncan returning to your own position in this situation Mister Bast especially as viewed in terms of the possibilities we have just discussed, I am of course fully aware that, were you guided by strictly mercenary considerations, you would hardly have disdained your original opportunity to lay claim to a share of the estate in question against which no doubt you could have borrowed forthwith, particularly since recent changes in the law would appear to obviate any problems regarding your emancipation . . .

—Like me to send you a few of those novelty rolls when I get back to Zanesville Cohen? The top man in the company he had cases sent out to all the division heads, sort of an encouraging word when you're in the middle of . . .

—No no thank you no, I wouldn't . . .

—Wouldn't deprive anybody there's a whole case there, just get fixed up and get back to Zanesville . . .

—I would heartily support that Mister Duncan yes, now Mister Bast if we could clear up this one essential point which has been a major obstacle to the logical and satisfactory conclusion of this entire matter since my initial confron, my first meeting with your aunts . . .

—Say Cohen, before you get into . . .

—Mister Duncan please! I, I just purchased those newspapers for you in the admittedly desperate hope that reading them to yourself might provide you with sufficient diversion to permit . . .

—Thanks that's just what I want to do what do I owe you.

—Nothing, only a brief period of si . . .

—I just wanted to ask you to reach across him in that night table there and hand me the bedpan.

—I, yes. Yes. Mister Bast? Under the circumstances . . .

—Not leaving are you Cohen?

—I think so yes I, I should get downtown for another probably equally futile here you are Mister Duncan, yes perhaps when I return tomorrow one of you will be discharged one of you, either one of you it almost ceases to matter . . .

—Wait do you want to take this story about this wetback with the five dollar Cadillac I'll tear it out for you, talking about wills and executors what this dumb millionaire did he made his wife executor so when he left the proceeds of this yacht and this Cadillac to some chip . . .

—No no thank you all the same Mister Duncan the Corpus Juris is filled with such follies goodnight, goodnight Mister Bast I trust . . .

—Thank you for the pencil Mister Coen.

—Cohen? Bring him some tomorrow sharp ones, he wants fifty sharp ones getting on this thing it's like riding a midget's surfboard, there. Bast? listen to this one, Davenport Iowa. The wife of a wealthy East Coast publishing executive who disappeared from her fashionable Scarsdale New York home last Christmas eve was discovered here today working as a waitress in a coffeeshop in order to help her husband out of the severe financial difficulties she was convinced had overtaken him, which she believed he feared to confide even to her how do you like that. Reached at Boca Raton where he is attending a publishing convention, the six figure a year executive good naturedly characterized as cigar money his wife's savings of nine hundred sixteen dollars and eleven cents in small bills and coins, discovered by chance when fire struck the four dollar a week room here in which she has no privacy in this place at all what do you want.

—You're Mister Duncan? You were to call the office about your insurance this health plan, is it all you have?

—What's wrong with it, I got it through those same son of a . . .

—It's very interesting, we've never seen one like it but it doesn't seem to cover you till you enter the nursing home.

—What makes you think I'm entering a nursing home.

—If you want to get your coverage page eleven, twelve it's down here miscellaneous provisions wait I brought a magnifying glass, approved nursing home care including specified prescription drugs and prosthetic devices in accordance with article sixteen paragraph twenty g, your departure by private hearse, plastic casket and complete service by the denomination of your choice with free plastic flower spray and your own personalized plot four by eight feet overlooking the picturesque leisure village of Union . . .

—Wait hand me that newspaper no, under there that one those son of a, look here, Eldercare bill passes they passed this Eldercare bill that should . . .

—But your age according to our . . .

—Then I'll just sit here till I qualify how do you like that, Waddles? Get this woman out of here she's upsetting me, and get me off this thing, what's that. Jello?

—It's your supper.

—It's Jello.

—Mister Bast? Let's just move all these papers and put your tray here, you have been busy today haven't you.

—Just hand me the financial page there before you go Waddles, read it while I eat this there's no sense being sick twice see that Bast? Life never lets you down does it, the Dow just hit four fifty-three the whole thing's finally going to pot how do you like that, wake up some morning and it just won't be there that's what I'm telling you Bast you can't call yourself a failure if you've never done anything. Run the whole country into the ground get thirty or forty thousand boys killed but they'll let you pretend it's not a war as long as you don't raise taxes to pay for it, son of a bitches who still think winning's what it's all about that's what would scare them this is worse than that fish I never tasted anything like it. Lie about taxes cheat on the federal budget a few years of that you've got the rate of private debt formation running double the real output it's all supposed to be paid back from, let the interest rates triple on top of that and they'll plant you a tree on the Perdinalies hand you a world bank or a three billion dollar foundation and give you ninety thousand a year walking around money while she sits in her four dollar a week room in Davenport and counts her tips that's what I'm telling you Bast, if you want to make a million you don't have to understand money, what you have to understand is people's fears about money that's what it's all about try your Jello right on top of the cauliflower see? That way you can't taste either one of them, you hear people crying about inflation that's the only thing that's kept it all going how else do they expect to pay back the two dollars they owe from the one they make here's another of these son of a bitches listen to this. In a strongly worded appeal following today's Senate hearings on the two hundred million dollar government loan guarantee favored by banking and investment interests engaged in reorganizing the complex corporate affairs of the same son of a bitches that got me out of the wallpap . . .

—Are you boys all finished?

—That's the word Waddles, I'm never going to eat another bite.

—You shouldn't say a thing like that Mister Duncan, you'll feel better after an enema.

—Coffee?

—You're not to have coffee, I'll get you some juice if you . . .

—I'm talking about the enema a coffee enema, Waddles? Colombian coffee did you hear me? Conjuring up the impending threat of unemployed constituents in numerous states where the corporate son of a bitches where was I here, corporate holdings are located, Senator Broos went on to emphasize the further threat to company stockholders and its proliferation in terms of the current market plunge with the consequent headlong flight of the small investor as a near fatal wound upon the nation's body politic son of a bitches never let you down do they, who said that Mark Twain a politician's an ass everything's sat on except a man? Stressing the vital necessity of expanded capital formation unimpeded by government restraints, Senator Broos' impassioned plea for a restoration of faith on the part of the common man in the free enterprise system as the cornerstone of those son of a bitches who still think winning's what it's all about give them a string of high p e ratios and a rising market it's all free enterprise all they howl about's government restraints interference double taxation, all free enterprise till they wreck the whole thing they're the first ones up there with a tin cup whining for the government to bail them out with a loan guarantee so they can do it all over again . . .

—Here we are Mister Duncan, now let's just . . .

—What's that, Waddles. I said coffee.

—It's just mineral oil it's not going to bite you, now just lie on your side and try to re . . .

—No such thing as free enterprise in this country since the Haymarket riots, the minute something threatens this expanding capital forma ow . . .

—That's it lie still now, just try to keep it in as long as you can that's it . . .

—Threaten this expanding capital formation and they're at the head of the line whining for loan guarantees against the, the taxes on those tips she's sitting out there counting at night on her four dollar davenport to, to . . .

—That's it now just keep it in . . .

—to bail them out because she's the only one who knows failure's what it's really all, all I don't know how much longer I . . .

—Just a little longer you're doing fine . . .

—See the debt burden rising twice as fast as income the price of chemicals today see that in the paper? Price of chemicals in the human body it's worth three dollars and a half used to be ninety-eight cents when I, I can't, good time to sell out try to slow down inflation the whole security market's co, collapsing credit shrinkage forcing a, can't . . .

—Just a minute longer . . .

—forcing a, a mass, massive outflow of . . .

—Wait here's the pan! here's the pan! my . . .

—I don't, don't feel too good Waddles . . .

—Just lie back now it's all right, let me change this sheet.

—Just let me, hand me that paper there something I wanted to read to Bast.

—He's had a busy day Mister Duncan, I don't think he even . . .

—Bast? you awake? I thought you'd want to hear about our brave little fourth grader listen. A brief rockthrowing disturbance erupted here this morning when hot coffee, frankfurter and novelty vendors clashed with signcarrying members of the MAMA organization over their line of march past Cyclone Seven on the windswept Cultural Plaza where, for the eighth straight day, a haggard member of the local fire department stands with his torch ready to reach the brave little eighth straight day it can't be, what day is it Waddles.

—I don't know is it Wednesday? let's move your feet . . .

—Where's the rest of this paper wait, Bast? how do you like this one. An elderly drifter who has made his home with a local family in recent years was found in critical condition here today being nursed by two small children, who have been administering a mixture of maple syrup and plaster of Paris to him following what appears to have been a fall some days ago. In the unexplained absence of both parents, stories pieced together from neighbors and authorities at the nearby school where both had taught until recently indicate that each of them believed their elderly guest to be the other's father, and during recent . . .

—Mister Duncan why don't you just rest now let me turn off the light, I think Mister Bast's already . . .

—He's a good listener aren't you Bast, that's the whole secret of making people like you be an American you want everybody to like you. I took a Dale Carnegie course once learned you can't trust anybody you can't even trust yourself how do you like that, son of a bitches blow off their hands and feet wreck the whole economy just wanted everybody to like him, you wouldn't believe I started out a Roman would you? Anything serious for confession sneak down to the slums and confess to the Franciscans they'd heard everything rape, incest, steal the household money that night you told me you'd had your chance and made a mess of it? Steal from the dime store the kind of things I did they'd hand out five hail Marys that story I told you about my boy, you didn't believe it did you? Something I read in the paper once that's why I told it to you Bast just get a good opinion of yourself that's all you need, reach the end of the line waiting for God to drop the other shoe that's all you've got . . .

—Let's just put your light out and settle down now Mister Duncan, I think you need . . .

—Get fixed up and get back to Zanesville . . .

—Don't worry we'll fix you up . . .

—Good night nurse. You don't hear that one anymore do you.

—Good night now, I'll see you boys in the morning . . . and the glow at the wall socket took up the loss of day, eyed the slow accumulation of the night.

—Bast? you awake? Bast? Will you help me over here?

—What, what is it. Mister Duncan?

—I can't find it help me over here will you?

—Yes but, wait a minute, yes. What's, but what are you reaching for . . .

—Not the eye of a needle.

—What?

—Those people at the next bed there are they, I can't understand them what are they Porto Ricans?

—Mister Duncan there's nobod . . .

—Do you want to split a beer? Split a beer with me will you?

—Well, well all right but . . .

—Never in the service were you Bast?

—No I, never . . .

—Fourteen years it took me to get out of the wallpaper business the first payday I was drafted down there at Dix I started a ten cent crap game, son of a bitches came raised it a dollar five dollars ten I got out and started another ten cent crap game the same thing happened, kept happening till I was standing there alone crap games going on all around me I'd started them all how do you like that. I said how do you like that.

—Well I, I'm sorry it ended that way maybe I'd better . . .

—It always does Bast it always does, life never lets you down the first night we were out there they put us out there in the Huertgen Forest Marty shouts over to us you guys want to see a dead German? Out there in the moonlight the moon was out half his head gone squatted there with his pants down I couldn't take a crap for five days after that, you'd better get a case, Bast? Better get a case, call home and get three dollars and twenty eight cents. Have you had your lunch?

—Well, well yes we . . .

—What are you going to have for supper.

—Well we, we just . . .

—Have you got the money? Let's see it . . .

—Mis, Mister Duncan I'd better ring for the nurse . . .

—Going at three fifty a good time to sell out I lost a daughter, did I tell you that Bast? Both of us get fixed up and go homesteading she could spell almost anything how do you like that, she was taking piano lessons when they took out her appendix son of a bitches never let you down do they it wasn't her appendix at all. I took a bride doll up to her that's the one thing she wanted, a bride doll, she'd keep missing the right notes keep trying it again she was learning a song called for Alise's something like that I never did hear it like it was supposed to be, she'd miss notes leave little parts out and start again I always thought maybe someday I'd hear it right hear what I was supposed to there was a delicatessen near us named Alise's then, that's why I can even remember the name of it still hear it like she played it though that's all I, all I want, I can still, hear it? hear it . . . ?

—Yes who rang in here?

—I did nurse it's Mister Duncan he's, I just wonder if he's all right he . . .

—Get back to bed I'll take care of him . . . the spot of light leaped, dropped shrunk close searching white from whites, darted, paused —just get to sleep he won't disturb you now . . . came up blinding and was gone, leaving the dark confirmed by the wall socket's glow until it faded with the rise of day.

—Mister Duncan? are you awake? Sun caught on water somewhere trembled on the ceiling —that reflection up there, can you see it throbbing? I think it's my pulse I've just been lying here watching it, I couldn't figure it out. I wasn't even trying to Mister Duncan? do you know what scares me? Just lying here watching it it's from that glass of water down there where my foot's resting I was thinking about all the things you've said, I was thinking there's so much that's not worth doing suddenly I thought maybe I'll never do anything. That's what scared me I always thought I'd be, this music I always thought I had to write music all of a sudden I thought what if I don't, maybe I don't have to I'd never thought of that maybe I don't! I mean maybe that's what's been wrong with everything maybe that's why I've made such a, why I've been thinking of things you've said as though just, just doing what's there to be done as though it's worth doing or you never would have done anything you wouldn't be anybody would you, you wouldn't even be who you are now, Mister Duncan? where's the, nurse? Miss Waddams is that you out there . . . ?

—Haven't you boys washed up yet?

—No but Mister Duncan is he, I guess he's still asleep I called the nurse for him last night when he . . .

—Mister Duncan . . . ?

—I was just telling him how much I, wait what are you closing the curtain . . .

—Joe? will you bring that chair in out there?

—Wait where's he going is he awake? Mister Duncan? I just remembered something is there a piano here someplace Miss Waddams? That piece of music you said your daughter used to practice the one you said you'd never heard right? I think I know what it . . .

—No over here Joe, Mister Bast's going down to the solarium would you like that Mister Bast?

—Well, well all right yes but I haven't even had breakfast I mean what's . . .

—We'll bring you some just get your feet down that's it, your friend Mister Coen called he said he's bringing your cousin up, the one whose husband's in intensive care now step back, that's it, that will be nice won't it sit back now, do you feel steady?

—Fine yes I feel fine but what wait, wait is he awake? I just wanted to tell him that piece your daughter used to practice Mister Duncan? I think I know what it was I'll play it for you later and see, I think it's a piano piece Beethoven wrote for . . .

—Go ahead Joe hurry up . . . she came after them —and come right back . . . but she paused there through the door, finding a tissue before she turned up the corridor. —Is there a doctor on the floor yet?

—Why what happened.

—They left me an expiration in three nineteen last night, you busy?

—I've got a pre-op in three eleven this nasty old . . .

—Would you change with me?

—What for three nineteen? sure what's . . .

—I just, you just get to like them sometimes . . .

—Don't worry you won't get to like this one watch out though, they said he's a trustee here . . .

—Thanks . . . she paused outside the door using the tissue, brought her weight against it. —Good morning, are we read . . .

—Where the two phones I ordered put in here.

—There's a telephone right there beside the bed sir, if you . . .

—Told them to put in two outside lines here can't waste half the day going through your damn switchboard every time I . . .

—Hold your water John you're just here to have a plug changed, nurse I told them at the desk out there to bring me some Bananx where is it.

—I don't know ma'am I don't think we . . .

—It's a hospital isn't it? You don't use drugs in a hospital?

—Yes ma'am but we can't hand them out to a visitor without any doc . . .

—Visitor! you'll see a visitor who'll hand you something hand you your ass if you can't, who's doing this implant, Handler? You call Doctor Han . . .

—Damn it Zona start this you better get a room of your own here where the devil's Beaton, should have been here three minutes ago.

—I wouldn't get a room of my own here for an ingrown toenail, I came in three years ago to have my tubes blown out and couldn't open my eyes till they painted these filthy green walls put up my own drapes and got rid of this atrocious furniture look at this chair, I feel like I'm sitting on a pot.

—Look like it too Zona just waiting for the barrage to start, here what the devil do you want.

—If you could get into your gown sir, we . . .

—Have to get out of my damn shirt first don't I? Get me the, here he is Beaton? Hang this up in the closet get hold of the director here what's his name get these phones put in get my arm here young woman, wasted one day getting this damn thing implanted waste another getting it replaced I told you to look into this company Beaton, Broos down there holding hearings on these research projects if they're as useless as this damn thing they should have stayed in toys let go of me girl!

—I've looked into it yes sir, it all sounds so prepos . . .

—Dried up old Raggedy Andy what makes you think they didn't stay in toys lift up his little gown Beaton, let's see if the toy heart they gave him says I love . . .

—Zona damn it be quiet I didn't ask you how it sounded Beaton I asked what you found out down there get this shoe off me will you?

—Yes sir I'm waiting for a call now from one of the Senator's staff people who's down at the company's Texas installation as an observer on this Teletrav . . .

—Careful damn it! want to take my foot off . . .

—Yes sir I'm sorry, he tells me the parent company's head of personnel who went down there to troubleshoot the project is scheduled to take part in a preliminary evaluation of its operational capabilities this morning as soon as they . . .

—Poor devil where they sending him.

—They have a phone company trunk line leased to an undisclosed receiving point somewhere in Maine sir I presume it's an Army base, the company's research director insists on establishing the system's long-range capacity at the outset although it hardly . . .

—What I saw in the papers sounds like the same stunt he pulled with this Frigicom project, gets the DOD to draw up an impact statement shut up these damn fish lovers could have settled it with a car horn but he starts off with some complicated damn fool piece of music . . .

—Yes sir however I've pointed out all the Committee has is his word that this music was actually . . .

—Told you to get onto him down there too didn't I? find out what the devil here put these in the closet . . .

—Yes sir I did quite inadvertently in fact, he joined me in a men's room in the Senate Office Building where he wet my, granted he was hampered by bandages he wet my leg thoroughly during a brief conversation which convinced me the man is certifiably insane frankly sir this idea of transporting people by cable is so utterly preposterous I . . .

—Sounds like he just wet down your pride a little Beaton damn it you're not a scientist neither am I, think how preposterous television sounded a few years ago now you can't get away from the damn thing ever see color television? One bawling idiot after another on the screen, send his bawling picture a thousand miles in color like that probably no reason you can't just go ahead and send the idiot himself is there?

—Possibly not sir but . . .

—Used to be the right people traveled all the idiots stayed put now nobody travels, haven't been anywhere myself since they took out the Berengaria here hang these up. Now the right people stay put all you see's the idiots and errand boys being flown around like bundles don't know where they're going don't even know where they've been line them up like an infantry regiment and telegraph them they wouldn't know the damn difference, don't cost us a nickel to sit things out while this reorganization gets underway see where Diamond fits in does it? Sounded like the reason that bunch had their eye on it's why I want this tender to go right through, see this project come up with something and we run into an antitrust ruling leave us standing there with a wish in one hand and where the devil's that young woman.

—Getting my Bananx while Beaton sits there with his . . .

—No I brought you some ma'am wait, it's right here in . . .

—Give it to me then don't just stand there with your thumb in your . . .

—Damn it Zona he's not your nursemaid who the devil got you up here this morning, one place I thought I'd have some priva . . .

—Beaton got me up here this morning get this open Beaton.

—Beaton you tell her after this get her damn free pills someplace else, those two hundred thousand shares of Diamond she was sitting on as Boody's guardian running around loose now no damn reason I have to listen to any more of her damn . . .

—Tell him to hold his water Beaton, what does he mean running around loose.

—Meant what I said what does she call Boody, the Bank of England? Damn law falling apart anyplace you look give these eighteen-year-olds the right to sue vote make contracts all the rest of it see Boody marry some black find some shyster lawyer get this sock off me Beaton, why I told you to look into those gossip items see if it was some corporate stunt they cooked up to start a raid on Diamond or just plain damn greed with this what's his name Bast? he's a black isn't he?

—I think not sir, that was a misapprehension you gained initially from a poor quality newspaper picture when their activities first came to our atten . . .

—No other damn reason anybody black or white want to marry Boody but these two hundred thousand shares is there? Anybody who could get near enough to her to . . .

—Beaton you tell him anybody who wants a smell of those shares can kiss mine tell him he gets both cheeks, tell him she's being committed I had the papers drawn up for Ude's signature to . . .

—Having his funeral Saturday ask her how the devil she's getting his signature, up there yesterday his wife and daughter pouring scotch down the drain hand over fist so damn scared of estate taxes . . .

—Well tell him Beaton!

—Yes ma'am the papers were drawn up last week sir, Judge Ude signed them the morning he fell into the . . .

—Excuse me sir could you lie back and give me your arm . . .

—Nurse get me some water.

—Damn it Zona she's . . .

—What are you strapping a radio on him for nurse he's not going anyplace, now get me some water.

—It's an external heart pacer ma'am just until he . . .

—Want somebody to wait on you hand and foot damn it Zona where's your black girl this is a hosp . . .

—That's what I want to know where is she Beaton, get me some water.

—Deleserea she's still in jail ma'am, she . . .

—What's she doing there, you proved she wasn't peddling her ass on that street corner didn't you? You said you could prove she was just asking directions dragging that city bus sign into court where nobody could understand it what's she doing in jail.

—She's been given a complete medical examination and placed in a rehabilitation program involving beauty school where she's able to spend her time having her hair and nails done taking showers and watching telev . . .

—What does she mean I have twelve at lunch tomorrow!

—I told her that yes ma'am that's when she abruptly changed her plea to guilty, she . . .

—That's the most the most ungrateful here give me that you're spilling it, what gets into these people no consideration at all as bad as Vida's girl last night she could have ruined the evening . . .

—Tell me how anybody could ruin one of Vida's evenings worst damn wastes of . . .

—You were standing right there when she went down with a tray of Vida's best Waterford and some busybody called the police who said not to move her, she had to be covered with a tablecloth till the coroner could . . .

—Had the crystal insured didn't they? Thought I heard something fall must have been when I was talking to Handler he's doing this job this morning isn't he nurse? Something to discuss with him when we get up there . . .

—The implant? Yes sir but you'll have a shot before you go up I don't think you'll be able to discuss anything with . . .

—You look into it then Beaton, Handler's damned annoyed said he was looking around for a good tax loss Crawley put him onto backing a play from some bunch called Angels East told him it was so bad it would fold overnight the damn thing opened it's sold out must be some way to get it closed, fire laws health laws unions contracts must have pulled a fast one somewhere never met anybody in that theater bunch wasn't a scoundrel a damn fool or both, one of them with no tie going on at me last night at Vida's thought he was making some sense about what the pound's been through rallies declines public turning its back turns out he's talking about some damn dead poet finally had to put him out the door, few free drinks he's insulting Vida tells her husband they betrayed literature selling out to this same damn bunch we're talking about, the bank acting as corporate trustee of this Duncan stock nobody tells me a damn thing about it how the devil'd they get hold of it.

—From what I've been able to piece together sir during their acquisition of Triangle Paper they took advantage of a bad debt situation involving an entirely different Duncan and Company, an Ohio wallpaper manufacturer, to mislead the . . .

—Other damn way round I'd understand it take the wallpaper any day something you can draw up a budget on, don't matter how ugly it is houses like a string of motel rooms you know how many damn rolls you can sell, these damn books you need a fortune teller in there doing your budget publish ten hold your breath waiting for one of them to bail out the other nine that any way to run a business?

—No sir in fact their major objective in this scheme to get control of the Duncan trade list and textbook line was obviously to use it as a readymade adver . . .

—Get into these mass paperbacks print an edition of five hundred thousand might as well ship three straight to the shredder one thing I hate it's waste, can't figure costs to sales too many unknowns too damn much waste . . .

—Yes sir what they've done is reduce the significance of the cost factor, largely write off the waste element and outrage traditional publishing convention by using the entire list as a readymade advertising enterprise, they . . .

—Have to advertise the damn things how else they going to sell them.

—No sir in the books I mean ads in the books themselves sir, textbooks and novels filled with columns of advertising the prime space goes to their own subsidiaries but most of them appear to be quite tastelessly solicited, what figures I've obtained from our sources indicate a startling amount in billings which no excuse me sir just my briefcase I, yes here are some of the figures, it's created a furor in publishing particularly the textbook area and drawn violent objections from some prominent writers who threat . . .

—Always objecting to something only damn reason they're writers, make their damn peace the country could get on with its business if this bunch hadn't done it somebody else would here what's these figures, haven't got my glasses . . .

—Those are, oh yes that's a children's encyclopedia they're bringing out sir, it's doing extremely well even though it seems to be teeming with inaccuracies and a number of prominent educators have demanded its withdraw . . .

—Didn't ask your editorial opinion Beaton I said what's the figures.

—Down here sir the initial outlay is in the neighborhood of a third of a million, two hundred sixty-six thousand on promotion sixty-six thousand in production and, yes and six hundred sixty dollars went in research writing and editorial costs yes no wonder the . . .

—Beaton what's that, that magazine give it to me.

—Where the, oh this ma'am yes this is their magazine She, they took over the old Her magazine and turned it into a . . .

—Don't stand there blubbering about it give it to me, the cover looks like Emily.

—Here let me see that, looks like Amy if she was some broken down two dollar . . .

—Two dollars worth of cold fish she wouldn't spread her toes for the King of . . .

—This Mister Katz's room?

—What the devil does he want.

—You Mister Katz?

—What Mister Katz get him out of here.

—Wait sir he, what's that name who . . .

—Room three eleven come to do the phones right on the order here, right here c, a, t e s. Katz.

—Never mind yes just put them in as quickly as you . . .

—Over here damn it! think I talk with my feet? See how much damn difference one more bungled encyclopedia's going to make Beaton? this boob what's his name Duncan's head of sales, thought he went out and set up his own company.

—This Skinner person yes sir he picked up that option but . . .

—Skinnerflix that's the name of it Skinnerflix what do you think they make, shoelaces? He's making a movie called Two Foxy Girls and Vida's psychia . . .

—Don't give a damn what they make Zona be quiet, just want to know how this bunch got in here Beaton.

—That piggish little man with glasses last night going around handing out his card that says he deals in women's underclothes plays the part of the psychi . . .

—Damn it Zona be quiet! Picked up this option to set up in publishing didn't he Beaton? now how the devil . . .

—Originally yes sir under this D and S imprint but according to a trade journal a novel he just published there, a Western called The Blood in the Red White and Blue had already been published elsewhere with the title Guns of God under different pseudonyms by the same writer who's now being sued for plagiarism by the producers of a motion picture called Dirty . . .

—Didn't ask for a lot of damn gossip I said how'd this bunch get in there!

—Yes sir he, they allowed this Skinner person to put up a small interest in another company against a loan to take up the Duncan option sir, when he couldn't meet the loan they exercised the option, seized his collateral and terminated his management con . . .

—Get something out of you's like pulling teeth what's this collateral.

—A small interest I think it's five percent sir in a company called General Roll, a small company out here in Astoria that makes . . .

—Don't matter if it makes paper dolls this same bunch grabbed up twenty percent of it here a while back in an estate tax bind you sit here talking about wallpaper and some fool encyclopedia this is what they were after the whole damn time, family owned outfit this twenty-five percent might control it that so hard to figure out Beaton?

—Yes well no sir but it's just a small comp . . .

—Don't matter if it's as big as your thumb it's sitting there on this old patent claims suit with JMI never read your damn law journals? Why the devil you think Stamper picked up JMI in that Dallas mortgage deal think he needed a million used jukeboxes? Get hold of this end of it in this receivership there's the whole punched tape industry by the short here young woman plug that in Beaton get me the price on Diamond.

—Yes sir but that's nurse what is it . . .

—It's this monitor to monitor the patient's heart so the pacer can be adjusted to . . .

—Told them to bring in a Quotron where the devil is it.

—A what did he say?

—Quotron damn it can't she . . .

—It's a machine to get current stock prices on nurse it was supposed to be . . .

—Like this little television? It's out there they said to don't use it it might interfere with the monitor just lie real still sir.

—By God lie here not know the price of anything what was the damn Dow when you came in Beaton?

—Two eighty sir they opened on another heavy selling wave but the . . .

—Two eighty by God where the damn bargain hunters call the ow!

—Just a small needle lie still sir . . .

—Hello operator trying a line here . . .

—See it's mainly like a precaution on account of the patient's age if the pacemaker's set wrong it could send him into . . .

—Why I want you to look right into this General Roll outfit hear me Beaton? What happens in most damn families probably split ten ways by now ready to cut each other's throats this twenty-five percent probably do it, want that cleared up before this hearing examiner's word comes down Stamper thought they stood a damn good chance leave us standing there with JMI in one hand and . . .

—This picture's not Emily at all it's some revolting nurse what's that smell.

—Got that clear have you Beaton?

—To a yes sir to a point but the, how we can expect Mrs Stamper's cooperation on the JMI end she's been quite belligerent since the . . .

—Don't need to know a damn thing about it does she? Crawley handled those Dallas mortgages picked up the JMI stock in his street name didn't he?

—Yes sir but . . .

—Could you move your briefcase sir I think maybe the patient had an accid . . .

—Right in with the rest of this street name collateral Crawley handed the bank when we were trying to bail him out of those damn bellies here what are you doing there young woman where's that damn phone, told Monty to call as soon as he . . .

—It's that package they just brought in nurse, open it.

—Like the Trimline phone with the Touch Tone Mister Katz? Have it in antique beige, aqua . . .

—Antique by God stand there asking damn fool questions just put in a damn phone!

—Company regulations have to ask the subscriber if . . .

—Look put in any of them just the quickest you can will you? I was going to say sir the estate's lawyers have asked for an accounting and Mrs Stam . . .

—It's this old cheese it came for the patient, it smells like . . .

—It's a Stilton you ninny who sent it.

—I had it sent ma'am, I knew he enjoyed . . .

—The patient can't have any now sir he's . . .

—That's no reason I can't is it nurse? Get me a plate.

—Installation on a WATS line operator? Authorization's three five nine sev . . .

—I said get me a knife and plate!

—By God somebody get her a spoon give her the whole damn jar Beaton? Want to hear this auditor's report get this whole thing settled before I go up hear me?

—WATS line operator party name Katz that's c, a . . .

—Beaton!

—Please ask the patient to lie still he's . . .

—Yes sir I was going to say indications that Mrs Stamper expects to litigate the . . .

—Litigate her damn head off she'd already filed for divorce hadn't she? Damn fool married six months tells her I don't know what you're going to do but I'm going fishing, clears out for the Indian Ocean so she leaves a note don't know what you're doing but I'm getting a divorce wants to litigate let her litigate with Crawley, join the rest of that gang trying to get blood out of a turnip lawyers know what's good for her they'll keep her out of court before that National Parks stunt of theirs comes up, fool movie million damn zebras running around tried to make it look like some conservation project Crawley's a big enough damn fool probably believed it himself, told you to call Frank Black on this new House bill didn't I?

—Yes sir but in light of this consumer group's action to force him to register as a lobbyist I thought you might want to wait until this X-L Lith . . .

—Wait till this bunch takes over the damn country? By God Beaton you're getting softheaded, only one damn consumer group it buys something or it don't buy it what the devil you think a market economy's all about, tell this bunch to go read that act again section three hundred eight no requirement there makes him a lobbyist don't pay him a lobbyist fee do we? Pay him a retainer for legal services what do you call this X-L Lithograph appeal a damn teaparty? Fined triple damages and costs in a pollution suit when this Mooneysomebody's drunk don't even show up to defend it told Frank Black to get a reversal come up with a consent order, lawyer yourself that what lawyers are for?

—Yes sir but . . .

—Always some damn but, you just get onto him hear me? Want to be damn sure this new House bill bars any more judicial reviews of this environmental nonsense on this gas line consortium Stamper's people put together before we pick up their offer on this Alsaka subsidiary, damn fool explosion that bunch set off out there's got every bleeding heart in the country wetting their damn pants tell that young woman to get me a handkerchief, monkey putting those phones in where the devil'd he go . . .

—Under the bed sir I think he . . .

—Didn't ask what you think just get them put in what's all this you're waving around.

—Yes sir you asked for the auditor's report on J R Cor . . .

—Can't waste time listen to it all now just want to know if they got the damn figures straightened out, told me down at the bank they never saw such accounting procedures, head of the company himself two places off with the damn decimal half the time SEC have him on fraud?

—No sir I understand they were unable to establish evidence of intentional wrongdoing since the errors were as frequently to the company's own disadvantage as not and the generally unortho . . .

—Had an accountant didn't they?

—Yes sir but apparently he was unused to dealing with transactions of these magnitudes, he seems to have been retained simply because he was the brother-in-law of the head of their public relations firm which in turn had been retained by his brother their general counsel Mister Piscator who is now handling Pomerance Associates' suit against the parent as a substantial creditor, so that the entire . . .

—Didn't ask for a lot of damn gossip Beaton take care of them like everybody else what the devil's this, flimsy damn tissue blow a hole right through it said a handkerchief didn't I? Perfectly good linen handkerchief in my coat there young woman told you to bring that stockholder letter Beaton, supposed to go out today it's not even finished?

—I have the final draft right here yes sir, do you . . .

—Quit wasting time gossiping and read it then.

—Nurse leave Mister Katz alone and get me some crackers.

—Got this WATS line open operator try the hey man this Doris?

—Beaton what are you waiting for.

—Yes sir. Agreement in principle concerning the restructuring of debt and recapitalization of the company was executed by the company and a banking consortium of the company's principal lending . . .

—Know that part get to the next paragraph.

—Hey man I thought you on long lines . . .

—Your company's new management proposed, as an alt . . .

—Damn it Beaton what's going on down there.

—Katz you mean him he's right in the bed here man, got a call from Wash . . .

—Beaton!

—Here give me that! hello . . . ? Yes sir he . . . this is Beaton yes sir he's right here. Mister Moncrieff sir, he's . . .

—Hold it to my ear damn it! can't hear him under there can I? Monty . . . ? No got your desk cleaned out there yet . . . ? No going up in a few minutes got Beaton in here on damn it hold that close can't blow my nose across the room can I? what . . . ? Got Beaton up here on it now trying to reach Broos find out what the devil's holding up this damn loan guarantee before we . . . don't know yet waiting to hear on this cable transport scheme, comes up with something I want that Diamond tender to . . . shouldn't have a problem Zona up here usual gracious self eating her way through a five pound Stilton says Boody's all taken care of hold on, Beaton? Didn't tell you to quit reading did I? Quit when I tell you hear me? Monty . . . ?

—Yes sir proposed, as an alternative to straight liquidating bankruptcy, that the company file a petition seeking an arrangement with creditors under chapter eleven of the Bankruptcy Act. A chapter eleven proceeding is one which permits a debtor to continue in possession of its property and to operate its bus . . .

—Saw all that in the paper Monty damn nonsense nobody ever won an interview why the devil'd you give them one, used to dealing with these nickel and dime politicians down there can't make up a new scandal try to rake up an old one see what they printed about me last week? Took off on this management contract with Pythian interlocking directorates went back a hundred years to the Bitterroot strike dragged in everything but the damn kitchen sink, leftwing press want to make it sound like this smaltite contract's why you're quitting what's the damn difference a contract's a contract, just want to be damn sure this one's honored see that smelter we built them over there's declared surplus sold back to Typhon, ought to be in operation right now finished their fool war country's running like a company town labor pool pulled in from . . . what? Place next door there Malwi yes I told Blaufinger to annex it while they were at it favor to . . . No no favor to Zona, having some trouble here parking her damn car simplest thing just to hold on what's that Beaton?

—The suspension from trading of the company's common stock and nine percent convertible subordinated debentures, at which time the securities of the company were delisted due to the company's inability to meet listing requi . . .

—Monty? didn't hear you got Beaton here babbling about this debt restructuring damn it Beaton hold it to my ear think I hear with my chin? was what . . . ? Annexed told them just to go in and . . . how the devil'd that happen said there wouldn't be any resistance, Blaufinger didn't think they had a damn slingshot between them said these Uaso troops just walk in and . . . well by God . . . Well by God decima . . . what? Poor buggers where'd they . . . thought they were real? Where the devil'd they get them never heard such a . . . don't know damn it means we'll have to drag in labor from Angola or some other damn hold on, what the devil do you want.

—Just sign here Mister Katz?

—Here here give me that I'll sign it. There. On that date . . .

—Monty? How secure's this damn phone you're on . . .

—City National Bank, the trustee under the indenture applicable to the nine percent convertible subordinated debentures declared an event of default and demanded payment of the outstanding principal amount together with the accrued int . . .

—Figured those deposits someplace upriver from the brewery where they get the trace of cobalt puts the head on their beer, damn fools tip their hand file for the mineral depletion allow . . . I know that no damn reason to broadcast it is there? Already hanging you with this Typhon contract cobalt stockpile's the whole damn basis for it, broadcast this every damn leftwing paper in . . . resignation don't take effect till tomorrow does it? Any damn reason you can't just stamp the whole damn thing classified before you clean out your desk there? Don't any . . . Management no don't know a damn thing about it good earnings record probably got it in to raise capital hold on, Beaton? Paragraph in there on this brewery sale?

—Yes sir it's the next para . . .

—Well read it.

—Yes sir. The operations of Wonder Brewery are continuing normally. The company has received and is entertaining several inquiries looking to the sale of this subsidiary. The chapter eleven proceeding poses certain technical difficulties but there does not appear to be any reas . . .

—Strike it out. Monty . . . ? No just sit on the whole damn . . . shouldn't make any trouble no, heard they locked him up chasing police around the brewery there with a damn gun right now just sit on it maybe tie it in later on the sale to this pipeline outfit soon as Broos gets this loan guaran . . . taking the original offer Stamper made before he went down that's right Alberta Western sites mining clai . . . Don't care how damn low it was bona fide offer wasn't it? Think we . . . because his outfit's already spent forty million studies surveys hearings impact statements litigation with these damn ecologists still haven't laid a damn inch of pipe . . . banking consortium underwriting every damn penny that's why, sell off this Alsaka subsidiary to them lock stock and barrel only way to keep the damn reins on it . . . SEC why should the damn SEC interfere, recapitalizing the parent company settle the creditors save the damn stockholders something, have to raise capital don't we? Cash flow level's projected to hold this paper complex together Triangle handful of satellites no damn reas . . . know that yes still mostly timber harves . . . well by God, Beaton?

—National Bankruptcy Act filed with the court a proposed arrangement with unsecured creditors specifying the manner in which claims against the comp . . .

—Beaton!

—In order for yes sir?

—Know anything about these damn mining claims? Monty says they just handed down a decision invalidates every damn one of them who the devil . . .

—Yes sir you may recall suggesting I initiate an action when they declined Mister Stamper's original offer. I was able to demonstrate that the claims laws clearly envisage placer mining which presumes large amounts of available water, whereas the entire area these claims comprise is dry as a . . .

—Monty? Beaton in there demonstrating again he . . . know you did yes, he . . . know it damn it forgot about it, any damn reason you can't leave a memorandum reverse your position before you clean out your desk there? Want this whole piece to hang together Alberta Western sites right straight down through the . . . Know it yes just that damn reserva . . . just arrested those damn Brook brothers didn't they? Picture in yesterday's paper had them dragged out of BIA in there tearing up the peapatch after that show they put on at the res . . . FBI what . . . ? Stolen car count all the damn FBI's ever good for, always find another fool salesman damn well think assault on a federal marshal they'd be . . . Claims to the whole damn thing wiped out weren't they? Supposed to revert to the Bureau of Land Management but they're in here suing Alsaka and the parent on those leases and damages biggest damn claim the company's got against it, leftwing press fanning the damn flames end up with a jury seen too many fool movies hand them every damn penny they . . . Win it they'd have the money to bid it in buy the whole damn thing back heard one of them on a phone tape shouting he'd . . . what? By God no didn't authorize didn't ask for it Monty how big a damn fool do you . . . don't know no tapes just turned up, phone at their uptown headquarters Beaton couldn't even find the damn place borrowed a couple of half-baked detectives from Zona came up with a lot of damn bits and pieces worst damn job of . . . Talking about what . . . ? Don't know no Beaton's heard them have to call you back, wade through this foulmouth secretary they had up there bring those tapes with you Beaton?

—Holders of the company's yes sir, nine percent convertible subordinated debentures provide for the issuance of eight shares of common stock for each one thousand dollar princip . . .

—BIA what? Have to talk louder Beaton holding the damn phone a mile away is . . . wards damn right they're government wards, been feeding at the public trough since Custer's last . . . good, damn good way to . . . need every damn cent they can get, handle it that way never even get near Appeals Court stop the whole damn thing in its tracks who's . . . good yes straighten Broos out when I get him Stamper's people scratching around said just lowgrade coal told them to talk to that little Jew on the power commission might gasify it set up a . . . who Stamper's outfit? Beaton no hasn't told me a damn word about it standing here bab . . . shouldn't be no just make damn sure Bureau of Land Management's signed this ninety-nine year lease with them before you clean out your desk there, less damn publicity the better Beaton here tells me that damn Stamper woman's kicking up her hee . . . Crawley? what's . . . Know he handled it but . . . Don't have a damn thing to do with this operation Monty no Stamper set him up on that National Parks stunt tried to get into the Everglades hundred thousand acres drilling rights Seminoles and Mickeysuckies sitting on there, district next door supplies fresh water to Miami broken down retired population only fun's flushing toilets lease that out they'd hand them their scalps damn it Beaton trying to mash my ear off? Told you Crawley don't know his elbow from . . . can't help it damn it crybaby called me too said he was being thrown to the . . . know that Monty but by God pulls a stunt like this goes under peak of this crisis in investor confidence no business getting into those damn bellies in the first place did he? Expects the Exchange to put up twenty-eight million bail him out doing their damndest down there right now just to hold things together, may get up two or three million settle his clients with eight or ten cents on the dol . . . No damn choice Monty let these small investors up to two three hundred thousand go under bank feeling the pinch had to put all Crawley's street name collateral every-thing Wiles could salvage into Emily Cates and Francis Joubert way the damn market's sliding faster we redeem them pay both foundations back the bet . . . Had to pull Wiles out didn't we? So damn much underwriting bring charges like that against him and Crawley see the whole thing go like a stack of dominoes, SEC in there wetting their damn pants just slapped their wrists on this know your client rule damn fools both of them get up at that hearing say they never laid their damn eyes on him heard even his own fool directors said they'd never . . .

—Excuse me could I just get the patient's arm again he shouldn't be . . .

—Who . . . ? No only one says he knows him well's that boob you had brown nosing around Typhon tried to give the damn company away David somebody, just won this fool Advertising Man of the Year award . . . same damn thing here got the bit in his teeth now he puts the blame upstairs tries to subpoena his boss in this Nobili hearing don't turn up for it FDC probably just let it . . . Wouldn't even show up to defend that erratic management suit handed over his whole damn company didn't he? think he'll show up to take this boob off the hook? Don't even defend that paternity suit picture of her in the paper jury take one look he would have won it hands dow . . . Don't know Crawley said Honduras thought he wanted to buy it damn nerve called me at the bank sounded like he was at the bottom of a rain barrel hardly hear what he . . . No some deal wanted me to help him out just this once set up a string of sounded like only banks your family ever need, said he still had a friend over at Chase . . . got off fast as I damn well could just told him to quit calling the press issuing these damn statements, reads the parent company's made debtor in possession tells me he's the damn parent says he's bringing countersuit next damn thing all he wants back's the corporate seal, says he . . . Not worth the damn trouble no, marshals sealed some off uptown picked some up at the Waldorf heard Zona's half-baked detectives found some hid in a school locker someplace but . . . He called who . . . ? Well by God can you . . . just says it looks like they followed the damn letter of the damn law damn it Monty IRS says his social security number's same one on a million sample cards in dime store wallets, filed under that don't constitute massive fraud does it? Only damn suit I know against him now's the short swing stock conversion he pulled in that mill takeover back at the start, disgruntled damn stockholder lost her drawers in it place a ghost town only ratable left's the damn cemetery since this bunch pulled the mills down shipped the looms to South America on a tax dodge and set up in Georgia with cheap equipment under deductible maintenance, too cheap to supervise it whole damn thing went up on some cracker's used car lot tried to hang onto their tax umbrella with a shipload of damn Hong Kong sweaters lawsuit don't touch him does it? Statement in the paper he was working for the stockhol . . . cut the whole damn thing loose cemetery's part of this fool health plan franchised it out to these funeral people some dancy cowboy Beaton picked up with, this junk car cracker down there wants to sue sitting duck let him sue the damn franchi . . . What I just said calls the Attorney General just sounds like he's trying to get his ex . . . says because that's what you do damn it that's what I mean! Sounds like he's just trying to get his executive officer off the damn hook Beaton here just hold on, Beaton? What's this damn suit against this what's his name executive officer just talking about him.

—Five. Cash payment in full to all general unsecured claimants whose allowable claims aggregate one hundred dol . . .

—Beaton! Zona belching over here can't hear a damn . . .

—lars or less yes sir, or who choose to reduce their claims to this amount the action against Mister Bast is an insider suit sir, rising from his sale of parent company stock at the . . .

—Damn insider suit Monty old stunt he pulled on the bank put up his stock as collateral forced us to sell it for him before the damn bottom fell out to get around his option terms, how the devil Crawley let him exercise the damn option before it matured class action is it Beaton?

—The issuance of yes sir both this and the suit against the company's president are class actions brought by the same plaintiff, since the mill properties were deeded over for a public park and speedway resentment has grown over the rising welfare burden in the town of Union . . .

—Didn't ask for a tour of the damn place Beaton just answer my questions after this hear me? Monty? Didn't tell you to quit reading did I Beaton?

—No sir issuance of eight hundred thousand shares of common stock to be distributed ratably to all other generally unsecured . . .

—Don't look like it no both class actions probably throw them right out, price of stamps don't sound like anybody can raise the damn postage run around notify all the potential claimants under this Eisen ruling first decent decision the damn Court's handed down since FDR packed his damn what's that Beaton?

—The arrangement is conditioned upon approval by the company's shareholders of a one for twenty-four reverse split of the shares of common stock presently outstan . . .

—Cut that make it one for twenty, trying to make a market in it at a half get this damn thing back on my ear, what's that Monty . . . ? No what damn good would . . . get's him barred from trading that's all, don't serve any damn purpose to . . . Well by God no, just make it look worse for the whole damn business community that's why damn it! SEC's civil complaint put the whole damn thing into the hands of a receiver didn't it? had this Bast and this J R what's his damn name barred from running any publicly owned companies didn't it? harshest penalty the damn SEC can ask for isn't it? Can't bring criminal charges by God Monty push this too far get every damn fool who ever lost a nickel in the market writing his damn congressman to . . . No but by God that's what the whole damn thing's all about! Civil complaints nothing but these damn lawyers having lunch fight over a few damn prepositions but by God push Congress too far like walking in a damn hencoop at night wake them all up, start cackling about criminal provisions pass a damn law before they know it only damn face you'll see in the Union Club be some black with a tray, already got these two barred from trading on any major exchange haven't they? do any damn good to add one more to the pile? Federal damn prisons already beginning to look like the damn Harvard Business School inside blacks running loose in the streets cutting throats but every damn paper you pick up's somebody in a Brooks suit on his way to Leavenouch! By . . .

—Please you're overexciting the patient he's going up in a few minutes, if this shot doesn't quiet him they . . .

—Get that damn phone back here! Monty? damn babying let go of me there, fifty other damn companies to worry about play nursemaid to this outfit taking too much of my damn time thought you could take on this recapitalization program when you get up here may have your hands full with Typhon ought to get right over there see where Pythian stands on the . . . don't know maybe Cutler could handle it, litigation coming in corporate structure like something a damn monkey put together think he'd be . . . haven't no not since they . . . not a damn word from her no got her picture on one of this outfit's magazines here damned if I can . . . hasn't mentioned it no, Beaton?

—Management appreciates your patience during this most trying and difficult period sincerely yours yes sir.

—Talked to Emily since they got back?

—Yes sir. In fact sir, I think you should prepare yoursel . . .

—Says he's talked to her just need some more time to come around she . . . Know that damn it but she's got the boy back don't she? Didn't think she'd be so damn mean about it either maybe Cutler can talk some damn sense to her now they're settled . . . only damn reason she wouldn't come in sign those powers when she took off for Geneva just had to prove she Beaton! damn phone ringing there have to tell you to pick it up? maybe's Broos, Monty . . . ?

—Yes sir but it's the room phone I, hello . . . ?

—Know she's Freddie's damn guardian on this well as you do Monty, anything went wrong no signature on these powers have the other trustees by the short hair give her leverage to control both foundations everything in them any damn reason something should go wrong . . . ?

—Then you're at the Maine end Colonel yes, what . . . They have? When do you ex . . .

—Planned to miss three dividends in the first place didn't we? No damn voting rights on it unless we miss the fourth one, pay that everything's under control got Beaton here keeping an eye on the . . . who Freddie? Any word on Freddie Beaton?

—You mean the actual reconstituting hasn't even excuse me, no sir Mrs Cutler is placing ads in the pap . . .

—Still out loose Monty no Wiles thought he saw him in Tripler's elevator while back with Emily must have been wrong, Beaton says she's got ads in the pap . . . must have got it from the doorman when she moved that drunk into their old place up on Seventy . . . Joubert no don't know she . . . don't know must have paid him off, damn lulu need it for lawyers job in a Swiss bank there dipped in the cash drawer bought back into Nobili when this outfit ran it up to nineteen turned right around wiped it out with their own Far East market nothing left but what . . . ?

—Lost in transmission but that's prepos . . .

—Same damn fool yes got the bit in his teeth there tried to give them away too, launched a big drug donation dates running out thought they'd deduct at retail, IRS disallows it lets them write off at cost under eighty thousand wholesale value damn near two million, drugs show up in every black market in the Pacific dates expire damn druggists returning them hand over fist get the wholesale price back nothing left of the company but this happy pill Zona's on lose that patent suit all they've got's this damn green aspirin FDA's got them up on not worth . . . Depends what Broos comes up with Beaton standing here gossiping on the damn phone trying to reach him on . . . what, called Broos . . . ?

—But he's, but by train . . . ?

—Must be that White some damn face was it? Whitefoot? Idiot we sent down there get him out of that damn bank when we took over stuck him in the FCC what's he . . . same little wop he was mixed up with was on the state banking committee just pushed this girl out a . . . Ask Broos when I get him try to straighten it out yes . . .

—No not unless something positive develops Colonel goodbye, thank you for . . .

—Hang this damn thing up Beaton think I want to lie here listen to it whistle? Who the devil was that.

—Yes sir that was a call from the . . .

—What about that stockholder letter didn't hear a damn thing about selling off that tobacco outfit.

—Yes sir that was deleted upon representation by the attorney for a Mrs Schramm that majority interest in Ritz Tobacco had not been conveyed in the acquisition of Triangle Paper in which she also had an interest as legatee, and while their earnings forecast based on the introduction of two new cigarette brands Ace and Mary Jane with extremely high promotion budgets is astronomical the company's past record hardly justif . . .

—Just trying to hold us up let her have it, one damn thing we don't need's another tax loss what the devil you standing there for told you to get hold of Broos didn't I? See where that damn new strip mining bill stands Monty tells me Stamper's people already in there scraping up lowgrade coal where those damn Indians were camping out set up to gasify it make electricity teach the buggers to smash those washing machines, told you to keep an eye on that didn't I?

—I have yes sir but apparently no electricity will be available in the vicinity of the reservation itself for, excuse me this phone line's caught here, it's intended to supply power for the city four hundred miles away where the power station itself is being located, and since all available water on the reservation will be needed to move the coal there by pipeline those who might attempt to stay on the reservation land would have to carry water some distance on their backs to irrigate the corn which has been their only excuse me sir, hello? I'm calling Senator Broos for Gov . . . pardon? Thank you yes as soon as possible he'll be here for a few more minutes I think yes, goodbye. They say the Senator will call right back sir he's on the floor for a rollcall vote on the arms procurement budg . . .

—Told him to hold that up till we see where these damn Ray-X projects come out thought they were calling you on this tellything.

—Yes sir this call a minute ago a Colonel Moyst at the designated receiving point in Maine sir, he . . .

—What the devil's going on stand here babbling about Indians watering their damn corn got him sent off did they?

—They yes sir at least they claim a successful sendoff at the Texas end but the receiving point is reporting severe difficulties with the reconstituting procedure they fear the, the passenger may have been lost or dissipated in transmission and are requesting someone be sent as a tracer but as yet no one has volun . . .

—Damn fools like that other project could have proved it with a car horn, couldn't just string a wire across the line to Arkansas where's the damn research director ought to send him.

—I'd certainly agree yes sir but it's too late, he just left the Texas installation by train and is expected at the designated receiving point in about three day . . .

—Three days by God arms budget be history, these DOD projects both collapse company's not worth an old shoe anybody fool enough to unload it on be left with these damn fixed price thermocouple contracts in one hand and get hold of Box, get him together with that who the devil general they had on their board there both go down talk to . . .

—General Haight yes sir but excuse me, I doubt that would work in light of the strong feeling remaining between them over which one stopped General Blaufinger's advance at Saint Fiacre in the Ardennes offensive of nineteen for . . .

—Had him up before Broos' committee with these other damn clowns didn't they?

—No sir General Haight was permitted to submit an interrogatory he won't leave his suite at the Waldorf, I understand he refuses to pay his bill there he's told them to file a claim against the company which contends the hotel invited him as a guest gratis for publicity purposes but he's begun his memoirs and moved in all his filing cab . . .

—Damn fool started the run on their stock got all these damn campus activists forcing universities to dump it didn't he? Showed up down there had them throwing rocks at him wanted the place named after him for some fast depreciation real estate deal they pulled didn't he?

—As I understand it sir he wanted the university renamed to honor his achievement in the arts in return for a collection of his own paintings, which he presented with extremely high evaluations for tax purposes supported by letters from a correspondence school comparing his brilliance to Norman Rockwell, apparently all the correspondence students got similar letters and of course since the law changed the IRS has flatly disallowed his paintings as . . .

—What changed what law Beaton what are you talking about.

—By God another county heard from she still here? thought she'd turned into a . . .

—The law which now permits him to deduct only the cost of his materials ma'am, paints brushes canv . . .

—What all I can deduct is the housepaint that ape used on those filthy atrocities I paid good money for? You mean the law changed while you stood there with your thumb in your . . .

—No no ma'am no, as a collector of course you may deduct the full market value of the paintings we've already established with your cousin on the museum's board this law applies to the artist himself, if Mister Schepperman were to donate his own paintings to the museum for instance, he would be allowed only the actual cost of the materials he used in producing them just as an author is allowed paper costs, erasers typewriter rib . . .

—Ape he wouldn't donate the sweat off his . . .

—Damn it Zona be quiet, got your damn cheese got your free pills don't you? Got your damn parking space back what the devil else . . .

—Parking space what am I supposed to do squat in it? You get Nick fired expect me to . . .

—Fired him when these fool detectives of yours said they kept seeing your damn car parked outside this outfit we're picking up the pieces of what the devil was he doing there, making pastoral calls? Boobs even carting off their trash said they had some more leads Beaton?

—I doubt it sir, they'd spent two days in Brooklyn tracing the owner of a car with license K four six six when this was identified as simply a concerto of Mozart's, and of course these tapes they . . .

—Told you don't want to know about that damn it say you brought them along?

—Yes sir but as you, I mean to say they're only fragments a few words and long gaps filled with splashing sounds that obliter . . .

—Just play them damn it see if Emily shows up anyplace, ever hear her voice on them?

—But, but no sir I, why why would . . .

—See how she was mixed up with this outfit got her picture all over their damn magazine there don't she?

—Oh, no no sir that's . . .

—It's not Emily I just told you that it's some revolting nurse I said get me some crackers, most disgusting magazine I've ever seen tummy bulge sagging tits laxatives this revolting creature doing yogi tricks in a body stocking here show him this Beaton. There, does that look like Emily?

—Here sir it's, there's a surface resemblance but I believe this is the wife of the parent company's personnel manager the man who's just been lost in, who's taking part in this Teletravel trial apparently he used his influence to get her this position with an aid program to Ind . . .

—Which position show him the top one Beaton show him el hedouli, can you see Emily doing that? Ninny wouldn't lift her leg for the king of . . .

—Shacked up with that drunk uptown didn't she? Sure he's out of the damn picture Beaton?

—According to information from the doorman he was never seen there again after she . . .

—Monty still mad how she flew the coop like that, told him maybe Cutler can talk some damn sense to her, why the devil she'd . . .

—Cutler's worse than she is, he wouldn't get into her pants without an engraved invitation why do you think she chose him she's still a cold ninny that's why, you've seen her since they came back isn't she Beaton?

—No she, I haven't seen her ma'am I've only talked to her on the pho . . .

—She still sounds like a cold ninny doesn't she? Did you hear what she said about me at the . . .

—She sounded very cold yes ma'am she, she sounded frozen inside in fact when . . .

—Go out spend fifty cents on their wedding present stack of damn placemats Zona what the devil you expect where's that handkerchief, damn it Beaton told you to . . .

—And I want my detectives back too they lost that ape when you took them and if anything happens to him Beaton I want to know it, his price could double and leave me sitting with my thumb in my . . .

—Yes ma'am of course in the event of his death his estate would be assessed the full market value you've established on any work remaining in his posses . . .

—Anything remaining anywhere belongs to me what about that heap of junk he went out and spent my good money on.

—Yes ma'am he sold a large section of it we immediately attached the bank dep . . .

—Unloaded it on this same damn outfit we're talking about Zona, fool art foundation they set up paid out twenty thousand for it handed ninety more to some damn band want that money put in escrow Beaton, find out how legal that damn founda . . .

—You put that money in escrow Beaton I'll put you in escrow I'll put Mister Katz there in escrow I'll . . .

—By God . . .

—Please I think you'll have to leave if the patient can't . . .

—Beaton you tell him if he tries that I'll sue him for, dried up old Raggedy Andy with his tin heart I'll sue him for impersonating himself for impersonating Mister Katz he's nobody, he's a lot of old parts stuck together he doesn't even exist he started losing things eighty years ago he lost a thumbnail on the Albany nightboat and that idiot classmate of his Handler's been dismantling him ever since, started an appendectomy punctured the spleen took it out then came the gall bladder that made it look like appendicitis in the first place now look at him, he's listening through somebody else's inner ears those corneal transplants God knows whose eyes he's looking through, windup toy with a tin heart he'll end up with a dog's brain and some nigger's kidneys why can't I take him to court and have him declared nonexistent, null void nonexistent why can't I Beaton.

—Well it, it would be a novel case ma'am I doubt if there are precedents and the time it would take to adjudi . . .

—By God Beaton shut that woman up get the damn phone!

—The patient's going up in a couple of minutes could you . . .

—Hold that damn thing closer! who's . . . Broos? What's holding up the damn vote on this loan guaran . . . who is? Do some horse trading damn it got the vote on his sugar support bill haven't you? Whole damn economy going to hell in a handbas . . . read your speech yes damn fine speech something don't turn the damn Dow around fast we . . . Know that damn it have to restructure their damn debt first don't we? Thought I'd turn it over to Monty once this smelter's off and . . . By God what's that got to do with it lot of damn . . . damn politician yourself don't know it's a lot of damn nonsense? Leftwing press drum something up smear anybody they can reach, Monty drew up that smaltite contract before he went into the damn government didn't he? still working for the damn stockholders when he drew it up wasn't he? Job he had running Typhon get the best damn deal he could for the stockholders just what he did, takes a salary cut goes to serve his damn country gets this leftwing press hounding him out of office any damn wonder Washington can't get one single damn good man to . . . Whole smelting operation over there declared surplus what the damn contract says don't it? None of their business in the first place, question of the damn national security cobalt stockpile requirements set up damn thing ought to be running right now only damn prob . . . labor force whole damn Malwi labor force decimated yes how the devil'd that happen, Dé's people supposed to annex it just heard they walked in these buggers meet them armed to the damn teeth Dé's bunch panic cut them down like flies go in to clean up find all they had's toys, pistols carbeens submachineguns rocket launchers every damn weapon you can think of plastic toys poor buggers must have . . . don't know damn it maybe Gandia what's left of it, heard that red regime collapsed when Nowunda cleared out probably find him hiding under Milliken's phone damn it Beaton have to tell you to pick the damn thing up? Way that damn fool stuck his neck out backing that UN resolution supporting interven . . . what?

—Yes . . . ? no this is a hospital room who . . .

—Who Milliken? Have to do some damn arm twisting, had his law firm out there retained by this Alsaka outfit of theirs didn't he? Still sore the way they blew the corner off his state didn't lose any damn constituents did he? few sheep and Indians no damn reason to get so . . . who that damn bunch camped out down below there? Whole treaty abrogated Bureau of Land Management's got every damn right to lease it out for ninety-ni . . . still wards of the damn government aren't they? Damn lawsuit even if they won it BIA still their guardian's got to give them permission to spend every damn nickel don't it? Meet their damn legal responsibilities litigation keep them busy the next ten years BIA break-in, stolen car transported across state lines did in a salesman out there even got his fine boy in the hospital heard one of them assaulted a federal marshal with a damn hair dryer, add on their court costs in this suit with these bankrupt cement companies over their original treaty reservation won't have a pot left to . . . Any that wants to stay there fine stay there and work, heard they're starting to pull out lowgrade coal plenty of damn work for everybody why I want this damn . . . no got Beaton up here on it now like something a damn monkey put to . . . know the figures are incomplete damn it that's the what . . . ? Never heard of it hold on, Beaton?

—I never have no, just a minute . . .

—Beaton! Wants the assets of J R Shipping Corp some query on a six percent subsidy, who the devil's that.

—A Mister just a minute I said! yes sir it's right here with, most of the parent company employees seem to have been on the payroll but the only asset I've uncovered is a here it is yes, a vessel under construction designated hull number three five nine seven now lying in damaged condition in the vicinity of Mile sixteen point six Galveston River approximately four mi . . .

—Broos? Beaton still digging up the figures on it sounds like the kind of stunt they tried to pull at the last minute there loading their Ray-X payroll with everybody in this damn fool family of companies right down to the scrubwomen build up their overhead on these cost-plus contracts looked like they had half the damn country working on them, they . . . Know that damn it so's the damn bank, can't expect us to keep nursing it can you? Thought maybe Typhon could take it on Beaton tells me we'd run straight into antitrust only other damn thing's DOD, already tied up in these cost overruns and . . . Well by God whose damn fault's that! DOD's projects aren't they? DOD contracts aren't they? So damn tied up in it cost overruns all the rest let them take over the whole shooting match can't expect the stockholders to . . . no reason the damn Army can't do it under the War Powers Act is there? buy up all the Ray-X preferred like the damn Navy did this Long Island defense plant here two or three years ago? No dividend nonvoting nonconvertible company redeems it in five years from after-tax prof . . . well why the devil'd you think I told you to hold up this damn vote, arms procurement budget this size you can damn well squeeze in this many million nobody look at it twice. . .

—Excuse me could we put up the phone now? The patient . . .

—Water somebody get me some water . . .

—Damn it Beaton come back here with that! Broos . . . Didn't hear you no, who . . . can't take time to open that damn can of worms now just had Monty on the phone here nuisance over this tv channel point is who's the damn applicants, stunt that peachy little wop just pulled probably expects to run for president stays out of jail we can stick him in a judgeship out here in . . . to call who? By God no wouldn't ask a dog to appoint him, just get him the damn nomination tenth judicial district march right up and elect him been voting the straight ticket out there since McKin . . . know that damn it but he's tied up with this Flo-Jan outfit that's applying for this damn tv channel out there isn't he? Him and this Whitefoot whatever his fool name is pull his damn bank out of the hole find him a berth on the FCC don't know enough to keep his damn fool mouth . . . Well by God don't talk to me about interference somebody has to hold things together that's why damn it! Most of the damn trouble in the world's made by damn fools with nothing to do have to give them something to do to keep them off the damn streets and I'm by God sick and tired of hearing them bite the damn hand that feeds them hear me? Only damn reason they think something's worth doing's they get paid to do it, make a nickel and they march around show off their damn cars ranch splits backyard pools outboard boats kids eating peanut butter take credit like they was the ones invented their success by their own damn selves don't see me in a damn backyard pool do you? don't see me taking vacations do you? Somebody don't spend every damn minute working to hold the whole damn thing together for them they'll be squatting in tents on the White House lawn make Coxey's Army look like a damn Sunday school picnic by God Broos don't talk to me about interference! Politicians can't make up your damn minds take your winnings with one hand got the other one out shaking every fool hand you can grab still want to be liked well by God I made that choice eighty years ago never been here damn it give me that!

—Now now let's act our age let go of the . . .

—Here nurse give me the, hello? Senator? Yes sir he's going up in just a minute, he's . . . to call you later sir I'm sure he will, goodbye . . .

—Some, water . . . !

—Go up when I'm damn ready! Beaton? What's that other call.

—That was Mister Leva again sir, he . . .

—Get that damn payment stopped?

—No sir it was too late Mister Crawley had already nego . . .

—Drop in the damn bucket won't do Crawley any good will it? Find out where he got the title to that damn music in the first place?

—No sir he said he'd commissioned it but . . .

—Could you get your briefcase out of the way sir? We're . . .

—Watch my damn foot there! What the devil'd this Leva want.

—He's furious because the new management has told Erebus to fire him sir, he insists this Mister Grynszpan assured him he . . .

—Thirty damn million not enough to waste on one picture goes out spends another sixty thousand on music for it I'm the one fired him damn it, thought we'd put this Grynszpan in there he bought them the damn outfit didn't he? Deals he worked out sound like he might have a crackerjack mind help untangle the whole damn thing told you to get me the story on him didn't I?

—Yes sir in fact there's been speculation he may have been the éminence grise behind the company's meteoric expansion, he seems to have led quite a varied career. According to yesterday's paper he developed the Grynszpan theory of common foci and was engaged in a major work on mechanization and the arts, he apparently worked his way through Harvard selling encyclopedias and has left them a vast sum in securities and real estate although when the will was probated both the IRS and the Edison Comp . . .

—Will was what? mean he's dead damn it?

—He's reported to have died suddenly in Yucatan of leuk . . .

—Dead what damn good is he! damn it Beaton what's . . .

—Joe just get the foot of the bed there and . . .

—Water . . . ?

—By God damn it Beaton? Where the devil are you, want you to get that damn stockholder letter out while I'm up there Beaton hear me? Want you to look into the ownership on the shirttail family outfit in that damn patent suit have it ready when I come down hear me? Get that damn JMI stock out where we can get at it hear me? Court decision goes the wrong way whoever's sitting on that JMI stock still give this shirttail outfit one hell of a fight on appeal, too damn much at stake here for any slipups you get that JMI out where we've got our damn hands on it hear me Beaton? Where the devil . . .

—Please if the patient doesn't lie dow . . .

—Get out of the damn way where is he, Beaton? Get over here where I can see you, you get that JMI out hear me?

—No sir.

—And you look into the own, what did you say?

—The current assets of both foundations have been frozen under an injunction, sir.

—What the devil do you, why didn't you tell me! what . . .

—You didn't ask me sir.

—Well by God I'm asking you now! Whose injunction!

—Mrs Cutler, sir.

—Mrs, Emily? by God what . . .

—Yes sir, she informed me this morning she had an injunction to freeze their assets pending resolution of control of both founda . . .

—Control the, Amy by God no damn question who controls the, when's that dividend told you to keep an eye on that damn fourth dividend didn't I?

—I have, yes sir.

—Well damn it when's it due!

—In about twenty minutes, sir. In fact I believe she may be meeting with the other trustees right now and of course if no dividend is declared, her failure to have signed over these last powers of attorney will give her the additional votes of both her brother's and her son's . . .

—I declare it hear me!

—No get his arm Joe here, get his arm! He'll go under in a . . .

—As their duly appointed guardian in each of these . . .

—Fourth damn dividend I declare it hear me! Hear me?

—Joe get the supervisor he's beginning to throw p v c's, I think you ought to leave sir the patient is . . .

—Yes I, I do too quickly where's the men's room . . .

—There's one out to the left, just . . .

—Oh and the lady here nurse . . . he made the door between rustles of white, —she seems to be in difficulty, I don't think I've ever seen her quite that color . . .

—Hear me . . . !

The door jarred behind him with the first surge and he caught the rim of the nearest basin, clung there brought down by heaves, clung there.

—Excuse me would you, would this help?

—What? oh, thanks . . . a hand came up freed for the wet towel —I'm, kind of you sorry I, I hope I didn't . . .

—No that's all right it's, I mean I just did the same thing do you need any help? Shall I send in a nurse or . . .

—No! no, thank you I'm, I'll be all right . . .

—Yes well, if you're sure . . . the door jarred again. ·

—Careful! the cartload of lunch trays clattered still, —don't get run over the day you're leaving us Mister Bast, still a little shaky? Your friend Mister Coen just came he's in your room waiting, that suit doesn't look bad on you at all . . . she came on up the greens behind him, pushed —here we are Mister Coen. You want to just sit on that empty bed while I pull the sheets off yours Mister Bast? That suit doesn't look bad on him does it Mister Coen, if he just keeps the jacket buttoned where the waist is doubled over? It's not the latest fashion but what he had on when you brought him in that night, it was so shrunk he couldn't wear it anyplace could you Mister Bast.

—No but, if you think it's all right for me to take this I . . .

—He would have wanted you to have it, he really liked you a lot Mister Bast the way he was always telling us to do things for you and reading you the papers . . . a sheet came billowing to the floor. —He was a real character wasn't he.

—But, yes but how did it happen!

—Don't let yourself get all upset again now Mister Bast, sometimes they just slip away like that . . . the second sheet followed in a heap —you can't blame anybody. Sometimes when you think they just really want to go and get it over with they hang on like your friend up in intensive care, you said his wife just came to see him Mister Coen he probably didn't even know her, did he.

—No, no he doesn't know anyone no, she should be down in a moment Mister Bast and I think she, I think you should be prepared for the fact that this ordeal has taken quite a toll. Her deeply exaggerated feelings of responsibility that led her to insist on being held by the police are not entirely dissipated, her appearance of cold calm I think may be deceptive and her reactions to certain situations are liable to be some-what, somewhat erratic, especially concerning these unresolved aspects of your family situation as they relate to her father's estate. The sooner your own position is clarified and your aunts' situation more clearly resolved . . .

—No but wait they, what happened where are they . . .

—Yes I was about to say, I was finally able to learn they seem to have somehow managed to return to that town in Indiana where they've entered a nursing home. I tried to call them there earlier in fact, but was told they'd just been temporarily evacuated when a small fire broke out in the upper story and I do owe you an apology Mister Bast. That was indeed your house we saw that night you became so understandably distraught. It now appears that when the property was condemned, the advertisement for the auction of the house itself appeared only in a newspaper in Poughkeepsie, when the auction was held in Albany by the State Department of Public Works the only bid submitted came from a Mister Cibo who heads the Catania Paving Company I believe it's called. On further inquiry his one dollar bid appears to have been submitted on behalf of a Father Haight with the understanding of a substantial fee for moving it down next to the church where we saw it that night, to serve as a teen center for . . .

—But no how could . . .

—I know it's not precisely what your aunts might have wished Mister Bast but you, they may be pleased to know it's been preserved . . .

—No but a dollar! how could . . .

—It does seem rather inequitable yes I agree, however in such cases the state feels it comes off well with any bid over a penny since the purchaser is obliged to remove the structure from the condemned property saving the state the costs of demolition, as occurred with the barn studio building there to the rear of the property where, oh Mrs, Mrs Angel come in I'm sorry, I didn't see you standing there please come in and, and sit down yes Mister Bast and I were just discussing . . .

—Hello Edward. I heard what you were discussing Mister Coen, please go on.

—There's really no more to it aside from the, the somewhat ironic circumstances of my discovery. The details just came to light when a woman of some means whose philanthropies include the preservation of the studios of prominent American artists learned inadvertently that the Bast property was razed to make way for a Cultural Center project of which she is also a sponsor, as a trustee of the Philharmonic her abrupt interest in James Bast seems to have been provoked by their decision to plead for his return from what I see referred to as his self-imposed exile as the only conductor capable of rescuing them from the severe difficulties into which they have recently . . .

—Excuse me Mister Coen, where shall I put all this music Mister Bast. Mister Bast . . . ?

—What.

—All this music you wrote here, where shall I . . .

—Just, just throw it away it's, throw it away.

—But the way you worked on it, I'd hate to just throw it away after how hard you . . .

—I said throw it, here! give it to me I'll throw it away! it's, it's . . .

—But you worked so hard remember how proud Mister Dunc . . .

—Look he didn't even, I told him this morning I don't have to anymore I don't have to try to write music . . . he had a foot up jamming the pages into the wastebasket —I never had to, it was just something I'd never questioned before I thought it was all I was here for and he, everybody thought that they thought I was doing something worth doing he did too but he, nothing's worth doing he told me nothing's worth doing till you've done it and then it was worth doing even if it wasn't because that's all you . . .

—Mister Bast please, you . . .

—There's no please no there's no please left! the, the damage I've caused because they all thought what I tried to do was worth doing and I haven't even done it . . . ! he was down picking up pages his foot had brought out of the basket with it, jamming them back in with his fist —I, I should have just done what you wanted me to in the first place Mister Coen that, signed that waiver or whatever it is for my claim to half the estate and just let everything . . .

—No but Mister Bast you, I'm afraid you mistake the purpose of a waiver it was simply, at this point the question is really irrelevant of course but if you do now intend to claim . . .

—Excuse me is, Mrs Angel . . . ?

—Yes I, I am doctor what . . .

—It's your husband in intensive care? Yes, I have a . . .

—But what is it what's happened!

—No no please sit down no he's, his condition is unchanged, I know this is an extremely difficult time for you Mrs Angel but we have a request which I hope you will be able to consider without . . .

—Well what is it!

—Yes you see the, of course you're aware that in spite of our efforts the possibility of your husband's failing to survive is a very real one it, it could happen very abruptly we have really no way of knowing. Aside from this traumatic injury however his health appears to have been, to be excellent there's no indication of damage sustained by any of his internal organs and . . .

—You mean he might, that you might be able to . . .

—No no I'm afraid I, you see Mrs Angel in the transplant of a vital organ the decision must be carried out as rapidly as possible following the expiration of the, the donor and you see as his wife we would need your prior authorization for the immediate remov . . .

—No.

—If I could add that another patient has just been taken to the operating room whose survival may depend . . .

—No! leave me alone no!

—Doctor I, as their attorney you might clarify matters for me if we stepped into the hall . . .

—Stella . . .

—I said leave me alone! Haven't you done enough Edward didn't you just say you'd done enough! You despised him you . . .

—I! I didn't even, no that night in the barn that night I can still hear his steps on the broken glass down there in the dark you didn't even move when he, everything smashed breaking in when I found you up there and you . . .

—You think, I did? that I broke in and smashed . . .

—Dishes that's not what I said I didn't say dishes! What difference are, are dishes no you broke in Stella you broke in and destroyed every, up there I can still see you those flashes of lightning I can still see you on the bed up there I can still see your throat your voice I can still hear it don't, you don't have to seduce me I can still feel your hand when you . . .

—Destroyed of course I did! You didn't think I, that I wanted you did you? You don't think I, that day up on the mountain that I didn't know you were watching me? that you'd followed me up the stream till I took off my bathing suit and were in the bushes there watching me? That this whole absurd, her bosom shaken by a sudden storm of sighs this whole frightened romantic nightmare you'd put me into all of it, all of it! that, that barn out there where these ideas these fantasies these, these obsessions could hide untouched unfinished till you opened the door on them again, on this fear you haven't inherited James' talent so you'll settle for money that's where it belongs all of it, with your music in the trashbasket all ot it!

—No you, you are aren't you Stella you're, he said you were yes you're a witch aren't you you're . . .

—Who did who!

—Your throat yes that scar I can still taste it in the dark those steps crushing glass you destroyed him you've tried to destroy . . .

—It was Jack wasn't it, it was Jack . . .

—Who Jack who it didn't have to be Jack you destroyed him too yes, you . . .

—Where is he!

—He's I don't know where he is he's, that place I've been working in uptown he's been trying to work up there no he didn't have to tell me no, no I could have told him since you were a child I've always heard it, what you could destroy I've always heard them talk about you that you made things up you spread stories because you hated her didn't you, one summer you were still a child one summer in Tannersville you hated my mother for what she'd done to your father didn't you! For leaving him to, when she left him for . . .

—Yours yes for yours! When she left my father and wanted James to marry her and he wouldn't because he was afraid for his work, even when you were born and she just wanted him to try and he wouldn't he was afraid for anything to come between him and his work when all of it happened and then they blamed me they all blamed me! That horrible woman that fair that summer in Tannersville that tent, I went in to have my fortune told it was almost dark inside she had scarves and earrings so much makeup and costume jewelry and I thought she was a real gypsy I was so excited, she told me some stupid flattering things she had a crystal ball it was just a fishbowl upside down looking into it and she said, she said you're really a very unhappy little girl aren't you and I started to talk, I didn't know what I was telling her I didn't even know she was asking me questions, my father and yours and Nellie what I'd seen what I'd heard everything I didn't even know I'd told her when it was over, when she said cross my palm with silver and I paid her the ten cents I saw her finger, the tip of one finger missing and I knew who she was I didn't even know why I was frightened, I ran out in the sun and fell down and your father found me behind the car being sick he took me back, they didn't know what had happened they never knew but they blamed me all of them, all of them and I never trusted any of them again!

—But I don't, I don't know what you . . .

—Because she took her own life! Nellie your mother she took her own life! When he wouldn't marry her, when James wouldn't marry her and she wrote a will she made him your guardian and he told Aunt Julia, he told them both afterwards he'd married her secretly so the scandal wouldn't hurt my father, now can you . . .

—Oh excuse me, Mrs Angel? I've talked with the doctor I think everything should, are you all right?

—Yes I'm all right! I, I'd like a glass of water.

—Of course yes let me, here, here you do look quite . . .

—Thank you. Now what is it you want to discuss Mister Coen.

—Yes well of course, of course this matter of the estate Mrs Angel but you've both been under severe strain and these are hardly ideal circumstances to discuss it in fact the nurses' supervisor just told me this room may be required momentarily but I did at least want to counsel you both, pending resolution of your own differences, that for the moment an appearance of family solidarity should be maintained in the face of the impending court decision in this old JMI suit, since I believe whoever emerges with controlling interest in General Roll must expect a rather fierce confrontation from them on appeal. In fact this was the reason for my attempt to reach your aunts directly as I mentioned earlier, having just learned that their attorney Mister Lemp has been dead for almost sixteen years I'm trying to help resolve their other affairs here and hope to recover six or seven cents on the dollar for them in the liquidation of their broker whose . . .

—Wait who Mis, Mister Crawley? What do you mean liquid . . .

—His firm yes, straight liquidating bankruptcy, as I think I've already told you your aunts' account was severely diminished when he began to buy and sell as rapidly as possible simply to generate as many commissions as he . . .

—But he owes me, he still owes me four hundred dollars he said he'd send the check what if, would they take his bank account?

—I can't say Mister Bast, perhaps if it were a personal account you might still, excuse me. Nurse . . . ?

—Joe bring in a chair to take Mister Bast down to the front door, you signed everything for him didn't you Mister Coen I have to hurry you out, we need this room immediately and Joe? Hurry right back it has to be scrubbed everything including the Venetian blinds, if she recovers we'll probably have to paint it too.

—Joe wait, wait that wastebasket . . .

—Please Mister Bast we're in a hurry . . .

—So am I! No just those papers on the top . . .

—But what . . .

—Because it's all I've got! Look I don't need a chair I have to get uptown to see if that check's there, I can't wait for . . .

—I'm sorry Mister Bast it's a hospital regulation and Joe, move that chair out she hates green and you'll have to change the curtains, she's one of the trustees we had her in once just for a tubal insufflation and practically had to rebuild the whole wing.

—Mrs Angel here let me get your coat, I hope one of you will be in touch with me as soon as you've been able to discuss Mister Bast's position in this entire . . .

—There's nothing left to discuss! There's nothing left is there? Stella? No, no I've failed enough at other people's things I've done enough other people's damage from now on I'm just going to do my own, from now on I'm going to fail at my own here those papers wait, give me those papers . . .

—And Joe tell the kitchen she'll bring her own silver and have her food brought in from outside, her maid will bring her jewelry and makeup and send in her hairdresser just see what color curtains we have, she'll send her maid out to Saks for a negligee and the color . . .

—You're finally leaving us Mister Bast, you'll miss our Christmas tree. Come back and see us . . .

—Yes well thank you for, for everything . . . the wheels spun down the corridor, swerved for the ponderous approach of a bed mounting an inert figure massed under sheets and veered through the bull's eye doors for the lull of the elevator, the swing of glass doors. —Thank you Mister Coen goodbye and, Stella goodb . . .

—I'm coming with you.

—Why what for! we don't . . .

—For Jack. That's where you're going isn't it?

—Yes but, all right I'm going up here for the bus if you . . .

—A bus don't be silly, Mister Coen could you call us that cab please. You can reach me at home when anything develops.

—Of course yes Mrs Angel any change in your husband's con . . .

—I don't think we need wait for that do we? If my acting for him presents any problem, I'm sure under the circumstances you can draw up papers enabling me to do so?

—Why, why yes if you . . .

—And incidentally yes there's no need to bother my aunts any further is there, surely my husband's interest in the company together with my father's estate is sufficient majority for any decisions I come to? this old lawsuit you mentioned for instance, I want the judgment on it the moment you learn it so we can act appropriately without any delay in fact, Mister Coen, on the chance it goes against General Roll you might begin to get material together for an appeal I don't intend to see it lost, I think that's all clear?

—Why, why yes Mrs Angel of course yes, yes here let me get the door . . .

—And thank you again you've been terribly helpful. Driver? we're going uptown, it's on Ninety-sixth Street isn't it Edward?

—Yes it's, it's between Second and Third yes, Ninety-sixth between Second and Third driver . . . he squared the pages loose against him at the lurch of the cab, knees tight holding him forward to the edge of the seat looking out as though aware that his back, the back of his head was being looked at, looking down as abruptly as the knee crossed under his elbow, crossing his own.

—Is there anything you can do about those trousers Edward, we could certainly stop and get you something and a coat, you haven't even a coat . . .

—No! I'm, I'm fine . . . he thrust the pages away pulling, tucking at his waist, paired his knees again coming forward —did you know that he, my father did you know he was coming back?

—I suggested it to them.

—Oh . . . he sat hunched to the window there staring at the massive side of a truck where five dwarfs heralding None Of Us Grew But The Business moved ahead, fell back for a hatless woman blowing her nose, U S Mail, Dumor Delivery Service, a brown dog muzzling glass.

—I didn't hear you.

—Nothing I didn't say anything . . . ! a bus bullied passage, fell away for Department of Correction, the woman wadding her handkerchief now, Ace Photo Service, Emergency —this next corner . . . National Casket Co, XL Cab —driver . . . ?

—You still don't understand do you! You think he, that he knew what would happen? the courage it took for him to go on facing the . . .

—Driver! it's, it's up behind that ambulance . . .

—Where's all the ashcans out front?

—That's it yes . . . he brought the papers close coming forward for the door —right here, yes . . . he was out, holding the cab's door open. —You'd better wait here till I see what's . . .

—I'd intended to.

—Yes well if he's, if Mister Gibbs is up there what shall I tell him you want.

—Nothing. Nothing! no you won't understand will you! that your own selfish suffering's easier than facing suffering you've caused and can never call back Edward don't you think I, Edward? Well you will . . . !

He caught balance as the door was pulled from him in his turn between the burned car hulk and the ambulance backed open at the curb, clattered through doors to linoleum mounting two steps at a time —sorry . . . ! he backed down a step, two, turned to wait at the foot as whites took shape descending, filling the narrow stairs.

—Want to hold that door for us there? That's it, little wider can you get it any wider?

—It's no, no this is as far as . . .

—Wait just lower your end a little Jim, should have used the window sling on this one.

—Only four stories of rope how could we.

—Mister?

—That's it a little harder now, that's it . . .

—Mister could I ride to the hospital with you Mister?

—Not going to no hospital, that's it, there. Got it now?

—But my wife Mister, I could ride with her where you're going?

The doors clattered. He held the cold metal of the newel and then climbed hand on the rail a step at a time to the top and the turn for the end of the hall, where the door stood leaning free against the wall there. —Hello? he knocked on it —is, oh Mister Eigen hello is Mis . . .

—Christ where have you been come in, I'm on the phone.

—I just got out of the hosp . . .

—What . . . ?

—Out of the hos . . .

—Look I'm not trying to rewrite the God damn agreement, I just asked if it would be convenient for me to come up and see him tomorrow afternoon instead of today, I've been . . . no I know he does but . . . Not used to what . . . ? No now wait listen, do you think you're granting me a privilege letting me see my own son? Do you ex . . . all right why shouldn't he have told you where we'd been, she's a perfectly nice woman who . . . he what . . . ? Look of course I never told him if I marry somebody else now and have more children that you'll get them too, now . . . Because I've been helping her clean up some of the details on Schramm's estate that's why! She's a perfectly ni . . . No, where . . . no I don't, look if he wanted it why didn't you just take it like you took everything el . . . yes Bruckner and the double God damn boiler I know it! Look if I find his crèche I'll bring it up whenever I . . . Well Christ I know he wants it there for Christmas don't I? What . . . because that's what the God damn court order says doesn't it? that we all have to spend Christmas together doesn't it? Now listen is David there? can I . . . Well can't you call him in for a minute . . . ? All right! Look will you just tell me what time to call so I can . . . Because I won't be at this number no, I just came up here to straighten some things out and get my papers as soon as this delivery service gets here to . . . well can you just tell him I called? I'll try later if . . . all right I'll just keep trying! Goodbye! Christ . . . !

—But Mister Eigen who . . .

—Bitch.

—Yes but I mean who, who's that man in there staring at me and that, that Chinese girl sitting on the box with the . . .

—Well who the hell is she! She came in from Hong Kong with a shipment of sweaters for that company of yours no return ticket no papers she can't even speak English, Immigration's sending somebody up to take her in as an illegal alien I mean do you know what's been going on here Bast? U S marshals postal inspectors IRS agents arguing jurisdiction over every scrap of paper I haven't been able to take anything of mine out till right now, valuable manuscripts all over the place just lucky as hell they didn't all go up in smoke these God damn matchbooks of yours dumped everyplace look at them! Five summonses from the fire deptment they brought in the public health people took one look in the refrigerator and . . .

—Yes but, well they're not really mine the matches I mean, they . . .

— They've got this God damn J R thing all over them same company you've been working for isn't it? He's been calling here too hardly hear him look get the corner of this box here will you? Just push it past the tub there, sounded like he said he had a cold couldn't meet you but he got some school to mail you a check you expected asked if you're mad and what the hell happened to you no wait, push it a little further so I can tape it closed can you? Lawyers reporters executive placement agencies civil liberties union some drunk general somebody trying to reach you I mean do you know what's been going on here Bast? Indian legal aid fund, some God damn television talk show civil beautification committee in some town where you painted their water tower want you at their award banquet? Somebody named Crawley who keeps calling and the phone company, I mean do you know this God damn phone bill's over eleven thousand dollars?

—No but wait, wait this Mister Crawley was it about a check he . . .

—Just said some slides he lent you sounds affronted as hell you haven't returned them look hand me that folder on the tub, finally found it stuffed under some boxes I'm not going to look no the one with stains all over it listen, where you going from here are you in a hurry?

—Well, no well no place exactly no I just came up to see if my . . .

—Fine then look there's something you can do, can you just get Freddie where he's supposed to go as soon as I get this call? There was an ad in the paper his sister's been looking for him for Christ knows how

long I've got an attorney checking the details now, I'm just waiting for
him to call me back I'd do it myself but I'm waiting for this messenger
service to, help me get this box up here will you?

—Well yes but I mean who's, is that Freddie in there on the . . .

—Yes he's fine look there's nothing to worry about, once we got the
bulb out of that lamp flickering on and off in there he thought it was his
mother sending him messages, just hold this closed while I tie it can you?
Been fine ever since they shot the God damn radio didn't even bother
him when the Jones boys had a fire in their clubhouse down there, the
only thing that's upset him was the drowned cat they found in the tub
when they came in to turn off the water look, can you pull that box out
while I hold back these film cans? This pain I've been getting it starts
here and goes right down to my knee I don't want to make it any worse.

—Well yes but, I mean Freddie where did he come from who . . .

—Pull it out a little further can you? Jack brought him in here out
of the rain one day knew him in boarding school, he's been here ever
since can you hand me that roll of tape? They found a practice golf course
someplace it's laid out all over those books and boxes in there, Jack's been
teaching him golf eating these freeze-dried chicken Marengos drinking
that God damn grape drink I just want to get him back safe to his family
before Jack starts wait, just hold this down so I can tape it closed and,
who . . .

—Yes but where's Mister Gib . . .

—Ello . . . ?

—Good God, who . . .

—Is Mister Grinspan ere? General Motor ave buy im a . . .

—He's not no but come in, come . . .

—I ave a busy schedule. Wen e's ere?

—Look he's not here he's gone he's dead but come in, I . . .

—E's dead? That's not nice no, I don do that. Goodbye . . .

—Good, God where did she come from . . .

—I don't know but I mean what happened to Mister Gryn . . .

—Too much damn trouble Jack just fixed up a nice obituary on him
and look, hand me that box on the tub maybe we can get these into it,
Britannica finally caught up with him worked his way through up there
selling them for twenty dollars a set Jack had us taking turns on his exams
to get him through with a summa they've been after him for twenty years
finally just more God damn trouble than he was worth, Edison Company
finds the meter bypass wants him on fraud the IRS shows up with his
track winnings list as long as your arm some old woman after him for a
concentration camp reunion, even had the Connecticut State Highway
Department building a road they stumbled on a family grave wait look
out, let me get the phone maybe the call I've been, hello . . . ? Yes, yes
fine . . . fine yes there's sombody here now who can bring him right down,
did she say whether . . . Sitting in there peaceful as can be look there

wasn't any violence just grabbed the inspector's gun when they broke off the Minuet in G for an aspirin commercial fired it down there till the thing finally . . . that's what I mean once he's in his sister's custody yes, he . . . Right now yes somebody here who can bring him right down, hold on a minute. Look can you take Freddie down there right now? Somplace in the Seventies . . .

—Well yes well as soon as I see if there's a letter for me I . . .

—Look back there in Appletons', GRIN-LOC Volume three Jack said he'd put some there. Hello? Fine yes, just picking up his mail here and they can get started, now what . . . I'll tell him that yes now what about this matter I called you on earlier, the . . . to sue him and this Walldecker too yes, look this is the way I reconstruct it. I gave a copy of my play to this young man Gall to read just to read, instead he sold it to this company Angels West for fifteen hundred dollars worth of their stock and they sold it to Angels East for a hundred thousand in stock that showed up as a ninety-eight thousand five hundred dollar profit on their books, when the . . . because no they're both Walldecker that's the point, Angels East and Angels West are both Walldecker and when he . . . No but it was produced that's the God damn point! ran for three days it was sold out and the backers suddenly stepped in and closed it without any explan . . . Wait no what do you mean a misdemeanor, they . . . No for defamation punitive damages anything you can think of all of them yes, the backers all of them and listen there's something else, I . . . No, no this is an ad in today's paper for a concert by some rock group called Baby Jeeter and the Three Wide Men, I . . . no it's Jeeter, Jeeter and I want an injunction to make them stop using that name I don't know how the hell they . . . Because they have no right to it's mine! I . . . it's not registered in my name no but it's, look it has personal associations it's mine and my son's and I won't let it be dragged through the . . . who my son? Look God damn it he's four years old how could he have a rock group he can't even . . . the same one yes David the only one I have that reminds me yes, when am I supposed to get these Letters of Guardianship I thought . . . No record of what . . . ? No, no I sent the estate a check for sixty-eight dollars the next morning, if there's no record of one from Mister Gibbs he probably never sent it he's, look I'd better just give it to you myself God knows when he'll be able to, he's got the IRS after him on some stock he gave his ex-wife in a settlement when she . . . didn't have any idea no he thought it might be worth a few hundred a few thousand, it was just a token severance he got from some small family company he'd worked for once, turned out they'd been putting all their earnings back into the company ever since. When he handed it over in this alimony settlement the IRS stepped in and figured his long-term capital gains tax around twenty-eight thousand dollars he's never seen a God damn penny of the . . . yes I know it but . . . He's here yes but he can't come to the phone, he's . . . Look it wouldn't do any good anyhow!

I just had to lend him twenty dollars to buy his daughter a pair of boots when he sees her this afternoon he can't even . . . Yes of course I'm aware you're attorney of record for the estate Mister Beamish but . . . in granite yes I know it was expen . . . I know she's upset yes I don't blame her either, we talked about it at breakfast this morn . . . what letter, from Arlington? No, no just that piece in the paper that called the epitaph a desecration to all who fought and lie buried in these hallowed . . . Well they can't prosecute him for that can they? He was named an executor in the will he says he was just carrying out what Schramm would have . . . All right look I'll talk to her again this evening, I think we can straighten it out before you leave for . . . what on that tobacco stock? I think she's decided to hold onto the whole thing yes, of course she's delighted at the remarkable recovery it made I'll talk to you tomorrow then, good . . . I wrote it down yes thanks for taking care of it, goodbye. Bast? find your mail?

—Yes but, but who's that back in the . . .

—Christ will you get away from that window!

—Yes but what happened back there who's, everything's covered with . . .

—What does it look like happened, the old man slammed the door brought down half the God damn ceiling when he look, look those papers jammed in with the paper bags right under your those yes, yes is that my, no, no Christ what a mess he must have jammed them back there himself here just just throw them wait, that box two-ply facial no right on the sink there, is it empty? Just throw them in that he might still want to keep them, hardly make out what the hell he ever thought he was trying to wait, wait where are you going . . .

—I think I just saw Mister Gibbs with somebody back there in Schramm, in the back apartment I have something to . . .

—Well God damn it I just told you didn't I? We just got him quieted down back there, portrait he's been trying to finish for years the old man knocked on the door one night he dragged him inside made him sit for it day and night fed him on boiled potatoes till it was done the old man just broke out, plaster in the wet paint we just got him quieted down Jack's in there reading him Broch's Sleepwalkers, been on page thirty-five for two hours if you go in he'll start the whole God damn thing again grab you and shout look! if you could have seen what I saw there! Listen they're waiting for you to bring Freddie, got your mail now . . .

—No but I have to tell Mister Gibbs something there's somebody waiting for him, a woman she's waiting for him downstairs in a cab she . . .

—Christ how did she, I mean do you know her too?

—Yes well she's . . .

—All right I'll tell him, I'll tell him now will you . . .

—No but if he doesn't come down I know she'll . . .

—Look I know all about it I'll tell him! Now . . .

—But why doesn't . . .

—Because he had some more blood tests they told him he'd live another fifty God damn years thats why! told him what had sent his white count through the roof and everything else was all this penicillin he'd taken for his throat when she finally called he wouldn't speak to her, heard her voice he pretended he was an old black retainer yas'm, yas'm, dat ole Mistah Gibbs he a genuine rascal to play de ladies so, say he clear out to a place yonder call Burmesquik set him up a little factory there hasn't answered the God damn phone since now look, here's the address it's his sister Mrs, where the hell's that ad . . .

—But I mean I still don't under . . .

—Look Bast you don't have to understand nobody expects you to! What you just threw in that box on the sink nobody expects you to know what it cost him, nobody expects you to see what he saw there all these papers, these boxes what we saw here that painting back there it's magnificent, the way it looks right now it's still magnificent he's down on his knees picking plaster out of it nobody expects you to see what he saw there! what Jack saw, what Schramm . . .

—Mister Eigen?

—Any of us! because you're just a young . . .

—Can you cash a check? I've got one here for four hundred dollars I'm not sure it's any good, one from Ascap for twenty-six fifty, one from a school for a dollar fifty-two and this torn one from Texas Gulf for fifteen cents. We need carfare.

—Christ just, here take this and wait here's the address, Mrs Cutler she's told the doorman to expect you, Mrs Richard Cutler here, address like that they might give you a tip. Freddie? Let's go, this young man is taking you down to your sister's she's waiting for you . . .

—And some papers, I put down some papers when I . . .

—Well Christ what do they look like.

—They don't look like anything Mister Eigen, just a lot of papers with crayon . . .

—Wait look under the, those?

—Yes, yes here they are look. They don't really look like anything do they.

—Yes fine, now . . .

—A lot of, like a lot of chickentracks don't they, look. I mean it's all still just what I hear there isn't it.

—Fine yes! now . . .

—I mean until a performer hears what I hear and can make other people hear what he hears it's just trash isn't it Mister Eigen, it's just trash like everything in this place everything you and Mister Gibbs and Mister Schramm all of you saw here it's just trash!

—Listen will you, God damn it will you just go do what you have to and . . .

—That's what I'm doing yes! Yes and, tell Mister Gibbs . . .

—I'll tell him . . . ! he bent with a twinge to lift Wise Potato Chips Hoppin' With Flavor! to the tub, stood there staring inside before he tied and then closed another box flap on the marionette in a tangle of strings, a laceless red sneaker, an arm lofting a bugle, legless sheep and the Virgin cropped in wild surmise muttering —bastards, young bastards . . . reached for the tape, turned for the phone —God damn it, hello? Yes wait a minute . . . and dropped it dangling on 24-One Pint Mazola New Improved. —Yes . . . ?

—Immigration, is this . . .

—She's right in there . . . he pressed back against Mazola New Improved for the brisk passage of serge.

————finally got you boy I mean holy shit where did you . . .

—Eigen?

—What? Yes what . . .

—Dumor Delivery, you the party called for a pickup?

—Finally got here yes, look . . .

—Holy, wait a minute buddy I can't take all this in my . . .

—Look I'm not buddy I'm not a party nobody asked you to! Just these boxes here and this pile on the tub they go to East Sixty-fourth Street here, care of Schramm here's the address on the top one I'll meet you down there wait, wait hand me that folder, I'm not going to lose it now . . . and he pulled aside 500 Novelty Rolls 1-Ply White for the constraint of nylon passing with the taut scorn of eyes gone under a fall of black hair, of serge to the floor crushing matchbooks, gray squares of film in perforated sequence, glass squares of stripes in flight.

————ca's all about like what we have to protect and how we're always going around helping everybody out and how they should do everything like us and all you know? but I mean would you ever think he would of actually wrote to me himself hey . . . ?

—Mind if I take some matches buddy? I'm . . .

—Take one take a thousand, Christ. Do you need toilet paper too?

—Now wait a . . .

—Look just do what you're paid for will you? God damn it can't, why can't people just shut up and do what they're paid for! I'll meet you down there.

————for all these here letters and offers I been getting because I mean like remember this here book that time where they wanted me to write about success and like free enterprise and all hey? And like remember where I read you on the train that time where there was this big groundswill about leading this here parade and entering public life and all? So I mean listen I got this neat idea hey, you listening? Hey? You listening . . . ?

A NOTE ON THE TYPE

The text of this book was set in Gael, a computer version of Caledonia, designed by William Addison Dwiggins for the Mergenthaler Linotype Company in 1939. Dwiggins chose to call his new type face Caledonia, the Roman name for Scotland, because it was inspired by the Scotch types cast about 1833 by Alexander Wilson & Son, Glasgow type founders. However, there is a calligraphic quality about Caledonia that is totally lacking in the Wilson types. Dwiggins referred to an even earlier type face for this "liveliness of action"—one cut around 1790 by William Martin for the printer William Bulmer. Caledonia has more weight than the Martin letters, and the bottom finishing strokes (serifs) of the letters are cut straight across, without brackets, to make sharp angles with the upright stems, thus giving a "modern face" appearance.

Composed by Haddon Craftsmen, ComCom, Allentown, Pa.
Printed and bound by American Book–Stratford Press, Saddlebrook, N.J.

Typography and binding design by Virginia Tan